Anglo-Saxon England 30

Her mon mæg giet gesion hiora swæð

ANGLO-SAXON ENGLAND
30

Edited by

MICHAEL LAPIDGE
University of Notre Dame

MALCOLM GODDEN
University of Oxford

SIMON KEYNES
University of Cambridge

PETER BAKER
University of Virginia

CARL BERKHOUT
University of Arizona

MARTIN BIDDLE
University of Oxford

MARK BLACKBURN
University of Cambridge

DANIEL DONOGHUE
Harvard University

ROBERTA FRANK
Yale University

RICHARD GAMESON
University of Kent at Canterbury

HELMUT GNEUSS
Universität München

PATRIZIA LENDINARA
Università di Palermo

ANDY ORCHARD
University of Toronto

PAUL REMLEY
University of Washington

FRED ROBINSON
Yale University

DONALD SCRAGG
University of Manchester

CAMBRIDGE
UNIVERSITY PRESS

Published by the Press Syndicate of the University of Cambridge
The Edinburgh Building, Cambridge CB2 2RU, United Kingdom
40 West 20th Street, New York, NY 10011-4211, USA
10 Stamford Road, Oakleigh, Melbourne 3166, Australia
Ruiz de Alarcón 13, 28014 Madrid, Spain

© Cambridge University Press 2001

First Published 2001

Typeset by
Servis Filmsetting Ltd
Manchester

Printed in the United Kingdom by
the University Press
Cambridge

ISBN 0 521 802105
ISSN 0263-6751

SUBSCRIPTIONS: Anglo-Saxon England (ISSN 0263-6751) is an annual journal. The subscription price including postage (excluding VAT) of volume 30 is £70 for institutions (US$115 in the USA, Canada and Mexico), £51 (US$78 in the USA, Canada and Mexico) for individuals ordering direct from the Press and certifying that the annual is for their personal use. EU subscribers (outside the UK) who are not registered for VAT should add VAT at their country's rate. VAT registered subscribers should provide their VAT registration number. Japanese prices for institutions are available from Kinokuniya Company Ltd., P.O. Box 55, Chitose, Tokyo 156, Japan. Orders, which must be accompanied by payment, may be sent to a bookseller, subscription agent, or direct to the publishers: Cambridge University Press, The Edinburgh Building, Shaftesbury Road, Cambridge CB2 2RU, UK. Orders from the USA, Canada or Mexico should be sent to Cambridge University Press, Journals Fulfillment Department, 110 Midland Avenue, Port Chester, NY 10573-4930, USA. Prices include delivery by air.

Back volumes: £70.00 (US$115.00 in the USA, Canada and Mexico) each available from Cambridge or the American Branch of Cambridge University Press.

A catalogue record of this book is available from the British Library.

Contents

v

Contents

Abbreviations listed before the bibliography (pages 247–249) are used throughout the volume without other explanation.

The editorial assistance of Clare Orchard and Peter Jackson is gratefully acknowledged.

Illustrations

PLATES

FIGURES

ACKNOWLEDGEMENTS

By permission of the Trustees of the British Museum the design on the cover is taken from the obverse of a silver penny issued at London in the early 880s, reflecting Alfred's assumption of political control over the city.

Permission to publish photographs has been granted by the Bibliothèque Nationale de France, Paris (pl. I); the British Library, London (pl. II); the Master and Fellows of Corpus Christi College, Cambridge (pls. III, IV, V, VI, VII and VIII); the Master and Fellows of Gonville and Caius College, Cambridge (pls. IX and X).

Material should be submitted to the editor most convenient regionally, with these exceptions: an article should be sent to Martin Biddle if concerned with archaeology, to Mark Blackburn if concerned with numismatics, to Daniel Donoghue if concerned with Old English metrics, to Richard Gameson if concerned with art history, to Simon Keynes if concerned with history or onomastics, and to Michael Lapidge if concerned with Anglo-Latin or palaeography. Whenever a contribution is sent from abroad it should be accompanied by international coupons to cover the cost of return postage. A potential contributor is asked to get in touch with the editor concerned as early as possible to obtain a copy of the style sheet and to have any necessary discussion. Articles must be in English.

The editors' addresses are:

Professor P. S. Baker, Department of English, University of Virginia, Charlottesville, Virginia 22903 (USA)

Professor C. T. Berkhout, Department of English, University of Arizona, Tucson, Arizona 85721 (USA)

Mr M. Biddle, Hertford College, Oxford OX1 3BW (England)

Dr M. A. S. Blackburn, Fitzwilliam Museum, Cambridge CB2 1RB (England)

Professor D. Donoghue, Department of English, Harvard University, 8 Prescott Street, Cambridge, Massachusetts 02138 (USA)

Professor R. Frank, Department of English, Yale University, New Haven, Connecticut 06520 (USA)

Dr R. Gameson, Faculty of Humanities, Rutherford College, University of Kent at Canterbury, Canterbury, Kent CT2 7NX (England)

Professor H. Gneuss, Institut für Englische Philologie, Universität München, Schellingstrasse 3, D-80799 München (Germany)

Professor M. R. Godden, English Faculty, St Cross Building, Manor Road, Oxford OX1 3UK (England)

Professor S. D. Keynes, Trinity College, Cambridge CB2 1TQ (England)

Professor M. Lapidge, Department of English, University of Notre Dame, Notre Dame, Indiana 46556 (USA)

Professor P. Lendinara, Cattedra di Filologia Germanica, Università degli Studi di Palermo, Facoltà di Magistero, Piazza Ignazio Florio 24, 90139 Palermo (Italy)

Professor A. Orchard, Centre for Medieval Studies, University of Toronto, 39 Queen's Park Crescent East, Toronto, Ontario M5S 1A1 (Canada)

Professor Paul G. Remley, Department of English, Box 354330, University of Washington, Seattle, WA 98195–4330 (USA)

Professor F. C. Robinson, Department of English, Yale University, New Haven, Connecticut 06520 (USA)

Professor D. G. Scragg, Centre for Anglo-Saxon Studies, University of Manchester, Manchester M13 9PL (England)

Place-name evidence for an Anglo-Saxon animal name: OE *pohha/*pocca 'fallow deer'

CAROLE HOUGH

It is well known that the extant corpus of Old English literature preserves only a proportion of the vocabulary that once existed. In some instances, terms for concepts that must have been familiar to the Anglo-Saxons have been lost without trace; in others, they may be reconstructed from non-literary forms of evidence such as the place-names coined by early settlers in the areas now known as England and southern Scotland. The main dictionary of place-name terminology, Smith's *English Place-Name Elements* of 1956,[1] includes many entries for words which are otherwise either unattested, or attested only with other meanings. Animal names in particular constitute an area of vocabulary which is under-represented in literary sources but common in place-names, and for which toponymic evidence often proves crucial. Old English animal names unattested in the extant literature but included in *English Place-Name Elements*[2] are *bagga 'badger',[3] *bula 'bull', *ean 'lamb', *gæten 'kid', *galt 'pig, boar', *græg 'badger',[4] *hyrse 'mare', *padde 'toad', *padduc 'frog', *pigga 'young pig', *stedda 'horse', *tacca and *tagga 'teg, young sheep', *tige 'goat', *todd 'fox' and *wiðer 'ram, wether'. Those identified more recently include *brun 'pig'[5] and *wearg 'wolf'.[6] As the English Place-Name Survey progresses, providing detailed coverage of the country's toponyms in a series of annual volumes inaugurated in the 1920s, further examples may be expected to come to light. The aim of this article is to offer a new addition to the corpus.

---

[1] A. H. Smith, *English Place-Name Elements*, 2 vols., EPNS 25–6 (Cambridge, 1956). Currently in preparation is a new edition, of which one fascicle has so far appeared: *The Vocabulary of English Place-Names (Á – Box)*, ed. D. Parsons and T. Styles with C. Hough (Nottingham, 1997).

[2] Smith, *English Place-Name Elements*, s.vv. Smith also treated OE *hogg* 'hog' as an unattested word, but this was corrected in the *Addenda and Corrigenda* published in *JEPNS* 1 (1968–9), 9–52, at 25.

[3] This interpretation was regarded as uncertain by Smith, but is placed on a securer footing by P. Kitson, 'Quantifying Qualifiers in Anglo-Saxon Charter Boundaries', *Folia Linguistica Historica* 14 (1993), 29–82, at 72–4. The most recent discussion is in *The Vocabulary of English Place-Names (Á – Box)*, ed. Parsons *et al.*, pp. 36–7.

[4] An alternative interpretation as 'wolf' is suggested by C. Hough, 'OE *græg* in Place-Names', *NM* 96 (1995), 361–5; and independently by C. P. Biggam, *Grey in Old English: an Interdisciplinary Semantic Study* (London, 1998), pp. 79–80.

[5] C. Hough, 'OE *brún* in Place-Names', *ES* 79 (1998), 512–21, notes that this sense may also be attested as a nonce occurrence in Riddle 92.

[6] C. Hough, 'OE *wearg* in Warnborough and Wreighburn', *JEPNS* 27 (1994–5), 14–20.

According to the entry in *English Place-Name Elements*, OE *pohha, pocca* 'a pouch, a bag' is 'used in some undetermined sense in p[lace-]n[ame]s, possibly as a by-name'.[7] The only other sense attested in literary sources is as a medical term 'sinus', and no additional light is thrown on the matter by the related adjective *pohhed* 'baggy, loose' or by the compound nouns *cramming-pohha* 'some sort of snare' and *nest-pohha* 'a bag for food, wallet'.[8] An attempt to establish the likely range of meaning in toponyms is made under the entry for Poughley Farm in the English Place-Name Survey for Berkshire,[9] where Gelling argues for a transferred topographical sense on the grounds that all known place-names from OE *pohha, pocca* have topographical terms as second elements, whereas a personal name or a by-name would be expected to compound with a wider range of generics.[10] This interpretation has been adopted in later volumes of the Survey, and currently holds the field. While disproving the by-name theory, however, the evidence adduced by Gelling is insufficient to establish a topographical sense beyond reasonable doubt.[11] Indeed, she herself raises the alternative possibility that the element may function as an animal name, having presumably developed along similar lines to OE **bagga* 'badger', an animal named from its bag-like shape. Either sense would appear to represent a native development, without recorded parallels in cognate languages. This article will support an interpretation as an animal name through a closer examination of the toponymic contexts in which OE *pohha, pocca* occurs, and will attempt to identify the type of animal in question.

Besides Poughley itself (OE *leah* 'wood, clearing'), place-names cited by Gelling in her discussion of OE *pohha, pocca* are Poughill (OE *hyll* 'hill') and Poflet (OE *hlype* 'leap, leaping place') in Devon,[12] Poffley in Oxfordshire (OE *wiella* 'spring, stream'),[13] and Poughill in Cornwall (either OE *hyll* 'hill' or OE

---

[7] Smith, *English Place-Name Elements* II, 68, s.v. *pohha, pocca*.

[8] J. Bosworth, *An Anglo-Saxon Dictionary*, ed. T. N. Toller (Oxford, 1898); T. N. Toller, *An Anglo-Saxon Dictionary: Supplement* (Oxford, 1921); A. Campbell, *An Anglo-Saxon Dictionary: Supplement: Enlarged Addenda and Corrigenda* (Oxford, 1972), s. vv. A. C. Amos and A. diP. Healey, *Dictionary of Old English* (Toronto, 1986–) defines the *hapax legomenon cramming-pohha* as '"a cramming bag or pouch" . . . or perhaps take as "bag of tricks"', but has not yet reached letters *N* or *P*.

[9] All references are to the county boundaries preceding the local government reorganization of 1974.

[10] M. Gelling, *The Place-Names of Berkshire*, 3 vols., EPNS 49–51 (Cambridge, 1973–6) II, 290–1.

[11] K. Cameron, *English Place Names*, new ed. (London, 1996), p. 181, notes cautiously: 'It has been usual to interpret Poughill . . . as "Pohha's hill", but a possible alternative meaning is certainly "pouch-shaped hill".' A. D. Mills, *A Dictionary of English Place-Names*, 2nd ed. (Oxford, 1998), p. 277, s.n. *Poughill*, also gives both alternatives.

[12] J. E. B. Gover, A. Mawer and F. M. Stenton, *The Place-Names of Devon*, 2 vols., EPNS 8–9 (Cambridge, 1931–2) II, 415; I, 216.

[13] M. Gelling, *The Place-Names of Oxfordshire*, 2 vols., EPNS 23–4 (Cambridge, 1953–4) II, 322.

wiella 'spring, stream').[14] The second elements of all these place-names are topographical terms used elsewhere of the habitat of wild creatures,[15] and there are three aspects of the group as a whole which point towards an interpretation of OE *pohha, pocca* as an animal name. The first is the incidence of identical formations within limited geographical areas. It is unclear whether or not a second occurrence of the place-name Poughley in the Berkshire parish of East Garston, some four miles from Poughley Farm in Chaddleworth, represents an independent formation.[16] Gelling's interpretation of the name as 'probably "wood by a feature resembling a bag"' makes it necessary to assume that both places were named from the same wood, which, as she points out, must in that case have been very extensive, lying on both sides of the river Lambourne. An alternative possibility that both *leah*s might have been named independently from the same type of animal is strengthened by the occurrence of another Poughley Farm in the Berkshire parish of East Hanney.[17] This is considerably further north than the other two, and cannot be taken to have been named from the same wood, although it could of course be a transferred name. Finally, a fourth compound with *leah* occurs as Pophley's Farm in the neighbouring county of Buckinghamshire.[18] Since all the attested spellings are from personal names, the Buckinghamshire editors suggest that this is a manorial name from the Berkshire Poughley; but it may well be the case that all four toponyms were named from an animal indigenous to the whole area. Similarly in Oxfordshire, a lost place-name *Pochwele* about four miles from Poffley again represents a second instance of the same formation with OE *wiella* 'spring, stream'.[19] Here it is highly unlikely that two springs or streams four miles apart would be named from a single topographical feature, but fully plausible that the same type of animal would be found throughout the district.

A second point against an interpretation as a topographical feature is the fact that such a term would be unlikely to occur exclusively as a qualifying element. Only two occurrences of OE *pohha, pocca* as a generic have been identified in volumes of the English Place-Name Survey published to date, both in Staffordshire field-names. The first is a lost field-name in Forton parish,

---

[14] O. J. Padel, *A Popular Dictionary of Cornish Place-Names* (Penzance, 1988), p. 145. A derivation from *hyll* is supported by the Domesday Book form, but all other early spellings are indicative of *wiella*. Since both generics are represented in other place-names from OE *pohha, pocca*, the matter is difficult to resolve.

[15] The entry for each of these terms in Smith, *English Place-Name Elements*, includes a section for animals or wild creatures.   [16] Gelling, *The Place-Names of Berkshire* II, 331.

[17] *Ibid.* II, 478. Unfortunately there are no early spellings, and so the etymology cannot be regarded as certain.

[18] A. Mawer and F. M. Stenton, *The Place-Names of Buckinghamshire*, EPNS 2 (Cambridge, 1925), 195.   [19] Gelling, *The Place-Names of Oxfordshire* II, 332.

recorded as *Scacherds pokkis* in a single spelling dating from 1487.[20] The second is Matthew's Pow Field in the nearby parish of Gnosall, for which no early spellings are available.[21] Neither can be regarded as secure. Even if these do represent topographical uses of the term, however, this would not rule out an alternative use as an animal name. The two possibilities are not mutually exclusive, since a term which developed an extended sense as an animal name may have developed another sense as a topographical feature. Again, comparison with OE *bagga* 'bag' is useful, as the sense 'badger', which is well evidenced in place-names, appears to have have existed alongside a sense 'bag-like feature', found for instance in the Dorset field-names Croam Bags (1838) and *Cleybagge* (1538),[22] and in the West Riding of Yorkshire field-names the Bag(s) (1575), *Bagg acre* (1636), *le Bagge* (1560), *Ruddge Bagge* (1575) and *Ruggbagge* (1640).[23]

Thirdly, and most crucially, it appears hitherto to have escaped notice in this connection that OE *hlype* 'leap, leaping place', the second element of Poflet in Devon, rarely appears as a place-name generic in combination with anything other than an animal name or a personal name. Smith's headword entry explains that the term is characteristically used in place-names of '"a place that can be crossed by leaping" such as "a chasm, a narrow defile, that part of a fence which some animals can leap over but which restrains others"', and he notes that 'in compounds the first el[ement] is usually (i) the name of an animal or bird . . . (ii) a word denoting people', citing three instances of the first type and one of the second, and also drawing attention to the charter spellings *swealewan hlypan* (KCD 739; S 960) and *presta hlype* (KCD 813; S 1036).[24] Several additional instances have been identified in post-1956 volumes of the English Place-Name Survey. Putting these together with Smith's examples and with others not cited by him from earlier county surveys, the following pattern emerges:[25]

---

[20] J. P. Oakden, *The Place-Names of Staffordshire: Part I*, EPNS 55 (Cambridge, 1984), 152.

[21] *Ibid.* p. 162.

[22] A. D. Mills, *The Place-Names of Dorset: Part I*, EPNS 52 (Cambridge, 1977), 236; A. D. Mills, *The Place-Names of Dorset: Part III*, EPNS 59/60 (Cambridge, 1989), 346.

[23] A. H. Smith, *The Place-Names of the West Riding of Yorkshire*, 8 vols., EPNS 30–7 (Cambridge, 1961–3) VII, 100.

[24] Smith, *English Place-Name Elements* I, 251, s.v. **hlēp, hlíep, hlӯp*. In references to Anglo-Saxon charters, S = P. H. Sawyer, *Anglo-Saxon Charters: an Annotated List and Bibliography*, R. Hist. Soc. Guides and Handbooks 8 (London, 1968), followed by the number of the document; BCS = W. de G. Birch, *Cartularium Saxonicum*, 3 vols. (London, 1885–93); KCD = J. M. Kemble, *Codex Diplomaticus Aevi Saxonici*, 6 vols. (London, 1839–48).

[25] Included in this corpus are place-names which may derive from later reflexes of the term, conventionally assigned to Old English etymons by the EPNS editors. The field-name Deelips in Rutland is attributed to ModE *deer-leap* 'a low place in a hedge or fence over which deer may jump' in B. Cox, *The Place-Names of Rutland*, EPNS 67/69 (Nottingham, 1994), 277, but has evidently been in existence long enough to undergo phonetic change.

Fig. 1   Occurrences of OE *hlype* 'leap, leaping place' as a second element in place-names

(i) References to wildlife

a) Deer

Hartlip, Kent (OE *heorot* 'hart, male deer')[26]

Hindleap, Sussex (OE *hind* 'hind, female deer')[27]

Hindlip, Worcestershire (OE *hind* 'hind, female deer')[28]

Horsley Bank, Cheshire (OE *heorot* 'hart, male deer')[29]

f.n. Dear Lips, Gloucestershire (OE *deor* 'deer')[30]

f.n. Dear Leap, West Riding of Yorkshire (OE *deor* 'deer')[31]

f.n. Deelips, Rutland (OE *deor* 'deer')[32]

f.n. Deer's Leap, Cheshire (OE *deor* 'deer')[33]

f.n. *Deere leape flatt* (1639), Staffordshire (OE *deor* 'deer')[34]

f.n. *Hindehlypan* (780), Gloucestershire (OE *hind* 'hind, female deer')[35]

f.n. *Hyndelepe dale* (1300), Nottinghamshire (OE *hind* 'hind, female deer')[36]

b) Other animals

f.n. *Catlephebbyll* (n.d.), West Riding of Yorkshire (OE *catt* 'cat')[37]

wulfhlype (1062), Essex (OE *wulf* 'wolf')[38]

c) Birds

Birdlip, Gloucestershire (OE *bridd* 'bird')[39]

swealewan hlypan (1023), Hampshire (OE *swealwe* 'swallow')

(ii) References to people

a) Personal names

Cudlipptown, Devon[40]

?St Lucas Leap, Dorset[41]

---

[26] J. K. Wallenberg, *The Place-Names of Kent* (Uppsala, 1934), pp. 249–50.

[27] A. Mawer and F. M. Stenton, *The Place-Names of Sussex*, 2 vols., EPNS 6–7 (Cambridge, 1929–39) II, 331.

[28] A. Mawer and F. M. Stenton, *The Place-Names of Worcestershire*, EPNS 4 (Cambridge, 1927), 139.

[29] J. McN. Dodgson, *The Place-Names of Cheshire*, 5 vols. in 7, EPNS 44–8, 54, 74 (Cambridge and Nottingham, 1970–97) [part 5.2 completed and ed. A. R. Rumble] II, 298.

[30] A. H. Smith, *The Place-Names of Gloucestershire*, 4 vols., EPNS 38–41 (Cambridge, 1964–5) IV, 139. (f.n. = field name.)   [31] Smith, *The Place-Names of the West Riding of Yorkshire* VII, 205.

[32] Cox, *The Place-Names of Rutland*, p. 277.

[33] Dodgson, *The Place-Names of Cheshire* II, 302.

[34] Oakden, *The Place-Names of Staffordshire: Part I*, p. 126.

[35] Smith, *The Place-Names of Gloucestershire* IV, 139.

[36] J. E. B. Gover, A. Mawer and F. M. Stenton, *The Place-Names of Nottinghamshire*, EPNS 17 (Cambridge, 1940), 284.

[37] Smith, *The Place-Names of the West Riding of Yorkshire* VII, 205.

[38] P. H. Reaney, *The Place-Names of Essex*, EPNS 12 (Cambridge, 1935), 65.

[39] Smith, *The Place-Names of Gloucestershire* I, 156–7.

[40] Gover *et al.*, *The Place-Names of Devon* I, 232.

[41] Mills, *The Place-Names of Dorset: Part I*, p. 49, suggests a link with Richard Lucas, rector of Studland 1536–78, but notes an alternative tradition that the allusion may be to 'a greyhound which fell from the cliff here while coursing a hare'.

Fig. 1 *(cont.)*

(ii) References to people *(cont.)*
a) Personal names *(cont.)*
Postlip, Gloucestershire[42]
Wintour's Leap, Gloucestershire[43]
Freobearnes hlype (1062), Essex[44]

b) Appellatives
Clerkenleap, Worcestershire (OE *clerc* 'cleric')[45]
Lad's Leap, Cheshire (OE **ladda* 'servant, youth')[46]
st.n. Counterslip, Gloucestershire (ME *contasse, -esse* 'countess')[47]
presta hlype (1062), Essex (OE *preost* 'priest')[48]

(iii) Others
Poflet, Devon (OE *pohha, pocca* '?')
Ruislip, Middlesex (?OE *rysc, risc* 'rush')[49]

Altogether, then, fifteen of the twenty-six known toponyms from OE *hlype* contain animal or bird names, eleven of which are terms for deer. All others refer to people, with the sole exception of Ruislip in Middlesex, the etymology of which is highly uncertain. There is thus a strong case for interpreting OE *pohha, pocca* in Poflet, Devon, as one of these types of word.[50] Since, as Gelling points out,[51] a personal name is unlikely to occur solely with topographical terms, the balance of evidence clearly favours an animal name.

---

[42] Smith, *The Place-Names of Gloucestershire* II, 34–5. The etymology of this place-name is uncertain. Alternative possibilities discussed by Smith include an unattested Old English personal name **Pott* or a transferred topographical use of OE *pott* 'pot' to refer to a pit or deep hollow. Since the latter would represent an anomalous formation out of line with all other known place-names from OE *hlep, hlype*, a personal name must be preferred.

[43] Smith, *The Place-Names of Gloucestershire* III, 267.

[44] Reaney, *The Place-Names of Essex*, p. 135.

[45] Mawer and Stenton, *The Place-Names of Worcestershire*, p. 145.

[46] Dodgson, *The Place-Names of Cheshire* I, 324.

[47] Smith, *The Place-Names of Gloucestershire* III, 87. (st.n. = street-name.)

[48] Reaney, *The Place-Names of Essex*, p. 73.

[49] J. E. B. Gover, A. Mawer and F. M. Stenton, *The Place-Names of Middlesex*, EPNS 18 (Cambridge, 1942), 46–7. The etymology of this place-name is uncertain. Gover *et al.* suggest a compound of OE *rysc, risc* 'rush' with OE *hlype* 'leap', but comment that 'the application of the second element here is uncertain'. E. Ekwall, *The Concise Oxford Dictionary of English Place-Names*, 4th ed. (Oxford, 1960), p. 396, s.n. *Ruislip*, prefers a derivation from OE *rysc, risc* 'rush' with OE *slæp* 'slippery spot', which is topographically more appropriate. The fact that Ruislip is outside the general pattern of place-names from OE *hlype* may throw further doubt on the EPNS etymology.

[50] P. H. Reaney, *The Place-Names of Cambridgeshire and the Isle of Ely*, EPNS 19 (Cambridge, 1943), 331, also identifies a usage of OE *hlype* 'in the special sense *Fyshynglepys* (1441), as in *Horescroft-, Newe-, Nordonelepes* (1240), *Vtlep* (1277)'.

[51] Gelling, *The Place-Names of Berkshire* II, 291.

Other possible occurrences of OE *pohha, pocca* have been identified in later volumes of the English Place-Name Survey. In Shropshire, a lost field-name recorded in 1301 as *Pogh Wenhale, Poghwenhale* is tentatively attributed to OE *pohha, pocca* 'bag' and OE *halh* 'nook' with the comment that 'the middle el[ement] and the structure of the name are obscure'.[52] In Staffordshire, a lost field-name *Powefeldes* (1570) is attributed to OE *pohha, pocca* and OE *feld* 'open country',[53] another element which more commonly combines with the names of wild than of domestic animals.[54] In Dorset, Bowridge Hill (*Poghrigge* 1292) is interpreted as 'probably "ridge shaped like a pouch or bag",' from OE *pohha, pocca* and OE *hrycg*,[55] but could equally well refer to a ridge frequented by a certain type of animal, as do place-names such as Bageridge in Dorset and Staffordshire and Baggridge in Somerset 'badger ridge', Hawkridge in Berkshire and Somerset 'hawk ridge', and Henstridge in Somerset 'stallion's ridge'.[56] Indeed, given the precision with which Old English topographical vocabulary is now known to have been used,[57] a reference to shape would appear to be redundant with this type of word. The Dorset editor also notes that Bowridge Hill 'gave name to *Powgh'rygge-*, *Pokeryge brygge* 1501', adding: 'the same bridge is apparently earlier called *Pough'fordebrig*' . . . from the same first el[ement] with **ford**'.[58] It strains credulity to believe that a bridge, as well as a nearby ridge, was considered to be bag-shaped; but again there are many instances of place-names combining OE *ford* with animal names, which as Gelling explains 'must have been mentioned because they were frequently seen in the vicinity of the ford'.[59]

There may in fact be more occurrences of OE *pohha, pocca* than have yet been identified. *A Microfiche Concordance to Old English* reveals a reference to *on Poholte* in the eighth-century bounds of an estate at Zoy in Somerset (BCS 143; S 251), and to *pohweg* in the eleventh-century bounds of an estate at Elmley Castle in Worcestershire (KCD 764; S 1396).[60] These appear to represent combinations of OE *pohha, pocca* with OE *holt* 'wood' and OE *weg* 'way' respectively. Again, both are terms which are recorded elsewhere in combination with animal names. The second element of the lost field-name *Poghole* (1313) in Berkshire is identified by the county editor as OE *hol* 'hole, hollow'.[61] No attention has as yet been paid to the first element, which bears a striking resemblance to certain early spellings of

---

[52] M. Gelling, *The Place-Names of Shropshire: Part II*, EPNS 70 (Nottingham, 1995), 118.
[53] Oakden, *The Place-Names of Staffordshire: Part I*, p. 66.
[54] M. Gelling, *Place-Names in the Landscape* (London, 1984), p. 244.
[55] Mills, *The Place-Names of Dorset: Part III*, p. 11.
[56] Gelling, *Place-Names in the Landscape*, p. 169.
[57] Cf. the many publications by M. Gelling and A. Cole, and in particular the survey of topographical vocabulary presented in Gelling's *Place-Names in the Landscape*.
[58] Mills, *The Place-Names of Dorset: Part III*, p. 11.   [59] Gelling, *Place-Names in the Landscape*, p. 71.
[60] A. diP. Healey and R. L. Venezky, *A Microfiche Concordance to Old English* (Toronto, 1980), s.vv. *poholte, pohweg, pohweges*.   [61] Gelling, *The Place-Names of Berkshire* I, 276.

place-names from OE *pohha, pocca*, including Poughley Farm in the same county (*Poghelye* (p), *Poghel', Poghele* 1241, *Pogheleg'* 1242–3, *Poghely* 1275–6, *Poghelee* 1297, *Pogh'ele* 1436–7),[62] Poflet in Devon (*Poghelippe* 1242, *Poghelyp(e)* 1296, *Poghlippe* 1303, *Poggelyp* 1346, *Poghlep, Poghlup* 1412)[63] and Poughill in Devon (*Poghelle* 1279).[64] It seems to me most likely that the field-name represents another occurrence of OE *pohha, pocca*. If this suggestion is correct, an interpretation as an animal name is again supported by the combination with OE *hol* 'hole, hollow', an element which very commonly designates the lair or den of a wild creature.[65]

It is also possible that some occurrences of OE *pohha, pocca* may have been wrongly attributed to OE *puca* 'goblin', since the two elements are sometimes difficult to distinguish and the latter has tended to be preferred on grounds of sense to the attested meaning of OE *pohha, pocca* as 'bag, pouch'. In Devon, for instance, the minor names *Pokemore* (1463), *Pokepytte* (1473) and *Pokemershe* (*c.* 1500)[66] could all formally derive from OE *pohha, pocca* rather than from OE *puca*, and the same applies to Pock Field in Cambridgeshire (*Pokefeld(e) c.* 1190, 1305, *Pock-, Pooke-feild(e)* 16th)[67] and the field-name *Pokefelde* (1513) in Essex.[68] Comparison with spellings such as *Pokeleia* 1176–7, *Pokel'* 1214, 1220, *Pokeleygh'* 1220 for Poughley Farm in Berkshire suggests a common derivation;[69] and again, the second elements are topographical terms found elsewhere in combination with animal names.

In other instances, there may be confusion with a personal name *Pohha* or **Poca*, the first element of place-names such as Pockthorpe in the East Riding of Yorkshire (*Pochetorp* 1086, *Poketorp, -thorp(e)* 1195–8 etc.),[70] Pockley in the North Riding (*Pochelaf, -lac* 1086, *Pokelai, -lay* 1184–98, 1279–81, *-le* 1232, 13th, *-ley(e)* 1282, 1301, *Pockeley(a)* 1252, 1259, *Poklee, Pockele* 1285),[71] Powick in Worcestershire

---

[62] Gelling, *The Place-Names of Berkshire* II, 290. ((p) = personal name or surname.)

[63] Gover *et al.*, *The Place-Names of Devon* I, 216.

[64] *Ibid.* II, 415. The page number is wrongly cited as 445 in Gelling, *The Place-Names of Berkshire* II, 290, s.n. *Poughley Fm.*

[65] As noted for instance by M. G. Williamson, 'The Non-Celtic Place-Names of the Scottish Border Counties' (unpubl. PhD dissertation, Edinburgh Univ., 1942), p. 234, and Kitson, 'Quantifying Qualifiers in Anglo-Saxon Charter Boundaries', p. 33. For further discussion, see C. Hough, 'Carolside in Berwickshire and *Carelholpit* in Lincolnshire', *Nomina* 23 (2000), 79–86.

[66] Gover *et al.*, *The Place-Names of Devon* II, 691.

[67] Reaney, *The Place-Names of Cambridgeshire and the Isle of Ely*, p. 272.

[68] Reaney, *The Place-Names of Essex*, p. 587.

[69] Gelling, *The Place-Names of Berkshire* II, 290.

[70] A. H. Smith, *The Place-Names of the East Riding of Yorkshire and York*, EPNS 14 (Cambridge, 1937), 95. However, G. Fellows-Jensen has recently suggested an alternative interpretation of this and similar formations from 'a derogatory compound appellative **pūkatorp* to denote an insignificant settlement' ('Scandinavian Settlement Names in East Anglia: Some Problems', *Nomina* 22 (1999), 45–60, at 53).

[71] A. H. Smith, *The Place-Names of the North Riding of Yorkshire*, EPNS 5 (Cambridge, 1928), 72. Pockley is not included in Gelling's discussion of names from OE *pohha, pocca*, and neither is

(*Poincguuic* 972 [*c*.1050], *Poiwic(h)(a)* 1086, etc.),[72] Poxwell in Dorset (*Poceswylle* 987 [13th], *Pocheswelle* 1086, *Pokeswel(l)e* 1188, etc.),[73] and the lost field-name *Poketorp* (1202) in Norfolk,[74] with a diminutive form **Pocel(a)* occurring in Pocklington in the East Riding of Yorkshire (*Poclinton* 1086, *Poc-*, *Poklington(a)*, *-y-* 13th *et freq.* to 1524, *Pochelinton* 1100–8, etc.).[75] The personal name is recorded independently (in the form *Pohta*) in the witness list to BCS 91 (S 22).[76] Although generally associated with OE *pocc* 'smallpox' by modern scholars,[77] it could well be based on an animal name, as are many other Anglo-Saxon eponyms. The diminutive might either constitute a hypocoristic form of the personal name or be adopted directly from a diminutive form of the appellative, apparently evidenced in a lost Shropshire field-name recorded as *Poklbroc* 1222–*c*. 1230, *Powelbrok* 1291–8, concerning which the county editor comments that the first element 'looks like a diminutive in *-el* of *pohha* "pouch"'.[78] Again, references to wild creatures are common in combination with OE *broc* 'brook, stream', and an OE **pohhel* could plausibly represent an animal name, possibly referring to the young or to a small variety of the species.[79] The same formation may occur in the Northamptonshire place-name Polebrook (*Pochebroc* 1086, *Pokebroc* 1207 *et passim* to 1428 with variant spelling *-brok(e)*, *Pokesbrok* 1314; *Pockebroc* 1203, *Pokbrok* 1229, *Pakebrok* 1428; *Polebroc* 1254, *-broke* 1428, *Polbrok* 1316; *Polebroke al. Pokebroke* 1608).[80] Initially attributed to OE

---

the derivation from a personal name challenged by Mills, *A Dictionary of English Place-Names*, pp. 274–5, s.n. *Pockley*. However, the place-name seems to me almost certain to represent a doublet of Poughley in Berkshire.

[72] Mawer and Stenton, *The Place-Names of Worcestershire*, pp. 223–4.

[73] Mills, *The Place-Names of Dorset: Part I*, pp. 143–4, suggests an OE **poc(c)e* 'frog' related to MLG, MDu *pogge* as an alternative possibility, and notes that the same first element may occur in the nearby Pixon Barn (*ibid.* p. 214). The second element is taken to be probably OE *(ge)swell(e)* 'steeply rising ground' rather than OE *wiella* 'spring, stream', but a combination of the latter with a strong personal name **Poc* is not entirely ruled out. OE **poc(c)e* 'frog' was proposed by Ekwall, *The Concise Oxford Dictionary of English Place-Names*, s.n. *Polebrook*, as the first element of Polebrook in Northamptonshire, and is at least as likely as a personal name in Pockington and *Pockham Moor* in Gloucestershire (*The Place-Names of Gloucestershire* II, 235). An interpretation as 'frog' may also be possible in some of the other place-names attributed to OE *pohha/pocca* – particularly those in combination with water-words – but does not fit the toponymic context in a majority of instances.

[74] K. I. Sandred, *The Place-Names of Norfolk: Part II*, EPNS 72 (Nottingham, 1996), 9.

[75] Smith, *The Place-Names of the East Riding of Yorkshire and York*, p. 182.

[76] W. G. Searle, *Onomasticon Anglo-Saxonicum: a List of Anglo-Saxon Proper Names From the Time of Beda to That of King John* (Cambridge, 1897), p. 390. Searle also cites *Pohanleah* from BCS 366, but this is an early spelling of Poughley Farm in Berkshire discussed above.

[77] Smith, *The Place-Names of the North Riding of Yorkshire*, p. 72; Mills, *The Place-Names of Dorset: Part I*, p. 144.   [78] Gelling, *The Place-Names of Shropshire: Part II*, p. 148.

[79] Compare for instance OE *puca*, *pucel* 'goblin', OE **putta* 'kite', *pyttel* 'hawk, mousehawk' (Smith, *English Place-Name Elements*, s.vv.).

[80] J. E. B. Gover, A. Mawer and F. M. Stenton, *The Place-Names of Northamptonshire*, EPNS 10 (Cambridge, 1933), 215. Additional spellings cited at 209 under the entry for Polebrook Hundred are *Pocabroc a*.1076, *Pochebroc* 1086, *Polebroke* 1316, 1346.

puca 'goblin' by the Northamptonshire editors, a subsequent *addendum* to the
Survey drew attention to Anderson's suggestion that 'in view of the absence of
any *u*-forms, ... the first element is OE *pohha, pocca*, "bag" used in some topographical sense or as a personal name'.[81] Again, the second element is OE *broc* 'brook,
stream', and here the alternative spelling traditions with /k/ or /l/ may reflect an
alternation between *pohha, pocca* and a diminutive form **pohhel, *poccel*.

To summarize the argument so far, I suggest that the range of second elements recorded in combination with OE *pohha, pocca* points towards an interpretation as an animal name, and that this is supported by occurrences of identical
formations within limited geographical areas. The type of animal in question is
difficult to establish, but it is at least suggestive that nearly half the known place-
names from OE *hlype* 'leap, leaping place' contain words for types of deer, referring, like the compound OE *hlyp-geat*, to 'a gate in a fence over which deer and
other animals can leap but which restrains others such as sheep and cattle'.[82]
Moreover, deer are also the commonest type of living creatures to appear in
place-names with OE *leah* 'wood, clearing'. This is demonstrated by Gelling,
who cites Darley (two occurrences) in Derbyshire, Durleigh in Somerset,
Durley in Hampshire, Hartley in Berkshire, Dorset, Hampshire (three occurrences) and Kent (two occurrences), Hurstley in Herefordshire, Hiendley in the
West Riding of Yorkshire and Hindley in Cheshire.[83] Compounds with OE *hyll*
include Harthill 'hart hill' in Cheshire, Derbyshire and the West Riding of
Yorkshire,[84] and with OE *wielle*, Hartwell 'harts' spring' in Buckinghamshire,
Northamptonshire and Staffordshire:[85] in both instances, these are the only for-
mations to occur more than twice in Gelling's corpus. Similarly with OE *ford*,
where out of twenty-two instances relating to wild creatures in the corpus of
names discussed by Gelling, no less than five refer to deer: Harford in
Gloucestershire, Hartford in Cheshire and Northumberland, Hartforth in the
North Riding of Yorkshire, and Hertford in Hertfordshire.[86] Compounds with
OE *feld* 'open country' appear in Darfield in the West Riding of Yorkshire[87] and
Hartfield in Sussex.[88] Deer are not particularly common in combination with
OE *hol* 'hole, hollow', but are represented in names such as Hartshole in
Devon[89] and Hart Holes and Harts Hole in the West Riding of Yorkshire,[90]

[81] Reaney, *The Place-Names of Essex*, p. lviii.
[82] Smith, *English Place-Name Elements* I, 252, s.v. *hliep-geat*.
[83] Gelling, *Place-Names in the Landscape*, p. 205. Another possibility is Hattersley in Cheshire, where
the first element may be OE *heah-deor* 'a stag, a deer' (Dodgson, *The Place-Names of Cheshire* I,
307).   [84] Gelling, *Place-Names in the Landscape*, p. 171.   [85] *Ibid.* p. 31.   [86] *Ibid.* p. 71.
[87] Smith, *The Place-Names of the West Riding of Yorkshire* I, 95.
[88] Mawer and Stenton, *The Place-Names of Sussex* II, 365–6.
[89] Gover *et al.*, *The Place-Names of Devon* I, 221.
[90] Smith, *The Place-Names of the West Riding of Yorkshire* II, 290.

while the only major place-names cited by either Smith or Gelling from OE *weg* 'way' with an animal name are Shipway in Kent (OE *sceap* 'sheep') and Hartington in Northumberland (OE *heorot* 'hart, male deer').[91] In short, it would be difficult to find a type of animal that fits the overall profile of *pohha*-names so well as does the deer.

The problem with such an interpretation is that the deer has no apparent connection with a pouch or bag. Unlike the badger, whose physical shape may be imagined to resemble that of a bag, the deer is generally long-legged and agile, with no obviously pouch-like characteristics to account for a development of meaning from OE *pohha, pocca* 'a pouch, a bag'. Indeed, the entry for 'Family Cervidae/deer' in the *Historical Thesaurus of English*, a major new research tool presenting a conceptual and chronological listing of all recorded words in the English language from Anglo-Saxon times to the present day, shows no instances of deer being named in this way, although other aspects of appearance such as colour of coat (e.g. *blue-coat, fallow-deer, menald, red deer, white-tail*) are frequently alluded to.[92] The *Historical Thesaurus* data make it possible to establish that not only has the deer never been likened to a bag or pouch at any time in the recorded history of the English language, but neither has it ever been named according to perceived characteristics of fatness or bagginess which might help to explain or reflect such a comparison. A description of the animal as 'pouch-like' would be both unaccountable and unprecedented.

It may none the less be worth approaching the question from a different angle. As noted above, the element *pohha, pocca* is formally difficult to distinguish from a personal name *Pohha* or **Poca*, taken to derive from OE *pocc* 'smallpox', presumably with reference to the disfiguring spots borne by victims of the disease. The two terms are closely related. They are represented in the standard dictionary of Old English by contiguous entries for *pocc* 'a pock, pustule, ulcer'

[91] Smith, *English Place-Name Elements* II, 249, s.v. *weg* (b) (iii); Gelling, *Place-Names in the Landscape*, p. 84. Smith also notes the Old English charter spellings *horsweg* (BCS 299; S 1556) and *swinweg* (BCS 801; S 496). Identified in post-1956 volumes of the English Place-Name Survey are the lost field-names *Sterisweye* (1309) in Derbyshire (K. Cameron, *The Place-Names of Derbyshire*, 3 vols., EPNS 27–9 [Cambridge, 1959] III, 754), *Catwaye* (1591), *Cat-* (1301) and *Rotherewey* (1319) in Gloucestershire (Smith, *The Place-Names of Gloucestershire* IV, 184) and *Necway* (l.13th), *-wey* (e.15th) in Dorset (A. D. Mills, *The Place-Names of Dorset: Part II*, EPNS 53 (Cambridge, 1980), 130: 'first el[ement] probably *nēat* "cattle" ').

[92] For a description of the *Historical Thesaurus*, which is currently in preparation in the Department of English Language at the University of Glasgow, see C. Kay and I. Wotherspoon, '*Historical Thesaurus of English*', *Dictionaries of Medieval Germanic Languages: a Survey of Current Lexicographical Projects*, ed. K. H. van Dalen-Oskam, K. A. C. Depuydt, W. J. J. Pijnenburg and T. H. Schoonheim, International Med. Research 2 (Turnhout, 1997), pp. 47–54. I am particularly grateful to Mrs Flora Edmonds for her expert help and advice in using the *Historical Thesaurus* database.

and *pohha, poha, pohcha, pocca* 'a poke, pouch, bag',[93] both of which appear to derive from a common root referring to 'that which is blown out, or inflated'.[94] The development from 'pustule' to 'spot or mark' is a logical one, paralleled in Modern English by the various documented uses of the term *pock*.[95] An extended meaning as an animal name could therefore have arisen from this sense, referring not to a bag-shaped animal but to a spotted one. The usage would thus be similar to that recorded in the *Oxford English Dictionary* for the term *dapple*, attested from *a.*1635 in the sense 'An animal, as a horse or ass, with a mottled coat.'[96]

It seems unlikely to be a coincidence that spots are a distinguishing feature of young deer – so much so that the *Oxford English Dictionary* defines *deer* as 'The general name of a family (*Cervidæ*) of ruminant quadrupeds, distinguished by the possession of deciduous branching horns or antlers, and by the presence of spots on the young.'[97] It is particularly interesting to note in this connection that no demotic term for a young deer is preserved in the extant corpus of Old English literature. Neither is there a general term for the fallow deer, the variety whose spotted coat serves to differentiate it from the other two native species, the red deer and the roe deer.[98] The main research tool here is the *Thesaurus of Old English*, an offshoot of the *Historical Thesaurus* which presents a classified listing of recorded Old English vocabulary, making it possible not only to establish a range of vocabulary for particular concepts, but also to identify gaps in the available evidence by revealing areas of vocabulary which must have been familiar to the Anglo-Saxons but are largely unrepresented in the extant sources.[99] The entry for deer in the *Thesaurus of Old English* reads as follows:[100]

02.06.03.01.06 Deer, hart: heorot
.Of/concerning deer: heorten°
.A deerskin: heorþa[g]
.A young deer: hindcealf[g]
..Skin of a young deer: næsc
.A male deer: bucca, bucheort°[g]
..A stag: hēahdēor, stagga

[93] Bosworth, *An Anglo-Saxon Dictionary*, ed. Toller; Toller, *Supplement*, with addenda by Campbell, s.vv. Mr Victor Watts points out in a private communication that Toller is wrong to postulate a Celtic origin on the basis of related terms in Irish and Gaelic, since Gaelic *pòca, pòcaid*, Irish *póca, pócait* are borrowed from Modern English *poke, poket*.
[94] W. W. Skeat, *An Etymological Dictionary of the English Language* (Oxford, 1882), p. 453, s.vv. *pock, poke*. [95] *Oxford English Dictionary*, 2nd ed. (Oxford, 1989), s.v. *pock* sense 1 (a) and (b).
[96] *Ibid.* s.v. *dapple sb.* sense 3. [97] *Ibid.* s.v. *deer* 2.a.
[98] I owe this point to Professor Richard Coates.
[99] J. Roberts and C. Kay with L. Grundy, *A Thesaurus of Old English*, 2 vols. (London, 1995).
[100] *Ibid.* I, 85. The flag [g] is used to indicate a word form recorded in glossed texts or glossaries; the flag ° to indicate a word form recorded very infrequently.

..**A roebuck**: rā, rāhdēor
.**A female deer**: dā, hind
.**An elk**: eolh^g
.**A reindeer**: dēor, hrān, wilddēor
..**A reindeer as decoy**: stælhrān°

Three things are clear from this: first, that the Anglo-Saxons had a wide range of terms for different types of deer; secondly, that those recorded in the surviving sources relate almost exclusively to adult animals; and thirdly, that the majority refer to the red deer or the roe deer as opposed to the fallow deer. The only term for a young deer is *hindcealf*, attested only by gloss evidence,[101] while the only term for a fallow deer is *da*, referring to the female of the species. Demotic names for both the fawn and the male fallow deer must have existed, and it would not be unusual for such terms to be preserved in the onomastic corpus.[102] A previous attempt to establish the Old English term for a fallow deer was made by Ekwall, who identified the first element of Fawley in Berkshire and Fawsley in Northamptonshire as a substantive use of the adjective *fealu* 'fallow, pale brown, reddish yellow', possibly used either as the name of a forest 'fallow-coloured wood' or as the name of an animal 'fallow deer'.[103] Sufficient evidence is lacking to confirm either interpretation, as Gelling makes clear in her discussion of Fawley in the English Place-Name Survey for Berkshire;[104] but it remains possible that some occurrences of OE *fealu* in place-names refer to the fallow deer. Given the plethora of different terms for common birds and animals in Anglo-Saxon England,[105] this need not rule out a similar meaning for OE *pohha, pocca*, although it seems likely that the two concepts would have been differentiated in some way. Possibly OE *fealu* may have represented the general term for the species, OE *pohha, pocca* a more specialized term for the adult male or for the fawn. Since the word *fawn* itself is of Old French origin, entering the English language after the Norman Conquest,[106] it is axiomatic that it must have replaced an existing Old English word. The latter may plausibly be identified

---

[101] See also *Oxford English Dictionary*, s.v. *hind-calf*.

[102] A similar interpretation to the one I propose here for OE *pohha, pocca* may well underlie the first element of a West Riding field-name recorded in the twelfth century as *Frakildakelda* and attributed by the county editor to ME *fracled* 'spotted', a term otherwise unknown in English place-names (Smith, *The Place-Names of the West Riding of Yorkshire* VII, 189). The second element, ON *kelde* 'spring, well', is found elsewhere in combination with animal names, as in the field-names *Gosekeld* (1202) and *Musekelde* (1210) in the same county (*ibid.* VII, 214). The combination 'spotted spring or well' makes little sense, and I suspect that this may be an instance of an adjective used substantively to represent a spotted animal.

[103] Ekwall, *The Concise Oxford Dictionary of English Place-Names*, s.n. *Fawsley*.

[104] Gelling, *The Place-Names of Berkshire* II, 298, s.n. *Fawley*; III, 867, s.v. *fealu*.

[105] See for instance the wide variety of terms listed under individual animal names in Roberts *et al.*, *A Thesaurus of Old English* I, 81–6.

[106] T. F. Hoad, *The Concise Oxford Dictionary of English Etymology* (Oxford, 1986), p. 167, s.v. *fawn*[1].

with the diminutive form *pohhel, *poccel discussed above, indicating that *pohha, pocca* was the general term for the (male) adult animal.[107]

In conclusion, occurrences of OE *pohha, pocca* in place-names support an interpretation as an animal name, most probably designating a type of deer. While difficult to account for as an extended meaning of OE *pohha* 'pouch, bag', this may rather be associated with OE *pocc* 'spot', a distinguishing feature of the fallow deer and of its fawn. No term is on record for either the adult male or the young of this type of deer, although the Anglo-Saxons are known to have had a wide range of terms for different varieties of animals, including the red deer and the roe deer. An unattested OE *pohhel, *poccel also occurs in some place-names, and appears to represent a diminutive. I therefore suggest that OE *pohha, pocca* refers to a (?male) fallow deer, with the diminutive form OE *pohhel, *poccel designating the fawn.[108]

---

[107] This sense may also be represented in a later formation from the Middle English reflex of OE *pohha, pocca*. The Middle English compound *poke-aver* is defined in the *Middle English Dictionary*, ed. H. Kurath and S. M. Kuhn (Ann Arbor, MI, 1952–), s.v. *pōke-āver*, as 'A type of manorial rent [perh[aps] orig[inally] a service rent requiring provision of bags or other containers for (or as well as) carriage of goods]; ?land held by payment of such rent.' To the best of my knowledge, there are no documented instances of rent paid in the form of bags or containers. The payment of food-rent, on the other hand, in the form of provisions including livestock, is widely attested and has a long history. It therefore seems possible that ME *poke-aver* may refer to food-rent payable in the form of deer or venison.

[108] A version of this paper was read by invitation at the annual meeting of the English Place-Name Society on Wednesday 14 July 1999 in the rooms of the British Academy, 10 Carlton House Terrace, London SW1. I am grateful to those present for their comments.

Old sources, new resources: finding the right formula for Boniface

ANDY ORCHARD

Of all the many Anglo-Saxons who travelled to the Continent, some never to return, Boniface, apostle to the Germans, arguably had the deepest and most enduring influence; for some, he is simply 'the greatest Englishman'.[1] But aside from Boniface's historical importance there is much of related interest for scholars of Anglo-Saxon literary culture too: not only does a wealth of hagiographical material survive relating to Boniface and his mission, but there remain a number of letters, poems, and other works written by Boniface himself, alongside a wide range of associated texts.[2] Yet while the literary contexts and merits of (for example) Boniface's poetry have been discussed a number of times in recent years,[3] the primary academic focus on the so-called 'Bonifatian correspondence' has tended to be historical, rather than literary. Such a focus has tended to privilege those letters with political or administrative implications above those that deal with more domestic or personal issues, yet it is precisely the latter category which shows the less formal aspects of Anglo-Saxon literary culture, and seems to invite closer comparison with a range of

---

[1] See the collection edited by T. Reuter, *The Greatest Englishman: Essays on St Boniface and the Church at Crediton* (Exeter, 1981). For the historical background, see too W. Levison, *England and the Continent in the Eighth Century* (Oxford, 1946); J. M. Wallace-Hadrill, 'A Background to St Boniface's Mission', *England before the Conquest: Studies in Primary Sources presented to Dorothy Whitelock*, ed. P. Clemoes and K. Hughes (Cambridge, 1971), pp. 35–48; T. Schieffer, *Winfrid-Bonifatius und die christliche Grundlegung Europas*, rev. ed. (Darmstadt, 1972). Still useful for bibliography and basic orientation is the volume of essays collected as *Sankt Bonifatius: Gedankengabe zum zwölfhundersten Todestag* (Fulda, 1954).

[2] For an overview, see G. Greenaway, 'Saint Boniface as a Man of Letters', *Greatest Englishman*, ed. Reuter, pp. 33–46; see too R. Sharpe, *A Handlist of the Latin Writers of Great Britain and Ireland Before 1540*, Publ. of the Jnl of Med. Latin 1 (Turnhout, 1997), 79–80 (no. 166); M. Lapidge, 'Anglo-Latin Literature', in his *Anglo-Latin Literature 600–899* (London, 1996), pp. 11–12. As a sidelight on Boniface's literary interests, it is intriguing to note that M. B. Parkes, 'The Handwriting of St Boniface: a Reassessment of the Problems', *Beiträge zur Geschichte der deutschen Sprache und Literatur* 48 (1976), 161–79, believes that he has identified Boniface's own hand in several manuscripts; for a wider and more cautious view, see M. Lapidge, 'Autographs of Insular Latin Authors of the Early Middle Ages', *Gli autografi medievali: problemi paleografici e filologici*, ed. P. Chiesa and L. Pinelli (Spoleto, 1995), pp. 103–36, at 108–15.

[3] A. Orchard, 'After Aldhelm: the Teaching and Transmission of the Anglo-Latin Hexameter', *Jnl of Med. Latin* 2 (1992), 96–133, at 103–7; *idem, The Poetic Art of Aldhelm*, CSASE 8 (Cambridge, 1994), 64–7 and 275–8.

15

other texts.[4] In particular, the innately repetitious and formulaic quality of much of the correspondence has much in common with that of several other areas of Anglo-Saxon literature in both Latin and Old English, whether in prose or verse, and this article seeks to explore those links in detail, in order to offer a broader literary context for the composition of the correspondence as a whole.

The term 'Bonifatian correspondence' is itself something of a misnomer:[5] the 150 texts edited by Tangl that still comprise the standard edition certainly focus on Boniface and his German mission, but in fact span almost a century, from the last quarter of the seventh century to the last quarter of the eighth.[6] Not all the texts edited are letters,[7] however, and Tangl's selection is idiosyncratic in other ways. The edited collection is mainly derived from three manuscripts,[8] of which the best-known and most relevant for the following discussion is Vienna, Nationalbibliothek, lat. 751 (Mainz, s. ix^med),[9] which seems to stem directly from material apparently collected at the instigation of Lul, Boniface's successor as archbishop of Mainz.[10] Tangl's arrangement of material obscures a number of important features of the individual manuscripts, and the edited collection is clearly derived from a number of disparate sources. So, for example, the Vienna manuscript contains none of the thirty letters from various

---

[4] See, for example, P. Dronke, *Women Writers of the Middle Ages* (Cambridge, 1984), pp. 30–5; U. Schaefer, 'Two Women in Need of a Friend: a Comparison of *The Wife's Lament* and Eangyth's Letter to Boniface', *Germanic Dialects: Linguistic and Philological Investigations*, ed. B. Brogyanyi and T. Krömmelbein (Amsterdam, 1986), pp. 491–524; C. E. Fell, 'Some Implications of the Boniface Correspondence', *New Readings on Women in Old English Literature*, ed. H. Damico and A. H. Olsen (Bloomington, IN, 1990), pp. 29–43; P. Sims-Williams, 'Letter-Writing', in his *Religion and Literature in Western England, 600–800*, CSASE 3 (Cambridge, 1990), 211–42.

[5] See Fell, 'Some Implications', pp. 30–1.

[6] *Die Briefe des heiligen Bonifatius und Lullus*, ed. M. Tangl, MGH, Epist. select. 1, 2nd ed. (Berlin, 1955). All citations from the Bonifatian correspondence below are taken from this edition, together with Tangl's suggested dating. Tangl's text is substantially adopted, with facing-page German translation, in *Bonifatii Epistulae. Willibaldi Vita Bonifatii. Briefe des Bonifatius, Willibalds Leben des Bonifatius*, ed. and trans. R. Rau, Ausgewählte Quellen zur deutschen Geschichte des Mittelalters 4b (Darmstadt, 1968). English translations of part of the Bonifatian correspondence are found in C. H. Talbot, *The Anglo-Saxon Missionaries in Germany* (London, 1954); E. Emerton, *The Letters of Saint Boniface* (New York, 1940); E. Kylie, *The English Correspondence of Saint Boniface* (London, 1911).

[7] Also included are (for example) synodal *acta* (Tangl 59), prayer-formulas (Tangl 149), formulas for the lists of the dead (Tangl 150), an oath attributed to Boniface (Tangl 16), and five *carmina rhythmica* attributed to Aldhelm and his pupil, Æthilwald (Tangl 6).

[8] For an overview of the manuscript tradition, see Tangl, *Die Briefe*, pp. vi–xxxi.

[9] There is a useful facsimile of the Vienna manuscript by F. Unterkircher, *Sancti Bonifacii Epistolae. Codex Vindobonensis 751 der österreichischen Nationalbibliothek*, Codices Selecti Phototypice Impressi 24 (Graz, 1971).

[10] Cf. Fell's description of Lul as 'the mastermind behind the assembling of materials which the compiler of this codex used' ('Some Implications', p. 35).

16

popes that Tangl includes in his tally,[11] but all bar one of the twenty-nine (some, indeed, in multiple copies) are found in one or both of the other two major manuscripts, Munich, Staatsbibliothek, lat. 8112 (Mainz, s. viii/ix), and Karlsruhe, Badische Landesbibliothek, Rastatt 22 (Mainz, s. ix^{med}).[12] Likewise, all four of the letters sent from Boniface to either Pope Zacharias or Pope Stephen II are in both the Munich and Karlsruhe manuscripts, but only two are also found in Vienna 751.[13] By contrast, of the nine signed letters from Lul in the collection, all are found in Vienna 751,[14] but only four in the Karlsruhe manuscript, and none at all in the Munich manuscript. Vienna 751 also contains some fifty-three letters which are unattested in either of the other two main manuscripts, including many of the personal and less formal letters that are the main focus of attention here.[15]

The letters found in the Vienna manuscript fall into three distinct sections, comprising some (but by no means all) of the extant letters that make up the Aldhelm correspondence,[16] those letters contemporary with Boniface himself, and a large number which might more properly be said to belong to the next generation of missionaries, of whom Lul himself is undoubtedly the most conspicuous. Broadly speaking, Tangl 1–6 comprise the Aldhelm (and Aldhelm-related) material: Tangl 6 constitutes the five separate octosyllabic *Carmina rhythmica* now attributed to Aldhelm and his pupil Æthilwald;[17] Tangl 9–109 largely constitute the collection of letters produced during Boniface's own lifetime, and span the period 716–54; Tangl 110–42 comprise letters produced after Boniface's death in 754; Tangl 143–50 are undated. Within the second of these major groupings of texts from the Vienna manuscript, namely the letters belonging to Boniface's own lifetime, Tangl has interleaved the thirty-three letters by or to a succession of popes.

The collection as a whole, therefore, while in one sense it clearly charts the history of the Anglo-Saxon mission in Germany, none the less seems also

---

[11]   The letters in question are Tangl 12, 17–26, 42–5, 51–3, 57–8, 60–1, 68, 77, 80, 82–3 and 87–9; Tangl 20 is in none of the three main manuscripts.

[12]   So, for example, Tangl 11 (Daniel to Boniface) and 22 (Charles Martell to his dependent nobles) are found on both 51v–52r and (in reverse order) 107v–108r of the Karlsruhe manuscript; Tangl 23 (Daniel to Boniface) is likewise found on 79v and 113v of the Munich manuscript.   [13]   The letters in question are Tangl 50, 86 and 108–9.

[14]   The letters in question are Tangl 70–2, 92, 100, 113, 125–6 and 128.

[15]   The letters in question are Tangl 1–5, 7–8, 37, 39, 55, 72, 92, 98, 102, 106, 110–27 and 129–48. I have not included Tangl 6 and 149–50 in this tally, although they too are not found in either of the other two main manuscripts, because they are not letters.

[16]   For a useful overview, with translations, see M. Lapidge and M. Herren, *Aldhelm: the Prose Works* (Cambridge, 1979), pp. 136–70 and 197–203; the letters themselves are edited by R. Ehwald, *Aldhelmi Opera*, MGH Auct. antiq. 15 (Berlin, 1919), 474–503.

[17]   For the attribution, see the remarks of M. Lapidge in *Aldhelm: the Prose Works*, pp. 16–18; see further Orchard, *Poetic Art of Aldhelm*, pp. 19–72.

(indeed primarily) to have been intended to offer a kind of epistolary pattern-book for a range of occasions.[18] This conclusion seems especially appropriate in the case of the Vienna manuscript. All sixteen of the letters where the sender is unnamed or indicated by the siglum '.N.' (for *nomen*, 'name', the Latin version of 'X' or 'insert name here'), are found in Vienna 751, but only two of these are also attested elsewhere;[19] likewise, all thirteen of the letters in which the recipient is unnamed or represented by '.N.' are witnessed in the Vienna manuscript, while only two of these are also found in one or other of the other main manuscripts.[20] Another letter to Boniface (Tangl 15, found in all three main manuscripts) explicitly underlines this point: here, Bugga asks Boniface to offer masses for the soul of her dear relative 'who was dearer to me than all others, whose name was .N.' ('similiter deposco, ut sanctarum missarum oblationes offere digneris pro anima mei propinqui, qui mihi pre ceteris carus erat, cui nomen erat .N.'). It seems safer to suppose that this letter has been preserved primarily as a literary model and that the person echoing the phrase was to fill in the blank than that at the crucial moment of naming her nearest and dearest, Bugga, overcome with emotion, simply forgot. Such a letter, in fact, offers a perfect template for a later writer wishing to spice up his or her own letter of grief or longing, and the range of stock situations encapsulated by the anonymous letters is certainly instructive. Among the topics covered in the letters in which one or both of the recipient or sender are unnamed are: consolation for illness (Tangl 37); a request for clothing and news (Tangl 79); news of a pilgrimage (Tangl 98); a request to be allowed study-leave (Tangl 103); discussions of a vision (Tangl 115) or of the art of poetry (Tangl 98); a reminder of former friendship (Tangl 135); further requests for prayers (Tangl 66, 102 and 140), parchment (Tangl 142), or books (Tangl 145); thanks for books (Tangl 31); general good wishes (Tangl 141); but mostly complaints about solitude, suffering and isolation (Tangl 98, 102, 143 and 147–8). But if the same general themes and situations tend to recur, the derivative, repetitious and innately formulaic

---

[18] For a useful overview of the function of medieval letter-collections, see G. Constable, *Letters and Letter-Collections*, Typologie des sources du moyen âge occidental 17 (Turnhout, 1971), and J. Haseldine, 'Epistolography', *Medieval Latin: an Introduction and Bibliographical Guide*, ed. F. A. C. Mantello and A. G. Rigg (Washington, DC, 1996), pp. 650–8.

[19] The letters in question are Tangl 4 (properly part of the Aldhelm correspondence), 37, 79, 98, 103, 110, 115, 135, 140–6 and 148. Tangl 79 is also found in the Karlsruhe manuscript, while Tangl 103 is also attested in both the Karlsruhe and Munich manuscripts. Tangl 143, uniquely preserved in the Vienna manuscript, has '.N.' for the recipent, and 'H.' for the sender; it seems most likely that in this case 'H.' represents a copying error for '.N.'. The letter itself is discussed in detail below, pp. 37–8.

[20] The letters in question are Tangl 31, 66, 98, 102, 110, 115 and 140–6; Tangl 31 is also found in the Karlsruhe manuscript, while Tangl 66 is also attested in both the Karlsruhe and Munich manuscripts.

nature of the surviving Bonifatian correspondence can likewise to some extent be gleaned from a glance at Tangl's extensive *apparatus fontium*,[21] and comparison with a number of recently produced electronic databases and machine-readable corpora of texts only highlights the complex nexus of traditional and formulaic phrasing employed.[22]

Recent research has tended to highlight the fact that formulaic composition, once thought a sign of oral composition, is in fact found widely in Anglo-Saxon literature, including that produced by highly literate authors composing in both Latin and Old English. Although the bulk of research still tends to focus on for-mulaic composition in Old English poetry, in fact the same techniques of analy-sis, employing machine-readable texts and computer-generated concordances, have been applied successfully to (for example) the Latin poetry of Aldhelm or the Old English prose of Wulfstan.[23] Such research has allowed direct compari-sons to be made between shared techniques of formulaic composition across the whole range of Anglo-Saxon literature, whether in Old English or Latin, and whether in prose or verse. There is at present abundant evidence of such tech-niques being employed in the composition of Old English poetry, Old English homiletic prose and Anglo-Latin hexameter verse; the Bonifatian correspon-dence, with its large and largely self-contained number of correspondents, many of whom were interrelated both literally and by letter, provides a perfect corpus for considering techniques of formulaic composition in Anglo-Latin prose.[24]

---

[21] For a useful preliminary analysis of repeated diction in the Bonifatian correspondence, see too H. Hahn, 'Ueber einige Briefe der Bonifazischen Sammlung mit unbestimmter Adresse', *Forschungen zur deutschen Geschichte* 21 (1881), 383–400.

[22] The most useful electronic tools for this purpose are *eMGH-2: Die elektronischen Monumenta Germaniae Historica auf CD-ROM* (Turnhout, 2000) [the Bonifatian correspondence is also on *eMGH-1* (Turnhout, 1996)]; *Fontes Anglo-Saxonici: a Register of Written Sources Used by Authors in Anglo-Saxon England* [http://fontes.english.ox.ac.uk/]; *Cetedoc Library of Christian-Latin Texts 4* (Turnhout, 2000); the *Patrologia Latina Database* [http://pld.chadwyck.com/].

[23] The potential bibliography on the topic is vast: see in particular M. Lapidge, 'Aldhelm's Latin Poetry and Old English Verse', *Comparative Lit.* 31 (1979), 249–314; J. M. Foley, *Oral-Formulaic Theory and Research: an Introduction and Annotated Bibliography* (New York, 1985); F. P. Magoun, Jr, 'The Oral-Formulaic Character of Anglo-Saxon Narrative Poetry', *Speculum* 28 (1953), 446–67; A. H. Olsen, 'Oral-Formulaic Research in Old English Studies: I', *Oral Tradition* 1 (1986), 548–606 and 'Oral-Formulaic Research in Old English Studies: II', *Oral Tradition* 3 (1988), 138–90; A. Orchard, 'Crying Wolf: Oral Style and the *Sermones Lupi*', *ASE* 21 (1992), 239–64; A. Orchard, 'Oral Tradition', *Approaches to Reading Old English Texts*, ed. K. O'Brien O'Keeffe (Cambridge, 1997), pp. 101–23; A. Orchard, 'Both Style and Substance: the Case for Cynewulf', *Anglo-Saxon Styles*, ed. C. E. Karkov and G. H. Brown (Albany, NY, forthcoming).

[24] I am in the process of compiling an extensive series of linked databases, provisionally entitled 'An Anglo-Saxon Formulary', which will exhaustively document formulaic phrasing in four key areas of Anglo-Saxon literature, namely: (1) Old English poetry; (2) Anglo-Latin hexameter verse; (3) the Old English sermons of Wulfstan; (4) the Anglo-Latin letters of the Bonifatian correspondence.

Now, of course letters are (even today) innately formulaic, and many of the conventional epistolary formulas are essentially just that; but, as will become clear, the Bonifatian circle (on the Continent at least) comprises a peculiarly tight and idiosyncratic group of essentially isolated correspondents, who in the course of the first three decades of their mission apparently developed what is effectively almost a private language, deliberately echoing and reshaping the same words and the same themes. It is as if a group of individuals had read precisely the same handful of books, from which they endlessly (and progressively loosely) quote, until they end up quoting not the original texts, but their own quotations. The overwhelming impression to be derived from these texts is the profound sense of exile and of isolation, precisely those stock themes which Anglo-Saxon poets were to develop so movingly (and so formulaically) in vernacular Old English verse.[25] It is perhaps not surprising, then, that the most recent literary studies of the Boniface correspondence should all point up parallels with Old English texts like *The Wife's Lament*, *Wulf and Eadwacer* and *The Wanderer*.[26] Like these texts, alongside which they certainly deserve further study, the letters of the Bonifatian correspondence offer the authentic voice of Anglo-Saxon angst.

We can see a number of these basic points illustrated in a brief letter from Boniface to Eadburg, formerly identified as the abbess of Minster-in-Thanet, although Patrick Sims-Williams has suggested that Wimbourne seems a more likely venue.[27] The text below (Tangl 30) is essentially that edited by Tangl,[28] who dates it to the period 735 × 736, with biblical quotations presented in italics, and some parallels with others of the extant letters of the Bonifatian correspondence underlined:[29]

---

[25] A useful collection of five articles on the theme of exile in Old English poetry appears in S. B. Greenfield, *Hero and Exile: the Art of Old English Poetry*, ed. G. H. Brown (London, 1989), pp. 197–228. See too L. H. Frey, 'Exile and Elegy in Anglo-Saxon Christian Epic Poetry', *JEGP* 62 (1963), 293–302; M. Rissanen, 'The Theme of "Exile" in *The Wife's Lament*', *NM* 70 (1969), 90–104.   [26] See above, n. 4.

[27] See P. Sims-Williams, 'An Unpublished Seventh- or Eighth-Century Anglo-Latin Letter in Boulogne-sur-Mer MS 74', *MÆ* 48 (1979), 1–22, at p. 22, n. 119.

[28] Here and for the other letters cited, I have silently corrected Tangl's *v* to *u* throughout, and in a number of cases preferred the readings of the Vienna manuscript, as checked against Unterkircher's facsimile edition (see above, n. 9).

[29] Parallels:

Lucerna pedibus meis uerbum tuum et lumen semitis meis	Ps. CXVIII.105
praeuenerunt me laquei mortis	Ps. XVII.6
Dominus Deus noster qui in excelsis habitans humilia respicit	Ps. CXII.5–6
sermo in apertione oris mei	Eph. VI.19
ut sermo Domini currat et clarificetur	II Thess. III.1
peccatis . . . exigentibus	Gregory, *Moralia in Job* XIV.xxxvii.9, XXXIV.xv.110, etc.
periculoso saeculi naufragio et grassante dirae tempestatis turbine . . . nauigantes ad portum	Aldhelm, Prose *De uirginitate* 238.18–19

Dilectissime sorori et iamdudum <u>spiritalis</u> clientele <u>propinquitate conexe</u> Eadburge
abbatisse Bonifatius <u>seruus seruorum Dei perennem in Christo salutem</u>. Carissimam
sororem <u>remunerator</u> aeternus iustorum <u>operum in superna</u> letificet <u>curia angelorum</u>,
quae sanctorum librorum <u>munera</u> transmittendo exulem Germanicum spiritali lumine
consolata est, quia, qui tenebrosos angulos <u>Germanicarum gentium lustrare</u> debet,   5
nisi habeat *lucernam pedibus et lumen semitis suis uerbum* Domini, in *laqueum mortis*
incidet. Preterea de caritate tua diligenter confidens obsecro, ut pro me orare
digneris, quia <u>peccatis</u> meis <u>exigentibus periculosi maris tempestatibus quatior</u>;
rogans, ut ille, qui *in altis habitat et humilia respicit*, indulgens flagitia prestet mihi
uerbum *in apertione oris mei, ut currat et clarificetur* inter gentes euangelium   10
gloriae Christi.

To the most beloved Abbess Eadburg, for long linked by the close bond of spiritual
dependency, Boniface, the servant of God's servants, sends endless greetings in Christ.
May the eternal rewarder of just deeds make the most dear sister joyful in the celestial
band of angels, since she has cheered up with spiritual light a Germanic exile by sending
gifts of sacred books, since, as he has to travel round [or 'enlighten'] the dark corners of
the Germanic gentiles, unless he had the Lord's word as a lamp for his feet and a light on
his paths, he would fall into death's snare. Trusting, moreover, faithfully in your love, I
beseech you to deign to pray for me, since I am buffeted by my exacting sins like the
storms of a perilous sea, asking that he who dwells on high and looks on the lowly
should pity my shame and grant me a word in the opening of my mouth, so that the
gospel of Christ's glory should course and shine among the gentiles.

This letter constitutes a typical piece of what might be termed 'off-duty' Boniface:
light, witty and learned. The whole text could be paraphrased: 'Dear Eadburg,
thanks for the books; pray for me. Best wishes, Boniface'; in short, it appears little
more than an elegant letter of thanks. But there is much more, of a much more
subtle nature, which Boniface apparently expected his learned correspondent to

Que sine ullo naufragio periculose tempestatis nauem animae nostrae gubernans deducet ad amoenissimi litus paradisi et ad perpetua supernorum gaudia angelorum	Boniface to Nithard (Tangl 9; dated 716 × 717)
adfinitatis propinquitate conexo	Leofgyth to Boniface (Tangl 29; dated 732)
Germanicum mare periculosum nauigantibus	Boniface to Pehthelm (Tangl 32; dated 735)
Germanicarum gentium tempestatum fluctibus quassatam	Boniface to Nothelm (Tangl 33; dated 735)
Germanici maris tempestatibus undique quassantibus	Boniface to Duddo (Tangl 34; dated 735)
ne fluctibus Germanicarum tempestatum submergatur	Boniface to Aldhere (Tangl 38; dated 732 × 754)
conuersatio peregrinationis nostrae uariis tempestatibus inliditur	Boniface to Eadburg (Tangl 65; dated 742 × 746)
remuneratorem omnium bonorum operum	Boniface to Eadburg (Tangl 35; dated 735)
in superna curia beatorum angelorum restituat	Boniface to Eadburg (Tangl 35; dated 735)
spiritalis germanitatis propinquitate conexo	Boniface to unknown (Tangl 31; dated 735 × 736)

comprehend. In only eleven printed lines (and only twelve lines in the Vienna manuscript), Boniface fits in no fewer than five separate biblical allusions, carefully divided into two groups, separating his allusions to those parts of the Old and New Testaments respectively which most closely echo his thoughts of exile and his request for support in his evangelizing mission, namely the Psalms and the Pauline Epistles.[30] These five biblical allusions are together found a total of fourteen times in the entire Bonifatian correspondence, but on all but one occasion are apparently cited by Boniface himself.[31]

In this letter there is also a likely nod towards patristic sources, in a single arresting stock phrase (*peccatis . . . exigentibus*, line 8), ultimately perhaps traceable to Gregory the Great,[32] whose name and works are explicitly mentioned by Boniface on a number of occasions, and whose role as sponsor of the Augustinian mission to the English must have made him a particularly attractive role-model for Boniface.[33] Boniface repeats the tag elsewhere in his own correspondence, and again it becomes almost his own personal trademark: five of the six examples of the phrase are his.[34] A further faint debt to Aldhelm, from

---

[30] Tangl, *Die Briefe*, pp. 315–17, lists almost 450 biblical parallels and quotations in the edited correspondence as a whole, of which more than a third occur in Boniface's own letters. Of these more than 150 citations, references to the Psalms (I count twenty-one examples) and to the (mostly Pauline) Epistles (I count sixty examples) clearly predominate, and demonstrate Boniface's (understandable) preferences and preoccupations.

[31] So, for example, alongside the five parallels noted here, allusions to Ps. CXII.5–6 are also found in Tangl 31 (Boniface to an unidentified correspondent); to Eph. VI.19 in Tangl 31, 76 (Boniface to Abbot Hwætberht of Monkwearmouth–Jarrow), and 101 (Wihtberht to the monks of Glastonbury); to II Thess. III.1 in Tangl 31, 46 (Boniface to the English bishops), 67 (Boniface to Leofgyth, Tecla and Cynehild), 76 and 106 (Boniface to Abbot Optatus of Montecassino).

[32] The *Patrologia Latina Database* also lists Augustine as a possible source: the phrase is widely quoted.

[33] So, for example, in a letter to Nothhelm (Tangl 33; dated 735), Boniface asks for a copy of the exchange between Gregory and Augustine, Apostle to the English; in a letter to Cuthbert, Boniface mentions Gregory's *Regula pastoralis* (Tangl 78; dated 747); Gemmulus writes to Boniface (Tangl 54; dated 742 × 743) apologizing for not sending a copy of Gregory's *Epistolae*, but Gemmulus (or another correspondent) appears to have been ultimately successful, since in another letter to Archbishop Ecgberht of York (Tangl 75; dated 746 × 747), Boniface mentions that he is sending copies of some of Gregory's *Epistolae* that he has obtained from the papal archives; and Gregory's name is invoked in both Boniface's letter of rebuke to King Æthelbald of Mercia (Tangl 73; dated 746 × 747) and a letter to Pope Zacharias (Tangl 50; dated 742); Pope Zacharias quotes Gregory back at Boniface in a later letter (Tangl 60; dated 745).

[34] The letters in question are Tangl 31 (Boniface to an unidentified correspondent; dated 735 × 736) and 65–7 (all dated 742 × 746, and consisting of a series of letters requesting prayers from a range of female correspondents, including Eadburg); all three of the group Tangl 65–7 are linked by parallel expressions, although interestingly Tangl 66 in fact reads *meritis* for *peccatis* at this point. The only other letter in the collected correspondence to include the phrase is among the earliest, from Ecgburg to Boniface (Tangl 13; dated 716 × 718), and it is intriguing

whom elsewhere Boniface borrows very frequently,[35] is likewise evident in the storm-image of line 8; but four further examples of the same theme in Boniface's own letters once more illustrate the extent to which Boniface adopted and adapted images and phrases from his sources to make them his own. It will be clear from Boniface's letter to Nithard (dated 715 × 717) that he has lifted much of Aldhelm's material verbatim (note in particular that the borrowed words *naufragio periculose tempestatis* appear in sequence); but the noted passages from Boniface's letters to Pehthelm, Nothhelm and Duddo, like the one to Eadburg, are more like each other than they are either to the letter to Nithard or to Aldhelm's original.

The other striking thing about this letter is the number of phraseological parallels it shares with other letters sent by Boniface to Eadburg; a number of such parallels are given in the note, but a wider tissue of reminiscences appears to link all his letters to Eadburg still further. It is almost as if Boniface has developed a series of private topics, themes and in-jokes which he shares with Eadburg alone. It is interesting in this respect that it is only in another letter to Eadburg that Boniface uses the Latin verb *lustro* (as here, line 5), since in this letter it would seem that Boniface is playing on the two senses of the verb, which means both to 'light up, to illuminate', and 'to travel around, to traverse'; the same pun is employed to great effect by both Aldhelm and Vergil, to name but two authors with whose works Boniface was well acquainted.[36] The twin notions of illumination and travel are very cleverly enshrined by Boniface in two biblical allusions, one from the Old Testament and one from the New Testament: *lucernam pedibus et lumen semitis*, line 6 and *currat et clarificetur*, line 10. The effect is further highlighted by the essentially chiastic arrangement of ideas. Such punning or wordplay is of course very common in Old English poetry alongside the repetition of words or word-roots that in classical rhetoric is called paronomasia or polyptoton,[37] so it is further interesting that Boniface should indulge in the same game here, repeating *Germanicum*, line 4 and *Germanicarum*, line 5, to stress (as he does frequently) the essential bond of racial brotherhood (*germanitas*) that links the Anglo-Saxon exile to his gentile charges, and changing the *sermo* of both his

(though perhaps unlikely, given its wide currency) to speculate that it is from Ecgburg that Boniface derives the phrase.

[35] See, for example, the *apparatus fontium* for Tangl 9, 10, 33, 66, 75, 78, 86 and 91; for Boniface's heavy reliance on Aldhelm in the composition of his metrical verse, see too Orchard, 'After Aldhelm', pp. 103–7, and *The Poetic Art of Aldhelm*, pp. 66–7 and 245–6.

[36] See, for example, Vergil, *Aeneid* IV.6 and VII.148; Aldhelm, *Carmen de uirginitate* 181 and *Praefatio* to the *Enigmata*, line 20.

[37] The standard study of paronomasia in Old English remains R. Frank, 'Some Uses of Paronomasia in Old English Scriptural Verse', *Speculum* 47 (1972), 207–26; see too the collection of related articles in F. C. Robinson, *The Tomb of Beowulf and Other Essays on Old English* (Oxford, 1993), pp. 185–235.

New Testament allusions to the (more appropriate) *uerbum* (line 10) presumably to echo the utterly biblical *uerbum* (line 6) of his first Old Testament citation.[38] It will be clear from the above discussion of one brief letter that (at least occasionally) Boniface was a rather splendid and subtle prose-stylist, whose works perhaps deserve more literary attention than they have received so far.

But if the qualities of this letter to Eadburg have eluded modern critics, the same cannot be said for Boniface's contemporaries: Tangl 30 is one of forty-four letters common to all three main manuscripts, preserved presumably, at least in part, for its stylistic qualities.[39] Interestingly, however, practically the same letter appears elsewhere in the Vienna and Karlsruhe manuscripts (Tangl 31, dated 735 × 736):[40]

Reuerentissimo fratri et spiritalis germanitatis propinquitate conexo Bonifatius exiguus seruus seruorum Dei perennem in Christo caritatis salutem. Clementiam fraternitatis uestrae intimis flagitamus precibus, ut nostrae mediocritatis memores intercedere dignemini, quia peccatis nostris exigentibus periculosi maris tempestatibus undique quatimur; rogantes, ut illae, qui in altis habitat et humilia respicit, indulgens flagitia prestet nobis uerbum in apertione oris nostri, ut currat et clarificetur inter gentes euangelium gloriae Christi.

5

To a most reverend brother and one linked by the bond of spiritual brotherhood, Boniface, the lowly servant of the servants of God, sends an eternal greeting of love in Christ. We beg the mercy of your brotherhood with heartfelt prayers, that, mindful of our mediocrity, you deign to intercede, since we are buffeted on all sides by our exacting sins like the storms of a perilous sea, asking that he who dwells on high and looks on the lowly should pity our shame and grant us a word in the opening of our mouth, so that the gospel of Christ's glory should course and shine among the gentiles.

The message is essentially the same as that of Boniface's letter to Eadburg quoted above (Tangl 30), focusing on the general request for prayers rather than thanks for books. Moreover, the second half of the letter to the anonymous correspondent (from line 4 onwards: *quia peccatis . . . gloriae Christi*) echoes that to Eadburg practically verbatim, with the substitution of four first-person plural forms (*nostris . . . quatimur . . . nobis . . . nostri*) for the corresponding first-person singular forms of the letter to Eadburg (*meis . . . quatior . . . mihi . . . mei*), to match two earlier first-person plural references in line 3 (*flagitamus . . . nostrae*),[41]

---

[38] One might also note the paronomastic juxtaposition of *remunerator* and *munera*.

[39] The relevant letters are Tangl 9–11, 13–15, 22–3, 27, 29–30, 32–6, 40–1, 47, 56, 63, 65–7, 69, 73–6, 78, 81, 91, 93–7, 99, 103–5 and 107–9; note that all four of Boniface's extant letters to Eadburg (Tangl 10, 30, 35 and 65) are included in this number.

[40] For parallels, see above, n. 29, and below, fig. 2, together with the following:
intercedere dignemini   Lul (?) to Boniface (Tangl 103; dated 739 × 741);
intercedere dignemini [*twice*]   Boniface to Daniel (Tangl 63; dated 742 × 746)

[41] Likewise the 'extra' forms *uestrae* and *dignemini* are (second-person) plural, and *rogantes* is in concord with *flagitamus*.

and the addition of the word *undique* in line 5.[42] The first few lines of the letter, however, are simply a confection of a number of Boniface's own opening epistolary formulas, as can be seen from fig. 2 below. Fig. 2 focuses on just two of a large number of opening formulas found in the Bonifatian correspondence, but again underlines the close interrelationships that extend throughout the collection; Tangl 31 is one of eight letters that is on both lists (Tangl 32–3, 38, 70, 76, 91 and 108 are the others). The first formula is restricted to the opening salutation of the individual letters, and is perhaps best described as the *exiguus*-formula, since besides the (almost) mandatory term *salutem*, the adjective *exiguus* is the only significant shared word.[43] The second formula, designated here the *clementiam*-formula, is considerably more complex, comprising as it does a combination of the key term *clementiam* in conjunction with an honorific abstract noun in the genitive, linked to a verb of asking or requiring which is itself combined with an adverbial phrase containing the form *precibus* (modified on sixteen out of seventeen occasions by the adjective *intimis*). Fig. 2 lists the significant examples of these two formulas in the entire corpus of the Bonifatian correspondence, and a number of interesting patterns emerge.

Of more than forty named individuals whose works comprise the Bonifatian correspondence, these particular opening formulas are all but restricted to Boniface and Lul (his successor as archbishop of Mainz):[44] nor are precise parallels for any of these formulas found in any earlier biblical, patristic or Anglo-Latin letters. With respect to the *exiguus*-formula, Boniface favours some form of *in christo . . . salutem* without exception,[45] while as part of this formula Lul adopts *in domino . . . salutem* twice (Tangl 70 and 100), and only takes over the

---

[42] Cf. the addition of the word *undique* in the parallel phrase in Boniface's letter to Duddo, noted above.

[43] A notable exception occurs in the opening to Lul's letter threatening excommunication to the Abbess Switha (Tangl 128; dated 754 × 786), which, presumably in keeping with its tone of stern rebuke, has no other salutation than 'Lul, a lowly and humble prelate, to Switha and her subordinates' ('Lullus exiguus atque humilis antestis Suithan eiusque subiectis').

[44] Apart from the letters cited, it is perhaps worth noting that Boniface describes himself as *exiguus* at the end of his oath of office (Tangl 16; dated 722). A simpler form of the *clementiam*-formula is found at the openings of Tangl 29 (*Rogo tuam clementiam* [Leofgyth to Boniface; dated 732]); Tangl 49 (*Agnoscere cupimus almitatis tuae clementiam* [Denehard, Lul and Burghard; dated 739 × 741]); Tangl 69 (*Obsecramus celsitudinis tuae clementiam* [Boniface to King Æthelbald; dated 745 × 746]); Tangl 107 (*Celsitudinis uestrae clementiae magnas gratias agimus* [Boniface to King Pippin; dated 753]). Versions of the *clementiam*-formula are also found within the body of the letter (generally signalling the beginning of a new section) in Tangl 73 (*obsecramus . . . clementiam tuam* [Boniface to King Æthelbald; dated 746 × 747]); Tangl 93 (*almitatis uestrae clementiae diligenter . . . deprecor* [Boniface to Fulrad; dated 752]); Tangl 117 (*omnipotentis Dei clementiam obnixis exorare precibus* [Bregowine to Lul; dated 759 × 765]).

[45] Indeed, thirty-two of the thirty-seven extant letters of Boniface begin with some form of *in Christo . . . salutem*; the exceptions are Tangl 40, 50, 69, 95 and 107.

Fig. 2   Two opening formulas in the Bonifatian correspondence

(a) The *exiguus*-formula

No.	Date	From	To	Formula
10	716	Boniface	Eadburg	Uuynfrethus exiguus in Christo Iesu intimae caritatis salutem
27	pre-738	Boniface	Bugga	Bonifatius exiguus indignus episcopus aeternam in Christo salutem
31	735 × 736	Boniface	[unknown]	Bonifatius exiguus seruus seruorum Dei perennem in Christo caritatis salutem
32	735	Boniface	Pecthelm	Bonifatius exiguus seruus seruorum Dei optabilem in Christo caritatis salutem
33	735	Boniface	Nothhelm	Bonifatius exiguus seruus seruorum Dei optabilem in Christo aeternae caritatis salutem
35	735	Boniface	Eadburg	Bonifatius exiguus seruus seruorum Dei optabilem in Christo caritatis salutem
38	732 × 754	Boniface	Aldhere	Bonifatius exiguus seruus seruorum Dei in Christo salutem
59	745	Boniface	Pope Zacharias	Bonifatius exiguus seruus seruorum Dei optabilem in Christo karitatis salutem
76	746 × 747	Boniface	Hwætberht	Bonifatius exiguus seruus seruorum Dei in Christo fraternae caritatis salutem
104	c.742 × 754	Boniface	Gemmulus	Bonifatius exiguus seruus seruorum Dei amabilem in Christo aeternae caritatis salutem
86	751	Boniface	Pope Zacharias	Bonifatius exiguus seruus uester . . . optabilem in Christo inmarcescibilis caritatis salutem
91	747 × 754	Boniface	Ecberht	Bonifatius exiguus episcopus . . . florentem in Christo inmarcescibilis caritatis salutem
108	752	Boniface	Pope Stephen	Bonifatius exiguus episcopus . . . optabilem in Christo caritatis salutem
109	753	Boniface	Pope Stephen	Bonifatius exiguus legatus . . . optabilem in Christo caritatis salutem
70	745 × 746	Lul (?)	Eadburg	.N. indignus et exiguus diaconus perennem in Domino salutem
100	c.739 × 754	Lul	Leofgyth	Lullus exiguus seruus domni Bonifatii discipulorum in Domino salutem
125	767 × 778	Lul	Coaena	Lullus exiguus seruus seruorum Dei perennem in Christo salutem
126	764 × 786	Lul	Cuthbert	Lullus exiguus seruus seruorum Dei perennem in Christo salutem
101	c.732 × 754	Wihtberht	[unknown]	Uietberht exiguus in Christo aeternae caritatis salutem

(b) The *clementiam*-formula

No.	Date	From	To	Formula
31	735 × 736	Boniface	[unknown]	Clementiam fraternitatis uestrae intimis flagitamus precibus
46	c.738	Boniface	[English bishops]	Fraternitatis uestrae clementiam intimis obsecramus precibus
38	732 × 754	Boniface	Aldhere	Caritatis uestrae clementiam medullatis et intimis precordium obsecramus precibus
66	742 × 746	Boniface	[a nun]	Caritatis uestrae clementiam intimis obsecramus precibus
63	742 × 746	Boniface	Daniel	paternitatis uestrae clementiam . . . intimis precibus diligenter rogare uelim
65	742 × 746	Boniface	Eadburg	Dilectionis uestrae clementiam intimis imploramus precibus
76	746 × 747	Boniface	Hwætberht	Fraternitatis uestrae pietatem intimis obsecramus praecibus

91	747 × 754	Boniface	Egberht	sanctitatis uestrae clementiam intimis postulamus precibus
95	732 × 754	Boniface	Reginbert	Dignitatis tuae clementiam obsecramus precibus
108	752	Boniface	Pope Stephen	Sanctitatis uestrae clementiam intimis ac uisceratis obnixe flagito precibus
106	750 × 754	Boniface	Optatus	Venerandam sanctitatis uestrae clementiam intimis obsecramus praecibus
32	735	Boniface	Pehthelm	Paternam sanctitatis uestrae clementiam intimis obnixe flagitamus precibus
75	746 × 747	Boniface	Ecgberht	intimis praecordiorum praecibus almitatis tuae clementiam obsecro
33	735	Boniface	Nothhelm	Almitatis uestrae clementiam intimis obsecro precibus
74	746 × 747	Boniface	Herefrid	Almitatis tuae clementiam intimis obsecro praecibus
70	745 × 746	Lul (?)	Eadburg	Almitatis tuae clementiam intimis obsecro precibus
71	745 × 746	Lul	Dealwine	Almitatis tuae clementiam intimis praecibus flagito

exiguus-formula with *in Christo . . . salutem* after Boniface's death in 754.[46] It will be noted that the form of the *exiguus*-formula used in Tangl 31 differs slightly from Boniface's customary usage; although elsewhere he certainly favours the (very common) combination *perennem . . . salutem,* this is the only occasion on which the phrase occurs as part of the *exiguus*-formula.[47] Such a point would be insignificant, were it not for the fact that Tangl 31 also offers a unique form of the *clementiam*-formula, being the only example of the seventeen cited in which the word *clementiam* opens the formula.

One is tempted to describe this letter as a simple example of what has been called the 'cut and paste' technique, a term often applied to Old English homilies.[48] It is perhaps significant that none of the puns, wordplay, and use of matching biblical quotations in the version to Eadburg has been included here, since the rest of the letter seems so utterly hackneyed. In the entire Bonifatian correspondence the only other cases in which there are letters so close in content and diction as Tangl 30 and 31 are two general letters, dated to the same day, and written to two different districts by Pope Zacharias (Tangl 52 and 53). If we accept the attribution, found in both manuscripts, that Tangl 31 is indeed a genuine letter of Boniface,[49] then we may assume that it was produced at around the same time as Tangl 30; but its utterly commonplace diction and (relatively speaking) unusual use of both the *exiguus-* and *clementiam*-formulas perhaps offer the possibility that Tangl 31 is not genuinely the work of Boniface himself, but rather the general later confection of a Boniface-imitator.[50]

For a similarly brief, general and utterly derivative piece, one might cite, for example, a short (presumably incomplete) letter attributed to Wihtberht, and found only in the Vienna manuscript, where the text in its entirety reads as follows (Tangl 102; dated *c.* 732 × 754):

[46] Of the eight letters definitely attributed to Lul, four begin with some form of *in Domino . . . salutem* (Tangl 71–2, 100 and 113), two with some form of *in Christo . . . salutem* (Tangl 125–6), and two with neither (Tangl 92 and 128); of the nine anonymous letters attributed to Lul, two begin with some form of *in Domino . . . salutem* (Tangl 70 and 114), three with some form of *in Christo . . . salutem* (Tangl 98, 103 and 142), and four with neither (Tangl 37, 49, 110 and 141).

[47] Boniface uses the combination *perennem . . . salutem* in the salutations of Tangl 30, 40, 73 and 93.

[48] For a useful discussion of the term (and its applicability), see D. Scragg, *Dating and Style in Old English Composite Homilies,* H. M. Chadwick Memorial Lectures 9 (Cambridge, 1998).

[49] The Karlsruhe manuscript describes Tangl 31 as a 'letter of Boniface' (*epistola bonifatii*); the Vienna manuscript specifies that it is a 'letter of Archbishop Boniface' (*item epistola bonifatii archiepiscopi*).

[50] One might cite similar reservations about a 'cut and paste' vernacular homily which draws heavily on the works of Wulfstan, discussed by Scragg, *Dating and Style,* pp. 18–21, who notes of one piece (pp. 20–1): 'the problem here is that everything is *too* Wulfstanian. It seems to me to be a perfect example of a scissors and paste exercise, but the scissors were, by chance or design, at work only on writings which are known to be by the archbishop'.

Dilectissimo fratri et conpresbitero .N. Uuietberht exiguus in Christo aeternae caritatis salutem. Intime caritatis obnixis precibus flagito, ut mei in tuis sacrosanctis orationibus memor esse digneris, quia mundanae temptationis malleo uanis rebus turbantibus percutior.

To the most beloved brother and co-priest, .N., lowly Wihtberht sends greetings of eternal love in Christ. I urge with the fervent prayers of devoted love, that you deign to remember me in your holy prayers, because with vain matters disturbing me I am struck by the hammer of worldly temptation.

As a glance at the preceding pages will show, the whole letter might be summarized as a combination of an *exiguus*-formula, a truncated *clementiam*-formula (omitting the element *clementiam* itself), and a general observation on being buffeted by worldly concerns which parallels Boniface's (rather more elaborate) storm-image. Comparison with the only other letter by Wihtberht extant only confirms the suspicion that he is composing by rote (Tangl 101; dated 732 × 754): he closes that letter with yet another variation on the *clementiam*-formula,[51] and incorporates into the body of the text two of Boniface's favourite quotations from the Pauline Epistles.[52]

More evidence, both direct and indirect, of Boniface's quite literally exemplary position is found in the following letter to Boniface (Tangl 29; dated 732) from the Anglo-Saxon missionary nun Leofgyth, who (as she explicitly mentions) was trained in Latin by Eadburg herself (line 20); again, significant verbal parallels are underlined:[53]

---

[51] 'Commoniter omnes obnixis precibus flagitto uicem instantiae orationis nostrae inpendere orantemque pro nobis beatitudinem uestram diuina tueatur clementia opto' ('I entreat all of you with humble prayers to alternate with us in earnest prayer, and I wish that divine mercy may guard your holiness as you are praying for us').

[52] The quotation from I Tim. II.4 is used by Boniface in Tangl 38, 46 and 65 (and by Pope Gregory II and Pope Gregory III in Tangl 21 and 24); the quotation from Eph. VI.19 is used by Boniface in Tangl 30, 31 and 76.

[53] Parallels:

iugum . . . leue	Matt. XI.30 [also Tangl 78 and 119]
annorum curriculum	Ambrose, Gregory, Bede, etc. [a patristic commonplace]
ex hac luce subtractus est	Gregory, *Dialogues* I.viii.34, IV.xxxvi.26, etc.
summi pontificatus infula praeditus	Aldhelm, *De metris* 65.1 [also prose *De uirginitate* 274.13]
ne . . . longa locorum intercapedine refrigescant	Aldhelm, *De metris* 75.4
uenenata . . . iacula . . . metrorum pelta . . . protegere	
digneris	Aldhelm, *De pedum regulis* 201.26–202.1
epistolarem perscrutans rusticitatem	Aldhelm, *De metris* 74.5–6
dilectionis ligatura . . . enixius . . . reliquum nodetur in aeuum	Aldhelm, *De metris* 75.13–14
inhianter satago audire	Aldhelm, *De pedum regulis* 152.10
aliquantula metrorum munuscula . . . fiducia fretus subiunxi	Aldhelm, *De metris* 75.16–17
prima ingenioli rudimenta exercitari cupiens	Aldhelm, *De metris* 76.5
indesinenter secundum poeticae traditionis disciplinam	Aldhelm, *De metris* 76.12
Arbiter omnipotens, nutu qui cuncta creauit	Aldhelm, *Enigmata* 91.1

Domino reuerentissimo et <u>summe</u> dignitatis <u>infula predito</u> Bonifatio atque in Christo
carissimo et mihi adfinitatis propinquitate conexo Leobgyda ultima *leue iugum*
Christi portantium famula perennem sospitatis salutem. Rogo tuam clementiam, ut
memorare digneris prioris amicitiae, quam iamdudum cum patre meo copulasti,
cuius uocabulum est Dynne, in occiduis regionibus, qui nunc ante .viii. <u>annorum</u>   5
<u>curriculum ab hac luce subtractus est</u>, ut pro anima illius preces offerre Deo non
rennues. Necnon et matris mee memoriam commendo tibi, quae cognominatur
Æbbe, que tibi, ut melius nosti, consanguinitatis nexibus copulatur et adhuc
laboriose uiuit et diu ualide ab infirmitate obpressa est. Ergo unica filia sum ambobus
parentibus meis; et utinam, licet sim indigna, ut merear te in fratris locum accipere,   10
quia in nullo hominum generis mei tanta fiducia spei posita est mihi quanta in te.
Hoc paruum munusculum mittere curaui, non ut dignum esset tue almitatis aspectui,
sed ut memoriam paruitatis meae retines, ne <u>longa locorum intercapidine</u> obliuione
tradas, quin immo uere <u>dilectionis ligatura reliquum nodetur in euum</u>. Hoc, frater
amande, <u>enixius</u> efflagito, ut tuarum orationum <u>pelta</u> muniar contra hostis occulti   15
<u>uenenata iacula</u>. Illud etiam peto, ut <u>rusticitatem</u> huius <u>epistole digneris</u> emendare et
mihi aliqua uerba tuae affabilitatis exempli gratia transmittere non recusses, quae
<u>inhianter audire satago</u>. Istos autem subter scriptos uersiculos conponere nitebar
<u>secundum poetice traditionis disciplinam</u>, non audacia confidens, sed <u>gracilis</u>
<u>ingenioli</u> rudimenta exercitare <u>cupiens</u> et tuo auxilio indigens. Istam artem ab   20
Eadburge magisterio didici, quae <u>indesinenter</u> legem diuinam rimare non cessat.
Vale, uiuens aeuo longiore, uita feliciore, interpellans pro me.

<u>Arbiter omnipotens</u>, solus <u>qui cuncta creauit</u>,
in regno patris semper qui lumine fulget,
qua iugiter flagrans sic regnet gloria Christi,   25
inlesum seruet semper te iure perenni.

To the most reverend master, endowed with the fillet of the highest dignity, to Boniface,
dearest in Christ and linked to me by the bond of affinity, Leofgyth, the lowest hand-
maid of those bearing the light yoke of Christ sends the endless greetings of the fortunate. I ask you in your mercy that you deign to recall the former friendship, which you
once had long ago with my father, whose name is Dynne, in the west country, and who
has been taken from the light eight years ago now, so that you do not refuse to offer
prayers to God for his soul. I also commend to you the memory of my mother, who is
called Æbbe, who is connected to you by bonds of blood, as you know quite well; she is
still alive, but in difficulty, and for a long time has been greatly afflicted with illness. I am
both my parents' only daughter, and although I am unworthy, I should like to be worthy
to take you as a brother, since of all mankind there is no one in whom I have such faithful confidence as you. I have taken care to send this small offering, not so that it should
be worthy of the aspect of your kindness, but so that you may keep a memory of my
worthlessness, and not consign me to oblivion because of the expanse of distance, but
instead so that the bond of true love should be tied for the rest of time. Beloved brother,
I earnestly request this quite urgently, so that I should be protected by the shield of your
prayers against the poisoned darts of the hidden enemy. I also ask this thing, namely that
you deign to correct the artlessness of this letter and that you do not refuse to send me

some words through your own courtesy as an example, since I eagerly long to hear them. I tried to compose these paltry verses written below according to the rules of the poetic discipline, with no confidence in my boldness, but wishing to exercise the beginnings of my fragile intelligence, desperate for your help. I learnt this skill from the teaching of Eadburg, who unceasingly strives to examine the divine law. Farewell: may you live for long, and live happy, and intercede for me. May the almighty judge, who alone created all things, who always shines in light in the kingdom of the father, where too may Christ's glory reign, keep you always unharmed by eternal decree.

In her letter, Leofgyth asks Boniface for his patronage (which, since she goes on to become abbess of Tauberbischofsheim, was evidently forthcoming), invites him to correct her 'artless prose' (*rusticitatem*, line 16), and, more importantly in the context of the present discussion, to send her some of his own work as a (presumably literary) example (*exempli gratia*, line 17). In return, she sends him a small gift (*munusculum*, line 12): some Latin verses of her own. In form and technique the letter closely echoes in its formulation Boniface's own, and contains a rather fleeting biblical allusion to Matthew XI.30 (line 2), a smattering of patristic tags and a clear debt to Aldhelm. Even the mixed epistolary form, concluding with a poem, can be matched in Boniface's own earlier compositions, such as his letter to Nithard (Tangl 9).[54]

But it is the material derived from Aldhelm which is perhaps most revealing of Leofgyth's training and background: every Aldhelmian phrase derives either from Aldhelm's *De metris* (on consecutive pages of Ehwald's edition!) or from his *De pedum regulis*: in other words, from precisely the two treatises which Aldhelm composed to teach metrical verse-composition, and circulated along with his *Enigmata*, the verse-riddles which he included to illustrate metrical features.[55] It is scarcely surprising, then, that the first line of verse she cites is entirely confected from several lines of the *Enigmata*, nor that all four verses have precisely the same metrical structure as three-quarters of Aldhelm's own: a fixed cadence preceded by three long syllables, leaving only the first third of the line to be negotiated.[56] Such a verse-technique provides a perfect template for formulaic composition, effectively breaking the hexameter line down into three

---

[54] It is interesting to note that in a later letter to Boniface, apparently requesting study-leave in Thuringia (Tangl 103; dated *c.* 739 × 741), the anonymous author (assumed to be Lul) should again employ the same basic pattern of combining Aldhelmian and biblical allusions, and concluding with a poem. Like Leofgyth's, that letter also uses the honorific phrase 'endowed with the fillet of the highest pontificate' (*summi pontificatus infula predito*) when addressing Boniface. In the case of Tangl 103, however, it is important to note that the author cites the phrase more fully in its original form as derived from Aldhelm, as does Lul elsewhere in a letter to Coaena (Tangl 125), and Boniface in letters to Nothhelm, Pope Zacharias and Ecgberht (Tangl 33, 50 and 91).

[55] On these texts and their role in teaching verse, see N. Wright's Appendix to M. Lapidge and J. L. Rosier, *Aldhelm: the Poetic Works* (Cambridge, 1985), pp. 183–219 and 263–8.

[56] See further Orchard, *The Poetic Art of Aldhelm*, pp. 84–91.

discrete units, each of which can be supplied by formulaic borrowing or repetition; it is, indeed, the same technique as that employed by Boniface himself.[57] Leofgyth, then, has simply echoed passages from her textbooks; in other words, this is a sort of undergraduate essay, albeit a rather superior one, a supposition strengthened considerably by her somewhat shaky grasp of Latin grammar: she has particular problems with deponent verbs, and we must remember that, after all, she did send this letter to Boniface for correction.[58]

Now, given that there is compelling evidence that Lul himself was responsible for compiling the collection that now travels under the name of the 'Bonifatian correspondence', it is particularly intriguing to consider passages from two letters of his own. In the first instance, one might simply cite the closing phrases of a letter in the name of Lul and two other brethren which, however, it has been argued was almost certainly penned by Lul himself (Tangl 49; dated 739 × 741):[59]

Parua quoque munusculorum transmisio scedulam istam comitatur, quae sunt tria, id est turis et piperis et cinnamomi permodia zenia, sed omni mentis affectione destinata. Huius muneris magnitudinem ut non consideres, sed spiritalis caritatis amorem adtende, poposcimus. Illud etiam petimus, ut <u>rusticitatem huius epistiunculae emendas</u> et nobis <u>aliqua uerba tuae</u> dulcedinis <u>non rennues</u> dirigere,   5 <u>quae inhianter audire</u> gratulabundi <u>satagimus</u>.
    <u>Vale uiuens</u> Deo <u>aeuo longiore et uita feliciore intercedens pro</u> nobis.

A small consignment of little gifts accompanies this letter, three in number, that is, small presents (yet indicating the heart's whole affection) of frankincense, pepper and cinnamon. We beg you not to consider the size of the gift but to pay attention to the love which is spiritual charity. We also ask you to correct the rusticity of this little letter and not to refuse to send us some words of your own sweet self, which we will be satisfied to hear eagerly and joyfully.
    Farewell: may you live for long in God, and live happy, and intercede for us.

It will be clear from a comparison with Leofgyth's letter (parallel phrases have been underlined) that in this case, Lul has borrowed from Leofgyth herself rather than from Aldhelm, her model: from Leofgyth we have the notion of

---

[57] See further Lapidge, 'Aldhelm's Latin Poetry and Old English Verse'; Orchard, 'After Aldhelm', pp. 103–7, and *The Poetic Art of Aldhelm*, pp. 102–25.

[58] There are a number of ways in which the grammar of the letter transgresses strict classical standards of correctness. For example, *ut . . . rennues* (lines 6–7) should probably read (ignoring the dittography) *ut rennuas; ut . . . retines* (lines 12–13) should probably read *ut . . . retineas; rimare* (line 21) should probably read *rimari; regnet* (line 25) should probably read *regnat*. It is perhaps amusing to note that in the manuscripts Tangl 29 has been repeatedly corrected by later hands: see Tangl, *Die Briefe*, pp. 52–3.

[59] For a discussion of Lul's authorship of unattributed letters, see, for example, Tangl, *Die Briefe*, pp. 218 and 279.

emending (Aldhelm simply says 'scrutinizing'); from Leofgyth we have the notion of sending *aliqua uerba* (entirely absent in Aldhelm); even the Aldhelmian phrase *inhianter satago audire* is given in the altered order of Leofgyth, while the verbatim copying of the final salutation has no parallel in Aldhelm.[60]

A still later letter from Lul to Dealwine of Malmesbury (Tangl 71; dated 745 × 746) is even more intriguing in this regard. The text of this letter reads as follows, with significant parallels again underlined:[61]

Reuerentissimo fratri Dealuuino iamdudum magistro Lul indignus diaconus sine prerogatiua meritorum diaconatus officio fungens optabilem in Domino salutem. Almitatis tuae clementiam intimis precibus flagito, ut meae mediocritatis carinam fulcire digneris tuis almis oraminibus, quatenus tuarum orationum intercessionibus pelta protectus ad portum salutis peruenire merear et piaculorum meorum in hoc 5 terreno ergastulo ueniam consequi, sicut iam praeterito anni circulo per Deneuualdum fratrem nostrum litterarum mearum portitorem deprecatus sum. Ergo uilium munusculorum transmissio scedulam istam comitatur non tam digna quam deuota mente directa. Similiter obsecro, ut mihi Aldhelmi episcopi aliqua opuscula seu prosarum seu metrorum aut rithmicorum dirigere digneris ad consolationem 10 peregrinationis meae et ob memoriam ipsius beati antestitis. Et mihi per aliqua uerba tuae affabilitatis indica, quid de istis ualeat precibus tua fraternitas perficere, quae inhianter audire satago.

Bene ualentem te et proficientem in prosperitate dierum et intercedentem pro me exopto longis temporibus. 15

To the most reverend brother Dealwine, his sometime teacher, Lul, an unworthy deacon discharging the office of the diaconate without the prerogative of merits, sends a hope for greeting in the Lord. I urge the generosity of your kindness with heartfelt prayers, so that you deign to support the keel of my mediocrity with your kindly prayers, so that protected by the shield of your prayers I may deserve to reach the post of salvation and to gain forgiveness for my sins in this earthly prison, just as in the past year I asked through Brother Denewald, the bearer of my letter. Therefore an offering of poor gifts

---

[60] It is interesting to note that the original Aldhelmian phrase, *inhianter satago audire*, appears in an order closer to that copied by Leofgyth (namely *inhianter audire satago*) in three of the nine manuscripts consulted by Ehwald; see Ehwald, *Aldhelmi Opera*, p. 152. Although none of these manuscripts is early enough to have been directly used by Leofgyth, they may well reflect the reading of her source. One might also point out that Lul is not the only one to echo Leofgyth's letter: Boniface himself apparently borrows the phrase *propinquitate conexo* (in the form *propinquitate conexe*), perhaps as a conscious form of literary flattery, in a his letter to Leofgyth's teacher Eadburg (Tangl 30), quoted above.

[61] Parallels:

sine praerogatiua meritorum	Boniface to the English (Tangl 46; dated *c.* 738)
sine praerogatiua meritorum	Boniface to Optatus (Tangl 106; dated 750 × 754)
almis orationibus fulcire	Milred to Lul (Tangl 112; dated 754)
dirigere digneris [*twice*]	Eangyth to Boniface (Tangl 14; dated 719 × 722)
dirigere digneris	Boniface to Ecgberht (Tangl 75; dated 746 × 747)
proficientem et bene ualentem	Boniface to Herefrid (Tangl 74; dated 746 × 747)

accompanies this epistle, not so much worthy as sent with a devoted heart. Likewise I ask, that you deign to send to me some works of Bishop Aldhelm, whether in prose or in metrical or rhythmical verse to cheer up my exile and in memory of that saintly prelate. And tell me through some words of your affable self, what your brotherliness can accomplish with respect to those prayers, since I eagerly long to hear them. I have the long-standing hope that you are faring well, and advancing in the prosperity of days, and interceding for me.

After the (by now) utterly formulaic opening, the notion of being protected by a shield of prayers (lines 4–5) again comes from the same letter of Leofgyth (line 15), as does the reference to *aliqua uerba tui affabilitatis* (Tangl 29, line 17; Tangl 71, lines 11–12), and the words *inhianter audire satago* (Tangl 29, line 18; Tangl 71, line 13). However, the words *munusculorum transmissio scedulam istam comitatur* (line 8) come from Lul's own earlier letter, and he has added a number of other echoes from elsewhere in the Bonifatian correspondence. It is almost as if he is writing with other letters on the table. The main point to make with respect to this letter to Dealwine is that Lul has moved far from Aldhelm, Leofgyth's ultimate source in his formulation, a somewhat ironic observation given that in this very letter Lul is requesting to be sent copies of Aldhelm's works. When we remember that Lul himself had been educated at Malmesbury (where, we are informed, his nickname at school had been Lytel ['little']),[62] and clearly had some (albeit by now evidently rather shaky) knowledge of Aldhelm, the poignancy (and urgency) of this letter becomes evident. In one of the two manuscript witnesses (the Vienna manuscript), a poem is appended to this letter to Dealwine, and one is tempted to conclude that this is one of the 'poor gifts' mentioned in the letter again, presumably in emulation of Leofgyth's poetic gift to Boniface.[63] But the appended verses are not even Lul's own, being simply a rather general call to moderation by the poet Ausonius (his *Epigram* 7); the relevance of these verses to the preceding letter seems slight, and they have been poorly copied in the Vienna manuscript: there are six substantial copying errors in only eight lines.[64] One cannot help but feel that the sooner they sent Aldhelm the better.

Later on, in a letter that Tangl dates to the period 767 × 778 (Tangl 125), Lul sends to Archbishop Coaena of York for the works of Bede in precisely parallel terms to those in which he had earlier requested Aldhelm's works: 'to

---

[62] So says a letter from an unnamed monk (Tangl 135; dated 754 × 786), recalling that the name was bestowed by Abbot Eaba ('Et hoc signum recordor, quod pro nomine uocauit te Lytel').

[63] Cf. Tangl 103, addressed to Boniface, attributed to Lul, and discussed above, in n. 54, which likewise ends with a poem.

[64] See Tangl, *Die Briefe*, p. 145. It is intriguing to note that in Ausonius' own poem, mention is made of someone receiving fortune 'from a place of exile' (*ab exili . . . loco*), but that the Vienna manuscript has 'from a lowly place' (*ab exiguuo loco*); both phrases might well have appealed to Lul, who, given his own penchant for using the adjective *exiguus* (see above, fig. 2), may even have been responsible for the metrical substitution himself.

console our exile' (*ad consolationem pereginationis nostrae*).[65] One might also note that around the same time Boniface himself had sent a letter to Hwætberht at Monkwearmouth–Jarrow for some works of Bede (Tangl 76),[66] but that in this case the request is couched more in the manner of an equal: 'we have heard that he shone like a candle in the investigation of Holy Scripture' ('Interea rogamus, ut aliqua de opusculis sagacissimi inuestigatoris scripturarum Bedan monachi, quem nuper in domo Dei apud uos uice candellae aecclesiastice scientia scripturarum fulsisse audiuimus, conscripta nobis transmittere dignemini'), says Boniface, immediately after a clever confection of three biblical allusions of his own,[67] the only such biblical references in the entire letter. It is as if Boniface is demonstrating that he too has some mastery of scripture. One remembers how in the letter from Boniface to Eadburg examined above (which was ostensibly written a decade earlier) Boniface had thanked his correspondent for sending him books, and one might note further an extant reply from Bugga to Boniface (Tangl 15; dated *c.* 720), apologizing for being unable to send him some *passiones martyrum* (a chillingly appropriate request for a man who went on to be horribly martyred as an octogenarian at Dokkum in 754). A further letter from Boniface to Eadburg (Tangl 35) requests a copy of the Epistles of Peter (again, a scarcely unusual request, given Boniface's often-stated identification of himself with St Paul, as illustrated by some of the borrowing we have already seen).[68] But this particular copy was requested to be illuminated with gold, to use 'before the eyes of the worldly in preaching' (*ante oculos carnalium in praedicando*). Indeed, much of the minutiae of the personal letters of the Bonifatian correspondence are taken

---

[65] Tangl 125 (p. 263, line 9); cf. Tangl 71 (p. 144, line 19: *dirigere digneris . . . ad consolationem peregrinationis meae*). It is also worth noting that when Abbot Cuthbert of Monkwearmouth–Jarrow does send Lul copies of Bede's works (Tangl 127), he too uses the same phrase (p. 265, lines 2–3: *ad consolationem tuae peregrinationi* [sic] *mittere curaui*).

[66] Two other letters from Boniface, both to Archbishop Ecgberht of York (Tangl 75 and 91), likewise make requests for works of Bede, each couched in broadly similar terms; Tangl 75 speaks of Bede's work in rather general terms ('Praeterea obsecro, ut mihi de opusculis Bedan lectoris aliquos tractatus conscribere et dirigere digneris, quem nuper, ut audiuimus, diuina gratia spiritali intellectu ditauit et in uestra prouincia fulgere concessit, et ut candela, quam uobis Dominus largitus est, nos quoque fruamur'), while Tangl 91 refers explicitly to Bede's *Homilies* and to various books of his exegesis ('Modo enim inhianter desiderantes flagitamus, ut nobis ad gaudium meroris nostri eo modo, quo et ante iam fecistis, aliquam particulam uel scintillam de candella aecclesiae, quam inluxit spiritus sanctus in regionibus prouinciae uestrae, nobis destinare curetis: id est ut de tractatibus, quos spiritalis presbiter et inuestigator sanctarum scripturarum Beda reserando conposuit, partem qualemcunque transmittere dignemini; maxime autem, si fore possit, quod nobis predicantibus habile et manuale et utillimum esse uidetur, super lectionarium anniuersarium et prouerbia Salomonis. Quia commentarios super illa eum condidisse audiuimus').

[67] The biblical references are I Cor. III.7, Eph. VI.19, and II Thess. III.1; for such a confection of references to the Pauline Epistles, see above, n. 30.   [68] See above, n. 29.

up with requests for books, regrets that books are unavailable, and thanks once books have been sent.[69]

One can conclude from all the above that the Bonifatian mission, at least for the first three decades, was effectively starved of books. Boniface apparently carried much of his own learning with him in his own head and took it with him when he died. Fresh blood (like that of Leofgyth) was sorely needed, and for the next generation even the most casual and commonplace letters appear to have been preserved with reverence for the learning and Latinity that they contained. The Bonifatian correspondence thus contains much more than simply a conspectus of the deeds of the good and the great, and offers to the literary scholars of both Anglo-Latin and Old English a largely untapped source of information about Anglo-Saxon attitudes towards literary style and structure. The creative tension between written, remembered and recycled words that is the hallmark of Anglo-Saxon literary culture is fully in evidence throughout the Bonifatian correspondence, in which the effects of isolation and distance become progressively more painful and clear.

Nowhere are these effects more starkly expressed than in the three undated letters attributed to the missionary nun Beorhtgyth and apparently written to her brother Balthard back in England,[70] which seem to symbolize not only the feeling of all those English exiles far from home, but also their seeming attitude to all the Latin learning and literature to which they must have felt they were slowly losing access; as Beorhtgyth asks (Tangl 147): 'and now I ask you, my dearest brother, to come to me or have me come to you so that I can see you before I die, because my deep love for you has never left my heart' ('Nunc ergo rogo te, dilectissime frater mi, ut uenias ad me aut me facias uenire, ut te conspiciam antequam moriar, quia numquam discedit dilectio tua ab anima mea'). The letter in which this plea appears is in one sense typical of the Bonifatian correspondence, consisting as it does of a chain of four biblical quotations, and concluding with some rhythmical octosyllables that are in form and diction greatly indebted to the *carmina rhythmica* of Aldhelm and Æthilwald that are uniquely found in the same Vienna manuscript.[71] Such clear evidence from the *carmina rhythmica* provides a poignant reminder of the tissue of borrowing that links so many of the texts in Vienna 751. A further letter from Beorhtgyth (Tangl 148) is of essentially the same form, and, in the fashion of so many of the letters of the Bonifatian correspondence, alludes to 'small gifts' (*munuscula parua*) that are to accompany the letter, just before a further octosyllabic composition, equally

[69] Among the letters which deal directly with books and learning, one might include Tangl 9, 29–30, 33–5, 54, 62–3, 65, 70–2, 75, 77, 91, 98, 103, 116, 119, 124–7, 131, 140, 142 and 145.
[70] These letters are discussed by Dronke, *Women Writers*, pp. 30–3, and Fell, 'Some Implications', pp. 37–41.
[71] See Tangl, *Die Briefe*, pp. 284–5, and Orchard, *The Poetic Art of Aldhelm*, pp. 65–7.

indebted to Aldhelm and Æthilwald. But it is the third of Beorhtgyth's letters that shows the tremendous chasm in literary sensibility that exists within the Bonifatian correspondence as a whole. The letter contains no literary allusions at all, and consists simply of a series of anguished questions (Tangl 143):

Fratri unico atque amantissimo .N., .N. ultima ancillarum Dei in Christo salutem. Quid est, frater mi, quod tam longum tempus intermisisti, quod uenire tardasti? Quare non uis cogitare, quod ego sola in hac terra et nullus alius frater uisitet me neque propinquorum aliquis ad me ueniet? Et si ideo facis, quia adhuc nihil potui, secundum quod mens mea diligenter uoluisset, aliquid beneficii inpendere, tamen 5 caritatis atque adfinitatis iura nullo alio suadente aut mens tua mutando debes obliuiscere. O frater, o frater mi, cur potes mentem paruitatis meae adsiduae merore fletu atque tristitia die noctuque caritatis tuae absentia adfligere? Nonne pro certo scies, quia uiuentium omnium nullum alium propono tuae caritati? Ecce non possum omnia per litteras tibi indicare. Iam ego certum teneo, quod tibi cura non est de mea 10 paruitate.

To my only and most beloved brother .N., .N., the least of God's handmaidens, [sends] greetings in Christ. Why is it, my brother, that you have let such a long time pass, that you have delayed coming? Why are you unwilling to consider that I am alone in this land and no other brother will visit me nor any kinsman come to me? And if for that reason, as I thus far have been unable to, according to what my mind would earnestly wish, you do some act of kindness, however with no one else urging the duties of love and kinship or changing your mind you must forget. Oh brother, oh my brother, why are you able to afflict the mind of little me with constant grief, weeping and sorrow, day and night through the absence of your love? Won't you know for sure that there is no one else alive that I would place above your love? Already I feel sure that you don't care for little me.

Although at times the letter verges on incoherence,[72] there are powerful patterns of rhyme, rhythm and repetition set up which underscore and highlight the depth of emotion expressed, in much the same way as similar patterns have been perceived in vernacular poems such as *Wulf and Eadwacer*, *The Wife's Lament* or *The Wanderer*.[73] In tone and temperament the letters of Beorhtgyth might

---

[72] Particularly problematic is the sentence *Et si ideo facis . . . obliuiscere*, in which although the parallel structure *mens mea . . . mens tua* seems clearly central, the precise grammatical function of the phrase *mens tua* is obscure (it can hardly be the subject of the verb *debes* as it stands: perhaps emend to *debet*?). Less troubling is the use of an apparently active infinitive *obliuiscere* for the deponent verb *obliuiscor*, since such forms can be paralleled elsewhere in the Bonifatian correspondence, but it is still perhaps significant that whereas Dronke, *Women Writers*, p. 33, states that Beorhtgyth 'uses lucid, uncomplicated vocabulary and syntax, and writes a Latin that seldom strays very far from classical correctness', he none the less omits to translate this very sentence.

[73] Dronke, *Women Writers*, p. 289, provides a helpful line-arrangement for the Latin text here, pointing out that 'the rhymes and assonances . . . while not completely regular, seem much too extensive to be fortuitous: they are [Beorhtgyth's] attempt at a particular kind of verbal artistry'.

seem light years from the polished elegance of Boniface's own letters to Eadburg, especially Tangl 30, which is about the same length, but what is most evident in all the letters of the Bonifatian correspondence is an earnest attempt to convey in literary terms the hardships and heartaches of the solitary missionary life, far from the books and learning of home. The correspondence captures perfectly the same elegiac spirit of loss and longing that pervades so much Anglo-Saxon literature, and represents a series of individual responses to the same sense of isolation so commonly expressed in vernacular verse; as the last line of *The Wife's Lament* aptly puts it (line 53): *Wa bið þam þe sceal of langoþe leofes abidan* ('it is hard for the one who has to wait in longing for what they love').[74]

---

[74] I am grateful to Michael Lapidge, Clare Orchard and Samantha Zacher for their helpful comments and suggestions in the writing of this paper.

The illnesses of King Alfred the Great

DAVID PRATT

It is an index perhaps of changing historiographical trends that the importance of Alfred's illnesses in the moulding of his outlook, both as a layman and as a king, now hardly needs to be emphasized.[1] In the course of the 1990s, Alfred became gradually better understood as a man of the 890s.[2] Yet Victorian sensibilities have died hard. Both Plummer and Stevenson detected an 'atmosphere of morbid religiosity' in Asser's account of Alfred's illnesses in ch. 74, and both refused to associate this atmosphere with the 'historical Alfred', in view of his well-attested military successes.[3] The recent resurrection of this approach by Alfred Smyth has only served, however, to emphasize the need for

[1] This paper was written in the first instance for the purposes of a colloquium held to commemorate the 1100th anniversary of Alfred's death on 26 October 1999 at the Institute of Historical Research, organized by the Centre for Late Antique and Medieval Studies, King's College London, in association with the Museum of London. In completing its revision, I would like to thank Simon Keynes for supplying me with numerous useful bibliographical leads; Katharine Scarfe Beckett, Rosalind Love, Andy Orchard and Oliver Padel, who provided advice on particular points of detail; Mayke de Jong, Paul Kershaw and Jonathan Shepard, who generously allowed me to take account of their forthcoming publications; and James Campbell, Paul Kershaw, Simon Keynes, Janet Nelson and Katherine O'Brien O'Keeffe, for helpful comments and discussion. In references to Anglo-Saxon charters, S = P. H. Sawyer, *Anglo-Saxon Charters: an Annotated List and Bibliography*, R. Hist. Soc. Guides and Handbooks 8 (London, 1968), followed by the number of the document; BCS = W. de G. Birch, *Cartularium Saxonicum*, 3 vols. (London, 1885–93). For Alfredian sources, translations are borrowed, where possible, from S. Keynes and M. Lapidge, *Alfred the Great: Asser's Life of King Alfred and other Contemporary Sources* (Harmondsworth, 1983).
[2] In addition to the work cited below by Scharer, Nelson and Kershaw, Alfred's illnesses have received further recent treatment from R. Abels, *Alfred the Great: War, Kingship and Culture in Anglo-Saxon England* (Harlow, 1998), pp. 96–102; M. Wood, *In Search of England: Journeys into the English Past* (London, 1999), pp. 137–42; and S. Hamilton, 'Review Article: Early Medieval Rulers and their Modern Biographers', *EME* 9 (2000), 247–60, at 252–5. Cf. now also M. Kempshall, 'No Bishop, No King: the Ministerial Ideology of Kingship and Asser's *Res Gestae Aelfredi*', *Belief and Culture in the Middle Ages: Studies presented to Henry Mayr-Harting*, ed. R. Gameson and H. Leyser (Oxford, 2001), pp. 106–27, published too late to be considered here.
[3] C. Plummer, *The Life and Times of Alfred the Great* (Oxford, 1902), pp. 24–8 (cf. addenda, p. 214); *Asser's Life of King Alfred, together with the Annals of St Neots, erroneously ascribed to Asser*, ed. W. H. Stevenson, new imp. (Oxford, 1959), pp. 294–6 (first published in 1904). Compare the sensitive handling of Alfred's illnesses by B. A. Lees, *Alfred the Great: the Truth Teller: Maker of England 848–899* (New York, 1915), pp. 103–4, 115–16 and 422–4.

greater sensitivity to the ideals and expectations of the society within which Alfred was operating. Smyth's unsuccessful attempt to expose Asser's *Life* as a later forgery relies heavily upon his assumption that the text is a work of hagiography, because it supposedly portrays Alfred as 'a saintly king, wrapt up in prayer [*sic*], and enduring some form of physical disease'.[4] It should therefore be stressed that royal sanctity was an entirely posthumous phenomenon in Anglo-Saxon England, and, in the case of kings, nearly always acquired through an appropriate manner of death.[5] Alfred's apparent preoccupation with his own bodily suffering rightly pertains to the sphere of lay devotion, as Anton Scharer first observed, rather than hagiography.[6] In about 884, Notker the Stammerer of St Gallen drew a particularly clear distinction between such lay devotion and outright sanctity, claiming that Louis the German 'closely resembled Saint [Ambrose], except in certain acts and occupations without which life on this earth cannot be carried on, namely marriage and the use of weapons'.[7] A different yet comparable distinction between saints and those endowed with worldly authority seems to have operated at Alfred's court, described by Pope Gregory the Great himself in Wærferth's relatively faithful translation of the preamble to bk I of the *Dialogi*. 'In positions of worldly responsibility (*worldscyrum*), we are very often compelled to do those things that we know well enough that we ought not to do':[8] this burden of worldly involvement feels all the heavier to Gregory when compared with the greater virtue of saints, who so 'pleased their Creator in a life of greater withdrawal' that Almighty God 'refused to occupy them with the toils of this world'.[9] On this evidence alone, Smyth's chapter entitled 'Neurotic Saint and Invalid King' entirely misses the point.

CAROLINGIAN CONNECTIONS AND CONTRASTS

It is revealing indeed to consider why this distinction between lay devotion and sanctity should have been particularly pertinent in the later ninth century. In

---

[4] A. P. Smyth, *King Alfred the Great* (Oxford, 1995), pp. 199–216, esp. 215. Among the many unfavourable reviews of this biography, criticism of Smyth's attitude towards Alfred's illnesses is central in that by J. L. Nelson, 'Review Article: Waiting for Alfred', *EME* 7 (1998), 115–24.

[5] S. J. Ridyard, *The Royal Saints of Anglo-Saxon England: a Study of West Saxon and East Anglian Cults* (Cambridge, 1981), esp. pp. 74–81.

[6] A. Scharer, 'The Writing of History at King Alfred's Court', *EME* 5 (1996), 177–206, at 187–91.

[7] *Gesta Karoli Magni Imperatoris* II.10 (*Notker der Stammler: Taten Karls des Grossen*, ed. H. F. Haefele, MGH SS rerum Germanicarum, nova series 12 (Berlin, 1959), 66).

[8] *Bischof Wærferths von Worcester Übersetzung der Dialoge Gregors des Grossen*, ed. H. Hecht, 2 vols. (Leipzig, 1900–7) I, 3. Cf. Gregory, *Dialogi* I.Prol.1 (*Grégoire le Grand: Dialogues*, ed. A. de Vogüé with P. Antin, 3 vols., Sources chrétiennes 251, 260 and 265 (Paris, 1978–80) II, 10–11).

[9] *Bischof Wærferths von Worcester Übersetzung*, ed. Hecht I, 6. Cf. Gregory, *Dialogi* I.Prol.6 (ed. de Vogüé II, 14–15).

general, lay practices seem to have fallen much further short of this borderline. Stuart Airlie has drawn attention to a range of thoroughly secular attributes and activities which were commonly considered to be the defining features of a Carolingian male lay aristocrat – including not only marriage and warfare, but also noble descent, office-holding, hunting and feasting.[10] Effective fulfilment of these secular 'markers' was also central to the very legitimacy of the Carolingian dynasty. Einhard's biography of Charlemagne propagated the notion that the last Merovingian king, Childebert III, had possessed only the *inutile nomen regis* ('empty name of king'), through his failure to exercise rulership; and as a result of these overtones, as Paul Kershaw has noted in this context, the language of *utilitas* acquired potent force as a means of judging subsequent rulers according to conventional secular expectations.[11] Hence Einhard presented Charlemagne himself as a war-leader par excellence, equally eager for hunting and feasting, and in Thegan's biography of Louis the Pious the brief summary of Charlemagne's reign states simply that he reigned *bene et utiliter*.[12] On the other hand, the grave implications of 'uselessness' could not be more clearly delineated in the case of Charles, the young king of Provence, who is reported to have suffered from epilepsy. This physical weakness provided the justification for an attempt to depose him in 861, on the basis that Charles was simply 'useless and unsuitable for the office and title of king'.[13] Although *inutilitas* seems to have originated as a specifically Carolingian political language, comparable secular expectations seem to have operated in early Anglo-Saxon England. This is illustrated most clearly in vernacular heroic poetry, which conveys a vivid impression of the social bonds which united a successful king with his aristocratic followers – not only the pursuit of glory and tribute on the battlefield, but

---

[10] S. Airlie, 'The Anxiety of Sanctity: St Gerald of Aurillac and his Maker', *JEH* 43 (1992), 372–95, at 376; cf. also K. Leyser, 'Early Medieval Canon Law and the Beginnings of Knighthood', *Institutionen, Kultur und Gesellschaft im Mittelalter: Festschrift für J. Fleckenstein*, ed. L. Fenske, W. Rösener and T. Zotz (Sigmaringen, 1984), pp. 549–66, repr. in his *Communications and Power in Medieval Europe: the Carolingian and Ottonian Centuries*, ed. T. Reuter (London, 1998), pp. 51–71.

[11] Einhard, *Vita Karoli*, c. 1 (*Einhardi Vita Karoli Magni*, ed. O. Holder-Egger, MGH SS rerum Germanicarum in usum scholarum separatim editi 25 (Hanover, 1911), 2–4). On 'usefulness', see P. Kershaw, 'Illness, Power and Prayer in Asser's *Life of King Alfred*', *EME* 10 (forthcoming, 2001); E. Peters, *The Shadow King: 'Rex Inutilis' in Medieval Law and Literature, 751–1327* (New Haven, CT, 1970), esp. pp. 53–4 and 69; and J. L. Nelson, 'Bad Kingship in the Earlier Middle Ages', *Haskins Soc. Jnl* 8 (1996), 1–26, at 4–9.

[12] Thegan, *Gesta Hludovici Imperatoris*, c. 5 (*Thegan: Die Taten Kaiser Ludwigs / Astronomus: Das Leben Kaiser Ludwigs*, ed. E. Tremp, MGH SS rerum Germanicarum in usum scholarum separatim editi 64 (Hanover, 1995), 180).

[13] *Annals of Saint-Bertin s.a.* 861, cf. 863 (*Les Annales de Saint Bertin*, ed. F. Grat, J. Vielliard and S. Clémencet (Paris, 1964), pp. 87 and 96; J. L. Nelson, *The Annals of St-Bertin* (Manchester, 1991), pp. 96 and 104).

also the hope of gifts and feasting in the mead-hall.[14] These practical criteria would seem to have played a particularly crucial role in determining the selection of kings, given the absence of any strict dynastic succession in early Anglo-Saxon England. Although documentary sources rarely record the particular shortcomings of unsuccessful kings, it is nevertheless significant that minors rarely seem to have been regarded as viable candidates for kingship.[15] War-leadership was simply too important to be entrusted to anyone other than a mature and able-bodied layman.

In this context of lay ideals, as Janet Nelson has persuasively argued, the Carolingian ecclesiastical reforms represented a major departure, especially those of the early ninth century.[16] Reform was dependent upon the harmony of Frankish political and ecclesiastical structures, and the overall aim was to correct every *ordo* of Frankish society according to its function, thus introducing more rigorous standards of behaviour not only for monks and clerics, but also for laymen. Where these new standards conflicted with the pre-existing expectations of aristocratic life, tensions understandably arose which could be psychological as well as social. These tensions reached their most extreme form in the sphere explored by Nelson – the upbringing of young aristocratic males, who were now confronted with two distinct and incompatible career-paths. On the one hand, the enforcement of monastic celibacy heralded the prospect of uncontaminated service to God within a Benedictine monastery, while on the other, life as a secular nobleman necessarily involved service to God *in saeculo*. Any uncertainty over which sort of career awaited a noble son in the formative stages of his youth might make it difficult for him to adapt to this career when it was eventually determined for him. Hence Gerald of Aurillac had initially been trained in 'secular pursuits', especially hunting, but was then struck down with so serious a skin disease that his parents applied him to *litterarum studia*, with the intention that he should become an ecclesiastic. When Gerald subsequently recovered, however, he resumed his military training.[17] It is this confusion in his youth, Nelson argues, that helps to explain why Gerald developed into such an anxious secular nobleman, celibate almost to the point of emasculation, even refusing to wear his sword in the appropriate manly way.[18] On the basis of several other

---

[14] See esp. K. O'Brien O'Keeffe, 'Heroic Values and Christian Ethics', *The Cambridge Companion to Old English Literature*, ed. M. Godden and M. Lapidge (Cambridge, 1991), pp. 107–25, and on the context for such poetry, P. Wormald, 'Bede, "Beowulf" and the Conversion of the Anglo-Saxon Aristocracy', *Bede and Anglo-Saxon England*, ed. R. T. Farrell, BAR Brit. ser. 46 (Oxford, 1978), 32–95.

[15] On succession practices, see D. N. Dumville, 'The Ætheling: a Study in Anglo-Saxon Constitutional History', *ASE* 8 (1979), 1–33, esp. 28–31, for some unusual exceptions.

[16] J. L. Nelson, 'Monks, Secular Men and Masculinity, *c.* 900', *Masculinity in Medieval Europe*, ed. D. M. Hadley (Harlow, 1999), pp. 121–42.

[17] Odo of Cluny, *Vita Geraldi*, I.4–5 (PL 133, cols. 644–5).   [18] *Ibid.* II.3 (PL 133, cols. 671–2).

Frankish examples, Nelson wonders whether Alfred's own anxieties might also be attributable to some similar period of youthful career confusion.

Nelson's explanatory framework demands further consideration, yet it is important to recognize that tensions no less significant, though perhaps less extreme, arose in other spheres of aristocratic life as a result of the Carolingian reforms. As Notker observed, marriage and warfare were incompatible with sanctity, and for this reason the Christianized code that Carolingian moralists directed towards aristocratic laymen represented something of an uncomfortable compromise between ascetic patristic ethics and the practical needs of the world. Admonitory texts known as 'mirrors for laymen' were ostensibly designed to reassure lay aristocrats that their *ordo* presented no insurmountable obstacle to the kingdom of heaven, yet the route they were offered was hardly straightforward.[19] Certainly, marriage received new positive affirmation as a holy institution, but the need for sexual restraint was stressed even within this monogamous relationship. After the example of the Old Testament patriarchs, Carolingian married men were expected to be prolific, but to achieve this through lust-free intercourse, thereby preserving chastity.[20] Sin was inevitable in such a regime, and appropriate escape-valves were therefore offered to laymen in the form of private prayer and secret confession, both originally of monastic origin. Yet precisely because these practices were so exacting, such reform was extremely difficult to implement. Though impressive, the surviving Carolingian corpus of 'mirrors for laymen' and other devotional compilations hardly suggests that these practices were adopted en masse.[21]

In one sphere of lay life, however, there were far stronger incentives to embrace these new disciplines. What made the message of reform so attractive to Louis the Pious and later Carolingian rulers was that it enhanced their rulership by defining their position as a *ministerium* or 'office'.[22] This *ministerium* exalted the ruler as a model of good conduct for the people beneath him to

[19] On this genre, see esp. J. M. H. Smith, 'Gender and Ideology in the Early Middle Ages', *Gender and Christian Religion*, ed. R. N. Swanson, Stud. in Church Hist. 34 (Woodbridge, 1998), 51–73, and M. Wallace-Hadrill, *The Frankish Church* (Oxford, 1983), pp. 283–6 and 403–11.

[20] Nelson, 'Monks', pp. 127–8.

[21] For surveys of the latter, see P. Salmon, *Analecta Liturgica: Extraits des manuscrits liturgiques de la Bibliothèque Vaticane*, Studi e testi 273 (Vatican City, 1974), 121–94; *idem*, 'Livrets de prières de l'époque carolingienne', *RB* 86 (1976), 218–34; and *idem*, 'Livrets de prières de l'époque carolingienne: nouvelle liste de manuscrits', *RB* 90 (1980), 147–9.

[22] Discussed in this context by M. de Jong, 'Power and Humility in Carolingian Society: the Public Penance of Louis the Pious', *EME* 1 (1992), 29–52, esp. 39–41, and by S. Airlie, 'Private Bodies and the Body Politic in the Divorce Case of Lothar II', *Past and Present* 161 (November 1998), 3–38, esp. 6–8. See also O. Guillot, 'Une ordinatio méconnue: le Capitulaire de 823–825', *Charlemagne's Heir: New Perspectives on the Reign of Louis the Pious*, ed. P. Godman and R. Collins (Oxford, 1990), pp. 455–86, and, more generally, H. H. Anton, *Fürstenspiegel und Herrscherethos in der Karolingerzeit*, Bonner Historische Forschungen 32 (Bonn, 1968).

imitate, and the ruler's ability to rule his people was therefore generally held to be dependent upon his prior ability to rule his own body and his household.[23] 'Ministerial' rulership enabled ecclesiastical reform to be harnessed even more effectively to the needs of royal power, and it also enabled individual Carolingians to claim moral superiority over their relatives whenever dynastic disputes arose, as inevitably they did. Yet, equally inevitably, these principles also enabled a ruler's opponents to seize upon any suspicion of personal royal short-comings as a 'devastating' new political weapon.[24] Hence one of the key accusa-tions levelled against Louis the Pious in 830 was that his empress, Judith, had committed adultery with Louis's godson, Bernard, and this charge resurfaced in 833 when Louis was temporarily deposed for neglecting his *ministerium* in a ritual stage-managed by a group of rebel bishops.[25] In 857, Lothar II first levelled a similar accusation of sexual perversion against his own queen, Theutberga, as a key part of his protracted efforts to divorce her. Yet as Airlie has shown, in the early 860s opponents of the divorce succeeded very effectively in reassigning the blame to Lothar himself, for failing to restrain his own bodily desire for his concubine, Waldrada.[26] In the hands of 'ministerial' rulers, newly vulnerable to such accusations, the recommended escape-valves of lay devotion acquired new and potent political significance. In this respect, Louis's humiliating public penance in 833 is exceptional: the admission of sins, however real or imaginary, more usually served to demonstrate that the royal *ministerium* was indeed being fulfilled. Louis himself had undertaken voluntary penance for these purposes in 822, and later in the ninth century, perhaps in reaction to these precedents, the model of David's secret confession to the prophet Nathan emerged as a less threatening means of regulating royal conduct.[27] It is surely no coincidence that this biblical episode was prominently displayed in ivory on the front cover of Charles the Bald's own pocket psalter.[28] The surviving personal prayerbooks of Carolingian rulers amply testify to the enhanced expiatory power of royal devo-tion.[29] Yet it should be stressed that such extreme demonstrations of Gregorian

[23] See esp. Sedulius Scottus, *Liber de rectoribus christianis*, cc. 2 and 5 (*Sedulius Scottus*, ed. S. Hellmann, Quellen und Untersuchungen zur lateinischen Philologie des Mittelalters 1(1) (Munich, 1906), 25–7 and 34–7). [24] Airlie, 'Private Bodies', p. 6.

[25] De Jong, 'Power and Humility', p. 29; Smith, 'Gender and Ideology', p. 69.

[26] Airlie, 'Private Bodies', esp. pp. 25–35.

[27] De Jong, 'Power and Humility', pp. 31 and 51–2; J. L. Nelson, 'Kingship, Law and Liturgy in the Political Thought of Hincmar of Rheims', in her *Politics and Ritual in Early Medieval Europe* (London, 1986), pp. 133–71, at 164–5.

[28] Paris, Bibliothèque Nationale de France, lat. 1152 (court school of Charles the Bald, 842 × 869; given to Metz in 869); see R. Deshman, 'The Exalted Servant: the Ruler Theology of the Prayerbook of Charles the Bald', *Viator* 11 (1980), 385–417, at 404–7, with figs. 17–18.

[29] For the psalter of Charles the Bald, see above, n. 28; for his prayerbook, see below, p. 46, n. 41. The psalter of Lothar I is London, British Library, Add. 37768 (court school of Lothar I, shortly after 842); see W. Koehler and F. Mütherich, *Die karolingischen Miniaturen*, IV: *Die*

or Christ-like humility seem to have been largely reserved for selected ecclesiastical audiences.[30] For example, an exclusive dialogue between Charles and the canons of Tours clearly lies behind the complex Davidic iconography of Charles' First Bible, recently decoded by Dutton and Kessler.[31] The ability of Louis the German to develop wider rituals of secular aristocratic unity from his own devotion to the True Cross seems to reflect the unusual 'frontier' conditions of the East Frankish kingdom.[32] In the wrong eyes, humble devotion could easily be reinterpreted as otherworldly withdrawal. Retrospective reports that Louis the Pious twice considered monastic withdrawal early in his career need to be interpreted in the light of his later determined refusal to accept monastic retirement in 830 and 833.[33] Yet as these tensions became increasingly internalized, at least one Carolingian ruler seems to have grown genuinely susceptible to the monastic calling. As Nelson notes, Charles the Fat's stated desire to abandon his wife and the world in 873 may represent his own personal verdict on the patent inadequacy of his childless marriage.[34]

As recent scholarship has rightly emphasized, this Carolingian tradition of royal devotion provides by far the clearest precedents for Alfred's own personal piety, described by Asser.[35] So rigorous is the daily liturgical regime attributed to Alfred that he is even said to have secretly visited churches at night for additional sessions of prayer.[36] Alfred thus maintained a constant dialogue with God, regulated fundamentally by the contents of the *libellus* which he is reported to have carried around with him at all times for the sake of prayer. Although this royal prayerbook has not survived, Asser reveals that its contents primarily consisted of the prayers of the hours, necessary for the celebration of the divine

---

Hofschule Lothars. Einzelhandschriften aus Lotharingien (Berlin, 1971), 35–46, with pls. 1–7. The psalter of Louis the German is Berlin, Staatsbibliothek Preußischer Kulturbesitz, Theol. Lat. fol. 58 (?Saint-Amand, *c.* 825 × *c.* 866, with subsequent augmentations); see E. J. Goldberg, '"More Devoted to the Equipment of Battle than the Splendor of Banquets": Frontier Kingship, Martial Ritual, and Early Knighthood at the Court of Louis the German', *Viator* 30 (1999), 41–78, at 67–71, with fig. 5.

[30] See the corrective remarks of J. L. Nelson, 'The Lord's Anointed and the People's Choice: Carolingian Royal Ritual', in her *The Frankish World, 750–900* (London, 1996), pp. 99–131, at 124–7.

[31] Paris, Bibliothèque Nationale de France, lat. 1 (Tours, 845; given to Metz in 869); P. E. Dutton and H. L. Kessler, *The Poetry and Paintings of the First Bible of Charles the Bald* (Ann Arbor, MI, 1997), esp. pp. 89–101.   [32] Goldberg, 'Frontier Kingship, Martial Ritual', esp. pp. 61–71.

[33] Astronomer, *Gesta Hludovici Imperatoris*, cc. 19, 32 and 44 (ed. Tremp, pp. 334–6, 392 and 458); Thegan, *Gesta Hludovici Imperatoris*, c. 43 (ed. Tremp, p. 230). See T. F. X. Noble, 'Louis the Pious and his Piety Re-Reconsidered', *Revue belge de philologie et d'histoire* 58 (1980), 297–316, at 308–10.

[34] Nelson, 'Monks', pp. 133–5.

[35] T. H. Bestul, 'Continental Sources of Anglo-Saxon Devotional Writing', *Sources of Anglo-Saxon Culture*, ed. P. E. Szarmach (Kalamazoo, MI, 1986), pp. 103–26, at 112 and 116–18; Scharer, 'Writing of History', pp. 187–91; Kershaw, 'Illness, Power and Prayer'.

[36] *Vita Alfredi*, cc. 74 and 76 (ed. Stevenson, pp. 55–6 and 59).

David Pratt

Office, together with certain selected psalms and many prayers.[37] Alfred's reported devotion to the office is here particularly significant, for this was an obligation of monastic origin, normally fulfilled only by ecclesiastics.[38] The unusual extension of the divine Office to laymen was a recent Carolingian trend, explicitly recommended in 'mirrors for laymen',[39] and this trend was suitably facilitated by the provision of psalters and prayerbooks specially designed for lay use, often personalized to meet the needs of their intended owners.[40] In this light, the similarities are all the more striking between Alfred's lost *libellus* and the surviving prayerbook of Charles the Bald.[41] The clipped pages of this tiny codex measure just 135 × 102 mm; the text itself begins with a preface recommending the services of the hours as a means of expiating sin (4v–5v);[42] and the prayers of the hours feature prominently in the compiled material which follows (40v–43r), in addition to many other prayers, directions for the use of psalms in different circumstances (19v–21r),[43] and a personalized litany (21r–28v). It may even be significant that this codex bears the title *Enchiridion precationum Caroli Calvi regis* (1r), for the word *enchiridion* is also employed by Asser to describe the *libellus* in which Alfred gathered his favourite passages from holy writings.[44] Asser's account leaves open the possibility that Alfred's *enchiridion* or *manualis liber* may have remained entirely separate from his prayerbook, however,[45] and

---

[37] *Ibid.* cc. 24 and 88, cf. 89 (ed. Stevenson, pp. 21 and 73–5).

[38] For the surviving manuscript evidence for the celebration of the divine Office in Anglo-Saxon England, see A. Corrêa, 'Daily Office Books: Collectars and Breviaries', and P. Pulsiano, 'Psalters', both in *The Liturgical Books of Anglo-Saxon England*, ed. R. W. Pfaff, OEN Subsidia 23 (Kalamazoo, MI, 1995), 45–60 and 61–85.

[39] Jonas of Orléans, *De institutione laicali* I.12 (PL 106, cols. 145–7); Dhuoda, *Liber manualis* II.3 and XI.1 (*Dhuoda, Handbook for her Warrior Son: Liber Manualis*, ed. M. Thiébaux, Cambridge Med. Classics 8 (Cambridge, 1998), 80–1 and 232–3).

[40] R. McKitterick, *The Carolingians and Written Word* (Cambridge, 1989), pp. 217–18, 244–57 and 264–9; P. Riché, *Les Écoles et l'enseignement dans l'Occident chrétien de la fin du Ve siècle au milieu du XIe siècle* (Paris, 1979), pp. 297–305; C. V. Leroquais, *Les Psautiers manuscrits latins des bibliothèques publiques de France*, 3 vols. (Mâcon, 1940–1) I, v–vii.

[41] The manuscript itself is housed in the Schatzkammer der Residenz, Munich, with original ivory plaques now in the Schweizerisches Landesmuseum in Zurich (court school of Charles the Bald, 842 × 869); see W. Koehler and F. Mütherich, *Die karolingischen Miniaturen, V: Die Hofschule Karls des Kahlen* (Berlin, 1982), 75–87, with pls. 1–3, and Deshman, 'Exalted Servant'.

[42] Originally composed by Alcuin for Charlemagne (?801 × 804): *Clavis des auteurs latins du Moyen Age: territoire français 735–987*, II: *Alcuin*, ed. M-H. Jullien and F. Perelman, CCCM (Turnhout, 1999), 344.

[43] Corresponding to the first seven groupings in Alcuin's *De psalmorum usu liber. ibid.* pp. 145–8.

[44] Cf. Scharer, 'Writing of History', pp. 190 and 200.

[45] Smyth, *Alfred the Great*, p. 232, raises this possibility in a very different context; cf. Keynes and Lapidge, *Alfred the Great*, p. 268 (n. 208). None of the preserved fragments of the text known at Worcester in the twelfth century as the *dicta Ælfredi regis* contain any devotional material; see D. Whitelock, 'William of Malmesbury on the Works of King Alfred', *Medieval Literature and Civilization: Studies in Memory of G. N. Garmonsway*, ed. D. A. Pearsall and R. A. Waldron

the use of the Greek word *enchiridion* to describe a small volume seems to have been something of an early medieval commonplace.[46] However one prefers to resolve these possibilities, the Carolingian character of Alfred's devotional behaviour remains inescapable.

Far from supplying answers, as has generally been assumed, however, such Carolingian precedents seem to raise still further questions in an Alfredian context. How unusual would Alfred's practices have seemed when viewed from an English perspective? Other precedents for Alfredian piety have recently been sought in the surviving English corpus of four pre-Alfredian devotional compilations, all written at Mercian centres in the late eighth or early ninth century.[47] Two of these compilations are believed to have been imported into Wessex in the later ninth century – the Book of Cerne and the Book of Nunnaminster – and the evidence for the latter depends upon an association with Alfred's Mercian wife, Ealhswith, whose ownership of this codex has often been suspected.[48] The important point, however, is that there is nothing in the content or conception of these four compilations to suggest original contexts anything other than highly learned and essentially ecclesiastical.[49] Particularly striking is the absence of any evidence for lay use remotely comparable to the personalized nature of material explicitly designed for Carolingian laymen. Michelle Brown has advanced good grounds for associating the production of the Book of Cerne with Ædeluald, bishop of Lichfield (*c.* 818–30),[50] and although the Royal Prayerbook has sometimes been identified as a physician's book, Patrick Sims-Williams plausibly suggests that the magico-medical material in question may derive from a double monastery in view of the closely related fragment, London, British Library, Harley 7653, which is largely

(London, 1969), pp. 78–93, at 90–1, repr. in her *From Bede to Alfred: Studies in Early Anglo-Saxon Literature and History* (London, 1980), no. VII.

[46] As noted by Stevenson (*Asser's Life of King Alfred*, p. 326), and by Scharer, 'Writing of History', p. 200.

[47] London, British Library, Harley 2965 ('Book of Nunnaminster'; Mercia, viii^{ex} or s. ix^{in}); London, British Library, Harley 7653 (Mercia, s. viii^{ex} or ix^{in}); London, British Library, Royal 2. A. xx (Mercia, s. viii^{ex} or ix^{in}); Cambridge, University Library, Ll. 1. 10 ('Book of Cerne'; Mercia, ?*c.* 818 × 830). See Scharer, 'Writing of History', p. 190; B. Raw, 'Alfredian Piety: the Book of Nunnaminster', *Alfred the Wise: Studies in Honour of Janet Bately*, ed. J. Roberts and J. L. Nelson, with M. R. Godden (Cambridge, 1997), pp. 145–53; Kershaw, 'Illness, Power and Prayer'.

[48] M. P. Brown, *The Book of Cerne: Prayer, Patronage and Power in Ninth-Century England* (London, 1996), pp. 157–61, 168 and 178–81; *idem* in *The Making of England: Anglo-Saxon Art and Culture AD 600–900*, ed. L. Webster and J. Backhouse (London, 1991), pp. 210–11 (nos. 164–5).

[49] For general discussion, see Bestul, 'Continental Sources', pp. 105–12; J. Morrish, 'Dated and Datable Manuscripts Copied in England during the Ninth Century: a Preliminary List', *MS* 50 (1988), 512–38, at 518–21; P. Sims-Williams, *Religion and Literature in Western England 600–800*, CSASE 3 (Cambridge, 1990), 273–327; Brown, *Book of Cerne*, pp. 103–15 and 129–61.

[50] Brown, *Book of Cerne*, pp. 131–6 and 181–4; cf. p. 114, where the possibility of lay patronage is briefly considered.

designed for female use.[51] In other words, the first clear English evidence for comparable lay devotion is Alfred's prayerbook itself.[52] It is of course quite conceivable that this watershed merely reflects the fuller nature of the Alfredian evidence, and certainly Alfred's behaviour raises important questions about the existing nature of West Saxon royal devotion in the period of his youth. It is interesting to note that it is also in the mid-ninth century that evidence first emerges for the existence of a small body of priests somehow attached to the West Saxon royal household,[53] and a tantalizing glimpse of their importance is provided by the actions of Alfred's brother, Æthelred, at the battle of Ashdown in 871, reportedly refusing to leave his tent before his priest had finished celebrating mass.[54] One is bound to wonder whether such militant royal devotion might not initially have arisen much earlier, perhaps in response to the intensification of the Viking attacks in the 830s; whether the example of Æthelred conveys a true sense of the significance accorded to the personal involvement of the king himself; and if so, whether Æthelred, or indeed his father Æthelwulf, might not also have possessed prayerbooks along Carolingian lines. Æthelred's attendance of mass is hardly in the same league as Alfred's more extreme devotions, however, and for what it is worth, the limited codicological evidence points to a slightly later turning-point in this respect. At least two high-status customized Carolingian psalters seem to have been imported into southern England in this period, of which the Psalter of Count Achadeus (Cambridge, Corpus Christi College 272) can be shown to have been originally constructed at some point between March 883 and May 884,[55] while the earliest English additions to the so-called 'Æthelstan' Psalter (London, British Library, Cotton Galba A. xviii) date from the early tenth century.[56] The

---

[51] Sims-Williams, *Religion and Literature*, pp. 281–2; cf. Brown in *The Making of England*, ed. Webster and Backhouse, pp. 208–10 (nos. 162–3), and *idem, Book of Cerne*, p. 152.

[52] As noted by Bestul, 'Continental Sources', pp. 116–18.

[53] S. Keynes, 'The West Saxon Charters of King Æthelwulf and his Sons', *EHR* 109 (1994), 1109–49, at 1131–7 and 1146–7.

[54] Asser, *Vita Alfredi*, cc. 37–8 (ed. Stevenson, pp. 28–30).

[55] Written in the diocese of Rheims for the personal use of Count Achadeus; in England by s. xi at the latest. The suspicion that the importation of this psalter might have been associated with Grimbald remains unproven; see M. R. James, *A Descriptive Catalogue of the Manuscripts in the Library of Corpus Christi College, Cambridge*, 2 vols. (Cambridge, 1912) II, 27–32; M. Lapidge, *Anglo-Saxon Litanies of the Saints*, HBS 106 (London, 1991), 64–5 and 110–14; D. N. Dumville, *English Caroline Script and Monastic History: Studies in Benedictinism, A.D. 950–1030* (Woodbridge, 1993), p. 131; P. P. O'Neill, 'On the Date, Provenance and Relationship of the "Solomon and Saturn" Dialogues', *ASE* 26 (1997), 139–68, at 162.

[56] Written in northern Francia, s. ix[1], with subsequent augmentations; in England by s. x[in] at the latest. The association with Æthelstan himself depends solely upon a sixteenth-century note; see S. Keynes, 'King Athelstan's Books', *Learning and Literature in Anglo-Saxon England: Studies presented to Peter Clemoes*, ed. M. Lapidge and H. Gneuss (Cambridge, 1985), pp. 143–201, at 193–6; *idem*, 'Anglo-Saxon Entries in the "Liber Vitae" of Brescia', *Alfred the Wise*, ed. Roberts

importation of these Gallican psalters clearly represented an unusual departure from the Roman version, hitherto used in England,[57] but a further explanation may be that comparable codices had simply never existed in England before this period. The possibility of earlier Carolingian influence must nevertheless be remembered at all times when one considers Alfred's own, better-documented devotions.

Whatever the extent of such Carolingian influence, the English church as a whole remained essentially untouched by any movement equivalent to the Carolingian reforms throughout the eighth and ninth centuries.[58] Certainly, conversion itself had relied heavily upon royal support, and there were indeed subsequent efforts on the part of kings to enforce ecclesiastical sanctions as a tool of royal power.[59] Yet these efforts were severely compromised by the fragmented nature of political authority among the English, when compared with the overarching diocesan structure of the wider English church.[60] In the absence of any firmer alliance between royal and episcopal authority, the English church continued to be dominated by the same proprietary aristocratic interests that had so facilitated its initial expansion. Tied to the world by the bonds of kinship, the majority of English monasteries seem to have been difficult to distinguish from other forms of noble residence, readily combining some form of religious observance with traditional aristocratic habits of clothing and entertainment, including feasting, gaming and the recitation of heroic poetry.[61] Family interests may also explain the high level of sexual activity apparently tolerated within such establishments. Abbots needed heirs, while unmarried aristocratic nuns remained vulnerable to the sexual advances of laymen or even ecclesiastics, tempted by the implications of blood and inheritance.[62]

and Nelson, pp. 99–119, at 117–19; R. Deshman, 'The Galba Psalter: Pictures, Texts and Contexts in an Early Medieval Prayerbook', *ASE* 26 (1997), 109–38.

[57] As argued by O'Neill, '"Solomon and Saturn" Dialogues', pp. 160–4.

[58] For a suggestive exploration of the many contrasts between Frankish and English ecclesiastical conditions in the ninth century, see J. L. Nelson, '"A King Across the Sea": Alfred in Continental Perspective', *TRHS* 5th ser. 36 (1986), 45–68, at 61–7, repr. in her *Rulers and Ruling Families in Early Medieval Europe: Alfred, Charles the Bald and Others* (Aldershot, 1999), no. I.

[59] Represented principally by the laws of Wihtred, king of Kent (695), and by the *capitulare* of the papal legates of 786.   [60] Nelson, '"A King Across the Sea"', p. 66.

[61] Wormald, 'Bede, "Beowulf" and the Conversion', esp. pp. 49–58; S. Foot, 'What was an Early Anglo-Saxon Monastery?', *Monastic Studies: the Continuity of Tradition*, ed. J. Loades (Bangor, 1990), pp. 48–57; A. Thacker, 'Monks, Preaching and Pastoral Care in Early Anglo-Saxon England', and J. Blair, 'Anglo-Saxon Minsters: a Topographical Review', both in *Pastoral Care before the Parish*, ed. J. Blair and R. Sharpe (Leicester, 1992), pp. 137–70 and 226–66; C. R. E. Cubitt, *Anglo-Saxon Church Councils c. 650–c. 850* (Leicester, 1995), esp. pp. 99–124.

[62] M. Clunies Ross, 'Concubinage in Anglo-Saxon England', *Past and Present* 108 (August 1985), 3–34, at 29–32.

These observations are necessarily dependent upon the criticisms of reformers, and it should therefore be stressed that the form of monasticism envisaged, for example, at the synod of *Clofesho* in 747 differed greatly from the model of Benedictinism enforced by Louis the Pious some seventy years later. Rather in the manner of Bede, the bishops of 747 seem to have been concerned to incorporate monasteries into an active, pastoral framework.[63] The strict isolation of *monachi* within monasteries would only be pursued during the Benedictine reform movement of the later tenth century, and it is revealing indeed that Louis' monastic reforms only seem to have interested the West Saxon dynasty at this late stage, after the creation of the kingdom of the English under Æthelstan and his successors.[64] It was far harder to maintain standards within monasteries of the eighth and ninth centuries, whose inhabitants were actively expected to provide pastoral care in the world at large. All these problems in turn served to shape the behaviour and religious practices of the English laity, in the absence of any more positive royal intervention in this sphere. In the case of marriage, for example, what is striking about the early English laws is the comparative rarity of explicit statements against concubinage.[65] Certainly, a distinction is increasingly implied in these texts between 'lawful matrimony', expressed by OE *rihtæw*, and intercourse outside the bonds of marriage, expressed by OE *unrihthæmed*;[66] but the actual practices of the English continued to attract regular criticism for their laxity, mainly from popes and other ecclesiastics based on the Continent.[67] Similarly in the case of penance, it clearly proved to be difficult to achieve any level of enforcement even within monasteries. Despite the hopes of Theodore and Bede, there is very little evidence for the lay application of penitential practices, even in

---

[63] Thacker, 'Monks, Preaching', pp. 164–6; C. R. E. Cubitt, 'Pastoral Care and Conciliar Canons: the Provisions of the 747 Council of *Clofesho*', *Pastoral Care*, ed. Blair and Sharpe, pp. 193–211.

[64] D. A. Bullough, 'The Continental Background of the Reform', *Tenth-Century Studies*, ed. D. Parsons (London, 1975), pp. 20–36, repr. in his *Carolingian Renewal: Sources and Heritage* (Manchester, 1991), pp. 272–96; N. Banton, 'Monastic Reform and the Unification of Tenth-Century England', *Religion and National Identity*, ed. S. Mews (Oxford, 1982), pp. 71–85.

[65] Laws of Wihtred, chs. 3–6 (*Die Gesetze der Angelsachsen*, ed. F. Liebermann, 3 vols. (Halle, 1903–16) I, 12); *capitulare* of the papal legates, cc. 15–16 (*Alcuini sive Albini epistolae*, no. 3, ed. E. Duemmler, MGH Epist. 2 (Berlin, 1895), 25).

[66] Clunies Ross, 'Concubinage', pp. 7–29, esp. 18–23.

[67] *Ibid.* pp. 25–9. See esp. the letters of Pope John VIII to Burgred, king of the Mercians (873 × 874), and to Æthelred, archbishop of Canterbury (877 × 878), and the letter of Fulk, archbishop of Rheims, to King Alfred (*c.* 890): *Councils and Synods and other Documents relating to the English Church*, I: *A.D. 871–1204*, ed. D. Whitelock, M. Brett and C. N. L. Brooke, 2 pts (Oxford, 1981) I, 1–2, 5 and 13 (nos. 1, 3 and 5); *English Historical Documents c. 500–1042*, ed. D. Whitelock, Eng. Hist. Documents 1, 2nd ed. (London, 1979), 880, 882 and 887 (nos. 220, 222 and 224). See also below, p. 54, n. 83.

limited form, before the tenth century.[68] Though undoubtedly vigorous in many cases, lay devotion before this period seems largely to have been restricted to a range of less extreme practices, including the veneration of saints, alms-giving and the commemoration of the departed by local religious houses.[69] The only evidence that widespread penance was ever considered as a means of forestalling Viking attack is preserved, significantly, in the form of an admonitory vision conveyed by English envoys to Louis the Pious in 839, clearly designed to affirm a sense of common purpose against this shared threat.[70]

The Carolingian character of Alfred's own piety thus seems to have been highly unusual in an English context, and any explanation of this unusual behaviour therefore needs to take full account of the very different English conditions to which it was being applied. This point is reinforced when one considers Nelson's recent attempt to explain Alfred's Carolingian behaviour according to parallel Carolingian mechanisms.[71] The notion that Alfred may once have been destined for an ecclesiastical career during his youth only seems to have gained some currency after this plot-line featured heavily in the 1969 film *Alfred the Great*. As Nelson concedes, Alfred's blessing at the hands of Pope Leo IV in Rome in 853 strongly suggests that his father Æthelwulf at least anticipated some future political role for his youngest son. Nelson suggests, however, that after Æthelwulf's death in 858, Alfred's older brothers may have proposed a monastic vocation for him, in order to exclude him from the succession, perhaps encouraged by any signs of ill-health that may then have been apparent. Yet this speculation rests on Nelson's claim that 'we have no idea where Alfred lived between 858 and 868 and what sort of future was mapped out for him', which apparently overlooks some important charter evidence to the contrary. Of the fifteen acceptable charters surviving from the period between 858 and 867, the year before Alfred's marriage, at least six, and perhaps seven, include Alfred as a witness, issued at locations which imply important meetings of the royal household not only in the West Saxon kingdom itself, but also in its eastern regions: *Freoricburna* in Surrey, *Willherestrio* in Kent, Micheldever in Hampshire, and Dorchester and Sherborne in

---

[68] Thacker, 'Monks, Preaching', pp. 157–64; A. J. Frantzen, *The Literature of Penance in Anglo-Saxon England* (New Brunswick, NJ, 1983), pp. 61–93 (on the eighth century) and 122–8 (on the three references to penance in Alfred's laws).

[69] Thacker, 'Monks, Preaching', pp. 160–70. On practices of commemoration, see *The Liber Vitae of the New Minster and Hyde Abbey Winchester*, ed. S. Keynes, EEMF 26 (Copenhagen, 1996), 49–65; *idem*, '"Liber Vitae" of Brescia'.

[70] *Annals of Saint-Bertin s.a.* 839 (*Annales de Saint Bertin*, ed. Grat *et al.*, pp. 29–30; J. L. Nelson, *Annals of St-Bertin*, pp. 42–3). For the possibility that these envoys might have been sent by King Ecgberht, prevented by death from fulfilling a planned journey to Rome, rather than King Æthelwulf, see Keynes, '"Liber Vitae" of Brescia', p. 113.   [71] Nelson, 'Monks', pp. 135–8.

Dorset.[72] Moreover, in five instances Alfred is given the title *filius regis*, which is precisely how Æthelwulf's other sons are described before they attain kingship of some sort.[73] Questions of succession, with the option of subdividing the realm always available, naturally tended to involve rivalry as well as agreement; but the brief period of acrimony that surrounded Æthelbald's usurpation in 855 seems to have given way to an extended period of co-operation between Æthelwulf's sons in the later 850s and throughout the 860s, in which younger brothers commonly received a share of governmental responsibility during the lifetime of the eldest. For a family which would lose three brothers in eleven years, all apparently dying of natural causes, such continuity and stability depended upon the fulfilment of agreed provisions for the future which had to be repeatedly renegotiated as circumstances changed.[74] Even if Alfred had indeed been regarded as a sickly youth, premature death was the norm among Æthelwulf's sons, and there is no hint in the charter evidence that the young Alfred remained anything other than a regular member of the royal household and a viable candidate to succeed his brothers if necessary.

Nelson's suggestion depends upon the broader assumption, moreover, that in England, as in contemporary Francia, ecclesiastical careers were commonly imposed upon potential candidates for kingship, with the intention of excluding them from succession.[75] Yet this assumption overlooks the important contrast –

[72] S 330, dated 861 (BCS 855; *The Charters of St Augustine's Abbey, Canterbury, and Minster-in-Thanet*, ed. S. E. Kelly, AS Charters 4 (Oxford, 1995), no. 22); S 331, dated 862 (BCS 506; *Charters of Rochester*, ed. A. Campbell, AS Charters 1 (London, 1973), no. 25); S 335, dated 862 (BCS 505; *The Charters of Abingdon Abbey*, ed. S. E. Kelly, AS Charters 7 (Oxford, 2000), no. 15); S 336, issued at Dorchester and dated 863 (BCS 508), where 'Ælfred dux', the second ealdorman in the witness-list, might be identified as the future king, rather than the ealdorman of Surrey of the same name; S 333, also issued at Dorchester, dated 863, with a subsequent endorsement at Sherborne, dated 864 (BCS 510; *Anglo-Saxon Charters*, ed. A. J. Robertson, 2nd ed. (Cambridge, 1956), no. 11; *The Charters of Sherborne*, ed. M. A. O'Donovan, AS Charters 3 (Oxford, 1988), no. 6); also S 1199 (BCS 515), a grant of land perhaps in Canterbury, which has no place of issue and can be dated no more closely than 858 × 866; and S327, dated '790', perhaps in error for 860 (BCS 502), a grant of land at Rochester, which also has no place of issue.

[73] S 327, S 331, S 1199, S 335 and S 333 (both grant and endorsement). This practice is demonstrated most clearly in the analysis of laymen attesting West Saxon charters of the ninth century presented by S. Keynes, *An Atlas of Attestations in Anglo-Saxon Charters, c. 670–1066*, rev. ed. (Cambridge, 1998), table XXI.

[74] These observations proceed initially from the examination of the charter evidence undertaken by Keynes, 'West Saxon Charters', pp. 1128–31; cf. also *idem*, 'The Control of Kent in the Ninth Century', *EME* 2 (1993), 111–31, at 120–31. This reinforces the impression of orderly re-negotiation that is otherwise conveyed by Alfred's will; see Keynes and Lapidge, *Alfred the Great*, pp. 314–16 (nn. 3, 4, 7 and 10), cf. also Dumville, 'The Ætheling', pp. 21–5.

[75] Alfred's younger son, Æthelweard, was certainly educated to a higher level than Edward the Elder (*Vita Alfredi*, c. 75, ed. Stevenson, p. 58), but there is no necessary implication that he may therefore originally have been destined for the church (cf. Nelson, '"A King Across the Sea"', p. 57). Edward himself may simply have been too old to benefit directly from the newly

first noted by Clare Stancliffe in her classic study of 'The Kings who Opted Out' – between continental experiences, in which 'the tonsuring of a prince or king and his confinement within a monastery was simply a political act, designed to remove a rival king', and the practice, particularly prevalent in Anglo-Saxon England, of kings who are said to have chosen the monastic life voluntarily, all six examples occurring in the age of Bede.[76] Naturally, one may wonder whether such accounts conceal any other political considerations than the desire to ensure the smooth succession of a chosen heir, and one should also acknowledge the three attested examples of Anglo-Saxon kings who do indeed seem to have been forcibly tonsured, all from eighth-century Northumbria: Bede's addressee Ceolwulf, tonsured and held for a time in a monastic centre in 731; Æthelwald, whose deposition from the throne in 765 involved tonsuring, according to Irish annals; and Osred II, who was deprived of the kingdom by his enemies in 789, tonsured at York and then expelled.[77] Yet these few exceptions still only serve to emphasize the marked contrast with Merovingian and Carolingian Francia, where deposed rulers, failed rebels and other noble victims were regularly tonsured and exiled within monasteries at the apparent behest of their opponents.[78] It is difficult to accept that this contrast should merely be ascribed to the comparative reticence of Insular sources. One explanation may lie in the extent to which Anglo-Saxon monasteries remained far less isolated from all kinds of lay encroachment than their Frankish counterparts, especially in the ninth century. In Anglo-Saxon England the demise of an opponent could perhaps only be achieved in general through physical mutilation or death, for the alternative of monastic exile would not usually have involved sufficiently serious a break with the secular world for his political neutralization to be even temporarily effective. Even if the young Alfred had indeed been installed in a monastery for a time, there is little reason to suppose that he would have experienced the same level of career confusion apparently suffered by the young Gerald of

founded court *schola*. In the event, Æthelweard clearly remained active as an ætheling in Edward's reign, and left two sons to succeed him after his death (*c.* 920); see Keynes and Lapidge, *Alfred the Great*, p. 256 (n. 147), and Keynes, *Atlas*, table XXXIa.

[76] C. Stancliffe, 'The Kings Who Opted Out', *Ideal and Reality in Frankish and Anglo-Saxon Society*, ed. P. Wormald, with D. Bullough and R. Collins (Oxford, 1983), pp. 154–76, at 154–6 and 158.

[77] See D. P. Kirby, *The Earliest English Kings* (London, 1991), pp. 147–9, 151 and 153–4. Cf. the case of Eadberht Præn, leader of Kentish resistance against Mercian domination in the 790s (*ibid.* pp. 176–9), whom Pope Leo III deemed to be ineligible for kingship on the basis that he had once been ordained as a priest, perhaps forcibly. This ruling gave the Mercian king Cenwulf carte blanche to have Eadberht captured, blinded and mutilated in 798; according to later tradition Eadberht survived and was imprisoned by Cenwulf for about thirteen years in the new royal monastery at Winchcombe.

[78] Now sensitively surveyed by M. de Jong, 'Monastic Prisoners or Opting Out? Political Coercion and Honour in the Frankish Kingdoms', *Topographies of Power in the Early Middle Ages*, ed. M. de Jong, F. Theuws and C. van Rhijn (Leiden, forthcoming).

Aurillac. All in all, Alfred's subsequent devotional behaviour can hardly be construed as positive evidence for some otherwise conjectural period of monastic exile in the time of his youth.

The fundamental contrast between English and Frankish conditions is further emphasized when one considers the status of royal sexual sin. In another context, Nelson has sought to associate Alfred's devotional behaviour with the possibility that he may have taken a concubine early in his career, by implication not later than *c.* 880.[79] Nelson's suggestion depends upon her identification of Osferth, an ealdorman of some importance during the reigns of Edward and Æthelstan, as Alfred's own illegitimate son, on the basis of his unusual attestation as *frater regis* in a cartulary copy of a charter dated 904, which others have tended to dismiss as a mistake.[80] Osferth was clearly related to Alfred in some way, for he is described as a 'kinsman' in the king's will and in a charter dated 909, and the question therefore hinges upon the significance of his leading-name, which rather seems to imply some relationship to Alfred's mother, Osburh, or to Oswald *filius regis*, who was probably the son of one of Alfred's brothers.[81] Yet Nelson raises the alternative possibility that Osferth may have received his leading-name from his father's maternal line as an indication of his illegitimacy and diminished suitability for kingship. Naturally, one may wonder which of these scenarios is more compatible with the literary evidence of Alfred's translations.[82] The more important question, however, is whether royal extra-marital relations of this kind would have been regarded as at all problematic from an English perspective. Of course, earlier ecclesiastical reformers, especially Boniface and Alcuin, had regularly threatened kings with divine punishment for adultery and concubinage, and on one occasion this concern even found formal expression, in the report of the papal legates of 786, where the sanctity of marriage is explicitly asserted in the context of a chapter prohibiting the succession of illegitimates.[83] Yet the exceptional nature of this canon is perhaps symptomatic of the degree of Frankish influence upon the report as a

[79] J. L. Nelson, 'Reconstructing a Royal Family: Reflections on Alfred, from Asser, chapter 2', *People and Places in Northern Europe, 500–1600: Essays in honour of Peter Hayes Sawyer*, ed. I. Wood and N. Lund (Woodbridge, 1991), pp. 47–66, at 59–61, repr. in her *Rulers and Ruling Families*, no. III.   [80] S 1286 (BCS 611).

[81] Keynes and Lapidge, *Alfred the Great*, p. 322 (n. 79); *Select English Historical Documents of the Ninth and Tenth Centuries*, ed. F. E. Harmer (Cambridge, 1914), pp. 15–19 and 49–53 (no. 11); S 378 (BCS 624).   [82] See below, pp. 75–81.

[83] Clunies Ross, 'Concubinage', pp. 25–8. Letter of Boniface to Æthelbald, king of the Mercians (*c.* 747): *Die Briefe der heiligen Bonifatius und Lullus*, ed. M. Tangl, MGH Epist. select. 1 (Berlin, 1916), 147–51 (no. 73); *English Historical Documents*, ed. Whitelock, pp. 816–22 (no. 177). Letters of Alcuin to Æthelred, king of the Northumbrians (793), and to an unnamed Mercian *patricius* (797): *Alcuini sive Albini epistolae*, ed. Duemmler, pp. 43 and 179 (nos. 16 and 122); *English Historical Documents*, ed. Whitelock, pp. 843 and 855 (nos. 193 and 202). Cf. *capitulare* of the papal legates, c. 16, cf. 12 (ed. Duemmler, pp. 23–5).

whole,[84] and in Wessex, as in other kingdoms, there is every sign that irregular royal unions continued to be tolerated or even encouraged. Donald Scragg has recently acquitted King Cynewulf of any improper sexual conduct on the occasion of his assassination later in 786,[85] while the unusually low status accorded to the king's wife in the ninth century can only have enhanced royal opportunities for marital flexibility. King Æthelwulf may conceivably have repudiated Osburh in order to marry the Carolingian princess Judith in 856;[86] Æthelbald seems to have had little difficulty in securing his own (uncanonical) marriage to Judith after his father's death in 858;[87] and in the tenth century, when better evidence is available, successive West Saxon kings can be shown to have practised serial monogamy, 'not always troubling to await the death of a previous wife before remarriage'.[88]

Even if Alfred had indeed taken a concubine, therefore, such behaviour would hardly seem to have demanded conspicuous expiation in a West Saxon context. In the absence of any more effective ecclesiastical regulation in the ninth century, Anglo-Saxon kingship seems to have conspicuously avoided the 'ministerial' disciplines that had so transformed expectations of rulership in the Carolingian world. Certainly, earlier ecclesiastical writers such as Bede and Alcuin had consistently promoted broadly Gregorian notions of humble rulership,[89] but these expectations hardly seem to have been shared by the Anglo-Saxon aristocracy as a whole, at least in any pure form, and by the mid-ninth century ecclesiastical priorities lay elsewhere. Of course, one must be alive to the possibility of Carolingian influence upon West Saxon kingship throughout the ninth century, given the long tradition of close diplomatic relations between the two dynasties. In particular, Æthelwulf's journey to Rome in 855–6 would have given Alfred himself first-hand experience of Carolingian kingship in action, at this vital early stage in his childhood. The problem, of course, is that it is very difficult to gain any sense at all of the established imagery of West Saxon kingship in the mid-ninth century. The impression derived from Alfred's Prose Preface at least, supported by the testimony of Asser, is that Alfred himself regarded his educational

---

[84] See J. E. Story, 'Carolingian Northumbria and the Legatine Mission of 786', *Conversion and Christianity in the North Sea World*, ed. B. E. Crawford, St John's House Papers 8 (St Andrews, 1998), 93–107.

[85] D. G. Scragg, '*Wifcyþþe* and the Morality of the Cynewulf and Cyneheard Episode in the Anglo-Saxon Chronicle', *Alfred the Wise*, ed. Roberts and Nelson, pp. 179–85.

[86] Nelson, 'Reconstructing a Royal Family', p. 54; *Asser's Life of King Alfred*, ed. Stevenson, pp. 222–5; cf. Abels, *Alfred the Great*, p. 71.

[87] *Asser's Life of King Alfred*, ed. Stevenson, pp. 214–15; Abels, *Alfred the Great*, pp. 90–1.

[88] P. Stafford, 'The King's Wife in Wessex 800–1066', *Past and Present* 91 (May 1981), 3–27, at 13. On the status of Edward the Elder's first partner, Ecgwynn, and the significance of his subsequent marriage to Ælfflæd, contracted by 901, see also Nelson, '"A King Across the Sea"', pp. 56–7, and *idem*, 'Reconstructing a Royal Family', p. 64.

[89] J. M. Wallace-Hadrill, *Early Germanic Kingship in England and on the Continent* (Oxford, 1971), pp. 72–123.

programme as a major new departure from the priorities of his immediate prede-
cessors, who are implicitly criticized for their general neglect of wisdom, and for
their failure to provide Alfred himself with skilled teachers during his youth.[90] It
is difficult to escape the conclusion that Alfred was probably establishing a new,
unfamiliar tone in presenting his own royal image so explicitly as the exemplary
fulfilment of a Gregorian *ðegnung* or 'ministry' (usually translating *officium*),[91] with
all the additional 'ministerial' disciplines that this implied.

All the forces that had served to sustain Carolingian royal devotion remained
essentially lacking, therefore, in an Alfredian context. The fundamental challenge posed by Alfred's piety is thus to explain how this unusual Carolingian
behaviour functioned in the very different conditions of Anglo-Saxon England,
and to identify alternative forces which might better account for this royal behaviour in the particular context of the West Saxon court. It is this broader challenge which in turn shifts the focus onto the specific question of Alfred's
medical history. Although Alfred himself clearly identified his sins as somehow
sexual, he also regarded his own bodily illnesses as a further consequence of
these sins, and the suspicion therefore arises that Alfred's piety may have been
primarily driven by the state of his health. It is therefore essential to consider the
medical reality of Alfred's illnesses, as well as his various interpretative
responses. It may be, for example, that Alfred's afflictions were sufficiently
debilitating to raise threatening doubts in some quarters about his very fitness to
rule, in which case his unusual piety might be interpreted as a direct attempt to
quell such doubts;[92] yet one must also consider the possibility that the afflictions
may have been 'in part psychological', in which case the unusual piety might
seem rather less immediately explicable.[93] Similarly, when one turns to the
sexual nature of Alfred's sinfulness, the possibility arises that this too may have
arisen primarily from the piety itself, not from the reality of any particular sexual
behaviour on Alfred's part. These possibilities make it all the more important,

[90] *King Alfred's West Saxon Version of Gregory's Pastoral Care*, ed. H. Sweet, 2 vols., EETS os 45 and 50
(London, 1871), 2–8; *Vita Alfredi*, cc. 22, 24 and 25 (ed. Stevenson, pp. 19–22). For an assessment of contemporary Latinity which lends substance to Alfred's rhetoric, see M. Lapidge,
'Latin Learning in Ninth-Century England', in his *Anglo-Latin Literature 600–899* (London,
1996), pp. 409–54. J. M. Bately, 'Old English Prose before and during the Reign of Alfred',
ASE 17 (1988), 93–138, throws the originality of Alfred's efforts into greater relief, by undermining the case for an established 'school' of Mercian vernacular writing earlier in the ninth
century.

[91] *Alfred's West Saxon Version of Gregory's Pastoral Care*, ed. Sweet, ch. VII, p. 46, line 20, p. 48, line
16, and p. 50, line 6; ch. VIII, p. 54, line 3; ch. XI, p. 64, line 2; ch. XIII, p. 74, line 20. Cf.
Gregory, *Regula pastoralis* I.7, I.8, I.11 and II.2 (*Grégoire le Grand: Règle pastorale*, ed. F. Rommel,
with B. Judic and C. Morel, 2 vols., Sources chrétiennes 381–2 (Paris, 1992) I, 150–2, lines 1, 17
and 30; I, 156, line 28; I, 164, line 2; I, 176, line 3).

[92] This view is approached by Nelson, 'Monks', p. 136, and by Kershaw, 'Illness, Power and
Prayer'.   [93] Keynes and Lapidge, *Alfred the Great*, pp. 255–6 (n. 143).

finally, to assess the manner in which Alfred's unusual royal image may have been understood by the wider nobility, in political circumstances which might otherwise seem to have placed a particular premium on the need for traditional secular behaviour. All these questions might seem speculative indeed, were it not for the exceptional quality of the direct evidence surviving from the West Saxon court, which deserves to be explored in full. Alfred's medical history can be reconstructed in detail which is quite unparalleled in the early Middle Ages, and this fact in itself bears witness to the great concern that the king's sufferings undoubtedly roused in contemporaries, not least in Alfred himself.[94]

THE TESTIMONY OF ASSER

Any assessment of Alfred's illnesses must initially proceed from the detailed account provided by Asser in ch. 74 of his *Life of King Alfred*. Marie Schütt was the first to rescue the coherence of this passage, in 1957, and her findings are lucidly summarized by Keynes and Lapidge:

[Asser] recounts the stages of Alfred's medical history in reverse order: (1) as a youth, Alfred was unable to suppress [his] carnal desire, and so prayed to God for an illness to strengthen his resolve, and contracted piles (*ficus*); (2) subsequently, on a visit to Cornwall, he asked God to replace the piles with a less severe illness but one not outwardly visible, whereupon he was cured of [the] piles; (3) at his wedding (aged nineteen, in 868) he was struck suddenly by [a] new, unidentified, illness which lasted from his twentieth to his forty-fifth year.[95]

In other words, this second illness was still afflicting Alfred in 893 when Asser was writing. The curious, regressive nature of Asser's account necessarily betrays an acute awareness of these troubling contemporary circumstances. Asser was an eyewitness to events at the West Saxon court only from about 885, and his knowledge of earlier West Saxon history was understandably more limited, which is why the *Anglo-Saxon Chronicle* provided such a useful framework.

---

[94] W. Bonser, *The Medical Background of Anglo-Saxon England*, Publ. of the Wellcome Hist. Lib. ns 3 (London, 1963), 109–13, briefly compares Alfred's case with what little is known about the medical histories of several other Anglo-Saxon individuals; C. Brewer, *The Death of Kings* (London, 2000), supplies later examples from Edward the Confessor to Queen Victoria.

[95] Keynes and Lapidge, *Alfred the Great*, pp. 255–6 (n. 143); M. Schütt, 'The Literary Form of Asser's *Vita Alfredi*', *EHR* 62 (1957), 209–20, at 214–15. J. Campbell, 'Asser's *Life of Alfred*', *The Inheritance of Historiography 350–900*, ed. C. Holdsworth and T. P. Wiseman, Exeter Stud. in Hist. 12 (Exeter, 1986), 115–35, repr. in (and cited from) his *The Anglo-Saxon State* (London, 2000), pp. 129–55, at 154–5, further reasserts the coherence of ch. 74 in specific response to the doubts raised by D. P. Kirby, 'Asser and his *Life of King Alfred*', *Studia Celtica* 6 (1971), 12–35, at 13–15. It is interesting to note that John of Worcester (*s.a.* 871) seems to have understood Asser's regressive chronology in precisely this manner, reordering his sentences accordingly: *The Chronicle of John of Worcester*, II: *the Annals from 450–1066*, ed. R. R. Darlington and P. McGurk, trans. J. Bray and P. McGurk (Oxford, 1995), 294–5.

Otherwise, Asser had to rely primarily on the testimony of others, most notably the king himself, his 'truthful lord', and the stories that he heard inevitably reflected retrospective perceptions current in 893. Hence, for example, the judicious account of Æthelwulf's return in the *Chronicle*'s entry for 855 prompts Asser to engage in a threefold regression into matters more murky: first, back to Æthelwulf's marriage to Judith, secondly, back to the establishment of the custom which this marriage flouted, and thirdly, back to the original story of Eadburh, upon which Alfred himself seems frequently to have brooded.[96] Asser's ch. 74 seems to preserve another retrospective story told by the king himself. In recording this story *praeposterato ordine* ('with the order reversed') as he self-referentially puts it, Asser is surely reflecting his own telescopic perception of the recent West Saxon past, and also the essential irony of Alfred's medical history, as the king himself saw it in 893.

Alfred's story would seem to represent his own rationalization of the second, mysterious, disease that had plagued him from his wedding feast right up to the present day. Some attributed this disease to the *fascinatio* ('enchantment') of the people around him, others to the intervention of the devil, others to 'some unfamiliar kind of fever', 'still others thought that it was due to "the fig" (*ficus*)', a disease which had afflicted him from the time of his childhood. Alfred had his own explanation, however, and any attempt to understand the thought processes involved must depend heavily upon one's interpretation of Alfred's first illness, *ficus*, which is normally understood to mean 'piles, haemorrhoids'. This is certainly the meaning implied in later medieval Latin texts,[97] and it is evident from medical texts that this was also the primary meaning of the vernacular equivalent, OE *fic*. This is clear enough from the description of a treatment for *fic adl* ('fig disease') included in a book of recipes which was appended to Bald's *Leechbook* at some point in the first half of the tenth century: 'Wyrc beþinge; nim þæt reade ryden, do on trig, hæt þonne stanas swiþe hate, lege on þæt trig innan, and he sitte on stole ofer þære beþinge þæt hio hine mæge tela gereocan; þonne feallað þa fic wyrmas on þa beþinge, him biþ sona sel.'[98] An even more direct approach is recommended in the late-tenth-century compilation, *Lacnunga*:

Gif se uic weorðe on mannes setle geseten: þonne nim ðu clatan moran, þa greatan, III oððe IIII, and berec hy on hate æmergean; and ateoh þonne ða ane of ðan heorðe and

---

[96] *Vita Alfredi*, cc. 13–15 (ed. Stevenson, pp. 10–14). For thought-provoking discussion of these chapters and of Asser's fondness for the technique of regression, see D. R. Howlett, *British Books in Biblical Style* (Dublin, 1997), pp. 374–81, esp. 380.

[97] R. E. Latham and D. R. Howlett, *Dictionary of Medieval Latin from British Sources* (London, 1975–), *s.v.*

[98] 'Work a fomentation; take the red ryden, put it in a trough, then heat stones very hot, lay them within the trough, and let him sit on a stool over the fomentation, that it may steam him well; when the fig worms fall on the fomentation, he will soon be well': *Leechdoms, Wortcunning, and Starcraft of Early England*, ed. O. Cockayne, 3 vols., RS 35 (London, 1864–6) II, 340–1.

cnuca and wyrc swylce an lytel cicel, and lege to þæm setle swa ðu hatost forberan mæge; þonne se cicel colige, þonne wyrc þu ma and lege to, and beo on stilnesse dæg oððe twegen.[99]

By no means all the occurrences of *fic* are so explicit, however, and it has long been recognized that the word could also refer to some more general form of ulceration.[100]

For example, in the *Leechbook* of Bald proper, a text with well-known Alfredian connnections,[101] *fic* is equated at one point with *seonde oman* ('oozing eruptions'), whose location is unspecified,[102] while at another point a rather unrevealing treatment for *fic* precedes another chapter of remedies for *wennas*, that is to say, swellings of some kind.[103] This may be significant, given that an eleventh-century medicinal fragment describes a salve that is effective 'wiþ wennas and wiþ þone flowendan fic'.[104] This usage of OE *fic* probably relates to a particular form of ulceration known in classical and late antique medical texts as *sycodes* or *syca*, by virtue of its resemblance to a fig, which is σῦκον (*sycon*) in Greek. Since some material composed by the fourth-century Greek medical writer Oribasius seems to have been available in Latin translation to the compiler of Bald's *Leechbook*,[105] it may be significant that according to Oribasius, 'Syca nominantur germina rotunda et subdura et subrobea, quas etiam sequitur dolor. Nascitur autem haec quam maxime in capite, quam in aliis corpore partibus.'[106] It would seem, therefore, that OE *fic* could also describe a sebaceous cyst, to which

---

[99] 'If the fig should become firmly established on a man's rump: take burdock roots – the large ones – three or four, and smoke them on hot embers; then pull out one from the hearth, and pound, and make like a little cake; and apply to the rump as hot as you can bear. When the cake cools, make more, and apply, and be in repose a day or two': J. H. G. Grattan and C. Singer, *Anglo-Saxon Magic and Medicine Illustrated Specially from the Semi-Pagan Text 'Lacnunga'* (Oxford, 1952), ch. LXXVIII, pp. 150–1; see also chs. XIX and LXXXIII, pp. 102–5 and 156–7.

[100] *Leechdoms*, ed. Cockayne II, 384; Bonser, *Medical Background*, pp. 411–12; L. Cameron, 'Bald's *Leechbook*: its Sources and their Use in its Compilation', *ASE* 12 (1983), 153–82, at 173; *idem*, *Anglo-Saxon Medicine*, CSASE 7 (Cambridge, 1993), 96.   [101] See below, pp. 67–72.

[102] *Leechbook* of Bald, bk I, ch. xxxix (*Leechdoms*, ed. Cockayne II, 10–11 and 102–3).

[103] *Ibid.* bk I, ch. lvii (*Leechdoms*, ed. Cockayne II, 128–9). Ch. lviii (pp. 128–9) supplies numerous 'leechdoms for a wen salve and for wen boils'.

[104] Lanhydrock, Bodmin, Collection of Lord Clifford B. 12. 16, fol. 144 (unknown provenance, s. x/xi); ptd as item III(d) by A. Napier, 'Altenglische Mitteilungen', *ASNSL* 84 (1890), 323–7, at 325–6.

[105] See Cameron, *Anglo-Saxon Medicine*, pp. 66–7, 77–9 and 83–92; cf. *idem*, 'Bald's *Leechbook*', pp. 154–6.

[106] 'Round and hardish and reddish growths, which also bring pain, are called figs. This arises most often on the head, but also on other parts of the body': Oribasius, *Synopsis* VII.39 (*Œuvres d'Oribase*, ed. U. C. Bussemaker, C. Daremberg and A. Molinier, 6 vols. (Paris, 1856–76) VI, 183). For *sycodes* ('fig-like inflammations') arising specifically in the beard, see VIII.47 (*ibid.* VI, 249), and Oribasius, *Euporistes* IV.53 (*ibid.* VI, 571). For a particularly clear account of such *sycosis*, in a text probably unknown in Anglo-Saxon England, see Celsus, *De medicina* VI.ii.3 (W. G. Spencer, *Celsus: De Medicina*, Loeb Classical Library, 3 vols. (Cambridge, MA, 1935–8) II, 180–1).

David Pratt

Modern English 'wen' still refers. Might the young Alfred have suffered from *fic* in this alternative sense? The potential disfigurement involved might fit rather well if one were to infer, from Alfred's stipulation that his second disease should not seem *corporaliter exterius*, that the *ficus* had indeed been externally visible. This inference is perhaps unwarranted, however, and one wonders whether a sebaceous cyst could have caused sufficient pain or lasted so long, unless perhaps it had become infected.

Under the meaning 'piles', the *Thesaurus of Old English* equates *fic* with another noun, *gefigo*, which is attested only three times, all in the context of a single chapter in bk I of Bald's *Leechbook*.[107] It is quite clear, however, that *gefigo* here refers to a disease of the eyes, for this is the area of the body discussed in this chapter, and the word itself is equated with *cimosis*, a transliteration of Greek χήμωσις.[108] Oribasius and other writers employed *cimosis* to describe an affliction of the eyes, when the cornea swells into the shape of a cockle-shell (Greek χήμη), so as to impede sight.[109] Toller reasonably suggested that *gefigo* may be an error for OE *gefligo*, and thus a version of OE *fleah*, a well-attested noun with the meaning 'a white spot in the eye, albugo'.[110] Might this have been Alfred's youthful affliction? This possibility might be supported by Alfred's subsequent stated fear of blindness,[111] and it is interesting to note that the young Gerald of Aurillac was reportedly struck blind for a year with a cataract, as a divine punishment, having earlier narrowly avoided the temptation of sleeping with the daughter of one of his tenants.[112] If Alfred had indeed suffered from an eye disease in his youth, this might also help to explain the emphasis that he would subsequently place in his translations upon the *modes eagan*, the 'mind's eyes', a spiritual faculty whose ability to 'see' wisdom would seem to be depicted with great

---

[107] J. Roberts and C. Kay, with L. Grundy, *A Thesaurus of Old English*, 2 vols., King's College London Med. Stud. 11 (London, 1995) I, 126; A diP. Healey and R. L. Venezky, *A Microfiche Concordance to Old English* (Toronto, 1980), *s.v.*

[108] 'Wiþ þeoradle on eagum þe mon gefigo hæt on læden hatte cimosis': *Leechbook* of Bald, bk I, ch. ii.23 (*Leechdoms*, ed. Cockayne II, 38–9). The term *þeor(adl)* occurs in other contexts associated with other parts of the body. Its precise meaning has been much discussed, and remains uncertain: see *Leechdoms*, ed. Cockayne II, 413; C. Lambert, 'The Old English Medical Vocabulary', *Proc. of the R. Soc. of Medicine* 33 (1939–40), 137–45, at 140; Grattan and Singer, *Anglo-Saxon Magic*, p. 119, n. 2; Bonser, *Medical Background*, pp. 409–11; Cameron, *Anglo-Saxon Medicine*, p. 96.

[109] See H. G. Liddell and R. Scott, with H. J. Jones and R. McKenzie, *A Greek-English Lexicon*, rev. ed., 2 vols. (Oxford, 1925) II, 1990.

[110] J. Bosworth, *An Anglo-Saxon Dictionary*, ed. T. N. Toller (Oxford, 1898), p. 285; cf. T. N. Toller, *Supplement* (Oxford, 1921), pp. 326 and 765. Cf. also A. Campbell, *An Anglo-Saxon Dictionary: Supplement: Enlarged Addenda and Corrigenda* (Oxford, 1972), p. 32.

[111] See Lees, *Alfred the Great*, pp. 115–16 and 423.

[112] Odo of Cluny, *Vita Geraldi*, I.9–10 (PL 133, cols. 647–9).

sophistication on the Fuller Brooch.[113] There are, however, virtually insurmountable difficulties in explaining how a disease commonly identified as *gefligo* by Old English speakers could possibly have given rise to Latin *ficus* in Asser's text.

The Latin tradition raises one further doubt over the straightforward interpretation of *ficus* as 'piles'. Although classical and late antique medical texts probably known in some form to the compiler of Bald's *Leechbook* do very occasionally employ Latin *ficus* to describe 'piles', the term generally favoured by Pliny, Oribasius, Marcellus and Isidore is *haemorrhoidae*, borrowed from Greek.[114] In the classical world at least, *ficus* seems to have been a vulgar alternative, often employed for defamatory purposes. In the standard guide to Latin sexual terminology, James Adams writes that 'the usual metaphorical sense of a sexual kind borne by Latin *ficus* and comparable words was "anal sore" (usually thought to have been induced by anal penetration)'.[115] The clearest instances occur in the *Epigrams* of Martial, who mocks a certain Laetilianus, for example, by preferring to use the fourth declension *ficus* for the fruit, and the second declension variant *ficos* for growths found elsewhere:

> Cum dixi ficus, rides quasi barbara verba
> et dici ficos, Laetiliane, iubes.
> Dicemus ficus, quas scimus in arbore nasci,
> dicemus ficos, Laetiliane, tuos.[116]

---

[113] See D. R. Pratt, 'Fuller Brooch', *The Blackwell Encyclopaedia of Anglo-Saxon England*, ed. M. Lapidge, J. Blair, S. Keynes and D. Scragg (Oxford, 1999), pp. 196–8, and *idem*, 'Persuasion and Invention at the Court of King Alfred the Great', *Court Culture in the Early Middle Ages*, ed. C. Cubitt (Turnhout, forthcoming).

[114] Pliny prefers *haemorrhois* for the disease, *ficus* and *marisca* for the tree and its fruit; see P. Rosumek and D. Najock, *Concordantia in C. Plinii Secundi Naturalem Historiam*, 7 vols. (Hildesheim, 1996), *s.v.* Both Oribasius and Marcellus regularly describe piles as *haemorrhoidae*: Oribasius, *Synopsis* IX.44 and IX.69 (*Œuvres d'Oribase*, ed. Bussemaker *et al.* VI, 306–8 and 348); Oribasius, *Euporistes* IV.81–3 (*ibid.* VI, 609–10); Marcellus, *De medicamentis liber*, c. 31 (*Marcelli De Medicamentis Liber*, ed. M. Niedermann, rev. E. Liechtenhan, 2 vols., Corpus Medicorum Latinorum 5 (Berlin, 1968) II, 540–50, but see 544, line 17 for an isolated reference to *ficus*). Cf. also Isidore, *Etymologiae* IV.vii.39 (*Isidori Hispalensis Episcopi Etymologiarum sive Originum Libri XX*, ed. W. M. Lindsay, 2 vols. (Oxford, 1911)).

[115] J. N. Adams, *The Latin Sexual Vocabulary* (London, 1982), p. 113. It would seem that in this context, the sores in question may have been anogenital warts, which are viral and sexually transmissible; this is the conclusion at least of J. D. Oriel, 'Anal and Genital Warts in the Ancient World', *Pathology Newsletter* 3 (September 1973).

[116] 'When I say "ficus", Laetilianus, you laugh as if at a barbarism and require that one say "ficos". We will say "ficus" for the kind we know grow on trees; we will say "ficos" for your kind, Laetilianus': Martial, *Epigrammata* I.65 (D. R. Shackleton Bailey, *Martial: Epigrams*, 3 vols. (Cambridge, MA, 1993) I, 88–9).

Thus in a similar vein:

> Ut pueros emeret Labienus vendidit hortos.
> Nil nisi ficetum nunc Labienus habet.[117]

It is rather unlikely, however, that Latin *ficus* would have retained such overtones in the ninth century, particularly since there is scarcely any evidence for the knowledge of Martial in Anglo-Saxon England.[118]

It is the essential irony of Alfred's story, however, which should ultimately persuade one to accept *ficus* straightforwardly as 'haemorrhoids'. Looking back from the perspective of the early 890s, Alfred seems to have regarded *ficus* as an affliction almost ideal for his own particular purposes. In his youth he had prayed for a disease which would restrain his carnal desire, without rendering him *indignum et inutilem in mundanis rebus* ('unworthy and useless in worldly affairs'). As a hidden disease, *ficus* met these conditions perfectly. Precisely because it did not *seem* to be 'outwardly visible on the body' – to quote from Alfred's subsequent stipulation – no one could accuse him of 'uselessness', as well they might if he had been afflicted by 'leprosy' or 'blindness'. The young Alfred suffered in silence, it would seem, and still went hunting. There is no implication here that Alfred was commonly *regarded* as a sickly youth – quite the opposite in fact.[119] The only problem was not external, but rather a lack of inner, spiritual strength, which rendered Alfred unable to cope with the pain of his hidden restraint. Hence Alfred's fateful prayer in the church of St Gueriir in Cornwall that God might exchange the *ficus* for a *levior infirmitas*, so long as this 'less severe illness' would be similarly hidden, *ne inutilis et despectus esset* ('lest he be rendered useless and contemptible'). Nothing else is known of this saint, and

---

[117] 'To buy boys, Labienus sold his garden villa. Now Labienus owns nothing but a fig plantation': Martial, *Epigrammata* XII.33 (*ibid.* III, 118–19).

[118] J. D. A. Ogilvy, *Books Known to the English, 597–1066* (Cambridge, MA, 1967), p. 199, might be taken as a starting-point. There is no significant manuscript evidence, nor does Martial seem to have been known by Anglo-Saxon authors who were otherwise widely read. Aldhelm's poetry betrays no obvious signs of his influence (see A. Orchard, *The Poetic Art of Aldhelm*, CSASE 8 (Cambridge, 1994), 220–1), nor do the works of Bede (see esp. *Bedae Venerabilis Opera. Pars VI. Opera Didascalica*, ed. C. W. Jones, 3 vols., CCSL 123A-C (Turnhout, 1975–8) III, 781), nor is Martial included by Alcuin in his list of authors who could be read at the school of York, though this list should not be regarded as comprehensive. Some indirect knowledge of Martial might have been gained from Priscian's *Institutiones grammaticae*, however, a text which enjoyed some limited circulation in the Insular world, and it should be noted that one of Priscian's five quotations from Martial is *Epigrammata* I.65, quoted above, p. 61, n. 116: *Institutiones grammaticae* VI.76 (*Grammatici Latini*, ed. H. Keil, 8 vols. (Leipzig, 1857–80) II, 261).

[119] Cf. M. J. Enright, 'Disease, Royal Unction, and Propaganda: an Interpretation of Alfred's Journeys to Rome, 853 and 855 AD', *Continuity* 3 (1982), 1–16, who argues that the young Alfred was taken to Rome because his ill-health was already apparent (at the age of four), in the hope that he might be cured through papal ministration.

the name *Gueriir* is also otherwise unattested, but a possible connection with Cornish *gweres* 'to help, to relieve, to heal' (cf. Welsh *gwared*), though problematic, would seem particularly appropriate in this context.[120] To Alfred's horror, however, divine mercy was not forthcoming, or perhaps merely temporary. The new illness which struck Alfred at his wedding feast turned out to be even *infestior* than the *ficus*, and although seemingly lacking in external symptoms, it was also unknown to all physicians. Worst of all, according to Alfred, even if the new illness ever abated, 'the fear and horror of this accursed pain' still rendered him *quasi inutilem . . . in divinis et humanis rebus* ('virtually useless for divine and human affairs'). 'If only I had stuck with the *ficus*', Alfred seems to have reflected: 'my unknown disease is far more severe because I once sought to lighten my affliction, and God was unfavourable towards me'.[121]

ALFRED'S DEVOTIONAL RESPONSE

Even if the essential framework of Alfred's story is accepted at face value, there is no need to suspect any period of monastic confinement if due account is taken of the reality of *ficus* as a recognized complaint in contemporary medical literature. It is not difficult in itself to imagine how any layman might have been driven to extreme levels of devotion by a bodily illness of sufficient persistence, and the West Saxon court itself would seem to provide an entirely appropriate context for such a transition, given the small body of priests attached to the royal household, and the reported piety of Alfred's brother, Æthelred. Although in later life Alfred recalled that the *ficus* had arrived in response to an initial prayer on his part 'when in the first flowering of his youth', the natural suspicion that this may represent a retrospective rationalization of events is considerably strengthened by Asser's report that 'by the shameful ignorance of his parents and tutors he remained ignorant of letters (*illiteratus*) until his twelfth year, or even longer'.[122] Asser's handling of the successive stages of Alfred's education is somewhat problematic,[123] but it seems that up to this point the young Alfred

---

[120] Cf. *Asser's Life of King Alfred*, ed. Stevenson, p. 296. I am extremely grateful to Oliver Padel for advice on this matter. Asser himself may conceivably have been responsible for the identification of the church of St Gueriir as the subsequent resting-place of St Neot (modern St Neot, Cornwall) in *Vita Alfredi*, c. 74 (ed. Stevenson, p. 55, lines 20–1), often regarded as a later interpolation; see Keynes and Lapidge, *Alfred the Great*, pp. 254–5 (n. 142). One can quite imagine how the memory of St Gueriir could have been totally lost over time; see now N. Orme, *The Saints of Cornwall* (Oxford, 2000), pp. 133–4.

[121] Smyth, *Alfred the Great*, p. 200, considers the irony of Alfred's bargaining all too briefly.

[122] 'Indigna suorum parentum et nutritorum incuria usque ad duodecimum aetatis annum, aut eo amplius, illiteratus permansit': *Vita Alfredi*, c. 22 (ed. Stevenson, p. 20; Keynes and Lapidge, *Alfred the Great*, p. 75).

[123] See Keynes and Lapidge, *Alfred the Great*, p. 239 (n. 46), and S. Kelly, 'Early Anglo-Saxon Society and the Written Word', *The Uses of Literacy in Early Medieval Europe*, ed. R. McKitterick (Cambridge, 1990), pp. 36–62, at 59–60.

had only received instruction orally, largely in the form of vernacular poetry. It is far from clear that Alfred's subsequent memorization of psalms and prayers necessarily occurred at this same early stage. *Illiteratus* usually denoted one unable to read or perhaps even to comprehend Latin,[124] but in Asser's hands the word seems more likely to imply an inability to read letters of any form, including the written vernacular.[125] In either case, the coincidence between Alfred's late acquisition of literacy and the initial onset of the *ficus* is striking, and it is difficult to see how Alfred could have made much direct use of his prayerbook before this time, even if he had indeed earlier received some basic instruction in Latin grammar. In other words, although the West Saxon court would certainly have provided a conducive atmosphere, the early education that Alfred received there seems likely to have been incapable in itself of generating such extreme levels of devotion, without the additional impact of a persistent physical affliction at around the age of twelve.

On this basis, the young Alfred's devotions would seem to reflect the limitations of contemporary medical expertise rather more than the inherent nature of his upbringing. Although Anglo-Saxon medical treatments were primarily 'rational' or 'conventional' in character, the surviving medical texts also include a range of 'ritualistic' treatments, and it is interesting to note that these are usually reserved for particularly intractable conditions, such as headaches, dysentery or infertility.[126] Some of these 'ritualistic' treatments include pagan elements – the *Nine Herbs Charm* in *Lacnunga*, for example, may have been a treatment for *fic*[127] – but many others are explicitly Christian, variously dependent upon the power of prayer, amulets or consecrated ingredients. As Kershaw points out, these pagan and Christian alternatives may help to explain why some contemporaries attributed the mysterious attack of Alfred's second illness either to popular 'enchantment' or to diabolic envy.[128] Certainly, such suspicions could only have exacerbated the need for Christian 'ritualistic' protection. The transition from leechbook to prayerbook would have been particularly smooth and seamless. Sims-Williams notes that similar Christian 'ritualistic' treatments are included peripherally in all four of the surviving Mercian prayerbooks, whereas such material is almost entirely lacking in ninth-century continental prayerbooks.[129]

Once prayer itself became established as the only possible remedy, it is again not difficult to imagine how the young Alfred, persistently afflicted with *ficus*

---

[124] H. Grundmann, '*Litteratus – illiteratus*: der Wandel einer Bildungsnorm vom Altertum zum Mittelalter', *Archiv für Kulturgeschichte* 40 (1958), 1–66, cited by R. McKitterick, 'Introduction', *Uses of Literacy*, ed. McKitterick, pp. 1–10, at 3.

[125] Grundmann, '*Litteratus – illiteratus*', p. 36. Cf. *Vita Alfredi*, c. 106 (ed. Stevenson, p. 94, line 42).

[126] Cameron, *Anglo-Saxon Medicine*, pp. 37–8, 130–58 and 180–1. [127] *Ibid.* pp. 144–9.

[128] Kershaw, 'Illness, Power and Prayer'.

[129] Sims-Williams, *Religion and Literature*, pp. 299–302.

'when in the first flowering of his youth', might have reached the conclusion that this disease represented a divine response to the excesses of his carnal desire.[130] The connection between illness and sin is emphasized in two modes of prayer in particular, and although this theme is especially dominant in the Royal Prayerbook and the Harley Fragment, these two modes are also well represented in continental collections. The first mode of prayer, particularly prevalent in the Royal Prayerbook, involves the common metaphor of the Godhead as 'the physician or *medicus* of man, for whom corporeal disease is the emblem of his sinful nature'.[131] Thus in one prayer, for example, the suppliant is to urge the Trinity 'to deign to defend me from threatening dangers and present contagions of sin, both of body and spirit, and from infesting enemies, whether of soul or body'.[132] Through his own suffering on the cross, Christ now has the power to heal the wounds of sin with spiritual medicines. 'O Christ', the suppliant is to ask in another prayer, 'through the wound of your side heal the wounds of all my vices through the medicines of your mercy, lest ever I be a guilty and unworthy receiver of your body and blood for the merits of my own sins'.[133] To any suppliant actually afflicted by some physical disease, this metaphorical connection between sin and bodily suffering might easily have seemed to be causal. The other mode of prayer, fully explored in this context by Kershaw, depends ultimately upon Cassian's identification of Ps. LXIX.2 as an *impenetrabilis lurica*, which had long been incorporated into the divine office as a prayer of personal protection, particularly associated with the moment of waking.[134] Inspired by this model, comparable Irish prayers for divine protection were strengthened by the listing of every conceivable part of the body, both internal and external;[135] and in turn, these Irish *loricae* seem to have inspired a more elaborate

---

[130] Medieval connections of this sort between illness and sin are placed in broader chronological context by D. W. Amundsen, *Medicine, Society, and Faith in the Ancient and Medieval Worlds* (Baltimore, MD, 1996), pp. 187–91.

[131] Morrish, 'Dated and Datable Manuscripts', p. 519. On the development of this theme, see the corrective remarks of Sims-Williams, *Religion and Literature*, pp. 298 and 306, and *idem*, 'Thoughts on Ephrem the Syrian in Anglo-Saxon England', *Learning and Literature*, ed. Lapidge and Gneuss, pp. 205–26, at 215–16.

[132] Royal 2. A. XX, 18r (ptd in *The Prayer Book of Aedeluald the Bishop, commonly called the Book of Cerne*, ed. A. B. Kuypers (Cambridge, 1902), p. 208). This prayer, beginning 'Sanctam ergo unitatem trinitatis', also occurs in the Book of Cerne itself (Cambridge Ll. 1. 10, 40v–41v; *ibid.* pp. 80–2).

[133] Royal 2. A. XX, 35v (ptd in *Prayer Book of Ædeluald*, ed. Kuypers, p. 216). This prayer, beginning 'O medicinae divinae mirabilis dispensator', also occurs in another version in the Book of Nunnaminster (Harley 2965, fol. 30; ptd in *An Ancient Manuscript of the Eighth or Ninth Century, formerly belonging to St. Mary's Abbey, or Nunnaminster*, ed. W. de G. Birch (London, 1889), p. 77).

[134] Kershaw, 'Illness, Power and Prayer'; Sims-Williams, *Religion and Literature*, pp. 277–9.

[135] *Lorica of Laidcenn* (*The Hisperica Famina*, ed. M. W. Herren, 2 vols. (Toronto, 1974–82) II, 76–89); *Leiden Lorica* (*ibid.* II, 90–3).

morning prayer, *Mane cum resurrexo*, in which God is urged to restrain another wide range of bodily parts, in this case in order to protect the suppliant from sin.[136] The emphasis here upon the division of the body into its constitutent parts leads one to suspect that the physical location of Alfred's *ficus* may have encouraged the identification of his sin as specifically carnal. The example of Gerald's blindness demonstrates the ease with which an affliction might be interpreted as physically appropriate. As Gerald's hagiographer, Odo of Cluny, reminded his readers, the eyes were the 'windows of the soul' itself (Jer. IX.21), and should therefore be directed with great caution.[137] It is tempting on this basis to imagine that the young Alfred's carnal desire might therefore have been directed specifically towards his own sex, but this interpretation should probably be resisted. It would certainly be misleading to support such an interpretation by appealing to the defamatory meaning of *ficus*. Even if Martial had indeed been known at the West Saxon court, this meaning would surely be entirely out of keeping with the autobiographical nature of the testimony upon which Asser is apparently relying. One further source of potential doubt about Alfred's sexuality has recently been analysed by Allen Frantzen in his sensitive review of the limited evidence for same-sex relationships in Anglo-Saxon England. Alfred's translation of Augustine's *Soliloquia* includes a strikingly sensual passage of paraphrase, in which the beautiful lady *sapientia* is transformed into OE *wisdom*, a masculine noun, and the (male) human interlocutor accordingly desires 'to see and feel wisdom fully naked', although 'he will seldom show himself so openly to any man'.[138] According to Frantzen's convincing reading, however, the vernacular translation is in fact appealing to the very chasteness of love between men, in deliberate contrast to the sexuality of love between opposing sexes.[139]

Perhaps in Alfred's case, therefore, it was significant enough that the *ficus* was located in the anogenital region. Certainly, the young Alfred's own anxieties, seemingly induced by a persistent disease, accord well with those experienced in adolescence by Carolingian youths, under different conditions. The fear of adolescence as a time of weakness and incontinence seems to have extended beyond the unusual examples cited by Nelson to afflict Carolingian youths apparently free from any career confusion. For example, giving testimony in his

[136] Fully translated and discussed by Kershaw, 'Illness, Power and Prayer'.
[137] Odo of Cluny, *Vita Geraldi*, I.9 (PL 133, col. 649).
[138] *King Alfred's Version of St Augustine's Soliloquies*, ed. T. A. Carnicelli (Cambridge, MA, 1969), p. 75, line 19, to p. 76, line 8. Cf. Augustine, *Soliloquiorum libri duo* I.xiii.22 (*Sancti Aurelii Augustini Opera: Sect. I Pars IV*, ed. W. Hörmann, CSEL 89 (Vienna, 1986), 34, lines 1–8). G. Watson, *Saint Augustine: Soliloquies and Immortality of the Soul* (Warminster, 1990), supplies a useful translation of the Latin text which is largely followed below.
[139] A. J. Frantzen, *Before the Closet: Same-Sex Love from 'Beowulf' to 'Angels in America'* (Chicago, IL, 1998), pp. 99–104.

own divorce-case in 860, Count Stephen blamed the 'fragile period of his youth' for the liaison with a young girl that had rendered his subsequent marriage uncanonical.[140] Bearing in mind the uncertain status of Osferth, one might therefore suppose that the young Alfred himself had perhaps engaged in behaviour comparable to that of the West Frankish king, Louis III, who died in 882 from injuries received while 'chasing a young woman on his horse for a joke (for he was a young man) while she fled into her father's house'.[141] Alternatively, one might suppose that Alfred's anxieties arose more simply, from the obvious coincidence between the attack of the *ficus* and the arrival of puberty. It should be stressed, however, that due allowances need to be made for the retrospective nature of Alfred's story, the whole point of which is to emphasize that the *ficus* itself was far less severe than the second, mysterious illness that first afflicted Alfred at the time of his marriage. One particularly plausible possibility is that it was only in response to this second illness that Alfred's devotions reached their full intensity, and that Asser's account may therefore be misleading in backdating the observable intensity of Alfred's adult behaviour to the obscure period of his youth.

One further, less obvious, feature of Alfred's devotional response involved the giving of alms. As is well known, bk II of Bald's *Leechbook* preserves an intriguing chapter of treatments, unfortunately acephalous, which ends with the explanation, 'All this Dominus Elias, patriarch in Jerusalem, ordered to be said to King Alfred.'[142] This chapter of treatments surely lends irrefutable support to Asser's claim that he has 'even seen and read letters sent to [Alfred] with gifts from Jerusalem by the Patriarch Elias'.[143] It has long been rightly assumed that these treatments represent a prescription for Alfred's second disease, perhaps conveyed from Jerusalem by pilgrims or other travellers.[144] Jerusalem had long aroused great interest among educated Anglo-Saxons. Bede had equipped his *Historia ecclesiastica* with extracts from Adomnan's *De*

---

[140] *Hincmari Archiepiscopi Remensis Epistolarum Pars Prior*, ed. E. Perels, MGH Epist. 6.1 (Berlin, 1939), 89 (no. 136), cited in this context by Airlie, 'Private Bodies', p. 25.

[141] *Annals of Saint-Vaast s.a.* 882 (*Annales Vedastini*, ed. B. von Stimson, MGH SS rerum Germanicarum in usum scholarum separatim editi 12 (Hanover, 1909), 52).

[142] *Leechbook* of Bald, bk II, ch. lxiv (*Leechdoms*, ed. Cockayne II, 288–91).

[143] 'Nam etiam de Hierosolyma ab Elia patriarcha epistolas et dona illi directas vidimus et legimus': *Vita Alfredi*, c. 91 (ed. Stevenson, p. 77; Keynes and Lapidge, *Alfred the Great*, p. 101). Stevenson's emendation of the transmitted 'Abel patriarcha' would be convincing even without the evidence of Bald's *Leechbook*. In a characteristic manoeuvre, Smyth attempts to develop this emendation into a smokescreen, without offering any plausible alternative reading, yet his inability to account for this corroborated detail is barely concealed (*Alfred the Great*, p. 208).

[144] Plummer, *Life and Times of Alfred*, pp. 33–4 and 132–4; *Asser's Life of King Alfred*, ed. Stevenson, pp. 328–9; A. L. Meaney, 'Alfred, the Patriarch and the White Stone', *AUMLA. Jnl of the Australasian Universities Lang. and Lit. Assoc.* 49 (1978), 65–79, at 67.

locis sanctis, an account based upon the eastern travels of the Frankish bishop, Arculf;[145] and in the later 720s the Anglo-Saxon monk Willibald had undertaken a pilgrimage to Jerusalem, via Rome and Constantinople, details of which were subsequently recorded at first hand by the nun Hygeburg in a text known as the *Hodoeporicon*.[146] Yet from recent work by Jonathan Harris and Jonathan Shepard it is now clear that Elias's prescription should also be seen in the context of sustained Carolingian contacts with the eastern Mediterranean region.[147] By cultivating friendly relations with the patriarchate and with the Abbasid caliph, Harun al-Rashid (786–809), Charlemagne had succeeded in establishing several communities of Frankish monks and nuns within Jerusalem.[148] This encouraged a steady stream of Frankish pilgrims to the east during the ninth century, including a monk, Bernard, who composed a detailed account of his journey to Jerusalem, via Rome and Alexandria, undertaken with two companions in 870.[149] Personal motivations of a similar kind would also seem to account for the pilgrimage of the three Irishmen who visited Alfred's court in 891, en route to Rome and Jerusalem.[150]

[145] Bede, *Historia ecclesiastica* V.15–17 (*Venerabilis Bedae Opera Historica*, ed. C. Plummer, 2 vols. (Oxford, 1896) I, 316–19); Adomnan, *De locis sanctis* (*Itineraria et alia geographica*, ed. P. Geyer, O. Cuntz, A. Francheschini, R. Weber, L. Bieler, J. Fraipont and F. Glorie, CCSL 175 (Turnhout, 1965), 175–234).

[146] Hygeburg, *Hodoeporicon* (*Vita Willebaldi*, ed. O. Holder-Egger, MGH SS 15 (Hanover, 1887), 86–106); *The Anglo-Saxon Missionaries in Germany*, ed. C. H. Talbot (London, 1954), pp. 153–77.

[147] J. Harris, 'Wars and Rumours of Wars: England and the Byzantine World in the Eighth and Ninth Centuries', *Mediterranean Hist. Rev.* 14.2 (December 1999), 29–46, at 37–40. In this article, which came to my attention after this paragraph was first written, Harris independently reaches similar conclusions on the immediate context for Alfred's contact with Elias, which he interprets as a conscious attempt to reopen contacts with wider Christendom, in reaction to the isolating experience of the Viking invasions. J. Shepard, 'The Ruler as Instructor, Pastor and Wise: Leo VI of Byzantium and Symeon of Bulgaria', *Alfred the Great: Proceedings of the Eleventh-Centenary Conferences*, ed. T. Reuter (Aldershot, forthcoming), raises the intriguing possibility that Alfred's posturing as a wise ruler may in part have been encouraged by some knowledge of similar efforts then being pursued by his counterparts in the east.

[148] M. McCormick, 'Byzantium and the West, 700–900', *The New Cambridge Medieval History*, II: *c. 700–c. 900*, ed. R. McKitterick (Cambridge, 1995), 349–80, at 376; M. Borgolte, *Der Gesandtenaustausch der Karolinger mit den Abbasiden und mit den Patriarchen von Jerusalem*, Münchener Beiträge zur Mediävistik und Renaissance-Forschung 25 (Munich, 1976), 45–107; J. Wilkinson, *Jerusalem Pilgrims before the Crusades* (Warminster, 1977), esp. pp. 10–11.

[149] Bernard, *Itinerarium* (*Itinera Hierosolymitana* I, ed. T. Tobler and A. Molinier, Publications de la société de l'orient latin, série géographique 1 (Geneva, 1879), 309–20); Wilkinson, *Jerusalem Pilgrims*, pp. 140–5.

[150] *Anglo-Saxon Chronicle* 891 AF, 892 BCD (= 891): *Two of the Saxon Chronicles Parallel*, ed. C. Plummer (Oxford, 1892–9) I, 82 (text); *The Anglo-Saxon Chronicle: a Revised Translation*, ed. D. Whitelock, with D. C. Douglas and S. I. Tucker (London, 1961), p. 53 (translation). Æthelweard, *Chronicon* IV.3 (*The Chronicle of Æthelweard*, ed. A. Campbell (London, 1962), p. 48).

It is nevertheless worth considering whether a more immediate context for Elias' prescription might not be sought in the West Saxon embassy to the east which is recorded under the year 883 in all manuscripts of the *Chronicle* except the A-text.[151] This passage was clearly added to the *Chronicle* at a very early stage in its transmission history, and Simon Keynes has advanced strong arguments for accepting that this material does indeed genuinely pertain to 883, rather than to 886, as had often been suggested.[152] The leaders of the embassy were 'Sigehelm and Æthelstan': Sigehelm may well have been the future western Kentish ealdorman of this name who first attests as *dux* in 889,[153] and it is tempting to follow Stevenson in identifying Æthelstan as the Mercian priest and chaplain whom Alfred enlisted in the early 880s,[154] though the name is also borne by three lay nobles of the period.[155] One important purpose of this embassy was evidently to cultivate friendly relations with the new pope, Marinus (882–4), whose predecessor, John VIII (872–82), had criticized Alfred by letter in the late 870s.[156] In return for Alfred's alms, Marinus generously restored the West Saxon dynasty to papal favour, freeing the Saxon quarter in Rome from all tribute and tax, and sending many gifts in return, including a fragment of the True Cross.[157] Yet alms were also taken further afield by Sigehelm and Æthelstan, 'to St Thomas and St Bartholemew', located either in 'India' (according to manuscripts DEF), or in 'Judea' (in manuscripts BC). Both these saints were indeed commonly thought to have been martyred in India, and stories to this effect are recorded in the *Old English Martyrology*,[158] but this reading might just as well have resulted from the intervention of a learned copyist, and in any case the term 'India' seems to have been employed

---

[151] *ASC* 883 BDE, 884 C (= 883): *Two Chronicles*, ed. Plummer I, 78–9 (text); *Anglo-Saxon Chronicle*, ed. Whitelock *et al.*, p. 50 (translation).

[152] S. Keynes, 'King Alfred and the Mercians', *Kings, Currency and Alliances: History and Coinage of Southern England in the Ninth Century*, ed. M. Blackburn and D. N. Dumville (Woodbridge, 1998), pp. 1–45, at 22–3.

[153] S 1276 (BCS 562); Sigehelm is also the beneficiary of S 350 (BCS 576), dated 898, and his death at the battle of the Holme is recorded in *ASC* 903 A, 904 CD (= 902). He is almost certainly the same as the king's thegn who attests S 1203 (BCS 539), dated 875.

[154] Asser, *Vita Alfredi*, c. 77 (ed. Stevenson, p. 62, cf. 290); on Æthelstan's career, see Keynes, 'West Saxon Charters', pp. 1136–7 and 1141.

[155] An Ealdorman Æthelstan attests S 1275, datable to the period 871 X 877; two king's thegns of this name attest S 352, dated '979' for 878, and S 345, dated 882.

[156] This letter itself has not survived, but its contents may be deduced from John's letter to Æthelred, archbishop of Canterbury (877 X 878): *Councils and Synods*, ed. Whitelock *et al.* I, 3–6 (no. 3); *English Historical Documents*, ed. Whitelock, pp. 881–3 (no. 222).

[157] *ASC* 883 BDE, 884 C (= 883); *ASC* 885 ABDE, 886 C (= 885); Asser, *Vita Alfredi*, c. 71 (ed. Stevenson, pp. 53–4).

[158] G. Kotzor, *Das altenglische Martyrologium*, 2 vols. (Munich, 1981) II, 186–8 and 264–6.

rather vaguely in this period.[159] It may therefore be significant that just two years earlier, in 881, the Patriarch Elias (878–907) had directed an open letter to the emperor Charles the Fat, sending greetings to all the secular and spiritual rulers of the world, and asking for financial aid to support a programme of church restoration.[160] There is no evidence that Charles himself responded, but it would hardly be surprising if news of this open letter had somehow reached Alfred's court, given his extensive foreign contacts. This would provide a plausible explanation for the embassy's otherwise curious decision to continue eastwards, when it would have been safer to return home immediately with the pope's gifts. It was probably in the context of this embassy, therefore, that Elias was first informed of Alfred's ill-health, whether at the king's own request, or on the individual initiative of his emissaries.

Alfred's indirect dealings with Elias would seem to provide a particularly vivid illustration of the problems posed when a disease was held to have been granted by God himself.[161] In these circumstances, it was somewhat unclear whether 'conventional' remedies should even be attempted, given that such bodily afflictions were merely external symptoms of some deeper spiritual malaise. For example, punished with blindness by God, the young Gerald 'neither refused bodily medicines, nor eagerly sought them', but waited patiently for the Lord to end his chastisement.[162] In contrast, Alfred would seem to have had rather less time to spare, for Asser gives the impression that his sufferings were closely monitored at every stage in their development by physicians (*medici*), who were

---

[159] See the doubts of Stevenson (*Asser's Life of King Alfred*, pp. 288–90). As Stevenson also demonstrates, William of Malmesbury erroneously conflated Sigehelm with a later bishop of Sherborne who held office in the 920s, so his claim that Sigehelm returned from India with gems and perfumes seems equally fanciful: William of Malmesbury, *Gesta regum* II.cxxii.2 (*William of Malmesbury: Gesta Regum Anglorum / The History of the English Kings* I, ed. R. A. B. Mynors, R. M. Thomson and M. Winterbottom (Oxford, 1999), 190–1); William of Malmesbury, *Gesta pontificum* II.80 (*Willelmi Malmesbiriensis Monachi De Gestis Pontificum Anglorum Libri Quinque*, ed. N. E. S. A. Hamilton, RS 52 (London, 1870), 177). In *The Old English Orosius*, ed. J. Bately, EETS ss 6 (Oxford, 1980), bk I, ch. i, p. 9, lines 29–31, the translator departs from his Latin source in identifying the Red Sea as the southern border of India; cf. Orosius, *Historiae aduersum paganos* I.ii.15 (*Pauli Orosii Historiarum adversum Paganos Libri VII*, ed. C. F. W. Zangemeister, CSEL 5 (Vienna, 1882), 12–13).

[160] Ptd by L. d'Achéry, *Spicilegium sive Collectio Veterum Aliquot Scriptorum qui in Galliae Bibliothecis delituerant*, 3 vols., new ed. (Paris, 1723) III, 363–4. Stevenson (*Asser's Life of King Alfred*, pp. 328–9) also draws attention to a later open letter, known to have been received by Pope Benedict IV (900–3), in which Elias asks for help in raising a ransom demanded by the Turks for some monks who had been captured along with Malacenus, bishop of Amasea (in Cappadocia): ptd by J. Mabillon, *Vetera Analecta*, new ed. (Paris, 1723), p. 428; cf. Benedict's encyclical on this subject (PL 131, cols. 43–4).

[161] For wider discussion of these problems, as old as Christianity itself, see Amundsen, *Medicine, Society, and Faith*, pp. 1–29 and 127–221.

[162] Odo of Cluny, *Vita Geraldi* I.10 (PL 133, col. 649).

perhaps attached to the royal court in some way.[163] Moreover, given the survival of Elias's prescription, it is not unreasonable to imagine that the collective expertise of these physicians or *læcas* may somehow be preserved in bks I and II of Bald's *Leechbook*, and indeed Alfred's efforts to revive wisdom would seem to provide a highly plausible context for the very compilation of this medical manual. Although the text itself is preserved in a single mid-tenth-century manuscript, together with a third book of recipes, a colophon reveals that bks I and II represented a pre-existing compilation which had first been written for 'Bald', probably a physician who is otherwise unknown.[164] Alfred was presumably subjected to every appropriate *læcedom* in his physicians' repertoire. Blood-letting was in fact employed very sparingly in Anglo-Saxon medicine;[165] but one common treatment for stomach complaints relied upon the equally unpleasant effects of a sweetened emetic draught or *spiwdrenc*.[166] This practice would seem to have left its own particular impression upon Alfred, for in a subtle alteration in his translation of Boethius he describes a medicine which is 'swiðe liðe on ðæm innoðe, and swiðe swiðe swete to bealcetenne'.[167]

The important point, however, is that the efforts of native physicians proved to be ineffective, and indeed this fact in itself may have further encouraged the view that only God himself could have inflicted such a disease. The embassy to Jerusalem seems particularly appropriate in this context. There could hardly be a better means of placating God than through a gift of alms to the very city of David and Solomon, the actual location of Christ's crucifixion and resurrection. Alfred's own role as an enthusiastic alms-giver is encapsulated above all by the remarkable surviving Alfredian silver offering-pieces, with the reverse inscription ELIMO[SINA], which are some seven times the weight of normal pennies, and probably represent gifts to the church.[168] The protective power of alms-giving is particularly emphasized in the opening of Ps. XL, which Alfred translates: 'Eadig bið se þe ongyt þæs þearfan and þæs wædlan, and him þonne gefultumað, gif hine to onhagað; gif hine ne onhagað, þonne ne licað him þeah his earfoðu;

---

163 *Vita Alfredi*, cc. 25 and 74 (ed. Stevenson, pp. 21 and 54).

164 See *Bald's Leechbook. British Museum Royal Manuscript 12. D. xvii*, ed. C. E. Wright, EEMF 5 (Copenhagen, 1955), esp. 13–14 and 17–18.

165 See Cameron, *Anglo-Saxon Medicine*, pp. 159–68.

166 *Leechbook* of Bald, bk II, ch. lii (*Leechdoms*, ed. Cockayne II, 269–73), cf. also chs. ix, xxiv, xxvii and xxix (*ibid.* pp. 188–9, 216–17, 222–4 and 226–7).

167 'Very agreeable to the stomach, and extremely sweet to bring up': *King Alfred's Old English Version of Boethius: De Consolatione Philosophiae*, ed. W. J. Sedgefield (Oxford, 1899), XXII.1, p. 51, lines 4–5. The 'remedia' in the Latin original are said to become sweeter only when received further inside: Boethius, *Consolatio philosophiae* III, pr. 1.3 (*Anicii Manlii Severini Boethii Philosophiae Consolatio*, ed. L. Bieler, CCSL 94, 2nd ed. (Turnhout, 1984), p. 37).

168 C. F. Keary and H. A. Grueber, *Catalogue of English Coins in the British Museum. Anglo-Saxon Series*, 2 vols. (London, 1887–93) II, xl–xli, 37, 55 and pl. V (nos. 14 and 15) (type xxii); J. J. North, *English Hammered Coinage* I, 3rd ed. (London, 1994), 126 (no. 648).

þone gefriþað Drihten on swylcum dæge swylce him swylc yfel becymð.'[169] To judge from the interesting qualification incorporated into Alfred's translation, it would seem that the ability to answer even distant requests for help such as that from Elias could also serve as a demonstration of practical political power.[170] It is also noteworthy that Alfred seems to empathize particularly strongly with David's bodily infirmity later in his translation of this psalm.[171] On this basis, the prescription sent by Elias would seem to have differed significantly from previous medicinal treatments, in that his expertise had in effect been obtained in return for an explicit gift of alms. This subtle exercise in gift-exchange may thus have represented a rather desperate attempt to justify the use of 'conventional' medicines, which might otherwise have seemed to contravene the will of God.

ELIAS'S PRESCRIPTION AND A MODERN DIAGNOSIS

The precious survival of the recommendations sent by Elias allows the physical symptoms of Alfred's mysterious second illness to be reconstructed in remarkable detail. Since all the recommended substances seem to have been readily available only in the eastern Mediterranean, Audrey Meaney has convincingly argued that Elias must have assembled a collection of appropriate medicines to accompany his oral or written advice.[172] Elias thus prescribed

... s[ca]monian wið innoþes forhæfdnesse, and gutomon wið milte wærce and stice, and spican wiþ utrihtan, and dracontian wiþ fule horas on men, and alwan wiþ untrymnessum, and galbanes wiþ nearwum breostum, and balzaman smiring wiþ eallum untrumnessum, and petraoleum to drincanne anfeald wiþ innan tydernesse and utan to smerwanne, and tyriaca is god drenc wiþ innoþ tydernessum, and se hwita stan wið eallum uncuþum brocum.[173]

---

[169] 'Blessed is he who perceives the needy and the poor man, and then supports him, if it is within his power; if it is not within his power, then his hardships will still not please him; the Lord will preserve him on the day when such evil befalls him': *Liber Psalmorum: the West Saxon Psalms, being the Prose Portion, or the 'First Fifty', of the So-Called Paris Psalter*, ed. J. W. Bright and R. L. Ramsay (Boston, MA, 1907), XL.1, p. 95. Quotations from this text have been corrected, where appropriate, to accord with the edition of P. P. O'Neill, 'The Old-English Prose Psalms of the Paris Psalter' (unpubl. PhD dissertation, Univ. of Pennsylvania, 1980), pp. 102–327. Cf. Ps. XL.1: 'Beatus qui intelligit super egenum et pauperem: in die mala liberabit eum Dominus' ('Blessed is he who understands concerning the needy and the poor: the Lord will deliver him on the evil day'). Alfred's translation is based upon the Roman text, which will be cited here from *Le Psautier romain et les autres anciens psautiers latins*, ed. R. Weber, Collectanea Biblica Latina 10 (Vatican, 1953). On occasion, however, Alfred follows the Gallican text, which will be cited where appropriate from *Biblia Sacra Iuxta Vulgatam Versionem*, ed. R. Weber, 4th ed. (Stuttgart, 1994).

[170] This addition may have been inspired by the exegesis of Theodore of Mopsuestia; see O'Neill, 'Old-English Prose Psalms', p. 277.   [171] See below, p. 76.

[172] Meaney, 'Alfred, the Patriarch', esp. pp. 67–70.

[173] 'Scammony [dried juice from a Syrian root] for constipation of the bowels; and ammoniacum [a type of tree gum] for pain in the spleen and stitch; and oil of spike [?] against diarrhoea; and

On the basis of the symptoms described in this prescription, and the periods of fearful remission which Asser implies, Gillian Craig, a trained nurse, has advanced the attractive hypothesis that Alfred may have been suffering from Crohn's disease.[174] This particularly unpleasant disorder is now thought to be caused by 'an abnormal immune response in the gut wall to an unidentified antigen', and typically involves intense abdominal pain, and diarrhoea some-times with mucus and blood, often alternating with periods of constipation. In one quarter of cases, Crohn's disease also causes anal lesions, and these may precede the onset of the intestinal disease by several years, which might explain Alfred's youthful *ficus*. It is particularly striking, moreover, that victims are usually first afflicted in their later teens or twenties, and typically suffer disturb-ing bouts of relapse and remission for much of their adult life (the disease may either burn itself out in early middle age, or ultimately prove terminal). Naturally, any attempt to diagnose the medical condition of an historical indi-vidual is necessarily speculative, especially in the absence of any physical remains. Prima facie, nevertheless, there is a strong case for Craig's diagnosis, and this would seem only to be reinforced by further consideration of the polit-ical circumstances.[175]

Above all, Crohn's disease would help to explain the discrepancy that has often been perceived between Asser's 'Invalid King', and the active war-leader who emerges from the pages of the *Chronicle*. It should be admitted that Alfred's personal involvement in warfare is less evident in the 890s, when his son Edward would seem to have played an increasingly important military role. Alfred regularly appears at the head of contingents in the 870s and 880s, never-theless, and there is no positive indication of the king ever being restricted or

---

tragacanth [another form of gum from Persia] for foul phlegm in a man; and aloes for infir-mities; and galbanum [another Persian gum] for oppression in the chest; and application of balsam [a resin from the Red Sea region] for all infirmities; and petroleum to drink unmixed for internal tenderness, and to apply externally; and theriac is a good drink for intestinal tender-ness [literally 'treacle' – a compound remedy of some kind], and the white stone [rock crystal] for all unfamiliar afflictions': *Leechbook* of Bald, bk II, ch. lxiv (chapter-heading) (*Leechdoms*, ed. Cockayne II, 174–5); further details are given in ch. lxiv itself (*ibid.* pp. 288–91). The transla-tion and identifications here follow Meaney, 'Alfred, the Patriarch', pp. 65 and 67–70.

[174] G. Craig, 'Alfred the Great: a Diagnosis', *Jnl of the R. Soc. of Medicine* 84 (1991), 303–5; cf. also a letter in response by F. I. Jackson, in vol. 85 (1992), 58. The website of the National Association for Colitis and Crohn's Disease is www.nacc.org.uk.

[175] Craig's findings are only tentatively considered by Abels, *Alfred the Great*, pp. 99–100, and by Kershaw, 'Illness, Power and Prayer'. C. N. L. Brooke, 'Historical Writing in England between 850 and 1150', *SettSpol* 17 (1970), 223–47, at 233, once promised to explore elsewhere the pos-sibility that Alfred might have been suffering from Henoch's Purpura, a blood disease whose symptoms include severe abdominal pain, vomiting and diarrhoea. Professor Brooke tells me that this diagnosis proved to be unlikely on further inspection; and indeed, this disease is not entirely internal, for one other symptom is a rash of purple spots on the skin.

incapacitated by illness. This is in marked contrast to the *Annals of Fulda*, for example, where attention is repeatedly drawn to the respective illnesses suffered by Charles the Fat and Arnulf of Carinthia, and to their incapacitating effects.[176] One must consider the possibility, of course, that mention of any periods of incapacity might have been deliberately omitted from the *Chronicle*, perhaps for political reasons. It is striking that Asser is no more forthcoming, however, despite his detailed account of the illnesses themselves. Furthermore, there were recognized contemporary methods of coping with an incapacitated ruler, which would have been far harder to conceal from posterity. Later sources claim that Æthelred, ealdorman of the Mercians had been laid low by a serious illness for several years before his death in 911, and this tradition would help to explain why his wife Æthelflæd seems to have played a leading role in Mercian affairs even during Æthelred's lifetime.[177] Equally, King Eadred is known to have suffered from a serious internal illness throughout his reign which rendered him unable to digest solid food,[178] and in the last few years before his death in 955 the power to produce charters seems to have been entrusted primarily to Dunstan, abbot of Glastonbury. The resulting 'Dunstan B' charters are highly unusual in that the king himself rarely appears as a witness, and the list of secular witnesses is commonly headed by Æthelstan 'Half King', a particularly powerful ealdorman whose territorial responsibilities reached their widest extent during this same period.[179] In the absence of such tell-tale signs in Alfred's case, it is reasonable to conclude that his second disease can hardly have prevented him from leading a full and active life, even though its symptoms may have been extremely unpleasant on occasion. Crohn's disease would fit these requirements perfectly, for although the attacks of diarrhoea and constipation are entirely incapacitating, these are typically separated by long periods of remission involving little or no physical discomfort.

In this light, the question of Alfred's 'usefulness' deserves serious reconsideration. Nelson simply assumes that the fear of an incapacitated king remained a live political issue in the 890s, and she then proceeds to interpret Asser's ch. 74

[176] *Annals of Fulda* (continuation in manuscripts of group 3) *s.a.* 883, 887, 896, 897 and 899 (*Annales Fuldenses*, ed. F. Kurze, MGH SS rerum Germanicorum in usum scholarum separatim editi 6 (Hanover, 1890), 109, 115, 129 and 132–3; T. Reuter, *The Annals of Fulda* (Manchester, 1992), pp. 107, 113, 134 and 139).

[177] F. T. Wainwright, *Scandinavian England*, ed. H. P. R. Finberg (Chichester, 1975), pp. 79–83, 141–2 and 308–9.

[178] *Vita Sancti Dunstani*, c. 20 (*Memorials of Saint Dunstan Archbishop of Canterbury*, ed. W. Stubbs, RS 63 (London, 1874), 31).

[179] See S. Keynes, "England, 900–1016', *The New Cambridge Medieval History*, III: *c. 900–c. 1024*, ed. T. Reuter (Cambridge, 1999), 456–84, at 474–6; *idem*, 'The "Dunstan B" Charters', *ASE* 23 (1994), 165–93, at 185–6; and C. Hart, 'Athelstan "Half King" and his Family', in his *The Danelaw* (London, 1992), pp. 569–604, at 579–83.

as a deliberate attempt to reassure a court audience that Alfred's mysterious illness was only intermittent and internal, and therefore posed no threat to his performance in the marriage-bed.[180] This had of course been Alfred's original hope in the church of St Gueriir, and this hope had indeed been at least partially realized; but court readers would surely have received comparatively little reassurance from such reports of Alfred's excessive despair at the pain and horror of his subsequent affliction. Asser's unguarded account reads much more naturally as a report for outsiders who knew little about Alfred's medical history, by an insider anxious to demonstrate the intimate level of his access to the king himself. As such, this chapter lends strong support to the view of Keynes, that Asser's intended audience remained essentially restricted to the Welsh readers for whose benefit the *Life* was clearly first conceived.[181] In any case, by 893 the king had amply demonstrated his 'usefulness' in a more appropriate way, by fathering his five surviving children. On this basis, any hypothetical doubts there may have been about Alfred's physical effectiveness would seem to have been firmly put to rest by the early 870s. Aristocratic opposition to Alfred is of course notoriously difficult to detect in the surviving evidence. The fact remains that only one clear example can be cited, however, and there is no particular reason to suppose that the rebellion of the ealdorman Wulfhere was in any way provoked by the state of Alfred's health.[182]

This revised view of Alfred's 'usefulness' is strongly reinforced, moreover, by the king's own evident concern to emphasize his afflictions. Of course, any attempt to identify Alfred's own voice in the translations attributed to him is inevitably fraught with difficulty. There is nevertheless a strong case for considerable royal involvement, and this is only further strengthened by the existence of numerous passages of expansion relating to the theme of ill-health and infirmity. These translations were clearly composed for various aristocratic audiences, and Alfred's own remarkable frankness would therefore seem to confirm the impression that his physical effectiveness at least was securely beyond question. On the contrary, indeed, the only doubt seems to have been the extent to which Alfred was perhaps exaggerating the severity of his illness. For example, at one point in the original *Soliloquia*, the persona of 'Ratio' rebukes Augustine for aggravating his chest disorder with tears. In rendering Augustine's reply, Alfred omits reference to the specific location of Augustine's complaint, and

---

[180] Nelson, 'Monks', p. 136.

[181] Keynes, 'King Alfred and the Mercians', pp. 41–4. Cf. Campbell, 'Asser's *Life of King Alfred*', who argues for an English audience (pp. 141–2), suggesting that 'the prime intended audience was the king himself' (pp. 149–50); and Scharer, 'The Writing of History', who suspects a court audience, with the *Life* serving either as a handbook for priests newly summoned to the royal household (pp. 186 and 189), or as a *speculum principis* for Alfred's sons (pp. 204–5).

[182] On Wulfhere, see Nelson, '"A King Across the Sea"', pp. 53–6.

translates loosely, 'ðu hæst me forlætan þa unrotnesse, ðy læst ic awðer oððe on mode oððe on lichaman þy mettrumra si, and ic ne ongyte nane trimðe ne on mode ne on lichaman, ac æom fulnah ormod'.[183] Alfred seems to have empathized in a similar way with David's sickness in Ps. XL. In the original Latin the psalmist's enemies ask allusively, 'Numquid qui dormit non adiciet ut resurgat?',[184] whereas Alfred emphasizes their derision: 'Nis him nan lað, he rest hine; eaðe he mæg arisan, þeah he slape and liccete untrymnesse.'[185] There is surely no necessary implication here that Alfred himself faced similar critical 'enemies': both these passages read more naturally as artful exercises in conspicuous self-mockery, in which the king is fishing for compliments from his aristocratic readers. Alfred presumably wants to be reassured that his afflictions are indeed real and yet, on the contrary, no cause for despair.

It is no coincidence, furthermore, that Alfred seems to have adopted precisely this same tactic of self-mockery in the account of his medical history that he related to Asser. Alfred blamed himself for his current mysterious illness, it will be recalled, because he had mistakenly exchanged a suitable hidden disease for a worse internal affliction, which now threatened his very 'usefulness' in divine and human affairs. This is surely not a serious threat to 'opt out', however, but rather a veiled request for support and reassurance. The irony of the story is clearly Alfred's own: Asser adds a subtle aside in the final sentence – *ut ei videtur* ('as it seems to him')[186] – the primary purpose of which is presumably to assure his (unfamiliar) readers that the doubt here apparently cast over Alfred's 'usefulness' is far from slanderous, because it emanates from the mind of the king himself.[187] This aside has the additional effect, nevertheless, of undercutting Alfred's story with another layer of irony: namely, that the only person to claim that the new disease rendered him 'virtually useless' was Alfred himself. A similar irony is implied in ch. 91, when Asser draws attention to

---

[183] 'You command me to abandon the sadness, lest I be weaker in mind or in body because of it, yet I perceive no strength either in mind or body, but am very nearly despondent': *Soliloquies*, ed. Carnicelli, p. 80, lines 16–19. Cf. Augustine, *Soliloquiorum libri duo* I.xiv.26 (ed. Hörmann, p. 39, lines 16–17: 'aut valetudinem corporis considerare me iubes, cum ego ipse tabe confectus sim?' ('and do you order me to take care for the health of my body when I am consumed by bodily decline?').   [184] 'Shall he who sleeps rise again no more?': Ps. XL.9.

[185] 'He has no pain, he rests; he is easily able to arise, yet he sleeps, and feigns infirmity': *Liber Psalmorum*, ed. Bright and Ramsay, XL.9, p. 96.

[186] 'Si aliquando Dei misericordia unius diei aut noctis vel etiam unius horae intervallo illa infirmitas seposita fuerat, timor tamen ac tremor illius execrabilis doloris unquam eum non deserit, sed quasi inutilem eum, ut ei videtur, in divinis et humanis rebus propemodum effecit' ('if at any time through God's mercy that illness abated for the space of a day or night or even of an hour, his fear and horror of that accursed pain would never desert him, but rendered him virtually useless – as it seemed to him – for divine and human affairs'): *Vita Alfredi*, c. 74 (ed. Stevenson, p. 57; Keynes and Lapidge, *Alfred the Great*, p. 90).

[187] I am extremely grateful to James Campbell for this observation.

Alfred's fear of his unknown *infestatio*, and then remarks, in implied contrast, that the effects of the pagan *infestationes* on the king were *non sine materia* ('not without cause'): is this just an unknown disease, or merely a figment of Alfred's imagination?[188] Asser leaves his readers entirely free to draw their own conclusions, and one imagines that he would have been rather more circumspect in a court context, especially when directly invited to offer sympathy by the king himself. This sophisticated dialogue of despair and encouragement lends additional support to the diagnosis of Crohn's disease. The attacks of diarrhoea and constipation are sufficiently unpleasant to render victims extremely fearful of future relapses, and this anxiety can often seem inordinate during the long periods of remission.

Crohn's disease seems even more likely in view of the strong sexual dimension that Alfred evidently emphasized in explaining his afflictions. An overwhelming sense of sinful fragility features prominently in Alfred's translations, and the sin in question is often explicitly sexual, especially when it is associated with bodily weakness. One typical example is a startling addition in the translation of the *Soliloquia*, where Alfred writes that 'gyf hyt me æfre on lust becymð, ic hyt ondrede swa þare nædram. hys me lyst swa læng swa læs; and simle swa ic ma wilnige þæt leoht to geseonne, swa me læs lest þara wisan.'[189] The significance of these words is uncertain, however, for they are spoken by the persona of Augustine soon after he has explicitly rejected the possibility of marriage, as a priest.[190] The persona of

---

[188] 'A vigesimo aetatis anno usque ad quadragesimum quintum annum, quem nunc agit, gravissima incogniti doloris infestatione incessanter fatigatur, ita ut ne unius quidem horae securitatem habeat, qua aut illam infirmitatem non sustineat aut sub illius formidine lugubriter prope constitutus non desperet. Praeterea assiduis exterarum gentium infestationibus, quas sedulo terra marique sine ullius quieti temporis intervallo sustinebat, non sine materia inquietabatur' ('from his twentieth year until his forty-fifth (which is now in course) he has been plagued continually with the savage attacks of some unknown disease, such that he does not have even a single hour of peace in which he does not either suffer from the disease itself or else, gloomily dreading it, is not driven almost to despair. Moreover, he was perturbed – not without cause – by the relentless attacks of foreign peoples, which he continually sustained from land and sea without any interval of peace'): *Vita Alfredi*, c. 91 (ed. Stevenson, p. 76; Keynes and Lapidge, *Alfred the Great*, p. 101).

[189] 'If lust ever comes to me, I fear it as a snake: just as it pleases me the longer, so it pleases me less, and ever the more do I desire to see the light, the less it pleases me in this way': *Soliloquies*, ed. Carnicelli, p. 73, lines 5–8. Cf. Augustine, *Soliloquiorum libri duo* I.x.17 (ed. Hörmann, p. 27, line 21, to p. 28, line 2): 'etiam cum horrore atque aspernatione talia recordor . . . Et hoc mihi bonum in dies crescit. Nam quanto augetur spes videndae illius cui vehementer aestuo pulchritudinis, tanto ad illam totus amor voluntasque convertitur' ('even when I remember such things I do so with horror and disgust . . . And this good attitude increases in me day by day: for the more the hope increases of seeing that beauty which I burn for so strongly, the more all my love and pleasure turn towards it').

[190] *Soliloquies*, ed. Carnicelli, p. 72, line 21, to p. 73, line 2. Cf. Augustine, *Soliloquiorum libri duo* I.x.17 (ed. Hörmann, p. 26, line 21, to p. 27, line 16).

Boethius poses no such problems, however, and gives Alfred a rare opportunity, unmatched in his other translations, to empathize with the devotions of married life. Translating loosely and expansively, Alfred captures the despair of Boethius's wife with eloquent pathos: 'Sio liofað nu þe, þe anum', *Wisdom* reminds the imprisoned Boethius, 'forðæmðe hio nonwuht elles ne lufað buton þe . . . For þinre æfweardnesse hire þincð eall noht þæt hio hæfð, forðæm hio is for þinum lufum ormod and fulneah dead for tearum and for unrotnesse.'[191] Earthly love of this sort, as well as true friendship, would therefore seem to have had its place among the various levels of royal intimacy available at Alfred's court.[192] Yet Alfred finds no corresponding opportunity to dwell upon the love offered by Boethius in return; and it is also striking that in bk III Alfred is equally concerned to emphasize Philosophia's denial that bodily pleasures can ever bring true happiness. *Voluptas* ('pleasure') becomes more explicitly *unrihthæmed* (Alfred's favoured word for 'unlawful intercourse'), and the king readily acknowledges the dangers of such sexual temptation: 'Hwæt, se yfela willa unrihthæmedes gedrefð fulneah ælces libbendes monnes mod. Swa swa seo beo sceal losian þonne heo hwæt irringa stingð, swa sceal ælc sawl forweorðan æfter þam unrihthæmede, buton se mon hweorfe to gode.'[193] It should be noted that in other contexts OE *unriht-hæmed* typically refers explicitly to intercourse outside the bonds of marriage, in direct opposition to OE *rihtæw*.[194] It would nevertheless be dangerous to interpret this passage as positive evidence that Osferth was indeed Alfred's own

---

[191] 'Now she lives for you alone, because she loves nothing else but you . . . Because of your absence all that she has seems nothing to her, for she is despondent in her love for you and very nearly dead with tears and sadness': *Alfred's Old English Version of Boethius*, ed. Sedgefield, X, p. 22, lines 16–22. Cf. Boethius, *Consolatio philosophiae* II, pr. 4.6 (ed. Bieler, p. 23): 'uiuit, inquam, tibique tantum uitae huius exosa spiritum seruat, quoque uno felicitatem minui tuam uel ipsa concesserim, tui desiderio lacrimis ac dolore tabescit' ('she lives, I say, and preserves her life only for you, hating this life, and I must concede that in this alone is your happiness diminished, that she wastes away in tears and pain with longing for you').

[192] Cf. Lees, *Alfred the Great*, pp. 423–4: 'His imagination was quick and vivid, but his intellectual powers were, probably, richer and fuller than his emotional capacity. He speaks much of friendship, but little of earthly love. He touches high passion only when he faces the mysteries of the spiritual world.' See also R. Thomas, 'The Binding Force of Friendship in King Alfred's *Consolation* and *Soliloquies*', *Ball State Univ. Forum* 29.1 (1988), 5–20.

[193] 'Behold, the evil desire for fornication afflicts the mind of very nearly every living man. Just as the bee has to perish when it stings anything angrily, so each soul has to die after fornication, unless the man returns to goodness': *Alfred's Old English Version of Boethius*, ed. Sedgefield, XXXI.2, p. 71, lines 4–8. Cf. *Philosophiae consolatio* III, met. 7 (ed. Bieler, p. 47): 'Habet hoc uoluptas omnis: / stimulis agit fruentes / apiumque par uolantum / ubi grata mella fudit / fugit et nimis tenaci / ferit icta corda morsu' ('Every pleasure has this [characteristic]: it urges those enjoying it with goads and, like flying bees, when it has poured forth pleasing honey, it flees [*or* dies] and with a too lasting sting, strikes smitten [*or* stung] hearts').

[194] Clunies Ross, 'Concubinage', pp. 18–23.

illegitimate son. Certainly, Alfred's characteristic emphasis upon the possibility of repentance might seem particularly appropriate in this context; yet this passage is directed as much against desire as against action, and Alfred's language might equally reflect a concern to exclude the duties of the marriage-bed from such unequivocal condemnation.

Alfred returns to the theme of sexual sin in his version of bk IV, metre 3, the story of Ulysses and Circe, which has been studied in rewarding detail by Susan Irvine. The Latin original follows the traditional version of the story, in which Circe turns Ulysses' men into various beasts, with Ulysses himself being spared through the intervention of Mercury. Alfred tells the story 'back to front', however, introducing a love affair between Ulysses and Circe, and placing this *before* Circe's magical transformation of Ulysses' men into beasts.[195] According to Alfred's lengthy and inventive reinterpretation, Ulysses loved Circe *swiðe ungemetlice* ('very immoderately'), entirely abandoning his realm and his kindred for the love of her, and it is for fear that his men are about to leave without him, in disgust, that Circe turns them into the shape of wild animals.[196] In Alfred's hands, Ulysses thus becomes an explicitly evil man immersed in bodily pleasures, and it is surely no coincidence that in the preceding prose section Alfred is particularly concerned to liken this particular type of man to foul swine: 'He bið anlicost fettum swinum þe symle willað licgan on fulum solum, and hy næfre nellað aspyligan on hluttrum wætrum; ac þeah hi seldom hwonne beswemde weorðen, þonne sleað hi eft on ða solu and bewealwiað hi þæron' (cf. II Peter

---

[195] S. Irvine, 'Ulysses and Circe in King Alfred's Boethius: a Classical Myth Transformed', *Studies in English Language and Literature. 'Doubt Wisely': Papers in honour of E. G. Stanley*, ed. M. J. Toswell and E. M. Tyler (London, 1996), pp. 387–401, esp. 391–4. Cf. also K. R. Grinda (trans. P. Battles), 'The Myth of Circe in King Alfred's *Boethius*', *Old English Prose: Basic Readings*, ed P. E. Szarmach, with D. A. Oosterhouse, Basic Readings in AS England 5 (New York, 2000), 237–65.

[196] 'Sona swa hio geseah þone fordrifenan cyning ðe we ær ymb spræcon, þæs nama wæs Aulixes, þa ongan hio hine lufian, and hiora ægþer oðerne swiðe ungemetlice, swa þætte he for hire lufan forlet his rice eall and his cynren, and wunode mid hire oð ðone first þæt his ðegnas him ne mihton leng mid gewunian, ac for hiora eardes lufan and for þære wræce tihodon hine forlætenne. Ða ongunnon lease men wyrcan spell, and sædon þæt hio sceolde mid hire drycræft þa men forbredan, and weorpan hi an wildedeora lic' ('As soon as she saw the shipwrecked king, about whom we spoke before, whose name was Ulysses, she loved him, and each loved the other very immoderately, so that he entirely abandoned his realm and his family for the love of her, and dwelt with her until the time when his thegns could not remain with him any longer, but intended to abandon him for the love of their native land and out of vengeance. Then false men made up the story, and said that she supposedly transformed the men with her witchcraft, and cast them into the shape of wild animals'): *Alfred's Old English Version of Boethius*, ed. Sedgefield, XXXVIII.1, p. 116, lines 6–15. Cf. *Philosophiae consolatio* IV, met. 3 (ed. Bieler, pp. 72–3).

II.21).[197] Boethius's original point is that the bodily transformation of Ulysses' men is harmless when compared with deeper poisons which transform the mind alone.[198] Alfred replicates this point in concluding that bodily weakness cannot affect the mind, as the example of Ulysses' men indeed demonstrates. Equipped with the new counter-example of Ulysses himself, however, Alfred is able to add a subtle twist: the reason why the mind's vices are more harmful than any bodily imperfection is that 'the mind's vices draw all the body into them', *in addition* to their effect upon the mind.[199]

This additional emphasis upon the bodily implications of mental sin presumably reflects Alfred's own personal outlook, not least because it accords closely with the story that he told to Asser. Alfred would thus seem to have regarded his own bodily illness as the sign of a further, inward bestial transformation on his part, comparable to that of Ulysses, and incurred in a similar way, through excessive indulgence in bodily pleasures. Quite how Ealhswith might have responded to such self-loathing is unfortunately hidden from view. Unlike Charles the Fat, Alfred had little difficulty in fathering children, and it is therefore unclear why carnal sin should have remained such a troubling problem, long after he had demonstrated his manhood. It is again tempting to invoke the uncertain status of Osferth, but this is perhaps unnecessary. A simpler explanation might rather be sought in the sheer persistence of Alfred's second illness, as the primary sign of his carnal sinfulness. This fateful symbolism might easily have arisen solely from the characteristic timing of Crohn's disease. Suddenly struck down at around the time of his marriage, Alfred would naturally have turned to his new marital duties

---

[197] 'He is most like the fat pigs that always want to lie in foul sloughs, and are never willing to wash themselves in pure water; but if, however rarely, they are made to bathe, they rush back to the sloughs and wallow there': *Alfred's Old English Version of Boethius*, ed. Sedgefield, XXXVII.4, p. 115, lines 6–10. Cf. *Philosophiae consolatio* IV, pr. 3.20 (ed. Bieler, p. 72): 'Foedis immundisque libidinibus immergitur: sordidae suis uoluptate detinetur' ('One is immersed in foul and unclean lusts: he is seized by the pleasure of the filthy pig'). It may be a measure of Alfred's own personal hygiene that he is reported to have given a particular legal judgement after washing his hands; see S. Keynes, 'The Fonthill Letter', *Words, Texts and Manuscripts: Studies in Anglo-Saxon Culture presented to Helmut Gneuss*, ed. M. Korhammer, with K. Reichl and H. Sauer (Cambridge, 1992), pp. 53–97, at 73–5.

[198] *Philosophiae consolatio* IV, met. 3, 35–9 (ed. Bieler, p. 73): 'Haec uenena potentius / detrahunt hominem sibi / dira quae penitus meant / nec nocentia corpori / mentis uulnere saeuiunt' ('These ominous poisons more powerfully draw a man away from himself which go deep inside and, not harming the body, vent their rage through a wound of the mind').

[199] 'Be swylcum and be swylcum þu miht ongitan þæt se cræft þæs lichoman bið on þam mode, and þætte ælcum men ma deriað his modes unþeawas. Ðæs modes unþeawas tioð eallne þone lichoman to him, and þæs lichoman mettrumnes ne mæg þæt mod eallunga to him getion' ('From such things you can understand that the virtue of the body is in the mind, and that the mind's vices harm each man more. The mind's vices draw all the body into them, and the body's weakness cannot entirely draw the mind to it'): *Alfred's Old English Version of Boethius*, ed. Sedgefield, XXXVIII.1, p. 116, lines 30–4.

as the most likely source of the sin to be restrained by his new mysterious affliction. This would represent an understandable internalization of the equivocal
patristic view of marriage, already familiar from Carolingian 'mirrors for
laymen'.[200] As Pope Gregory himself had warned in the influential *Libellus responsionum*, quoted by Bede, 'even lawful intercourse cannot take place without fleshly
desire', and 'desire itself can by no means be without sin'.[201] In other words, whatever Alfred's activities in his youth, it was undoubtedly this second, mysterious
affliction which was the immediate cause of all the anxieties of his adult life. It
should therefore be stressed that the initial emergence of Crohn's is an entirely
physical process, although indeed a psychological dimension may later develop,
with subsequent attacks partially induced by fear and worry. Looking back in 893
at least, Alfred chose to trace the chain of causality back to the time of his youth,
with a degree of hindsight which can only be imagined. At the very least, the far
greater severity of Alfred's mysterious illness is enough to suggest that his devotions may only have reached their full intensity at this later stage, after his marriage. Yet even Alfred's recollection of the *ficus* itself seems likely to be coloured in
some way by the impact of his subsequent illness, equally hidden yet far more
severe. It is therefore ironic that this earlier attack of *ficus* is probably best interpreted in medical terms as the anal lesions that are often the first sign of Crohn's,
rather than some unrelated attack of haemorrhoids or anogenital warts.[202]

ALFREDIAN 'MINISTERIAL' DISCIPLINES

It is now possible, finally, to consider the overall implications of Alfred's
unusual image as king, and the nature of its dependence upon those two linch-
pins of Carolingian 'ministerial' rulership: Gregory's *Regula pastoralis* and the
psalms. The former in particular would have held obvious attractions for any
ruler regularly afflicted by bodily illness. Gregory himself had suffered from a
painful disease of the internal organs for much of his life,[203] and it was partly for
this reason that bodily suffering came to play such a prominent function in his
political and pastoral theology.[204] The *Regula pastoralis* was originally written as a

---

[200] See above, p. 43.
[201] Bede, *Historia ecclesiastica* I.27 (*Opera Historica*, ed. Plummer I, 57), quoted by Clunies Ross,
'Concubinage', p. 7. Cf. *The Old English Version of Bede's Ecclesiastical History of the English People*,
ed. T. Miller, 2 vols., EETS os 95–6 and 110–11 (London, 1890–8) I, pp. 82–3. On the translator's repositioning of the *Libellus responsionum*, between bks III and IV, see D. Whitelock, 'The
Old English Bede', *PBA* 48 (1962), 57–90, at 70, repr. in her *From Bede to Alfred*, no. VIII.
[202] Cf. above, p. 61, n. 115.   [203] As noted by Scharer, 'The Writing of History', p. 188.
[204] On this theme, see esp. C. Straw, *Gregory the Great: Perfection in Imperfection* (Berkeley, CA, 1988),
pp. 107–46. I am grateful to Paul Kershaw for drawing my attention to the significance of
Straw's analysis. Other recent accounts of Gregorian thought include R. A Markus, *Gregory the
Great and his World* (Cambridge, 1997); B. Judic, 'Introduction', *Règle pastorale*, ed. Rommel, pp.
15–111; and G. R. Evans, *The Thought of Gregory the Great* (Cambridge, 1986).

guide to the episcopal ministry, but Gregory conceived of power in such universal terms that his advice was often held to apply equally to those in positions of secular authority. Locating the origins of power in the need to prevent sins from being committed, Gregory therefore presents the position of *rector* as a responsibility so heavy that it should only be undertaken by persons of outstanding merit and virtue.[205] This responsibility represents the highest fulfilment of Christ's two injunctions, requiring not only the love of God through contemplation and study, but also the active life of service to one's fellow men in the world.[206] It is this latter necessity of worldly involvement which makes power so inherently dangerous to possess. For power presents inevitable temptations to the ruler, which Gregory often characterizes, significantly, in bodily terms, as the *carnalis uitae operatio*, for example, or *carnis petulantia*, or *carnis delectatio*.[207] The great danger is that the ruler's mind may yield to these temptations, and thus become enslaved to the body in pride.[208] The ruler should therefore welcome all forms of tribulation, including bodily suffering, as an essential means of restraining his desire and of retaining his humility.[209] It is for this reason that in tackling the fundamental question, 'What sort of man ought to come to rule', Gregory answers immediately, 'the man who, dying in all the sufferings of the flesh, still lives spiritually'.[210] One can quite imagine, then, why Alfred should have chosen to place the principles of the *Regula pastoralis* at the very heart of his distinctive royal image. Certainly, these principles played a profound role in shaping Alfred's retrospective account of his own afflictions. The dangers of *carnale desiderium* were clearly heightened in a Gregorian context, while elsewhere in the *Regula pastoralis* Gregory interprets bodily illness in precisely the same terms as in Asser's ch. 74 – as a gift from God in response to sin, designed to restrain the mind, through pain, from the contemplation of future sins.[211]

Now in the Carolingian world, it will be recalled, discourse of this kind had rendered rulers newly vulnerable to any suspicion of sexual sin. Self-rulership was the first hallmark of a true king, and any king who proved to be incapable of ruling his own body also ran the risk of being deemed unworthy to rule his kingdom as a whole.[212] In this sense, Carolingian 'ministerial' rulers prefigured

---

[205] *Regula pastoralis* II.6 (ed. Rommel I, 202–18).   [206] *Ibid.* I.7 (ed. Rommel I, 150–4).

[207] *Ibid.* I.11 and II.2 (ed. Rommel I, 168, lines 63–4; I, 170, line 82; and I, 180, lines 48–9).

[208] *Ibid.* I.4, II.5 and II.7 (ed. Rommel I, 140–4; I, 196–202; and I, 218–30).

[209] *Ibid.* I.3 and II.3 (ed. Rommel I, 136–40 and 180–6).

[210] 'Ille igitur, ille modis omnibus debet ad exemplum uiuendi pertrahi, qui cunctis carnis passionibus moriens iam spiritaliter uiuit': *ibid.* I.10 (ed. Rommel I, 160–2, lines 1–4).

[211] *Ibid.* III.12 (ed. Rommel II, 330–2, lines 115–138). Alfred's translation is even more explicit on this point: *Alfred's West Saxon Version of Gregory's Pastoral Care*, ed. Sweet, ch. XXXVI, p. 256, line 19, to 260, line 1.

[212] Airlie, 'Private Bodies', pp. 7–8 and 31–5; Sedulius Scottus, *Liber de rectoribus christianis*, cc. 2 and 5 (ed. Hellmann, pp. 25–7 and 34–7).

later medieval developments in effectively presiding over two bodies, one physical, the other political,[213] though in the later ninth century the mechanisms sustaining this parallel were primarily moral, with legal dimensions which were rather less tightly defined.[214] It is perhaps for this reason that in rightly emphasizing this Gregorian context, Scharer and Nelson both choose to interpret Alfred's internal illness as an explicit mark of divine favour, largely on the basis that 'The Lord scourgeth every son whom he receiveth' (Heb. XII.6), an explanation of Job-like suffering particularly favoured by Gregory and also frequently cited in the context of Carolingian lay ideals.[215] The alternative image of a king openly unable to rule his own body is startling indeed from a Carolingian perspective.[216] Yet this is precisely the implication of Alfred's reflections upon Ulysses and Circe, and it will shortly become clear that this is also the implication in his translation of the psalms. In other words, even though Gregorian thought did indeed offer the comforting explanation of humble chastisement, Alfred himself was far more concerned by the implication that his illness had been necessitated by the uncontrollable state of his *carnale desiderium*. Alfred's greatest fear was that his hidden illness actually represented a mysterious indictment of his own inability to rule the body beneath him, and thus a perplexing sign of divine disfavour. No wonder, then, that Alfred's devotions were so strenous and extreme. Yet one is bound to ask quite how it could possibly have been advantageous to Alfred to draw open attention to his own sexual sinfulness, and thus to depart so significantly from Carolingian orthodoxy.

The curious answer would seem to lie in the political realities of Alfred's military struggle against the Vikings, and in the distinctive rhetoric that Alfred adopted in order to persuade his nobles to unite behind his ambitious programme of military reform. Although this rhetoric is preserved most fully in Asser's portrayal of Alfred as a suffering king, it is deployed in a form so overtly critical of Alfred's nobles that the *Life* itself could hardly have aided this particular process of persuasion, but could easily have served another purpose, in conveying a frank view of the burghal programme to Welsh

---

[213] Airlie, 'Private Bodies'; J. L. Nelson, 'Carolingian Royal Funerals', *Rituals of Power: From Late Antiquity to the Early Middle Ages*, ed. F. Theuws and J. L. Nelson (Leiden, 2000), pp. 131–84, at 136. Cf. E. H. Kantorowicz, *The King's Two Bodies: a Study in Mediaeval Political Theology* (Princeton, NJ, 1957), esp. pp. 45–86, in which the Carolingian period is explored solely for the development of Christocentric and Davidic models of kingship.

[214] Cf. Kantorowicz, *The King's Two Bodies*, pp. 87–192, on the impact of Roman and canon law in the twelfth and thirteenth centuries.

[215] Scharer, 'The Writing of History', pp. 186–91; Nelson, 'Monks', p. 137. See esp. *Regula pastoralis* III.12 (ed. Rommel II, 326, lines 64–5).

[216] It was Lothar II's unusual attempt to adopt such an image which rendered him so vulnerable to attack; see Airlie, 'Private Bodies', pp. 24–6 and 31–5.

readers.[217] One should be in no doubt that Alfred's nobles received this rhetoric more directly from the king himself, in the language that they could all
understand – explicitly, from his own mouth, and implicitly, via his own translations of the *Regula pastoralis* and the psalms, which supplied all the fundamental principles to which the king evidently sought to appeal. Asser's *Life*
nevertheless offers an invaluable impression of this rhetoric, written by an
insider entirely committed to the cause, in which the practical implications of
Alfred's Gregorian and Davidic posturing are fully revealed. At the very heart
of this rhetoric is the close parallel that Asser in particular emphasizes
between Alfred's bodily sufferings and the many other difficulties that he is
facing as king. As Asser frequently reminds the reader, Alfred is forced to fulfil
his royal duties *inter omnia praesentis vitae impedimenta* ('among all the hindrances
of this present life'), of which the king's mysterious illness is certainly the most
obvious example, but perhaps not the most threatening:[218] Alfred is also dis-
quieted by the external *infestationes paganorum*, which are rather more cease-
less;[219] and Alfred receives still further *perturbatio*, second only to his bodily
pain, from the reluctance of his own people to undertake his orders, especially
with regard to the building of fortifications.[220] The entire business of ruling is
thus portrayed as a constant struggle against hindrances and distractions, in
which the extent of the king's own commitment is all the more conspicuous:
Alfred is the great helmsman of his kingdom, yet he is sailing against the tide,
'transfixed by the nails of many tribulations' in Christ-like self-sacrifice.[221] All
these numerous burdens clearly demonstrate Alfred's fulfilment of his active
obligations as a Gregorian *rector*, and these are matched by equally strenuous
efforts on Alfred's part to fulfil the contemplative obligations of reading and
study. Alfred thus seems to have exhibited an unusually practical form of
humility, rather more compatible with his position as king, in which any
dangers of excessive asceticism or otherworldly withdrawal were entirely
avoided. The more Alfred could be shown to suffer, the greater the emphasis
that could then be placed upon his own active efforts to overcome the practical
difficulties of his rule, and the greater the obligation then incumbent upon

---

[217] See esp. *Vita Alfredi*, c. 91 (ed. Stevenson, pp. 76–9). Cf. Campbell, 'Asser's *Life of Alfred*',
p. 142, who cites this chapter in support of his case for an English audience, judging that it
'seems concerned to drive home a lesson about the need to co-operate in Alfred's programme
of fortification'.   [218] *Vita Alfredi*, cc. 22, 24, 25 and 76 (ed. Stevenson, pp. 19–22 and 59).
[219] *Ibid.* c. 91 (ed. Stevenson, p. 76), quoted above, p. 77, n. 188.
[220] 'Qui[d de] maxima, excepto illo dolore, perturbatione et controversia suorum, qui nullum aut
parvum voluntarie pro communi regni necessitate vellent subire laborem?' ('And what of the
mighty disorder and confusion of his own people – to say nothing of his own malady – who
would undertake of their own accord little or no work for the common needs of the
kingdom?'): *ibid.* (ed. Stevenson, p. 77; Keynes and Lapidge, *Alfred the Great*, p. 101).
[221] *Ibid.* (ed. Stevenson, p. 77, lines 28–35; cf. p. 76, lines 1–2).

Alfred's nobles to co-operate with these efforts, in order to defeat the Vikings. It was evidently in this way that Alfred promoted the building of the burhs, above all, through selfless service to the *communis utilitas*, as Asser puts it.[222] Alfred's frequent expressions of despair at his own 'uselessness' could only have reinforced this message.

This rhetoric clearly endowed the king's body with wider symbolic significance, and this transformation is equally implicit in his own translation of the psalms. Although the renderings themselves are generally quite faithful and literal, Alfred also provides an introduction for each psalm, explaining its significance in terms of the circumstances in which it was first composed; and these introductions regularly draw attention to David's numerous struggles against both enemies and other forms of hardship.[223] In Ps. XXVII, for example, David is said to have urged the Lord to preserve him 'against all hardships, both of mind and body', and to protect him 'from all his enemies, both visible and invisible'; and in the same way Hezekiah is said to have repeated this psalm in the hope of deliverance 'both from his infirmity and from his enemies'. In accordance with his systematic exegetical scheme, Alfred then explains that 'each righteous man' should sing this psalm in similar circumstances, thus establishing a close parallel between the struggles of David and Hezekiah and his own predicament as king.[224] The overall effect is thus to imply a further symbolic parallel between the physical attacks of Alfred's bodily illness and the military attacks of his Danish enemies. The destructive effects of the Danish attacks on Alfred's kingdom are replicated deep inside the king's own body by the equally unpredictable attacks of his mysterious illness. The extent of Alfred's own sacrificial commitment to the needs of his kingdom could hardly be more directly demonstrated. It is therefore no surprise that both forms of royal affliction seem to

---

[222] *Ibid.* (ed. Stevenson, pp. 76–9).

[223] See P. P. O'Neill, 'The Old English Introductions to the Prose Psalms of the Paris Psalter: Sources, Structure, and Composition', *Eight Anglo-Saxon Studies*, ed. J. S. Wittig, Stud. in OE Philol. 78 (no. 5: Texts and Studies) (Chapel Hill, NC, 1981), 20–38.

[224] 'Dauid sang þisne seofon and twentigoþan sealm: on þæm sealme he was cleopiende to Drihtne; wilnode þæt he hine arette and gefriðode wiþ eallum earfoðum, ægðer ge modes ge lichaman, and wið ealle his fynd gescylde, ge wið gesewene ge wið ungesewene. And eac Ezechias on þam ylcan sealme hine gebæd þæt hine God alysde, ægðer ge æt his mettrumnesse ge æt his feondum, swa he þa dyde. And þæs ylcan wilnað ælc þara þe hine singð, oþþe for hine sylfne oððe for oþerne. And swa ylce dyde Crist, þa þa he þysne sealm sang' ('David sang this twenty-seventh psalm: in this psalm he called out to the Lord, and petitioned that he might cheer him and preserve him against all hardships, both of mind and body; and that he might protect him against all his enemies, both visible and invisible. And likewise Hezekiah in the same psalm prayed that God might deliver him, both from his infirmity and from his enemies, just as he then did. And each of those who sing it desires the same thing, either for himself or for another; and likewise did Christ, when he sang this psalm': *Liber Psalmorum*, ed. Bright and Ramsay, p. 57.

have been primarily explained in the same terms, as divine punishment in response to sin, rather than the testing of Job-like innocence. According to Alfred's Prose Preface to his translation of the *Regula pastoralis*, the English had deserved to be punished by the Danish attacks, because of their neglect for the pursuit of wisdom; and it was upon such powerful incentives to unite in the placation of God that Alfred's entire programme of reform fundamentally depended.[225] Both body and kingdom were sinful, therefore, and the embassy of 883 demonstrates just how easily these two subjects could be equated within a single expiatory framework. Alfred is said to have promised his gift of alms while his troops were encamped against a Viking army at London, and the chronicler then emphasizes that 'there, by the grace of God, their prayers were well answered after that promise'.[226] In contrast, however, Asser reports that Alfred's illness still remained unknown to all those who had inquired into its origins even 'up to the present day', and the implication, surely, is that even the remedies sent by Elias proved to be ineffective.[227] In this respect the embassy ended in failure: the Lord may well have rewarded his people with victory on this occasion, but evidently remained unfavourable towards Alfred himself. This open demonstration of divine disfavour can only have reduced Alfred to new levels of despair and self-loathing. 'Deus Deus meus respice in me: quare me dereliquisti?', asks David in Ps. XXI.[228] In a considerable expansion upon the Latin original, Alfred continues: 'Ic clypige dæges and nihtes to ðe, and andette mine scylda, and seofige min ungelimp, and þu hit ne gehyrst; ac ne understand þu hit me to unrihtwisnesse, for ðæm ic þe nane oðwite þæt þu me ne gehyrst, ac minum agnum scyldum ic hit wite.'[229]

Alfred's sexual sinfulness thus implicated the king himself in the spiritual cause of the Danish attacks, just as his bodily suffering enabled him to share in their physical effects. It is perhaps for this reason that Alfred's clearest allusions to his own illness in his translation of the psalms similarly occur in the straightforward

---

[225] 'Geðenc hwelc witu us þa becomon for ðisse worulde, þa þa we hit nohwæðer ne selfe ne lufedon ne eac oðrum monnum ne lifdon' ('Remember what punishments befell us in this world when we ourselves did not cherish [wisdom] nor transmit it to other men'): *Alfred's West Saxon Version of Gregory's Pastoral Care*, ed. Sweet, p. 4.

[226] *ASC* 883 BDE, 884 C (= 883). Keynes, 'King Alfred and the Mercians', pp. 22–3, persuasively interprets this attack as a response to a recent and short-lived Viking occupation of the city.

[227] *Vita Alfredi*, c. 74 (ed. Stevenson, p. 54, lines 6–7).

[228] 'O God, my God, look upon me: why have you forsaken me?': Ps. XXI.2.

[229] 'I call out to you day and night, and confess my sins, and lament my adversity, and you do not hear it: but you do not perceive it as an unrighteousness to me, for I do not reproach you at all that you do not hear me, but I blame it on my own sins': *Liber Psalmorum*, ed. Bright and Ramsay, XXI.2, p. 43. Cf. Ps. XXI.3: 'Deus meus clamabo per diem nec exaudies: et nocte et non ad insipientiam mihi' ('O my God, I shall cry by day, and you will not hear: and by night, and it shall not be reputed as folly in me').

context of divine punishment, for sins which are often sexual. In Ps. XXXVII, for example, David is said to have lamented 'his ungelimp þæt he ær mid his scyldum geearnode'.[230] Begging the Lord to end his punishments, the psalmist then identifies his own physical infirmity as the primary consequence of his sins: 'Nis nan hælo on minum flæsce, for þære andweardnesse þines yrres; ne nan sib, ne nan rest nis minum banum, beforan þære ansyne minra synna . . . Mine wunda rotedan and fuledon for minum dysige.'[231] Apparently struck by the explicitly sexual nature of the sins being punished, Alfred then translates loosely, 'For þæm eall min lichama is full flæslicra lusta; for þam nis nan hælo on minum flæsce.'[232] The nocturnal *inlusiones* of the Latin original have become less specific, as *flæsclice lustas*, perhaps more appropriate to Alfred's status as a married man. Similar thinking seems to lie behind Alfred's translation of Ps. XV, which David is said to have sung 'about his hardships, both of mind and body', and likewise Hezekiah 'about his infirmity'.[233] In its original form, this psalm is essentially a request to the Lord for further support, on the basis that the psalmist's righteousness has always been justly rewarded in the past. At one point, however, there is an allusive reference to bodily weakness of some kind: 'Benedicam Dominum qui mihi tribuit intellectum: insuper et usque ad noctem increpauerunt me renes mei.'[234] With revealing royal empathy, Alfred detects a contrast here between David's earthly success and his personal infirmity, and translates expansively, 'Ic bletsige þone Drihten þe me sealde andgit; ac þeah he me þara uterrena gewinna gefreode, þeah winnað wið me þa inran unrihtlustas dæges and nihtes, þæt ic ne eom þeah eallunga orsorh.'[235]

---

[230] 'The adversity that he had earlier merited with his sins': *Liber Psalmorum*, ed. Bright and Ramsay, p. 86.

[231] 'There is no health in my flesh, because of the presence of your anger; nor any peace nor any rest in my bones in the face of my sins . . . My wounds have rotted and decayed because of my foolishness': *ibid.* XXXVII.3 and 5, pp. 86–7. Cf. Ps. XXXVII.4 and 6: 'Nec est sanitas in carne mea a uultu irae et non est pax ossibus meis a facie peccatorum meorum . . . conputruerunt et deteriorauerunt cicatrices meae a facie insipientiae meae' ('There is no health in my flesh, because of your anger, and there is no peace for my bones, because of my sins . . . My sores are putrified and corrupted, because of my foolishness').

[232] 'For all my body is full of fleshly desires; for there is no health in my flesh': *ibid.* XXXVII.7, p. 87. Cf. Ps. XXXVII.8: 'Quoniam anima mea conpleta est [Gallican reads 'lumbi mei impleti sunt'] inlusionibus et non est sanitas in carne mea' ('For my soul is [loins are] filled with illusions, and there is no health in my flesh').

[233] 'þone fifteoðan sealm Dauid sang be his earfoðum, ægðer ge modes ge lichaman. And eft swa ilce Ezechias hine sang be his mettrumnesse; wilnode him to Gode sumre frofre' ('David sang this fifteenth psalm about his hardships, both of mind and body; and again likewise Hezekiah sang it about his infirmity, and petitioned to God for a certain consolation'): *ibid.* p. 27.

[234] 'I will bless the Lord who has given me understanding: moreover my loins also have corrected me even until night': Ps. XV.7.

[235] 'I will extol the Lord who has given me understanding; but although he has freed me from outer strifes, nevertheless the inner wrongful desires strive against me, day and night, so that I am never entirely free from care': *Liber Psalmorum*, ed. Bright and Ramsay, XV.7, pp. 28–9.

In other words, despite the Lord's general approval, the psalmist himself is still suffering internally, as a result of sins which are implicitly sexual.

Far from undermining his position as king, therefore, Alfred's inability to rule his own body seems rather to have enhanced his fulfilment of the royal office, in this unusual context. Through his open protestations of sexual sin, Alfred asserted his own heavy degree of responsibility for the Viking attacks, thus participating bodily in the collective guilt of his entire kingdom. This shared sense of sinfulness can only have improved the opportunities for appropriate collective action in response, not only on the battlefield but also at burghal building sites. In the new context of defensive warfare against the Vikings, nobles could hardly be expected to rally to the traditional heroic model of the king as an aggressive tribute-taker.[236] This is surely why the opening of Alfred's Prose Preface was so devastating, as an evocation of the very different circumstances of the late seventh century, when kings 'extended their territory outside', thereby succeeding 'both in warfare and in wisdom'.[237] In the course of the ninth century, the old incentives of tribute and conquest had been increasingly displaced by the new, heavy burdens of mobilization and burghal construction, and Alfred's nobles rather needed to be convinced of the necessity of their own practical sacrifices, as the only possible means of collective salvation.[238] This was precisely the message conveyed by Alfred's own bodily sacrifice in seeking to restrain his carnal desire. For Alfred's nobles, to observe the king's unusual devotions was to be reminded of the need for restrained desires of a more general kind within the kingdom as a whole, while the sight of the king's bodily suffering acted as a salutary warning against disobedience or complacency. To express sympathy for the king in his pain was to confirm a wider commitment to Alfred's own political agenda. It was far easier for Alfred to draw attention to the shortcomings of his nobles when he himself had openly acknowledged his own sinfulness, and was busily devoting himself to God and his wisdom, day and night, in the hope of deliverance. By posing as a tainted reformer in this way, rather in the manner of his favourite biblical models, David and Solomon, Alfred thus seems to have transformed his own body into a remarkably effective tool of practical political power. The very relentlessness of Alfred's role-playing

---

[236] Cf. *Beowulf* 1–11.
[237] *Alfred's West Saxon Version of Gregory's Pastoral Care*, ed. Sweet, p. 2, lines 7–8. See esp. T. A. Shippey, 'Wealth and Wisdom in King Alfred's *Preface* to the Old English *Pastoral Care*', *EHR* 94 (1979), 346–55.
[238] See esp. N. P. Brooks, 'The Administrative Background to the Burghal Hidage', *The Defence of Wessex: the Burghal Hidage and Anglo-Saxon Fortifications*, ed. D. Hill and A. R. Rumble (Manchester, 1996), pp. 128–50, at 143–5, repr. in his *Communities and Warfare, 700–1400* (London, 2000), pp. 114–37, at 134–7.

strongly suggests that his message was properly understood by the nobility, and their willingness to embrace it can only be judged from the improved security of Alfred's kingdom in the 890s, evidently transformed by the immediate impact of the nascent burghal network.[239]

Although clearly of vital significance, the Carolingian character of Alfred's devotional behaviour should not be allowed to distract attention from the very different English conditions under which this behaviour came to be adopted. All the anxieties of Alfred's adulthood did indeed proceed from an extreme internalization of prayer and Gregorian thought, but without the infrastructure of the Carolingian reforms to support it, Alfred's behaviour cannot be explained according to parallel Carolingian mechanisms. It is certainly unlikely that Alfred was ever installed in a monastery during his youth, and it seems rather more reasonable to attribute the emergence of his unusual devotions to the sheer persistence of his two consecutive medical complaints, as interpreted within the existing religious environment of the West Saxon court. All the circumstantial evidence suggests that Alfred's second illness should be identified as the internal attacks of Crohn's disease, raising the attractive possibility that the earlier attack of *ficus* might be ascribed to the same cause, as the anal lesions that are often the first sign of Crohn's. The medical reality of these two afflictions strongly suggests that the Carolingian character of Alfred's devotions arose as a remedial response, and in this sense Alfred fell victim to the understandable limitations of Anglo-Saxon medicine, rather than to the disciplines of his early education. Whatever his activities in his youth, it is clear that the anxieties of Alfred's married life were driven not by any career confusion, but by the unpredictable, unpleasant nature of his second illness, and one therefore suspects that Alfred's devotions may only have reached their full intensity in response to the sudden emergence of this condition, at around the time of his marriage. It was only at this stage that Alfred's health became a matter of wider concern at court, when there was an immediate prospect that he might become king; and it was then only after Alfred's succession itself that the attacks of his second illness came to acquire additional significance, as a symbolic parallel to the Viking attacks upon his kingdom as a whole. It is this context of a king struggling against both bodily and military hardships which helps to explain the fundamental importance accorded to the *Regula pastoralis* and the psalms in Alfred's educational programme. The Alfredian 'ministerial' disciplines that resulted were not a sign of weakness, but rather served to assert the king's own bodily and political power. In effect, Alfred's achievement was to harness all the expiatory force of Carolingian royal prayer to the wider needs of his kingdom as a whole, thus to

---

[239] Keynes and Lapidge, *Alfred the Great*, pp. 42–3.

adapt and extend the existing West Saxon tradition of militant royal devotion. 'Uselessness' itself was incorporated within the king's own grim, ironic rhetoric, and all the dangers of episcopal regulation were entirely avoided. Punished yet invulnerable, like his kingdom, Alfred's body lay subject to the judgement of God alone.

The social context of narrative disruption in
The Letter of Alexander to Aristotle

BRIAN McFADDEN

David Williams has recently argued that medieval representations of the monster give humans an image of divinity, but one which can never be totally understood or described. Positive theology, the *via positiva*, attempts to take what is known of divinity and then to derive more precise statements about the nature of God; it attempts to contain God in human thought and language. The *via negativa*, by contrast, forces humans to discard the idea of any positive knowledge about God, since reason and language are inadequate to the task of containing or describing a being so totally other to humans.[1] Alexander the Great, the narrator of the Old English *Letter of Alexander to Aristotle*, experiences such a negation in his campaign in India; he attempts to describe the wondrous beings and races which he encounters with his army, and his narrative of conquest functions as a metaphor for containing the encountered world in thought, description and mental order. However, he is resisted at every turn by natives, monsters and classical divinities; he is forced to realize that his reason and his force are incapable of containing divine power as manifested in the natural world of India. This narrative, I argue, had a chilling resonance for the English; the Viking attacks and the marvels recorded in the *Anglo-Saxon Chronicle* were taken by some as signs that the English had incurred divine displeasure at not having placed their faith in civil or ecclesiastical authority and that resistance to the Vikings would be futile without improvement in the beliefs and behaviour. In light of the historical context of the *Beowulf* manuscript,[2] the *Letter* may also be viewed as a site for expression of the anxieties caused by tenth- and early-eleventh-century Viking invasions, the Benedictine Reform, and eschatological concerns provoked by the coming millennium; it highlights the resistance of foreign others to containment in either a social or narrative order.

The *Letter's* military narrative betrays several social anxieties about the encroachments of the Vikings from the mid-tenth to early eleventh centuries.[3]

---

[1] D. Williams, *Deformed Discourse: the Function of the Monster in Mediaeval Thought and Literature* (Montreal, 1996), pp. 32–4, 40–8 and 93–103.

[2] London, British Library, Cotton Vitellius A. xv (s. x/xi); see N. R. Ker, *A Catalogue of Manuscripts Containing Anglo-Saxon* (Oxford, 1957), pp. 281–3 (no. 216), and the facsimile edition of K. Malone, *The Nowell Codex: British Museum Cotton Vitellius A.XV*, EEMF 12 (Copenhagen, 1963).

[3] F. M. Stenton, *Anglo-Saxon England*, 3rd ed. (Oxford, 1971), pp. 320–93; E. John, 'The Age of Edgar', *The Anglo-Saxons*, ed. J. Campbell (Oxford, 1982), pp. 160–91.

Edgar's reign was relatively peaceful with no major Viking incursions due to his consolidation of power and his acknowledgement as supreme king of England in 973;[4] it appeared that Bede's idea of a *gens Anglorum* had come to a certain degree of fruition.[5] However, on Edgar's sudden death in 975, the succession was contested between his sons Edward and Æthelred. Edward succeeded to the throne but was murdered in 978; Æthelred then succeeded to the throne but always ruled under a cloud of suspicion about his involvement in the murder, which contributed to his reputation as a weak king.[6] Within two years, Viking activity was renewed and lasted for the next thirty years, leading to numerous defeats; English antipathy toward the 'other' erupted in 1002 when Æthelred ordered the St Brice's Day massacre of all Danes in England,[7] which resulted in severe Viking retributions. With the accession of Cnut to the throne in 1016, the English found themselves overcome by the 'other' they had tried to defeat or eradicate.

Another factor contributing to the social unrest in England during this period was the repercussions of the Benedictine reforms. The English monastic system had long been tied into local family structures;[8] Eric John notes that Iona was run by Columba's kinsmen in Bede's time, that Alcuin inherited a monastic community by being related to St Willibrord, and that even Oswald (d. 992), the noted reformer, began his career with an abbacy purchased by Archbishop Oda of Canterbury (d. 958), his uncle.[9] The English reformers proposed to create a clerical status group which would command more loyalty than the families who currently influenced the monasteries. The reform movement had begun on the Continent in the early tenth century in Burgundy and Lorraine, especially at Cluny and Fleury; Oda took his vows at Fleury, as did his nephew Oswald, later one of the three main reformers with Dunstan (d. 988) and Æthelwold (d. 984), all of whom looked to the Continent for broader learning and examples of monastic practice. Edgar's succession in 959 resulted in the appointment of Dunstan to the see of Canterbury, Æthelwold to

---

[4] Stenton, *Anglo-Saxon England,* pp. 367–71. See *Two of the Saxon Chronicles Parallel,* ed. C. Plummer, 2 vols. (Oxford, 1892–9) I, 119: '⁊ þær him comon ongean .vi. cyningas, and ealle wið trywsodon þæt hi woldon efen wyrhton beon on sæ ⁊ on lande'.

[5] P. Wormald, '*Engla Lond*: the Making of an Allegiance', *Jnl of Hist. Sociology* 7 (1994), 1–24, at 14–16.

[6] Stenton, *Anglo-Saxon England,* p. 374; but see S. Keynes, 'A Tale of Two Kings: Alfred the Great and Æthelred the Unready', *TRHS* 5th ser. 36 (1986), 195–217.

[7] See Keynes, 'A Tale', pp. 211–13.

[8] B. Yorke, 'Æthelwold and the Politics of the Tenth Century', *Bishop Æthelwold: His Career and Influence,* ed. B. Yorke (Woodbridge, 1988), pp. 65–88, at 65–8 and 73. See also D. Knowles, *The Monastic Order in England,* 2nd ed. (Cambridge, 1963), pp. 16–30.

[9] John, 'The Age of Edgar', pp. 183–4.

Winchester and Oswald to Worcester, but Edgar's motives were as political as the reformers' were religious.[10] Monastic communities in these dioceses had to accept the Benedictine Rule or lose their property;[11] the families who had been influencing the monasteries lost power and status to bishops more loyal to the king than to any kinship structure. On Edgar's death in 975, a brief but violent anti-monastic reaction broke out[12] and the church was drawn into the succession dispute;[13] on Æthelred's succession, the Vikings took advantage of the disorder to resume raiding. To some, the weakness of the state could thus be traced not only to foreign invasion but also to foreign-inspired church reforms. The second generation of reformers, including Ælfric and Wulfstan, often spoke against this belief by encouraging support of and obedience to both church and crown.[14]

The social and political context in which the *Beowulf* manuscript was copied in the first decade of the eleventh century[15] may be the key to understanding its treatment of marvels; the texts become a site for the expression of cultural anxieties about uncertain times. In a society used to seeing the divine hand in history, these social disorders give rise to reports of wonders in the *Anglo-Saxon Chronicle*, such as the appearances of 'stars with hair' (comets), a 'bloody cloud . . . in fire's likeness . . . which was shaped like parti-coloured beams', and 'fiery

---

[10] E. John, *Orbis Brittaniae* (Leicester, 1966), pp. 178–80. See also A. Thacker, 'Membra Disjecta: the Division of the Body and the Diffusion of the Cult', *Oswald: Northumbrian King to European Saint*, ed. C. Stancliffe and E. Cambridge (Stamford, 1995), pp. 97–127, at 124.

[11] E. John, *Reassessing Anglo-Saxon England* (Manchester, 1996), pp. 113–17, *Orbis Brittaniae*, pp. 162–3; P. Wormald, 'Æthelwold and his Continental Counter parts: Contact, Comparison, Contrast', in *Bishop Æthelwold*, ed. Yorke, pp. 13–42, at 34–5; and Knowles, *Monastic Order*, p. 41. See also annal 964 in *The Anglo-Saxon Chronicle MS A*, ed. J. Bately, The AS Chronicle: a Collaborative Edition 3 (Cambridge, 1986), 75–6: 'Her dræfde Eadgar cyng þa preostas on Ceastre of Ealdanmynstre 7 of Niwanmynstre 7 of Ceortesige 7 of Middeltune 7 sette hy mid munecan.'   [12] Stenton, *Anglo-Saxon England*, p. 455.

[13] For the legitimacy controversy and the anti-monastic reaction, see John, *Reassessing*, pp. 119–20, *Orbis Brittaniae*, p. 158, and Yorke, 'Æthelwold', pp. 85–8. Although many authors note 'anti-monastic' sentiments at this time, it is more proper to say that monks were opposed more as Edgar's beneficiaries than as monks themselves.

[14] For the effects of the reform on the political, social and ecclesiastical establishments of the late tenth and early eleventh centuries, see P. Clemoes, 'Ælfric', *Continuations and Beginnings: Studies in Old English Literature*, ed. E. G. Stanley (London, 1966), pp. 176–209, at 179; in the same volume, see also D. Bethurum, 'Wulfstan', pp. 210–46, at 211–12; M. Clayton, 'Homiliaries and Preaching in Anglo-Saxon England', *Peritia* 4 (1985), 207–42, at 220–1; M. Gatch, 'Basic Christian Education from the Decline of Catechesis to the Rise of the Catechisms', *A Faithful Church: Issues in the History of Catechesis*, ed. J. H. Westerhoff III and O. C. Edwards Jr (Wilton, CT, 1981), pp. 79–108, at 94; and M. K. Lawson, 'Archbishop Wulfstan and the Homiletic Element in the Laws of Æthelred II and Cnut', *EHR* 107 (1992), 565–86, at 574–9.

[15] D. Dumville, 'Beowulf Come Lately: Some Notes on the Palaeography of the Nowell Codex', *ASNSL* 225 (1988), 49–63.

Brian McFadden

dragons'.[16] Given this mindset, it seems natural for ecclesiastical writers to defuse the unsettling effect of perceived wonders by containing their meanings in Christian contexts or using this fear to urge support for the failing English defence.[17] Unlike earlier works such as the *Liber monstrorum* (*c.* 750–850), which leaves the truth of marvels to the reader, the *Letter* accepts their existence but emphasizes the lack of human capacity to control and contain wonders. I do not wish to suggest that the *Letter* is an allegory consciously composed to reflect the events of the times;[18] rather, I argue that the times raised concerns which found their way into the *Letter* or which influenced the decision to include this work in the manuscript, since the text expresses unease at being unable to control or understand the unknown. Marvels raise fears which must be contained somehow, and the *Letter* uses a military narrative in an attempt to understand and thereby resist the source of the fear which uncertain times produce.

The narrator of the *Letter*, Alexander the Great, opens with a formal greeting to Aristotle, his former instructor, stating his desire to expand the boundaries of knowledge just as he has attempted to expand the boundaries of his empire:

Ond for þon þe ic þe wiste wel getynde in wisdome, þa geþohte ic for þon to þe to writanne be þæm þeodlonde Indie 7 be heofenes gesetenissum 7 be þæm unarimdum cynnum nædrena 7 monna 7 wildeora, to þon þæt hwæthwygo to þære *ongietenisse* þissa niura þinga þin gelis 7 gleawnis to geþeode. þeoh to þe seo gefylde gleawnis 7 snyttro 7 naniges fultumes abæded sio lar þæs rihtes hwæþere ic wolde þæt þu mine dæde *ongeate*,

---

[16] See *ASC MS A*, ed. Bately, p. 55, for the 'feaxede steorra' in 891 (892 BCD). The 'blodig wolcen . . . on fyres gelicnesse . . . on mistlice beamas wæs gehiwod' appears in 979 C; see *The Anglo-Saxon Chronicle MS C*, ed. K. O'Brien O'Keeffe, The AS Chronicle: a Collaborative Edition 5 (Cambridge, 2001), 84. For the 'fyrene dracan' in 793 E, see *Two Chronicles*, ed. Plummer I, 55. Comets also appear before major events in 678 ABCE, 729 ABCDE, 744 DE, 905 D, 975 ABCDE, 995 CDE (= 994?) and 1066 CD; see *The Anglo-Saxon Chronicle, MS B*, ed. S. Taylor, The AS Chronicle: a Collaborative Edition 4 (Cambridge, 1983), and *The Anglo-Saxon Chronicle MS D*, ed. G. P. Cubbin, The AS Chronicle: a Collaborative Edition 6 (Cambridge, 1996).

[17] See *Ælfric's Lives of Saints*, ed. W. W. Skeat, 4 vols. in 2, EETS os 76, 82, 94 and 114 (London, 1881–1900) II, 114, for the four types of war: just war is 'wið ða reðan flot-menn / oþþe wið oðre þeoda þe eard willað fordon'. See also J. E. Cross, 'The Ethic of War in Old English', *England Before the Conquest: Studies in Primary Sources presented to Dorothy Whitelock*, ed. P. Clemoes and K. Hughes (Cambridge, 1971), pp. 269–82, at 272.

[18] K. Sisam, *Studies in the History of Old English Literature* (Oxford, 1953), pp. 83–96, argues that the *Letter's* Latin text (from a Greek original) was originally translated into Old English in the late ninth century during Alfred's reign. If so, I wish to suggest that a ninth-century text expressing fear of the other would still be culturally relevant enough during Æthelred's reign to be copied into the *Beowulf* manuscript. See A. Orchard, *Pride and Prodigies: Studies in the Monsters of the 'Beowulf'-Manuscript* (Cambridge, 1995), pp. 116–39, for the Latin text's history in Anglo-Saxon England and the English translator's adaptation of the Latin military narrative to focus on Alexander's pride.

þa þu lufast 7 þa þing þe ungesewene mid þe siond, þa ic in Indie geseah þurh monig-feald gewin 7 þurh micle frecennisse mid greca herige (emphasis added).[19]

Alexander wishes to expose the novelties of India to the intellectual talents of his teacher so that Aristotle can incorporate them into his intellectual frame of reference. The idea of the necessity of perception to understanding is brought out in the passage by the words *ongietenisse* and *ongeate*, from *ongietan* ('to perceive or understand');[20] through this letter, Aristotle can perceive the things he has not seen personally in order to understand the marvellous beings and peoples Alexander has seen in his travels. However, Alexander qualifies the degree to which this mediated text can give adequate knowledge; he notes that Aristotle's knowledge can only contribute 'somewhat' (*hwæthwygo*) to understanding the marvels of India.[21] This may be an acknowledgement that Aristotle's personal experience of these marvels would be more intellectually acceptable than an indirectly related account in a letter; however, it may also be the author's first hint that the things which Alexander has seen defy containment in any intellectual category. The word *gelicnesse*, 'likeness', for example, occurs seven times in the text, and the adjective *gelic(e)* occurs four times;[22] Alexander cannot describe the objects he sees as they really are, and his inability to interpret suggests again his inability to complete his conquest. Alexander has attempted to know too much and to put into words what he knows; his attempt to conquer India has also been an attempt to contain it in narrative, and the strange things which he has seen not only resist his attempts at conquest but defy his descriptive powers.

The primary difficulty that Alexander foresees with respect to his account is that it may seem incredible. He is insistent about his truthfulness:

Ne gelyfde ic æniges monnes gesegenum swa fela wundorlicra þinga þæt hit swa beon mihte ær ic hit self minum eagum ne gesawe. Seo eorðe is to wundrienne hwæt heo ærest

---

[19] *Letter of Alexander to Aristotle* (hereafter *Letter*), p. 224 (§2): 'And because I know you to be well established in wisdom, because of that I thought to write to you about the land and people of India and of the arrangement of the heavens and of the uncountable breeds of serpents and men and wild beasts, in order that your learning and knowledge might serve the understanding of these new things somewhat. Although complete knowledge and wisdom and the learning of what is right requires no help in you, yet I would that you should understand my deeds, which you love, and those things which are unseen by you, which I saw in India through many struggles and through great strife along with the Greek army.' I cite the *Letter* from Orchard's edition in *Pride and Prodigies*, pp. 224–53. All translations are my own. See also L. Gunderson, *Alexander's Letter to Aristotle about India* (Meisenheim, 1980), pp. 48–9.

[20] See M. J. Menzer, 'Ælfric's *Grammar*: Solving the Problem of the English Language Text', *Neophilologus* 83 (1999), 637–52, at 644–6.

[21] J. J. Cohen, 'Old English Literature and the Work of Giants', *Comitatus* 24 (1993), 1–32, at 1–4, for understanding monsters as a means of controlling them.

[22] 'Gelicnesse' occurs in *Letter*, pp. 230, 236, 238 and 240 (§§ 11, 19, 21 and 25); 'gelic(e)' on pp. 236, 238 and 242 (§§ 18, 20 and 27).

oþþe godra þinga cenne, oððe eft þara yfelra, þe heo þæm sceawigendum is æteowed. Hio is cennende þa fulcuþan wildeora 7 wæstma 7 wecga oran, 7 wunderlice wyhta, þa þing eall þæm monnum þe hit geseoð 7 sceawigað wæron uneþe to gewitanne for þære missenlicnisse þara hiowa. Ac þa ðing þe me nu in gemynd cumað ærest þa ic þe write, þy læs on me mæge idel spellung oþþe scondlic leasung beon gestæled. Hwæt þu eac sylfa const þa gecynd mines modes mec a gewunelice healdon þæt gemerce soðes 7 rihtes. Ond ic sperlicor mid wordum sægde þonne hie mid dædum gedon wærun. Nu ic hwæþre gehyhte 7 gelyfe þæt þu þas þing ongete swa þu me ne talige owiht gelpan 7 secgan be þære micelnisse ures gewinnes 7 compes. For ðon ic oft wiscte 7 wolde þæt hyra læs wære swa gewinfulra.[23]

Alexander seems to anticipate a reaction like the one of the narrator of the *Liber monstrorum*, who attributes the creatures described to the lies or fictions of the poets and philosophers:

Et dum sermo de his per multarum scripturarum auctoritatem uelud excelsi sideris fulgore olim humano generi paene ubique refulsit, mendacia ea nemini iteranda putassem nisi me uentus tuae postulationis a puppi praecelsa pauidum inter marina praecipitasset monstra. Ponto namque tenebroso hoc opus aequipero, quod probandi si sint uera an instructa mendacio, nullus patet accessus eaque per orbem terrarum aurato sermone miri rumoris fama dispergebat, quorum maximam partem philosophorum et poetarum scriptura demonstrat, quae semper mendacia nutrit. Quaedam tantum in ipsis mirabilibus uera esse creduntur, et sunt innumerabilia quae si quis ad exploranda pennis uolare potuisset et ita rumoroso sermone tamen ficta probaret, ubi nunc urbs aurea et gemmis aspersa litora dicuntur, ibi lapideam aut nullam urbem et scopulosa cerneret. Et de his primum eloquar quae sunt aliquo modo credenda et sequentem historiam sibi quisque discernat, quod per haec antra monstrorum marina puellae quandam formulam sirenae depingam, ut sit capite rationis quod tamen diuersorum generum hispidae squamosaeque sequuntur fabulae.[24]

---

[23] *Letter*, p. 226 (§§3–4): 'I should not believe the speech of any man that so many wonderful things could exist before I had seen them myself with my own eyes. The earth is to marvel at, first for what she bears of good things, then again for the evil things, by which she is revealed to onlookers. She is the bearer of well-known wild beasts and plants and nuggets of ore, and of wonderful creatures, those things which to all men who see and examine them are difficult to understand for the variety of their shapes. But I will now write to you about those things which first come into my mind, lest empty story-telling or shameful lying be imputed to me. Behold, you yourself know that the form of my mind has ever customarily held me within the boundaries of truth and right. And I have told in words more sparingly than they were done in deeds. Now I yet think and believe that you should understand these things so that you should not account to me to boast in any way and to speak about the greatness of our struggles and battles, because I often wished and would that fewer of them were so difficult.' See D. Green, *Medieval Listening and Reading: the Primary Reception of German Literature 800–1300* (Cambridge, 1994), p. 266, and B. Guenée, 'Histoires, annales, chroniques: essai sur les genres historiques au Moyen Age', *Annales: Économies, Sociétés, Civilisations* 28 (1973), 997–1016, at 1000–3.

[24] Orchard, *Pride and Prodigies*, pp. 254–6: 'And while speech on these things on the authority of many writings shone as with the brightness of a high star once almost everywhere to the

One of the ways of dealing with things that do not fit intellectual categories is to relegate them to the world of fantasy or fiction; however, as Alexander reminds the reader, many things which cannot be explained, both good and evil, occur in the world. Alexander's plea to be believed recalls Augustine's answer to the pagan philosophers in *De civitate Dei*, in which he states that pagans and Christians alike do not understand wonders and yet accept the testimony of witnesses:

Sed cum Deus auctor sit naturarum omnium, quur nolunt fortiorem nos reddere rationem, quando aliquid uelut inpossibile nolunt credere eisque redditionem rationis poscentibus respondemus hanc esse uoluntatem omnipotentis Dei? qui certe non ob aliud uocatur omnipotens, nisi quoniam quidquid uult potest, qui potuit creare tam multa, quae nisi ostenderentur aut a credendis hodieque dicerentur testibus, profecto inpossibilia putarentur, non solum quae ignotissima aput nos, uerum etiam quae notissima posui. Illa enim quae [aput nos] praeter eos, quorum de his libros legimus, non habent testem et ab eis conscripta sunt, qui non sunt diuinitus docti adque humanitus falli forte potuerunt, licet cuique sine recta reprehensione non credere.[25]

Alexander also echoes his characterization of Aristotle as a master of what is right by suggesting that his master's tutelage has made him desire to stay within the bounds of truth. However, Alexander's mention of boundaries suggests that understanding in the way that Aristotle conceives of it has its limits; one

human race, I thought them fictions to be repeated to no one, except that the wind of your question knocked me from the high stern, trembling among the marine monsters. For I compare this work to the dark sea, because there is no plain way of proving if this report which is dispersed through the world with the golden speech of marvellous rumour is true or furnished with lies, of which the writings of poets and philosophers, which always nourish falsehood, show the greatest part. Only certain things among these wonders are believed to be true, and there are innumerable ones which, if someone could fly with wings for exploration, would nevertheless prove to be made of rumorous speech; where now is said to be a city of gold and beaches strewn with gems, there he would see a stony city or no city and a pebbly beach. And first I will speak of those things which should be believed in some way, and let everyone decide for himself about the following story, because through these caverns of monsters I will depict a small picture of a marine siren-girl, that if there should be a head of reason, hairy and scaly tales of all types nevertheless follow.' See also M. Lapidge, '"Beowulf", Aldhelm, the "Liber Monstrorum", and Wessex', *SM* 23 (1982), 151–92, at 167.

[25] *De civitate Dei* XXI.7, ed. E. Hoffmann, CSEL 40 (Vienna, 1900), 528: 'But since God is the author of all natures, why do [pagan philosophers] not allow that we give them a better account when they do not believe in anything as if impossible, and with them seeking an account we respond that this is the will of God Almighty? He certainly is not called almighty on account of anything unless he can do whatever he wills, who was able to make so many things not only unknown among us but also those well-known things which I have established, which, unless they had been pointed out or reported by current and credible witnesses, would surely be thought impossible. Concerning those things which have no testimony among us beyond that of those in whose books we read of them and were written by those who were not divinely inspired and were surely able to err humanly, it is permitted to anyone to disbelieve them without just blame.'

may perceive something but still be unable to understand it fully. Just as Alexander's conquest of India will prove incomplete, so will his reason and his narrative attempt to contain the marvels of India.

Alexander mentions an unknown previous letter in which 'ic þe cyþde 7 getacnode be þære asprungnisse sunnan 7 monan 7 be tungla rynum 7 gesetenissum 7 be lyfte tacnungum. þa ðing eall ne magon elcor beon buton micelre gemynde swa geendebyrded 7 fore stihtod.'[26] The contents of the previous letter contrast with what is to come in the *Letter*; some parts of the natural world are predictable and understandable to people with the proper knowledge, while others resist attempts to contain them in an intellectual order. The word choices subtly suggest a distinction between ambiguous wonders and significant wonders, *wundra* and *tacna*. In a direct communication to Aristotle, Alexander has indicated (*getacnode*) clear and understandable information; he has also mentioned the signs in the heavens (*tacnungum*, presumably the constellations), which indicate the presence of some intelligence, presumably divine, who has something to reveal to human beings through signs in nature.[27] However, the world is for marvelling at (*to wundrienne*); the things Alexander is about to reveal to Aristotle exist without explanation or obvious significance. Obvious signs of order in the world are *tacna*, but the strange races of humans or strange creatures are marvels, *wundra*, which confound all attempts to contain them in orderly intellectual categories, including narrative. English people around the year 1000 would have perceived the tumultuous events surrounding them in the light of the reports of wonders, as mentioned above; clerics such as Ælfric and Wulfstan might attribute them to divine displeasure at the ecclesiastical and civil disorders which had disrupted the relative stability of church and state in Edgar's reign, making the wonders into signs.[28] An English translator clinging to the hope that the Vikings would be turned back might want to foreshadow the ultimate failure of Alexander's conquest; a pessimistic author, however, might well choose the narrative voice of a warrior writing with knowledge of his impending death. The intention behind the Alexander-narrative is ambiguous, which reflects the English situation and makes their anxiety present in the text.

Despite acknowledging the difficulty of containing marvels in narrative, however, Alexander sets out to do just that. Having defeated Darius of Persia,

---

[26] *Letter*, p. 226 (§6): 'I made known to you and indicated about the eclipse of the sun and the moon and of the courses and ordering of the stars, and of the signs in the heavens. All these things cannot be otherwise but so established and foreordained by a great mind.'

[27] C. Lecouteux, *Les Monstres dans la pensée médiévale européenne* (Paris, 1993), pp. 75–6, notes that all creation would have been seen as potentially significant. For English views of astrology, see A. Meaney, 'Ælfric's Use of His Sources in His Homily on Auguries', *ES* 66 (1985), 477–95, at 483.

[28] See E. Duncan, 'Fears of the Apocalypse: the Anglo-Saxons and the Coming of the First Millennium', *Religion and Literature* 31.1 (1999), 15–23, at 18–21, and L. Carruthers, 'Apocalypse Now: Preaching and Prophecy in Anglo-Saxon England', *EA* 51 (1998), 399–410, at 406–8.

Alexander turns his army east and defeats Porus in the land of Fasiacen. After describing the men and material he has captured, Alexander describes the wonders of Porus's palace:

þær wæron gyldene columnan swiðe micle 7 trumlice 7 fæste, ða wæron unmetelice greate heanisse upp, ðara wæs þe we gerimdon be þæm gemete .CCCC. þa wagas wæron eac gyldene mid gyldnum þelum anægled fingres þicce. Mid þy ic ða wolde geornlicor þa þing geseon 7 furðor eode þa geseah ic gyldenne wingeard trumlicne 7 fæstlicne, 7 þa twigo his hongodon geond þa columnan. Ða wundrode ic þæs swiðe. Wæron in þæm wingearde gyldenu leaf 7 his hos 7 his wæstmas wæron cristallum 7 smaragdus, eac þæt gimcyn mid þæm cristallum ingemong hongode. His brydburas 7 his heahcleofan ealle wæron eorcnanstanum unionibus 7 carbunculis þæm gimcynnum swiðast gefrætwode. Uton hie wæron elpendbanum geworhte þa wæron wunderlice hwite 7 fægere 7 cypressus styde 7 laurisce hie uten wreþedon, 7 gyldne styþeo 7 aþrawene ðær ingemong stodon, 7 unarimedlicu goldhord þær wæron inne 7 ute 7 monifealdlicu hie wæron 7 missenlycra cynna. 7 monig fatu gimmiscu 7 cristallisce dryncfatu 7 gyldne sestras ðær wæron forð borenne. Seldon we þær ænig seolfor fundon. Siðþan ic þa me hæfde þas þing eall be gewealdum, þa wilnode ic Indeum innanwearde to geseonne.[29]

The wealth and the sumptuousness of Porus's quarters is amazing due to its intricacy and the sheer amount of precious material necessary to build it. However difficult this degree of wealth and workmanship is to imagine, though, it is still within the realm of possibility; human skill and effort created, and can explain, the things which Alexander sees. As a result, he is able to take possession of it, and his appetite for more conquest is whetted.[30]

Once Alexander has expanded the boundaries of his empire, he desires to push his military, intellectual and narrative borders farther into the centre of India, where he is warned that he may encounter many unpleasant beings.

þa sægdon us ða bigengean þæs londes þæt we us warnigan scoldon wið þa missenlican cynd nædrena 7 hrifra wildeora þy læs we on ða becwomon. þæra mænego in ðissum

---

[29] *Letter*, p. 228 (§§8–9): 'There were golden columns very great and tall and strong, which were of an immeasurable upward height, of which we counted a number of four hundred. The walls were in addition golden, covered with gold plating to a finger's thickness. When that I would see these things more earnestly and went farther, then I saw a golden vineyard, strong and firm, and the twigs hung over the columns. Then I wondered greatly at this. There were golden leaves in the vineyard and its vines and fruits were of crystals and emerald, and also gems hung in among the crystals. His women's quarters and his high chambers were all very greatly adorned with precious stones, with pearls and carbuncles the gemstones. Outside they were worked with elephant tusks which were wonderfully white and fair, and posts of cypress and ivory wreathed them on the outside, and supports golden and twisted stood in among them, and there were inside and outside uncountable gold hoards, and they were many and of various types. And many gem-adorned cups and crystal drinking vessels and golden vessels were borne forth from there. We seldom found any silver. After I had all of these things in my control, then I wished to see the inner part of India.' See also Gunderson, *Alexander's Letter*, pp. 49–50.

[30] Orchard, *Pride and Prodigies*, pp. 120–5.

Brian McFadden

dunum 7 denum 7 on wudum, 7 on feldum eardigeað 7 in stanholum hie selfe digliað. Ac hwæþre ma ic wolde þæm frecnan wege 7 siðfatum foeran ðonne þæm gehyldrum wegum, to ðon þæt ðone fleondon Porrum of þæm gefeohte þæt ic hine gemette ær he on þa westenu middangeardes gefluge. Ic me ða mid genom .CC. ladþeowa 7 eac .L. þe ða genran wegas cuðan þara siðfato. Ða ferde we in Agustes monþe þurh þa weallendan sond, 7 þurh þa wædlan stowe wætres 7 ælcere wætan. 7 ic mede gehet þæm us cuþlice gelæddon þurh þa uncuðan land Indie 7 mec wolde mid mine herige onsund gelædon in Patriacen þæt lond. 7 swiðast ic wilnade þæt hie me gelæddon to þæm dioglum godweb-wyrhtum, ða þonne wunderlice of sumum treowcynne 7 of his leafum 7 of his flyse, þæs treowes spunnon 7 swa eac to godewebbe wæfon 7 worhton. Ac hie þa londliode tiolodon ma ussa feonda willan to gefremmanne þonne urne, for þon þe hie us gelæddon þurh þa lond þe þa unarefnedlican cyn nædrena 7 hrifra wildeora in wæron. Ða ongeat ic selfa 7 geseah of dæle þæt me þa earfeðu becwoman. For þon ic ær forlet 7 ne gymde þara nytli-cra geþeahta minra freonda 7 þara monna þe me þæt logon þæt ic þæm wegum ferde.[31]

Alexander is spurred on by hearing of this wondrous cloth[32] which can be controlled by humans; as with the golden palace of Porus, Alexander believes that he can conquer the land because the human effort involved in making the cloth makes his objective understandable. He does not take into account until too late, however, that the process of reaching Patriacen will take him to where he will encounter creatures over which he has no control other than the sword. He also does not take into account that his guides might be willing to deceive him; his belief in the power of treasure overrides his caution as a general regarding unfamiliar territory and people. Andy Orchard has argued that disregard for others' advice is a sign of pride in Alexander,[33] but while this is certainly true, Alexander

---

[31] *Letter*, pp. 228–30 (§§9–10): 'Then the dwellers in that land said to us that we should beware of the various kinds of serpents and fierce wild beasts, should we come upon them. A great many of them live in the hills and dens and in the woods, and dwell in fields and conceal themselves in stone holes. And yet I wished more to go on the fierce ways and paths than on the more secure ways, so that I could encounter Porus, fleeing from the fight, before he should flee to the wastes of the earth. I then took with me 250 guides who knew the shorter paths of that journey. Then we went in the month of August through the boiling sand, and through the places poor in water or any moisture. And I promised treasure to those who would lead us knowingly through the unknown land of India and would lead me with my army safely into the land of Patriacen. And most strongly I wished that they should lead me to the hidden workers of good cloth, who spun it wonderfully from a certain type of tree and of its leaves and its fleece, and also wove it and worked it into a good cloth. But the native guides worked more to help the will of our foes than our own, because they led us through the lands in which were intolerable kinds of serpents and fierce wild beasts. Then I myself saw and perceived on my part that afflictions would come to me, because I earlier ignored and disregarded the helpful thoughts of my friends and the men who had opposed me that I should travel those ways.' See also Gunderson, *Alexander's Letter*, p. 51.

[32] Possibly silk; see M. L. Cameron, 'Aldhelm as Naturalist: a Re-Examination of Some of his Enigmata', *Peritia* 4 (1985), 117–33, at 124, and 'Bald's *Leechbook* and Cultural Interactions in Anglo-Saxon England', *ASE* 19 (1990), 5–12, at 8.

[33] Orchard, *Pride and Prodigies*, p. 118. See also H. Tristram, 'More Talk of Alexander', *Celtica* 21 (1990), 658–63, at 660, and P. J. Frankis, 'The Thematic Significance of *enta geweorc* and Related Imagery in *The Wanderer*', *ASE* 2 (1973), 253–70, at 254–8.

is also not so foolish that he does not recognize his error. This first episode of the situation escaping Alexander's control has begun a process of recognition that the things and beings of the world are not readily contained, either by bribery, conquest or narrative itself.

Alexander's army, close on Porus's trail, encounters its first major setback in the desert. The first water they encounter is undrinkable, but they proceed through the desert in full battle array because 'ic wiste hwæþre þæt ure for 7 siðfæt wæs þurh þa lond 7 stowe þe missenlicra cynna eardung in wæs, nædrena 7 rifra wilde-ora. Ond we we ðe þæs londes ungleawe 7 unwise wæron, þæt usic ðonne sem-ninga hwelc earfeðo on becwome.'[34] Alexander is aware of the dangers which the land contains, although he does not know just how fierce nature's resistance will be. Alexander's army next encounters a village of Indians whom Alexander wishes to ask about fresh water, but the sight of a host of armed and edgy Macedonians drives them to their houses. Alexander orders a few threatening arrows to be shot into the village, but the villagers hide more securely; Alexander relies on the threat of force rather than peaceful attempts at communication, and it fails him. When Alexander finally sends two hundred of his thanes to swim over in order to ask them about the water, his men receive a deadly surprise:

þa hie ða hæfdon feorðan dæl þære ea geswummen, ða becwom sum ongrislic wise on hie. þæt wæs þonne nicra mengeo on onsione maran 7 unhyrlicran þonne ða elpendas in ðone grund þære ea 7 betweoh ða yða þæs wæteres þa men besencte 7 mid heora muðe hie sliton 7 blodgodon 7 hie ealle swa fornamon, þæt ure nænig wiste hwær hiora æni cwom. Ða wæs ic swiðe yrre þæm minum ladþeowum, þa us on swylce frecennissa gelæddon. Het hiera ða bescufan in þa ea .L. 7 .C. 7 sona þæs ðe hie inne wæron, swa wæron þa nicoras gearwe tobrudon hie swa hie þa oðre ær dydon, 7 swa þicce hie in þære ea aweollon swa æmettan ða nicras, 7 swilc unrim heora wæs. þa het ic blawan mine byman 7 þa fyrd faran.[35]

---

[34] *Letter*, p. 232 (§14): 'I knew, however, that our travel and journey was through the lands and places in which the dwelling of various types of serpents and fierce wild beasts was, and because we were unfamiliar and unwise about the land, then any affliction might suddenly come to us.' See A. Kennedy, 'Byrhtnoth's Obits and Twelfth-Century Accounts of the Battle of Maldon', *The Battle of Maldon, A.D. 991*, ed. D. G. Scragg (Manchester, 1991), pp. 59–80, at 67–8 and 73–5, for narrative parallels between Byrhtnoth and Alexander. See also Gunderson, *Alexander's Letter*, pp. 51–2.

[35] *Letter*, p. 234 (§15): 'When they had swum a fourth part of the way over the river, then a terrible thing happened to them, which was that then a great host of water monsters came into sight, larger and more fierce than elephants, from the bottom of the river and drew the men between the waves and with their mouths bit them and bloodied them and seized them all away, so that none of us knew where any of them had gone. Then was I very angry with my guides, who had led us into such peril. I commanded 150 of them to be shoved into the river then, and as soon as they were in it, the water monsters were eager and they dragged them off as they had done to the others before, and the water monsters welled up in the river as thickly as ants, and just as uncountable as them. Then I ordered my trumpets to be blown, and the army departed.' See J. B. Friedman, 'The Marvels-of-the-East-Tradition in Anglo-Saxon Art', *Sources of Anglo-Saxon Culture*, ed. P. Szarmach (Kalamazoo, MI, 1986), pp. 319–41, at 321, and Gunderson, *Alexander's Letter*, pp. 52–3.

Alexander's reaction is swift and severe. He kills the guides for not warning the army of the danger, not taking into account that they might be just as surprised as he is; he reacts where he can, against the men under his command. However, the action is too little, too late; he has lost two hundred of his best men and has not found fresh water, so he abandons the attempt. The water monsters, which Orchard identifies as hippopotami,[36] prevent Alexander from achieving knowledge; the natural world again resists Alexander's attempt to learn something about it and to appropriate it for his purposes.

After this disastrous encounter, Alexander meets natives in reed boats who tell him 'in heora gereorde' ('in their own language')[37] where fresh water can be found; significantly, Alexander must deal with the natives on their terms instead of his own. The army travels all night, but 'symle leon 7 beran 7 tigris 7 pardus 7 wulfas ure ehtan'.[38] When Alexander reaches the water, he orders trees felled so that his army and their pack animals can more easily reach the water. However, the land turns on Alexander yet again that night; all sorts of beings who also want water find their way to the lake and attack the encamped army. Alexander is first visited by scorpions and serpents:

Ða toforan monan upgonge þa cwomon þær Scorpiones þæt wyrmcyn swa hie ær gewunelice wæron toweard þæs wætersciepes. Wæs þæra wyrma micel mænegeo 7 heora wæs unrim 7 hie swiðe on þa ure wic onetton 7 in þa feollon. Ða æfter þon cwoman þær hornede nædran Carastis þæt nædercyn. þa wæron ealle missenlices hiwes, for þon hie wæron sume reode, sume blace, sume hwite. Sumum þonne scinan þa scilla 7 lixtan swylce hie wæron gyldne þonne mon onlocode. Eall þæt lond hleoðrade for þara wyrma hwistlunge, 7 us eac noht lytel ege from him wæs. Ac we þa mid scyldum us scyldan, 7 eac mid longsceaftum sperum hie slogan 7 cwealdon monige eac in fyre forburnon. þas ðing we þus drugon þæt we swa wið þam wyrmum fuhtan 7 wunnan huru twa tida þære nihte.[39]

Alexander's next problem comes from various large serpents 'wunderlicran þonne ða oðre wæron 7 egeslicran', as large as columns with poisonous breath:

---

[36] Orchard, *Pride and Prodigies*, p. 235.   [37] *Letter*, p. 234 (§16).
[38] *Ibid.*: 'All together lions and bears and tigers and leopards and wolves attacked us.' See also Gunderson, *Alexander's Letter*, pp. 53–4.
[39] *Letter*, p. 236 (§17): 'Then at the moonrise came there the type of serpent called Scorpions toward the water as they had usually done before. There was a great host of these serpents and they were innumerable and they greatly hastened and fell upon our camp. Then after them came there the horned serpent of the type of snake called Carastis. These were all of various colours, because some of them were red, some black, some white. On some of them the scales shone and gleamed as if they were gold that men looked on. All that land resounded with the hissing of the serpents, and in addition there was no small terror to us from them. But we defended ourselves with shields and also with the long-shafted spear we struck them and killed many, and also burned them in fire. We thus endured these things to such a degree that we fought and struggled against the creatures for two hours of the night.'

'Hæfdon hie þa wyrmas þrie slite tungan 7 þonne hie eðedon þonne eode him of þy muðe mid þy oroþe swylce byrndende þecelle. Wæs þæra wyrma oroð 7 eðung swiþe deadberende 7 æterne.'[40]

After losing twenty thegns and thirty soldiers to the serpents, the army endures another combined assault:

þa hit wæs seo fifte tid þære nihte, þa mynton we us gerestan, ac þa cwoman þær hwite leon in fearra gelicnesse swa micle 7 hie ealle swiðe grymetende ferdon. Mid þa ða leon þyder cwoman þa ræsdon hie sona on us 7 we us wið him sceldan þæs ðe we mihton 7 us wæs swælc geswencnis 7 swilc earfeþo mid deorum becymen in þære sweartan niht 7 in þære þystran. Swelce eac eoforas þær cwoman unmætlicre micelnisse, 7 monig oþer wildeor 7 eac tigris us on þære nihte þar abisgodon. Swelce þær eac cwoman hreaþemys þa wæron in culefrena gelicnesse swa micle, 7 þa on ure ondwlitan sperdon 7 us pulledon. Hæfdon hie eac þa hreaþmys teð in monna gelicnisse, 7 hie mid þæm þa men wundodon 7 tæron.[41]

As if Alexander's men have not suffered enough, the onslaught continues with a Dentestyrannus, or rhinoceros: 'Ðis deor mid þy ðe hit þæs wætres ondronc, þa beheold hit þa ure wicstowe, 7 þa semninga on us 7 on ure wicstowe ræsde. Ne hit for þæm bryne wandode þæs hatan leges 7 fyres þe him wæs ongean, ac hit ofer eall wod 7 eode.'[42] The rhino kills twenty-six of Alexander's thegns and maims a further fifty-two; after much effort, the rhino is killed, but the men endure yet another hardship of 'wolberende lyft hwites hiowes, 7 eac missenlices wæs heo on hringwisan fag, 7 monige men for heora þæm wolberende stence swulton'.[43] The horrors continue with a plague of 'Indisce mys ... in foxa gelicnisse and in heora micle. Ða þonne ure feþerfotnietenu bitan 7 wundedon 7 monige for hiora wundum swultan.'[44] Last comes a flock of black night-ravens;

---

[40] *Ibid.* p. 236 (§18): 'More marvellous than the others were, and more terrible'; 'These worms had three-pronged tongues and when they breathed the breath came out of their mouths like a burning torch. The breath and exhalation of these worms was very deadly and venomous.'

[41] *Ibid.* p. 236 (§19): 'When it was the fifth hour of the night, then we thought to rest ourselves, but then there came white lions shaped like and in the size of bulls, and they came grunting greatly. When the lions came there then they immediately rushed on us and we shielded ourselves against them as best we could, and there was great affliction to us, and also such torment with the beasts coming in the black night and the darkness. Also boars of immeasurable size came there, and many other wild beasts and also tigers tormented us there in the night. Also there came "quick mice" [bats] which were like doves in shape and size, and they slashed our faces and pulled at us. These bats had teeth like men's and they wounded and tore up the men with them.'

[42] *Ibid.* p. 238 (§20): 'When this beast had drunk the water, then it saw our camp, and then it suddenly rushed on us and on our camp. It was not frightened by the burning of the hot fire and flame that was against it, but it went and trampled over everything.'

[43] *Ibid.* p. 238 (§21): 'A poisonous vapour of a white colour, and it was also full of circular swirls, and many men died due to its poisonous stench.'

[44] *Ibid.*: 'Indian mice ... in the shape of foxes and their size. Then they bit our four-footed beasts and wounded them and many [beasts] died of their wounds.'

mercifully, however, the birds only take water and eat fish, '⁊ þa fuglas us nænige laðe ne yfle ne wæron . . . Ac hi him selfe eft gewiton þonon.'[45] Alexander's first act the next morning is to break the legs of his guides 'ðæt hie on niht wæron from þæm wyrmum asogone þe þæt wæter sohton. ⁊ ic him het eac þa honda of aheawan, þæt hie be gewyrhtum þes wites wite drugon, þe hie ær hiora þonces us on gelæddon ⁊ gebrohton.'[46]

Alexander's incredible afflictions may indeed be the result of deliberate treachery by his guides; on the other hand, he has knowingly taken the risk of going on the dangerous paths, and although the army is able to kill some of the creatures, it cannot defeat them. Alexander is explicit about the losses he has suffered, paying special attention to the thegns from his personal guard who have died. Rather than accept responsibility for their deaths himself, however, he once again puts the blame on his guides and executes them; the creatures and the poisonous fog are beyond Alexander's control, a fact he cannot accept, so he takes vengeance where he can do so, on human beings. Again we see India resisting Alexander's attempts to go farther; as a result, he decides to take the safe paths, which lead him to Patriacen where the natives 'us þær fremsumlice ⁊ luflice onfengon'.[47] Once back in well-defined bounds, Alexander and his army encounter humans whom they can deal with in a peaceful way. For Alexander, attempting to cross boundaries into the unknown results in an unwinnable strife; staying within the bounds of what is known results in co-operation and safety.[48] This contrast suggests that attempting to impose one's own categories on the marvellous does violence to it and only reveals one's own weakness and incapacity.

Trying to reach these known borders, however, means trouble for Alexander; when the army reaches 'þa londgemæro Medo ⁊ Persa, þa we ðær eft edniowunga hæfdon micle gefeoht. ⁊ .XX. daga ic þær mid minre fyrde wið him wicode.'[49] Having finally caught up with Porus and reached a stalemate, Alexander devises a stratagem to spy out his camp; he dresses as a cattle-herd and goes to Porus, claiming to have information about Alexander. He tells

[45] *Ibid.*: 'And the birds did us no harm and were not evil to us . . . But they departed from there all by themselves.'
[46] *Ibid.* p. 238 (§22): 'That they should suffer torment from the serpents who would seek water there in the night. And I also commanded that their hands should be cut off, that they who worked the torment should endure the torment to which they had by plan led us and brought us.' [47] *Ibid.* p. 238 (§23): 'Received us in a gracious and kind manner.'
[48] P. Sorrell, 'The Approach to the Dragon-Fight in *Beowulf*, Aldhelm, and the "traditions folkloriques" of Jacques Le Goff', *Parergon* 12 (1994), 57–87, at 82–5, for the implications of boundary crossing; see also M. K. Lafferty, 'Nature and Unnatural Man: Lucan's Influence on Walter of Châtillon's Concept of Nature', *Classica et Mediaevalia* 46 (1995), 285–300, for nature's attempts at self-defence.
[49] *Letter*, p. 238 (§23): When they reached 'the boundaries of the Medes and Persians, then there we had a great battle one more time. And for twenty days I camped there with my force opposite them.'

Porus that Alexander is old and weak; Porus pays him to take a message back to Alexander, which he eventually reads with amusement. Unexpectedly, however, Porus surrenders the next morning 'þa he hæfde ongieten þæt he wið me gewinnan ne meahte'.[50] Alexander receives Porus's kingdom from him and promptly returns it; the grateful Porus gives treasure to the Macedonians and shows Alexander two gold statues of Hercules and Bacchus, which Alexander tests by drilling holes in them. Two key things become apparent in this episode. First, if monstrousness consists of crossing borders between identifiable physical categories, as David Williams argues,[51] then Alexander becomes like a monstrous being when he assumes his disguise and enters Porus's camp; he appears to cross the boundaries between nobility and servitude by changing his appearance, crosses in fact the boundaries between friend and enemy, and thus confuses Porus's conception of him. From a military standpoint, Alexander gains the intelligence which he sought, but he does so by temporarily trading his customary identity for 'uncuþe hrægl 7 … lyþerlice gerelan';[52] ironically, by confusing Porus's knowledge, Alexander has increased his own, which suggests that appearance can be deceptive to human reason and that one must therefore move beyond reliance on the perceptible and transcend the known to achieve understanding. Secondly, Alexander also seems to be learning that discourse is more powerful than the sword; by talking to Porus and exchanging kingdoms, 'of þæm feondscipe þe us ær betweonum wæs þæt he seoðan wæs me freond 7 ealle greca herige 7 min gefera 7 gefylcea'.[53] When Alexander cannot establish a discourse with someone he encounters, he tends to fight; once he learns he can reason with someone, there is a greater chance to avoid bloodshed. Again we see that lack of discourse tends to be one of Alexander's major factors in determining monstrosity. If Alexander can talk with a race of beings, he sees them as human and feels he can ally with them, containing them in his narrative and his empire; if he cannot talk to them, he usually – and more often than not, unsuccessfully – sets out to destroy them.

Alexander's military failure and verbal success have an important implication for the *Letter* in the context of the Viking invasions. First, the text may have been translated or copied because it struck a chord, resonating with echoes of the

[50] *Ibid.* p. 240 (§25): 'When he had perceived that he could not fight against me.' See also Gunderson, *Alexander's Letter*, pp. 54–6.   [51] Williams, *Deformed Discourse*, pp. 107–11.
[52] *Letter*, p. 240 (§24): 'Unknown garments and … lowly clothes.'
[53] *Ibid.* p. 240 (§25): 'Out of that enmity which had been between us, he afterwards became a friend to me and all of the Macedonian army, and my companion and ally.' See G. Bunt, 'An Exemplary Hero: Alexander the Great', *Companion to Middle English Romance*, ed. H. Aertsen and A. MacDonald (Amsterdam, 1990), pp. 29–55, at 30. See also R. I. Page, 'The Audience of *Beowulf* and the Vikings', *The Dating of Beowulf*, ed. C. Chase (Toronto, 1981), pp. 113–22; the Danish settlers (as opposed to raiders) and the English had a relatively peaceful coexistence as long as they could negotiate.

English failure to unite and defeat the Vikings and Æthelred's preference to negotiate and pay tribute rather than to fight and be defeated.[54] Secondly, Alexander
describes his adventures but does not interpret them; the ability to interpret an
event and fully understand it would be a fuller method of containment than conquest, but Alexander cannot grasp the significance of his failure to conquer. As
noted above, from the perspective of clerics such as Wulfstan, the English do not
see the connection between the Viking terror and their own personal and social
sins; the English have pushed God too far by failing to unite in ecclesiastical and
political reform and in standing against the Vikings, and in return, God is allowing
the Vikings victory. The *Letter* is a site for the expression of such concerns;
Alexander in his pride fails to see that he is opposing divinity in the form of the
marvellous, and his quest to know and to conquer more will be punished.

After his alliance with Porus, Alexander sets out to learn more about India,
but he is once again frustrated: 'Ac þa ne gesawon we swa swa we geferdon noht
elles buton þa westan feldas 7 wudus 7 duna be þæm garsecge, ða wæron
monnum ungeferde for wildeorum 7 wyrmum.'[55] Alexander then wishes to continue along the sea to see if he can go around the world, but the natives tell him
that the sea is 'to þon þiostre . . . þæt hine nænig mon mid scipe geferan ne
meahte';[56] he is thwarted by the topography, suggesting again that nature refuses
knowledge of itself to human reason. He turns inland into a marshy region to
determine whether or not 'me owiht in þæm londe beholen oððe bedegled
wære', and his army is immediately attacked by a crocodile, 'þæt deor hatte *quasi
caput luna* 7 him wæron þa breost gelice niccres breastum 7 heardum toðum 7
miclum hit wæs gegyred 7 geteþed. Ond hit þa þæt deor ofsloh mine þegnas
twegen.'[57] In Alexander's attempt to explore, specifically to find anything which
some agency has tried to keep from him, he again encounters a monster which
impedes his efforts, but he cannot or will not interpret these repeated hindrances as a divine warning to proceed no farther.

The difficulty of knowing the country of India is next symbolized by a place-
name; after moving on and camping by the river Biswicmon (which may mean
'deceive the man', 'evade the man', or 'be free from man'),[58] Alexander's army is

[54] Keynes, 'A Tale', pp. 203–4. See also John, *Reassessing*, p. 145.
[55] *Letter*, p. 242 (§26): 'But we did not see anything else as we journeyed except for waste fields and woods and hills by the ocean, which were untravelled by men due to the wild beasts and serpents.'
[56] *Ibid.*: 'Too dark . . . so that no man could sail over it by ship.' See also Gunderson, *Alexander's Letter*, p. 56.
[57] *Letter*, p. 242 (§26): 'Anything in that land should have been hidden or concealed from me'; p. 242 (§27): 'That beast which is called "head like the moon", and the breast on it was like the breast of a water monster, and it was equipped and toothed with hard and great teeth. And that beast then killed two of my thegns.' See also Gunderson, *Alexander's Letter*, p. 56.
[58] J. Bosworth, *An Anglo-Saxon Dictionary*, ed. T. N. Toller (Oxford, 1898), p. 93, for *beswican* and

attacked by a herd of elephants, which Alexander repels by releasing a herd of pigs which then panic the elephants. Even creatures known to Alexander become opponents in India; just as the wild elephants cannot be contained, the countryside frustrates Alexander's attempts to conquer and narrate. Alexander's next encounter is with the Ictifafonas, nine-foot, hairy, naked people who live by eating whales: 'Mid þy ic þa wolde near þa men geseon 7 sceawigon, ða flugon hie sona in þa wæter 7 hie þær in þæm stanholum hyddon.'[59] Alexander does not have any harmful intent toward the Ictifafonas, but his attempt to learn something about them is frustrated by their flight to inaccessible places; again, the world resists observation and knowledge by escaping or eluding him. The army is then attacked by Cynocephali, dog-headed men, 'ða cwomon to þon þæt hie woldon us wundigan';[60] they are repelled with arrows and flee back into the woods. The narrator makes an explicit judgement about the enmity of the dog-heads and notes that they flee into the woods; once again, difficult territory resists attempts at human penetration and harbours enemies of human knowledge and power.

The land gives one last reminder of its harshness to Alexander before he returns to Fasiacen. As his army camps, there arises a great wind which 'ura getelda monige afylde, 7 he ða eac usse feþerfotnietenu swiðe swencte'; next, a heavy snowfall hits which causes Alexander to worry 'þæt he wolde ealle þa wicstowe forfeallan'; last, the skies grow dark and fire falls from the skies 'swelce byrnende þecelle 7 for þæs fyres byrne eall se feld born. Ða cwædon men þætte hie wendon þæt þæt wære goda eorre þæt usic on becwome.'[61] Apparently, Alexander's men can understand what their general cannot or will not see. Five hundred of Alexander's thegns are killed that evening; after burying them, the army sets out toward Fasiacen again, where they come upon the cave of Bacchus. Alexander wishes to test the legend of the cave that one must enter it with an offering to the god or else die; he sends condemned men in without offerings, and they die within three days. Alexander then 'eaþmodlice 7 geornlice bæd þa godmægen þæt hie mec ealles middangeardes kyning 7 hlaford mid hean sigum geweorþeden, ond in

---

beswician. The Latin text gives the river's name as 'Buemar'. See Orchard, *Pride and Prodigies*, p. 215 (§28), and W. W. Boer, *Epistola Alexandri ad Aristotelem*, Beiträge zur klassischen Philologie 50 (Meisenheim, 1973), 30.

[59] *Letter*, pp. 242–4 (§29): 'When I wanted to go nearer these people to see and observe them, then they flew immediately to the water and hid themselves in stone caves.' See also Gunderson, *Alexander's Letter*, pp. 56–7; Boer, *Epistola Alexandri*, p. 32, gives *faunos* in his edition, but lists several variant spellings.

[60] *Letter*, p. 244 (§29): 'Who came because they wanted to wound us.' See also Gunderson, *Alexander's Letter*, pp. 56–7.

[61] *Letter*, p. 245 (§30): the wind 'felled many of our tents, and it also greatly harmed our four-footed beasts'; 'That it would cover over all of the campsite'; 'Like a burning torch, and by reason of that fire all the field was burning. Then the men said that they believed that this was the gods' anger that had come upon us.' See also Gunderson, *Alexander's Letter*, pp. 57–9.

Brian McFadden

Macedoniam ic eft gelæded wære to Olimphiade minre meder 7 to minum geswus-trum 7 gesibbum'.[62] The army fears divine vengeance manifested in the forces of nature, and Alexander himself provokes some of it by allowing his men to die; it seems somewhat ironic, then, that Alexander should pray for success in his military exploits when he has apparently misinterpreted all that has happened to him. What he does not seem to see is that his attempt to conquer the unknown in India is an attempt to know more than divinity will allow; Alexander has offended by entering the land of India without offering, only with a desire to take, and by praying for such success, he seeks to exceed the bounds of human knowledge and will be resisted regardless of what he asks.

The last episode in the *Letter*, Alexander's encounter with the talking trees, suggests that the divine response to Alexander's effrontery will be his own death. Alexander encounters two men on the road to Fasiacen who tell him of two trees, the male tree of the Sun and the female tree of the Moon, which prophesy in Greek and in Indian. At first sceptical, Alexander succumbs to curiosity, and he takes a force of three thousand through 'þa wædlan stowe wætres 7 þurh þa unarefndon lond wilddeora 7 wyrma þa wæron wunderlicum nomum on Indisc geceged';[63] once again, his desire to learn is resisted by both the land and also by his difficulty with the words which name its wonders. When he arrives at the land where the trees are, Alexander praises its beauty and the abundance of incense and balsam; he meets and talks with 'ægþer ge wif ge wæpned-men mid panthera fellum 7 tigriscum þara deora hydum gegyrde 7 nanes oðres brucon'.[64] Dressing in skins was regarded as a sign of savagery throughout the Middle Ages,[65] but Alexander's speech with them suggests that the narrator regards them as more human than beast. He is then introduced to the high priest, similarly dressed, who '[w]æs he se bisceop .X. fota upheah, 7 eall him wæs se lichoma sweart buton þæm toþum ða wæron hwite. 7 þa earan him þurh þyrelode, 7 earhringas onhongedon of mænigfealdan gimcynne geworhte.'[66]

---

[62] *Letter*, p. 244 (§31): '[I] eagerly and humbly prayed the mighty gods that they should make me worthy with high victories as the king and lord of all earth, and that I should be led back to Macedonia to my mother Olympias and to my sisters and kin.' See also Gunderson, *Alexander's Letter*, p. 59.

[63] *Letter*, p. 246 (§33): 'The place poor in water, and through a land unbearable due to wild beasts and serpents which were named with marvellous names in Indian.'

[64] *Ibid.* p. 246 (§34): 'Both men and women were dressed in skins of panthers and of beasts named tigers and wore nothing else.' See also Gunderson, *Alexander's Letter*, pp. 59–60.

[65] J. B. Friedman, *The Monstrous Races in Medieval Art and Thought* (Cambridge, MA, 1981), pp. 31–2; see also D. Sprunger, 'Wild Folk and Lunatics in Medieval Romance', *The Medieval World of Nature: a Book of Essays*, ed. J. E. Salisbury (New York, 1993), pp. 145–63, at 147.

[66] *Letter*, p. 248 (§35): 'The bishop was ten feet in height, and all of his body was black except the teeth which were white. And his ears were pierced through, and earrings hung down made with many types of gems.' The Latin reads *antistes* ('priest') in Boer, *Epistola Alexandri*, p. 41, which the English translator renders as 'bisceop'.

108

Again, the priest displays a monstrous excess of height and outlandish bodily adornment, but Alexander treats him respectfully; he can hold discourse with him. The priest makes certain conditions to enter the grove of the trees: the supplicants must be virgin,[67] must not offer any form of blood sacrifice, and must enter the grove naked. Alexander also notes that unusual circumstances surround the trees; despite their great growth, no rain ever falls in the grove, nor do bird, beast or serpent ever approach, and during eclipses, the trees fear that they are losing their power.[68] It seems as if the laws of nature are temporarily suspended here in the presence of divinity; again, by encountering the trees on their own terms, Alexander will receive the knowledge he seeks.

Alexander's questioning, however, yields something unexpected that he may not have wanted to know:

Mid þy we þa wel neah stodan þam bearwum 7 þæm godsprecum, þa ðohte ic on minum mode hwæþer ic meahte ealne middangeard me on onweald geslean . . . Ða ondswarode me þæt triow Indiscum wordum 7 þus cwæd: 'ða unoferswyðda Alexander in gefeohtum þu weorðest cyning 7 hlaford ealles middangeardes, ac hwæþre ne cymst þu on þinne eþel ðonan þu ferdest ær, for þon ðin wyrd hit swa be þinum heafde 7 fore hafað aræded.' Ða wæs ic ungleaw þæs geþeodes þara Indiscra worda þe þæt triow me to spræc, ða rehte hit me se bisceop 7 sægde. Mid þy hit mine geferan gehyrdon þæt ic eft cwic ne moste in minne eþel becuman, ða wæron hie swiðe unrote for þon.[69]

The message itself is beyond Alexander; he must have it translated, again showing his dependence on others and suggesting his lack of power. Translation has not been an issue before Alexander traverses this region of India in the narrative; the Indian speakers are assumed to be translated by Alexander's guides, and this is the first time that Alexander notes explicitly that he does not speak the language. Unfortunately, he learns that he will win a pyrrhic victory; he will conquer the known world but will not live to enjoy it. The 'wyrd' which decrees Alexander's fate, however, does not always mean 'fate', and can often be translated as 'the course of events';[70] several scholars have noted

---

[67] J. Bugge, *Virginitas: an Essay in the History of a Medieval Ideal* (The Hague, 1975), p. 50, notes that sex would have been held to diminish Alexander's strength.

[68] Gunderson, *Alexander's Letter*, pp. 61–2.

[69] *Letter*, pp. 248–50 (§§36–7): 'When we stood well near the grove and the oracles, then I thought in my mind whether I might take all the world in my control . . . Then the tree answered me in the Indian tongue and thus said: "Alexander, you will be undefeated in battle and king and lord of all the world, but yet you will not come again to your homeland which you earlier left, since your fate has so decided it on your head already." When I was ignorant of the words in the Indian language which the tree spoke to me, then the bishop translated it for me and told me. When my companions heard that I would not come back alive to my homeland, they were then very unhappy about it.' See also Gunderson, *Alexander's Letter*, pp. 62–5.

[70] Bosworth, *Anglo-Saxon Dictionary*, ed. Toller, pp. 1287–8. *Wyrd* comes from *weorþan*, 'to be, become, happen'; cf. German *werden*. See F. Robinson, *The Tomb of Beowulf and Other Essays on Old English* (Cambridge, MA, 1993), pp. 102–3.

that *wyrd* may not imply a deterministic fate but something that can change depending on one's actions.[71] The implications of *wyrd* suggest that what Alexander has already done has started the chain of events which will end in his death. His attempt to contain the known world has consistently been resisted; death, the ultimate resistance, will prevent him from further conquest.

Still not content with what he has already learned, Alexander seeks the trees again that evening with three trusted friends, Perticas, Clitus[72] and Pilotas. The tree of the moon answers the request this time:

Ða þohte ic on minum mode 7 on minum geþohte on hwelcre stowe ic sweltan scolde. Mid þy ða ærest se mona upeode þa gehran he mid his sciman þæm triowum ufeweardum 7 þæt triow ondswarode þæm minum geþohte 7 þus cwæð: 'Alexander fulne ende þines lifes þu hæfst gelifd, ac þys æftran geare þu swyltst on Babilone on Maius monðe from þæm þu læst wenst from þæm þu bist beswicen.' Ða wæs ic swiðe sariges modes, 7 þa mine frynd swa eac þa me þær mid wæron. 7 hie weopon swiðe, for þon him wære min gesynto leofre þonne hiora seolfra hælo.[73]

Alexander receives his specific information about the time and place of his death, but even the specifics come with more uncertainty; the knowledge that he is to be murdered by a person whom he least suspects opens up a vast range of possibilities for the source of his death. Now, in addition to knowing that he is going to die, Alexander knows that someone supposedly in his power is going to kill him; Alexander's conquest and containment of the world can neither keep death away nor guarantee his safety. It is perhaps ironic that Clitus accompanies Alexander to hear the tree and that he values Alexander's safety; in some versions of the Alexander legend, Alexander in a drunken rage murders Clitus when, out of family loyalty, Clitus says that Philip of Macedonia, Alexander's

---

[71] For various discussions of the nature of *wyrd*, see T. P. Dunning and A. J. Bliss, *The Wanderer* (New York, 1969), pp. 71–4; K. Lochrie, '*Wyrd* and the Limits of Human Understanding: a Thematic Sequence in the Exeter Book', *JEGP* 85 (1986), 323–31; P. Cavill, '*Beowulf* and *Andreas*: Two Maxims', *Neophilologus* 77 (1993), 479–87, at 482–3; J. M. Hill, *The Cultural World of Beowulf* (Toronto, 1995), pp. 56–8 and 80; C. T. Majors, 'A Christian *Wyrd*: Syncretism in *Beowulf*', *ELN* 32 (1995), 1–10; and E. Wilson, 'The Blood-Wrought Peace: a Girardian Reading of *Beowulf*', *ELN* 34 (1996), 7–30, at 20–1. Cf. *Beowulf*, ed. F. Klaeber, 3rd ed. (Lexington, MA, 1950), lines 572–3: 'Wyrd oft nereð / unfægne eorl þonne his ellen deah.'

[72] The Old English text reads 'Clitomus' and several Latin versions read 'Clitonas', which may be a way of rendering the Greek accusative Κλειτόν, from Κλειτός (Clitus). Boer, *Epistola Alexandri*, p. 47, reads 'Ditoricam', but the texts do not use capitals and it is possible that a scribe may have taken the initial 'cl' as a 'd' and mistaken the 'n' for an 'r'.

[73] *Letter*, p. 250 (§38): 'Then I thought in my mind and in my thoughts in which place I should die. When the moon first rose it brushed with its beam the uttermost top of the tree, and the tree answered my thoughts and thus said: "Alexander, the full end of your life you have lived, and this next year you will die in Babylon in the month of May by one from whom you least expect to be betrayed." Then was I very sorry of heart, and also my friends who were there with me, and they wept greatly because my safety was dearer to them than their own safety.'

father, was the greater conqueror of the two.[74] Clitus certainly does not expect to die at Alexander's hand, and the gods may be setting Alexander up for horrible retribution in the way that other mythological figures lose their lives in an attempt to flee their fates.

In fact, Alexander does think to escape his fate. He goes to the trees one more time in order to hear more about his death, but the trees spurn him:

þa ondswarode me þæt treow on grecisc 7 þus cwæð: 'Gif ic þe þone gesecge þines feores yþelice þu ða wyrde oncyrrest 7 his hond befehst. Ac soð ic þe secge þæt yb anes geares fyrst 7 eahta monað þu swyltst in Babilone, nalles mid iserne acweald swa ðu wenst ac mid atre. Ðin modor gewiteð of weorulde þurh scondlicne deað 7 unarlicne, 7 heo ligeð unbebyrged in wege fuglum to mete 7 wildeorum. þine sweostor beoð longe gesæliges lifes. Ðu þonne ðeah þu lytle hwile lifge hweþre ðu geweorðest an cyning 7 hlaford ealles middangeardes. Ac ne frign ðu unc nohtes ma ne axa, for þon wit habbað oferhleoðred þæt gemære uncres leohtes, ac to Fasiacen 7 Porre þæm cyninge eft gehworf þu.'[75]

The tree's use of the word *wyrd* in a way which implies its changeability suggests again the idea of a course of events instead of fixed fate. In the Latin text, the tree begins answering Alexander by saying 'Si matris tuae tibi insidiatorem prodidero, sublato eo facile instantia facta mutabis nam mihi tres irascentur sorores, quod ueridico oraculo earum pensa inpedierim, Clothos Lachesis Atropos.'[76] This implies that fate is changeable, despite the appearance of the classical Fates; however, it is only changeable if one knows what is going to happen. Since the tree withholds different information from Alexander, we may suppose that Alexander's *wyrd* is changeable, the result of his own actions, and that too much information will allow him to avoid his death. Seen in this light, Alexander's continued aggressive pursuit of knowledge has sealed his fate. With respect to his mother and sisters, he can know their fates since he can do nothing

---

[74] Orchard, *Pride and Prodigies*, pp. 123–4. The historical Alexander killed his general Clitus the Black before he attacked India; however, this may be a different general, Clitus the White. See also Gunderson, *Alexander's Letter*, pp. 66–71.

[75] *Letter*, p. 252 (§40): 'Then that tree answered me in Greek and said thus: "If I tell to you that about your life, then easily could you change your destiny and hold back its hand. But truly I tell you that in the time of about a year and eight months you will die in Babilon, killed not at all as you thought by the sword, but by poison. Your mother will depart the world by a shameful and honourless death, and she will lie unburied in the way, food for birds and wild beasts. To your sisters will be long and happy lives. You then, although you will only live for a little while, will still become the one king and lord of all the earth. But do not seek or ask any bit more of us two, for we have spoken more than the boundary of our light, but turn yourself again to Fasiacen and King Porus."' See Meaney, 'Ælfric's Use', pp. 492–5, for Ælfric's views of augury.

[76] Orchard, *Pride and Prodigies*, p. 221: 'If I come forth to you with what lies in wait for your mother, having done away with it you would change easily the impending deeds [*facta*], with the result that the three sisters Clothos, Lachesis and Atropos will grow angry with me, because by the truly-spoken oracle I would impede their plan.' Boer, *Epistola Alexandri*, p. 50, shows that only two manuscripts read 'facta'; the rest have 'fata'.

about them; his own fate, on the other hand, seems to be avoidable, but the gods are not allowing him to change it.

The final rebuff of the trees is the last episode in the *Letter*; Alexander's attempt to contain knowledge and the attempt to contain the world is again thwarted by uncertainty. At the end, Alexander accepts his fate, symbolized by his last act in the narrative; he withholds the information of his death,

þy læs þa elreordegan kyningas ðe ic ær mid nede to hyrsumnesse gedyde, þæt hie on þæt fægon þæt ic swa lytle hwile lifgean moste. Ne hit eac ænig mon þære ferde ðon ma ut mæran moste þy læs hie for ðon ormode wæron 7 þy sænran mines willan 7 weorð-myndo, ðæs hie mid mec to fromscipe geferan scoldon. Ond me næs se hrædlica ende mines lifes swa miclum weorce swa me wæs þæt ic læs mærðo gefremed hæfde þonne min willa wære. Ðas þing ic write to þon, min se leofa magister, þæt þu ærest gefeo in þæm fromscipe mines lifes 7 eac blissige in þæm weorðmyndum. Ond eac swelce ecelice min gemynd stonde 7 hleouige oðrum eorðcyningum to bysne, ðæt hie witen þy gearwor þæt min þrym 7 min weorðmynd maran wæron, þonne ealra oþra kyninga þe in middangearde æfre wæron.[77]

Alexander has been driven and thwarted by his lack of knowledge of the world; ironically, he now secures the drive of his army and the peace of his conquered territory by withholding the knowledge of his impending death. Alexander is most vexed by his inability to go farther; there will always be something that prevents the general and the narrator from completing the narrative and the conquest.[78] He sends the *Letter* back to Aristotle so that posterity may know what Alexander has done and seen; however, the example which Alexander sets for future kings cautions them about their inability to conquer the world completely. The implicit message to the audience is that human knowledge and narrative are also unable to withstand divine power and that divinity should not be provoked. Reason, like force, is ultimately inadequate to contain marvels and will be resisted by things yet unseen and unthought; only a being with which communication can be established can be contained.

Given the political and social milieu of the *Beowulf* manuscript, the compiler may have felt that English sins had reached the point where divine vengeance was provoked; as Wulfstan notes in the *Sermo Lupi ad Anglos*,

---

[77] *Letter*, p. 252 (§41): 'Lest any of the foreign kings whom I had forced into obedience should rejoice that I would only live so little a time. Nor was anyone permitted to make it known further to the army, lest they become sad, and the less eager for my will and honour, which they had to carry to success with me. And it was not the end of my life that was such a torment to me as it was that I had earned less honour than was my will. These things I write to you, my dear master, that you first may rejoice in the glory of my life, and also rejoice in the honour, and also that my memory will stand and loom eternally as an example to other earthly kings, that they should know the more clearly that my power and my honour were greater than that of all the other kings who ever were on the earth.'

[78] See F. Kermode, *The Genesis of Secrecy* (Cambridge, MA, 1979), p. 66.

The Letter of Alexander to Aristotle

[a]n þeodwita wæs on Brytta tidum Gildas hatte. Se awrat be heora misdædum hu hy mid heora synnum swa oferlice swyþe God gegræmedan þæt he let æt nyhstan Engla here heora eard gewinnan 7 Brytta duguþe fordon mid ealle. And þæt wæs geworden þæs þe he sæde, þurh ricra reaflac 7 þurh gitsunge wohgestreona, ðurh leode unlaga 7 þurh wohdomas, ðurh biscopa asolcennesse 7 þurh lyðre yrhðe Godes bydela þe soþes ges- wugedan ealles to gelome 7 clumedan mid ceaflum þær hy scoldan clypian . . . Ac utan don swa us þearf is, warnian us be swilcan; 7 soþ is þæt ic secge, wyrsan dæda we witan mid Englum þonne we mid Bryttan ahwar gehyrdan.[79]

Clerics such as Wulfstan might have seen the English failure to support the ecclesiastical reforms and to unify under Æthelred as having cut off discourse between God and England, and the irruption of the Vikings as the temporal manifestation of the English state of enmity with God. By citing Gildas on the Britons, Wulfstan would probably have recalled Bede's *Historia ecclesiastica* I.22 to learned Anglo-Saxon minds:

Qui inter alia inenarrabilium scelerum facta . . . et hoc addebant, ut numquam genti Saxonum siue Anglorum, secum Brittaniam incolenti, uerbum fidei praedicando com- mitterent. Sed non tamen diuina pietas plebem suam, quae praesciuit, deseruit; quin multo digniores genti memoratae praecones ueritatis, per quos crederet, destinauit.[80]

In this case, the physical event of conquest is interpreted as a manifestation of divine displeasure with human behaviour; the lack of British effort to convert the Angles and Saxons results in a lack of divine effort to protect the Britons. To Bede, anything which causes physical or social disruption suggests spiritual dis- order as well, and the move towards disorder becomes a sign of inward fault which ecclesiastical and social unity can cure, in this case by divinely sanctioned subjugation of the offending people. Bede interprets historical events in the context of salvation history; they are more believable as signs in a rhetorical and

[79] Bethurum, *Homilies of Wulfstan*, pp. 274–5: 'There was a learned man in the time of the Britons named Gildas. He wrote of their misdeeds, how they by their sins so very greatly angered God that he at last allowed the invading army of the Angles to conquer their land and to destroy the British host utterly. And what he said was brought about, through plunder of the nation and through greed for ill-gotten gains, through the people's lawlessness and through unjust judge- ments, by the sloth of bishops and by the corrupt dereliction of God's ministers who kept silent about the truth all too often and muttered with their jaws where they should have cried out . . . But let us do what is needful for us, to take heed of such things; and what I say is true, that we know of worse deeds among the English than we ever heard of among the Britons.'
[80] *Bede's Ecclesiastical History of the English People*, ed. B. Colgrave and R. A. B. Mynors (Oxford, 1969), p. 68: '[The Britons] added this too among other deeds of unspeakable crime, that they never began preaching the word of faith to the peoples of the Saxons or the Angles dwelling with them in Britain. But divine grace nevertheless did not desert his people whom he fore- knew; but he ordained a more worthy people as heralds of the remembered truth.' See A. Gransden, *Historical Writing in England c. 550 to c. 1307* (Ithaca, NY, 1974), pp. 2–4 and 93; J. M. Wallace-Hadrill, *Bede's Ecclesiastical History of the English People: a Historical Commentary* (Oxford, 1988), pp. 11–30; and N. Wright, 'Did Gildas Read Orosius?', *CMCS* 9 (1984), 31–42.

theological sense. Wulfstan attempts to bring the English back into line with their previous story of obedience to God; unfortunately, as history tells, they ended by playing the role of the defeated Britons. As with Alexander, the conquerors became the conquered.

The narratives of the *Beowulf* manuscript all deal with uncertain situations in which powerful figures may lose their struggles: St Christopher will not deconvert despite torture, the Danes and Geats in *Beowulf* face the loss of their political and military power in the face of assaults by others, the Assyrian army is defeated by a smaller group of Bethulians and a courageous woman in *Judith*, and neither Alexander nor the narrator of *The Wonders of the East* can create a coherent narrative or mount a successful campaign due to monstrous resistance. Again, I do not wish to suggest that the texts were consciously composed to set a specific mood; the texts reflect the doubtfulness of their time and are sites for playing out anxiety rather than allegories for the English situation. The *Letter*, in the context of the *Beowulf* manuscript, reveals an English fear about foreign persons and ideas, and it reminds the reader that success is never a permanent state.[81]

---

[81] I would like to acknowledge with thanks the assistance of Katherine O'Brien O'Keeffe and Michael Lapidge in the preparation of this essay.

Broken bodies and singing tongues: gender and voice in the Cambridge, Corpus Christi College 23 *Psychomachia*

CATHERINE E. KARKOV

The relationship between the book and the body in the Middle Ages is complex and has been the focus of much recent attention.[1] At a most basic level the dead, dismembered, yet living body of the book was united with the bodies of author, scribe, artist and reader in the act of reading. Medieval readers from the age of Augustine on left their marks in books in the form of glosses, personal comments, sketches, signatures, and the traces of kisses, caresses, or of simple repeated readings that have worn away parts of numerous illustrations. Michael Camille, in particular, has explored the sensual nature of the relationship between book and reader in the act of reading.[2] Perhaps nowhere is this union of bodies so vividly enacted as in the works of the fourth-century Spanish poet Prudentius, whose poems remained extremely popular for centuries. They were copied, translated, rearranged and illustrated to suit the needs of a variety of patrons and readers across medieval Europe.

The poems of Prudentius were particularly popular in Anglo-Saxon England, where thirty-nine copies of various poems survive in a total of twelve manuscripts produced between the late ninth and mid-eleventh century.[3] Three

---

[1] See, for example, the essays in *The Book and the Body*, ed. D. Frese and K. O'Brien O'Keeffe (Notre Dame, IN, 1997), and *Women, the Book and the Worldly*, ed. L. Smith and J. H. M. Taylor (Woodbridge, 1995).

[2] Following André Green, Camille suggests ways in which reading was closely related to sex and voyeurism, noting that 'the very act of reading was a libidinal experience, of penetrating the bound volume, that dangerously ductile opening and shutting thing': M. Camille, 'The Book as Flesh and Fetish in Richard de Bury's *Philobiblon*', *The Book and the Body*, ed. Frese and O'Brien O'Keeffe, pp. 34–77, at 41 and 47.

[3] See also G. R. Wieland, 'Prudentius', *Sources of Anglo-Saxon Literary Culture: a Trial Version*, ed. F. M. Biggs, T. D. Hill and P. E. Szarmach (Binghamton, NY, 1990), pp. 150–6; A. Orchard, *The Poetic Art of Aldhelm*, CSASE 7 (Cambridge, 1994), 171–8. The manuscripts in question are: Oxford, Bodleian Library, Rawlinson C. 697; Cambridge, Corpus Christi College 223; Cambridge, Trinity College O. 2. 51; Durham, Cathedral Library, B. IV. 9; Oxford, Oriel College 3; London, British Library, Add. 24199; London, British Library, Cotton Cleopatra C. viii; Cambridge, Corpus Christi College 23; Boulogne, Bibliothèque Municipale, 189; Munich, Staatsbibliothek, Clm. 29031/1; Oxford, Bodleian Library, Auct. F. 3. 6; Cambridge, University Library, Gg. 5. 35.

115

manuscripts contain the complete works,[4] while echoes of individual poems have been identified in the writings of Bede, Alcuin, Boniface and, most especially, Aldhelm.[5] Without doubt the most popular and influential of Prudentius's poems was the *Psychomachia*. It survives in nine of the twelve manuscripts (two of them imported from the Continent),[6] and is the sole work of Prudentius included in six of those nine.[7] It is followed in popularity by the *Peristephanon*, or 'Concerning the Crowns of the Martyrs', and *Contra Symmachum*, each included in six of the twelve manuscripts. The date and provenance of the surviving corpus suggest that they were first imported from the Continent either during or shortly after the reign of Alfred, or during the late-tenth-century Benedictine Reform.[8]

One of the most interesting features of the Anglo-Saxon Prudentius manuscripts is the relationship which they exhibit between the *Psychomachia* and bk X of the *Peristephanon* (the *Passio S. Romani*). In all extant copies of the *Peristephanon* bk X does not appear in tenth position, leading to speculation that it was never intended to be an integral part of that work. In continental manuscripts it can appear in first position or last, or just about anywhere other than tenth among the fourteen poems of the *Peristephanon*; or it could be separated from the other thirteen poems altogether, standing as a separate work in the Prudentius corpus.[9] It has no clearly established relationship to the text of the *Psychomachia*. Only in Anglo-Saxon England does it consistently appear either directly following the *Psychomachia* (as in Cambridge, Corpus Christi College 223; Durham, Cathedral Library, B. IV. 9; and Cambridge, Corpus Christi College 23) or directly preceding it (Oxford, Bodleian Library, Auct. F. 3. 6). Admittedly, this is a small group, but a suggestive one none the less. Since there is no earlier evidence for a tradition of ordering the texts in this manner, it is likely to be an Anglo-Saxon innovation, although the reasons for its development are unclear. In Prudentius's version of the story, Romanus was a deacon of the church in Caesarea and was martyred in Antioch in 303, along with the child Barulas. He

---

[4] CCCC 223; Durham, Cathedral Library, B. IV. 9; Oxford, Bodleian Library, Auct. F. 3. 6.

[5] Wieland, 'Prudentius'; Orchard, *Aldhelm*, pp. 171–8; G. H. Brown, *Bede the Venerable* (Boston, MA, 1987), p. 66. See also G. R. Wieland, 'Aldhelm's *De Octo Vitiis Principalibus* and Prudentius' *Psychomachia*', *MÆ* 55 (1986), 85–92.   [6] Rawlinson C. 697; CCCC 223.

[7] Rawlinson C. 697; Cambridge, Trinity College O. 2. 51; BL, Add. 24199; Cleopatra C. viii; Munich, Staatsbibliothek, CLM 29031/1 (a fragment consisting of only one folio); CUL, Gg. 5. 35.

[8] G. R. Wieland, 'The Anglo-Saxon *Psychomachia* Illustrations', *ASE* 26 (1997), 169–86, at 173–4. See also G. R. Wieland, 'The Anglo-Saxon Manuscripts of Prudentius's *Psychomachia*', *ASE* 16 (1987), 213–31.

[9] See *Aurelii Prudentii Clementis Carmina*, ed. M. P. Cunningham, CCSL 126 (Turnhout, 1966), x–xlvii; M. Manitius and K. Manitius, *Handschriften antiker Autoren in mittelalterlichen Bibliothekskatalogen*, Beiheft zum Zentralblatt für Bibliothekswesen 67 (Leipzig, 1935), 213–20. All citations in the text that follows are from Cunningham's edition of Prudentius.

does not appear to have been a particularly popular saint in Anglo-Saxon England. A Romanus is known to have been recorded in four litanies of the saints, but all have continental associations – three were imported from the Continent and the fourth is a 'scholarly compilation' produced at Leofric's Exeter in the third quarter of the eleventh century.[10] There is no guarantee that this Romanus is Romanus the martyred fourth-century deacon and not the third-century soldier Romanus who was martyred with St Laurence. Both are commemorated in Anglo-Saxon calendars, Romanus the deacon four times and Romanus the soldier three or four times (he is a later addition to one manuscript).[11] Romanus the soldier martyr is the only Romanus included in the Old English Martyrology,[12] while both Romani appear in continental martyrologies.[13] It is likely, then, that commemoration of St Romanus of Antioch came to England with the Benedictine Reform, at about the same time, it appears, as the illustrated *Psychomachia*.[14] His popularity after the mid-tenth century does seem to increase. Oxford, Bodleian Library, Auct. F. 3. 6, a Prudentius manuscript produced at Exeter in the mid-eleventh century, opens with fourteen elegiac lines from the *Passio S. Romani*, suggesting some sort of special appreciation for that work – at least at Exeter.[15]

Whatever the popularity of Romanus, there are formal and contextual reasons for juxtaposing the *Passio S. Romani* and the *Psychomachia*. Both deal with the battle between paganism and heresy – the theme is at the heart of the *passio*,

[10] London, British Library, Harley 863; Oxford, Bodleian Library, Bodley 579; a lost manuscript from Rheims; and Salisbury, Cathedral Library, 180. See *Anglo-Saxon Litanies of the Saints*, ed. M. Lapidge, HBS 106 (London, 1991), nos. XXIII.50, XXIX.ii.34, XXXVIII.55 and XLIV.75.

[11] Romanus of Antioch is listed on 18 November in: Bodley 579 (Glastonbury, c. 970); London, British Library, Add. 37517 (St Augustine's, Canterbury, s.x²); London, British Library, Cotton Nero A. ii (Winchester or Sherborne, s.xi¹); Cambridge, University Library, Kk. 5. 32 (Glastonbury, s.xi¹). Romanus the soldier martyr is listed on 9 August in: CUL, Kk. 5. 32 (Glastonbury, s.xi¹); Vatican City, Biblioteca Apostolica Vaticana, Reg. Lat. 12 (Bury St Edmunds or Christ Church, Canterbury, s.xi¹); Oxford, Bodleian Library, Douce 296 (Crowland, s.xi^med); London, British Library, Cotton Vitellius A. xviii (Wells, 1061 × 1088), according to Sarah Keefer (pers. comm.) the name in this last manuscript is added in a later hand. See F. Wormald, *English Kalendars Before AD 1100*, HBS 72 (London, 1934); H. Gneuss, 'A Preliminary List of Manuscripts Written or Owned in England', *ASE* 9 (1981), 1–60.

[12] G. Kotzor, *Das altenglische Martyrologium*, 2 vols. (Munich, 1981) I, 297; II, 175.

[13] Both appear in the Martyrology of Florus (c. 837) and the Martyrology of Ado (c. 855). See *Édition pratique des martyrologes de Bède, de l'anonyme lyonnais et de Florus*, ed. J. Dubois and G. Renaud (Paris, 1976). I would like to thank George Hardin Brown for drawing this edition to my attention.

[14] As evidenced by the two imported manuscripts, unillustrated copies of the *Psychomachia* were present in England during the reign of Alfred, or shortly thereafter. See further Wieland, '*Psychomachia* Illustrations', pp. 173–4.

[15] Salisbury, Cathedral Library, 180, which contains one of the litanies of the saints in which Romanus the deacon appears, is also an Exeter manuscript.

while the battle of the *Psychomachia* is framed by the defeat of *Veterum cultura deorum* and *Discordia/Heresis*. The *Psychomachia* closes with the poet's call for the rejection of the body for the sake of the spirit. In the illustrated manuscripts the poem is accompanied by a drawing of Prudentius kneeling before an altar and the enthroned Virtue *Sapientia* within her temple, the latter an image of the church. The *Peristephanon* opens with the poet's plea to St Romanus, also a symbol of the church, to bestow on him the power of song. If Prudentius casts Romanus as God's tool for speech,[16] he identifies himself as the vehicle through which Romanus speaks. Moreover, Romanus's tongue, now finally silent in the prologue to his passion, is given a new voice through the words of Prudentius:

> Romane, Christi fortis adsertor dei,
> elinguis oris organum fautor moue,
> largire comptum carmen infantissimo,
> fac ut tuarum mira laudum concinam,
> nam scis et ipse posse mutos eloqui.[17]

This is a standard humility topos, and somewhat ironic since it directly follows the lengthy song of the *Psychomachia*. One might also wonder if such an account of divinely inspired song from the lips of the speechless might not have reminded an Anglo-Saxon audience of the story of Caedmon, the birth of English poetry, and their own process of christianization. If it was indeed the motifs of words and speech that most interested Prudentius in the story of St Romanus,[18] it may have been the same motifs that captured the imagination of the Anglo-Saxons, especially if they enabled them to connect the birth of Anglo-Saxon poetry with the birth of Christian poetry.

One Prudentius manuscript in particular merits special attention, namely Cambridge, Corpus Christi College 23. Three aspects of the manuscript in particular will be examined: the way in which the *Psychomachia* and *Peristephanon* relate to each other; how their juxtaposition affects our reading of both texts; and the relationship of the reader to these texts. Gender will be a major concern in all three areas, since the gendered nature of the imagery constructs a gendered position for its audience. CCCC 23 is a luxury manuscript possibly produced at Christ Church Canterbury, possibly for a secular patron, and later

---

[16] C. Hahn, 'Speaking without Tongues: the Martyr Romanus and Augustine's Theory of Language in Illustrations of Bern, Burgerbibliothek Codex 264', *Images of Sainthood in Medieval Europe*, ed. R. Blumenfeld-Kosinski and T. Szell (Ithaca, NY, 1991), pp. 161–80, at 163–4.

[17] 'Romanus, stout defender of the divine Christ, grant thy favour and stir up the tongue within my speechless mouth, bountifully bestow grateful song on the mutest of men and enable me to sing the wonders of thy glory; for thou knowest, thyself too, that the dumb can speak.' Unless otherwise indicated, all translations are from H. J. Thomson, *Prudentius* (London, 1949).

[18] A.-M. Palmer, *Prudentius on the Martyrs* (Oxford, 1989), p. 264.

owned by Malmesbury Abbey.[19] Its donation to Malmesbury and its special status are commemorated in its grand, full-page dedicatory inscription written in verse and in display capitals at the opening of the manuscript.[20] The dedication begins with an anathema against anyone who might damage the book or attempt to remove it from the library or sell it, and requests prayers for Æthelweard the donor.[21] The bodies of donor, book, library and church are here inextricably linked in a chain that is not to be severed, while the body of the reader is placed under divine scrutiny and threatened with eternal damnation by the words of the curse. The voices of all give new life to the dead flesh. In addition to the prefatory material, the manuscript contains the *Psychomachia* (1v–40v), the *Passio S. Romani* (41r–60r), the remaining thirteen poems of the *Peristephanon* (60r–104r), and the first page of the *Contra Symmachum* (104v).[22] It is the work of three scribes and one artist. Only the text of the *Psychomachia* is illustrated, although sketches, some possibly by the original artist, have been added to various pages including two pages of the *Passio S. Romani* (44v and

---

[19] R. I. Page argues that the lavishness of CCCC 23 and the manner in which the vernacular glosses focus on the illustrations indicate that it was likely to have been produced for a wealthy secular patron ('On the Feasibility of a Corpus of Anglo-Saxon Glosses: the View from the Library', *Anglo-Saxon Glossography: Papers Read at the International Conference Held in the Koninklijke Academie voor Wetenschappen, Leteren en Schone Kunsten von België*, ed. R. Derolez (Brussels, 1992), pp. 77–95, at 91). Although he refrains from assigning it to a secular patron, R. Gameson does comment on the *de luxe* nature of the manuscript (*The Role of Art in the Late Anglo-Saxon Church* (Oxford, 1995), pp. 8 and 10), while M. Budny believes that the small number of additions and corrections indicate that it could not have been a classbook (*Insular, Anglo-Saxon, and Early Anglo-Norman Manuscript Art at Corpus Christi College, Cambridge: an Illustrated Catalogue* (Kalamazoo, MI, 1997), p. 279). Wieland, on the other hand, argues against lay ownership, pointing out that glossed Latin manuscripts are more at home in a monastic milieu than a private library ('*Psychomachia* Illustrations', p. 185). He does, however, admit that the earliest surviving imported manuscripts may be associated with the royal court at Winchester, and that the text may well have been popular among aristocratic laymen as well as within the monastery (*ibid.* pp. 173–4 and 184).

[20] Fol. iiv, with the *Psychomachia* starting on 1r. See Budny, *Illustrated Catalogue*, no. 24. Budny's observations on the gender of the Virtues and the Vices in her commentary on the manuscript are inaccurate.

[21] Æthelweard is often identified with one of the two Malmesbury abbots of that name, of which the first was abbot *c.* 977–85, and the second abbot *c.* 1043–4, but there is no guarantee that either was in fact the donor.

[22] The texts of the poems in CCCC 23 are distinguished from each other only by their titles and incipits; there are no spaces or blank pages separating one from the next. In Durham, Cathedral Library, B. IV. 9 and CCCC 223, the *Psychomachia* and *Passio S. Romani* are paired, but at least half a page is left between the end of the *Passio S. Romani* and bk I of the *Peristephanon*. CCCC 223 was written in the monastery of Saint-Bertin and is among the earliest of the Prudentius manuscripts surviving from Anglo-Saxon libraries. It is therefore possible that the practice of reading the *Psychomachia* and *Passio S. Romani* together was developed in northern France and imported into England through this or similar manuscripts. Surviving continental manuscripts, however, display no such links between the two texts.

45r).[23] It was later bound with a twelfth-century copy of Orosius's *Historiae adversum paganos*, an appropriate addition to the manuscript not only because of its theme of the fight against heresy, but also because of what it has to say about gender. The *Historiae* contain the story of Sardanapallus 'uir muliere corruptior'.[24] Orosius tells us that, 'qui inter scortorum greges feminae habitu purpuram colo tractans, a praefecto suo Arbato, qui tunc Medis praerat, uisus atque exsecrationi habitus, mox etiam excitis Medorum populis ad bellum prouocatus, et uictus, ardenti pyrae se iniecit'.[25] Allen Frantzen notes that Sardanapullus's effeminacy is a sign of his moral corruption and weakness rather than of sexual preference.[26] Like the feminine Vices defeated by the manly Virtues in the *Psychomachia*, Sardanapallus's Assyrians yield inevitably to the Medes.

Even without Orosius, the combination of texts in CCCC 23 is interesting. The *Peristephanon*, a collection of saints' martyrdoms, was perceived as a synactic text and rarely illustrated; while the *Psychomachia* was used primarily as a textbook, its copious illustrations functioning in part as visual mnemonics to the episodes of moral triumph. CCCC 23 does not seem to have been designed for use either within the synaxis of the Anglo-Saxon church, or as a textbook. It is a large manuscript (365 × 287 mm), of extremely high quality and certainly not intended for everyday use. If, as has been speculated, it was produced for a secular patron,[27] this manuscript indicates that the message of the *Psychomachia* and *Peristephanon* found (or continued to find) an audience outside the Anglo-Saxon church and classroom – or continued to do so if Alfred's court at Winchester was indeed responsible for the earliest imported manuscripts.

The *Psychomachia* records the eternal battle between the Virtues and the Vices enacted within the soul, hence within the body, of each man and woman. Anglo-Saxon authors differed on the details of the relationship of the soul to the body,

---

[23] The sketches throughout the manuscript consist of drapery folds, body parts, foliate and interlace motifs. See Budny, *Catalogue*, p. 280.
[24] 'A man more corrupt than any woman.' *Pauli Orosii Historiarum Aduersum Paganos Libri VII*, ed. C. Zangemeister, CSEL 5 (1882), 70 (I.19).
[25] *Ibid.* 'While he was wearing purple cloth in the garb of a female in the midst of a flock of harlots, he was seen by his prefect, Arbatus, who was then in command of the Medes and he was cursed by him. Soon also, when the people of the Medes rose in revolt, he was called forth to war and when conquered cast himself upon the burning pyre.' Translation from *Orosius: Seven Books of History against the Pagans*, trans. R. J. Defarrari (Washington, DC, 1964), p. 38.
[26] A. J. Frantzen, *Before the Closet: Same-Sex Love from 'Beowulf' to 'Angels in America'* (Chicago, IL, 1998), pp. 89–90. The king's effeminacy is even more pronounced in the Old English translation of the passage which says that he was very indulgent, wanton (or effeminate) and lustful, and that he preferred the conduct of women to that of men: 'He wæs swiþe furþumlice mon, and hnesclic and swiþe wræne, swa þæt he swiðor lufade wifa gebæro þonne wæpnedmonna.' See *The Old English Orosius*, ed. J. Bately, EETS ss 6 (London, 1980), 32, lines 16–17.
[27] See above, n. 19.

what exactly constituted the soul, when it entered the body and where within the body it was located; however, all agreed that it was housed somewhere within the body and that it left the body at death.[28] Alcuin, Alfred and Ælfric all portray the soul as permeating the body,[29] and terms such as *sawulhus* extended the notion of the body as a container for the soul across the literate Anglo-Saxon world. The Anglo-Saxon poetic tradition, however, was more specific, locating the soul within the heart or chest of the body.[30] The poems *Soul and Body I* and *II* reveal that the soul and body were thought of as separating at death, the soul remaining a living speaking entity, the body a voiceless shell, but that the two would be physically reunited at the time of final judgement.[31] They also reveal the power of the body to affect the fate of the soul and, while largely ambiguous as to the gender of either soul or body, do contain hints that the damned body was sometimes read as female.[32]

For the reader of the *Psychomachia*, the body whose soul was opened up for view within the pages of the book was, in theory, his or her body, and the violence depicted on the pages of dead flesh was something experienced daily in his or her own living soul. I emphasize the *his or her* of the reader because gender is crucial to any reading of the *Psychomachia*. The problem of gender in CCCC 23 is introduced in the preface to the poem, which focuses on stories of male conflict and triumph. It narrates in summary fashion Abraham's rescue of Lot and the birth and sacrifice of Isaac. Abraham's battle is presented as an Old Testament type of the battle of the Virtues against the Vices and, by extension, the battles of St Romanus in the *Peristephanon* and of each virtuous Christian in the manuscript's audience.[33] More specifically, Abraham's battle is against barbarian kings, but Prudentius also carefully notes that Lot was taken captive while 'dwelling in the wicked cities of Sodom and Gomorrah' ('inmorantem criminosis urbibus Sodomae et Gomorrae'). The naming of the cities is no doubt significant as *Libido* is later identified as the 'Sodomite' Vice (*Sodomita Libido*) at the

---

[28] On the relationship between the soul and body in Anglo-Saxon England, see *Soul and Body I* and *Soul and Body II*, both edited in *The Old English Soul and Body*, ed. D. Moffatt (Wolfeboro, NH, 1990); see also M. Godden, 'Anglo-Saxons on the Mind', *Learning and Literature in Anglo-Saxon England: Studies presented to Peter Clemoes on the Occasion of his Sixty-Fifth Birthday*, ed. M. Lapidge and H. Gneuss (Cambridge, 1985), pp. 271–98; *The Vercelli Homilies and Related Texts*, ed. D. Scragg, EETS os 300 (Oxford, 1992), Homilies IV and XXII; A. J. Frantzen, 'The Body in *Soul and Body I*', *Chaucer Rev.* 17 (1982), 76–88; R. Willard, 'The Address of the Soul to the Body', *PMLA* 50 (1935), 957–83.   [29] Godden, 'Anglo-Saxons on the Mind', p. 290.
[30] *Ibid.*   [31] The poems are most recently edited by Moffat, *Soul and Body*.
[32] See below, p. 135.
[33] See A. Orchard, 'Conspicuous Heroism: Abraham, Prudentius, and the Old English Verse *Genesis*', *Heroes and Heroines in Medieval English Literature: a Festschrift presented to André Crépin on the Occasion of his Sixty-Fifth Birthday*, ed. L. Carruthers (Cambridge, 1994), pp. 45–58, at 54–7.

opening of her battle against *Pudicitia*.[34] It seems likely that Prudentius wished to establish a contrast between the manly and impenetrable bodies of Abraham and the Virtues, and the penetrable, doomed, and feminized bodies of *Libido* and the Sodomites, with Lot, the body trapped by desires,[35] caught between them. The introduction of the Sodomites does offer the possibility of complicating the issue of gender in the poem by introducing what might be read as a warning against male homosexuality, perhaps aimed at a male monastic audience, but that possibility is denied by the way in which the illustrations interpret the text and position the reader. The masculine body is never destroyed, only its feminine, or feminized, counterpart.

The preface both opens and closes with references to patriarchy and fatherhood as the reward for Abraham's faith. Sarah is mentioned only in her capacity to 'give the Father's household a worthy heir'.[36] On a purely structural level, in CCCC 23 the offering but ultimately non-sacrifice of Isaac, the patriarch's son, both looks forward to and forms an interesting contrast with the prolonged and bloody sacrifice of the infant Barulas plucked from his mother's arms at the wish of Romanus in the *Passio S. Romani*.[37] Like Sarah, the infant's mother is a type of Ecclesia, allowing her son to be offered to God and even catching his blood in her cloak.[38] Unlike Sarah, she plays an active role in the poem, voicing her support of her son's sacrifice, chastising him when he asks for a drink to

---

[34] The Vice's doomed attack on the Virtue is reminiscent of the punishment of the Sodomites:
   quam patrias succincta faces Sodomita Libido
   adgreditur piceamque ardenti sulpere pinum
   ingerit in faciem pudibundaque lumina flammis
   adpetit et taetro temptat suffundere fumo (lines 42–5).
   ('On her falls Lust the Sodomite, girt with the fire-brands of her country, and thrusts into her face a torch of pinewood blazing murkily with pitch and burning sulphur, attacking her modest eyes with flames and seeking to cover them with the foul smoke.'
[35] See M. Smith, *Prudentius's Psychomachia: a Reexamination* (Princeton, NJ, 1976), p. 145.
[36] Lines 67–8. 'Tunc sera dotem possidens puerpera herede digno Patris inplebit domum.'
[37] Lines 656–86.
[38] Talia retexens explicabat pallium
   manusque tendebat sub ictu et sanguine,
   uenarum ut undam profluam manantium
   et palpitantis oris exciperet globum (lines 841–4).
   'While repeating the words, she spread out her robe and stretched forth her hands beneath the stroke and the blood to catch the stream that ran from the flowing veins, and the round head as the mouth breathed its last; and catching it she pressed it to her breast.' In Bern, Burgerbibliothek, 264, written and illustrated at Reichenau or St Gallen in the second half of the ninth century, the infant's mother's identification with Ecclesia is heightened by her blue cloak and her position within the doorway of the church (fol. 131): see Hahn, 'Speaking without Tongues', pp. 166–8. The Bern manuscript is the only illustrated text of the *Passio S. Romani* to survive from the early medieval period. There are two later illustrated manuscripts, one from thirteenth-century France and the other from Byzantium (*ibid.* p. 163, n. 5). See also O. Homburger, *Die illustrierten Handschriften der Burgerbibliothek Bern* (Bern, 1962), pp. 136–58.

relieve his thirst, and reminding him of the model set by Abraham and Isaac, about whom she had told him often.[39] Like Sarah, she overcomes her female nature, here defined as maternal feelings, obediently turning her son over to the will of his father. But Barulus's mortal father is not named, and his mother's words instruct us to think only of God as his Father.[40] Moreover, her active participation in the sacrifice establishes a parallel between her and Abraham above and beyond her typological relationship with Sarah, and indirectly between her and the Virtues (for whom Abraham is a type), all emerge triumphant in their battle against sin and heresy.

The battle between the Virtues and the Vices that follows the story of Abraham is above all an engendered battle – both within the poem and across the history of its illustration. Even though Latin grammatical gender dictated that both Vices and Virtues be feminine, that was not the way their bodies were always represented. In most early medieval *Psychomachia* manuscripts the Vices are both described and depicted as monsters, and the Virtues as heavily armoured warriors – the one clearly not human, the other clearly male (see, for example, pl. I).[41] The Anglo-Saxon manuscripts are the first group to depict both

---

[39] Scis, saepe dixi, cum docenti adluderes
et garrulorum signa uerborum dares,
Isac fuisse paruulum patri unicum,
qui, cum inmolandus aram et ensem cerneret,
ultro sacranti colla praebuerit seni (lines 746–50).
'You know I have often told you, when you used to turn my lessons into play and prattle sounds that stood for words, that Isaac was a little boy, his father's only child, and how, when he was to be sacrificed and saw the altar and the sword, of his own will he stretched out his neck to the old man who was making the offering.'

[40] 'Quanam arte nobis uiuere intus coeperis
nihilumque et illud unde corpus nescio,
nouit animator solus et factor tui.
Inpendere ipsi cuius ortus munere es,
Bene in datorem quod dedit refuderis' (lines 786–90).
'"How your life began within me, that nothingness from which your body grew, I know not; only he who quickened you, he who is your creator knows. Devote yourself to him by whose gift you were born. You will do well if you restore to the giver that which he gave."'

[41] R. Stettiner, *Die illustrierten Prudentiushandschriften*, 2 vols. (Berlin, 1895–1905), divided the *Psychomachia* illustrations into two groups. Group II manuscripts contain representations of the Virtues as mail-clad and helmeted warriors, while the Vices wear flame-skirts. Group I manuscripts have Virtues dressed in long robes, their heads often covered by a mantle, and the Vices are in long or short tunics. Group I contains only the four Anglo-Saxon manuscripts, Paris, Bibliothèque Nationale de France lat. 8318 (from tenth-century Tours), and Leiden, Bibliotheek der Rijksuniversiteit, Voss lat. O. 15 (produced in the ninth century at Limoges or Angoulême). Group II consists of: Leiden, Bibliotheek der Rijksuniversiteit, Codex Burmannorum Q. 3; Paris, Bibliothèque Nationale de France, lat. 8085; Brussels, Bibliothèque Royale, 9987–91; Valenciennes, Bibliothèque publique, 563; Lyons, Bibliothèque du Palais des Arts, 22; Paris, Bibliothèque Nationale de France, lat. 18554; Brussels, Bibliotheque Royale, 10066–77; Brussels, Bibliothèque Royale, 9968–72; Bern, Burgerbibliothek, 264; Cologne, Dombibliothek,

as primarily, if not entirely, female. Paris, Bibliothèque Nationale de France, lat.
8318, a tenth-century illustrated Prudentius from Tours, preserves a similar iconography, although its drawings are sufficiently different in detail to indicate that
it was not a model for the Anglo-Saxon manuscripts.[42] However, even if the
Anglo-Saxons did not invent the tradition they certainly developed it, and we can
see both Virtues and Vices appearing more and more feminine in these manuscripts. Only occasionally will a Virtue *look* male, or a Vice monstrous, suggesting
a model in the process of transformation, or modernization. CCCC 23 is the
least consistent of the three complete Anglo-Saxon illustrated *Psychomachiae*, the
other two being London, British Library, Cotton Cleopatra C. viii (pl. II) and
London, British Library, Add. 24199.[43] In the one surviving English
Romanesque *Psychomachia* manuscript (London, British Library, Cotton Titus D.
xvi, made at St Albans *c*. 1120) the Virtues and Vices all wear female dress, while
Ottonian depictions of Virtues and Vices are distinctly and consistently feminine.[44] By the late thirteenth century the Virtues had come to be depicted as nuns
and the Vices as contemporary townswomen.[45] In other words, it is in the Anglo-
Saxon manuscripts that the monstrous Vices become women while the warrior

81; Hamburg, Museum für Kunst and Gewerbe, 542. Three manuscripts are considered to fall
  somewhere between the two groups: St Gallen, Stiftsbibliothek, 135; London, British Library,
  Cotton Titus D. xvi; Paris, Bibliothèque Nationale de France, lat. 15158. See also H. Woodruff,
  'The Illustrated Manuscripts of Prudentius', *Art Studies, Medieval Renaissance and Modern*
  (Cambridge, MA, 1929), pp. 33–79. Woodruff refines Stettiner's criteria for classification, but
  does not change the two major groupings.
[42] Stettiner and Woodruff also place Leiden, Bibliotheek der Rijksuniversiteit, Voss. lat. O. 15 in
  this group, but its illustrations are grouped together at the beginning of the text and the drawings of individual scenes crowded together on the page. More importantly, the gender of both
  Virtues and Vices is often ambiguous. As Wieland notes, the manuscript is also likely to have
  been produced too late to have had much of an influence on the Anglo-Saxon manuscripts:
  'Illustrated Manuscripts', p. 172.
[43] Munich Clm. 29336/1 is just a fragment preserving only three illustrations. Budny, *Catalogue*,
  reproduces all of the illustrated pages from CCCC 23 (her manuscript no. 24). For Cleopatra C.
  viii, see *Anglo-Saxon Textual Illustration*, ed. T. Ohlgren (Kalamazoo, MI, 1992), no. 15.
[44] For Titus D. xvi, see *Romanesque Manuscripts 1066–1190*, ed. C. M. Kauffmann (London, 1975),
  no. 39 (ills. 69–71). For Ottonian manuscripts, see the illustration of the four kingly Virtues and
  their representatives in the Bamberg Apocalypse (Bamberg, Staatsbibliothek, Bibl. 140, fol. 60,
  illustrated in H. Mayr-Harting, *Ottonian Book Illumination: an Historical Study*, 2 vols. (London,
  1991), II, ill. 3. The Bamberg Apocalypse was produced at Reichenau *c*. 1001. Fol. 4 shows the
  four kingly Virtues and their Old Testament representatives. The Virtues are dressed in long
  gowns and veils and stand on top of the naked Vices, their spears aimed directly at the Vices'
  mouths. Gameson, *Role of Art*, p. 13, credits Anglo-Saxon and Ottonian artists with 'moderniz-
  ing' classical and late antique modes of representation.
[45] E.g. BNF, lat. 15158, produced in 1298. See Stettiner, *Prudentiushandschriften*, pp. 144–8 and pls.
  197–200; Woodruff, 'Prudentius', p. 47, figs. 123 and 126; A. Katzenellenbogen, *Allegories of the
  Virtues and the Vices in Medieval Art from Early Christian Times to the Thirteenth Century* (Toronto,
  1989), p. 7.

soldiers become the traditional saintly women who overcome their gender to become spiritually male, like Sarah in the Preface or the mother of Barulas in the *Passio S. Romani*.[46] This is a model of spirituality that Jerome perhaps more than any other patristic author helped to popularize. In his *Commentaria in epistolam ad Ephesios*, for example, he writes 'Quamdiu mulier partui servit et liberis, hanc habet ad virum differentiam, quam corpus ad animam. Sin autem Christo magis voluerit servire quam saeculo mulier esse cessabit et dicetur vir.'[47]

The inconsistency of the CCCC 23 drawings very effectively captures the dual nature of both the Virtues and Vices. In the text of the *Psychomachia* the attitudes expressed verbally and visually pertaining to the body, desire, the physical world and to proper Christian conduct gender the Vices as 'feminine' and the Virtues as 'masculine'. The fact that most of the Virtues and Vices wear the dress of contemporary Anglo-Saxon women may have been a part of the modernization of the classical model, an attempt to make the battle more accessible to the manuscript's tenth- or eleventh-century audience. The text, however, makes it clear that beneath the feminine exteriors of the Vices lurk monsters, while the Virtues have the faith and power of men. Indeed, when the Virtues are temporarily weakened by the temptations of *Luxuria*, *Sobrietas* upbraids them for adorning their 'manly hair' with gilded and yellow headdresses.[48] In CCCC 23, these manly Virtues are echoed by the figure of Barulas's mother in the *Passio S. Romani*, and also in the figures of SS. Eulalia and Agnes, whose martyrdoms are recorded in poems III and XIV of the *Peristephanon*, and who overcame their female bodies to become soldiers for Christ.[49] In the text of the *Psychomachia* Prudentius draws the appearance of the warriors to our attention by prefacing the first battle with the words,

---

[46] On the theme of the saintly woman become male, see M. Miles, *Carnal Knowing: Female Nakedness and Religious Meaning in the Christian West* (New York, 1989), pp. 53–77; P. E. Szarmach, 'Ælfric's Women Saints', *New Readings on Women in Old English Literature*, ed. H. Damico and A. H. Olsen (Bloomington, IN, 1990), pp. 146–57; G. Roy, 'A Virgin Acts Manfully: Ælfric's *Life of St Eugenia* and the Latin Versions', *Leeds Stud. in Eng.* 23 (1992), 1–27; P. E. Szarmach, 'St Euphrosyne: Holy Transvestite', *Holy Men and Holy Women: Old English Prose Saints' Lives and Their Contexts*, ed. P. E. Szarmach (Albany, NY, 1996), pp. 353–65; C. Lees, 'Engendering Religious Desire: Sex, Knowledge, and Christian Identity in Anglo-Saxon England', *Jnl. of Med. and Early Mod. Stud.* 27 (1997), 17–45; and Frantzen, *Before the Closet*, pp. 72–89.

[47] PL 26, 533C: 'As long as woman is in the service of childbirth and children, she remains as different to man as body is to soul. But if she desires to serve Christ more than the world, she ceases to be a woman and will be judged a man.'

[48] Lines 358–9: 'Ut mitra caesariem cohibens aurata uirilem / conbibat infusum croceo religamine nardum.'

[49] Poems III and XIV of the *Peristephanon*. See also M. A. Malamud, *A Poetics of Transformation: Prudentius and Classical Mythology* (Ithaca, NY, 1989), pp. 149–80; *idem*, 'Making a Virtue of Perversity: the Poetry of Prudentius', *Imperial Roman Lit. II* 19.1 (1990), 64–88.

Vincendi praesens ratio est, si comminus ipsas
uirtutum facies et conluctantia contra
uiribus infestis liceat portenta notare.[50]

This statement focuses our attention on the pictures, on what we see,[51] and what
we see at this point is the first drawing of the battle sequence, the fight between
Fides and *Veterum cultura deorum* (pl. III). The drawing depicts a sequence of
events that will be repeated throughout the poem. *Fides* stands firm while
Veterum cultura deorum, dressed as an Amazon in this case, lunges at her with a
spear. Lethal men become women, and since Amazons were women who
behaved as men the transformation is particularly appropriate. The Amazon
who behaves like a man is the opposite of the female saint who overcomes her
nature to become male; the female saint fights *with* good Christian men, the
Amazon fights against them – at least in the *Psychomachia* tradition. (There is also
a tradition of understanding the Amazons as noble and honourable monsters,
but the illustrated *Psychomachia* manuscripts invariably equate them with the
Vices.)[52]

Fides lacks a veil, a detail which has led to her being interpreted as literally
male.[53] This is understandable in the light of the Virtues' position as warriors
for Christ. However, the lack of a veil alone is not sufficient grounds for considering her a male figure particularly, since the poet mentions her untrimmed hair
and lack of armour.[54] Moreover, men in CCCC 23 are all depicted with short
hair and, with the exception of Prudentius himself, short tunics. The artist
shows the Vice's spear touching the breast of *Fides*, but Prudentius assures us

---

[50] Lines 18–20: 'The way of victory is before our eyes if we may mark at close quarters the very
features of the Virtues, and the monsters [here literally unstable or lethal men] that close with
them in deadly struggle.'

[51] A point made by M. Carruthers, *The Craft of Thought: Meditation, Rhetoric, and the Making of Images
400–1200* (Cambridge, 1998), p. 145.

[52] J. B. Friedman, *The Monstrous Races in Medieval Art and Thought* (Cambridge, MA, 1981), pp.
129–30 and 170–1.

[53] Budny, *Catalogue*, pp. 278 and 312.

[54]   'Prima petit campum dubia sub sorte duelli
pugnatura Fides agresti turbida cultu
nuda *umeeros* intonsa comas exerta lacertos.
Namque repentinus laudis calor ad noua feruens
proelia nec telis meminit nec tegmine cingi;
pectore sed fidens ualido membrisque retectis
prouocat insani frangenda pericula belli' (lines 21–7).
'Faith first takes the field to face the doubtful chances of battle, her rough dress disordered, her
shoulders bare, her hair untrimmed, her arms exposed; for the sudden glow of ambition,
burning to enter fresh contests, takes no thought to gird on arms or armour, but trusting in a
stout heart and unprotected limbs challenges the hazards of furious warfare, meaning to break
them down.'

that despite her unprotected limbs the Virtue remains unharmed. Similarly, *Patientia* withstands the attack of *Ira* because she had prudently donned a corselet of mail and a bronze helmet (pl. IV). In this case the artist has depicted the helmet, but otherwise the Virtue is protected only by her pious stance of prayer. The poet tells us that

> Inde quieta manet Patientia, fortis ad omnes
> telorum nimbos et non penetrabile durans.[55]

In this drawing it is *Ira* who does not look particularly feminine, although she is clearly female in the drawing of her suicide that follows (pl. V). Unlike *Patientia*, *Ira* has a feminine body which is easily penetrated by the point of her sword, and blood flows dramatically from her death wound. Her changing appearance is echoed by that of a number of the other Vices and may be the artist's way of suggesting the ever-shifting and monstrous nature of the Vices, all of whom are shown as female in death. A monster is by its very nature uncontrollable and indefinable, something that is neither one thing nor another. The author of the seventh- or eighth-century *Liber monstrorum* draws attention to this at the very opening of bk I:

Me enim quendam hominem in primordio operis utriusque sexus cognouisse testor, qui tamen ipsa facie plus et pectore uirilis quam muliebris apparuit; et uir a nescentibus [*sic*] putabatur, sed muliebria opera dilexit, et ignaros uirorum more meretricis, decipiebat; sed hoc frequenter apud humanum genus contigisse fertur.[56]

Ira, more than any other of the Vices, is uncontrolled and uncontainable. She foams at the mouth and shows her teeth, her eyes are shot with blood and gall, and Prudentius labels her a 'monster' who 'rages in ungoverned frenzy'.[57] In the illustrations she shifts from a helmeted figure in a long cloak (9r, top) to a short-haired figure in a long cloak (9r, bottom), to a figure with hair of flames (9v, top), back to a short-haired figure with a long cloak (9v, bottom), then to a short-haired amazon (10r), and finally to a long-haired feminine body in death (11r). Details of the Virtues' attire, helmets for example, may change, but otherwise

---

[55] Lines 128–9: '[She] abides undisturbed, bravely facing all the hail of weapons and keeping a front that none can pierce.'

[56] 'Indeed I bear witness at the beginning of the work that I have known a person of both sexes, who although they appeared more masculine than feminine from their face and chest, and were thought male by those who did not know, yet loved feminine occupations and deceived the ignorant amongst men in the manner of a whore; but this is said to have happened often amongst the human race.' A. Orchard, *Pride and Prodigies: Studies in the Monsters of the Beowulf-Manuscript* (Cambridge, 1995), pp. 258–9. I quote Orchard's translation. See also Friedman, *Monstrous Races*, pp. 149–53.

[57] 'Nec mota est iaculo monstri sine more furentis,
opperiens propriis perituram uiribus Iram' (lines130–1).

they remain consistent in appearance from one drawing to the next. It might be argued that the change in the appearance of the Vices is due simply to the artist's model, or models, but CCCC 23 contains blank spaces where drawings were never completed, and for which there are no parallels in the other surviving manuscripts. This suggests that this manuscript was meant to diverge from the traditional pictorial narrative in a unique and now irretrievable way, and that the artist was not simply blindly copying his exemplar.[58]

The pictorial narrative in CCCC 23, as in most, but not all, of the illustrated *Psychomachia* manuscripts, is particularly important because the drawings directly precede the textual accounts of the individual battles. They are dramatic, frequently gruesome, and always memorable.[59] For an Anglo-Saxon reader, as for a modern one, the image would have had an influence over the way in which the following text was understood. Prudentius might tell us in his account of *Avaritia* that

> Cura Famis Metus Anxietas Periuria Pallor
> Corruptela Dolus Commenta Insomnia Sordes,
> Eumenides uariae, monstri comitatus aguntur.
> Nec minus interea rabidorum more luporum
> crimina persultant toto grassantia campo
> matris Auaritiae nigro de lacte creata.[60]

However, we read these lines with the image of a placid (though half-naked) mother with a lap full of children before us.

The violence of the *Psychomachia* is disturbing, particularly so when read in conjunction with the text of the *Peristephanon*. The bodies of the Vices are not just feminine in appearance but also in their permeability. Their bodies are repeatedly penetrated, and repeatedly overflow their boundaries. The Vices eat, drink, give birth and disgorge themselves when penetrated by the weapons or hands of the Virtues, but they are powerless and unable to penetrate the bodies of the Virtues. The action within the text is paralleled by the act of reading in which the gaze of the reader penetrates the book, as well as the bodies depicted within it, making the reader a participant in the action described and depicted on the page. Moreover, the battles in the *Psychomachia* are not just gendered but sexualized battles in which the impenetrable Virtues quite clearly become male in order to triumph, piercing the bodies of the Vices with their enormous phallic

[58] *Pace* Wieland, 'Illustrated Manuscripts', pp. 181–2. See Gameson, *Role of Art*, p. 10; Budny, *Catalogue*, p. 276. On the transformation of pictorial exemplars in Anglo-Saxon England, see also W. Noel, *The Harley Psalter* (Cambridge, 1995).
[59] On Prudentius and memory, see Carruthers, *Craft of Thought*, pp. 143–50.
[60] 'Crime, Hunger, Fear, Anguish, Perjuries, Pallor, Corruption, Treachery, Falsehood, Sleeplessness, Meanness, diverse fiends, go in attendance on the monster; and all the while Crimes, the brood of their mother Greed's black milk, like ravening wolves go prowling and leaping over the field' (lines 464–9).

N uda humeros intonsa comas exerta lacertas
N unq; repentinus laudis calor, adnoua feruens
[roelia netrolis meminit nec tegmine cingi
[ectore sed fidens ualido membrisq; retectis
[rouocat insani frangenda pericula belli
E cce lacessentem conlatis uiribus audet
[rima ferire fidem ueterem cultura deorum

FIDES IDOLATRIAM COHCULCAT.

[xultat uictrix legio quam mille coactam
Mastyrib; regina fides animarat inhostem
N unc fostes socios pasta prolaude coronat
[lorib; ardentiq; iubet uestirier ostro

PUDICITIA CONTRA LIBIDINE
ARMIS PUG NAT.

[Uahostile caput faleratraq; reporauit us
N laor insurgens labefactat et oraciruore
D epecudum satiatalo adplicat et pede calcat
L isos immosto oculos animaq; malignam
[raeant tortæ pti conmerta guttutis astant
D ifficilem q; obitem suspitalonga fatigat

FIDES POST UICTORIAM UIRTUTIS
COROLLAT.

Pudicitia contra Libidine

[xim grammineo incampo concurrere promptae
U irgo pudicitia speciosis fulget inarmis
Q uam patrias succincta faces sodomitalibido
A dgreditur piceamq; ardens sulphurepinu
I ngerit infaciem pudibundaq; lumina flammis
A dpetit et retro temptat subfundere sumo

PUDICITIA LIBIDINE CU SAXO PCUTIT.

II London, British Library, Cotton Cleopatra C. viii, 7v. *Fides* crowns the Virtues; *Pudicita* and *Libido*

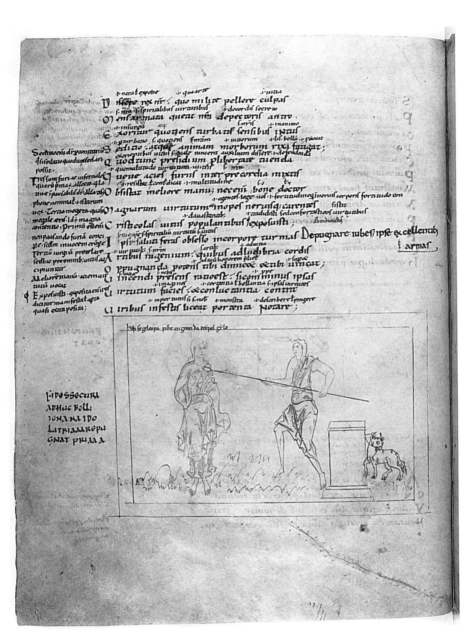

III Cambridge, Corpus Christi College 23, 4v. *Fides* and *Veterum cultura deorum*

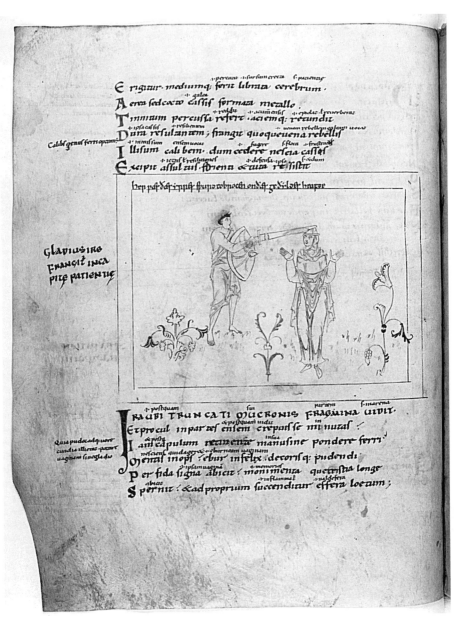

IV Cambridge, Corpus Christi College 23, 10v. *Ira attacks Patientia*

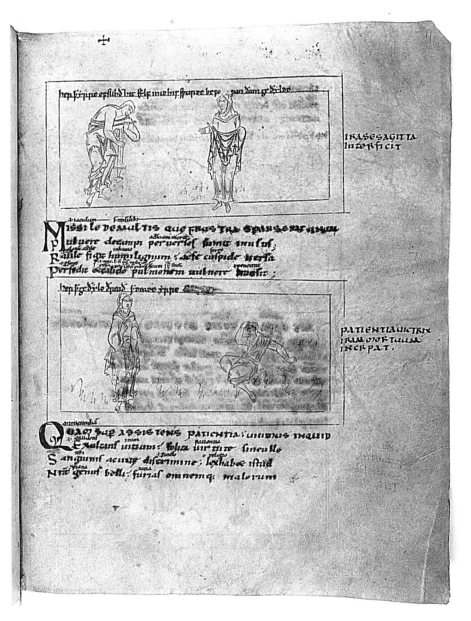

hep firæpe epfilıdlıc fele mıelıtſ ſtupτe bep̄o   panðam gſtılꝰ

IRASESAGITTA
INTERFICIT

Miſsıle ꝺemultıs que fruſtra ſpınſeraꝫum
Puluere ꝺecampı peruerſoſ ſumıt ınuſuſ;
Riſıle ſıgnır humıl lıgnum; acte culpıꝺe uerſa
Perfoꝺır oculıde pulmonem uulnore noxıt;

hep fıgeꝺ̃ile ẍpꝰ fraıuoppe

PATIENTIA UICTRIX
IRAM ORTUUM
INCREPAT.

Quoꝺ ſuꝑ aꝺgıſ tens patıentıa; uıuıꝰus ınquıt
Exultaſ uıtıum; foıa uıꝛ tuꝛe ſıneullo
Sanguını ſ acuıꝰ ꝺıſcꝛımıne; lexhabet ıſtuꝺ
Nꝛe genuſ bellı; furıaſ omnemꝗ malorum

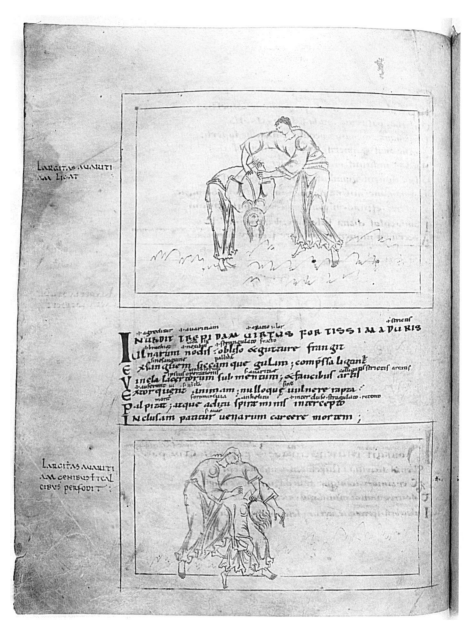

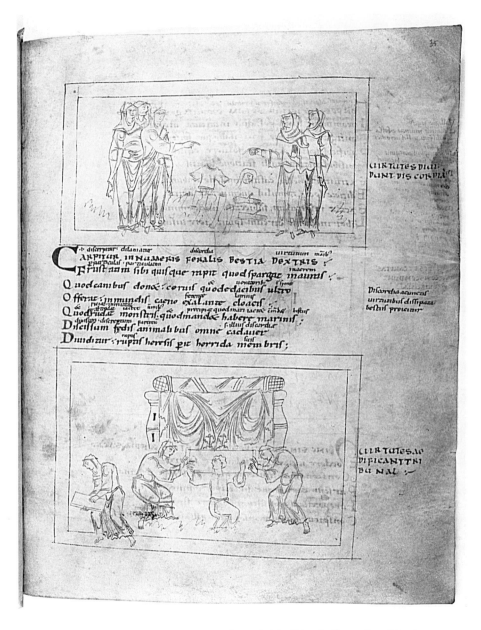

CIRTUTES DII
UANT UIS CORPLT

C·s discerpitur dilaniana·   discordia   uirtutum masc̅

CARPITUR INNUMERIS FERALIS BESTIA DEXTRIS ;
Frustatim sibi quisque rapit quod spargit inanis ;
Quodcumbus donec cotui quodecdacibus ultro
Offerut inmunehis caeno exalante cloacis ;
Quodrudat monstris quodmandet habere marinis ;
Decissum fedis animalibus omne cadauer
Dimiditur rupus heresis pie horrida membris ;

Discordia acuncas
uirtutibus dissipata
bestus proiciatur

CIRTUTESAC
DIFICANITRI
BUNAL :

VII Cambridge, Corpus Christi College 23, 35r. *Discordia* dismembered (top)

TUNC EX AR MA TE IUGULUM MERETRICIS ADACTO
Transfigit gladio; calidos uomit illa uapores
Sanguine con cretos eo e noso ipsi inde
Sordidus exhalans uicinas polluit auras;

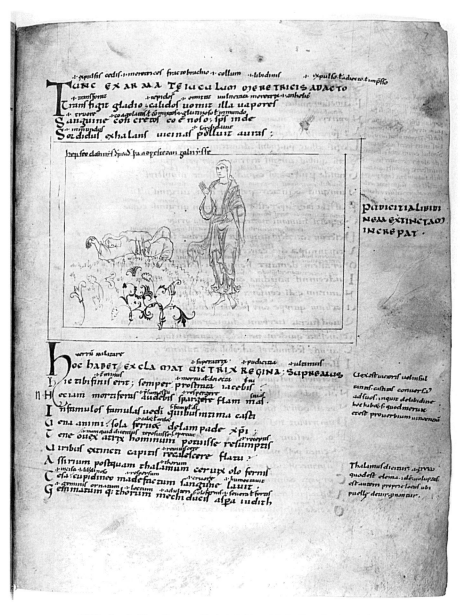

PUDICITIA LIBIDI
NEM EXTINCTAM
INCREPAT·

Hoc HABET EXCLA MAT UICTRIX REGINA; SUPREMUS
Die tibi finis erit; semper prostrata iacebis
Hec etiam mortiferas audebis spargere flam mas·
Insimulos famulas uedi quibus intima casti
Lena animi sola feruex delampade xpi
Tene ouex atrix hominum potuisse resumptis
Timbus examen capiti recalescere flatus·
Asirium postquam thalamum ceruix olo feruit
Esta cupidinee madefactum sanguine luuit·
Gemmarum q; thorum mechi ducis alba iudith

VIII Cambridge, Corpus Christi College 23, 7r. Death of *Libido*

swords, and waving their Medusa-like severed heads as tokens of victory.[61] *Pudicitia*'s sword is stained by the blood of *Libido*, previously a sinner and 'stainer' of men's bodies, and can only be cleansed by dipping it into the waters of the river Jordan and inserting it into the virginal body of the church. *Avaritia* is dispatched by *Operatio* in a confrontation that is close to that of violent rape (pl. VI):

> Inuadit trepidam Virtus fortissima duris
> ulnarum nodis, obliso et gutture frangit
> exsanguem siccamque gulam; conpressa ligantur
> uincla lacertorum sub mentum et faucibus artis
> extorquent animam, nullo quae uulnere rapta
> palpitat atque aditu spiraminis intercepto
> inclusam patitur uenarum carcere mortem.
> Illa reluctanti genibusque et calcibus instans
> perfodit et costas atque ilia rumpit anhela.[62]

There is a relationship between this passage and the eroticized language of female martyrdom. In the *Passio S. Agnetis* (poem XIV of the *Peristephanon*) Agnes's executioner has been worked up to a bloodthirsty wrath ('iram nam furor incitat hostis cruenti', lines 63–4), and Agnes, looking at him and his 'naked sword', cries out:

> 'Exulto, talis quod potius uenit
> uaesanus atrox turbidus armiger,
> quam si ueniret languidus ac tener
> mollisque ephebus tinctus aromate,
> qui me pudoris funere perderet.
> Hic, hic amator iam, fateor, placet.
> Ibo inruentis gressibus obuiam
> nec demorabor uota calentia;
> ferrum in papillas omne recepero
> pectusque ad imum uim gladii traham'.[63]

---

[61] In fact, as is generally acknowledged, the Virtues take on some of the attributes of the Vices in order to defeat them. Hope and Humility, for example, gleefully wave the severed head of Pride at their moment of triumph. See Malamud, *Poetics*, pp. 65–7, and J. P. Hermann, *Allegories of War: Language and Violence in Old English Poetry* (Ann Arbor, MI, 1989), pp. 14–15.

[62] 'The brave Virtue sets upon her with the iron grip of her arms and strangles her, crushing the blood out of her throat till it is dry. Her arms pressed tight like bands beneath the chin, squeeze the gorge and wrest the life away; no wound ravishes it in the agony of death; the breath-passage stopped, it suffers its end shut up in the prison of the body. As she struggles, the victor presses hard on her with knee and foot and stabs her through the ribs and pierces the heaving flanks' (lines 589–97).

[63] '"I rejoice that there comes a man like this, a savage, cruel, wild man-at-arms rather than a list-less, soft, womanish youth bathed in perfume, coming to destroy me with the death of my honour. This lover, this one at last, I confess it pleases me. I shall meet his eager steps half-way and not put off his hot desires. I shall welcome the whole length of his blade into my bosom, drawing the sword-blade to the depths of my breast"' (lines 69–78). See also Malamud, 'Virtue of Perversity', pp. 78–82; *idem*, *Poetics*, pp. 149–80.

Of course Agnes, like Romanus, is a saint rather than a Vice; she dies willingly while *Avaritia* does not; and she has the power of speech right up to the moment of her death. It is the power of speech more than anything else that separates the bodies of the *Psychomachia* from those of the *Peristephanon*, especially those of the *Passio S. Romani*. The Vices are not only gruesomely dispatched, but silenced: *Avaritia* has her throat crushed, *Discordia* her tongue pierced with a spear, *Veterum cultura deorum* is choked, *Libido*'s throat is slit, *Superbia* decapitated. *Luxuria* is the most dangerous of the Vices, and she temporarily wins over the Virtues by literally unmanning them:

> Inde eblanditis uirtutibus halitus inlex
> inspirat tenerum labefacta per ossa uenenum
> et male dulcis odor domat ora et pectora et arma
> ferratosque toros obliso robore mulcet.[64]

Luxuria is also the most feminine of the Vices, fighting with perfume and flowers rather than spears and swords. As a result she is not only silenced, but forced to consume her own mouth and tongue:

> Dentibus introrsum resolutis lingua resectam
> dilaniata gulam frustis cum sanguinis inplet.
> Insolitis dapibus crudescit guttur et ossa
> conliquefacta uorans reuomit quas hauserat offas.[65]

The silencing of the feminine voice and dismembering of the feminine body is reinforced by the tension created between text and illustration. What we see in the drawings is not always in accord with what we read in the text. The text tells us that the Vices are monsters, but we see women. The *Psychomachia* is, as Mary Carruthers has recently stated, 'designedly disgusting and morbid because it is those qualities that make it memorable, particularly for the novice schoolboy minds for which it was written'.[66] But Carruthers ignores the gendering of the violence in the poem, and it is the gendering of the violence, particularly in the Anglo-Saxon illustrated manuscripts, that makes the *Psychomachia* disturbing rather than merely memorable, whether intended for the minds of schoolboys, monks or kings. Each female body in CCCC 23 is made, to borrow one of Carruthers' own phrases, 'dead, dead, dead'.[67]

---

[64] 'So the Virtues are won over by her charms; the alluring breath blows a subtle poison on them that unmans their frames, the fatally sweet scent subduing their lips and hearts and weapons, softening their iron-clad muscles and crushing their strength' (lines 328–31).

[65] 'The teeth within are loosened, the gullet cut, and the mangled tongue fills it with bloody fragments. Her gorge rises at the strange meal; gulping down the pulped bones she spews up again the lumps she swallowed' (lines 423–6).   [66] Carruthers, *Craft of Thought*, p. 144.

[67] *Ibid.* p. 148.

Gender and voice in the CCCC 23 Psychomachia

Both the Anglo-Saxons and Prudentius were well aware of the power of images. Bede tells us that even the illiterate were moved to examine their conscience by the image of the Last Judgement at Wearmouth,[68] while Alfred was spurred to memorization, if not literacy, by his desire for the beautiful initial in his mother's book.[69] In the *Passio S. Cassiani* (poem IX of the *Peristephanon*), Prudentius describes himself as moved to tears by a painting of Cassian's martyrdom, 'a pitiful sight' (*miserabile uisu*, line 13).[70] In poem XI of the same text, concerning the martyrdom of Hippolytus, Prudentius's description of a painting of the martyr, torn to pieces by wild horses, merges imperceptibly with his narrative account of the martyrdom, so that life and art become one.[71] Modern readers of the *Psychomachia* have noted the potential of the illustrations to 'enhance rather than diminish the didactic potential of the manuscript'.[72] In CCCC 23 the vivid illustrations that accompany the violent battles of the *Psychomachia* form a significant contrast to the unillustrated battle of St Romanus. In the former the female body is dismembered before and with our eyes – we see it, sense it, join in the battle – while in the latter the death and triumph of Romanus are seen only with the mind's eye. If narrative voice can serve to establish the reader's perspective, so can the narrative strategies of illustration.[73] The text of the *Passio S. Romani* invites us to adopt the martyr's voice, while the illustrations of the *Psychomachia* invite us to adopt the Virtues' actions, and we become one of their warrior troop. Yet despite its lack of illustration, imagery and drawing are crucial to Romanus's triumph. At the end of the *Passio S. Romani* Prudentius writes:

> Excepit adstans angelus coram deo
> et quae locutus martyr et quae pertulit;
> nec uerba solum disserentis condidit,
> sed ipsa pingens uulnera expressit stilo
> laterum, genarum pectorisque et faucium.
> Omnis notata est sanguinis dimensio,
> ut quamque plagam sulcus exarauerit
> altam patentem proximam longam, breuem,

---

68 *Venerabilis Baedae opera historica*, ed. C. Plummer, 2 vols. (Oxford, 1896) I, 369–70.
69 S. Keynes and M. Lapidge, *Alfred the Great: Asser's 'Life of King Alfred' and Other Contemporary Sources* (Harmondsworth, 1983), p. 75.
70 Cassian's body was literally transformed into text by being beaten with wax tablets and opened up with the styluses of his students.
71 A point noted by M. Roberts in his *Poetry and the Cult of the Martyrs* (Ann Arbor, MI, 1993), p. 154.
72 Wieland, 'Illustrated Manuscripts', p. 184. See also Carruthers, *Craft of Thought*, pp. 144–8.
73 On narrative voice, see esp. P. Ricoeur, *Time and Narrative*, trans. K. McLaughlin and D. Pellauer, 3 vols. (Chicago, IL, 1984) II, 99.

quae uis doloris, quiue segmenti modus;
guttam cruoris ille nullam perdidit.[74]

As in the *Passio S. Agnetis* the language is both gruesome and erotic in its desire
for blood and its probings of the body, here dismembered into its constituent
parts and wounds and reassembled in the words and pages of the angel's book.
In the passage quoted above, language embodies the passion of the martyr and
the longing for the divine embrace that fuels it. The angel's drawing is one of the
acheiropoietai, the images 'not made by human hands'. The unseen image of
Romanus becomes a type of lost icon, taking its place beside such other lost and
miraculous icons as the veil of Veronica, or Luke's portrait of the Virgin and
Child. In this case the reader does not see the body, but follows the actions of
the unseen angel, tracing the body with the mind. In CCCC 23 the flawed female
body and its destruction can be represented by human hands, while the triumph
of the saintly male body cannot. The martyr's battle is transitory, but the
triumph of the martyr is eternal, as are his soul, unseen image and story. While
we cannot read the angel's book we can follow it as it is mirrored by Prudentius's
text and by the verbal portrait which he traces of Romanus's words and wounds
with Romanus's borrowed tongue.

But Romanus too has a voice, and in this respect he could not be more
directly opposed to the Vices. In fact both Romanus and the *Passio S. Romani* are
almost entirely voice. The martyr speaks over half (640) of the *passio*'s 1140
lines. The Vices, on the other hand, while they do speak, are more akin to the
blank pages of a book with the story inscribed or carved on their silenced
bodies by the Virtues, Prudentius and the reader. Romanus's wounds actually
magnify his voice, they become 'quod multa pandens ora iam Christum
loquor'.[75] He tells his tormentors 'Tot ecce laudant ora quot sunt uulnera.'[76] But,
again, we do not see the mouth, we hear it speaking. Even with his face torn
open and his tongue cut out he cannot be silenced, but says:

'Christum loquenti lingua numquam defuit;
nec uerba quaeras quo regantur organo,
cum praedicatur ipse uerborum dator.
'Qui fecit ut uis uocis expressa intimo
pulmone et oris torta sub testudine

[74] 'An angel standing in the presence of God received both what the martyr said and what he
endured; he did not write down the words of [the martyr's] discourse alone, but tracing with his
pen he portrayed the very wounds of his sides, breast, cheeks, and jaws. Every drop of his
blood was written down, how the furrow ploughed every wound, deep, searching, near, long or
short; the force of the pain, the manner of each cut; he did not waste a speck of blood' (lines
1121–30). The translation is that of K. O'Brien O'Keeffe (*Book and the Body*, pp. x–xi).
[75] 'Many mouths to speak of Christ' (line 563).
[76] '"For every wound I have, you see a mouth uttering praise"' (line 570).

nunc ex palato det repercussos sonos,
nunc temperetur dentium de pectine
sitque his agendis lingua plectrum mobile'.[77]

As the angel's pen will reassemble his body, so Romanus's words here reassemble his shattered face and missing tongue, the very bits of the anatomy that *Luxuria*, her face smashed with a stone, was forced to swallow. In the *Passio S. Romani* wholeness is created out of fragmentation. The process, in Michael Roberts's words, 'is like reading inscriptions, in which the intelligible text must be pieced together from the constituent strokes (*apices*) of which the whole is made up'.[78] But here it is Romanus who is reading his own body to us. Moreover, the bodies of Romanus, the angel and Prudentius are all united in the process of creating text – and one could add the bodies of the Anglo-Saxon scribe who copies that text, and the reader who recreates it at each reading. The breaking of the martyr's body creates a never-ending multiplication of text and voice, proving Prudentius's statement at the beginning of the *passio* that 'Vox ueritatis testis extingui nequit.'[79]

The first-person voice of Prudentius is not present in the *Psychomachia*, but the image of the praying Prudentius is. On CCCC 23, 4r, he prays before an enormous altar, his back turned to the battle of the Virtues and the Vices that begins on the verso of the same page, and his pose and gesture directing us back to the story of Abraham and Isaac that precedes it. The cross on the altar represents Christ's body, like that of Romanus both broken and whole, unseen in bodily form and with a voice that cannot be annihilated.[80] On 40r of the same manuscript, Prudentius stands praying and offering thanks to God before the church and the enthroned Wisdom, thereby offering continuity with the text of the *Passio S. Romani* which begins on 41r with the poet's prayers. But how do the body and voice of both poet and martyr change our reading of the *Psychomachia*, and how do they position the reader in relation to the body of the book and the bodies it contains?

Michael Roberts notes that 'The reduction of an individual body to his physical *membra* provides an appropriate contrast to the martyr, whose spiritual integrity survives the dismemberment of his body.'[81] In the *Psychomachia* the

---

[77] '"Tongue never failed him who spoke of Christ, and you need not ask what organ controls the speech when it is the giver of speech himself who is proclaimed. He who brought it to pass that the potency of the voice, forced out from the depths of the lung and launched in the vault of the mouth, now gives out sounds that reverberate from the palate, and again is modified by the rows of teeth, and that for these processes the tongue plays the part of the nimble quill"'(lines 928–35).   [78] Roberts, *Poetry*, p. 156.

[79] Line 9: 'The voice that bears witness to the truth cannot be annihilated.'

[80] On the changeable nature of Christ's body, see M. Rubin, *Corpus Christi: the Eucharist in Late Medieval Culture* (Cambridge, 1991). Ch. 1 deals with the eucharist *c.* 1000.

[81] Roberts, *Poetry*, p. 65.

female bodies that we see dismembered remain just that, body parts and bodies forever in the process of being torn to pieces (pl. VII). Framed by stories of male agency, the stories of Abraham and Romanus, and unseen images of the male body, Christ and Romanus, the sexual violence towards and silencing of the female body in the *Psychomachia* are all the more disturbing. The ultimate message of the two texts may be the same – one must overcome the body for the sake of the spirit – but it is the female body that is shown to be dangerous, lethal and in need of being overcome. The stories of Eulalia and Agnes also teach that for women the whole process of overcoming the body is doubled. While male saints like Romanus transcend their bodies, women must first conquer and deny their feminine sexed and gendered bodies before they can transcend them.[82] The *Psychomachia* shows us that sin and the body are not only feminine, but monstrous things, and it keeps vice and bodiliness firmly tied to the female and the feminine, and the 'dead, dead, dead' (pl. VIII). Romanus's body is strangely absent from his martyrdom. Prudentius focuses not on the bodily wounds produced by his tormenters, but on the persistent voice that results from his torments. He does not allow his body to be read or penetrated by the gaze of earthly readers, but deflects our eyes with his incessant mono-logue. In fact at one point the prefect Asclepiades vainly attempts to torture Romanus's words by tearing open his face.[83] Man and the masculine are voice and spirit rather than body. By the eleventh century this binary division was a commonplace, and one that both hagiography and poetry make clear was famil-iar to the Anglo-Saxons. The poem *Soul and Body I* contains an interesting refer-ence to the body's *bryde beag* ('bride's ring'), suggesting that even when dealing with the abstract, some Anglo-Saxon authors identified body, following

---

[82] Lees, 'Engendering Religious Desire', p. 32, describes the tradition in Anglo-Saxon England: 'Ælfric's male saints take many paths to that *imitatio (Christi)*; the female saints in the collection, however, live lives of the sexed body, centering on their virginity and chastity, whether as brides of Christ (Agatha, Agnes, Lucy), monks (the two transvestite saints, Eugenia and Euphrosyne), chaste wives (Æthelthryth, Cecilia), or as ascetics (Mary of Egypt). The transformation of sex-uality is the prime component of the female saint's life. Women have sexuality where men don't, and women who become saints redirect it toward God.'

[83] 'Vertat ictum carnifex
in os loquentis inque maxillas manum
sulcosque acutos et fidiculas transferat.
Verbositatis ipse rumpatur locus,
scaturrientes perdat ut loquacitas
sermonis auras perforatis follibus.
Quibus sonandi nulla lex ponit modum.
Ipsa et loquentis uerba torqueri uolo' (lines 548–55).
'"Let the executioner turn the stroke on to his mouth and stop his speech, to his jaws transfer hands and sharp cuts and cords. Shatter the seat of his verbosity, puncture the bellows so that his loquacity may lose the gushing winds of words since no law puts a stop to their sounding. I will have the very words tortured even as he speaks"'.

Jerome, as the feminine half of the soul and body pair.[84] The *Psychomachia* clearly reinforces this message.

The juxtaposition of the *Passio S. Romani* with the *Psychomachia* emphasizes the division between the masculine spirit (or mind) and the feminine body all the more forcefully and, in CCCC 23, it does so with the help of the illustrations. As we participate in the action of the *Psychomachia*, so we participate in the mind and voice of Romanus. In reading the story, the first-person voice of Romanus merges with the voice of the reader. We may not undergo his torments, but we can speak his words. And because Prudentius tells us at the beginning of the *Passio S. Romani* that it is Romanus's tongue that has loosened his own, it becomes difficult to separate authors and texts: Prudentius's words are Romanus's words, and become our words as we read. The lack of illustration makes it all the easier to associate our voice with their voices, since we have no image to pin those voices to. Yet these are masculine voices. Even the mother of the child Barulas, the one female character in the *Passio S. Romani*, is portrayed as overcoming her feminine maternal nature in order to glory in the martyrdom of her son. The *Psychomachia*, on the other hand, is all about body, the body of the

---

[84] Line 59. The *Soul and Body* poems present us with what is for the most part an ambiguously gendered soul and body. *Soul and Body I* opens with a reference to *æghwylc hæleða* ('each man or warrior') who will be responsible for the fate of his soul. The word is masculine, but may be used here in reference to the reader of whatever gender as a warrior in the battle against sin. Jerome, as already noted, makes this point, and Aldhelm refers to both male and female readers of his *Carmen de virginitate* as chaste soldiers: see M. Lapidge and J. L. Rosier, *Aldhelm: the Poetic Works* (Cambridge, 1985), p. 102. In *Soul and Body I* soul and body are sundered at death and the words used to describe them from this point on range across all three grammatical genders. The damned soul berates the silent and dead body for the state to which body has brought it, and one of the earthly treasures soul tells body that it can no longer enjoy is *þinre bryde beag*. While men might have received rings as part of the marriage 'ceremony' in Anglo-Saxon England, the first documented occurrence of a dual-ring ceremony is in two prayers for a *Benedicto anuli sponsi et sponse* printed in the Appendix to H. A. Wilson's 1910 edition of the twelfth-century Magdalen Pontifical (HBS 39, 222). The prayer is found in two slightly earlier twelfth-century pontificals (Cambridge, Trinity College B. 11. 10 and Cambridge, University Library, Ll. 2. 10) and Wilson interprets its wording as suggesting that the ceremony included two rings (p. 293). I would like to thank R. W. Pfaff for drawing this text to my attention. Pfaff also notes (pers. comm.) that Wilson's interpretation of the text is problematic but, if correct, suggests that the two-ring ceremony *might* have developed in England before the Norman Conquest. Most, if not all, references to rings and marriage in Anglo-Saxon poetry are to women (*Maxims I*, 129; *Maxims II*, 45, *Genesis*, 1875, *Christ I*, 290). Indeed, Aldhelm lists the desire for rings as one of the things that differentiates the sensual married woman from the pious virgin: M. Lapidge and M. Herren, *Aldhelm: the Prose Works* (Cambridge, 1979), p. 73. We might also consider the possibility that the ring is a symbol of body's former union with soul, a state referred to in the opening lines of the poem. In lines 104–22 the poet of *Soul and Body I* goes on to relate in language reminiscent of the violent battles of the *Psychomachia* (and looking forward to the Last Judgement) how the body will be torn apart and chewed to pieces by worms.

135

reader and the opening up of the bodies within the text. If the battle for the soul is something experienced on a daily basis, the dangers dramatized in the *Psychomachia* were likewise experienced on a daily basis. Here, too, the reader is positioned as masculine. We must resist Vice, gendered as feminine and labelled as monstrous, and triumph through Virtue, which though it may look feminine is always gendered masculine by its actions – like Agnes, or Eulalia, or the saved soul of *Soul and Body I*. To the good Christian reader of whatever sex, Self in CCCC 23 is masculine and Other is feminine. Wieland asks, 'What would monks and priests do with the explicit violence of the *Psychomachia*?' He neatly sidesteps the issue of gender by first assuming an exclusively male audience, and then associating the battle of the *Psychomachia* with monastic desire to take up arms against the Viking invaders after the sack of Lindisfarne.[85] This theory fails to explain both the chronological gap between the Viking attacks on monastic houses and the production of the illustrated manuscripts, and the transformation of the warriors into women. Wieland's assumption of a male readership is likely to be correct as, in addition to the way in which text and illustration position the reader, there is no evidence that women either produced or read the *Psychomachia* in Anglo-Saxon England.[86] The absence of a female audience, the nature of the imagery, and the fact that the illustrated manuscripts appear only in the wake of the Benedictine Reform, suggest that we might relate the production of the manuscripts to the curtailing of female power within the church that has come to be seen as a feature of the late-tenth and eleventh-century church across Europe.[87] This seems a highly plausible explanation as long as we bear in mind that the historical reality was likely to have been far more complex than the propagandistic nature of the manuscripts suggests. Nevertheless, in reading CCCC 23 it is hard to deny that the masculine voices of Romanus, Prudentius and the manuscript's audience are eternal, while the female body remains broken and earth-bound, like so many pages of dead flesh.

---

[85] Wieland, 'Illustrated Manuscripts', p. 185.

[86] Though they certainly did read texts influenced by it, such as Aldhelm's *De uirginitate* and *Carmen de uirginitate*, both written for the nuns and monks of Barking Abbey. See Lapidge and Herren, *Aldhelm: the Prose Works*, pp. 51–132, and Lapidge and Rosier, *Aldhelm: the Poetic Works*, pp. 97–167.

[87] C. Lees and G. Overing, 'Before History, Before Difference: Bodies, Metaphor, and the Church in Anglo-Saxon England', *Yale Jnl of Criticism* 11 (1998), 315–34, at 319; Lees, 'Engendering Religious Desire', p. 36; J. T. Schulenburg, 'Women's Monastic Communities, 500–1100', *Signs* 14 (1988–9), 261–92.

The prodigal fragment: Cambridge, Gonville and Caius College 734/782a

REBECCA RUSHFORTH

Two fragments of an important eleventh-century manuscript, missing for some years, were recently rediscovered by the staff of Gonville and Caius College library.[1] The manuscript is significant both because of its attribution to the hand of 'Eadwig Basan', a major figure in the history of eleventh-century English script, and because it constitutes evidence for the use in late Anglo-Saxon England of a mass lectionary, a rare type of liturgical book. The fragments have now been assigned the class-mark 734/782a, in order both to associate them with and distinguish them from manuscript 734/782, a seventeenth-century paper catalogue of a bequest of books to the college, in whose binding they were originally preserved.[2]

DESCRIPTION OF THE FRAGMENTS

All that survives of this manuscript is two vertical strips which fit together to make between a half and two-thirds of an original leaf (see pls. IX–X). Each fragment is 271 millimetres tall, and between approximately 55 and 58 millimetres wide. I will refer to that side of the leaf of which the left-hand margin survives as the recto; this side still bears traces of having been pasted into the spine of the binding of 734/782. Although it is difficult to be certain because of its worn and battered state, it seems that the recto is the hair side of the leaf, and that the leaf was ruled from this side. The text on the verso follows on directly from that of the recto of the leaf: this shows that the surviving margin was an inner margin, in the middle of a bifolium, and therefore the absence of visible prickings suggests that the leaf was ruled before folding.

Two large initials survive on the recto of this leaf, both the letter **I** for *in*. The first (4–5 lines in height, line 8) is green and the parchment has perished in its centre making a long thin hole. The second initial **I** (5 lines in height, line 21) is red and has tarnished somewhat, as have the three lines of red majuscules (lines 7 and 20 on the recto and 9 on the verso), making it hard to read the minuscules on the corresponding line on the other side.

---

[1] I would like to express my gratitude to the librarians of Gonville and Caius College, especially Lyn Bailey and Mira Beaglehole, for their helpfulness and patience.

[2] Neither the fragments nor the volume from which they came are included in M. R. James, *A Descriptive Catalogue of the Manuscripts in Library of Gonville and Caius College*, 2 vols. (Cambridge, 1907–8).

THE SCRIPT OF THE FRAGMENTS

Discussion of these fragments has necessarily been severely limited by their erstwhile unavailability. The only reference to them published before their loss is in T. A. M. Bishop's *English Caroline Minuscule*, where he included them in his list of surviving specimens in the hand of 'Eadwig Basan',[3] and all subsequent mention of them has centred on this attribution.[4] 'Eadwig Basan' is an important and interesting figure of early-eleventh-century script history: not only can a name and self-portrait be attached to him (in both cases, tentatively),[5] but he seems to have been instrumental in developing a new style of script the influence of which had spread throughout England by the time of the Norman Conquest.[6] The name 'Eadwig Basan' comes from a colophon in one of his manuscripts, Hanover, Kestner-Museum W.M. XXIa, 36, and is therefore subject to the usual proviso applicable to colophons that it may have been copied from the exemplar.[7] Whatever his name, this scribe can be confidently located at Christ Church, Canterbury, for at least part of his career: all the charters in his hand are in favour of this house,[8] and he also wrote London, British Library, Arundel 155 and part of London, British Library, Harley 603, both

---

[3] T. A. M. Bishop, *English Caroline Minuscule* (Oxford, 1971), nos. 24–5, p. 22. He refers to the fragments by the classmark 732/754 in his text, p. 22, and by the then correct classmark 734/782 in his index, p. 25.

[4] D. N. Dumville, *English Caroline Script and Monastic History* (Woodbridge, 1993), pp. 131, n. 90, and 139; R. W. Pfaff, 'Eadui Basan: Scriptorum Princeps?', *England in the Eleventh Century*, ed. C. Hicks, Harlaxton Med. Stud. 2 (Stamford, 1992), 267–83, at 268, n. 8, refers to the fragment by the classmark 732/734. This manuscript is no. 120.6 in Helmut Gneuss, *Handlist of Anglo-Saxon Manuscripts* (Tempe, AZ, 2001), a revision of his 'A Preliminary List of Manuscripts Written or Owned in England up to 1100', *ASE* 9 (1981), 1–60. I am extremely grateful to Professor Gneuss for discussing this manuscript with me.

[5] This possible self-portrait is on 133r of London, British Library, Arundel 155. It is reproduced in colour in *The Golden Age of Anglo-Saxon Art: 966–1066* ed. J. Backhouse, D. H. Turner and L. Webster (London, 1984), no. 57, pl. XVIII; see also the discussions in N. Brooks, *The Early History of the Church of Canterbury: Christ Church from 597 to 1066* (Leicester, 1984), p. 264; Dumville, *English Caroline Script*, p. 122, n. 60; R. Gameson, *The Role of Art in the Late Anglo-Saxon Church* (Oxford, 1995), pp. 84–6, 136 and 172; T. A. Heslop, 'The Production of *De Luxe* Manuscripts and the Patronage of King Cnut and Queen Emma', *ASE* 19 (1990), 151–95, at 175; W. Noel, *The Harley Psalter* (Cambridge, 1995), p. 143; and Pfaff, 'Eadui Basan', pp. 279–80.

[6] Bishop, *English Caroline Minuscule*, p. xxiii; Dumville, *English Caroline Script*, pp. 125–6.

[7] For discussion of this colophon, see Dumville, *English Caroline Script*, pp. 120–2; Heslop, 'The Production', pp. 175–6; Pfaff, 'Eadui Basan', pp. 267–9. A manuscript colophon probably copied from the exemplar is found in Oxford, Bodleian Library, Junius 121 (5232), 101r.

[8] London, British Library, Royal 1. D. IX, 44v (P. H. Sawyer, *Anglo-Saxon Charters: an Annotated List and Bibliography* (London, 1968) [here after S], no. 985); Stowe Ch. 2 (S 22); and Stowe Ch. 38 (S 950). London, British Library, Cotton Claudius A. iii, 2r–6r (S 914), also a Christ Church, Canterbury, document, has been attributed to the hand of 'Eadwig Basan'; see below, n. 14.

Christ Church, Canterbury, books.[9] Some of his work is datable. The calendar in Arundel 155 includes the martyrdom of St Ælfheah in 1012, but his translation in 1023 is added in a later hand; it is therefore likely that 'Eadwig' wrote between these two dates, since the translation of Archbishop Ælfheah was of great importance to the Christ Church community.[10] Of the documents in the hand of 'Eadwig', one is dated to 1018,[11] and two are probably datable between 1017 and 1020.[12] 'Eadwig' presumably finished his small contribution to York, Minster Library, Add. 1, before the death in 1023 of Wulfstan, archbishop of York, to whom it belonged.[13] Therefore the dates of the identified script-specimens of 'Eadwig Basan' centre on the year 1018.[14] 'Eadwig' seems to have written mostly high-grade texts: his surviving work consists of luxurious biblical manuscripts, texts of charters, and additions to valuable books, all in his own distinctive, calligraphic, and much imitated hand.[15]

Bishop's attribution of Cambridge, Gonville and Caius 734/782a to 'Eadwig Basan' needs re-examining: David Dumville, the only person to have reconsidered the attribution so far, suggested in 1993 on the grounds of a previous inspection that the identification might be erroneous, but was unable at the time to view the manuscript, which was still missing.[16]

The majuscule script used in these fragments is Uncial, not the distinctive Rustic-Capital-based mixed majuscules that we associate with 'Eadwig

[9] See E. Temple, *Anglo-Saxon Manuscripts 900–1066* (London, 1976), p. 86, and Noel, *The Harley Psalter*, pp. 130–45, respectively.   [10] Brooks, *The Early History*, pp. 265 and 291–2.

[11] Stowe Ch. 38 (S 950).

[12] Royal 1. D. IX, 44v (S 985), and Stowe Ch. 2 (S 22); see Brooks, *The Early History*, pp. 288–90.

[13] Dumville, *English Caroline Script*, p. 123; S. D. Keynes, 'The Additions in Old English', *The York Gospels*, ed. N. Barker (London, 1986), pp. 81–99; D. N. Dumville, 'On the Dating of Some Late Anglo-Saxon Liturgical Manuscripts', *Trans. of the Cambridge Bibliographical Soc.* 10 (1991–5), 40–57, at 53–4.

[14] The text of another document which has been attributed to 'Eadwig', Claudius A. iii, 2r–6r, can be shown to have been forged in the mid-1030s; however a close comparison of this script with that of 'Eadwig' reveals many differences between them in both letter-forms and aspect. I think this attribution is mistaken, and there is, therefore, no evidence for the extension of the career of 'Eadwig' beyond the second and third decades of the eleventh century. See P. Chaplais, 'The Anglo-Saxon Chancery: from the Diploma to the Writ', *Prisca Munimenta*, ed. F. Ranger (London, 1973), pp. 43–62, at 59; Brooks, *The Early History*, pp. 257–9; and Dumville, *English Caroline Script*, p. 126, n. 75. Reproduced by W. Noel, 'The Division of Work in the Harley Psalter', *Making the Medieval Book: Techniques of Production*, ed. L. L. Brownrigg (London, 1995), pp. 1–15, fig. 1.

[15] As well as the charters mentioned above, n. 8, 'Eadwig' wrote two gospelbooks (Hanover, Kestner-Museum W.M. XXIa, 36, and London, British Library, Add. 34890), a gospel lectionary (Florence, Biblioteca Laurenziana, Plut. XVII.20), and a psalter (Arundel 155, fols. 1–191), as well as adding material to three valuable biblical manuscripts (London, British Library, Cotton Vespasian A. i; London, British Library, Harley 603; and York, Minster Library, Add. 1).

[16] Dumville, *English Caroline Script*, p. 131, n. 90.

Basan'.[17] 'Eadwig' did use Uncials for the rubrics in some of his manuscripts, most often in Florence, Biblioteca Laurenziana, Plut. XVII.20[18] and the Grimbald Gospels (London, British Library, Add. 34890).[19] The Uncial script in these two manuscripts does not exhibit any distinguishing idiosyncrasies, and bears close comparison with the majuscules surviving in 734/782a. The back of the letter **D** is kept very flat, but letters such as **L, P** and **Q** are allowed to extend beyond the script's notional two lines. **A** is the form with an open eye in the left-hand stroke, and **E** has the widened finials typical of English Uncial. The small amount of surviving material, and its canonical nature, neither allows nor disallows an attribution to the hand of 'Eadwig Basan'.

The characteristics of the minuscule hand of 'Eadwig' have been well established.[20] In aspect it is very round, and the use of wedges makes it look substantial; it is neatly written, with a high degree of internal consistency. Ascenders have tapering wedges, while the wedges on minims are heavy. The feet of letters have small turned-up finishing strokes. **a** has a narrow, often rectangular compartment, and occasionally there is a trailing-headed **a** at the beginning of a word. **e** has a small compartment, usually slanting upwards slightly; **g** has a small downwards stroke linking the body to the tail, and the tail is open; **r** has an angular top stroke, like a brief horizontal zigzag. **s** has a very heavy shoulder, and is noticeably shorter than ascenders. 'Eadwig' uses the **r**+**a** ligature with an Insular half-uncial **a** ('two **c**' **a**), and his **c**+**t** ligature is tall and narrow; sometimes there is a gap between the top of the **c** and the **t**, and sometimes they meet. He tends to use a small, minim-height, majuscule **H** in the **ihc** abbreviation for 'Iesus'.

A close examination of the script of the Caius fragments reveals subtle differences from the distinctive hand written by 'Eadwig'.[21] The most immediate is in the aspect of the script of 734/782a; though round, it does not make such heavy use of wedges. The ascenders are not as tall (*galilea*, line 5) and the feet of letters are not usually finished in the same way; sometimes the feet of letters are not finished at all (*formidinis*, line 16). The script has a slight forward slant. Many of the important letter-forms are the same: **a** (*ad iesum*, line 1) and **e** (*galilea*, line 5) have narrow compartments; **g** usually has a small downwards stroke in the middle (*galilea*, line 5); and **r** (*nrm*, line 24) has an angular top-stroke. However, **s** is not the markedly heavy-shouldered form used by 'Eadwig' (*esset*, line 25). Trailing-headed **a** is occasionally used in initial position (*a galilea*, line 5), as is small majuscule **H** in the 'Iesus' abbreviation (line 1). The **c**+**t** ligature (*nocte*,

---

[17] *Ibid.* p. 128.   [18] Script reproduced by Dumville, *English Caroline Script*, pl. XII.

[19] Script reproduced by M. P. Brown and P. Lovett, *The Historical Source Book for Scribes* (London, 1999), pp. 82–3.

[20] Bishop, *English Caroline Script*, nos. 24–5; Dumville, *English Caroline Script*, pp. 128–30; Pfaff, 'Eadui Basan', pp. 267–8.   [21] See pls. IX–X; line numbers refer to pl. IX.

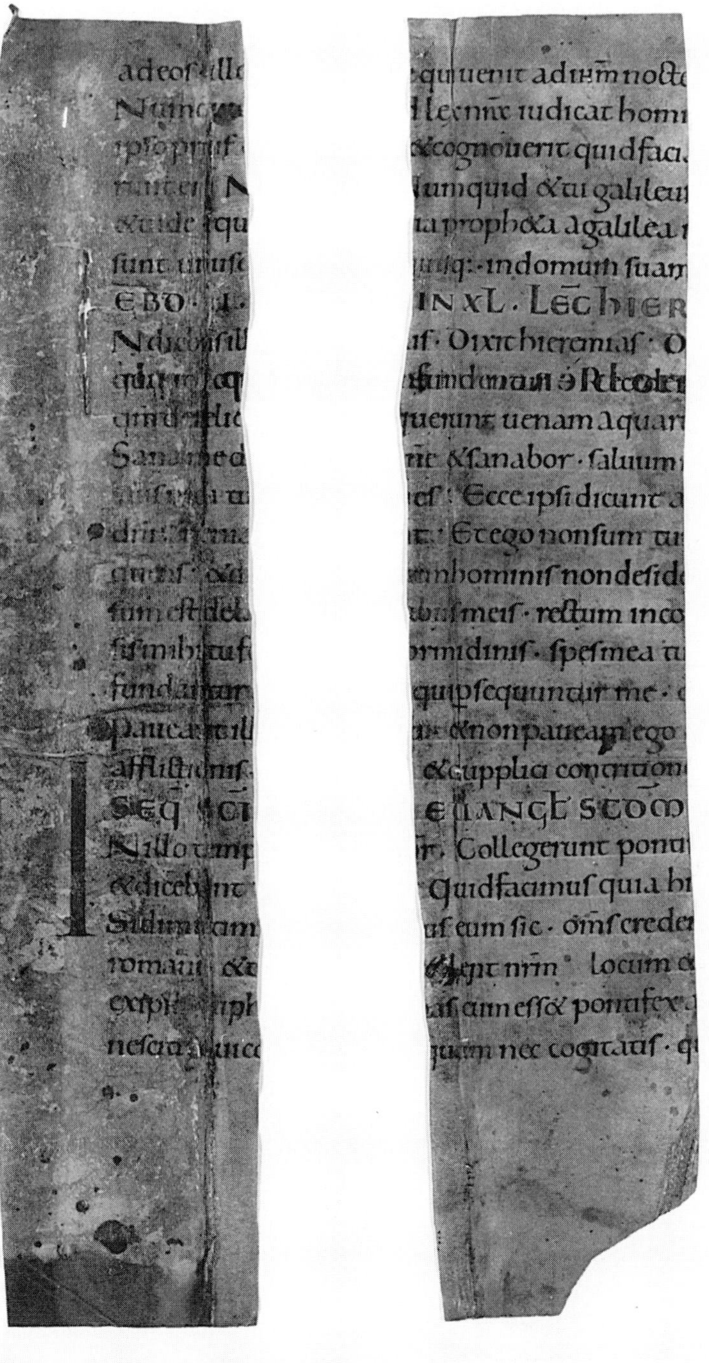

IX Cambridge, Gonville and Caius College 734/782a, *recto*

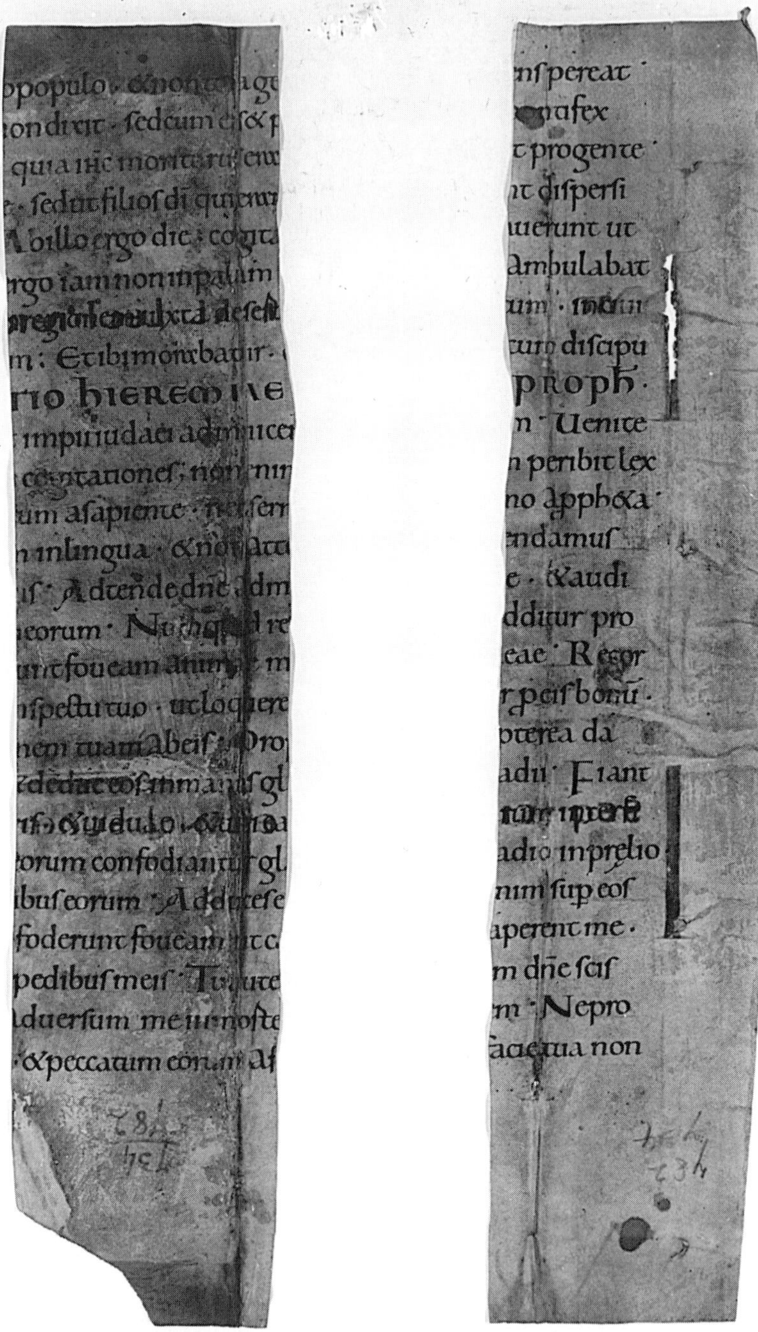

X Cambridge, Gonville and Caius College 734/782a, *verso*

line 1) is similar to that of 'Eadwig', but is neither as tall nor as laterally compressed. Although the script of the Caius fragments resembles that of 'Eadwig Basan', I do not think that it can safely be attributed to him because of these small differences in aspect and practice.[22] The similarities can be accounted for by the 'lasting and wide influence' of the hand developed by 'Eadwig' on later English script,[23] an influence so considerable that after the Norman Conquest the style he originated 'became a scribal mark of Englishness'.[24]

The attribution of these fragments to 'Eadwig Basan' has allowed in the past for an easy dating and localization of its production, but since this attribution cannot be maintained it is necessary to reconsider both when and where it might have been written. This specimen of script certainly shows the influence of the style developed by 'Eadwig', but since this influence was so widespread, I do not think I can be any more precise than to attribute it to England in the middle fifty years of the eleventh century.

THE TEXT OF THE FRAGMENTS

The Anglo-Saxons used three different ways of recording what mass lection was assigned to each date in the Christian year: the date appropriate to a particular passage could be written beside that passage in a gospelbook or a manuscript of some other part of the Bible; a separate list could be made of the beginnings and ends of the lections in date order; or a type of manuscript known as a lectionary could be produced, listing each reading in full in date order.[25] A lectionary made it a very simple task to find and read the correct lection for each day, although the production of such a book would have required some investment of both time and materials. There were two set readings from the Bible; one was from the gospels, and the other, although known as the epistle reading, was from anywhere in the remainder of the New and Old Testaments. There were three different types of lectionary: a gospel lectionary contained only the gospel readings and an epistolary contained only the epistle readings, whereas a mass lectionary contained both the gospel readings and the epistle readings.

Four Bible excerpts survive on this leaf, two of which are entire and two partial. The first is from ch. VII of the gospel of John: the surviving text starts at *ad eos*, which is in the middle of verse 50, and continues until the end of the chapter at verse 53. The second and third readings are whole and consist of Jer.

[22] I am very grateful to both David Dumville and Michael Gullick for discussing with me the question of the attribution of the Caius fragments to 'Eadwig Basan'.
[23] Bishop, *English Caroline Minuscule*, p. xxiii.   [24] Dumville, *English Caroline Script*, pp. 125–6.
[25] The meanings of terms for liturgical books are explained by H. Gneuss, 'Liturgical Books in Anglo-Saxon England and Their Old English Terminology', *Learning and Literature in Anglo-Saxon England: Studies presented to Peter Clemoes on the Occasion of his Sixty-Fifth Birthday*, ed. M. Lapidge and H. Gneuss (Cambridge, 1985), pp. 91–141.

XVII.13 (starting at *Domine*) to 18 and John XI.47–54. The last reading is from Jeremiah, starting at XVIII.18: the legible text on this leaf finishes in the middle of verse 23 at *tua non*.[26] The inclusion of readings both from the gospel of John and from Jeremiah, an Old Testament book, shows that this was a mass lectionary. The rubric before the second text starts *EBDU. IN XL.*, meaning that these were the readings for the fifth week in Lent. Although the customary texts of epistle readings have not been well established,[27] it is possible to compare these gospel readings with those found in other witnesses to Anglo-Saxon liturgical practice.[28] The second gospel lection on these fragments, John XI.47–54, is the reading given for the Friday of the fifth week in Lent in almost all Anglo-Saxon liturgical sources, and is therefore uninformative. However, the gospel reading for the Thursday of the fifth week in Lent, John ch. VII, up to verse 53, is less common than the alternative text for the same day, Luke VII.36–47: five manuscripts give both lection texts, ten give only the Luke text, and three have only this text from John. The gospel-list written by 'Eadwig' in the Grimbald Gospels (BL, Add. 34890) gives only the other reading, Luke VII.36–47; and the Florence gospel lectionary (Florence, Biblioteca Laurenziana, Plut. XVII.20), which 'Eadwig' wrote, gives a different reading from any other Anglo-Saxon witness, preferring Luke XX.1–8. The text found in the Caius fragments, from John chapter VII, was certainly available in early-eleventh-century Christ Church, as London, British Library, Royal 1. D. IX, the book to which 'Eadwig' added a document in Old English, gives both lections; it is also the only reading given in London, British Library, Cotton Tiberius A. ii, a book of continental origin given to the cathedral by King Æthelstan. So although the lection given in this fragment is different from the two distinct readings given in liturgical books written by 'Eadwig Basan', this discrepancy cannot be used as additional evidence that he did not write it, since this lection was certainly available at Christ Church in the period when he was there, from two very important books belonging to that house. The other two manuscripts which contain only this gospel reading for the Thursday of the fifth week in Lent are Cambridge, University Library, Ii. 2. 11, from eleventh-century Exeter; and London, British

---

[26] There are a few variants from the text of the Vulgate edited by R. Weber, *Biblia sacra iuxta vulgatam versionem*, 2 vols. (Stuttgart, 1969). These are *ad Iesum nocte* for *ad eum nocte* in John VII.50; the omission of *ergo* in John XI.47; the omission of the *et* between *nostrum* and *locum* in John XI.48; and the insertion of *in* between [*eu*]*m* and *lingua* in Jer. XVIII.18. Of these, only the omission of *et* in John XI.48 is listed by Weber as occurring in significant manuscripts, in his sigla Z and P, which are both sixth-century Italian manuscripts.

[27] The two 'epistle' readings, Jer. XVII.13–18 and XVIII.18–23, are those given for the Friday and Saturday respectively of the fifth week in Lent in the Sarum use, ed. J. W. Legg, *The Sarum Missal* (Oxford, 1916), pp. 90–1.

[28] U. Lenker, *Die westsächsische Evangelienversion und die Perikopenordnung im angelsächsischen England* (Munich, 1997), pp. xviii–xxi and 315–16.

Library, Add. 40000, written on the Continent in the tenth century, but with later provenance at Thorney; hence no evidence for the location of the Caius fragments can be gleaned from the places of origin of other manuscripts containing this uncommon reading.

Only three other mass lectionaries survive from pre-1100 England and all, like 734/782a, survive only in fragments.[29] One, Durham, Cathedral Library, A. IV. 19, fol. 89, is from eighth-century Northumbria,[30] and the other two – Oslo, Riksarkivet, Lat. fragm. 201 + Oslo, Universitetsbiblioteket, Lat. fragm. 9, and London, Society of Antiquaries 154* – were both written in the tenth century.[31] Cambridge, Gonville and Caius College 734/782a is the only manuscript evidence we have for the use of a mass lectionary in eleventh-century England. The use of a lectionary would seem to be the most straightforward way to obtain the correct lections for each day of the church year; this single book combined the functions of a gospel-list, a gospelbook and an epistolary. Consequently it is surprising that the Caius manuscript is only the fourth fragment of such a book, and that none survives entire. Liturgical books were, of course, even more at risk of destruction than other Anglo-Saxon manuscripts in the later Middle Ages and Early Modern period; first, their texts could soon become obsolete, and therefore valueless; secondly, their workaday nature and the amount of use which they received could make them physically less attractive than other manuscripts. However, gospel lectionaries, although presumably subject to the same vagaries of survival as mass lectionaries and epistolaries, are represented by six whole surviving manuscripts from Anglo-Saxon England, as well as fragments of others.[32] There is no manuscript evidence at all for the use of epistolaries in Anglo-Saxon England, as not even a fragment of one survives.[33] However, Ælfric includes them in a list of books which all priests should own, which suggests that at least some existed.[34] It is possible that the number of liturgical books surviving from Anglo-Saxon England is simply too small for us safely to be able to read anything into comparison of numbers of different types; but there is certainly very little surviving evidence for the epistle lections used by the Anglo-Saxons.

The rediscovery of Cambridge, Gonville and Caius College 734/782a makes it possible to see that the primary significance of these fragments is after all liturgical rather than palaeographical. It may not be a specimen of the hand of 'Eadwig Basan', that innovative and much-imitated figure of eleventh-century

---

[29] Gneuss, 'Liturgical Books', p. 106. [30] Gneuss, 'A Preliminary List', no. 224.

[31] *Ibid.* nos. 870 and 522 respectively. [32] Gneuss, 'Liturgical Books', pp. 106–9.

[33] *Ibid.* p. 110.

[34] B. Fehr, *Die Hirtenbriefe Ælfrics in altenglischer und lateinischer Fassung*, repr. with supplement by P. Clemoes (Darmstadt, 1966), p. 51, lines 20–2: 'Presbyter debet habere etiam spiritalia arma, id sunt diuinos libros, scilicet missalem, lectionarium, quod quidam uocant epistolarium ...'

script history, but the unearthing of this manuscript is still noteworthy for the contribution it makes to our knowledge of late Anglo-Saxon liturgical practice. Manuscript fragments continue to be found in the bindings of early modern printed books, especially in Scandinavia, and further discoveries will probably add to our knowledge of those manuscripts, such as liturgical volumes, whose everyday and easily superseded nature made them less likely to survive to us entire.[35]

---

[35] I am very grateful to David Dumville for his help and advice on this paper.

Contextualizing the *Knútsdrápur*: skaldic praise-poetry at the court of Cnut

MATTHEW TOWNEND

It is generally recognized that during the reign of Cnut the Danish king's court came to represent the focal point for skaldic composition and patronage in the Norse-speaking world. According to the later Icelandic *Skáldatal* or 'List of Poets', no fewer than eight skalds were remembered as having composed for Cnut: Sigvatr Þórðarson, Óttarr svarti, Þórarinn loftunga, Hallvarðr háreksblesi, Bersi Torfuson, Steinn Skaptason, Arnórr Þórðarson jarlaskáld, and Óðarkeptr.[1] Comparing this list with the extant poetic remains, one arrives at the following collection of skaldic praise-poems (some fragmentary) in honour of Cnut: Sigvatr Þórðarson's *Knútsdrápa*;[2] Óttarr svarti's *Knútsdrápa*;[3] Hallvarðr háreksblesi's *Knútsdrápa*;[4] Þórarinn loftunga's *Hǫfuðlausn*[5] and *Tøgdrápa*;[6] and (probably) a fragment by Arnórr jarlaskáld.[7] Of the other poets cited in *Skáldatal*, no verse in honour of Cnut is extant by Bersi Torfuson, and none at all by Steinn Skaptason and Óðarkeptr.[8] However, an extant anonymous poem in honour of Cnut is

---

[1] For the *Skáldatal* list, see *Edda Snorra Sturlusonar*, ed. Sveinbjörn Egilsson, Jón Sigurðsson and Finnur Jónsson, 3 vols. in 4 (Copenhagen, 1848–87) III, 251–86, at 282–3.

[2] For text, see *Den Norsk-Islandske Skjaldedigtning*, ed. Finnur Jónsson, 4 vols. (Copenhagen, 1912–15) IB, 232–4. For (almost complete) translation, see *English Historical Documents c. 500–1042*, ed. D. Whitelock, Eng. Hist. Documents 1 (London, 1955), 310–11 (no. 16, where the poem is titled *Tøgdrápa*).

[3] For text, see *Skjaldedigtning*, ed. Finnur Jónsson IB, 272–5; M. Ashdown, *English and Norse Documents Relating to the Reign of Ethelred the Unready* (Cambridge, 1930), pp. 136–9 (text and translation). For translation, see *English Historical Documents c. 500–1042*, ed. Whitelock, pp. 308–9 (no. 15).

[4] For text, see *Skjaldedigtning*, ed. Finnur Jónsson IB, 293–4; R. Frank, 'King Cnut in the Verse of his Skalds', *The Reign of Cnut: King of England, Denmark and Norway*, ed. A. R. Rumble, Stud. in the Early Hist. of Britain (London, 1994), pp. 106–24, at 119–21 (text and translation).

[5] For text, see *Skjaldedigtning*, ed. Finnur Jónsson IB, 298. For translation, see Frank, 'King Cnut in the Verse of his Skalds', p. 116.

[6] For text, see *Skjaldedigtning*, ed. Finnur Jónsson IB, 298–9. For translation see *English Historical Documents c. 500–1042*, ed. Whitelock, p. 312 (no. 19).

[7] For text, see *Skjaldedigtning*, ed. Finnur Jónsson IB, 326 (strophe 3); D. Whaley, *The Poetry of Arnórr jarlaskáld: an Edition and Study*, Westfield Publ. in Med. Stud. 8 (Turnhout, 1998), 134 and 308–10 (text and translation). For the grounds for believing this fragment is from a poem on Cnut, see *ibid.* pp. 34–5.

[8] Even the name of this obscure skald is uncertain: see *Edda Snorra Sturlusonar*, ed. Sveinbjörn Egilsson *et al.* III, 736–7.

Liðsmannaflokkr,[9] and one is justified in also bringing into general consideration an extant poem in honour of one of Cnut's earls, namely Þórðr Kolbeinsson's *Eiríksdrápa*.[10] There are also a number of *lausavísur* or 'loose verses' believed to have been addressed to Cnut or associated with him, which do not seem to derive from larger poems and whose provenance may thus be less secure:[11] the most important of these is (in Finnur Jónsson's numbering) Óttarr's *lausavísa* 2,[12] while the fragment by Arnórr should also possibly be listed here rather than among the *drápur*. There is also, of course, a good deal of poetry which either mentions Cnut or is, at some remove, composed about him, the most important of which is Sigvatr's *Vestrfararvísur*,[13] but the discussion that follows is concerned only with the poetry composed directly for and in honour of him.

As an initial observation, one may note that such an extant collection of skaldic praise-poetry is remarkable in terms of its sheer quantity: Cnut can be ranked alongside Earl Hákon Sigurðarson, Óláfr Haraldsson and Haraldr harðráði as one of the most prominent of patrons for extant skaldic verse, and without question he is the most important non-Norwegian according to such terms. As has been acknowledged, therefore, skaldic verse associated with Cnut represents a substantial, and reasonably discrete, subject for investigation – a body of poetry which I shall collectively refer to by the shorthand label of 'the *Knútsdrápur*'.[14] In what follows I wish to consider in particular the context or contexts in which these poems in honour of Cnut were originally produced and received, and in doing so to explore more generally the role of original context in the generation of literary meaning for skaldic praise-poetry.

By 'original context' here is meant the circumstances of composition and delivery in the reign of Cnut itself, rather than the manuscript context in which

---

[9] For text, see *Skjaldedigtning*, ed. Finnur Jónsson IB, 391–3; R. Poole, 'Skaldic Verse and Anglo-Saxon History: Some Aspects of the Period 1009–1016', *Speculum* 62 (1987), 265–98, at 281–3 (text and translation); R. G. Poole, *Viking Poems on War and Peace: a Study in Skaldic Narrative*, Toronto Med. Texts and Translations 8 (Toronto, 1991), 86–90 (text and translation); also Ashdown, *English and Norse Documents*, pp. 140–3 (partial text and translation).

[10] For text, see *Skjaldedigtning*, ed. Finnur Jónsson IB, 203–6. For (partial) translation, see *English Historical Documents c. 500–1042*, ed. Whitelock, p. 307 (no. 14).

[11] So, for example, such verses are excluded from Bjarne Fidjestøl's fundamental study of the corpus of skaldic praise-poetry: B. Fidjestøl, *Det Norrøne Fyrstediktet*, Universitetet i Bergen Nordisk Institutts Skriftserie 11 (Øvre Ervik, 1982).

[12] For text, see *Skjaldedigtning*, ed. Finnur Jónsson IB, 275. For translation, see B. Hudson, 'Knútr and Viking Dublin', *Scandinavian Stud.* 66 (1994), 319–35, at 319.

[13] For text, see *Skjaldedigtning*, ed. Finnur Jónsson IB, 226–8; for translation of the stanzas relating to Cnut, see *English Historical Documents c. 500–1042*, ed. Whitelock, p. 311 (no. 17).

[14] The most important studies are D. Hofmann, *Nordisch-Englische Lehnbeziehungen der Wikingerzeit*, Bibliotheca Arnamagnæana 14 (Copenhagen, 1955), 59–101 (§§52–109); Poole, 'Skaldic Verse and Anglo-Saxon History'; and Frank, 'King Cnut in the Verse of his Skalds'. See also A. Campbell, *Skaldic Verse and Anglo-Saxon History*, Dorothea Coke Memorial Lecture (London, 1971); and M. Townend, *English Place-Names in Skaldic Verse*, EPNS es 1 (Nottingham, 1998).

such poetry is preserved. As is well known, virtually all skaldic verse survives only within the prose of later Icelandic sagas (some details of which will have to be attended to later in the discussion), and most long poems have had to be reassembled by gathering together strophes scattered through a number of works, or at least through a number of chapters of one particular work. In doing this there are evidently two major methodological assumptions operative, the first pertaining to accurate oral (and scribal) transmission and the second to accurate editorial reassembling; but both are reasonable and generally accepted. On the first point, the formal complexity of skaldic metre, *dróttkvætt* or otherwise, is famously – and justifiably – held as a protection against garbling or misremembering in the process of oral and memorial transmission.[15] On the second point, the procedures and practice of reassembling longer skaldic poems have been subjected to rigorous and sustained assessment, and seem methodologically secure,[16] though inevitably problems can arise in the (mis-)attribution of particular strophes to particular works, and above all in the ordering of strophes.[17] Strophes which are presented as *lausavísur*, rather than as coming from longer *drápur*, are more problematic, however, and in some cases there is no clear evidence from within the strophes themselves as to whom the verses were addressed, meaning that we only have the opinion of later sagawriters to depend on: an example from among possible *Knútsdrápur* would be Þormóðr Kolbrúnarskáld's *lausavísur* 10 and 11,[18] especially since *Skáldatal* does not reckon Þormóðr among Cnut's poets.[19]

In this article I shall therefore subscribe both to the general practice of reassembling longer skaldic poems – a practice which is, of course, enshrined in Finnur Jónsson's standard edition of the skaldic corpus – and also, in broad terms, to the specific configurations of the *Knútsdrápur* as presented by Finnur Jónsson and refined by later scholars such as Russell Poole. But a belief in the importance of recovering original texts does not necessarily go hand-in-hand with a desire to recover their original contexts, and the ambition here to contextualize the *Knútsdrápur* as closely as possible is motivated by two related

---

[15] See, for example, E. O. G. Turville-Petre, *Scaldic Poetry* (Oxford, 1976), pp. lxvi–lxxiv; B. Fidjestøl, 'Norse–Icelandic Composition in the Oral Period', in his *Selected Papers*, ed. O. E. Haugen and E. Mundal, Viking Collection 9 (Odense, 1997), 303–32.

[16] See, above all, Fidjestøl, *Det Norrøne Fyrstediktet*, and Poole, *Viking Poems on War and Peace*.

[17] See, for example, Poole's discussion of *Liðsmannaflokkr* (*Viking Poems on War and Peace*, pp. 90–8). [18] For texts, see *Skjaldedigtning*, ed. Finnur Jónsson IB, 262–3.

[19] For the episode of Þormóðr's encounter with Cnut (in which these two *lausavísur* are quoted), see *Olafs Saga hins Helga: die 'Legendarische Saga' über Olaf den Heiligen (Hs. Delagard. Saml. Nr.8¹¹)*, ed. A. Heinrichs, D. Janshen, E. Radicke and H. Röhn (Heidelberg, 1982), pp. 124–8; and *Óláfs saga helga* in *Flateyjarbók*, ed. S. Nordal, V. Bjarnar and Finnbogi Guðmundsson, 4 vols. (Akranes, 1944–5) II, 291–4; for discussion, see further below. For discussion of the verses, see Hofmann, *Nordisch-Englische Lehnbeziehungen*, pp. 100–1 (§109).

impulses, which may be crudely characterized as those of literary history and of literary criticism. The first of these needs little justification: since, as indicated above, the collection of skaldic poetry in honour of Cnut is one of the three or four most important collections in the entire skaldic corpus, there is plainly much to be gained from an attempt to explore some of the literary-historical aspects of the original production and reception of such a collection. The literary-critical impulse, on the other hand, derives from the conviction that attention to original context is an essential activity for the study of the literary meaning of skaldic praise-poetry in general, not just for the study of the *Knútsdrápur* (indeed, it is arguably essential for the study of all praise-poetry). Skaldic praise-poetry is, in literary terms, a genre that has not survived its contexts at all well, as so much of its meaning appears to be contingent on the environment of original production and reception, and hence one might cogently argue that the literary meaning of skaldic praise-poetry is most fully accessible only by the fullest possible attention to original context. In such a view, context is not something prior or ancillary to literary meaning, as in much traditional literary study, but rather is itself a substantial part of the meaning. As the historical sociologist Norbert Elias writes, albeit with regard to the more long-lasting artistic productions of later French court culture:

Much that court people thought worthy of endeavour has paled and seems almost worthless now. But by no means everything. Closely bound up with court values that have lost their meaning and lustre are others that have lost very little. They include a large number of works of art and literature that are characteristic of the special cultivation of taste in court society; they also include a large number of buildings. We understand the language of forms better if we also understand the type of compulsion to display and of aesthetic sensibility characteristic of this society in conjunction with status competition. Thus social phenomena that have not lost value are connected to others that have.[20]

One can therefore readily observe an integral connection between the formal qualities of skaldic praise-poetry and its function as a social (or socio-political) phenomenon, and so for simple reasons such as these it seems mistaken, or at the very least inadequate, to consider skaldic praise-poetry in decontextualized isolation, with purely aesthetic criteria taking precedence over more functional ones.

The possible contexts within which to consider the *Knútsdrápur* are multifarious, and the most important can, for the sake of clarity, be formulated as a series of unnecessary dichotomies (unnecessary because in most instances it is not a case of either/or but rather, in varying degrees, of both/and). One might ask for example whether one should be thinking about these poems in terms of the

---

[20] N. Elias, *The Court Society* (Oxford, 1983), pp. 76–7.

Skaldic praise-poetry at the court of Cnut

political situation in the early years of Cnut's reign or the later; whether one should locate them to England or Denmark, and if – as is generally thought – to the former, whether to London or Winchester; whether one should consider them within the literary framework of Old Norse poetic tradition, or of Anglo-Saxon, and whether one should postulate for them a mixed or a homogeneous audience. To these one must add such broader contexts as the established traditions of Norse praise-poetry and the corpus of pre-existing verse in memorial circulation in the early eleventh century,[21] as well as Cnut's political circumstances as conqueror of England and the West Saxon dynasty[22] and occupier of an ascendant position over his great Scandinavian rival Óláfr Haraldsson of Norway.[23] Depending on the trust one chooses to place in later saga-accounts, one can attend to the biographies and careers of Cnut's poets, and to their positions in the literary field of skaldic culture; at the least one can partially reconstruct careers from extant works. As usual, everything depends on the perspective one adopts: here, the contexts in which one views the *Knútsdrápur* will substantially determine one's insights and emphases, and in what follows I shall primarily endeavour to contextualize the poems in terms of their date of composition and their geographical and physical place of delivery.

Cnut was king of all England from 1017 to 1035. With the possible exception of Sigvatr's poem (discussed below) there is no reason to believe that any of the *Knútsdrápur* are *erfidrápur* or memorial lays, and so by the very fact of Cnut's regnal dates one can position these poems within a fairly narrow eighteen-year band. Such ready datability may seem an obvious and fortuitous quality of praise-poetry, but in the study of early medieval vernacular poetry such a quality is all too rare and therefore not at all to be taken for granted. In attempting to date the *Knútsdrápur* more closely one must substantially ignore the chronological and narrative sequences in which their verses occur in later Icelandic sagas, since in many cases those sequences are likely to have derived (whether correctly or not) from the verses themselves, and in general terms saga chronology is a famously inexact instrument; in particular, the saga accounts of Cnut's reign tend to misplace verses within their chronological framework, so that for example verses belonging either before or after Cnut's Holy River campaign are sometimes intermingled.[24] None the less, and as will be seen below, the

---

[21] On the steady accumulation of a memorized corpus, see B. Fidjestøl, 'Icelandic Sagas and Poems on Princes: Literature and Society in Archaic West Norse Culture', in his *Selected Papers*, ed. Haugen and Mundal, pp. 228–54, at 246.

[22] See M. K. Lawson, *Cnut: the Danes in England in the Early Eleventh Century* (London, 1993), pp. 9–48.

[23] See *ibid.* pp. 95–102; P. Sawyer, 'Cnut's Scandinavian Empire', *The Reign of Cnut*, ed. Rumble, pp. 10–22.

[24] B. T. Hudson, 'Cnut and the Scottish Kings', *EHR* 107 (1992), 350–60, at 357.

saga-accounts must not be ignored wholly, and if one attends to them carefully then some intriguingly self-consistent patterns emerge.

There are also two notorious cruces of Cnut chronology which must be attended to,[25] namely the date of the battle of Holy River, and the question whether Cnut made one or two pilgrimages to Rome. MS E of the *Anglo-Saxon Chronicle* (the only version to mention it) ascribes Holy River to the year 1025, but there are no entries for 1026 and 1027 and so the 1025 entry may well be misplaced.[26] Later saga accounts of the reign of Óláfr Haraldsson suggest a date three years before Óláfr's death in 1030, so giving 1027.[27] But Cnut's 1027 Letter to his subjects indicates that Holy River occurred shortly before his time in Rome, in the course of which he attended the coronation of Conrad II; this occurred in early 1027, so late 1026 results as the most probable date for the Holy River campaign. Recent historiography seems to have reached a consensus over this date, and it will be followed here.[28] As for a possible second pilgrimage to Rome (subsequent to the first, securely dated to early 1027), this has primarily been suggested on account of the *Anglo-Saxon Chronicle*:[29] MSS DE give 1031 as the year in which *for Cnut cyng to Rome*.[30] However, no version of the *Chronicle* records Cnut's 1027 pilgrimage, and so it is generally agreed that 1031 is a mistake, plausibly arising from a misreading of MXXVI as MXXXI:[31] 1026 would then be an acceptable date for Cnut's departure on pilgrimage, as he was certainly in Rome in time for Conrad's coronation on 26 March 1027, and indeed may well have proceeded directly to Rome from the Holy River campaign in late 1026. In what follows, therefore, it will be assumed that Cnut made only one pilgrimage to Rome; again, although less clear-cut than in the case of Holy River, this seems to be the consensus in modern historiography.[32]

---

[25] For a helpful chronological table, see A. Rumble, 'Introduction: Cnut in Context', *The Reign of Cnut*, ed. Rumble, pp. 1–9, at 3–5.

[26] On the value and shortcomings of the *Chronicle* as a source for Cnut's reign, see Lawson, *Cnut*, pp. 49–54.

[27] *Encomium Emmae Reginae*, ed. A. Campbell, Camden 3rd ser. 72 (London, 1949), 82.

[28] Lawson, *Cnut*, pp. 96–7; Rumble, 'Introduction', p. 5; Sawyer, 'Cnut's Scandinavian Empire', pp. 18–19; S. Keynes, 'Cnut's Earls', *The Reign of Cnut*, ed. Rumble, pp. 43–88, at 86.

[29] *Encomium Emmae*, ed. Campbell, p. lxii.

[30] *The Anglo-Saxon Chronicle MS D*, ed. G. P. Cubbin, The AS Chronicle: a Collaborative Edition 6 (Cambridge, 1996), 65 ('King Cnut went to Rome'). (Unless indicated, all translations are my own.) One late tradition, however, suggests 1035: see F. Barlow: 'Two Notes: Cnut's Second Pilgrimage and Queen Emma's Disgrace in 1043', *EHR* 73 (1958), 649–56, at 650–1.

[31] Lawson, *Cnut*, p. 102.

[32] *Ibid.* pp. 102–4; Rumble, 'Introduction', p. 5; S. Keynes, 'Introduction to the 1998 Reprint', *Encomium Emmae Reginae*, ed. A. Campbell, Camden Classic Reprints 4 (Cambridge, 1998), lxi–lxii. MSS DE also mention under 1031 an expedition to Scotland by Cnut and the submission to him of a number of Scottish kings: as this is not of great importance in determining the dates of the *Knútsdrápur* there is no need to engage here with this lesser crux of Cnut chronology (see Hudson, 'Cnut and the Scottish Kings'; Lawson, *Cnut*, pp. 104–5).

Let us then review the various *Knútsdrápur* one at a time, to see how precisely they can be dated within Cnut's reign, before proceeding to an assessment of the literary significance of the resultant datings: what follows will be unavoidably detailed in many places, not least on account of the general difficulties in accurately dating skaldic poems, but it constitutes an essential stage of the argument. The two earliest poems appear to be the anonymous *Liðsmannaflokkr* and – though not a *Knútsdrápa* proper – Þórðr's *Eiríksdrápa*, and the dating of both has been cogently discussed by Russell Poole. Poole's conclusion with regard to *Liðsmannaflokkr* is that the poem 'is what it purports to be, an expression of rank-and-file jubilation at Knútr's conquest, composed almost contemporaneously with the events it describes':[33] this conclusion is derived from the Old English linguistic influence on the poem,[34] and the poem's diplomatic handling of the relationship between Cnut and Þorkell.[35] In other words, *Liðsmannaflokkr* should most plausibly be dated to 1017, or even late 1016.[36] In his discussion of the date of *Eiríksdrápa* Poole draws attention to lines 5–6 of the eleventh strophe, which read (following his text and translation) *regn þorins rekka / rann of þingamonnum* 'the rain of the dwarf's comrade [= poetry] ran over the retainers' – seeming to indicate that the poem was indeed recited to Cnut's élite followers (the *þingamenn*).[37] The *terminus post quem* is provided by the poem's celebration of the military events of 1016, and the *terminus ante quem* (since there is no indication that the poem is an *erfidrápa* or memorial lay) by the date of Eiríkr's death – apparently 1023.[38] Poole therefore reasonably concludes that '[t]he burden of proof rests with those who wish to place the poem significantly later than 1024',[39] and on account of the poem's subject matter the likelihood is for a date closer to 1016 than 1023.

Of the other *Knútsdrápur* the easiest to deal with is Arnórr's. In dating the probable fragment from Arnórr's poem on Cnut one naturally trusts in Diana Whaley's explication of the chronology of Arnórr's career: on the basis of Arnórr's likely date of birth (*c.* 1011) she suggests a date somewhere between *c.* 1031 and 1035 (Cnut's death),[40] but there is nothing in the single extant *helmingr* or half-strophe to permit any closer dating.

For Hallvarðr háreksblesi there is no saga evidence at all, and nothing is known of the poet beyond the eight stanzas said to come from his *Knútsdrápa* (of

[33] Poole, 'Skaldic Verse and Anglo-Saxon History', p. 286.
[34] Hofmann, *Nordisch-Englische Lehnbeziehungen*, pp. 59–71 (§§52–61); Poole, 'Skaldic Verse and Anglo-Saxon History', pp. 284–6.   [35] Poole, *Viking Poems on War and Peace*, pp. 99–107.
[36] *Ibid.* p. 108; see also Ashdown, *English and Norse Documents*, p. 206.
[37] Poole, 'Skaldic Verse and Anglo-Saxon History', pp. 270–1.
[38] *Encomium Emmae*, ed. Campbell, p. 70; Keynes, 'Cnut's Earls', p. 58.
[39] Poole, 'Skaldic Verse and Anglo-Saxon History', p. 271.
[40] Whaley, *The Poetry of Arnórr jarlaskáld*, pp. 41–3.

151

Matthew Townend

which five are *helmingar* and one is a *stef* or refrain): six of the eight are preserved only in Snorri's *Edda*, and hence lack the biographical or anecdotal framework which preservation in kings' sagas tends to impart.[41] The exceptions are the two complete eight-line stanzas: following Finnur Jónsson's numbering, stanza 3 is preserved in *Knýtlinga saga* (where it is introduced *Svá segir Hallvarðr Háreksblesi í Knútsdrápu*),[42] and stanza 6 in various sagas of Óláfr Haraldsson (*Svá segir Hallvarðr Háreksblesi, er hann orti um Knút konung*).[43] If one adds in his mention in *Skáldatal*, then such is the sum of circumstantial knowledge of Hallvarðr and his *Knútsdrápa*. However, internal evidence suggests Hallvarðr's poem should be dated after Cnut's acquisition of Norway, and probably quite soon after. For although the early stanzas look back to Cnut's conquest of England, with a particular emphasis on Cnut's status as a sea-king, stanza 6 declares:

> Englandi ræðr Yngvi
> einn (hefsk friðr at beinni)
> bǫðrakkr bœnar nǫkkva
> barkrjóðr ok Danmǫrku;
> ok hefr (odda Leiknar)
> jalm-Freyr und sik malma
> (hjaldrǫrr haukum þverrir
> hungr) Nóregi þrungit.[44]

Ok in line 5 would seem to suggest a recent addition: to his long-standing domains of England and Denmark, the great king has now added Norway. The date of 1028 for Cnut's Norway expedition is supplied by the *Anglo-Saxon Chronicle* (MSS CDE), as is the return to England in 1029 (MSS DE), and such a dating correlates exactly with later saga chronology for the reign of Óláfr Haraldsson. While its scattered preservation means that we can be even less than usually sanguine about possessing the complete poem, it is notable that Hallvarðr's extant verses make no mention of Sweden, again perhaps suggesting that it is Norway that constitutes the most impressive – and most recent – glory to be celebrated. One may therefore suggest a date of *c.* 1029 for Hallvarðr's *Knútsdrápa*, though the only real *terminus ante quem* is Cnut's death in 1035.

---

[41] *Skjaldedigtning*, ed. Finnur Jónsson IA, 317–18; Fidjestøl, *Det Norrøne Fyrstediktet*, p. 125. All six are in *Skáldskaparmál*, and in Faulkes' edition are Verses 115, 239, 258, 311, 348 and 388 (Snorri Sturluson, *Edda: Skáldskaparmál*, ed. A. Faulkes, 2 vols. (London, 1998)).

[42] *Danakonunga Sǫgur*, ed. Bjarni Guðnason, Íslenzk Fornrit 35 (Reykjavík, 1982), 103 ('As Hallvarðr háreksblesi says in *Knútsdrápa*').

[43] Snorri Sturluson, *Heimskringla*, ed. Bjarni Aðalbjarnarson, Íslenzk Fornrit 26–8 (Reykjavík, 1941–51) II, 311 ('As Hallvarðr háreksblesi says, when he composed about King Cnut').

[44] *Skjaldedigtning*, ed. Finnur Jónsson IB, 294. 'The prince, the battle-bold bark-reddener of the ship of prayer [= warrior], alone rules England and Denmark; peace comes to pass without trouble; and the noise-Freyr of weapons [= warrior] has subdued under him Norway; the battle-eager one diminishes hunger for the hawks of the Leikn of spears [= ravens].'

152

Sigvatr's *Knútsdrápa* is essentially concerned with three events, and would appear to be able to be dated fairly narrowly, perhaps even to a particular year: stanzas 1 and 2 deal briefly with Cnut's conquest of England, stanzas 2 to 9 (the main substance of the poem) with the Holy River campaign in 1026, and stanzas 10 and 11 with Cnut's pilgrimage to Rome. As has been noted, this pilgrimage took place in early 1027. Since Sigvatr was back in the service of Ólafr Haraldsson by the time of Cnut's 1028 expedition to Norway, this would appear to date his *Knútsdrápa* to (most probably) mid- or late 1027. Approximate corroboration for such a date comes in Sigvatr's own collection of verses known as *Vestrfararvísur*, which record the poet's trading and diplomatic journeys in western Europe on behalf of Ólafr: in the course of these journeys he visited Cnut's court in England. The content of these important verses will be returned to later; for present purposes what matters is the datability of the travels described in them to the mid-1020s. Finnur Jónsson dates the verses (and therefore the travel) to 1025–6,[45] presumably because he is following Snorri, who in his *Heimskringla* account places Sigvatr's visit to Cnut before Holy River, and his return to Ólafr after it.[46] But the *Vestrfararvísur* themselves refer only to Cnut's preparations for war against Norway and Ólafr, not against Sweden and Ǫnundr, and so they could equally well be concerned with Cnut's preparations for his 1028 campaign rather than his 1026 one: indeed, such a date would be more plausible on account of the attention given in stanzas 3 and 4 to Hákon Eiríksson, shortly to become Cnut's regent in Norway. The *Vestrfararvísur* therefore supply a reasonably secure date for Sigvatr's visit to Cnut's court, and this date corresponds perfectly well with the date for Sigvatr's *Knútsdrápa* arrived at by internal analysis of its contents. Everything would thus seem to point very clearly to a composition in 1027 or thereabouts.

There are, however, three problems, the first of which is a very strange statement in *Magnúss saga góða* in *Heimskringla*, concerning Sigvatr's movements after returning from his pilgrimage to Rome (which occurred in 1030):

Sigvatr fór ǫndverðan vetr austr um Kjǫl til Jamtalands ok þá til Helsingjalands ok kom fram í Svíþjóð ok fór þegar til Ástríðar dróttningar ok var með henni í góðu yfirlæti langa hríð. Ok var hann ok með Ǫnundi konungi, bróður hennar, ok þá af honum tíu merkr brenndar. Svá segir í Knútsdrápu.[47]

---

[45] *Ibid.* IB, 226.
[46] Snorri Sturluson, *Heimskringla*, ed. Bjarni Aðalbjarnarson II, 271–3 and 292–3.
[47] *Ibid.* III, 17–18. ('At the beginning of winter Sigvatr went eastwards over "the Keel" into Jamtaland, and then into Helsingjaland, and arrived in Sweden and went at once to Queen Ástríðr, and remained with her in her good favour for a long time. And he was also with King Ǫnundr, her brother, and received from him ten marks of pure silver. So it [or 'he'] says in *Knútsdrápa*.')

It is difficult to know what to make of this. If taken at face value, it would indicate that Sigvatr's poem must postdate this visit to Qnundr in the early 1030s; but no verse is quoted and, as Bjarni Aðalbjarnarson points out,[48] no extant stanza of Sigvatr's poem says anything remotely of this kind (though Qnundr is mentioned in stanza 4 as one of Cnut's enemies at Holy River, and both Sigvatr and Óttarr are enigmatically listed as Qnundr's poets in *Skáldatal*). Can Snorri have made a mistake here? One hesitates to suggest so; but as Judith Jesch has demonstrated, there are some odd things going on in this section of *Magnúss saga*, and the material and verses employed by Snorri in this episode are found in no other source.[49] A second, more coherent problem in dating Sigvatr's *Knútsdrápa* to *c.* 1027 is that *Fagrskinna* and the *Legendary saga* of St Óláfr both describe the poem as an *erfidrápa*. In these two works the poem is not explicitly titled *Knútsdrápa*, and the first quotation from it is introduced as follows: *sva sem sægir Sighuatr skalld i ærvisdrapo, þæirri er hann orte um Knut* (*Legendary saga*) and *sem segir Sighvatr skáld í erfidrápu þeiri, er hann orti um Knút gamla* (*Fagrskinna*).[50] However, that these two sources are not independent witnesses, but are here drawing on a common source (at whatever remove) is confirmed by their almost identical introduction of stanza 3: *I þesse samu drapo orte Sighvatr um norðanfærð Olafs konongs* (*Legendary saga*) and *Í þessi sǫmu drápu sagði Sighvatr frá norðanferð Óláfs konungs* (*Fagrskinna*).[51] In all other texts – *Óláfs saga helga*, *Heimskringla*, *Knýtlinga saga* and the *þáttr af Ragnars sonum* – Sigvatr's poem is given the title *Knútsdrápa*, and without any indication that it is a memorial lay.[52] The third objection, and itself possibly the reason why the author of a source antecedent to the *Legendary saga* and *Fagrskinna* thought the poem to be an *erfidrápa*, is the use of the past tense in the refrain-like opening lines of stanzas 3 and 7, which state that *Knútr var und himnum*.[53] Such a reading is by no means universal in the saga manuscripts

[48] *Ibid.* III, 18, n. 1.
[49] J. Jesch, 'In Praise of Ástríðr Óláfsdóttir', *SBVS* 24 (1994), 1–18, at 11–13.
[50] *Olafs Saga hins Helga*, ed. Heinrichs *et al.*, p. 140 ('As Sigvatr the poet says in the memorial lay which he composed about Cnut'); *Ágrip af Nóregskonungasǫgum. Fagrskinna-Nóregs Konunga Tal*, ed. Bjarni Einarsson, Íslenzk Fornrit 29 (Reykjavík, 1985), 183 ('As Sigvatr the poet says in the memorial lay which he composed about Cnut the Old').
[51] *Olafs Saga hins Helga*, ed. Heinrichs *et al.*, p. 142 ('In the same poem Sigvatr composed about King Óláfr's journey from the north'); *Fagrskinna*, ed. Bjarni Einarsson, p. 184 ('In the same poem Sigvatr told about King Óláfr's journey from the north'). On the complex textual relations between the works with regard to their Cnut material, see further A. Campbell, '*Knúts Saga*', *SBVS* 13 (1946–53), 238–48.
[52] Snorri Sturluson, *Saga Óláfs konungs hins helga: Den store saga om Olav den hellige*, ed. O. A. Johnsen and Jón Helgason, 2 vols., Norsk Historisk Kjeldeskrift-Institutt (Oslo, 1941) I, 425 and 428; Snorri Sturluson, *Heimskringla*, ed. Bjarni Aðalbjarnarson I, 270 and 274; *Danakonunga Sǫgur*, ed. Bjarni Guðnason, pp. 82 (*þáttr af Ragnars sonum*) and 120 (*Knýtlinga saga*).
[53] *Skjaldedigtning*, ed. Finnur Jónsson IB, 232 and 233 ('Cnut was under the heavens').

preserving these stanzas, and some fairly authoritative ones (such as Jöfraskinna) have present tense *er* 'is';[54] but none the less *var* remains the majority reading.[55] Several responses are possible, though, if one wishes to argue that the use of the past tense here does not necessarily indicate composition after the death of Cnut. Firstly, the past tense is the normal tense for skaldic praise-poetry anyway (though normally, of course, for actions that have been completed rather than states that are continuing). Secondly, and more sceptically, the degree of variability inherent in the oral transmission of skaldic verse is such as to make *var* an unauthoritative reading, even though it is the majority form: *var* and *er* could be in free variation depending on whether the poem was being presented as a contemporary praise-poem or an *erfidrápa*.[56] Thirdly, and most tellingly, metrical considerations would cast severe doubt on the majority reading: since the *tøglag* metre of Sigvatr's *Knútsdrápa* requires only four syllables to the line, past tense *Knútr var und himnum* does not scan, whereas present tense *Knútr er und himnum* does (with elision),[57] so forming a parallel with Þórarinn's *Knútr es und sólar*.[58]

Collectively, though, these three objections cannot be entirely explained away, and opinions can be found from eminent skaldicists for both dating positions: Bjarni Einarsson for example characterizes Sigvatr's *Knútsdrápa* as 'a eulogy of Canute the Great made in that king's lifetime',[59] while Russell Poole states that the poem 'was composed after Knud's death (1035), perhaps on the occasion of Magnús's reconciliation with Hardacnut (1038)'.[60] But the reasons given above for composition in Cnut's lifetime and at his court remain the more persuasive, and in addition to the certainty of Sigvatr's visit to Cnut's court and the apparent datability of the poem by its own internal coherence, two further general points may be made in support. The first is metrical: as noted above, Sigvatr's poem is composed in the innovative metre of *tøglag*, in which each line has only four syllables but otherwise fulfils most of the same stringent requirements of alliteration and rhyme

---

54 *Ibid.* IA, 249–50.   55 Fidjestøl, *Det Norrøne Fyrstediktet*, p. 120.
56 For an illuminating discussion of skaldic variability, see R. Poole, 'Variants and Variability in the Text of Egill's *Hǫfuðlausn*', *The Politics of Editing Medieval Texts: Papers Given at the Twenty-Seventh Annual Conference on Editorial Problems, University of Toronto, 1–2 November 1991*, ed. R. Frank (New York, 1993), pp. 65–105.
57 Hence Roberta Frank silently emends to *Knútr's und himnum* (Frank, 'King Cnut in the Verse of his Skalds', p. 116), a reading also adopted by Kock (E. A. Kock, *Notationes Norrænæ: Anteckningar till Edda och Skaldediktning*, 28 vols., Lunds Universitets Årsskrift ns (Lund, 1923–44) XX, 15 (§2516)).
58 *Skjaldedigtning*, ed. Finnur Jónsson IB, 298 ('Cnut is under the sun's . . .').
59 Bjarni Einarsson, 'De Normannorum Atrocitate, or on the Execution of Royalty by the Aquiline Method', *SBVS* 22 (1986), 79–82, at 79.
60 R. Poole, 'Sighvatr Þórðarson', *Medieval Scandinavia: an Encyclopedia*, ed. P. Pulsiano (New York, 1993), pp. 580–1, at 581.

as *dróttkvætt*.[61] The only other early poem in this metre is Þórarinn loftunga's *Tøgdrápa*, and hence it appears that this metrical development is one that comes directly out of Cnut's court.[62] The second point is linguistic. Dietrich Hofmann firmly aligns himself against those who would regard Sigvatr's *Knútsdrápa* as an *erfidrápa*: Hofmann notes that the poem makes more sense as praise for a living king, but his crucial demonstration is of the extensive degree of English influence on the language of the poem – far greater than is to be found in the rest of Sigvatr's work, and which in Hofmann's view is only explicable in terms of a mixed Anglo-Norse milieu for the poem.[63] There are thus strong internal grounds for believing that Sigvatr's poem is contemporary after all, from *c*. 1027, whereas the incompatible signals that it is a later work are (with the possible exception of the use of the past tense in the refrain lines) external and far from contemporary. Have the memories of two poems become confused in the course of transmission? Possibly so, though it seems a desperate counsel.[64] *Skáldatal* places Sigvatr at the top of the list of all Cnut's poets, and this would seem an odd position to occupy on the basis of an *erfidrápa* alone, implying again that Sigvatr was famous for composing in honour of Cnut during the king's lifetime. At the very least one can conclude that Sigvatr visited Cnut's court at the time of his travels recorded in *Vestrfararvísur* and composed poetry in his honour: that the extant *Knútsdrápa* is the poetry that Sigvatr composed then is a separate assumption, but on the whole it seems more likely than that it is an *erfidrápa* that somehow also managed to take in the generosity of Qnundr in the 1030s.

The dating of Þórarinn's *Tøgdrápa* – the companion *tøglag* poem to Sigvatr's *Knútsdrápa* – can be more easily achieved. The prime subject of the poem is Cnut's 1028 expedition to Norway in which he drove out Óláfr Haraldsson and so gained authority over that country, and the poem presents a place-name-driven itinerary of the progress of Cnut's fleet (*Limafjǫrðr*, *Agðir*, and so on), at the end of which the penultimate stanza 7 declares:

> Þá gaf sínum
> snjallr gǫrvallan
> Nóreg nefa

---

[61] On *tøglag* (also called *tøgdrápulag*), see further Turville-Petre, *Scaldic Poetry*, pp. xxxv–xxxvi; Snorri Sturluson, *Edda: Háttatal*, ed. A. Faulkes (Oxford, 1991), pp. 29–30, 66–7 and 84–5; A. Faulkes, 'The Use of Snorri's Verse-Forms by Earlier Norse Poets', *Snorrastefna: 25.–27. júlí 1990*, ed. Úlfar Bragason, Rit Stofnunar Sigurðar Nordals 1 (Reykjavík, 1992), 35–51, at 44.

[62] Frank, 'King Cnut in the Verse of his Skalds', p. 109.

[63] Hofmann, *Nordisch-Englische Lehnbeziehungen*, pp. 87–93 (§§86–97); see also R. Frank, 'Viking Atrocity and Skaldic Verse: the Rite of the Blood-Eagle', *EHR* 99 (1984), 332–43, at 339.

[64] Lee Hollander suggested that there were indeed two *Knútsdrápur* by Sigvatr, that the *Knútsdrápa* composed in the mid-1020s should be carefully distinguished from the *Knútsdrápa* composed in the mid-1030s, and that the extant *Knútsdrápa* is the latter (L. M. Hollander, 'Sigvat Thordson and his Poetry', *Scandinavian Stud.* 16 (1940), 43–67, at 55).

njótr veg Jóta,
ok gaf sínum
(segik þat) megi
dals dagvélir
Danmǫrk svana.[65]

The son to whom Cnut entrusted Denmark was presumably Harthacnut, his only son by Emma of Normandy.[66] Cnut's *nefi* was Hákon Eiríksson, with *nefi* here specifically meaning 'nephew' and not simply 'male relative': Hákon's father, earl Eiríkr Hákonarson (the subject of þórðr's *Eiríksdrápa*), married Cnut's sister, Gyða (daughter of Sveinn Haraldsson), and so Hákon was Cnut's sister's son.[67] He was also probably the husband of Cnut's niece: John of Worcester records that Hákon married Gunnhildr, the daughter of another of Cnut's sisters (and so, if true, Hákon and Gunnhildr would be first cousins).[68] However, Hákon was drowned in the Pentland Firth in 1030; and since þórarinn's *Tøgdrápa* seems to be composed soon after Cnut's Norway expedition, and certainly before Hákon's death, one arrives at the narrow dating band for the poem of 1029–30, with the likelihood of being earlier rather than later within that period. As for *Hǫfuðlausn*, þórarinn's other extant poem for Cnut, the fragmentary state of the poem (a single two-line *stef*) does not permit dating from internal references as *Tøgdrápa* does, and so the question is whether or not the two poems are roughly contemporaneous – or at least, were composed in the same period of service to Cnut. For what it is worth, saga evidence presents *Hǫfuðlausn* as the poem with which þórarinn escaped punishment and so entered Cnut's service, and *Tøgdrápa* as the fruit of that service, a poem arising from þórarinn's actual presence on Cnut's 1028 expedition.[69] It is probable that this sequence is derived from the titles and contents of the poems themselves; but as a deduction from such evidence the sequence remains inherently likely, and a reasonable supposition. This would mean that one should provisionally date þórarinn's *Hǫfuðlausn* to *c.* 1027–8.

Turning lastly to the work of Óttarr svarti, his single *lausavísa* on Cnut is as follows:

---

[65] *Skjaldedigtning*, ed. Finnur Jónsson IB, 299. 'Then the bold land-enjoyer of the Jutes gave to his nephew all Norway; and – I declare it – the distributor of the sun of the dale of swans [= gold] gave to his son Denmark.' For an alternative translation of the kenning in the second *helmingr*, see *English Historical Documents c. 500–1042*, ed. Whitelock, p. 312, which follows the reading preferred in Kock, *Notationes Norrænæ* XI, 103 (§1792).
[66] See N. Lund, 'Cnut's Danish Kingdom', *The Reign of Cnut*, ed. Rumble, pp. 27–42, at 39.
[67] Keynes, 'Cnut's Earls', pp. 57 and 61–2.
[68] *The Chronicle of John of Worcester*, ed. R. R. Darlington and P. McGurk, 3 vols. (Oxford, 1995–) II, 510–11.
[69] Snorri Sturluson, *Heimskringla*, ed. Bjarni Aðalbjarnarson II, 307–10; *Danakonunga Sǫgur*, ed. Bjarni Guðnason, pp. 124–5.

Svá skal kveðja
konung Dana
Íra ok Engla
ok Eybúa,
at hans fari
með himinskautum
lǫndum ǫllum
lof víðara.[70]

This strophe has recently received helpful discussion from Benjamin Hudson, who reviews evidence for possible political connections between Cnut and the Scandinavian colonies in Ireland, and concludes that '[t]he assembled evidence, some of which is open to different interpretations, is sensible in the light of a submission by the king of Dublin to Knútr'.[71] Hudson offers the date of 1026–9 for this verse,[72] but in doing so he is simply elaborating on Finnur Jónsson's earlier proposal of *c.* 1026,[73] and in fact none of the material Hudson reviews is able to supply a precise date. The king of Dublin in Cnut's time was Sigtryggr silkiskegg, and the closest Hudson comes to demonstrating an explicit and datable connection between the two kings is in his suggestion that Sigtryggr is to be identified with the *Sihtric dux* who attests three of Cnut's English charters in the late 1020s and early 1030s:[74] unfortunately, such an identification is unlikely, and Keynes's proposal that *Sihtric dux* was an earl established in Hertfordshire is clearly preferable.[75] The result is thus a compilation of disparate hints that collectively make the Cnut-Sigtryggr connection a plausible proposal but are unable to supply a closely datable context for Óttarr's *lausavísa*; none the less, the material that Hudson gathers tends to congregate in the second rather than the first half of Cnut's reign. Lesley Abrams contrasts this verse with Cnut's Letter of 1027, and observes that in the 1027 document Cnut is proclaimed as the king of England, Denmark, Norway and some of Sweden – but not of Dublin or Ireland.[76] This is true, but on the other hand Óttarr's strophe does not mention the Norwegians or Swedes. Two possible explanations therefore suggest themselves: that the Óttarr strophe predates Cnut's claims to dominion over Norway and Sweden (that is, it is pre-1026); or that the choice of peoples and territories

---

[70] *Skjaldedigtning*, ed. Finnur Jónsson IB, 275 ('I shall so greet the king of the Danes, of the Irish and English and Island-dwellers, that his fame will travel more widely through all the lands under the regions of heaven'). It should be noted that *himinskautum* represents an emendation by Finnur Jónsson: the reading of the manuscripts is the perfectly acceptable *himinkrǫptum* '(under) the pillars of heaven' (*ibid.* IA, 299; Hudson, 'Knútr and Viking Dublin', p. 319, n. 1).
[71] Hudson, 'Knútr and Viking Dublin', p. 335.   [72] *Ibid.* p. 319.
[73] *Skjaldedigtning*, ed. Finnur Jónsson IB, 275.
[74] Hudson, 'Knútr and Viking Dublin', pp. 330–2; see also Lawson, *Cnut*, p. 106.
[75] Keynes, 'Cnut's Earls', p. 65.
[76] L. Abrams, 'The Conversion of the Scandinavians of Dublin', *ANS* 20 (1998), 1–29, at 27.

is not primarily governed by chronology or a census-like exhaustiveness, but rather by geographical unity – that is, that Óttarr is deliberately restricting his range of reference to the British Isles.[77]

The strophe cannot be (or at least is very unlikely to be) part of Óttarr's *Knútsdrápa* proper (although it would make an attractive opening stanza), as it is in a different metre, and the extant *Knútsdrápa*, as reassembled, is metrically homogeneous; none the less, it would be a sound working assumption to suppose that *Knútsdrápa* and *lausavísa* are roughly contemporary, and derive from the same period of service at Cnut's court. It is however a difficult task to determine the likely date of Óttarr's *Knútsdrápa*, and for this reason it has been left till last of all. Traditionally the poem has been ascribed to the period after the battle of Holy River in 1026, as the last stanza (of eleven) celebrates that conflict (*Svíum hnekðir þú, . . . þars ǫ en helga . . . heitir*);[78] furthermore, a phrase in stanza 5 describes Cnut as the *Svía þrengvir* 'oppressor of the Swedes'. So for Óttarr's poem Finnur Jónsson suggests 1026, and Russell Poole any time after Holy River.[79] This dating may well be correct, but it is worth noting how little the poem as a whole is concerned with Holy River, and indeed with events occurring after 1016. This may be the result of loss of stanzas in the course of transmission, but as it now survives (and is reassembled) stanzas 1 to 10 celebrate Cnut's conquest of England, while only stanza 11 celebrates Holy River. So stanzas 1 and 2 are concerned with preparation and the voyage to England, and stanzas 3 and 4 with first attacks; while stanzas 5 to 10 are place-name-specific in their account of battles in or near (*inter alia*) the Ouse and the Tees, Sherston, Brentford, Ashingdon and the Thames.[80] It is therefore worth raising the possibility that the final stanza of Óttarr's *Knútsdrápa* does not belong here, and is either not by Óttarr or else is an Óttarr *lausavísa* that has been misidentified as deriving from the *Knútsdrápa*. For if one detaches the last stanza, Óttarr's poem becomes a focused and unified celebration of Cnut's conquest in 1016 – a poem that belongs in many of its concerns with *Liðsmannaflokkr* and Þórðr's *Eiríksdrápa*, but is distinguished from them in the importance it attaches to specificity in terms of battles and place-names. Certainly there is evidence in the saga distribution of the stanzas to suggest that the last stanza does not seem to have circulated and been preserved in association with the other stanzas, in that there

---

[77] For the possibility that the *Eybúar* are the inhabitants of Orkney, see J. Jesch, 'England and Orkneyinga saga', *The Viking Age in Caithness, Orkney and the North Atlantic: Select Papers from the Proceedings of the Eleventh Viking Congress, Thurso and Kirkwall, 22 August–1 September 1989*, ed. C. E. Batey, J. Jesch and C. D. Morris (Edinburgh, 1993), pp. 222–39, at 229–35 and 236, n. 14.

[78] *Skjaldedigtning*, ed. Finnur Jónsson IB, 275 ('you repulsed the Swedes, at the place called the Holy River'). [79] *Ibid.* IB, 272; Poole, 'Skaldic Verse and Anglo-Saxon History', p. 271.

[80] For a sustained explication of the poem, see *ibid.* pp. 272–80; on the place-names cited, see Townend, *English Place-Names in Skaldic Verse*.

is a clear split between stanzas 1–10 on the one hand, and stanza 11 on the other: 1–10 are all preserved in *Knýtlinga saga* and nowhere else, whereas stanza 11 is absent from *Knýtlinga saga*, and instead is preserved partially in *Fagrskinna* (first *helmingr*) and Snorri Sturluson's *Edda* (second *helmingr*) and completely only in sagas of Óláfr Haraldsson.[81] Such a distribution would seem to indicate that at some stage in the oral transmission of Óttarr's *Knútsdrápa*, stanza 11 became detached from the rest and circulated independently; or else that stanza 11 never was part of *Knútsdrápa*, but rather became attached to it at a later point. It is therefore also interesting to note that in the Codex Trajectinus version of Snorri's *Edda* the second *helmingr* of stanza 11 is not attributed to Óttarr at all but rather to Arnórr jarlaskáld; Whaley (no doubt rightly) rejects this attribution to Arnórr on the grounds that all other manuscripts specify Óttarr, but the incident again raises doubts about the connection between the last stanza of Óttarr's *Knútsdrápa* and the rest of the poem.[82] Indeed, it is possible to add further to the uncertainty regarding the transmission and inviolability of Óttarr's *Knútsdrápa* by noting that stanza 9 is also likely to be misplaced: it is probably an immigrant from an earlier Óttarr poem on Cnut's father, Sveinn.[83] Finally, and more generally, there are no clear intertextual connections that can assist in dating Óttarr's *Knútsdrápa*: although Poole suggests that Óttarr's poem draws on *Eiríksdrápa* (which, as has been seen, he dates to *c.* 1016–23), this argument only arises from the belief that the common features between the two poems cannot be independent, and therefore that a post-Holy-River *Knútsdrápa* must be the borrower.[84] Taking all these factors together, two related but separable points can be concluded: first, that it is far from certain that stanza 11 properly belongs in Óttarr's *Knútsdrápa*; and second, that if it does not, then the traditional dating of the poem to *c.* 1026–7 loses its cornerstone, and a date soon after Cnut's conquest in 1016 becomes a possibility.

There are, however, two substantial objections to such a revised dating, both of which continue to apply even if one accepts the first point above and removes the problematic last stanza. The first is the reference in stanza 5 to Cnut as the *Svía þrengvir* 'oppressor of the Swedes', a phrase which would only appear to make sense – indeed, would perhaps only be possible – after the battle of Holy River. It is true that the crucial word *Svía* is not guaranteed by metre (it par-

---

[81] *Skjaldedigtning*, ed. Finnur Jónsson IA, 296–8; Fidjestøl, *Det Norrøne Fyrstediktet*, p. 124.
[82] Whaley, *The Poetry of Arnórr jarlaskáld*, p. 38. The *helmingr* is Verse 314 in *Skáldskaparmál*: Snorri Sturluson, *Edda: Skáldskaparmál*, ed. Faulkes I, 86.
[83] This stanza refers to a battle at Norwich: see Campbell, *Skaldic Verse and Anglo-Saxon History*, p. 13; Poole, 'Skaldic Verse and Anglo-Saxon History', pp. 276–80. In *Skáldatal* Óttarr is one of only two poets recorded as having composed for Sveinn, the other being Þórleifr Rauðfeldarson: see *Edda Snorra Sturlusonar*, ed. Sveinbjörn Egilsson *et al.* III, 282.
[84] Poole, 'Skaldic Verse and Anglo-Saxon History', pp. 269–71.

ticipates in neither rhyme nor alliteration), but there is no real reason to doubt the genuineness of the locution. However, it should perhaps not be automatically assumed that the phrase must be a post-Holy-River coinage: Cnut's father Sveinn appears to have enjoyed overlordship of Sweden, and while there are signs of simmering Swedish–Danish hostility in the early years of Cnut's reign, this did not become overt until after the accession of Ǫnundr in *c.* 1022;[85] and so the period between Ǫnundr's accession and the battle of Holy River remains the only time when to describe Cnut as the *Svía þrengvir* would unquestionably be, in Snorri's celebrated phrase, *háð, en eigi lof*.[86] None the less, it must remain probable that the phrase does indeed allude to the Holy River campaign, and certainly in terms of the competitive dynamics of praise-poetry the allusion makes much more sense after that battle. The second objection to an early date for Óttarr's *Knútsdrápa* is the principle articulated earlier, namely that it is methodologically doubtful to needlessly multiply the number of visits made by Óttarr to Cnut's court. The problematic stanza 11 of *Knútsdrápa* is thus crucial after all: cogent reasons have been given for doubting that stanza's attribution to the *Knútsdrápa*, but there are not really any reasonable grounds for doubting its attribution to Óttarr himself, and to do so would smack of special pleading. So, since the date of stanza 11 must be post-Holy-River, and since none of Óttarr's verses for Cnut allude to his 1028 acquisition of Norway, a date of 1027 must be the most likely one for Óttarr's service at Cnut's court. This would thus be the date for Óttarr's *Knútsdrápa*, for stanza 11 (whether a *lausavísa* or part of *Knútsdrápa*), and for the Irish *lausavísa* (it will be recalled that Hudson argues for the second half of Cnut's reign). The probability is therefore that the traditional dating for Óttarr's *Knútsdrápa* (*c.* 1027) is the correct one after all, but the case is by no means as open and shut as previous commentators have suggested, and an earlier date of *c.* 1016–22 (post-conquest, pre-Ǫnundr) would be possible if one either rejected stanza 11 as not being by Óttarr and/or assumed that Óttarr made at least two visits to Cnut's court. Indeed, even if one accepts the traditional date for Óttarr's *Knútsdrápa* (post-Holy-River), the possibility remains strong that the last stanza does not belong in the poem, or that several other Holy River strophes may have been lost: in other words, it would arguably make most sense to regard the last stanza as a *lausavísa* – for which Óttarr's Irish stanza would be the obvious parallel and precedent – and to regard the *Knútsdrápa* proper as a poem deliberately restricted in scope to a celebration of Cnut's conquest of England.

This lengthy and detailed discussion therefore brings us eventually to the following likely chronology for the *Knútsdrápur*: *Liðsmannaflokkr c.* 1016–17;

---

[85] Sawyer, 'Cnut's Scandinavian Empire', pp. 14–15 and 18; Lawson, *Cnut*, p. 96.
[86] Snorri Sturluson, *Heimskringla*, ed. Bjarni Aðalbjarnarson I, 5 ('mockery, and not praise').

Þórðr's *Eiríksdrápa c.* 1016–23; Óttarr's *Knútsdrápa* (with or without stanza 11) *c.* 1027 and *lausavísa c.* 1027; Sigvatr's *Knútsdrápa c.* 1027 (probable date); Þórarinn's *Hǫfuðlausn c.* 1027–8 and *Tøgdrápa c.* 1029; Hallvarðr's *Knútsdrápa c.* 1029; and Arnórr's fragment *c.* 1031–5. For a number of these poems – especially, perhaps, Hallvarðr's and Arnórr's – it is the *terminus ante quem* that is lacking or weakly established, with Cnut's death forming the only real end-point. Stenton famously remarked that Cnut's reign in England was 'so successful that contemporaries found little to say about it';[87] and while this may or may not be true for chronicles and other documentary sources, the observation is quite aptly applicable to the genre of praise-poetry. Peaceful times give little cause for celebration in such a competitive and militant literature, and the *Knútsdrápur* mention no event later than the 1028 expedition to Norway: in terms of Cnut's own activities these years are blank too in all manuscripts of the *Anglo-Saxon Chronicle*.[88] Hence the poets look back to the empire-making battles and wars, either to the most recent campaign or (presumably) the most important: Óttarr's *Knútsdrápa*, perhaps the most militant of all of the praise-poems for Cnut, looks back some ten years to the winning of the English throne. It should be acknowledged, though, that the exception to this battle-driven poetry is, as a number of commentators have explored, the concern with Christian kingship which appears in a number of the *Knútsdrápur*, and which can be expressed in terms which are not event-specific.[89] It may be the case that Sigvatr presents the pilgrimage to Rome as a fame-making kingly action in his *Knútsdrápa* (forming the third of a trio, after the English wars and Holy River), but the related terms in which Hallvarðr and Þórarinn draw a (skaldically innovative) connection between royal and divine guardianship are plainly not event-driven in the same way: *Knútr verr jǫrð sem ítran / alls dróttin salfjalla* (Hallvarðr) and *Knútr verr grund sem gætir / Gríklands himinríki* (Þórarinn, *Hǫfuðlausn*).[90]

The literary and cultural implications of this chronology for the *Knútsdrápur* will be discussed in more detail after consideration has been given to the geographical and physical contexts for the poems; but one or two points are worth making at this stage. Above all, it is notable how the poems fall into two groups,

---

[87] F. M. Stenton, *Anglo-Saxon England*, 3rd ed. (Oxford, 1971), p. 399.

[88] For ease of reference, see Lawson, *Cnut*, pp. 231–2. As noted above, the entry for 1031 in MSS DE is very probably misplaced from 1026. The one event which may be correctly dated to 1031 is the submission of the Scottish kings.

[89] See Hofmann, *Nordisch-Englische Lehnbeziehungen*, pp. 96–7 (§104); B. Fidjestøl, 'Pagan Beliefs and Christian Impact: the Contribution of Scaldic Studies', *Viking Revaluations: Viking Society Centenary Symposium 14–15 May 1992*, ed. A. Faulkes and R. Perkins (London, 1993), pp. 100–20, at 106 and 118–19; Frank, 'King Cnut in the Verse of his Skalds', pp. 116–17.

[90] *Skjaldedigtning*, ed. Finnur Jónsson IB, 294 ('Cnut defends the earth just as the lord of all [defends] the glorious hall of the mountains [= heaven]') and 298 ('Cnut defends the land just as the guardian of Greece [defends] the kingdom of heaven').

with *Liðsmannaflokkr* and *Eiríksdrápa* coming soon after the conquest of England, but the rest of the poems after Holy River and (in some cases) the Norway expedition. One might also suggest that the two early poems are by insiders, those who had already thrown in their lot with Cnut's assault on England (especially *Liðsmannaflokkr*), whereas the later poems are by outsiders, those who came seeking Cnut's court at a subsequent point. And chronologically that point is clearly Cnut's establishment of a pan-Scandinavian hegemony, after Holy River and the Norway expedition: it is this creation of a wider Scandinavian empire that shifts the centre of skaldic culture to Cnut's court and that makes the Danish king the crucial patron for poets to seek out and cultivate. There is only a tiny amount of Viking Age verse extant for any Danish kings prior to Cnut; but the events of 1026 and 1028 reorientate the axis of skaldic composition, and so lead to the type of chronology established above. Such a reorientation is not however an automatic consequence of Cnut's political hegemony: as Pierre Bourdieu has emphasized, one must be careful to pay proper attention to the autonomy and career-making strategies of authors themselves, a factor which is lost in both an internalist analysis of style and an externalist emphasis on the social function of literature. For as Bourdieu observes, cultural objects fulfil functions for the persons who produce them, as well as for their recipients and users:[91] in this instance it is the combination of political factors, royal patronage and career-making possibilities that leads to the explosion of skaldic activity at Cnut's court. In or around 1030 it clearly made sense for a poet launching his international career to seek out Cnut first of all as the most important of patrons – as, from Whaley's chronology, Arnórr appears to have done when leaving Iceland for the first time.[92] Cnut's poetic hegemony thus resulted from his political one: as Roberta Frank has pointed out, Cnut's poets show a curious reluctance to describe Cnut in plain terms as *konungr* 'king', as if they understood very clearly 'that the title was not sufficiently grand or customized' for a widely dominant ruler with imperial aspirations.[93]

The two early poems are also distinctive in having a dual focus of praise: *Liðsmannaflokkr* celebrates the activities of both Cnut and Þorkell, *Eiríksdrápa* of Cnut and Eiríkr. In the later poems, on the other hand, the focus is exclusively on Cnut, and so for example neither Þorkell nor Eiríkr receive a single mention in Óttarr's *Knútsdrápa*, even though that poem represents the fullest

---

[91] P. Bourdieu, 'Principles for a Sociology of Cultural Works', in his *The Field of Cultural Production: Essays on Art and Literature* (Cambridge, 1993), pp. 176–91, at 181.

[92] Whaley, *The Poetry of Arnórr jarlaskáld*, pp. 41–7. Arnórr's choice of destination may also have been governed by the earlier career-successes of his father, Þórðr Kolbeinsson.

[93] R. Frank, 'When Poets Address Princes', *Sagnaþing helgað Jónasi Kristjánssyni sjötugum 10. apríl 1994*, ed. Gísli Sigurðsson, G. Kvaran and Sigurgeir Steingrímsson, 2 vols. (Reykjavík, 1994) I, 189–95, at 194.

skaldic account of the Anglo-Danish wars in which they played such crucial roles. Poole has explored how *Liðsmannaflokkr* is careful to balance and co-ordinate the relationship between Cnut and Þorkell, implying that at the time of composition the maintenance of such co-operative solidarity remained of signal importance.[94] In fact, both *Liðsmannaflokkr* and *Eiríksdrápa*, unlike the rest of the *Knútsdrápur*, can be profitably viewed as exemplifying the type of kingship termed 'charismatic' by Norbert Elias (here following Max Weber) in contradistinction to 'absolutist' rule.[95] The absolutist ruler, Elias argues, seeks to maintain the *status quo* by playing court factions and ambitions against one another, by 'allow[ing] opposed pressures to interpenetrate each other and hold[ing] them in equilibrium';[96] the charismatic leader, on the other hand, is attempting to overturn that *status quo* and so bring himself and his own faction to power:

Observing him during his rise to power one sees that, in his case, jealousies, rivalries and the tensions they produce are dangerous within the central group. They are doubtless always present. But they should not show themselves too clearly. They have to be suppressed. For what matters here, as we have said, is to direct the strength, the aims and thus the social pressure of all the people united in this group outwards, against the disturbed social field, against the wider dominion that is to be conquered.[97]

Broadly speaking, then, the two early *Knútsdrápur* demonstrate Cnut's 'charismatic' leadership; by the time of the rest of the poems in his honour Cnut was in much more of an 'absolutist' position. Þorkell was exiled in 1021 (though he and Cnut were briefly reconciled in 1023) and, as noted earlier, Eiríkr appears to have died in 1023;[98] but the diplomatic balancing-acts of *Liðsmannaflokkr* and *Eiríksdrápa* make much more sense when placed in the context of the early years of Cnut's reign and the need for the suppression of those internal tensions which were clearly able to be released by the time of 1021 and later.

Other perspectives that emerge from the chronology presented above will be explored once attention has been given to the geographical and physical contexts of the *Knútsdrápur*. In turning to this, the first question is whether one should locate the activities of Cnut's poets to England rather than to Denmark (or even Norway), and the usual ascription to England seems securely based on a number of convergent strands of evidence: above all, on the historical record of Cnut's movements, the centrality of England in his Anglo-Danish empire, and the marked linguistic influence on the poems from Old English. The first

---

[94] Poole, *Viking Poems on War and Peace*, pp. 99–107; see also R. Poole, 'Skaldic Praise-Poetry as a Marginal Form', *Poetry in the Scandinavian Middle Ages: the Seventh International Saga Conference, Spoleto, 4–10 September 1988*, ed. T. Pàroli (Spoleto, 1990), pp. 169–85, at 171–2.
[95] Elias, *The Court Society*, pp. 121–6. [96] *Ibid.* p. 122. [97] *Ibid.*
[98] *Encomium Emmae*, ed. Campbell, pp. 70 and 75–6; Keynes, 'Cnut's Earls', pp. 56–8.

two of these factors point to the localization of Cnut's court, while the third would seem to indicate that such a localization is correct with regard to the composition of court poetry. Between 1017 and 1035 there is record of Cnut being absent from England on no more than four or five occasions: in 1019–20, when he assumed the Danish throne after the death of his brother Haraldr and sent back his first letter to England; in 1022 or 1023, when he appears to have been in Denmark to stifle trouble caused by Þorkell;[99] in late 1026, for the Holy River campaign; in early 1027, when he made his pilgrimage to Rome and sent back his second letter; and in 1028–9, for the Norway expedition that resulted in the expulsion of Óláfr Haraldsson. If, as seems almost certain, Cnut did not return to England between Holy River and Rome, then these two absences should be counted as one. Two other possible absences are the fleet's 1022 expedition to *Wihtland* (almost certainly the Isle of Wight, but conceivably Wendland)[100] and, conceivably, a second 1031 pilgrimage to Rome (if that is not a confused replication of the earlier visit, as suggested above). Cnut's Scottish expedition (in either 1026 or 1031) should also be added to this list, but what is apparent is the dominant proportion of his reign which Cnut spent in England, and how this would appear to signal England rather than Denmark as the centre of his empire. Furthermore, between 1029 and 1035 there is (with the possible exception of Scotland in 1031) no record of Cnut being out of England; and the chronology of Cnut's presence in England correlates well with the chronology proposed above for the composition of the *Knútsdrápur*. The value of the linguistic evidence catalogued by Hofmann has been invoked earlier in consideration of Sigvatr's *Knútsdrápa*:[101] as Frank remarks, this is indeed the 'most persuasive' indicator that the poems were originally 'addressing Danes resident in England'.[102] It is this linguistic evidence which also suggests that the poems should not be ascribed to Cnut's few occasions of campaign in Scandinavia: the poems are coming out of an Anglo-Norse milieu, rather than one that is wholly Scandinavian.

In this regard it is also worth noting briefly that later saga accounts of the period are more or less unanimous in locating Cnut's court to England, and it is therefore in England that such sources locate their accounts of the Icelandic poets who sought patronage from Cnut, so giving rise to the *Knútsdrápur*. Óttarr's visit to Cnut's court in England is recorded in the *Legendary saga* of St Óláfr, Sigvatr's in *Heimskringla*, and Þórarinn's in *Knýtlinga saga*.[103] Perhaps the only exception to this English localization is the account (in the *Legendary saga*

---

[99] *ASC* 1023 C. See Keynes, 'Cnut's Earls', pp. 56–7.   [100] See Lawson, *Cnut*, pp. 92–4.
[101] Hofmann, *Nordisch-Englische Lehnbeziehungen*, pp. 59–100 (§§52–108).
[102] Frank, 'King Cnut in the Verse of his Skalds', p. 108.
[103] *Olafs Saga hins Helga*, ed. Heinrichs *et al.*, pp. 130–2; Snorri Sturluson, *Heimskringla*, ed. Bjarni Aðalbjarnarson II, 271–3; *Danakonunga Sǫgur*, ed. Bjarni Guðnason, pp. 124–5.

and *Óláfs saga helga* in *Flateyjarbók*) of Þormóðr Kolbrúnarskáld visiting Cnut in Denmark; but significantly, *Skáldatal* does not reckon Þormóðr among Cnut's poets, and the chronology of the episode will not stand up to scrutiny.[104] Saga accounts also record the presence at Cnut's court in England of those poets whose works in honour of Cnut have not survived, but whose compositions for the king are vouchsafed by *Skáldatal*: thus Bersi Torfuson's visit is recorded in *Heimskringla* and *Knýtlinga saga* (both drawing on Sigvatr's *Vestrfararvísur*), and Steinn Skaptason's in the *Legendary saga* and *Óláfs saga helga* in *Flateyjarbók*.[105]

More intriguing is the question of whereabouts in England one should locate this culture of courtly patronage. Hans Kuhn assumes that London was the prime location of Cnut's court and therefore in Cnut's reign constituted '*the* centre in the North for the production and distribution of skaldic poetry'.[106] However, courts of late Anglo-Saxon kings were still to a significant degree itinerant,[107] and during his reign Cnut is variously recorded engaged in legal or political activity in Kingston, Oxford, Abingdon, Cirencester, Ashingdon, Canterbury and Shaftesbury.[108] In essence, though, the search for the centre of poetic patronage in Cnut's reign comes down to a straight choice between the two other places where Cnut's presence is recorded, namely London (as Kuhn assumes) and Winchester – that is, between the emergent economic powerhouse of eleventh-century England and the ancient ceremonial seat of the West Saxon monarchy.

As usual, this is not really a case of either/or, and in fact the two cities appear, to some degree, to have been in what might be termed complementary distribution. As noted earlier, Poole has demonstrated persuasively that

---

[104] *Olafs Saga hins Helga*, ed. Heinrichs *et al.*, pp. 124–8; *Flateyjarbók*, ed. Nordal *et al.* II, 291–4. This anecdote, which incorporates the two *lausavísur* mentioned earlier, presents Þormóðr's visit as coming after Þórarinn's. However, Þórarinn's *Tøgdrápa* postdates Cnut's 1028 Norway expedition, and Cnut does not appear to have left England after that date; so an encounter in Denmark between Cnut and Þormóðr is chronologically impossible.

[105] Snorri Sturluson, *Heimskringla*, ed. Bjarni Aðalbjarnarson II, 224; *Danakonunga Sǫgur*, ed. Bjarni Guðnason, p. 126; *Olafs Saga hins Helga*, ed. Heinrichs *et al.*, pp. 138–40; *Flateyjarbók*, ed. Nordal *et al.* II, 368. Óðarkeptr, however, remains obscure.

[106] H. Kuhn, *Das Dróttkvætt* (Heidelberg, 1983), p. 267. The phrase quoted is Roberta Frank's, though Frank herself would not localize the poems so precisely: R. Frank, 'Skaldic Poetry', *Old Norse-Icelandic Literature: a Critical Guide*, ed. C. J. Clover and J. Lindow, Islandica 45 (Ithaca, NY, 1985), 157–96, at 179, and Frank, 'King Cnut in the Verse of his Skalds', p. 107.

[107] See, for example, S. Keynes, *The Diplomas of King Æthelred 'the Unready' 978–1016: a Study in their Use as Historical Evidence*, Cambridge Stud. in Med. Life and Thought, 3rd ser. 13 (Cambridge, 1980), 269–73 ('Appendix 2: Meeting places of the king's councillors during the tenth and eleventh centuries'); D. Hill, *An Atlas of Anglo-Saxon England* (Oxford, 1981), pp. 90–1 and 94 (maps 160–3 and 167–9); M. Biddle, 'Seasonal Festivals and Residence: Winchester, Westminster and Gloucester in the Tenth to Twelfth Centuries', *ANS* 8 (1986), 51–72, at 69–72.

[108] Hill, *An Atlas of Anglo-Saxon England*, p. 91 (map 163); reprinted in D. Hill, 'An Urban Policy for Cnut?', *The Reign of Cnut*, ed. Rumble, pp. 101–5, at 103.

Liðsmannaflokkr 'is what it purports to be, an expression of rank and file jubilation at Knútr's conquest, composed almost contemporaneously with the events
it describes',[109] and the geographical centre of the poem is London (referred to
in stanza 7 in Poole's ordering, as is the Thames in stanzas 3 and 6).
Liðsmannaflokkr appears to be coming directly out of the newly occupied city,
and the poem's concerns are thus emblematic of London's status under Cnut:
on account of its successful resistance in the preceding wars it became a
guarded and garrisoned city, the main focus for Cnut's punitive measures in
terms of geld-raising and forceful political action. So, for example, it was in
London (according to John of Worcester) that Cnut in 1017 executed the dangerous Eadric streona;[110] it was upon London that Cnut placed the burden of a
distinctive geld of £10,500 in 1018;[111] and it was from London that Cnut
removed the relics of the martyred Archbishop Ælfheah in 1023.[112] Above all,
and quite apart from individual events such as these, London was a city under
careful military occupation. It never fell in the Anglo-Danish wars, and its citi-
zens had preferred Edmund Ironside to Cnut in 1016:[113] post-1017, therefore,
it could not be relied upon to support the new Danish king, and might potentially become the crucible of anti-Danish rebellion. Hence the punitive taxes
and political gestures of potency; hence also it appears to have been the base for
Cnut's *liðsmenn* or standing fleet,[114] one of whom may be commemorated by
two of his comrades in the Ringerike-style St Paul's rune-stone,[115] while the

---

[109] Poole, 'Skaldic Verse and Anglo-Saxon History', p. 286.

[110] *The Chronicle of John of Worcester*, ed. Darlington and McGurk II, 504–5; Lawson, *Cnut*, pp.
83–4. For later versions of the event (which continue to place the action in London), see C. E.
Wright, *The Cultivation of Saga in Anglo-Saxon England* (Edinburgh, 1939), pp. 205–12.

[111] *ASC* 1018 CDE (though MS E states £11,000); Lawson, *Cnut*, p. 83; Hill, 'An Urban Policy for
Cnut?', p. 103.

[112] *ASC* 1023 CDE (with a particularly lengthy account in MS D); Lawson, *Cnut*, pp. 140–2 and
180–2; A. R. Rumble, 'Textual Appendix: *Translatio Sancti Ælfegi Cantuariensis archiepiscopi et mar-
tyris* (*BHL* 2519): Osbern's Account of the Translation of St Ælfheah's Relics from London to
Canterbury, 8–11 June 1023', *The Reign of Cnut*, ed. Rumble, pp. 282–315.

[113] *ASC* 1016 CDE.

[114] J. Campbell, 'Some Agents and Agencies of the Late Anglo-Saxon State', *Domesday Studies*, ed.
J. C. Holt (Woodbridge, 1987), pp. 201–18, at 204–5; N. Hooper, 'Military Developments in
the Reign of Cnut', *The Reign of Cnut*, ed. Rumble, pp. 89–100, at 98–100.

[115] The inscription reads (in normalized form) *Ginna lét leggja stein þensi auk Tóki* 'Ginna and Tóki
had this stone raised'. See D. M. Wilson and O. Klindt-Jensen, *Viking Art* (London, 1966), pp.
135–6; S. H. Fuglesang, *Some Aspects of the Ringerike Style: a Phase of 11th Century Scandinavian Art*,
MScand Supplements 1 (Odense, 1980), 189 (no. 88); *The Vikings in England and in their Danish
Homeland*, ed. E. Roesdahl, J. Graham-Campbell, P. Connor and K. Pearson (London, 1981), pp.
136 and 163 (no. I 19); Lawson, *Cnut*, pp. 206–7; M. Barnes, 'Towards an Edition of the
Scandinavian Runic Inscriptions of the British Isles – Some Thoughts', *Twenty-Eight Papers presented to Hans Bekker-Nielsen on the Occasion of his Sixtieth Birthday 28 April 1993* (Odense, 1993),
pp. 21–36, at 33 (no. E 2); K. Holman, *Scandinavian Runic Inscriptions in the British Isles: their
Historical Context*, Senter for Middelalderstudier Skrifter 4 (Trondheim, 1996), 19–20 and 28–38;

appearance of strategically positioned churches dedicated to Scandinavian saints may well indicate that they functioned as garrison chapels.[116] The signs therefore are that London was a closely guarded city in the reign of Cnut, and that presumably the king had some sort of base there.[117] As early garrison poetry, *Liðsmannaflokkr* – the *flokkr* or poem of the *liðsmenn* – should clearly be localized there; but it must be doubtful whether London represented the centre of court culture for the Danish king and his followers.

Instead one may look to Winchester, and it is in Winchester, arguably, that one should primarily contextualize the *Knútsdrápur*. David Hill has observed that 'any ... punishment of London would also explain the efforts to embellish Winchester as "capital", a policy that is certainly discernible in the reign of Cnut':[118] as Martin Biddle remarks, '[t]he evidence we have for the residences and itineraries of English kings before the Norman conquest is all too thin, but there is just enough to show that Winchester was for Cnut a principal, possibly the principal seat, as it was certainly for his wife Emma, after his death'.[119] So it was in Winchester at Christmas 1020 or 1021 that Cnut promulgated the law-codes now known as I and II Cnut,[120] and it was in the Old Minster at Winchester that Cnut was to be buried.[121] It is also, of course, from Winchester that the supreme image of Cnut derives, in the form of the frontispiece to the New Minster *Liber Vitae* (London, British Library, Stowe 944, 6r), commemorating his and Emma's donation of a gold cross to be placed on the foundation's altar.[122] For Emma herself the evidence is more extensive, in that she held property in Winchester from 1012 up till her death in 1052: there are

K. Holman, 'Scandinavian Runic Inscriptions as a Source for the History of the British Isles: the St Paul's Rune-Stone', *Runeninschriften als Quellen interdisziplinärer Forschung: Abhandlungen des Vierten Internationalen Symposiums über Runen und Runeninschriften in Göttingen vom 4.–9. August 1995*, ed. K. Düwel, Ergänzungsbände zum Reallexikon der Germanischen Altertumskunde 15 (Berlin, 1998), 629–38.

[116] P. Nightingale, 'The Origin of the Court of Husting and Danish Influence on London's Development into a Capital City', *EHR* 102 (1987), 559–78, at 566–9.

[117] A. Vince, *Saxon London: an Archaeological Investigation* (London, 1990), p. 57.

[118] Hill, 'An Urban Policy for Cnut?', pp. 103–4.

[119] M. Biddle, 'Capital at Winchester', *The Vikings in England*, ed. Roesdahl *et al.*, pp. 165–70, at 165.

[120] F. Liebermann, *Die Gesetze der Angelsachsen*, 3 vols. (Halle, 1898–1916) I, 278–371; Lawson, *Cnut*, pp. 61–3; M. K. Lawson, 'Archbishop Wulfstan and the Homiletic Element in the Laws of Æthelred II and Cnut', *The Reign of Cnut*, ed. Rumble, pp. 141–64, at 157–61; P. Wormald, *The Making of English Law: King Alfred to the Twelfth Century*, I: *Legislation and Its Limits* (Oxford, 1999), pp. 345–66.

[121] *ASC* 1036 E. See J. Crook, '"A Worthy Antiquity": the Movement of King Cnut's Bones in Winchester Cathedral', *The Reign of Cnut*, ed. Rumble, pp. 165–92.

[122] For discussion, see R. Deshman, '*Benedictus Monarcha et Monachus*: Early Medieval Ruler Theology and the Anglo-Saxon Reform', *FS* 22 (1988), 204–40, at 223–5; J. Gerchow, 'Prayers for King Cnut: the Liturgical Commemoration of a Conqueror', *England in the Eleventh Century:*

documentary records of Emma's presence there, and her house in the High Street was still able to be identified in the twelfth century.[123] She too was buried in the Old Minster, as was her and Cnut's only son, Harthacnut,[124] so confirming its status as (in Pauline Stafford's phrase) a 'dynastic mausoleum'.[125]

To this discussion of Cnut (and Emma) in Winchester one should add two other more general factors: the status of Winchester as late West Saxon 'capital', and evidence for a Danish presence in late West Saxon Winchester. Our extensive knowledge of Winchester derives substantially, of course, from the programme of excavations conducted there in the 1960s and the accompanying publication project.[126] Winchester's trajectory involves its development as the ceremonial royal centre of Wessex in the seventh to ninth centuries, its urban renovation in the late-ninth-century burghal system, and its confirmation as the royal and cultural centre of the unified kingdom of England in the tenth and eleventh centuries, before it declined in status at the rise of Westminster.[127] Thus in the early eleventh century Winchester was 'the principal royal city of England', centred upon its three royally endowed monasteries and 'the principal palace of the Anglo-Saxon kings'.[128] So for instance Winchester appears to have been the central repository of the king's treasure,[129] and upon Cnut's death in 1035 *ealle þa betstan gærsaman þe Cnut cyng ahte* were taken from Emma there by Harold Harefoot.[130] The royal palace itself (in which, one may assume, the treasury was located) was positioned directly to the west of the Old Minster and south of the New Minster cemetery, though the form of the buildings themselves is unknown as the area itself has not

Proceedings of the 1990 Harlaxton Symposium, ed. C. Hicks, Harlaxton Med. Stud. 2 (Stamford, 1992), 219–38, at 222–30; R. Gameson, *The Role of Art in the Late Anglo-Saxon Church* (Oxford, 1995), pp. 22, 74, 82–3, 230–1 and 263; *The Liber Vitae of the New Minster and Hyde Abbey Winchester*, ed. S. Keynes, EEMF 26 (Copenhagen, 1996), 38–9 and 79–80. On the gold cross itself, see *ibid.* pp. 35–7.

[123] See *ibid.* p. 34; P. Stafford, *Queen Emma and Queen Edith: Queenship and Women's Power in Eleventh-Century England* (Oxford, 1997), esp. p. 252 (fig. 9); Keynes, 'Introduction to the 1998 Reprint', pp. xix, xxvi–xxviii and lxxv.   [124] *ASC* 1041 EF, 1051 C.

[125] Stafford, *Queen Emma and Queen Edith*, p. 96.

[126] See M. Biddle, 'The Study of Winchester: Archaeology and History in a British Town, 1961–1983', *PBA* 69 (1983), 93–135; revised version reprinted in *British Academy Papers on Anglo-Saxon England*, ed. E. G. Stanley (Oxford, 1990), pp. 299–341.

[127] M. Biddle, 'Winchester: the Development of an Early Capital', *Vor- und Frühformen der europäischen Stadt im Mittelalter*, ed. H. Jankuhn, W. Schlesinger and H. Steuer, 2 vols. (Göttingen, 1975) I, 229–61.   [128] *Ibid.* pp. 258 and 257.

[129] M. Biddle and D. J. Keene, 'Winchester in the Eleventh and Twelfth Centuries', in F. Barlow, M. Biddle, O. von Feilitzen and D. J. Keene, *Winchester in the Early Middle Ages: an Edition and Discussion of the Winton Domesday*, ed. M. Biddle, Winchester Stud. 1 (Oxford, 1976), 241–448, at 290–1; Stafford, *Queen Emma and Queen Edith*, p. 99.

[130] *ASC MS D*, ed. Cubbin, p. 65 ('all the best treasures which King Cnut owned').

been excavated;[131] none the less, Biddle and Keene suggest that 'the evidence available for rural palaces, and the illustrations in the Bayeux Tapestry of the Confessor's palace at Westminster, may lead us to suppose a considerable complex of stone structures, probably not out of scale beside the two great churches of the Old and New Minsters'.[132] Of the form of the monasteries abutting the palace, on the other hand, a very great deal is known, and in the Benedictine reforms of the late tenth century, a mere generation before Cnut, both had experienced ambitious building programmes: the tower of the New Minster was completed sometime between 980 and 987, while the Old Minster was wholly rebuilt between 971 and 994, with its westworks in particular being completed in 980.[133] These were formidably impressive structures: the Old Minster westworks, centred upon the tomb of St Swithun, was probably over thirty-five metres in height, while the New Minster tower comprised six storeys, and its exterior was decorated with different carvings at every level.[134]

In such an environment it is perhaps surprising to find a variety of forms of evidence for a conspicuous Danish presence in the early eleventh century.[135] Funeral evidence is supplied in the form of a number of 'essentially Scandinavian' burials in the New Minster cemetery,[136] and in the hogback-shaped gravestone from the east of the Old Minster bearing the inscription HER L[I]Ð G[VN]N[I :] EORLES FEOLAGA.[137] *Gunni* is an Old Norse personal name,[138] and although the inscription itself is in Old English it shows

---

[131] M. Biddle, '*Felix Urbs Winthonia*: Winchester in the Age of Monastic Reform', *Tenth-Century Studies: Essays in Commemoration of the Millennium of the Council of Winchester and Regularis Concordia*, ed. D. Parsons (London, 1975), pp. 123–40, at 132–3.

[132] Biddle and Keene, 'Winchester in the Eleventh and Twelfth Centuries', p. 292.

[133] Biddle, '*Felix Urbs Winthonia*', pp. 134–9.

[134] R. N. Quirk, 'Winchester New Minster and its Tenth-Century Tower', *JBAA*, 3rd ser. 24 (1961), 16–54; *The Liber Vitae of the New Minster*, ed. Keynes, pp. 29–30. For artists' reconstructions, see *The Vikings in England*, ed. Roesdahl *et al.*, pp. 167 and 170 (no. J 14); T. B. James, *Winchester*, English Heritage (London, 1997), p. 49 (fig. 25).

[135] For summaries, see B. Yorke, *Wessex in the Early Middle Ages*, Stud. in the Early Hist. of Britain (London, 1995), pp. 143–5; *The Liber Vitae of the New Minster*, ed. Keynes, p. 40, n. 227.

[136] M. Biddle, 'Excavations at Winchester 1962–63: Second Interim Report', *AntJ* 44 (1964), 188–219, at 211.

[137] M. Biddle, 'Excavations at Winchester 1965: Fourth Interim Report', *AntJ* 46 (1966), 308–32, at 325; B. Kjølbye-Biddle and R. I. Page, 'A Scandinavian Rune-Stone from Winchester', *AntJ* 55 (1975), 389–94, at 390–2; E. Okasha, *Hand-List of Anglo-Saxon Non-Runic Inscriptions* (Cambridge, 1971), pp. 126–7 (no. 138) ('Here lies Gunni, the earl's [or possibly 'Eorl's'] comrade').

[138] E. H. Lind, *Norsk-Isländska Dopnamn ock Fingerade Namn från Medeltiden* (Uppsala, 1905–15), cols. 411–13. For the name's occurrence in England, see E. Björkman, *Nordische Personennamen in alt- und frühmittelenglischer Zeit*, Studien zur englischen Philologie 37 (Halle, 1910), 56; G. Fellows Jensen, *Scandinavian Personal Names in Lincolnshire and Yorkshire*, Navnestudier udgivet af Institut for Navneforskning 7 (Copenhagen, 1968), 116–17.

Norse influence in the presence of the loanwords *eorl* (strictly speaking, a semantic loan) and *feolaga*;[139] and if EORL is not a loanword but a personal name, then it too is thought to be an Old Norse one.[140] Beside this stone one should therefore set the rune-stone found at St Maurice's church in Winchester but almost certainly coming originally from the New Minster cemetery.[141] The stone is only fragmentary, and the inscription correspondingly difficult to read, but it is plainly in Scandinavian runes and enough is extant to indicate that the language of the inscription is Old Norse:[142] the writing of Old Norse in eleventh-century Winchester would thus seem to presuppose an audience for the reading thereof, and also an Old Norse speech community.

To this epigraphical evidence one may add visual evidence in the form of the controversial frieze sculpture found among the rubble resulting from the demolition of the Old Minster in 1093.[143] This has been interpreted as deriving from a narrative stone frieze depicting episodes from the legend of Sigmundr in the Vǫlsung cycle, and Biddle suggests that 'it was Cnut who had this frieze erected', since 'it celebrate[s] the shared traditions of England and Denmark': hence '[t]here could be no more suitable setting for such a frieze than the eastern arm of the Old Minster, in which . . . the royal burials probably lay' – including, in time, Cnut's own.[144] Less speculative is the so-called Winchester 'weathervane' – now relabelled as a 'decorative casket mount' – which was found beneath the south transept of the present cathedral and exemplifies the Ringerike style of decoration.[145] Half-a-dozen bone spoons also show influence from the Ringerike style,[146] while other small Scandinavian-style artifacts include over a dozen combs and an isolated (and possibly pre-Cnut) silver-gilt strap-end in the

---

[139] E. Björkman, *Scandinavian Loan-Words in Middle English*, Studien zur englischen Philologie 7 (Halle, 1900–2), 209 and 236; Hofmann, *Nordisch-Englische Lehnbeziehungen*, pp. 161 and 215–16 (§§221 and 331); H. Peters, 'Zum skandinavischen Lehngut im Altenglischen', *Sprachwissenschaft* 6 (1981), 85–124, at 89 and 94.

[140] However, ON *Iarl* is arguably not recorded as a personal name in Scandinavia itself: all documentary examples are from place-names, where it is more likely to be a title or term of rank (Lind, *Norsk-Isländska Dopnamn*, cols. 614–15), and the same applies to its occurrence in England (Fellows Jensen, *Scandinavian Personal Names*, pp. 154–5).

[141] Kjølbye-Biddle and Page, 'A Scandinavian Rune-Stone from Winchester', p. 389.

[142] *Ibid.* pp. 392–4; Barnes, 'Towards an Edition of the Scandinavian Runic Inscriptions', p. 33 (no. E 12); Holman, *Scandinavian Runic Inscriptions in the British Isles*, pp. 23–5 and 41–3.

[143] Biddle, 'Excavations at Winchester 1965', pp. 329–32 ('Appendix: a Late Saxon Frieze Sculpture from the Old Minster'); *The Golden Age of Anglo-Saxon Art 966–1066*, ed. J. Backhouse, D. H. Turner and L. Webster (London, 1984), pp. 133–5 (no. 140).

[144] Biddle, 'Excavations at Winchester 1965', p. 331.

[145] Wilson and Klindt-Jensen, *Viking Art*, p. 141; Fuglesang, *Some Aspects of the Ringerike Style*, pp. 170–1 (no. 54); *The Golden Age of Anglo-Saxon Art*, ed. Backhouse *et al.*, p. 107 (no. 102).

[146] *The Vikings in England*, ed. Roesdahl *et al.*, p. 168 (no. J 5); *The Golden Age of Anglo-Saxon Art*, ed. Backhouse *et al.*, p. 129 (no. 134).

Jellinge style.[147] Finally, and more generally, one may note the unusually high number of Old Norse personal names recorded in Winchester: in the surveys of the city made in the eleventh and twelfth centuries, approximately one in twenty of the persons recorded bore Old Norse personal names.[148] This cumulative collection of evidence therefore leads Barbara Yorke to conclude that in the reign of Cnut 'Winchester was probably the place in Wessex where the greatest concentration of Danish settlers was to be found',[149] and there are indications that in the post-Cnut years also Winchester continued to be regarded as the centre of Danish (or Anglo-Danish) interests.[150] What all these signs of Scandinavian culture in Winchester have in common, however, is their high or aristocratic status: as Birthe Kjølbye-Biddle observes, '[the] finds showing Scandinavian influence do not occur among common household goods, but reflect the upper ranges of the social hierarchy, as might be expected with a Danish king on the throne and his men at court'.[151]

I would suggest therefore that Winchester is the physical location in which one should primarily contextualize the *Knútsdrápur* – in particular, in which one should contextualize the main group of poems from the late 1020s, after Cnut's establishment of a Scandinavian hegemony, though inevitably the argument for Winchester must fall some way short of total proof. No doubt poetry in honour of Cnut was recited in the king's presence in places other than Winchester alone; and the case of London and *Liðsmannaflokkr* has already been reviewed. But the extensive evidence for aristocratic Danish culture in Winchester would seem to establish the city as almost certainly the most important centre for court culture in the reign of Cnut, and therefore as the primary context for the *Knútsdrápur* (if not, in an age of itineration, the only one); and the remainder of this article will accordingly proceed under this assumption.

In fact, such a context was proposed long ago by L. M. Larson, who suggested that Sigvatr and Óttarr came to Winchester in 1027, Þórarinn in 1029.[152] Larson's dates may need a little fine-tuning (though not much), but he appears to have been correct in believing that it was most probably the court at

---

[147] Kjølbye-Biddle and Page, 'A Scandinavian Rune-Stone from Winchester', p. 390; *The Vikings in England*, ed. Roesdahl *et al.*, pp. 168–9 (nos. J 6 and J 8); *The Golden Age of Anglo-Saxon Art*, ed. Backhouse *et al.*, p. 106 (no. 101).

[148] O. von Feilitzen, 'The Personal Names and Bynames of the Winton Domesday', *Winchester in the Early Middle Ages*, ed. Biddle, pp. 143–229, at 179–91.

[149] Yorke, *Wessex in the Early Middle Ages*, p. 144.

[150] *The Liber Vitae of the New Minster*, ed. Keynes, pp. 39–40. In Harthacnut's reign the *Encomium Emmae Reginae* may well have been written at Winchester in the service of precisely such interests: see Keynes, 'Introduction to the 1998 Reprint', pp. xxxix–xli and lxx–lxxi, and see further E. M. Tyler, '"The Eyes of the Beholders were Dazzled": Treasure and Artifice in *Encomium Emmae Reginae*', *EME* 8 (1999), 247–70.

[151] Kjølbye-Biddle and Page, 'A Scandinavian Rune-Stone from Winchester', p. 390.

[152] L. M. Larson, *Canute the Great 995 (circ)–1035, and the Rise of Danish Imperialism during the Viking Age*, Heroes of the Nations (London, 1912), p. 294.

Winchester that briefly, in the reign of Cnut, came to be the prime centre for skaldic composition in the Norse-speaking world. After Holy River and the Norway expedition, it was to Winchester that the poets came, and so in this respect it is worth briefly recalling Sigvatr's *Vestrfararvísur*, supplying as they do a contemporary account of a skald's visit to Cnut's court: in the course of his report Sigvatr draws particular attention to the processes of etiquette required to gain access to the king (*Útan varðk, áðr Jóta / andspilli fekk stillis,* ... / ... *húsdyrr fyrir spyrjask*), and to the king's great generosity (*Knútr ..., mætra / mildr* ... / ... *hringa*), especially as a benefactor to the poets who seek him (*Knútr hefr okr ... / ... bǫðum / hendr, es hilmi fundum, / ... skrautliga búnar*).[153] In this context, therefore, it is also interesting to note that Snorri's prose account of Cnut's court emphasizes the unparalleled activity and physical splendour of his palace buildings: *Mátti þar ok sjá tígn miklu meiri en í ǫðrum stǫðum, bæði at fjǫlmenni því, er þar var sídœgris, ok umbúnaði þeim ǫðrum, er þar var í þeim herbergjum, er hann átti ok hann var sjálfr í.*[154]

We return, therefore, to the literary-critical observations with which this discussion began, and to the role of context in the generation of meaning for praise-poetry. The royal palace at Winchester, right up close to the enclosure and tower of the New Minster, and directly overshadowed by the Swithun-centred westworks of the Old Minster, seems an astonishing place for the Norse poets to be saying what they do:[155] for Sigvatr to be declaring that *senn sonu / sló, hvern ok þó, / Aðalráðs, eða / út flæmði, Knútr,*[156] for Óttarr to be reminding the king that *ætt drapt, Jóta dróttinn, / Játgeirs í fǫr þeiri;*[157] for Hallvarðr to be

153 *Skjaldedigtning*, ed. Finnur Jónsson IB, 226 (*Vestrfararvísur* 2.1–2 and 4: 'I had to engage in enquiries outside, before the hall door, before I obtained conversation with the governor of the Jutes') and 227 (7.1–3: 'Cnut, generous with precious rings'; 5.1–4: 'Cnut has splendidly adorned the arms of both of us [i.e. Sigvatr and Bersi] when we met the prince').

154 Snorri Sturluson, *Heimskringla*, ed. Bjarni Aðalbjarnarson II, 222 ('There one could also see much greater pomp than in other places, both in terms of the many people who were there each day, and in those other decorations which were in the buildings which he owned and he himself occupied').

155 As Biddle observes, '[t]he west-work stood only a few metres from the royal palace immediately to the west, and their juxtaposition is still as striking in plan as it must have been to a contemporary observer' (Biddle, 'Winchester: the Development of an Early Capital', p. 256).

156 Sigvatr, *Knútsdrápa* 2.1–4 (*Skjaldedigtning*, ed. Finnur Jónsson IB, 232; 'Cnut soon killed the sons of Æthelred or drove out every one'). For the reality behind this phrase, see S. Keynes, 'The Æthelings in Normandy', *ANS* 13 (1991), 173–205, at 174. Curiously, a similar idiom is found in the *Anglo-Saxon Chronicle* for 1017 (7 *Cnut cining aflymde ut Eadwi æþeling 7 Eadwi ceorla kyning* 'And King Cnut drove out Eadwig the atheling and Eadwig king of peasants': *ASC MS D*, ed. Cubbin, p. 63; Hofmann, *Nordisch-Englische Lehnbeziehungen*, pp. 88–90 (§§89–90)), while the sentiment is echoed in the 1065 *Chronicle* poem on the death of Edward (*Cnut ofercom kynn Æðelredes* 'Cnut conquered the kin of Æthelred': *The Anglo-Saxon Minor Poems*, ed. E. V. K. Dobbie, ASPR 6 (New York, 1942), 26, line 18).

157 Óttarr, *Knútsdrápa* 3.5–7 (*Skjaldedigtning*, ed. Finnur Jónsson IB, 273; 'Lord of the Jutes, you struck the race of Edgar on that expedition').

describing him as the *bǫr . . . / . . . holmfjǫturs leiðar* or *jalm-Freyr . . . malma.*[158] The precincts of the royal palace are a remarkable location for Sigvatr and Óttarr to be celebrating Cnut's triumph over named West Saxon kings, the skyline of the monastic complex an unlikely backdrop for Hallvarðr's mythological kennings. For those who have ears to hear, this is a radically different image of King Cnut: in praise-poetry like this, context is an essential part of meaning.

Naturally, therefore, the question of audience arises: to whom are these poems speaking in such a culturally charged environment? Roberta Frank suggests that Cnut's poets were directing their message 'to one identifiable group at court' – namely, of course, the king's Danish followers.[159] Localizing the poems to Winchester, the presence of such a group is indicated by the archaeological and anthroponymical evidence cited above, and one may justifiably employ the term 'housecarls' here. From the work of Nicholas Hooper it has become clear that the housecarls should not, unlike the *liðsmenn*, be conceived of as some kind of bodyguard or standing army, but rather as Cnut's aristocratic followers and courtiers,[160] and Hooper observes that '[i]f a prince was to maintain fitting dignity and keep around him a retinue he would have to provide food and lodging, entertainment and, by this time, a monetary stipend':[161] one may therefore suggest that the *Knútsdrápur* should be ranked among the entertainments for Cnut's Danish followers at court. Names can of course be put to some of these followers, as can be readily seen from Simon Keynes's prosopographical survey of Scandinavians who attest Cnut's charters;[162] and one may also note the four benefactors entered into the New Minster *Liber Vitae* who each receive the label *Danus*, apparently indicating the perception of a distinctive group at the court in Winchester.[163]

In Cnut's Winchester one should therefore predicate a thriving Scandinavian culture at the higher levels of court society, and this includes verbal culture: the *Knútsdrápur* clearly indicate that the Old Norse language continued to be spoken at Cnut's court, and Old Norse literary traditions to be highly prized, while the writing of Old Norse is demonstrated by the runic inscription cited earlier; however, that none of the manuscript documents from Cnut's reign are in Old Norse is not significant, as there is no evidence that Old Norse was ever written in the Roman alphabet in Viking Age England, and one must therefore imagine

---

[158] Hallvarðr, *Knútsdrápa* 4.1–2 and 6.6 (*ibid.* IB, 294; 'tree of the Midgard serpent's path', 'noise-Freyr of weapons').　　[159] Frank, 'King Cnut in the Verse of his Skalds', p. 110.

[160] N. Hooper, 'The Housecarls in England in the Eleventh Century', *ANS* 7 (1985), 161–76; Hooper, 'Military Developments in the Reign of Cnut'; see also Campbell, 'Some Agents and Agencies of the Late Anglo-Saxon State', pp. 203–4.

[161] Hooper, 'The Housecarls in England', pp. 170–1.　　[162] Keynes, 'Cnut's Earls', pp. 54–66.

[163] *Liber Vitae: Register and Martyrology of New Minster and Hyde Abbey Winchester*, ed. W. de G. Birch, Hampshire Record Soc. (London, 1892), p. 55 (nos. xlvii–l); *The Liber Vitae of the New Minster*, ed. Keynes, pp. 40 and 94.

the coexistence of written English (and Latin) and spoken Norse (and English).[164] M. K. Lawson suggests that the law-codes I and II Cnut 'were perhaps read out by Wulfstan at a Christmas court at Winchester';[165] in such a society, in which two vernaculars were being spoken, and literary works in those two vernaculars being recited, one may reasonably postulate a variety of different audiences, correlating, in some degree, with different court-groupings.[166] The question of the possible intelligibility of skaldic verse to monolingual Anglo-Saxons is an old imponderable,[167] but even here one may propose a scale of difficulty: Hallvarðr's *Knútsdrápa*, for example, is especially dense in terms of language and allusions,[168] but Sigvatr's verse is much less intractable, and Russell Poole has even suggested with regard to Óttarr's *Knútsdrápa* that '[t]he relative simplicity of the style may indicate a special effort toward intelligibility in a mixed English-Scandinavian milieu'.[169] If this is so, then the poem's stance and subject would seem to presuppose that any such English audience must have aligned their interests with the Danish perspective of the conquerors.

For the chronology established earlier is significant here, in that most of the *Knútsdrápur* are from the latter half of Cnut's reign: except for *Liðsmannaflokkr* and *Eiríksdrápa*, they indicate that skalds came seeking Cnut's court after Holy River and the Norway expedition, and could expect a profitable reception when they arrived. In other words, these poems would seem to indicate that on Cnut's part there was no jettisoning of Norse traditions – whether suddenly or gradually – as his reign in England progressed: on the contrary, Cnut's reputation in the Scandinavian world as a patron of Norse culture appears to have been at its height in the late 1020s. It may therefore be worth drawing in Hooper's observation that the first extant grant of land to a housecarl dates from as late as 1033, and the resultant suggestion that until that point in his reign Cnut may well have had a greater number of Scandinavian followers about him at court.[170] The earliness (or otherwise) of the *Knútsdrápur* is therefore not the issue here, as it would

---

[164] See M. Townend, 'Viking Age England as a Bilingual Society', *Cultures in Contact: Scandinavian Settlement in England in the Ninth and Tenth Centuries*, ed. D. M. Hadley and J. D. Richards, Stud. in the Early Middle Ages 2 (Turnhout, 2000), 89–105, at 95.

[165] Lawson, 'Archbishop Wulfstan and the Homiletic Element', p. 161.

[166] Jeff Opland has suggested of Cnut that '[i]t is quite likely that this king of England's reputation was perpetuated in English eulogies, though none has survived': J. Opland, *Anglo-Saxon Oral Poetry: a Study of the Traditions* (New Haven, CT, 1980), p. 188.

[167] See M. Townend, 'Pre-Cnut Praise-Poetry in Viking Age England', *RES* 51 (2000), 349–70, at 361. Pauline Stafford makes the intriguing suggestion that if Emma was raised at the Norman court, then she quite possibly knew Old Norse – 'a tremendous advantage in 1016/17' (Stafford, *Queen Emma and Queen Edith*, p. 204).

[168] See Frank, 'King Cnut in the Verse of his Skalds', pp. 119–23, who writes of its 'decidedly *ancien régime* iconography' (p. 119).

[169] R. Poole, 'Óttarr svarti', *Medieval Scandinavia*, ed. Pulsiano, pp. 459–60, at 459.

[170] Hooper, 'Military Developments in the Reign of Cnut', pp. 94–5.

be if one were primarily interested in the poems as historical sources: Alistair Campbell, for instance, had no very high opinion of Óttarr's *Knútsdrápa* as a source since it probably dates from some ten years after the Anglo-Danish wars it describes and may be dependent in some of its details on earlier skaldic verse;[171] but if one is concerned, as here, with tracing the continuing literary culture of Cnut's court, then it becomes extremely interesting to see what forms the telling of those wars had assumed at Cnut's court a decade later, and what stories about the gaining of the throne the conqueror was pleased to hear. Much modern historiography on Cnut's reign stresses the care with which an Anglo-Danish *rapprochement* was achieved: it is therefore salutary to note that Óttarr's *Knútsdrápa* is instead concerned with celebrating the Danish military triumph over the English, even ten years after the accession.

Another strand in recent historiography on Cnut emphasizes the degree to which the king assumed an English persona, and the rapidity with which he did so: this is especially apparent in his dealings with the church, in which his conspicuous acts of patronage earned the famous praise from Fulbert of Chartres that *te quem paganorum principem audieramus, non modo Christianum, uerum etiam erga ecclesias atque Dei seruos benignissimum largitorem agnoscimus.*[172] So, for instance, Lawson notes that '[i]n matters of religion he was largely obliged to play an English game, with English men, and by English rules',[173] and Susan Ridyard has suggested that in his dedication to the cult of St Edith, Cnut appears as 'almost more West Saxon than the West Saxons'.[174] T. A. Heslop has sought to explain the increase in the number of sumptuous illustrated manuscripts in eleventh-century England by attributing their production to the patronage of Cnut and Emma.[175] In the light of such an ecclesiastical emphasis, the *Knútsdrápur* therefore constitute an invaluable reassertion of the continuing 'Norseness' of Cnut's court, and of the continuing importance to Cnut of his Scandinavian inheritance: as praise-poems they can 'imply much about the ways in which [Cnut] wanted to be seen',[176] and this was as

---

[171] Campbell, *Skaldic Verse and Anglo-Saxon History*, pp. 12–14.

[172] *The Letters and Poems of Fulbert of Chartres*, ed. F. Behrends (Oxford, 1976), pp. 66–9 ('you, whom we had heard to be a pagan prince, we now know to be not only a Christian, but also a most generous donor to churches and God's servants'). For an account of Cnut's relations with the church, see Lawson, *Cnut*, pp. 117–60.   [173] *Ibid.* p. 130.

[174] S. J. Ridyard, *The Royal Saints of Anglo-Saxon England: a Study of West Saxon and East Anglian Cults*, Cambridge Stud. in Med. Life and Thought, 4th ser. 9 (Cambridge, 1988), 195. Gregory F. Rose similarly claims that Cnut's self-presentation in his reign was 'more English than the English', and in fact goes so far as to argue, *contra* Kevin Kiernan, that *Beowulf* cannot have come from Cnut's court as it is too Scandinavian (G. F. Rose, 'The Kiernan Theory Revisited: *Beowulf* at the Court of Cnut?', *Envoi* 6 (1997), 135–45, at 140).

[175] T. A. Heslop, 'The Production of *de luxe* Manuscripts and the Patronage of King Cnut and Queen Emma', *ASE* 19 (1990), 151–95; however, for important reservations, see Gameson, *The Role of Art in the Late Anglo-Saxon Church*, pp. 258–9.

[176] Lawson, *Cnut*, p. 75; see also pp. 130 and 221–2.

the gold-giving warrior-king, proud of his Danish origins and by no means meta-morphosing into an honorary Englishman. This sense of the continuing impor-tance to Cnut of his Scandinavian inheritance is of course observable in other ways: for example in the way in which Cnut does not choose to give his children English names – which would have been an obvious gesture of *rapprochement* – but rather names his three sons Sveinn, Harald and Harthacnut, following in sequence the names of his father, grandfather and (probably) great-grandfa-ther.[177] But it is the *Knútsdrápur* that provide the fullest and clearest evidence for this alternative image of a Scandinavian Cnut.[178] It is not that the image of the 'English Cnut' is incorrect – clearly it is not – but simply that such a portrait is partial, and privileges one perspective on Cnut's reign over other possible views. It is therefore interesting to return again to the chronology of the *Knútsdrápur*, and to note that the supreme images of both the Scandinavian and English Cnuts co-exist exactly in time and space: the Norse poems derive from Winchester in the late 1020s or early 1030s, and the frontispiece to the New Minster *Liber Vitae* was produced in Winchester in 1031.[179]

Patronage and generosity are the motors for both these images. Richard Gameson has remarked that 'King Cnut expressed his aspirations no less through artistic patronage than by law codes and pronouncements',[180] and while Gameson is obviously thinking in terms of visual art, the dictum holds equally good of skaldic. As has been suggested above, the *Knútsdrápur* supply a unique insight into how Cnut wished to be seen and remembered by Scandinavian contemporaries, and the sheer scale of Cnut's patronage of skaldic verse indicates the importance he placed on the medium. In a study that exemplifies well the intriguing self-con-sistency of saga-literature, Bjarne Fidjestøl gathered together all the passages in the kings' sagas which record a king rewarding a poet for a praise-poem, and he demonstrated that in such saga accounts Cnut was remembered as by much the most generous, in terms of sheer monetary value, of all patrons of skaldic verse; and Fidjestøl suggested there is a direct correlation to be traced between the pos-session of movable wealth and the patronage of poets.[181] That the pre-eminence of Cnut in this regard is not simply a later medieval fiction is indicated by

---

[177] *Ibid.* pp. 114–15; Stafford, *Queen Emma and Queen Edith*, pp. 86–7 and 233. That Cnut's great-grandfather Gorm was also called Harthacnut is stated by Adam of Bremen (Adam of Bremen, *Gesta Hammaburgensis Ecclesiae Pontificum: Hamburgische Kirchengeschichte*, ed. B. Schmeidler, 3rd ed. (Hanover, 1917), p. 56).

[178] With regard to the value placed on Danish ancestry, Frank points out that his skalds did not 'hesitate to observe that Cnut was his father's son', and that the *Knútsdrápur* are peppered with references to Sveinn Haraldsson (Frank, 'King Cnut in the Verse of his Skalds', p. 112).

[179] For the date of the *Liber Vitae*, see *The Liber Vitae of the New Minster*, ed. Keynes, pp. 37–8.

[180] Gameson, *The Role of Art in the Late Anglo-Saxon Church*, p. 5.

[181] B. Fidjestøl, '"Have you Heard a Poem Worth More?" A Note on the Economic Background of Early Skaldic Praise-Poetry', in his *Selected Papers*, ed. Haugen and Mundal, pp. 117–32.

þórarinn's *Tǫgdrápa*, which specifies the receipt of fifty (silver) marks for his earlier *Hǫfuðlausn* (*Gjǫld hefk marka / malmdyns fyr hlyn / framm fimm tǫgu / forvist borit*).[182] As Fidjestøl notes, although this may seem an 'implausibly large sum', it is 'as well attested as anyone could wish' through its recording in the *Tǫgdrápa*.[183] So one may set the extent of Cnut's skaldic patronage beside that of his ecclesiastical patronage, and in conclusion observe again the coexistent diversity of the court culture to be found in Cnut's Winchester during the years of his reign.

To conclude: in this article I have not endeavoured to give a close reading or stylistic analysis of the *Knútsdrápur*, not least on account of the excellence of Roberta Frank's 1994 undertaking to that effect;[184] nor have I attempted to probe them for historical information, as has been done for some of the poems in Russell Poole's invaluable studies.[185] Rather, I have attempted to recover something of the immediate physical context in which these poems were originally delivered, and to sketch out some of the ways in which context and meaning are inseparable in an emphatically social type of literature such as praise-poetry. It is worth closing, therefore, with the observation that the *Knútsdrápur* are remarkable, even unique, in the degree to which one can specify the circumstances of production and reception. For these poems can be dated to particular phases in the reign of the king, and some of them to a particular year or two; they can be localized not just to a region or place, but perhaps even (for those with a Winchester provenance) to a particular, locatable building, surrounded by other identifiable and well-recorded buildings; they can be attributed to named poets, for some of whom we have biographical information and by nearly all of whom we have other works; and their genesis can, of course, be ascribed to a particular patron, whose court-followers can be postulated as the wider audience for the poems' oral delivery.

There is more or less no other vernacular poetry from Anglo-Saxon England – and certainly no other corpus of poetry – that can be contextualized as well as this; and this, as I have tried to argue, is fortuitously for a type of poetry that is deeply dependent on original context for generating its meaning, and for which we must attend to context if we are to recapture its effects. The *Knútsdrápur* might thus arguably be ranked among the most important of poetic remains from Anglo-Saxon England, and so I would conclude by asserting that these Old Norse poems from Cnut's court are just as much a part of Anglo-Saxon

---

[182] þórarinn, *Tǫgdrápa* 1.1–4 (*Skjaldedigtning*, ed. Finnur Jónsson IB, 298; 'I have certainly carried away a payment of fifty marks before the tree of the noise of weapons [= warrior]'). Later prose accounts of the episode can be found in *Heimskringla* and *Knýtlinga saga*: Snorri Sturluson, *Heimskringla*, ed. Bjarni Aðalbjarnarson II, 307–8; *Danakonunga sǫgur*, ed. Bjarni Guðnason, pp. 124–5.   [183] Fidjestøl, '"Have you Heard a Poem Worth More?"', p. 119.
[184] Frank, 'King Cnut in the Verse of his Skalds'.
[185] Poole, 'Skaldic Verse and Anglo-Saxon History'; idem, *Viking Poems on War and Peace*.

England's literary history as, say, Latin works composed at the time – though one may look in vain for them in the standard handbooks of Anglo-Saxon literature.[186]

[186] The work for this article was begun during a period of research funded by the British Academy. For help of various kinds I am also grateful to John Barrell, Katy Cubitt, Heather O'Donoghue and Elizabeth Tyler.

Anglo-Saxon prognostics in context: a survey and handlist of manuscripts

ROY MICHAEL LIUZZA

The various Latin and Old English texts which have come to be called 'prognostics' have not, in general, been well served by scholars. For some texts the only available edition is Oswald Cockayne's *Leechdoms, Wortcunning, and Starcraft of Early England* from 1864–6; most others are available only in the broad but somewhat unsystematic series of articles published by Max Förster in *Archiv für das Studium der neueren Sprachen und Literaturen* in the 1910s and 1920s.[1] Anselm Hughes does not include the eight prognostic texts in Cambridge, Corpus Christi College 391 in his otherwise fairly thorough edition of much of that manuscript;[2] Peter Baker and Michael Lapidge omit any discussion of such texts from their excellent survey of the history of the computus in the preface to their edition of Byrhtferth's *Enchiridion*.[3] The mid-eleventh-century Christ Church manuscript now known as London, British Library, Cotton Tiberius A. iii[4] has attracted the notice of many fine scholars, including liturgists, linguists and monastic and art historians, who have been drawn to the series of texts at the beginning of the manuscript (fols. 117–73 and 2–27), including two magnificent full-page drawings (117v and 2v)[5] and glossed copies of the *Benedictine Rule* and the *Regularis Concordia*.[6] Helmut Gneuss describes this carefully presented series

---

[1] See the appendix, p. 212, for a list of editions cited by author's name and date in these notes.

[2] *The Portiforium of Saint Wulfstan*, ed. A. Hughes, HBS 89–90 (1958–60).

[3] *Byrhtferth's Enchiridion*, ed. P. S. Baker and M. Lapidge, EETS ss 15 (Oxford, 1995).

[4] For contents and recent editorial history, see H. Gneuss, 'Origin and Provenance of Anglo-Saxon Manuscripts: the Case of Cotton Tiberius A. iii', *Of the Making of Books: Medieval Manuscripts, their Scribes and Readers. Essays presented to M. B. Parkes*, ed. P. R. Robinson and R. Zim (Aldershot, 1997), pp. 13–48.

[5] See F. Wormald, *English Drawings of the Tenth and Eleventh Centuries* (London, 1952), no. 31, and E. Temple, *Anglo-Saxon Manuscripts 900–1066: a Survey of Manuscripts Illuminated in the British Isles* (London, 1976), pp. 118–19 (item 100) and pls. 313–14.

[6] See M. Gretsch, *Die Regula Sancti Benedicti in England und ihre altenglische Übersetzung*, Texte und Untersuchungen zur Englischen Philologie 2 (Munich, 1973), L. Kornexl, *Die Regularis Concordia und ihre altenglische Interlinearversion* (Munich, 1993); see also T. Symons, *Regularis Concordia: the Monastic Agreement of the Monks and Nuns of the English Nation* (New York, 1953); and L. Kornexl, 'The *Regularis Concordia* and its Old English Gloss', *ASE* 24 (1995), 95–130. Between these texts is a glossed Latin 'Admonition concerning the Rule' by Pseudo-Fulgentius, ed. P. Pulsiano, 'BL Cotton Tiberius A. iii: Fulgentius, *Injunction*', *ANQ* ns 1 (1988), 43–4, and H. Sauer, 'Die Ermahnung des Pseudo-Fulgentius zur Benediktregel und ihre altenglische Glossierung', *Anglia* 102 (1984), 419–25; an epitome of the Rule known as the *Memoriale qualiter*, ed. A. S. Napier, *An Epitome of Benedict of Aniane*, EETS os 150 (London, 1916), pp. 119–28; *De festivitatibus anni*; and

of interrelated texts as 'a compendium of the Benedictine Reform movements in Carolingian Francia and in tenth-century England';[7] Robert Deshman has argued that the very sequence of texts is 'laden with meaning'.[8] Despite their appreciation of these manuscript sequences, however, few scholars have included in their study of this material the eighteen prognostic texts which follow the *Regularis Concordia* in the manuscript (27v–47), though most of these are in the same hand and are arranged, it may be argued, with equal care.

At the same time the Anglo-Saxon prognostics suffered a kind of enthusiastic overproduction at the hands of their early editors. Förster's determination to demonstrate the classical origins of these texts led him to provide an abundance of analogues and parallels ranging from the ninth to the sixteenth centuries – in Latin, Greek, German, French and Middle English – often in the notes and variants to one text. Such editorial abundance, however illuminating it may be for the history of traditions, makes it sometimes difficult to understand individual texts in their local contexts. Förster's practices may perhaps be explained by the attitude he and other scholars brought to the prognostics; they have generally been studied from the viewpoint of what Förster called *Volkskunde* 'folklore' or *Aberglaube* 'superstition',[9] sometimes qualified as 'monastic superstition'[10] to distinguish it from the pure products of folk belief.[11] To classify a certain sort of text as 'folklore', even the apparent oxymoron 'learned folklore', is not only to perform some interpretative work upon it, it is to place it as it were outside the realm of literary analysis, removing the text from a situation in a manuscript and a textual history, and into the precincts of anthropology, the domain of the local, the peculiar and the marginal. 'Folklore' (in the traditional sense that Förster and other early editors employed it)[12] inevitably implies a distinction between 'popular' ways of thinking, writing and acting and the ways of 'high' or 'élite' culture, but in effect it is a diachronic category: it is the label affixed to what one might call the 'recessive genes' of a culture, the practices whose theory was discarded or supplanted on the way to modernity. But this is certainly a *post hoc* characterization of little use in literary or historical analysis; it tells us nothing of

---

the Capitula of Aachen of 818/819, ed. H. Mordek, *Bibliotheca capitularum regum Francorum manuscripta*, MGH Hilfsmittel 15 (Munich, 1994), 223–5.

[7] Gneuss, 'Origin and Provenance', p. 15.

[8] R. Deshman, '*Benedictus Monarcha et Monachus*: Early Medieval Ruler Theology and the Anglo-Saxon Reform', *FS* 22 (1988), 204–40, at p. 229.

[9] It must be admitted that Förster used these words in a qualified sense and with some regret; see Förster 1908a, p. 43.   [10] Henel 1934–5.

[11] They are still so classified; in the subject index of Ker's *Catalogue* one finds '**Prognostics**. See **Folklore**'; in Karen and Kenneth Quinn's *Manual of Old English Prose* (New York, 1990) prognostics are grouped with charms in a section also labelled 'Folklore'. Cockayne even printed the Old English prognostic texts in Tiberius A. iii without the Latin texts they glossed, perhaps to make them seem more 'folkloric' and less learned.

[12] Changing definitions of the term are explored in *Jnl of Folklore Research* 33.3 (1996).

how such texts were used. Viewing texts from the diachronic perspective of the 'history of . . .' a subject (whether science, religion – even popular religion – or astrology) tends subtly but inevitably to expropriate them from the context in which they were written and copied, from which they contributed to lived experience. A prayer for safety addressed to the cross, for example, would be assigned without hesitation to the history of religion; a quasi-liturgical ritual 'charm' against cattle theft in the same manuscript is regarded as 'folklore'.[13] But prognostic texts are found in the same manuscripts as the Psalms, scientific works such as Ælfric's *De temporibus anni*, or penitential prayers; if we hope to understand the role such texts played in later Anglo-Saxon culture we might begin by assuming that they operated in the same world as their companion texts, were used by the same readers, and were regarded with something of the same respect. A consideration of the context, both material and cultural, of Anglo-Saxon prognostic texts may help us move beyond the misleading distinction between 'high' and 'low' culture which we bring to them, and which has coloured our understanding both of these texts and of Anglo-Saxon religious practice in general.

Since many of these works are not well known or readily available, it may be best to preface a discussion of their context with a brief survey of texts and their distribution.[14] The texts which we group together under the rubric 'Prognostics' may be divided into several different groups, nearly all of which are found in both Latin and English versions:

1. Predictions of the *if . . . then* type based on the calendar:

(i) *Revelatio (or Supputatio) Esdrae*, predicting the year's weather and other events, mostly agricultural, based on the day of the week on which New Year's Day falls.[15] Latin versions are found in **T4** (with Old English gloss),

---

[13] S. Hollis, 'Old English "Cattle Theft Charms": Manuscript Contexts and Social Uses', *Anglia* 115 (1997), 139–64, and see T. Hill, 'The Theme of the Cosmological Cross in Two Old English Cattle Theft Charms', *N&Q* ns 25 (1978), 488–90.

[14] The following typology is based upon my own survey of MSS but is indebted to S. Hollis and M. Wright, *Old English Prose of Secular Learning*, Annotated Bibliographies of Old and Middle Eng. Lit. 4 (Cambridge, 1992), 257–69. The proliferation of MS sigla is a necessary evil in a study like this; see below, pp. 212–30, for a list of editions, sigla, MSS and brief descriptions. In the following notes, MSS listed without intervening commas contain variant versions of the same text; MSS separated by commas contain different versions. A full survey of surviving texts and their relationships, towards which this list is only a gesture, is much to be desired.

[15] Ptd Förster 1908b, pp. 296–301. See L. Thorndike, *A History of Magic and Experimental Science*, 8 vols. (New York, 1923–58) I, 677–8; E. A. Matter, 'The "Revelatio Esdrae" in Latin and English Traditions', *RB* 92 (1982), 376–92, who notes its earliest Latin appearances in ninth-century MSS from Fleury (**F**) and Lorsch (Vatican City, Biblioteca Apostolica Vaticana, Pal. Lat. 1449, fols. 119–20); and *Sources of Anglo-Saxon Literary Culture: a Trial Version*, ed. F. M. Biggs, T. D. Hill and P. Szarmach, Medieval and Renaissance Texts and Stud. 74 (Binghamton, NY, 1990), 29–30. It also appears among Bede's writings in PL 90, col. 951; see C. W. Jones, *Bedae Pseudepigrapha: Scientific Writings Falsely Attributed to Bede* (Ithaca, NY, 1939; repr. in *Bede, the Schools, and the Computus* (Aldershot, 1994)), p. 87.

Æ67, Æ32, F8; all are similar though none is identical to another. A different Latin version, probably post-Conquest, is found in J13; a version based on Christmas rather than 1 January is found in S10. English versions in T16, V1 and H4 (the last based on Christmas rather than 1 January) are all similar both to Latin versions and to one another, but not identical.

(ii) Prognostic for a newborn child based on the day of the week on which the child is born:[16] a Latin version in T20 Æ62 J4, an English version in W3, H3 (the two are similar to the Latin version and to one another, but not identical).

(iii) A general prognostic in English based on the weekday of the new moon is found in T13.[17]

2. Predictions based on some natural occurrence:

(i) A forecast in English of various sorts of death and disaster based on the occurrence of wind in the twelve days after Christmas is found in H5.[18]

(ii) A forecast in English of various sorts of good fortune based on the occurrence of sunshine in the twelve days after Christmas is found in H6 and W1 (the two are closely similar but not identical).[19]

(iii) Brontologies (prognostics based on thunder):[20]

a. By hours of the night and day: a Latin version is found in T7 (with Old English gloss) Æ66.

b. By day of the week: an English version appears in T12 H9.

c. By month of the year: a Latin version is found in R1; an unrelated English version in V2.[21]

d. A composite brontology in English is found in W2; the first part = T12 H9; there follow indications of the meaning of thunder at the hours of the Night Office, then from different directions, then at the hours of monastic daily prayer.

---

[16] Ptd Förster 1912b, pp. 296–308. A version of this text is printed among Bede's pseudepigrapha in PL 90, col. 960.   [17] Ptd Cockayne 1864–6, III, 180–2.

[18] Ptd Förster 1912a, pp. 55–64. A Latin version exactly similar is found in Oxford, Bodleian Library Ashmole 345 (s. xiv), 69rv, which also includes a Latin version of H4. A different text on the same principle is found in Paris, Bibliothèque Nationale de France, nouv. acq. 1616 (Fleury, s.x), 12v, beginning *Si in nocte fuerit uentus in natali domini nostri iesu christi, in hoc anno reges & pontifices peribunt. Si in nocte .ii. fuerit uentus uiri ingrati deficient. Si in nocte .iii. fuerit uentus orfani & mulieres peribunt*; see Thorndike, *History of Magic* I, 678.

[19] Ptd Förster 1912a, pp. 64–71. In both cases Förster notes Latin analogues in later MSS.

[20] Middle English versions of these are ptd Förster 1912b, pp. 285–95. See also Thorndike, *History of Magic* I, 679–80.   [21] Ptd Warner 1917, p. 91.

3. Lists of lucky and unlucky days in the year (sometimes called 'Egyptian'),[22] usually for medical purposes:

(i) 'Three marvellous days' on which only male children are born, and these with incorruptible bodies:[23] a Latin version in **Æ57 J2**; an Old English version in **W6 C6 Vi5**.[24] The Old English versions are nearly identical and are closely similar to the Latin, but while **Æ57 J2** name the three days as *novissimus de thebet et duo primi de sabath* (i.e. January and February in the Jewish calendar), the Old English version says they are 'an þære daga on æftewardan decembre and tweigen on foreweardan Ianuarii' and adds, 'feawe men synd þe þas dagas cunnon'.

(ii) 'Three critical Mondays' on which it is not good to let blood:[25] Latin versions in **J1, G5, G6 Æ18b** and called 'Egyptian days' in **G8 Æ56 F6 Di1 Sa1**; a similar text is added to **D2**;[26] one English version in **W7 Vi6**, another in London, British Library, Cotton Vitellius C. viii, 22rv and London, British Library, Harley 585 (the *Lacnunga*), 190rv.[27] The days are the first Monday of August and the last Monday of March and December; warnings are included against taking medicines, and in some texts eating gooseflesh.

(iii) 'Twenty-four critical days', two in each month, on which it is not good to let blood; days are counted forward from the beginning of the month and backward from the end:
a. A Latin version in hexameters, beginning *Iani prima dies et septima fine timetur*, in **Æ18 G6 S9 Tr1** and the gloss to **G4**;[28] the same text is distributed

---

[22] Several different sorts of days – groups of three in the year or two per month – are labelled 'Egyptian'; see Thorndike, *History of Magic* I, 685–96. See also J. Loiseleur, 'Les Jours egyptiens. Leur variations dans le calendriers du moyen âge', *Memoires de la Société des antiquaires de France* 33 (1872), 198–253, and R. Steele, '"Dies Aegyptiaci"', *Proc. of the R. Soc. of Medicine* 13, supplement (1919), 108–21. For an early version of this tradition (unrelated to surviving Anglo-Saxon versions), see H. Stuart, 'A Ninth Century Account of Diets and *Dies Aegyptiaci*', *Scriptorium* 33 (1979), 237–44.   [23] A Latin version appears falsely attributed to Bede in PL 90, col. 960.
[24] Ptd Förster 1929, pp. 259–61; Henel 1934–5, pp. 346–7.
[25] Versions of this appear among Bede's pseudepigrapha in PL 90, cols. 955 and 960; see Jones, *Bedae Pseudepigrapha*, pp. 88–9. For background, see G. Keil, 'Die verworfenen Tage', *Sudhoffs Archiv* 41 (1957), 27–58.
[26] F. E. Wallis, 'MS Oxford St John's College 17: a Mediaeval Manuscript in its Context' (unpubl. PhD dissertation, Univ. of Toronto, 1984), p. 192, n. 24, notes other versions of this text in continental MSS of the tenth and eleventh centuries.
[27] Both versions are ptd Förster 1929, pp. 270–7.
[28] Ptd as a Bedan text in PL 90, col. 955; see Jones, *Bedae Pseudepigrapha*, p. 73. It is no. 7597 in D. Schaller and E. Könsgen, *Initia carminum Latinorum saeculo undecimo antiquiorum* (Göttingen, 1977) and is printed, each line distributed across the twelve months, in Baker and Lapidge's reconstruction of the calendar of Byrhtferth's Computus (*Byrhtferth's Enchiridion*, ed. Baker and Lapidge, pp. 391–416). See also L. Thorndike and P. Kibre, *A Catalogue of Incipits of Mediaeval*

throughout the calendar in **Vi1 A2 J9** (and in Oxford, Bodleian Library, Douce 296, fols. 1–6, an eleventh-century manuscript).

b. Versions in prose in **G4** (includes the prose portion of Æ**18**, with the verses added between the lines), **F5**, **Di1**, **J10c**, and **C3**;[29] an English version in **Vi7 C5 G1–2** (the latter has the two parts of the text in **C5** reversed).[30] The English version begins the year in March, but notes the same days as the Latin version; it includes a warning against letting blood on the fourth and fifth days of the lunar month, and on All Saints' Day; **G1** adds a warning against eating gooseflesh on the last day of March or December (cf. 3.ii above). Most Latin versions include a warning against letting blood in the *dies caniculares* and on the fourth, fifth, tenth, fifteenth, twentieth and twenty-fifth days of the month.

c. The Latin text of **J10a Th1**, which lists one unlucky day in each month, is unusual.

(iv) 'Twenty-four unlucky days', not specifically related to bloodletting. A Latin version in Æ**59** calls the days *aegiptiaci*; another Latin version, listing days in the lunar month, is found in **J10b**. An English version (with different days) is found in **Vi2 C4**.[31]

(v) *Dies caniculares* in which bloodletting is prohibited, from eighteen days before Lammas until thirty-five days after (i.e. 14 July until 5 September).[32] These dates are often noted in calendars.[33] These are included among other prohibitions in Latin in Æ**18b G4 G7**, **F7** and separately in Æ**58 G10–11**. An Old English version is found in **Vi3**; another version is found in London, British Library, Royal 12. D. XVII, 'Bald's Leechbook', 54v–55v.[34] Both Latin and Old English versions include a warning against letting blood on every fifth day of the lunar month.

4. Lunar hemerologies or 'lunaria', a list of days of the lunar month[35] for various actions. These are ultimately based on the principles of lunar astrology,

Scientific Writings in Latin (Cambridge, MA, 1963), no. 651. The days in question are 1, 25 January; 4, 26 February; 1, 28 March; 10, 20 April; 3, 25 May; 10, 16 June; 13, 22 July; 1, 30 August; 3, 21 September; 3, 22 October; 5, 28 November; 12, 15 December.
29 The same text is found added in a hand of s. xii to London, British Library, Cotton Tiberius C. vi, 114r.   30 Ptd Förster 1929, pp. 265–70; Henel 1934–5, pp. 335–46.
31 Ptd Förster 1929, pp. 261–5. Förster prints Greek analogues, and Förster 1903, p. 352 lists Latin analogues. A version of this text is found added in Norman French to Tiberius C. vi, 114r.   32 Ptd Henel 1934–5, pp. 331–3.   33 See Henel 1934–5, p. 331, for a partial list.
34 See *Bald's Leechbook: British Museum 12 D. xvii*, ed. C. E. Wright, EEMF 5 (Copenhagen, 1955).
35 According to Bede, *De temporum ratione* xxxvi.8–12, ed. C. W. Jones, *Bedae Opera de Temporibus*, Med. Acad. of America Publ. 41. (Cambridge, MA, 1943), the moon takes twenty-seven days, eight hours to complete its circuit around the earth, but because the earth is also moving while the moon revolves around it, the time from one new moon to the next – the synodical lunar

the transit of the moon through its 'mansions' from one new moon to another, but the system on which they were based was not included in the simple lists of days.[36] Such calendars are at least as old as Hesiod's *Works and Days*,[37] and are perhaps ultimately of Babylonian origin;[38] the earliest extant Latin texts, however, are no earlier than the ninth century.[39] Formal similarity conceals considerable variation within each type of text.

(i)   Bloodletting, with instructions for good and bad times of day.[40] A Latin version is found, usually in chart form, in Æ1 A1 G3 D1 T19 Æ61 J3; a different and simplified version is found in L2.[41]

(ii) Birth, predicting the fortune of a child born on a given day.[42] A Latin version is found in T5 (with Old English gloss) T21 Æ63 F4 J5; the latter three have the title *Incipit Lunaris sancti danielis de natitutate*. Old English versions, similar but not identical to one another and to the Latin, are in T15 C8, H2 (days 1–14 only), and W4.

(iii) Medical, offering prognoses on a patient who falls sick on a given day.[43] A Latin version is in T6 C2 (the former with Old English gloss, the latter with the Old English alongside the Latin in chart form) T22 (days 1–7

---

month or 'lunation' – is slightly longer, traditionally twenty-nine-and-a-half days. This was balanced out by alternating lunar months of twenty-nine and thirty days; lunaria have thirty days.

[36] The idea of lunar 'mansions' passed into the west with the recovery of Arabic astrology such as the works of Messahall's *De lune mansionibus* and Haly Embrani's *De electionibus horarum*; see S. J. Tester, *A History of Western Astrology* (Woodbridge, 1987), pp. 81–4, L. Means, *Medieval Lunar Astrology: a Collection of Representative Middle English Texts* (Lewiston, NY, 1993), pp. 60–8, and S. Weinstock, 'Lunar Mansions and Early Calendars', *Jnl of Hellenic Stud.* 69 (1949), 48–69. None of these Arabic works was known to the Anglo-Saxons; for their textual history, see F. J. Carmody, *Arabic Astronomical and Astrological Sciences in Latin Translation: a Critical Bibliography* (Berkeley, CA, 1956). See also Thorndike and Kibre, *Catalogue of Incipits*, no. 1093.

[37] Hesiod, *Theogony and Works and Days*, trans. M. L. West (Oxford, 1988); see lines 765–828.

[38] Tester, *History of Western Astrology*, pp. 82–3 and P. Yampolsky, 'The Origin of the Twenty-Eight Lunar Mansions', *Osiris* 9 (1950), 62–83. See also the numerous Babylonian lunar prognostics published by M. Jastrow, *The Religion of Babylonia and Assyria* (Boston, MA, 1898), pp. 375–79; or *Die Religion Babyloniens und Assyriens*, 2 vols. (Giessen, 1905–12) II, 457–577. A brief introduction to the subject may be found in U. Koch-Westenholz, *Mesopotamian Astrology: an Introduction to Babylonian and Assyrian Celestial Divination* (Copenhagen, 1995).

[39] See Svenburg 1936 and *Lunaria et Zodiologia Latina*, Studia Graeca et Latina Gothoburgensia 16 (Stockholm, 1963); E. Wistrand, *Lunariastudien*, Göteborgs Hogskolas Arskrift 48 (Göteborg, 1942).

[40] Ptd Förster 1912c, pp. 36–7, Henel 1934–5, pp. 333–5, and cf. the version falsely attributed to Bede, PL 90, cols. 961–2.   [41] S7 is a list of favourable hours in each day for bloodletting.

[42] Ptd Förster 1912c, pp. 16–30.

[43] Ptd Förster 1912c, pp. 30–6. See C. Weisser, *Studien zum mittelalterlichen Krankheitslunar*, Würzburger medizin-historische Forschungen 21 (Würzburg, 1982).

only) Æ64 F3 J6; Old English versions, apparently unrelated, are in T11, W5.[44]

(iv) Dreams, giving advice on the reliability of a dream.[45] Latin versions are in T3 (with Old English gloss), Æ65 J7, W8 (the latter includes verses of Psalms for each day of the month);[46] an Old English version is found in T8 C7 W8, and a somewhat similar version in H1.

(v) General, offering advice and predictions for various conditions. Latin versions are found in T2[47] (titled *De observatione lune et quae cavenda sunt*, with Old English gloss), S8, and Æ35 (titled *Argumentum lunare ad requirendum quomodo luna qualiter observitur*);[48] an unrelated Old English version is found in T10 (days 1–3 only) H11 (days 1–17 only).[49] Förster leaves open the question of whether the general lunaria are the source of the various lists for individual purposes or the product of their compilation;[50] evidence favours the latter possibility, but in their medieval transmission the lunaria were highly susceptible to various kinds of textual alteration and the two types of lists probably influenced one another almost equally.

5 Lists of the significance of objects seen in dreams, the so-called *Somniale Danielis*.[51] Latin versions, all similar but none identical, are found in T1 (with

---

[44] London, British Library, Cotton Nero A.ii contains a brief note at the bottom of 7r: 'Luna .i. 7 .iii. 7 .v. 7 .ix. 7 .xi. 7 .xv. qui inciderit in eis cito morietur.' Though the language is that of a medical lunarium, the dates given are not particularly those of the surviving Latin text. This part of the MS (fols. 3–13) was almost certainly once part of London, British Library, Cotton Galba A. xiv, a private prayerbook written 1029–47 at Winchester, probably Nunnaminster; see A. N. Doane, *Early English Manuscripts in Microfiche Facsimile* 1 (Binghamton, NY, 1994), 15, and B. Muir, *A Pre-Conquest English Prayer-Book (BL MSS Cotton Galba A.xiv and Nero A.ii (ff. 3–13))*, HBS 103 (Woodbridge, 1988).   [45] Ptd Förster 1925–6, pp. 58–93.

[46] A somewhat similar arrangement of Psalm verses for each day of the month is found in a general lunarium in St Gallen, Stiftsbibliothek MS 44 (s. ix), fols. 226–8 (pr. Weisser, *Studien zum Mittelalterlichen Krankheitslunar*, pp. 373–80; see pp. 446–7 for a list of later texts which also include Psalms); Förster 1925–6, p. 67, notes a similar text in Vatican City, Biblioteca Apostolica Vaticana, lat. 642, fol. 91 (s. xii; ed. Svenberg 1936, pp. 88–95).

[47] Ptd Förster 1944, pp. 79–129.   [48] Ptd Günzel 1993, pp. 117–20.

[49] Ptd Förster 1912c, pp. 37–45. Förster also prints a general lunarium from Vatican lat. 642, 91v–94r (ed. Svenberg 1936, pp. 30–41). It begins like the Old English version (*Luna .i. mari pleno uade ad regem & pete ab eo, quod uis, hora tercia, & dabitur tibi*) but quickly diverges. In general it lists different activities for each day of the month, including lost or stolen items, propitious activities, and birth and medical prognostics.   [50] Förster 1944, pp. 8–9.

[51] See L. T. Martin, *Somniale Danielis: an Edition of a Medieval Latin Dream Interpretation Handbook* (Frankfurt, 1981). The work itself was apparently written in Greek in the fourth century (see F. Drexl, 'Das Traumbuch des Propheten Daniel nach dem cod. Vatic. Palat. gr. 319', *Byzantinische Zeitschrift* 26 (1926), 290–314; a Greek text in a sixteenth-century redaction is published by E. DeStoop, 'Oneirocriticon du prophète Daniel dédié au roi Nebuchodonosor', *Revue de philologie, de littérature et d'histoire anciennes* 33 (1909), 93–111) but was translated into Latin early in its life. This version circulated throughout the medieval west and survives in nearly seventy MSS. It is a strikingly polymorphous work, no two copies of

Old English gloss), **F1, S11, Æ68**. Versions in Old English are found in **T9 H10** (the two are identical), **T17**. The former Old English version is clearly derived from a Latin source similar to the *si videris* list appended to **T1** (items 271–302): it follows that list in relatively good order, and its own order is, for the most part, alphabetical according to Latin but not Old English. But the number and scope of interpolations indicate that it is not a close relative of that text, and its immediate source is unknown.

6. Devices for divination. Unlike prognostics, which simply provide information to correlate natural phenomena and human activities, divinations require action, usually the manipulation of numbers, to answer a question.

(i) The 'Sphere of life and death', usually attributed to 'Apuleius' or 'Pythagoras'. A form of iatromathematical divination, the sphere predicts the outcome of a disease using the day of the month and/or week on which the patient falls sick and the numerical value of the patient's name.[52] Various forms of this diagrammatic device are found in Latin; a full study of their dissemination in Anglo-Saxon England remains to be done, but surviving examples include **C1 F2 J8 J11 Th2 Th4 L1 Th3 S6 Vi4 Vi8**; see also London, British Library, Cotton Tiberius C. vi, 6v.

(ii) Other devices: an Old English divinatory alphabet, untitled and without accompanying text in its manuscript but probably a version of the *sortes*

which are the same; essentially a catalogue of one-line items, it was naturally subject to a great deal of editing and expansion. Martin discerns 'two radically distinct versions' (p. 4) of the Latin text of the *Somniale*, with different dreams and different interpretations for the same dreams; surviving English texts are all versions of the A-text but none is the exemplar of another (p. 65). The version in **T1**, the fullest early version of the text, is in fact a composite list from at least two different sources and textual traditions; the first 249 entries follow alphabetical order, then a group (nos. 250–70) includes items with initials c–v (most of these are found in Æ68 but not in the first part of **T1**), then a third group (nos. 271–302) contains entries beginning with *si* (e.g., *si videris draconem . . .*, the usual formula being *draconem viderit*). Æ68 has 154 dreams; **F**, a fragment from Fleury, has 76. See also Thorndike, *History of Magic* II, 290–302; S. R. Fischer, *The Complete Medieval Dreambook. A Multilingual, Alphabetical Somnia Danielis Collation* (Frankfurt, 1982); and E. O. G. Turville-Petre, 'An Icelandic Version of the Somniale Danielis', *Nordica et Anglica: Studies in Honor of Stefán Einarsson*, ed. A. H. Orrick (The Hague, 1968), pp. 19–36.

52 Ptd among Bede's works in PL 90, cols. 963–6; Jones, *Bedae Pseudepigrapha*, p. 90, says the table is 'common in Fleury *computi*'. See Thorndike, *History of Magic* I, 682–4 and 692–4; Thorndike and Kibre, *Catalogue of Incipits*, nos. 1315, 1522 and 1542; and *Byrhtferth's Enchiridion*, ed. Baker and Lapidge, p. 427. Further background may be found in E. Wickersheimer, 'Figures médico-astrologiques des IXe, Xe, et XIe siècles', *Janus* 19 (1914), 164–7; H. E. Sigerist, 'The Sphere of Life and Death in Medieval Manuscripts', *Bull. of the Hist. of Medicine* 11 (1942), 292–303; L. Voigts, 'The Latin Verse and Middle English Prose Texts on the Sphere of Life and Death in Harley 3719', *Chaucer Rev.* 21 (1986), 291–305, and *idem*, 'The Golden Table of Pythagoras', *Popular and Practical Science of Medieval England*, ed. L. M. Matheson (Lansing, MI, 1994), pp. 123–39.

biblica,[53] is found in Æ40. A Latin divination for casting lots known as the *sortes sanctorum*[54] (though not so titled) is found in **J12**, but is probably post-Conquest.

Most texts, as can be seen, are astrological only in the broad sense, lists of fortunate or unfortunate days; seldom is any celestial rationale offered for a given day's character. Though these texts can be divided into groups based on several different considerations, such as the ends to which a prediction is made (agricultural, medical, natal and so forth) and the means by which the prediction is reached (dream interpretation, observation of some natural phenomenon or consultation of the calendar), no such division is seen in the manuscripts containing them. What they share is a conviction that certain times and days have symbolic content or physiological significance, a belief in the relationship between celestial phenomena – thunder, the phases of the moon, or the course of the solar year – and human life, and a hope that through care and knowledge one can foresee, and to that extent control, the unfolding of fortune. The popularity of such texts extended well into the Middle English period[55] and beyond and is a strong, though often overlooked, link of continuity between Anglo-Saxon and later English literature, indeed between antiquity and the modern world.

Belief in various forms of divination and dream interpretation, and a pragmatically fatalistic belief in the influence of the heavens on lucky and unlucky days, were apparently widespread in late classical culture at every level. The roots of these practices are of incalculable antiquity. Their condemnation is an equally ancient tradition, and most early Christian writers simply repeated the

[53] A form of divination in which a question is asked and the Bible is opened at random; either a verse is read or the first letter on the page is compared to a chart of divinatory meanings. See E. Sievers, 'Bedeutung der Buchstaben', *ZDA* 21 (1877), 189–90; A. Schönbach, 'Bedeutung der Buchstaben', *ZDA* 34 (1890), 1–6; and V. Flint, *The Rise of Magic in Early Medieval Europe* (Princeton, NJ, 1991), pp. 273–87.

[54] Some background on this work may be found in W. L. Braekman, 'Fortune-Telling by the Casting of Dice: a Middle English Poem and its Background', *SN* 52 (1980), 3–29. See also *Sortes Sangallensis,* ed. H. Winnefeld (Bonn, 1887), esp. pp. 53–60. Other versions of this work in twelfth-century English manuscripts include London, British Library, Egerton 821, 54v–56r and Los Angeles, Getty Museum Ludwig XII.5, 48r–49v.

[55] Useful surveys of texts available in England in later centuries, helpful also in understanding earlier material, are L. Means, 'Electionary, Lunary, Destinary, and Questionary: Toward Defining Categories of Middle English Prognostic Material', *SP* 89 (1992), 367–403; *idem,* 'Popular Lunar Astrology in the Late Middle Ages', *Univ. of Ottawa Quarterly* 48 (1978), 187–94 and *idem,* 'The Moon and Medicine in Chaucer's Time', *Stud. in the Age of Chaucer* 8 (1986), 145–56; see also I. Taavitsainen, 'The Identification of Middle English Lunary Manuscripts', *NM* 88 (1987), 18–26, and *Middle English Lunaries: a Study of the Genre* (Helsinki, 1988).

criticisms of earlier pagan authors;[56] Augustine's condemnations of astrological prediction and fatalism are unusual only in their breadth and in the frequency with which they were imitated.[57] A single example may suffice:[58] *Letter 55* to Januarius is largely devoted to explaining why Christian feasts were calculated by the solar and lunar calendars; in it Augustine presents his views on the appropriate and inappropriate uses of forecasting. The observation of signs and seasons was the legitimate concern of the mariner and the farmer as well as the cleric, he admits. The consummate orderliness of the heavens is a guide to earth's changing seasons, but must not be consulted as a guide to man's changing fate:

Se quantum intersit inter observationes siderum ad aerias qualitates accommodatas, sicut agricolae vel nautae observant, aut ad notandas partes mundi cursumque aliquo et alicunde dirigendum, quod gubernatores navium faciunt et hi, qui per solitudines arenosas in interiora austri nulla certa semita gradiuntur, aut ad aliquid in doctrina utili figurate significandum si fit nonnullorum siderum aliqua commemoratio – , quantum ergo intersit inter has utilitates et vanitates hominum ad hoc observantium sidera, ut nec aeris qualitates nec regionum vias nec solos temporum numeros nec spiritalium similitudines sed quasi fatalia rerum eventa perquirant, quis non intellegat?[59]

Yet faith in signs and portents was sound doctrine, and the broadly astrological principles on which many practices of divination and prediction were based

---

[56] See D. Amand, *Fatalisme et liberté dans l'antiquité grecque* (Louvain, 1945); Thorndike, *History of Magic* I, 268–86, notes classical attacks on magic and astrology. Useful summaries of early medieval attitudes may be found in M. L. W. Laistner, 'The Western Church and Astrology during the Early Middle Ages', *Harvard Theol. Rev.* 34 (1941), 251–75; Tester, *History of Western Astrology*; T. O. Wedel, *The Medieval Attitude to Astrology, particularly in England*, Yale Stud. in Eng. 60 (New Haven, CT, 1920); V. Flint, 'The Transmission of Astrology in the Early Middle Ages', *Viator* 21 (1990), 1–27; and D. Harmening, *Superstitio. Überlieferungs- und theoriegeschichtliche Untersuchungen zur kirchlich-theologischen Aberglaubensliteratur des Mittelalters* (Berlin, 1979), pp. 76–95.

[57] Laistner, 'Western Church and Astrology', pp. 259–60; see also Thorndike, *History of Magic* I, 504–22. A useful survey of Augustine's attitude is found in L. Smoller, *History, Prophecy, and the Stars: the Christian Astrology of Pierre d'Ailly, 1350–1420* (Princeton, NJ, 1994), pp. 25–9.

[58] To it might be added *City of God* V.1–9, *Confessions* VII.6, *De doctrina Christiana* II.21, *De Genesi ad litteram* II.17. The letter is discussed by Flint, *The Rise of Magic*, p. 96.

[59] Augustine, *Letter* 55.8.15 (*S. Aureli Augustini Hipponiensis Episcopi Epistulae*, ed. A. Goldbacher, 5 vols. in 4, CSEL 34, 44, 57 and 58 (Vienna, 1895–1923) I, 186): 'Everyone understands that there is a great difference between observing the stars as natural phenomena, in the way that farmers and sailors do, either to verify geographical areas, or to steer their course somewhere, as pilots of ships do, and travelers, making their way through the sandy wastes of the south with no sure path; or to explain some point of doctrine by mentioning some of the stars as a useful illustration – as I said, there is a great difference between these practical customs and the superstitions of men who study the stars, not to forecast the weather, or to find their way, or for spiritual parables, but to peer into the predestined outcome of events.' Trans. W. Parsons, *Saint Augustine: Letters*, 5 vols., The Fathers of the Church 12, 18, 20, 30 and 32 (New York, 1951–6) I, 272–3.

were scientifically valid – as the moon and other heavenly bodies sympathetically influenced the movements of seas and the growth of plants, so they were thought to affect the minds and bodies, health and fortune, of men.[60] No one doubted the influence of the stars and planets on weather, health, chemical processes and other natural phenomena; 'this was not superstition', says Tester; 'it was good science'.[61]

It is not at all clear to what extent the astrological sciences of the late classical world were known among the early Anglo-Saxons, nor what sort of auguries and prognostic practices might have been common among the English before their conversion;[62] most references to the subject in Anglo-Saxon England seem dependent upon the condemnations of the Church Fathers and early councils. The *Penitential of Theodore* XV.4 provides sanctions for those performing auguries or divinations by dreams, for example, but this is a copy of a canon of Ancyra and many have little to do with actual Anglo-Saxon practices.[63] And yet it may be argued that these condemnations were repeated for some reason, though they may have been directed less to a fully articulated astrological practice than to popular belief in fate, portents and unlucky days.[64] Ælfric's Homily

[60] See J. D. North, 'Celestial Influence – the Major Premiss of Astrology', *'Astrologi hallucinati': Stars and the End of the World in Luther's Time*, ed. P. Zambelli (Berlin, 1986), pp. 45–100, and 'Medieval Concepts of Celestial Influence: a Survey', *Astrology, Science and Society: Historical Essays*, ed. P. Curry (Woodbridge, 1987), pp. 5–18; See further K. Jolly, *Popular Religion in Late Saxon England: Elf Charms in Context* (Chapel Hill, NC, 1996), pp. 110–13; Flint, *The Rise of Magic*, pp. 129–30.

[61] Tester, *History of Western Astrology*, p. 178; see also S. Jenks, 'Astrometeorology in the Middle Ages', *Isis* 74 (1983), 185–210.

[62] Among the most important studies of western astrology since Thorndike's monumental *History of Magic and Experimental Science* are Tester, *History of Western Astrology*; F. Boll, C. Bezold and W. Gundel, *Sternglaube und Sterndeutung: Die Geschichte und das Wesen der Astrologie* (Darmstadt, 1974); R. Bonnaud, 'Notes sur l'astrologie latine au VIe siècle', *Revue belge de philologie et de l'histoire/Belgische tijdschrift voor philolgie en geschiedenis* 10 (1931), 557–77; A. Van de Vyver, 'Les plus anciennes traductions latines médiévales (x–xi siècles) de traités d'astronomie et d'astrologie', *Osiris* 1 (1936), 658–91; and Flint, 'The Transmission of Astrology' and *The Rise of Magic*. Although Flint's 'Transmission of Astrology' has reopened the question of the use of astrology in the early medieval west, Tester's arguments (*History of Western Astrology*, pp. 112–14) against the survival of the mathematical and astronomical competence required to use astrology in any sophisticated way seem beyond dispute.

[63] J. T. McNeill and H. M. Gamer, *Medieval Handbooks of Penance. A Translation of the Principal Libri Poenitentiales and Selections from Related Documents* (New York, 1938; rept. 1990), p. 198. The *Pseudo-Bede Penitential* X.1–4 (McNeill and Gamer, *Medieval Handbooks*, pp. 228–9) also forbids divination.

[64] Even in the absence of a fully developed theory of astrological influence the English may have held some tradition of lucky and unlucky days related to the calendar and the days of the week; see H. Henel, 'Planetenglaube in Ælfrics Zeit', *Anglia* 58 (1934), 292–317, and A. Meaney, 'Ælfric and Idolatry', *Jnl of Religious Hist.* 13 (1984), 119–35. Likewise evidence has been seen in some texts for the observance of New Year's Day (whether celebrated on 25 December or 1 January), including prognostications and rituals for securing good luck. See Harmening,

on the Epiphany (*Catholic Homilies* I.7) suggests as much when he condemns astrology:

Us is eac to witenne þæt wæron sume gedwolmen. þe cwædon þæt ælc man beo acenned. be steorrena gesetnyssum: and þurh heora ymbrynum him wyrd gelimpe; And namon to fultume heora gedwylde þæt niwe steorra asprang þe ða drihten lichamlice acenned wearð. and cwædon þæt se steorra his gewyrd wære; Gewite þis gedwyld fram geleaffullum heortum. þæt æni gewyrd sy. buton se ælmihtiga scyppend se þe ælcum menn foresceawað. lif be his geearnungum;[65]

This is in fact a fairly close translation of a passage in Gregory the Great's homily for that occasion[66] condemning the Priscillianist heresy, and Ælfric's use of the past tense suggests that he is not thinking of contemporary practice. He goes on, however, to add a lengthy warning against fatalism which is not in Gregory: 'Nu cweþað oft stunte menn þæt hi be gewyrde lybban sceolon: swilce god hi neadige to yfeldædum: ac we wyllað þissera stuntra manna ydele leasunge adwæscan mid deopnysse godcundra gewrita';[67] which suggests that he was concerned with general tendencies towards fatalism and determinism of the sort that may have led to a belief in omens and unlucky days.

English condemnations of augury and divination were more often directed not against its theoretical underpinnings but against its cultural setting. The *Pseudo-Ecgbert Penitential* situates a belief in lunar forecasting alongside the use of charms over medicinal plants as parallel practices:

Nis na soðlice nanum cristenum men alyfed þæt he idela hwatunga bega swa hæðene men doð, þæt is þæt hi gelyfen on sunnan and on monan and on steorren ryne and secen tida hwatunga hira þing to beginnenne, ne wyrta gaderunga mid nanum galdre butan

Superstitio, pp. 117–45 on prohibitions against New Year's prognostics and folk rites; on the date of New Year's Day in England, see D. Whitelock, 'On the Commencement of the Year in the Saxon Chronicles', *Two of the Saxon Chronicles Parallel*, ed. C. Plummer (1892–3; repr. Oxford 1952), II, cxxxix–cxlii; K. Harrison, 'The Beginning of the Year in England, *c.* 500–900', *ASE* 2 (1973), 51–70; and M. R. Godden, 'New Year's Day in Late Anglo-Saxon England', *N&Q* ns 39 (1992), 148–50. Other evidence for popular practices may be found in A. Meaney, 'Women, Witchcraft and Magic in Anglo-Saxon England', *Superstition and Popular Medicine in Anglo-Saxon England*, ed. D. G. Scragg (Manchester, 1989), pp. 9–40.

[65] 'We should also know that there were some heretics who said that each man was born as the stars ordained, and his fate befell through their courses; and they took as corroboration of their heresy the fact that a new star sprang up when the Lord was born in human form, and they said that the star was his fate. Let this heresy be banished from faithful hearts, that there be any fate but the almighty Creator, who provides life to each man according to his deserts' (*Catholic Homilies* I.7, lines 116–23). *Ælfric's Catholic Homilies. The First Series*, ed. P. Clemoes, EETS ss 17 (Oxford, 1997), 235–6. Unless otherwise noted, all translations are my own.

[66] See D. Hurst, *Gregory the Great: Forty Gospel Homilies* (Kalamazoo, MI, 1990), pp. 54–61, at 57.

[67] 'Now foolish men often say that they must live by fate, as if God constrained them to evil deeds; but we wish to dispel the empty lies of these foolish men with the profundity of divine writings' (*Catholic Homilies* I.7, lines 137–9; the defence of free will continues to line 201).

mid *pater noster* and mid *credo* oððe mid sumon gebede þe `to´ gode belimpe. Gif hwa þas idelan þing bega, geswice and andette and fæste XL daga, and gif he eft to þære idelnesse gehwyrfe, þonne fæste he III lengten.[68]

Wulfstan's homilies include divination among a list of sins to be avoided, placing it in the context of pagan practices involving unauthorized places of worship:

Scyldað eow wið gitsunga and wið gifornessa, and ðæt ge ahwar ne beon manswican ne manswaran, wedlogan ne wordlogan, ne on leasre gewitnesse ahwar standan. And scyldað eow wið galscypas and swyðe georne wið æwbrecas, and wið oferfylle beorgað eow georne. And ne gyman ge galdra ne idelra hwata, ne wigelunga ne wiccecræfta; and ne weorðian ge wyllas ne ænige wudutreowu, forðam æghwylce idele syndon deofles gedwimeru.[69]

Likewise the collection of canons made for Wulfstan specifies five years' penance for anyone bringing *diuinos et sortilegos* into his house.[70] Wulfstan's concern with the suppression of divination as part of the regulation of the state is seen in his reiteration of the legal sanctions against it in the *Laws of Edward and Guthrum* 11:

Gif wiccan oððe wigleres, mansworan oððe morðwyrhtan oððe fule, afylede, æbære horcwenan, ahwar on lande wurðan agytene, ðonne fyse hi man of earde and clænsie þa þeode, oððe on earde forfare hy mid ealle, buton hig geswican and þe deoppor gebetan.[71]

---

[68] 'Indeed it is not permitted that any Christian man practise idle divination like the heathens do, that is, they believe in the sun and the moon and the course of the stars, and seek divination of time to begin their business; nor the gathering of plants with charms, except with the *paternoster* and the *credo* or with some prayer pertaining to God. If anyone practises these idle things, let him desist and confess and fast for forty days, and if he returns to that idleness, then let him fast three Lents.' *Die Altenglische Version des Halitgar'schen Bußßuches (sog. Poenitentiale Pseudo-Ecgberti)*, ed. J. Raith, Bibliothek der angelsächsischen Prosa 13 (1933; 2nd ed., Darmstadt, 1964), II.23.

[69] 'Guard yourself against greed and avarice, and never be a deceiver or perjurer, pledgebreaker or oathbreaker, nor anywhere stand in false witness. And guard against lechery and very zealously against adultery, and protect yourself well against gluttony. And take no notice of spells and empty sorcery, nor of prognostication or witchcraft; and do not honour wells or trees of the forest, because all such empty things are the devil's deceptions.' *Wulfstan Homilies* 8C, lines 161–8. *The Homilies of Wulfstan*, ed. D. Bethurum (Oxford, 1957), pp. 183–4.

[70] Recension A, no. 71: 'Si quis paganorum consuetudinem sequens, diuinos et sortilegos in domum suam introduxerit, quasi ut malum foras mittant, aut maleficia inueniant uel lustrationibus paganorum seruiant, quinque annos penitant' ('if anyone, following the custom of the heathens, has brought diviners and seers into his house, as if to get them to drive evil outside, or discover spells, or assist at the heathens' purification ceremonies, he is to do five years' penance'). *Wulfstan's Canon Law Collection*, ed. J. E. Cross and A. Hamer (Cambridge, 1999), p. 96. Another canon (no. 72) prescribes penance for those who assist at *auguriis uel incantationibus*.

[71] 'If witches or diviners, perjurers or murderers or foul, filthy, open whores are caught anywhere in the land, then let them be driven out from the land and cleanse the people, or let them be completely destroyed in the land, unless they desist and atone all the more deeply.' (*Councils and Synods, with Other Documents relating to the English Church*, I: *A.D. 871–1204*, ed. D. Whitelock,

194

In such laws the forbidden practices of divination are seen as a species of licence; the breaking of oaths, sexual irregularity and improper religion are all equated and equally suppressed.[72]

In most prohibitions divination is associated with pagan survivals or practices of popular religion – charms over herbs, the consultation of a *wicce* or *wiglere* for advice on medical matters, cursing of cattle, abortion and infanticide, offerings at stones and trees and wells. The context in which divination was imagined is captured by the *Canons of Edgar*, no. 16:

[R]iht is þæt preosta gehwylc cristendom geornlice lære and ælcne hæþendom mid ealle adwæsce; and forbeode wyllweorðunga, and licwigelunga, and hwata, and galdra, and treowwurðunga, and stanwurðunga, and ðone deafles cræft þe man dryhð þær man þa cild þurh þa eorðan tihð, and ða gemearr þe man drihð on geares niht on mislicum wig-elungum and on friðsplottum and on ellenum, and on manegum mislicum gedwimerum þe men on dreogað fela þæs þe hi ne sceoldon.[73]

In effect Wulfstan and the authors of the penitentials, like modern scholars, sought to marginalize such practices by regarding them as 'folklore', remnants of an earlier system of belief and symptoms of incomplete conversion. But the manuscript context of prognostic texts suggests otherwise. Most surviving texts are found in at least one Latin version, and English versions are in nearly all cases obviously derived from a Latin original.[74] The earliest prognostic texts, from the ninth century, appear in French manuscripts such as **F**; for the most part they do not appear in English manuscripts before the eleventh century. The absence of such texts from English manuscripts before this time, the prevalence of Latin versions over English ones, and their appearance in collections of

M. Brett and C. N. L. Brooke, 2 vols. (Oxford, 1981), p. 312. This sanction is repeated almost verbatim in other laws, *V Ethelred* and its Latin paraphrase *VI Ethelred* (*ibid.* pp. 350 and 366) and the *Laws of Cnut* (*ibid.* p. 488).

[72] The Latin *VI Ethelred* inserts *sortilegia* in a list of crimes including *fornicationes, periuria, sacrilegia*, and *ebrietates* (*ibid.* p. 371). Some of these prohibitions may have arisen as a consequence of the proximity of pagan Danish settlers to the Christian English; see A. Meaney, 'Æthelwold, Ælfric, the Norse Gods and Northumbria', *Jnl of Religious Hist.* 6 (1970), 105–32. Others, however, are at least as likely to be directed at the Christian English themselves.

[73] 'It is right that each priest zealously teach the Christian faith and extinguish all heathenism among all people, and forbid the worship of springs and necromancy, and divination and incantation, and the worship of trees and stones, and the devilish practice in which a child is dragged through the earth, and the error which is practised on New Year's Night with various spells and in meeting-places (?) and elder trees, and many various delusions which men perform far more than they should.' *Wulfstan's Canons of Edgar*, ed. R. Fowler, EETS os 266 (London, 1972), 5. See Harmening, *Superstitio*, pp. 49–75 on the long history of forbidding worship at trees, wells and crossroads in conciliar canons and penitentials.

[74] The existence of close Latin analogues from slightly later periods or from continental MSS corroborates the probable existence of Latin sources for texts surviving only in English versions.

impeccable monastic provenance such as Tiberius A. iii (**T**) and London, British Library, Cotton Titus D. xxvi + xxvii (Æ), all suggest that the proliferation of prognostics in England must be considered as a consequence, though no doubt an unintended one, of the tenth-century monastic reform – not at its margins but in its midst.

To appreciate the complex place of such texts in later Anglo-Saxon England it may be useful to compare two monks from Winchester: Ælfric, abbot of Eynsham, and Ælfwine, abbot of New Minster. Ælfric was educated at the cathedral school in Winchester by Æthelwold in the 960s and 970s;[75] Ælfwine, of whom much less is known, was the commissioner and owner of the prayer-book which has survived as Titus D. xxvi + xxvii (Æ).[76] He became abbot of New Minster in 1031 or 1032[77] (his name appears in code in Titus D. xxvii, 13v, where he is described as *monachus* and *decanus*, monk and dean, thus fixing the date of the manuscript before 1031); his death in 1057 is recorded in the Easter Table of his own prayerbook. Much can be known of Ælfric's thought and opinion from his writings, and it is usual to cite Ælfric (as I have done here) as a voice, if not *the* voice, of reason and intellectual authority in later Anglo-Saxon England; Ælfwine's psychological portrait can only be inferred from the contents of his prayerbook. Together these two monks, a generation apart, offer a striking contrast in Anglo-Saxon attitudes towards divination and prognostication.

Ælfric's opposition to prognostication (*wiglung*) and other *wiccecræft* was adamant; he devoted one entire Rogationtide homily, *De auguriis*, to its condemnation, and touched upon the subject in several other works, including his homily for the Octave of Christmas (*Catholic Homilies* I.6), the Epiphany homily already cited, and his *De temporibus anni*. The source of *De auguriis* is, for the most part, Homily 54 of Caesarius of Arles,[78] though Ælfric adapts his source, interpolates apparently original material, and generally makes the homily his own. Its

---

[75] A recent synopsis of Ælfric's life is found in J. Wilcox, *Ælfric's Prefaces*, Durham Medieval Texts 9 (Durham, 1994), 1–15.
[76] Most of the manuscript has been edited by B. Günzel, *Ælfwine's Prayerbook (London, British Library, Cotton Titus D.xxvi + xxvii)*, HBS 108 (Woodbridge, 1993). See also W. de Gray Birch, 'On Two Anglo-Saxon Manuscripts in the British Museum', *Trans. of the R. Soc. of Lit.* 2nd ser. 11 (1878), 463–512.
[77] D. Knowles, C. N. L. Brooke and V. C. M. London, *The Heads of Religious Houses: England and Wales 940–1216* (Cambridge, 1972), p. 81.
[78] *Sancti Caesarii Arelatensis, Sermones*, ed. D. G. Morin, 2nd ed., CCSL 103–4 (Turnhout, 1953) I, 235–40; trans. M. M. Mueller, *Sermons*, 3 vols., The Fathers of the Church 31, 47 and 66 (Washington, DC, 1956–73) I, 265–70. The homily appears in Boulogne-sur-Mer, Bibliothèque Municipale, 63, fols. 29–31; for connections between this collection and Ælfric, see E. Raynes, 'MS Boulogne-sur-Mer 63 and Ælfric', *MÆ* 26 (1957), 65–73; M. McC. Gatch, 'MS Boulogne-sur-Mer 63 and Ælfric's First Series of Catholic Homilies', *JEGP* 65 (1966), 482–901; and J. Trahern, 'Caesarius of Arles and Old English Literature', *ASE* 5 (1976), 105–19.

comments on local customs and practices must be read cautiously and may not always reflect actual practices in Ælfric's own day;[79] what is beyond dispute in any reading, however, is Ælfric's rejection of divination:

Nu alyse ic me sylfne wið God, and mid lufe eow forbeode, þæt eower nan ne axie þurh ænigne wiccecræft be ænigum ðinge oððe be ænigre untrumnysse, ne galdras ne sece to gremigenne his scyppend; forðan se ðe þys deð, se forlysð his Cristendom, and bið þam hæðenum gelic þe hleotað be him sylfum mid ðæs deofles cræfte þe hi forðeð on ecnysse.[80]

It is permissible to cast lots in secular matters, he admits ('þis nis nan wiglung, ac bið wissung foroft'),[81] but divination in any form is prohibited:

Eall swa gelice se ðe gelyfð wiglungum oððe be fugelum oððe be fnorum oððe be horsum oððe be hundum, ne bið he na Cristen, ac bið forcuð wiðersaca. Ne sceal nan man cepan be dagum on hwilcum dæge he fare, oððe on hwylcum he gecyrre, forðan þe God gesceop ealle ða seofan dagas, þe yrnað on þære wucan oð þysre worulde geendunge. Ac seðe hwider faran wille, singe his paternoster, and credan, gif he cunne, and clypige to his Dryhten, and bletsige hine sylfne, and siðige orsorh þurh godes gescyldnysse, butan ðæra sceoccena wiglunga.[82]

Ælfric's *Homily on the Octave of the Nativity* (*Catholic Homilies* I.6) similarly condemns those who avoid business or bloodletting on Monday, or postpone journeys and voyages because of the position of the moon:

Nu wigliað stunte men menigfealde wigelunga on þisum dæge. mid micclum gedwylde æfter hæðenum gewunan ongean hyra cristendom: swilce hi magon heora lif gelengan. oððe heora gesundfulnysse mid þam ðe hi gremiað þone ælmihtigan scyppend; Sind eac manega mid swa micclum gedwylde befangene. þæt hi cepað be ðam monan heora fær. and heora dæda be dagum. and nellað heora þing wanian on monandæge: for angynne þære wucan: ac se monandæg nis na fyrmest daga on þære wucan: ac is se oþer; se sunnandæg is fyrmest on gesceapenysse: and on endebyrdnysse: and on wurþmynte; [. . .] Nis þæs mannes cristendom naht þe mid deoflicum wiglungum his lif adrihð: he is

---

[79] A. Meaney, 'Ælfric's Use of his Sources in his Homily on Auguries', *ES* 66 (1985), 477–95.

[80] 'Now I absolve myself before God, and with love forbid that any of you seek through any witchcraft to enquire after any business or any illness, or seek spells to provoke his Creator, because whoever does this abandons Christianity and becomes like the heathens, who cast lots concerning themselves with the devil's skill, which destroys them eternally.' *Ælfric's Lives of Saints*, ed. W. W. Skeat, 4 vols. in 2, EETS os 76, 82, 94 and 114 (Oxford, 1881–1900) I, 368–70.

[81] 'often that is not divination, but guidance' (*Ælfric's Lives of Saints*, ed. Skeat I, 370).

[82] 'Likewise whoever believes in divination, whether by means of birds or sneezes or horses or dogs, is no Christian, but is an infamous apostate. Let no one take heed according to days to see which day he will journey, or on which he should return, because God made all the seven days which run in the week until the end of this world. But whoever wishes to travel should sing his *paternoster* and creed, if he knows them, and cry out to his Lord, and bless himself, and journey carefree with God's protection, and without the devils' divinations' (*Ælfric's Lives of Saints*, ed. Skeat I, 370).

gehiwod to cristenum menn. and is earm hæþengylda. swa swa se ylca apostol be swylcum cwæð; [. . .] Nu ge cepað daga and monða mid ydelum wiglungum;[83]

The fact that Ælfric returns to these condemnations on several occasions may suggest how widespread such practices were; moreover, Malcolm Godden has suggested that Ælfric is condemning not lay belief but clerical practices.[84] He may have had in mind something like the learned texts which make up a significant portion of Ælfwine's prayerbook.

Titus D. xxvi + xxvii (Æ) is a miscellaneous collection of Latin and English prayers, offices, religious texts, a calendar and computus. It is a personal and pastoral book which seems to reflect the interests of its owner; it includes both private prayers, such as those for recitation while washing the hands and eyes (69),[85] and offices of the Trinity (49), the Holy Cross (50) and the Virgin Mary (51), as well as collects for various feasts and offices (73) in the public liturgy, and bits of lore and learning, such as the names of the Seven Sleepers (15) and parts of Ælfric's De temporibus anni (36).[86] The first part of the book, most of what is now Titus D. xxvii, is taken up with calendrical and computistical material (and one penitential prayer, 34, on 26r–27r) among which appear a number of prognostics and lunaria of precisely the kind Ælfric preached against.[87] As in other New Minster manuscripts like Cambridge, Corpus Christi College 422 (D) and London, British Library, Arundel 60 (A), the computus in Titus D. xxvii begins (1, 2r) with a lunarium for bloodletting,[88] and continues with a calendar (2, 3r–8v)

---

[83] 'Now foolish men work various kinds of divination on this day [i.e. 1 January] with great error, after the manner of the heathens against their Christian faith, as if they could lengthen their lives or health by offending the almighty Creator. There are also many who are caught up in such great error that they plan their journeys by the moon, and their deeds by days, and will not let blood on Monday because it is the beginning of the week. But Monday is not the first day of the week but rather the second; Sunday is first in Creation and in order and in dignity; [. . .] A person's Christianity is worth nothing if he rules his life by devilish divination; he has only the appearance of a Christian, and is a wretched idolater, just as the same apostle [i.e. Paul] said of such men: "You observe days and months with idle sorcery"' (Catholic Homilies I.6, lines 161–91. Ælfric's Catholic Homilies. The First Series, ed. Clemoes, pp. 229–30). For the expression þing wanian as 'let blood', see A. Meaney, 'Ælfric and Idolatry', pp. 124–5, and see the entry on bloodletting in Bald's Leechbook, 54v–55r: 'blodlæs is to forganne fiftyne nihtum ær hlafmæsse and æfter fif and þritig nihtum forþon þonne ealle æterno þing fleogaþ and mannum swiðe deriað. Læcas lærdon þa þe wisoste wæron þæt nan man on þam monþe ne drenc ne drunce ne ahwær his lichoman wanige butan his nydþearf wære' (emphasis added).

[84] 'The people who call 1 January "year's day" and the foolish people who practise auguries on that day are perhaps not the common people continuing old pagan celebrations but Ælfric's own ecclesiastical colleagues': Godden, 'New Year's Day', p. 150.

[85] Numbers refer to texts in Günzel's edition.

[86] Not included in Günzel's edition; it is collated as D in Ælfric's De Temporibus Anni, ed. H. Henel, EETS os 213 (London, 1942).   [87] See the appendix for a fuller description of these texts.

[88] The same bloodletting lunarium is found in Harley 3271 (G), but not at the beginning of the MS.

that marks critical days for bloodletting and the beginning and end of the *dies caniculares* in late summer. An incomplete diagram of the relation between the moon and sea is followed by a list in hexameters of the two critical days in each month for bloodletting, a warning against bloodletting and the eating of goose-flesh on the first Mondays of August and March and the last Monday of December, a warning against bloodletting during the *dies caniculares*, and a warning against bloodletting on certain days of the lunar month (**18**). This in turn is followed by a note on the threefold incarnation of Christ (conception, nativity and resurrection), giving not only the date but the age of the moon (twenty-six days, seventeen days and seventeen days, respectively) on each stage of the incarnation (**19**).[89] A collection of more computistical material (**20–31**) on the *saltus lunae*, the date of Easter, the equinoxes, the length of the seasons, and so forth, is followed by a 'Revelatio Esdrae' prediction for the year based on the day of the week on which the first of January falls (**32**); a penitential prayer (**34**) is followed by a general lunar hemerology (**35**) offering information on illness, dreams, and the fortunes of children born on each day of the lunar month, and other information for some days, including a list of good actions, the likelihood of catching a thief, and the possibility of finding lost objects. This in turn is followed by a copy of Ælfric's *De temporibus anni*, which includes the warning (44r) 'ne sceal nan cristen-mann nan þing be þam monan wiglian. gif he hit deð his geleafa nis naht'. At the end of the quire, on originally blank leaves, two scribes have added brief notes on indulgences and feasts, and an alphabetic divination (**40**).

The first two quires of what is now Titus D. xxvi also contain a number of prognostic texts, including a note on the three critical Mondays (**56**) similar to **18**, the three marvellous days (**57**), another note on the *dies caniculares* and other lunar days titled *Quali tempore aperienda sit uena* (**58**), again similar to **18**, but which encourages bloodletting on the fourth, fourteenth and twenty-fourth day of the month, and warns against it on the fifth, tenth, fifteenth, twentieth, twenty-fifth and thirtieth, a list of two unlucky days in each month (**59**) called *dies aegiptiaci*,[90] lunaria for bloodletting (**61**), birth (**63**), illness (**64**) and dreams (**65**),[91] a thunder prognostic (**66**), a birth prognostic based on the day of the week on which a child is born (**62**), another calendrical weather prognostic of the 'Revelatio Esdrae' type (**67**) similar to **32**, and a version of the dream-dictionary known as the *Somniale Danielis* (titled *Alphabetum somniale excerptum ex Danielis libro* by a later hand) containing 151 dreams (**68**). These are then followed by prayers, a recipe against boils, and, after two blank pages, a collectar. Clearly Ælfwine did not share Ælfric's disdain for prognostication. The idea that an abbot of New

---

[89] Günzel 1993, p. 112. Günzel notes (p. 200) that the same text is found in Royal 2. B. V (**R**), 187r.
[90] The days given are different from those in the calendar, and no mention is made of bloodletting: warnings are given against travel, planting, harvesting and making legal claims.
[91] **61–5** are found in the same sequence in Tiberius A. iii (**T**).

199

Minster in the second quarter of the eleventh century used this collection of texts, as he apparently did, in his practices of daily devotion – reading his dreams along with his offices, calculating times for letting blood along with liturgical feasts – drives us to speculate on the place which lunar and calendar divination, to which Ælfric was so opposed only a generation before, might have occupied in the monastic life, and the reasons for the survival and use of prognostic texts alongside more orthodox works.

We may assume that such texts survived in the first instance because, in an important sense, the science of the time authorized and underwrote them; even those who condemned them did not entirely reject their efficacy. Like Augustine, Ælfric makes a concession in the course of his condemnation of calendar prognostication and celestial forecasting; in his homily on the Epiphany he admits:

Is hwæþere æfter gecynde on gesceapenysse ælc lichamlic gesceaft þe eorðe acenð fulre and mægenfæstre on fullum monan þonne on gewanedum; Swa eac treowa gif hi beoð on fullum monan geheawene hi beoð heardran and langfærran to getimbrunge and swiþost gif hi beoð unsæpige geworhte; Nis þis nan wiglung ac is gecyndelic þing þurh gesceapenysse; Hwæt eac seo sæ wunderlice geþwærlæcð þæs monan ymbrene: symle hi beoð geferan on wæstme: and on wanunge; And swa swa se mona dæghwomlice feower pricum lator arist: swa eac seo sæ symle feower pricum lator fleowð;[92]

His information is from Bede's *De temporum ratione* c. XXVIII; in this chapter Bede draws together excerpts from Ambrose, Basil and Vegetius. Quoting Ambrose, *Hexameron* IV.7, Bede says that the moon has the same offices as the sun, 'ut illuminet tenebras, foveat semina, augeat fructus'.[93] He goes on to examine the effects of the moon's cycles on living things, again quoting Ambrose nearly verbatim:

In quo grande mysterium est – nam et defectui eius compatiuntur elementa et, processu eius quae fuerint exinanita, cumulantur ut animantium cerebra maritimarum humida. Siquidem pleniores ostreae reperiri ferantur multaque alia cum globus lunaris adolescit. De arborum quoque internis idem allegant, qui hoc usu proprio compererunt.[94]

Later, quoting Basil's *Hexameron*, he repeats these ideas.[95]

---

[92] 'It is however natural that each physical created thing which the earth brings forth is fuller and stronger in the full moon than in the waning; likewise trees, if they are cut down during the full moon, are harder and more durable for building, and strongest if they are worked on while sapless. This is no divination but is a natural thing in creation. So also the sea wonderfully agrees with the circuit of the moon: they are always companions in growth and in waning, and just as the moon arises four points [of an hour] later each day, so the sea always flows four points later.' (*Catholic Homilies* I.6, lines 191–9. *Ælfric's Catholic Homilies. The First Series*, ed. Clemoes, p. 230.)   [93] 'Illuminate the darkness, nurture seeds, and cause fruit to grow.'
[94] 'In this there is a great mystery – the elements are affected by the waning of the moon and, when they are exhausted by its course, grow again, as for example the humid brains of sea creatures. In fact, oysters and many other kinds of shellfish are said to be larger at the time when the moon is waxing. The same is said of the internal structure of trees by those who have made a special investigation of it.' Jones, *Bedae Opera de Temporibus*, p. 231.
[95] 'Opinor autem quod et animalibus creandis ceterisque omnibus quae terra producit non parva

200

In his English work drawn from Bede Ælfric omits most of this material; as
he again warns against lunar forecasting, however – specifically the belief that
the weather can be predicted by the horns of the crescent moon – he again
follows his warning with an admission that the moon does influence the earth,
and its phases must be observed for success in some enterprises:

(8.7) Ne sceal nan cristenman nan ðing be ðam monan wiglian. Gif he hit deð, his
geleafa ne bið naht [. . .] (8.11) Nu cweðað sume men þe ðis gescead ne cunnon þæt se
mona hine wende be ðan ðe hit wedrian sceall on ðam monðe, ac hi[ne] ne went næfre
naðor, ne weder ne unweder, of ðam ðe his gecynde is. (8.12) Men magon swa ðeah þa
ðe fyrwite beoð cepan be his bleo and be ðære sunnan, oððe þæs roderes, hwilc weder
toweard bið (8.13) Hit is gecyndelic þæt ealle eorðlice lichaman beoð fulran on weaxen-
dum monan þonne on wanigendum (8.14) Eac ða treowu þe beoð aheawene on fullum
monan beoð heardran wið wyrmætan and langfærran, þonne ða þe beoð on niwum
monan aheawene (8.15) Seo sæ and se mona geðwærlæcað him betweonan, æfre hi beoð
geferan on wæstme and on wanunge, and swa swa se mona dæghwomlice feower pricon
lator arist, ðonne he on ðam oðrum dæge dyde, swa eac seo sæ symle feower pricon lator
flewð.[96]

confertur ex lunae mutatione formatio; modo enim laxiora eorum corpora videntur et vacua
cum senescit, modo integra et repleta cum crescit, quoniam humorem quemdam cum calore
permixtum interius his latenter infundit. Quod ita esse demonstrant hi qui sub divo dormientes
lucente luna postquam surrexerint; inveniunt capita sua largissimo rore madentia. Sed et
recentes carnes, si sub luna iacuerint, fluida mox putredine corrumpuntur. Idemque significat
pecorinum cerebrum vel etiam viscera marinorum animalium quae sunt humectiora, necnon
arborum medullae' ('I believe that the changes in the moon exert no small influence upon
animals and all other living things which the earth produces; when it wanes their bodies seem to
lose their density and become empty, when it waxes they seem full and strong, since the moon
pours imperceptibly a certain moisture mixed with heat into their inward parts. This is proved
by the way those who sleep outdoors when the moon is shining find their heads drenched with
dew when they wake up; and by the way fresh meat, if left under the moon, is quickly turned
and corrupted; likewise the brain of cattle, the moist interior part of sea creatures, and the pith
of trees'). Jones, *Bedae Opera de Temporibus*, p. 232; see Basil, *Hexameron* VI.10.

[96] 'No Christian should divine any thing by the moon; if he does so, his faith is worth nothing.
[. . .] Now some men who do not understand this distinction say that the moon turns itself
according to how the weather shall be in a month, but it never turns, for good weather or bad,
from its nature. Curious men may, however, take heed by its colour and by the sun, or the
heavens, what sort of weather is coming. It is natural that all earthly bodies are fuller in the
waxing moon than in the waning, and trees that are cut in the full moon are harder against
worms and more durable than those that are cut in the new moon. The sea and the moon agree
between themselves – they are always companions in waxing and waning, and just as the moon
arises four points later each day than it did the day before, so the sea always flows four points
later.' *Ælfric's De Temporibus Anni*, ed. Henel, VIII:7–15. It is possible, as Meaney suggests
('Ælfric and Idolatry', p. 126), that this belief in the moon's influence on the durability of
timber was not in fact a common idea in England at the time; it was copied by Bede from
Ambrose, from Bede by Ælfric, and from Ælfric by Byrhtferth (*Enchiridion* III.ii.123–40), and
seems to have circulated as a morsel of learned science rather than popular lore. Nor is the
belief that the direction of the moon's horns predicts the weather found in any other Anglo-
Saxon source.

Like Augustine, Ælfric is caught between science and faith: lunar influence is an accepted fact of nature, but forecasting specific events or actions based on celestial influence is a dangerous practice best avoided by any pious Christian. Lunar calendars apparently slipped through this gap between science and prudence.

This is suggested by the fact that the most common prognostic texts, whether lunar or calendrical, are those devoted to medical matters. Though Ælfric condemned those who 'nellað heora þing wanian on monandæge', he followed Bede in recognizing the analogy between the veins of the body in the microcosm and rivers and seas in the macrocosm: 'Swa swa æddran licgað on þæs mannes lichaman swa licgað ða wæteræddran geond þas eorðan.'[97] A natural corollary of this analogy is a belief in the influence of the moon upon the body's humours, including of course the blood; reckoning this influence was an obvious and accepted part of medical practice. Bede, like Isidore of Seville,[98] believed that the moon's phases should be consulted for appropriate times for bloodletting. In his *Historia ecclesiastica* V.3 Bede relates that St John of Beverley healed a nun who has been imprudently bled on an inappropriate day; the saint chides: 'Multum insipienter et indocte fecistis in luna quarta flebotomando. Memini enim beatae memoriae Theodorum archiepiscopum dicere, quia periculosa sit satis illius temporis flebotomia, quando et lumen lunae et reuma oceani in cremento est.'[99] Bede offers a self-consciously rational reason for the prohibition, but it is not difficult to imagine that such belief served to permit, with, as it were, Bede's *imprimatur*, a broader range of less rational medical calendars. Among the texts which appear to have circulated under Bede's name is *De flebotomia*, whose various parts are found in manuscripts as early as the Carolingian period: it gives not only the best times for bloodletting (9 Kal. April to 9 Kal. July) but the times to be avoided – every fifth day of the lunar month, and the *dies caniculares* of summer – and cautions that the phases of the moon must be observed for bloodletting.[100] Theodore was not the only cleric learned

---

[97] *De temporibus anni* V.8: 'Just as the veins lie in the human body, so the streams of water lie across the earth.'

[98] See J. Fontaine, 'Isidore de Séville et l'astrologie', *Revue des études latines* 31 (1953), 271–300. Isidore's advocacy of medical astrology can be found in *Etymologiae* IV.13–14.

[99] 'You have acted foolishly and ignorantly to bleed her on the fourth day of the moon; I remember how Archbishop Theodore of blessed memory used to say that it was very dangerous to bleed a patient when the moon is waxing and the Ocean tide flowing.' *Bede's Ecclesiastical History of the English People*, ed. B. Colgrave and R. A. B. Mynors (Oxford, 1969), pp. 460–1. General information on the widespread Anglo-Saxon faith in the curative and prophylactic power of bloodletting may be found in M. L. Cameron, *Anglo-Saxon Medicine*, CSASE 7 (Cambridge, 1993), 159–68.

[100] See C. Singer, 'A Review of Medical Literature of the Dark Ages', *Proc. of the R. Soc. of Medicine* 10 (1917), 107–60, at pp. 130–3. Singer's text must be read with extreme caution. The text is similar to the pseudo-Bedan *De minutione sanguinis siue de phlebotomia*, PL 90, col. 959. It is also found in J, 1v; see Wallis, 'MS Oxford St John's College 17', p. 170.

in the medical arts who sought to observe proper times for bloodletting; prognostics on this topic appear in continental medical manuscripts as early as the ninth century.[101] An English version of a table of twenty-four unlucky days for bloodletting in London, British Library, Cotton Caligula A. xv, 130v (**C3**), is careful to assert, practically in Ælfric's own words, that such observance is not magic, but science:

Ða ealdan læces gesetton on ledonbocum, þæt on ælcum monðe beoð æfre twegen dagas, þa syndon swiðe derigendlice ænigne drenc to drincanne oþþe blod to lætenne, forþamþe an tid is on ælcum þara daga, gif man ænige æddran geopenað on þara tide, þæt hit bið lifleast oððe langsum sar. Þæs cunnede sume læce and let his horse blod on þære tide, and hit læg sona dead . . . Nu eft be þam monan is mycclum to warnienne, þæt man on IIII nihta ealdne monan oþþe on V nihta menn blod ne læte, swa us bec seggað, ærþamþe se mona and seo sæ beon anræde. Ac we gehyrdon seggon sumne wisne mann, þæt nan mann ne leofode, þe him blod lete on ealra halgena mæssedæg, oþþe gif

---

[101] A. Beccaria, *I codici di medicina del periodo presalernitano (secoli IX, X e XI)* (Rome, 1956), notes lunaria in the following medical MSS (most of which I have not yet seen), mostly from the ninth century: Bamberg, Staatbibliothek, med. 1 (s. ix); Berlin, Preussische Staatbibliothek, Phillipps 1790 (s. ix); Berlin, Preussische Staatbibliothek, Phillipps 1870 (s. xi/xii); Copenhagen, Royal Library, G.K.S. 1653 (s. xi); Herten, Bibliothek des Grafen Nesselrode-Reichenstein, 192; Karlsruhe, Badische Landesbibliothek, Reichenau CLXXI (s. ix); Lucca, Biblioteca Governativa 296 (s. ix); Paris, Bibliothèque Nationale de France, lat. 11218 (s. viii/ix); Paris, Bibliothèque Nationale de France, lat. 6882 A (s. ix); Vatican City, Biblioteca Apostolica Vaticana, lat. 4418 (s. xi); Uppsala, K. Universitetsbiblioteket, C. 664 (s. ix); St Gall, Stiftsbibliothek, 44 (s. ix); St Gall, Stiftsbibliothek, 751 (s. ix). E. Wickersheimer, *Les Manuscrits latins de médicine du haut moyen âge dans les bibliothèques de France* (Paris, 1966), notes texts concerning Egyptian days, Spheres of life and death, and lunaria in the following MSS which are not entirely devoted to medical texts: Angers 91 (Fleury, s. x; Egyptian days); Chartres 113 (Chartres, s. ix; 'Sphere of Apuleius'); Dijon 448 (Dijon, s. xi[in]; Egyptian days); Laon 426 *bis* (NE France, s. ix[4]; Egyptian days); Orléans 276 (Fleury, s. xi; 'Sphere of life and death'); Paris, Bibliothèque Nationale de France, 820 (s. xi; Egyptian days); Paris, BN, lat. 1338 (s. xi, Saint-Martial, Limoges, s.xi; Egyptian days); Paris, BN, lat. 2113 (Notre-Dame de Puy, s. x/xi; medical lunarium); Paris, BN, lat. 2825 (s. x; medical lunarium, Egyptian days, *dies caniculares*); Paris, BN, lat. 5239 (Saint-Martial, Limoges, s. x; Egyptian days, 'Sphere of Petosiris'); Paris, BN, lat. 5600 (Saint-Martial, Limoges, s. x; Egyptian days); Paris, BN lat. 6882 (Saint-Hilaire, Poitiers, s. ix[1]; medical lunarium); Paris, BN, lat. 8663 (Burgundy?, s. xi; 'Sphere of Apuleius'); Paris, BN, lat. 10233 (s. vii[ex]; medical lunarium); Paris, BN lat. 11411 (Echternach, s. ix; 'Sphere of Pythagoras'); Paris, BN, lat. 17868 (Paris, s. x; 'Sphere of Petosiris'); Paris, BN, lat. nouv. acq. 1073 (s. xi, xii; Egyptian days); Paris, BN, lat. nouv. acq. 1525 (Saint-Amand, s. ix–x; Egyptian days); Paris, BN, lat. nouv. acq. 1616 (Fleury, s. x; but Wickersheimer adds 'originaire de Bretagne ou d'Irlande', *Les Manuscrits*, p. 140; 'Sphere of Pythagoras', general lunarium, Egyptian days); Poitiers 184 (France, s. xi; Egyptian days); Reims 304 (Saint-Thierry, s. x; Egyptian days); Reims 438 (Saint-Thierry, s. ix; *dies caniculares*); Rouen 496 (Jumièges, s. x; Egyptian days); Strasbourg, Bibliothèque Nationale et Universitaire, 326 (Angoulême, s. x–xi; Egyptian days). The great variety of texts is as remarkable as their wide distribution in ninth- and tenth-century MSS.

he gewundod wære. Nis þis nan wiglung, ac wise menn hit afunden þurh þone halgan wisdom, swa heom god ælmihtig gedihte.[102]

Divination (*wiglung*) was wrong, but apparently few who used lunar and other calendars considered them *wiglung*. Prognostication as a forbidden practice was imagined in a cultural context among other forbidden practices such as the worship of trees and wells; under the rubric of medical science, in the respectability of the monastic or clerical world and the learned company of Latin texts, presumably, these acts were not regarded as heterodox or diabolical by those who performed them.

The lunarium was only one of several devices for determining favourable days for phlebotomy; Ælfwine's prayerbook contains no less than six texts related to bloodletting, and only three are based on the lunar cycle. Moreover, the lunar science endorsed by Bede and Ælfric offered a basic two-phase hydraulic principle of lunar influence (the waning and waxing of the moon influences earthly moisture), but lunar calendars are more complex, built around a thirty-day cycle which depended on astrological subtleties unavailable to the Anglo-Saxons. The result was an apparently arbitrary allotment of favourable and unfavourable days with no obvious relationship to the phases of the moon. Other prognostics for bloodletting, such as the warnings against 'Egyptian days', note only certain days of the year without any regard for the phase of the moon. Nor do the various calendars agree – while the notes on 'critical days' warn against bloodletting on any day of the month which is a multiple of five, the common lunarium for bloodletting notes that *luna x bonum est* and *luna xx tota die bona est*. But the science of lunar influence and the medical theory of the humours underwrote and authorized the lunar calendars, which in turn helped authorize other sorts of calendar prognostics. Given such beliefs about lunar influence on bodily fluids and health, it was apparently difficult to segregate lists of good and bad days for bloodletting from lists of good and bad days for general illness, childbirth or the reliability of one's dreams, all of which might be thought to depend, to one degree or another, on the proper balance of the humours.

A further assistance to the legitimization of prognostics, particularly those which involved lunar observation, was undoubtedly the fact that the method of

---

[102] 'Old doctors set out in Latin books that there are always two days in each month that are very dangerous for taking any potion or letting blood, because there is one hour in each of those days in which, if one opens any vein during that hour, the result will be death or lengthy illness. A certain doctor tested this and let blood from his horse in that hour, and it immediately fell dead ... Now concerning the moon be very careful not to let blood when the moon is four or five nights old, as books tell us, before the moon and the sea are in harmony. We have also heard a certain man say that no one could live who had blood let on All Saints' Day, even if he were wounded. This is no sorcery, but wise men have discovered it through holy wisdom, as God almighty directed them.'

calculating the age of the moon on any given day was an important part of clerical training, and texts explaining this method were part of most computus collections.[103] To calculate the date of Easter (on which depended, of course, the dates of the liturgical season from Septuagesima to Pentecost) one had to be able to reckon the relationship between the lunar month, the solar year, and the days of the week. One by-product of this astronomical attention would be a strong sense of the lunar month, a sense which could then be turned to more mundane uses by the inclusion in computus collections of texts of practical value relating to the moon's phases and the course of the calendar; for this reason medical material came to be included in computus collections.[104] While apparently not a part of the early Irish computus such as that found in Oxford, Bodleian Library, 309,[105] or the eighth-century French computus bound with later material in Caligula A. xv (**C**), prognostic texts found their way from a medical context into later French manuscripts of the Fleury computus such as **F** and into the computus developed in Winchester at the end of the tenth century represented by **Æ**, **D**, **A**, and **Vi**,[106] and later Christ Church manuscripts such as **T** and the closely related **C**. A Winchester-derived manuscript from Worcester,

[103] The monastic computus was not a single book, though works such as Bede's *De temporum ratione*, Hrabanus' *De computo*, and Helperic's *De computo ecclesiastico* were sometimes included in it. Rather it was a collection of relatively short texts and tables whose composition varied from one manuscript to another: letters, tables of Easter dates, instructions, and brief tracts relating to the calendar. For an overview, see F. Wallis, 'Chronology and Systems of Dating', *Medieval Latin: an Introduction and Bibliographical Guide*, ed. F. A. C. Mantello and A. G. Rigg (Washington, DC, 1996), pp. 383–7, and references cited there. *Byrhtferth's Enchiridion*, ed. Baker and Lapidge, pp. xl–lx, provide a useful introduction to the subject; H. Henel, *Studien zum altenglischen Computus* (Leipzig, 1934), A. Cordoliani, 'Les Traités de comput du haut moyen âge (526–1003)', *Bulletin du Cange* 17 (1943), 51–72, and Jones, *Bedae Opera de Temporibus*, remain the most complete studies. Hollis and Wright, *Old English Prose of Secular Learning*, pp. 185–95, offer a summary of manuscripts and contents for vernacular items, and see further P. McGurk, 'Computus Helperici: its Transmission in England in the Eleventh and Twelfth Centuries', *MÆ* 43 (1974), 1–5, and A. Borst, 'Computus: Zeit und Zahl im Mittelalter', *DAEM* 44 (1988), 1–88. Günzel, *Ælfwine's Prayerbook*, pp. 16–30, discusses the computus in that manuscript, and in the process provides an introduction to computus texts; pp. 203–4 of the same work offers a list of Anglo-Saxon MSS containing computus materials. F. Wallis's translation of *Bede: the Reckoning of Time* (Liverpool, 1999) came to hand as this work was being readied for publication; for introduction to the computus, see esp. pp. xviii–lxxxv.

[104] See Wallis , 'MS Oxford St John's College 17', pp. 156–63, and 'Medicine in Medieval Calendar Manuscripts', *Manuscript Sources of Medieval Medicine: a Book of Essays*, ed. M. R. Schleissner (New York, 1995), pp. 105–43, on the relationship of medical and computistical material in manuscripts.

[105] On the Irish origins of the computus see Jones, *Bedae Opera de Temporibus*, pp. 75–7 and 105–13, and idem, 'The "Lost" Sirmond Manuscript of Bede's "Computus"', *EHR* 52 (1937), 204–19; D. Ó Cróinín, 'A Seventh-Century Irish Computus from the Circle of Cummianus', *Proc. of the R. Irish Acad.* 82C (1982), 405–30; *Byrhtferth's Enchiridion*, ed. Baker and Lapidge, pp. xl–xli.

[106] Vitellius E. xviii; this contains no lunar calendar but several lists of unfortunate days for bloodletting.

CCCC 391 (**W**),[107] also has a rich collection of prognostics; in general this material seems to be from a different source than that in Winchester collections, and its inclusion at the end of the manuscript separate from the computus is perhaps significant. Not all English computus collections contain prognostics,[108] nor do all prognostics appear in a computistical context – both 'Bald's Leechbook' (Royal 12. D. XVII) and the *Lacnunga* (Harley 585), for example, contain warnings against bloodletting on certain days (the latter of which appears in Vitellius C. viii among computus material), and **S** is entirely a medical manuscript; London, British Library, Cotton Vespasian D. xiv (**V**) and the added material in Oxford, Bodleian Library Hatton 115 (**H**), both s. xii, show prognostics in a broadly homiletic context. But it is an inescapable conclusion that the spread of this body of literature in Anglo-Saxon England cannot be separated from the development of the Winchester computus.

One indication of the degree of interest in prognostics is the evidence that their texts, like the various texts which made up the computus, were collected, adapted, organized and developed. The large collection of texts in **T** is carefully arranged with a set of glossed Latin texts preceding a set of mostly parallel English ones;[109] it derives at least in part from previous collections, for the same subgroup of Latin prognostics is found in **Æ61–64**, **T19–22** and **J3–6**, though none can be shown to be copied from the others. **H** contains versions of **T8, 9, 10, 12** and **15**, though not in that order; its source may be a collection of English items similar to that which contributed to **T**, here added to an anthology of vernacular homilies. Prognostic material is found in the company of a note on the Six Ages of the World in **L, J, T, C, Ti, R**: though the notes are not all the same, the conjunction suggests that these sorts of material travelled together in manuscript collections. Like the texts of the computus, prognostics were portable and multiform; considerable variation is found within texts and in collections of texts, as one would expect from a work of practical use.

This coexistence, what one might perhaps unfairly call the 'parasitical' nature of the prognostic on the computus, may suggest something about the psychology of monastic life: to enter a monastery was to enter into a new relationship to time. By far the majority of Anglo-Saxons at every period lived according to the

---

107 Hughes, *Portiforium*, suggests that similarities to Galba A. xv, and the general character of the calendar, argue that the exemplar of the MS was from Winchester.

108 The computus in London, British Library, Cotton Tiberius B.v, fols. 2–19 (Winchester, s. xi¹), for example, has no prognostic material; see the discussion by P. McGurk in *An Eleventh-Century Anglo-Saxon Illustrated Miscellany, British Library Cotton Tiberius B.v Part I*, ed. P. McGurk, D. N. Dumville, M. R. Godden and A. Knock, EEMF 21 (Copenhagen, 1983), 51–4, and the discussion in *Byrhtferth's Enchiridion*, ed. Baker and Lapidge, pp. xlv–xlviii. Other MSS with significant computus material but no prognostics include Cambridge, University Library, Kk. 5. 32, fols. 49–78 (Glastonbury, s. xi¹) and London, British Library, Cotton Julius A. vi (Canterbury?, Durham, s. xi).   109 See the appendix for the sequence of texts.

rhythms of rural or village life; 'labor time', as characterized by Jacques le Goff, 'was still the time of an economy dominated by agrarian rhythms, free of haste, careless of exactitude, unconcerned by productivity'.[110] This is no doubt something of an exaggeration, but it may stand to emphasize the contrast between agricultural and monastic life: a life of orderly calendar time, in the course of which the soul is habituated to the rhythm of the liturgical day and year. Monastic discipline is first and foremost a temporal discipline of punctuality and accurate timekeeping. The spiritual life was shaped by the cycles of the calendar – fasts and feasts, psalms and prayers, repentance and celebration were all performed according to calendrical calculations, and their observance was an outward sign of the universal unity of the church. The *Regularis Concordia*, whatever else it may be, is an elaborate timetable. Ælfric's *Letter to the Monks of Eynsham*, to take only one example, is explicit about the conformity of the calendar and the monk's soul: 'Ergo regularium monachorum consuetudo non sinit ut aliquis frater neglegenter occurrat horis canonicis, sed facto signo conueniant omnes ad orationem, et intenti incipiant simul sinaxim simulque finiant.'[111] Hours were counted and seasons reckoned not by dawn and dusk, seedtime and harvest, but by liturgical observance; the calendar regulated both habits of the body and states of the mind. As the farmer feels the alternation of summer and winter, so the monk feels the succession of Advent and Christmas, Lent and Easter, not just in his mind but in his heart and in his bones. The monastic calendar, however, unlike the agricultural one, requires a fairly precise attention to the calculation of lunar and solar time.

It is this precise attention to time – bordering perhaps on the obsessive – coupled with the confidence that the soul moved to the changes of the calendar that makes late-classical survivals like lunar dream calendars and calendrical prohibitions against the eating of gooseflesh comfortable in their monastic setting; monastic timekeeping creates a context in which these texts could flourish.[112] In

---

[110] J. le Goff, 'Labor Time in the "Crisis" of the Fourteenth Century', in his *Time, Work and Culture in the Middle Ages*, trans. A. Goldhammer (Chicago, IL, 1980), p. 44. See J. Leclercq, 'Experience and Interpretation of Time in the Early Middle Ages', *Stud. in Med. Culture* 5 (1975), 9–19, S. C. McCluskey, 'Gregory of Tours, Monastic Timekeeping, and Early Christian Attitudes to Astronomy', *Isis* 81 (1991), 9–22, and the more general discussion in D. Landes, *Revolution in Time: Clocks and the Making of the Modern World* (Cambridge, MA, 1983), pp. 53–66.

[111] 'The custom of monks living under the *Rule*, then, does not permit any brother to be negligent in attending the canonical hours; but at the bell they shall all assemble for prayer and attentively begin the Office together and finish it together.' *Ælfric's Letter to the Monks of Eynsham*, ed. C. A. Jones, CSASE 24 (Cambridge, 1998), 113–15, trans. Jones.

[112] Henel, surveying the various lists of lucky and unlucky days for bloodletting which survive in many monastic manuscripts, suggests that 'Unglückstage, die man beachten muss, Heiligentage, die man ebenfalls beachten muss – das scheint den Schreibern der Hss Harley und Bodley 579 "Wissen" von ziemlich derselben Bedeutung gewesen zu sein' ('Altenglische Mönchsaberglaube', p. 344).

Roy Michael Liuzza

a manuscript like Æ ecclesiastical observance and lunar observation intersect; they are treated, in effect, as two aspects of the same thing. Egyptian days and canicular days were marked on many monastic calendars alongside saints' days;[113] the lunar dream calendar in W contains verses of Psalms for each day, making explicit this link between lunar observation and monastic observance of the Hours. Computing the date of Easter, finding the duration of moonshine, figuring unlucky days for bloodletting, calculating time for the recitation of the Divine Office and reckoning the effect of the moon on the validity of dreams are all interrelated skills; all call upon the clerical familiarity with pastoral, medical, chronometric and astronomical practice.[114] In T, organized around the two poles of monastic and pastoral concerns,[115] the largest series of prognostic material is placed, perhaps significantly, after the monastic rules but before the penitential material: while the former regulates the social body, prescribing a practice of routine and conformity for the good of the soul and the peace of the

---

113 Egyptian days, *dies malae*, and/or *dies caniculares* are indicated in or added to all but one (no. 17, CCCC 391 = W) of the nineteen calendars printed in F. Wormald, *English Kalendars before A.D. 1100*, HBS 72 (London, 1934). Henel 1934–5, p. 331, n. 1, lists MSS in which the *dies caniculares* are indicated; in addition to those printed in Wormald he notes Durham, Cathedral Library, Hunter 100 and Rouen Y. 6 (the Missal of Robert of Jumièges).

114 Two brief texts in Caligula A. xv, 130v, illustrate this point: the first, a note on the extreme dates of Easter, begins 'Ealde witan and wise romane gesetton on gerimcræfte þæt næfre ær. xi. kal. Aprelis. Ne naht æfter .vii. kal. maius. eastor tid gewurðan sceal' ('Old scholars and wise Romans set down in their computi that Easter time must never occur before the 11th Kalends of April or after the 7th Kalends of May'). The following text, a warning against unlucky days in each month, begins 'Ða ealdan læces gesetton on ledon bocum þæt on ælcum monðe beoð æfre twegen dagas þa syndon swiðe derigendlice ænigne drenc to drincanne oþþe blod to lætenne' ('The old doctors set down in their Latin books that in each month there are two days that are very dangerous for drinking potions or letting blood'). The similar appeal to venerable textual authority suggests that the two sorts of information were regarded as in some respect parallel.

115 Many of the texts in this MS, in Gneuss's words, are 'meant to serve the needs of a monastic community' ('Origin and Provenance of Anglo-Saxon Manuscripts', p. 28); in addition to the series of texts with which the manuscript begins Gneuss points to (Ker's) items 10a (Vespers and Lauds for an office of All Saints), 22 (*Monasteriales indicia*), 25 (ch. 4 of the Benedictine *Rule* in Latin and Old English), 29 (Ælfric's *Pastoral Letter* III) and 30 (Office of the Virgin). Together this sort of material makes up roughly two-thirds of the whole book. Other items, particularly items 9 and 21, are penitential and confessional in nature. One penitential prayer (item 9i, ed. H. Sauer, 'Zwei spätaltenglische Beichtermahnungen aus Hs. Cotton Tiberius A.iii', *Anglia* 98 (1980), 1–33, as *Exhortation of a Confessor III*) is essentially a vernacular adaptation of ch. 4 of the *Rule*, a text found elsewhere in the same MS in Latin with a different Old English prose translation (item 25); it concludes with another lengthy absolution and benediction, and directions for fasting. The use of a chapter from Benedict's *Rule* suggests that the confessional material in Tiberius A. iii should stand alongside the Benedictine material as a distinctly monastic form of penitential aid, reflecting the pastoral duties of the monks of Christ Church.

community, and the latter heals the moral body, confessing the sins of the flesh and prescribing routines of corporeal penance, prognostics, particularly lunar calendars, chart the health of the physical body seen as a theatre of cosmic influence, a fluid system whose ebbs and flows – whether in the blood, in the course of good and bad fortune, or in the shifting images found in dreams – must be recognized in order to be managed. Prognostics exist, as it were, at the intersection of medical theory, the penitential and the computus, between the care of the body and soul (the confessor is a *gastlican læce*)[116] and the observation of the heavens.

Valerie Flint suggests that prognostics and related texts were 'controlled compromises', deliberate accommodations of Christianity to paganism; she argues that 'the monks made their rather simpler efforts in the direction of astrological divination . . . primarily to make friends, and indeed Christians, of the people in the countryside in which they settled, and among whom the old magic persisted in so many of its forms'.[117] This may be true in some cases, as Flint's extensive survey suggests, but eventually one must hesitate over the ascription of intentionality implied by the word 'primarily'; it may be more accurate to say that so-called 'magical' practices flourished in Christian contexts because they were, to put it plainly, congruent with the world-view of monks and priests. Many churchmen, after all, were born and raised in the towns and villages and farms of their own region, and certainly shared with their lay neighbours a worldview which included a belief in celestial influence on earthly life, the existence of days of various qualities, and a desire to use knowledge of such things to one's advantage whenever possible.[118] The monastic life, with its careful attention to and sophisticated instruction in reckoning the passage of time, simply allowed them access to better technology for doing so. It would not be surprising if prognostics were employed in the exercise of pastoral duties; they spoke to the everyday anxieties of people's lives such as illness, weather, agriculture and childbirth. In their local setting priests and monks were authority figures, confessors and occasional secular authorities, their status enhanced by their use of literacy and Latinity. It may well be that collections of prognostics such as that found in **T** offered a canonically acceptable alternative, with learned pseudo-biblical and textual authority and

---

[116] The metaphor is too common to need citation, but the phrase in this case comes from R. Fowler, 'A Late Old English Handbook for the Use of a Confessor', *Anglia* 83 (1965), 1–34, at p. 17, citing a text which follows the prognostic material in Tiberius A. iii. Elsewhere in the same text (p. 26) the analogy is explicit: 'On wisum scryfte bið swiðe forðgelang forsyngodes mannes nydhelp, ealswa on godan læce bið seoces mannes lacnung.'

[117] Flint, *The Rise of Magic*, pp. 142 and 145.

[118] Jolly, *Popular Religion in Late Saxon England*, p. 21.

pretensions to scientific objectivity, to more popular forms of augury – 'be fugelum oððe be fnorum oððe be horsum oððe be hundum', as Ælfric scornfully characterized them – and to the advice of local healers or wise women and men. But such texts were not directed entirely or in the first instance to the laity; they appear in personal and devotional manuscripts like **Æ**, **W** and **D** whose primary use appears to have been securely within the monastic walls. Nor, undoubtedly, were such texts directed only to rural parishes or the lower classes: in a later period (1101) Matilda, wife of Henry I, summoned Faritius, abbot of Abingdon, to care for her during her pregnancy and interpret the prognostications – 'curam impendere, prognostica edicere' – as a kind of outside specialist, and we may imagine that monks of Winchester or Christ Church might have been called on to do the same.[119] In effect it is not the laity but the clergy who were susceptible to a belief in the efficacy of complex lunar calendars; prognostics are not a relic of popular belief but a by-product of the monastic reform itself.

Flint attributes the proliferation of lunar prognostics to 'a division in the Christian ranks, and . . . a greater willingness at the local level than at a central one to make compromises with older beliefs', but such statements might mislead one into thinking that these lunar calendars were some attenuation of orthodoxy which crept in far from the centres of ecclesiastical authority.[120] They were not. Nor were they deployed simply as a pragmatic alternative to popular belief; they are most widespread in the later rather than the earlier Anglo-Saxon period, and appear to emanate from Winchester, one of the centres of the monastic reform. Prognostics were copied because they were trusted, and because, no doubt, they were used. If they found their way into a pastoral setting, as an alternative to local *wiccan* or diviners, they were no less used, on the evidence of the manuscripts, by monks and priests as part of their private devotion and regulation of personal health. There is nothing rustic or 'folkloric' about **Æ**; its general tenor is not 'compromise with older beliefs' but the up-to-date practices of a learned monk in the generation before the Conquest.

It may be described, however, as a portrait of monastic culture from the bottom up, not from the top down – not the orderly world of Æthelwold's Benedictine Reform movement but the private world of monastic preoccupation with times and seasons, interior movements and exterior portents, spiritual and physical hygiene, in which 'superstitious' practices existed comfortably

---

[119] F. Getz, *Medicine in the English Middle Ages* (Princeton, NJ, 1998), p. 13, citing *Chronicon monasterii de Abingdon*, ed. J. Stephenson, 2 vols. RS 2 (London, 1858) II, 50. I am grateful to Professor Lea Olsan for calling this reference to my attention.

[120] Flint, *The Rise of Magic*, pp. 135.

alongside orthodox religious devotions. The mingling of 'high' and 'low' culture represented by such manuscripts challenges our notions of religious practice among the Anglo-Saxons. Recent studies by scholars such as Natalie Zemon Davis, Karen Jolly, Eamon Duffy and Richard Kieckhefer suggest, however, that medieval religious practices cannot easily be separated into simple dichotomies of 'Christian' and 'pagan', 'orthodox' and 'heterodox', 'religion' and 'magic', 'faith' and 'superstition'.[121] These new studies ask us to view medieval Christianity as an intersection of 'official' and 'popular' cultures rather than an opposition. Just as prayers to the cross merge imperceptibly into a 'charm' in the form of a prayer to the cross,[122] so the practice of observing times and seasons for the liturgical year tends gradually towards the observance of lunar seasons for dreams, good and bad fortune, medical predictions and the forecasting of one's fate at birth. Just as ritual and sacramental action might embrace attitudes and activities we now sceptically regard as 'magical', so medical science and personal devotion might include areas now labelled 'superstition', such as the interpretation of dreams and the forecasting of dangerous days. In this respect, as in many others, our modern categories cut across the grain of the medieval world. The same mentality that could attune itself to the elaborate prescriptions of the *Rule* and the *Regularis Concordia* for the days and seasons of liturgical practice could consult the lunar calendar to learn whether those days were favourable for bloodletting, childbearing or trusting one's dreams. The corpus of prognostic texts suggests that the later Anglo-Saxon conception of the orthodox spiritual life was more capacious than many modern scholars have imagined. If we are to understand these texts properly, we may need to unlearn some of our modern distinctions.[123]

---

[121] N. Z. Davis, 'Some Tasks and Themes in the Study of Popular Religion', *The Pursuit of Holiness in Late Medieval and Renaissance Religion*, ed. C. Trinkhaus and H. Oberman (Leiden, 1974), pp. 307–36; Jolly, *Popular Religion in Late Saxon England*; *idem*, 'Anglo-Saxon Charms in the Context of a Christian World View', *JMH* 11 (1985), 279–93; and *idem*, 'Magic, Miracle, and Popular Practice in the Early Medieval West: Anglo-Saxon England', *Religion, Science, and Magic: in Concert and in Conflict*, ed. J. Neusner, E. S. Frerichs and P. V. McC. Flesher (New York, 1989), pp. 166–82; E. Duffy, *The Stripping of the Altars: Traditional Religion in England, 1400–1580* (New Haven, CT, 1992); R. Kieckhefer, *Forbidden Rites: a Necromancer's Manual of the Fifteenth Century* (University Park, PA, 1997). See also J. Van Engen, 'The Christian Middle Ages as an Historiographical Problem', *AHR* 91 (1986), 519–52.
[122] As in Cotton Tiberius A. iii, fols. 57–60 (Ker's no. 10a-g). The latter is ptd P. Pulsiano, 'British Library, Cotton Tiberius A. iii, fol. 59rv: an Unrecorded Charm in the Form of an Address to the Cross', *ANQ* ns 4 (1991), 3–5; and cf. J. Zupitza, 'Kreuzzauber', *ASNSL* 88 (1892), 364–5.
[123] I am grateful to Peter Baker, Sandor Chardonnens, Christopher Jones, Sarah Larratt Keefer, Lea Olsan, Sharon Rowley and Leslie Stratyner for their help and advice during the writing of this paper. Part of the research for this essay was made possible by a stipend from the Barbara Greenbaum Newcomb Fellows program.

Roy Michael Liuzza

APPENDIX

Anglo-Saxon manuscripts containing prognostics[124]

EDITIONS

Cockayne, O., *Leechdoms, Wortcunning, and Starcraft of Early England*, 3 vols., RS 35 (London, 1864–6).

Förster, M., 'Die Kleinliteratur des Aberglaubens im Altenglischen', *ASNSL* 110 (1903), 346–58.

Förster, M., 'Beiträge zur mittelalterlichen Volkskunde I', *ASNSL* 120 (1908), 43–52 (cited as Förster 1908a).

Förster, M., 'Beiträge zur mittelalterlichen Volksunde II', *ASNSL* 120 (1908), 296–305 (cited as Förster 1908b).

Förster, M., 'Beiträge zur mittelalterlichen Volkskunde III', *ASNSL* 121 (1908), 30–46 (cited as Förster 1908c).

Förster, M., 'Beiträge zur mittelalterlichen Volkskunde IV', *ASNSL* 125 (1910), 39–70.

Förster, M., 'Beiträge zur mittelalterlichen Volkskunde V', *ASNSL* 127 (1911), 31–84.

Förster, M., 'Beiträge zur mittelalterlichen Volkskunde VI', *ASNSL* 128 (1912), 55–71 (cited as Förster 1912a).

Förster, M., 'Beiträge zur mittelalterlichen Volkskunde VII', *ASNSL* 128 (1912), 285–308 (cited as Förster 1912b).

Förster, M., 'Beiträge zur mittelalterlichen Volkskunde VIII', *ASNSL* 129 (1912), 16–49 (cited as Förster 1912c).

Förster, M., 'Beiträge zur mittelalterlichen Volkskunde IX', *ASNSL* 134 (1916), 264–93.

Förster, M., 'Die altenglischen Traumlunare', *Englische Studien* 60 (1925–6), 58–93.

Förster, M., 'Die altenglischen Verzeichnisse von Glücks- und Unglückstagen', *Studies in English Philology. A Miscellany in Honor of Frederick Klaeber*, ed. K. Malone (Minneapolis, MN, 1929), pp. 258–77.

Förster, M., 'Vom Fortleben antiker Sammellunare im Englischen und in anderen Volkssprachen', *Anglia* 67/68 (1944), 1–171.

Günzel, B., *Ælfwine's Prayerbook (London, British Library, Cotton Titus D.xxvi + xxvii)*, HBS 108 (Woodbridge, 1993).

Henel, H., 'Altenglischer Mönchsaberglaube', *Englische Studien* 69 (1934–5), 329–49.

Svenburg, E., *De Latinska Lunaria* (Gothenburg, 1936).

Warner, R. D.-N., *Early English Homilies, from the Twelfth Century MS. Vesp. D. XIV*, EETS os 152 (London, 1917).

SHORT LIST OF MS SIGLA

A   London, British Library, Arundel 60
Æ   London, British Library, Cotton Titus D. xxvi, xxvii

---

[124] See Hollis and Wright, *Old English Prose of Secular Learning*, pp. 257–69, for partial descriptions. The list of MSS that follows includes some non-English MSS (such as **F**) which may have been in England before the eleventh century and some English MSS from the twelfth century such as **J** and **V** which might preserve pre-Conquest material. It is not, however, a complete list.

C   London, British Library, Cotton Caligula A. xv
D   Cambridge, Corpus Christi College 422, pt II
Di Oxford, Bodleian Library, Digby 63
F   London, British Library, Harley 3017
G   London, British Library, Harley 3271
H   Oxford, Bodleian Library, Hatton 115
J   Oxford, St John's College 17
L   Oxford, Bodleian Library, Bodley 579
R   London, British Library, Royal 2. B. V
S   London, British Library, Sloane 475, fols. 125–231
Sa London, British Library, Cotton Vitellius A. xii
T   London, British Library, Cotton Tiberius A. iii
Th London, British Library, Cotton Tiberius C. i, fols. 2–42 + London, British Library, Harley 3667, fols. 2–18
Tr Cambridge, Trinity College R. 15. 32
V   London, British Library, Cotton Vespasian D. xiv
Vi London, British Library, Cotton Vitellius E. xviii
W   Cambridge, Corpus Christi College 391

MANUSCRIPTS

CCCC 391 (W). Ker, *Catalogue*, no. 67; Gneuss, 'Preliminary List', no. 104; Budny, *Manuscript Art*, no. 43.[125] Worcester Cathedral Priory, s. xi². May have belonged to St Wulfstan of Worcester (*c.* 1008–95); one of only a few witnesses to the early development of the breviary in England. Contains a Gallican Psalter and Canticles (pp. 24–294), Collectar (pp. 295–560), Latin calendar and computus material (pp. 1–23), and other liturgical items.[126] At the end of the MS (pp. 713–21) is a series of eight prognostic texts, all in English, in the same hand as the Latin of the main text; it begins incompletely:

> 1. p. 713. General prognostic based on sunshine during the twelve days of Christmas, beginning imperfectly 'kiningum and ricum mannum bið mycel syb þy geare'. (Frank and Cameron, 'List of Old English Texts', B23.3.1.1). Similar to H6. Ptd Förster 1912a, pp. 65–6.
>
> 2. pp. 713–15. General prognostics by thunder based on the day of the week, time of day, and direction in which thunder is heard, beginning 'On anweardne gear gif

---

[125] N. R. Ker, *A Catalogue of Manuscripts Containing Anglo-Saxon* (Oxford, 1957); H. Gneuss, 'A Preliminary List of Manuscripts Written or Owned in England up to 1100', *ASE* 9 (1981), 1–60; M. Budny, *Insular, Anglo-Saxon, and Early Anglo-Norman Manuscript Art at Corpus Christi College, Cambridge: an Illustrated Catalogue*, with a foreword by David M. Wilson and an Introduction by R. I. Page (Kalamazoo, MI, 1997). Other works commonly cited below include: R. Frank and A. Cameron, 'A List of Old English Texts', *A Plan for the Dictionary of Old English* (Toronto, 1973), pp. 25–306; A. Beccaria, *I codici di medicina del periodo presalernitano (secoli IX, X e XI)* (Rome, 1956).

[126] Most of the liturgical material is ed. Hughes, *Portiforium*.

hit þunreð ærest on sunnandæg se becnað kyninges oððe biscopes deað oððe mænige ealdermen on þam geare sweltað' (Frank and Cameron, 'List of Old English Texts', B23.3.1.2). Partly = **T12 H9**. Ptd Förster 1908a, pp. 46–8.

3. p. 715. Birth prognostic by day of the week, beginning 'Gif mon bið acennen [*sic*] on sunnandæg oððe on nihte swa wer swa wif swahweðer hit þonne bið nafað he na mycle sorge and he bið gesælig be his gebyrde' (Frank and Cameron, 'List of Old English Texts', B23.3.1.3). Ptd Förster 1912b, pp. 297–300.

4. p. 716. Birth lunarium, beginning 'Onre [*sic*; for On] .i. nihte ealdne monan þæt cild þæt swa bið acenned þæt bið liflic.On .ii. nihte aldne monan þæt bið seoc and sicle' (Frank and Cameron, 'List of Old English Texts', B23.3.1.4). Ptd Förster 1912c, p. 21.

5. p. 717–18. Medical lunarium, beginning 'Se ðe onre [*sic*; for on anre] nihte monan weorðeð untrum se bið on ðære adle swiðe geswenced. [O]n .ii. nihta monan hraðe æfter sare he ariseð' (Frank and Cameron, 'List of Old English Texts', B23.3.1.5). Ptd, except for the last sentence, Förster 1912c, pp. 34–6.

6. p. 718. A list of the three marvellous days, beginning 'Ðry dagas synd on .xii. monðum mid iii nihtum on ðam ne bið nan wif acenned' (Frank and Cameron, 'List of Old English Texts', B23.2.1.1). = **C6 Vi5**. Ptd Förster 1929, p. 260.

7. p. 718. A list of three unlucky days for bloodletting, beginning 'Ðry dagas synd on xii. monðum þa synd swiðe unhalwende monnum oððe nytenum blod on to forlætene oððe drenc to drincane' (Frank and Cameron, 'List of Old English Texts', B23.2.1.2). = **Vi6**. Ptd Förster 1929, p. 273.

8. pp. 718–21. Dream lunaria: first in Latin, including verses from Psalms for each day of the month, beginning *Luna .i. quicquid uideris in gaudium conuertitur. Beatus uir qui non abiit* [Ps I.1]; *Luna .ii. luna. iii. effectum habent nec in animo ponas. Adstiterunt reges terre.* [Ps II.2] *Tu autem domine susceptor* [Ps III.4], then in English, beginning 'þonne se mone bið anre nihte eald swa hwæt swa þu gesihst. þæte kymð to gefean. On twam nihtum and on .iii. ne bið on þam swefne ne god ne yfel' (Frank and Cameron, 'List of Old English Texts', B23.3.1.6). The Latin is collated in Förster 1925–6, pp. 67–74; the Old English – not a translation of the Latin – is ptd Förster 1925–6, pp. 79–86.

CCCC 422, pt II, the 'Red Book of Darley' (D). Ker, *Catalogue*, no. 70; Gneuss, 'Preliminary List', no. 111; Budny, *Manuscript Art*, no. 44. *c.* 1061. 'Made probably at New Minster, Winchester, for use at Sherborne Cathedral Priory, Dorset, or perhaps made at Sherborne from Winchester material' (Budny, *Manuscript Art*, p. 647). Possibly owned by the Church of St Helen at Darley Dale in Derbyshire as early as the twelfth century, when a mass for St Helen was added on p. 49. A 'decorated, small-format copy of Masses and other Offices, with some Old English texts and headings, and with prefatory calendrical and computistical tables . . . a portable breviary in partial or primitive form' (Budny, *Manuscript Art*, p. 645). The calendar is similar to other New Minster calendars such as those in **A** and **Vi**. Prognostic material is found among computistical texts and includes:

1. p. 27. Bloodletting lunarium, damaged but legible, described in Ker as a 'table of lucky and unlucky days of the moon', in Latin and Old English, beginning '*Luna. i.*

Bona est her hit i<s god tima.> *Luna. ii. Non est bona* nis hi<t her god tima.> (Frank and Cameron, 'List of Old English Texts', B23.2.2). = Æ1. Ptd Henel 1934–5, pp. 334–5.

2. p. 49. Added prognostic text (s. xii), beginning *Isti sunt tres dies anni pre aliis obseruandi.* A version of the 'Three Critical Days'.

Cambridge, Trinity College R. 15. 32 (Tr). Ker, *Catalogue*, no. 90; Gneuss, 'Preliminary List', no. 186. Winchester, New Minster; later in St Augustine's Canterbury, s. xi^in. Pp. 13–36, containing computus and calendar material, were written by one of the scribes of Titus D. xxvi/xxvii.[127]

1. fol. 37r. A list of two critical days in each month for bloodletting, in hexameters, beginning *Iani prima dies. & septima fine timetur.* = Æ18a.

Arundel 60 (A). 'Arundel Psalter'. Ker, *Catalogue*, no. 134; Gneuss, 'Preliminary List', no. 304. Probably from New Minster, Winchester, s. xi².[128] Prefatory computistical material, fols. 1–12, contains:

1. fol. 1r. Bloodletting lunarium titled *Ad sanguinum minuendum.* Closely similar to Æ1 G3.
2. 2r–7r. Distributed throughout the calendar are the verses on twenty-four unlucky days for bloodletting, beginning *Iani prima dies et septima fine timetur.* = Æ18a.

Caligula A. xv, fols. 120–53 (C). Ker, *Catalogue*, no. 139A; Gneuss, 'Preliminary List', no. 411. Christ Church, Canterbury, s. xi².[129] 'Three quires containing notes on computus and the calculation and observance of church services, a table of years and annals of Christ Church, Canterbury, lunar prognostics, charms and other notes' (Ker, *Catalogue*, p. 173). Closely related to the texts in **T**, and bound together with extracts (142–53v) from Ælfric's *De temporibus anni* from the same textual family as **T**,[130] and notes on ferial regulars, concurrents and epacts:

1. 125v. Diagram and text, beginning *Spera apulei platonici de uita et morte.* Ptd Förster 1912c, pp. 45–9.
2. 125v–126. Medical lunarium in Latin and Old English, beginning *Luna prima Qui inciderit difficile euadet* 'Se þe afealð earfoðlice he ætwint' (Frank and Cameron, 'List of Old English Texts', B23.3.2.1). = **T6**. Ptd Förster 1912c, p. 34; Latin ptd Henel, *Studien*, p. 51; English ptd Cockayne 1864–6 III, 150.

---

[127] Contents are noted by M. R. James, *The Western Manuscripts in the Library of Trinity College, Cambridge: a Descriptive Catalogue*, 2 vols. (Cambridge, 1900–2) II, 363–6, and see T. A. M. Bishop, 'Notes on Cambridge Manuscripts', *Trans. of the Cambridge Bibliographical Soc.* 2 (1954–8), 185–99, at 189–92.

[128] Facsimile ed. P. Pulsiano, *Anglo-Saxon Manuscripts in Microfiche Facsimile* 2 (Binghamton, NY, 1994); a description is on pp. 13–18.

[129] See also P. J. Willetts, 'A Reconstructed Astronomical MS from Christ Church Canterbury', *Brit. Museum Quarterly* 30 (1966), 22–9.

[130] *Ælfric's De Temporibus Anni*, ed. Henel, pp. xxxv–xxxviii.

Roy Michael Liuzza

3. 129v–130r. Latin list of twenty-four days on which it is not good to let blood, beginning on 129r. *Non interficias. nec sangius relaxetur*, and on 130r, *Mense Ianuari .i. et antequam exeat dei .vii.* The days are the same as no. 5.

4. 130r. A list of twenty-four unlucky days, beginning 'Syndon twegen dagas on æghwylcum monðe swa hwæt swa on þam dagum ongyð ne wurð hit næfre geendod' (Frank and Cameron, 'List of Old English Texts', B23.2.3.1). Ends 'And swa hit bið gyme se þe wylle.' = **Vi2**. Ptd Förster 1929, p. 262; Cockayne 1864–6 III, 224.

5. 130v–131r. A list of the twenty-four days on which it is not good to let blood, beginning 'Ða ealdan læces geseetton on ledon bocum þæt on ælcum monðe beoð æfre twegen dagas' (Frank and Cameron, 'List of Old English Texts', B23.2.3.2). = **Vi7**. The list begins in March. Ptd Förster 1929, p. 266.

6. 131r. A note on the three marvellous days, beginning 'Ðreo dagas syndon on .XII. monðum mid þrim nihtum. on þam ne bið nan wifmann akenned' (Frank and Cameron, 'List of Old English Texts', B23.2.3.3). = **W6 Vi5**. Ptd Förster 1929, p. 260; Cockayne 1864–6 III, 154.

7. 131v–132. Dream lunarium, beginning 'On anre nihta eald monan swa hwæt swa þe mæteð.' = **T8 W8**. Ptd Förster 1925–6, p. 79; Cockayne 1864–6 III, 154–6.

8. 132. Birth lunarium, beginning 'Gif mann biþ akenned on anre nihtne ealne [*sic*] monan. se bið lang lifes ond welig. Gif he bið on tweigra nihta akenned, se bið a seoc ond unhal' (Frank and Cameron, 'List of Old English Texts', B23.3.2.3). = **T15**. Ptd Förster 1912c, p. 21; Cockayne 1864–6 III, 156–8.

Tiberius A.iii (T). Ker, *Catalogue*, no. 186; Gneuss, 'Preliminary List', no. 363. Christ Church, Canterbury, s. xi. A monastic miscellany containing, *inter alia*, the glossed Benedictine Rule and *Regularis Concordia*. Prognostic material is in two groups; the first (Ker's no. 7) is 27v–43 between the *Regularis Concordia* and a group of penitential material, and the second (Ker's item 12) 65rv before Ælfric's *De temporibus anni*. The Latin of the first set of prognostics is in the same hand as the monastic material preceding it; the gloss is a different hand from the gloss to the preceding material.

1. fols. 27v–32v. *Somniale Danielis*, Latin with Old English Gloss, titled *DE SOM-NIORUM DIUERSITATE SECUNDUM ORDINEM ABCHARII DANIE-LIS PROPHETE* and beginning '*Aues in somnis qui uiderit et cum ipsis pugnauerit. lites aliquas significat.* fugelas on swefenum se þe gesyhð ond mid him winneð saca sume hit getacnað' (Frank and Cameron, 'List of Old English Texts', C16.1). Ed. Förster 1910, pp. 39–70. Errors in Latin which are glossed correctly (e.g. no. 230 *scola*, an apparent error for *scala*, is glossed correctly 'læddran') suggest that the gloss may not be original to this MS.

2. 32v–35v. General lunarium, Latin with Old English gloss, titled *De observatione lune et quae cauenda sunt*, beginning *Luna prima; omnibus rebus agendis utilis est* 'mona se forma. on eallum þingum dondum nytlic ys' (Frank and Cameron, 'List of Old English Texts', C16.2). Ptd Förster 1944, pp. 79–129.

3. 35v–36. Dream lunarium, Latin with Old English gloss, beginning *Luna prima quicquid uideris. in gaudium erit. et si uideris te uinci. tu tamen uinces omnes inimicos tuos*

216

Anglo-Saxon prognostics in context

annuente deo. 'swawætswa þu gesihst on blisse biõ ond gif þu gesihst þe beon ofercumene ofercymst ealle feond þine geunnendum gode' (Frank and Cameron, 'List of Old English Texts', C16.3). Ptd Förster 1925–6, pp. 67–74.

4. fol. 36rv. Calendar prognostic for New Year's Day (a version of the *Revelatio Esdrae*), Latin with Old English gloss, beginning *Si fuerit kalendas Ianuarius die dominico, hiems bona erit et suauis, ac calida, uer uentuosus, et sicca estas, uindemia bona, oues crescent, mel habundabit, senes morientur, et pax fiet* 'Gif biõ on dæg drihtenlicum winter god biõ ond wynsum ond wearm windhladen ond drige wingeard god, sweap [*sic*] weaxaõ hunig genihtsumaõ ealde swealteõ ond sib gewyrõ' (Frank and Cameron, 'List of Old English Texts', C16.4). Ptd Förster 1908b, pp. 296–7.

5. 36v. Birth lunarium, Latin with Old English gloss, beginning *Luna .i. qui natus fuerit. uitalis erit* 'se þe acenned biõ liflic he biõ' (Frank and Cameron, 'List of Old English Texts', C16.5). = Æ63. Ptd Förster 1912c, pp. 18–21.

6. 36v–37. Medical lunarium, Latin with Old English gloss, beginning *Luna .i. qui inciderit difficile euadet*. 'se þe afeallaõ earfoõlice he ætwint' (Frank and Cameron, 'List of Old English Texts', C16.6). = C2 Æ64. Ptd Förster 1912c, pp. 32–4.

7. 37rv. Thunder prognostic based on the hours of the night and day, Latin with Old English gloss, beginning *Si tonitruauerit hora uespertina significat natiuitatem cuiusdam magni* 'Gif hit þunraõ on tide æfen hit getacnaõ cennednysse sumes miceles' (Frank and Cameron, 'List of Old English Texts', C16.7). = Æ66. Ptd Förster 1908a, pp. 50–1.

8. 37v–38. Dream lunarium in Old English, beginning 'On anre nihte ealdne monan swa hwæt swa þe mæteõ þæt cymõ to gefean. [O]n tweigra nihte monan. 7 on þreora. næfþ þæt swefen nænige fremednesse godes ne yfeles.' (Frank and Cameron, 'List of Old English Texts', B23.3.3.1). = C7 W8. Ptd Förster 1925–6, pp. 79–86.

9. 38–39v. Dreambook in Old English, beginning 'Gif mann mæte þæt he geseo earn on his heafad ufan. þæt tacnaõ wurþmynt. Gif him þince. þæt he feala earna ætsomne geseo. þæt byþ yfel niõ ond manna sætunga ond seara' (Frank and Cameron, 'List of Old English Texts', B23.3.3.2). = H10. Ptd Förster 1916, pp. 270–93.

10. 39v–40. General lunarium in Old English, beginning 'On anre nihte ealdne monan far þu to cinge. bidde þæs þu wille. he þe þæt gifõ. gang in to him on þa þriddan tide þæs dæges oõõe þænne þu wene. þæt sæ sy full' (Frank and Cameron, 'List of Old English Texts', B23.3.3.3). = H11. Imperfect, ending after only three days. Ptd Förster 1912c, p. 43.

11. fol. 40. Medical lunarium in Old English, beginning 'On anre nihte ealdne monan seþe hine adl gestandeõ. se biõ frecenlice gestanden. Gif hine on .ii. nihta ealdne monan adl gestandeþ. sona he ariseþ' (Frank and Cameron, 'List of Old English Texts', B23.3.3.4). Ptd Förster 1912c, p. 34.

12. 40rv. Thunder prognostic based on the days of the week, beginning 'On anweardan geare gif se forma þunor cymõ on sunnan dæge þonne tacnaõ þæt cyme bearna cwealm' (Frank and Cameron, 'List of Old English Texts', B23.3.3.6). Very similar to H9 and the first part of W2. Ptd Cockayne 1864–6 III, 180.

13. 40v. General prognostic based on the weekday of the new moon, beginning 'Ðonne se mona bið acenned on sunnan dæig þæt tacnað .iii. þing on þam monþe. þæt is ren ond wind ond smyltnys ond hit tacnað nytena wædla ond manna gesynto ond hælo' (Frank and Cameron, 'List of Old English Texts', B23.3.3.7). Ptd Cockayne 1864–6 III, 180–2.

14. 40v–41. A note on the growth of the fetus, beginning 'Her onginð secgan ymbe mannes gecynde. hu he on his modor innoþe to men gewyrðeð' (Frank and Cameron, 'List of Old English Texts', B21.4). Ptd Cockayne 1864–6 III, 146.

15. 41rv. Birth lunarium in Old English, beginning 'Gif mann biþ acenned on ane nihtne ealdne monan. se lang lifes ond welig bið. Gif he bið on tweigra nihta acenned. se bið a seoc ond unhal' (Frank and Cameron, 'List of Old English Texts', B23.3.3.5). Similar to **C8 H2**. Ptd Förster 1912c, pp. 21–4.

16. 41v–42. Calendar prognostic for New Year's Day of the *Revelatio Esdrae* type, beginning 'Kalendas Ianuarius gif he byþ on monandæg. þonne biþ grimm 7 gemenged winter, 7 god lencten, 7 windig sumor, 7 hreohfull gear biþ, 7 adlseoce menn beoð on þam geare' (Frank and Cameron, 'List of Old English Texts', B23.3.3.9). Ptd Förster 1908b, pp. 297–8.

17. fol. 42rv. Dreambook in Old English, beginning 'Gif man mæte þæt his mon ehte. yfel þæt bið. Gif him mæte. þæt his onsyne fæger si. god þæt bið. and him bið wurðmynt toweard. and gif him þince unfæger. yfel þæt bið' (Frank and Cameron, 'List of Old English Texts', B23.3.3.10). Ptd Förster 1908b, p. 302; corrections in Förster 1908c, p. 37.

18. 42v–43. Omens in pregnancy, beginning 'Eft is oðer wise be þissum þingum þæt þu meht witan on bearn eacenum wife hwæþeres cynnes bearn heo cennan sceal' (Frank and Cameron, 'List of Old English Texts', B23.3.3.8). Ptd Cockayne 1864–6 III, 144.

19. 65r. Bloodletting lunarium, in Latin, beginning *Luna .i. tota die bonum est. Luna .ii. non est bonum. Luna tertia bona est.* = **Æ61**.

20. 65r. Birth prognostic by day of the week, in Latin, beginning *Die dominico hora diuturna siue nocturna utilis erit qui nascetur. magnusque et splendidus.* = **Æ62**.

21. 65rv. Birth lunarium, in Latin, beginning *Luna .i. qui natus fuerit. uitalis erit. Luna ii mediocris erit.* = **T5 Æ63**.

22. 65v. Medical lunarium, in Latin, beginning *Luna .i. qui inciderit difficile euadet. Luna .ii. cito consurget.* Ends at day 7. = **T6 Æ64**.

Tiberius C. i, fols. 2–42 + Harley 3667, fols. 2–18 (Th). Ker, *Catalogue*, no. 196. Peterborough, *c.* 1120. Surviving quires vi, vii and xxi of a large collection of computistical and astronomical works closely related to **J**.[131] Prognostic material is likewise largely shared with that MS:

---

[131] Discussed in *Byrhtferth's Enchiridion*, ed. Baker and Lapidge, pp. lv–lvii; a detailed list of contents is found in Wallis, 'MS Oxford St John's College 17', pp. 693–6. See also F. Saxl and H. Meier, *Catalogue of Astrological and Mythological Illuminated Manuscripts of the Latin Middle Ages*, III: *Manuscripts in English Libraries* (London, 1953), pp. 128–34, and N. R. Ker, 'Membra Disiecta', *Brit. Museum Quarterly* 12 (1937–8), 130–5.

1. Tiberius C. i, 7r. List of one unlucky day in each month, surrounding a diagram of the *syzygia elementorum* (= **J10a**).
2. Tiberius C. i, 7v. Two versions of the 'Sphere of Pythagoras' (= the first part of **J11**).
3. Harley 3667, 4v. A version of the 'Sphere of Pythagoras' with personified 'Vita' and 'Mors' figures. Similar in some respects to **L1**.
4. Harley 3667, 5r. A diamond-shaped prognostic diagram probably similar to that excised in **J**, 41r, with rules for its use, beginning *De quacumque re scire uolueris vel consulere.* (= **J11**).

Titus D. xxvi, xxvii (Æ). Ker, *Catalogue*, no. 202; Gneuss, 'Preliminary List', no. 380. Written for Ælfwine, dean (later abbot) of New Minster, Winchester, s. xi[1]. Two small volumes, originally one book in the order D. xxvii–D. xxvi. Contains Latin prayers, offices, religious texts, a calendar and computus. The same scribe wrote some of the same material in **Tr**. Prognostic material appears in several places throughout the manuscript (item numbers follow Günzel's edition):

1. Titus D. xxvii, 2r. Bloodletting lunarium, titled *Ad sanguinem minuendam*, beginning *Luna i. Tota die bona est. Luna .ii. Non est Bona.* = **A1 D1 T19 Æ61** etc. Ptd Günzel 1993, p. 89.
18. Titus D. xxvii, 22rv. (a) A list of the two critical days in each month for bloodletting, in hexameters, beginning *IANI PRIMA DIES ET SEPTIMA FINE TIMETUR. Periculosum est flebotomari in principio mensis ianuarii.* The verses are ptd PL 90, col. 955. (b) A warning against bloodletting and the eating of gooseflesh on the first Mondays of August and the last Monday of March and December, beginning *Super omnes hos sunt etiam isti obseruabilis.* (c) A warning against bloodletting during the canicular days, and against bloodletting on the fourth, fifth, tenth, fifteenth, twentieth, twenty-fifth and thirtieth day of the lunar month. = **G4 G6**. Ptd Günzel 1993, pp. 110–11.
32. Titus D. xxvii, 25rv. Prognostic of the *Revelatio Esdrae* type, based on the day of the week on which the Kalends of January falls, beginning *Kal. Ianuarii si fuerit in prima feria, hiems bona erit et uentus* [sic: for *uernus*] *uentosus.* Ptd Günzel 1993, p. 115.
35. Titus D. xxvii, 27r–29v. A general lunarium, titled *Argumentum Lunare ad Requirendum Quomodo Luna Qualiter Observitur*, beginning *Luna .i. hec dies ad omnia agenda utilis est. In lecto qui inciderit diu languescet et longa infirmitate patietur. Et quidquid uideris in gaudium conuertetur. Et si uideris te uinci, tu tamen uinces omnes inimicos tuos. Infans si fuerit natus, uitalis erit.* Provides information on illness, dreams and the fortunes of children for every day of the lunar month; other information, including a list of good actions, the likelihood of catching a thief, and the possibility of finding lost objects, appear for some days. The first fifteen days are more fully discussed than the last fifteen. Ptd Günzel 1993, pp. 117–20.
40. Titus D. xxvii, 55v–56v. Old English alphabet prognostic with a verse doxology, added by a different hand on blank leaves at the end of a quire, beginning 'A. He gangeþ. 7 biþ his siðfæt gesund. B. God þu fintst gif ðu hit onginst. 7 ðe bið

wel' (Frank and Cameron, 'List of Old English Texts', B23.3.4).[132] Ends with a metrical doxology. Ptd Günzel 1993, pp. 121–2.

56. Titus D. xxvi, 3v–4r. The three critical Mondays (see **18b** above), titled *hic noctantur* [sic] *dies egiptiaci, qui obseruandi sunt per omnia ne quis sanguinem in eis minuere*, beginning *Dies enim aegyptiaci, in quibus nulliusmodi nec per ulla necessitate non licet hominem nec pecus sanguinem minuere.* Ptd Günzel 1993, p. 144.

57. Titus D. xxvi, 4rv. The three marvellous days, beginning *Tres dies sunt in anno cum totidem noctibus.* The days are here listed as 1 Thebet and the first two days of Sabath (i.e., January and February in the Jewish calendar). = **J2.** Ptd Günzel 1993, p. 145.

58. Titus D. xxvi, 4v. Canicular days and other lunar days, titled *Quali tempore aperienda sit uena* and beginning *Incipiente artucanis* [sic] *uel arcturi adque Siria stella* (cf. **18b** above, and see Thorndike and Kibre, *Catalogue of Incipits*, no. 726). In addition to the canicular days the text encourages bloodletting on the fourth, fourteenth and twenty-fourth day of the month, and warns against it on the fifth, tenth, fifteenth, twentieth, twenty-fifth and thirtieth. = **G10–11.** Ptd Günzel 1993, p. 145.

59. Titus D. xxvi, 5r. A list of twenty unlucky days in the year, beginning *Incipiunt dies aegiptiaci, qui in anno obseruandi sunt, per unumquemque mensem .ii. duo.* The days given are different from those in the calendar, and no mention is made of bloodletting: warnings are given against travel, planting, harvesting and making legal claims. Ptd Günzel 1993, p. 145.

61. Titus D. xxvi, 6rv. Bloodletting lunarium, titled *De flebotomatione uel de minuendo sanguine*, beginning *Luna prima Tota die bonum est. Luna .ii. Non est bonum.* Nearly identical to item **1**, and = **T19.** Ptd Günzel 1993, p. 146.

62. Titus D. xxvi, 6v–7v. Birth prognostic based on the day of the week on which a child is born, titled *De natiuitate infantium*, beginning *Die domenico hora diuturna* [sic; for *diurna*] *siue nocturna uti<..>li erit. qui nascetur magnusque et splendidus.* = **T20.** Ptd Günzel 1993, p. 147.

63. Titus D. xxvi, 7v–8r. Birth lunarium, titled *Incipit lunaris sancti Danielis de natiuitate*, beginning *Luna .i. Qui natus fuerit, uitalis erit. Luna .ii. Mediocris erit.* = **T21.** Ptd Günzel 1993, pp. 147–8.

64. Titus D. xxvi, 8r–9r. Medical lunarium, titled *Incipit lunares* [sic] *de aegris*, beginning *Luna .i. Qui inciderit, difficule euadet. Luna .ii. Cito consurget.* = **T22.** Ptd Günzel 1993, pp. 148–9.

65. Titus D. xxvi, 9rv. Dream lunarium, titled *Incipit lunaris de somnis*, beginning *Luna .i. Quicquid uideri* [sic], *ad gaudium pertinet. Luna .ii. et .iii. Affectus erit.* = **T3.** Ptd Günzel 1993, pp. 149–50.

[132] Described as a 'dream chancebook' by Kruger, *Dreaming in the Middle Ages*, p. 8, this is more likely a version of the *sors biblica*, as much a prayer practice as a method of divination: a prayer is said, then the querent opens the Bible or Psalter at random, and the first letter on the left-hand page is compared with an alphabetical list of divinatory meanings. Günzel 1993, pp. 61–3, doubts that this is a prognostic: the work is untitled and includes no instructions for its use. But Günzel offers no alternative explanation for this text, and its similarity to other such works is undeniable.

66. Titus D. xxvi, 9v–10v. Thunder prognostic, titled De *tonitruis dierum uel trium* [sic: for *noctium*], beginning *Si notauerit* [sic; for *tonituraueri*] *hora uespertina, significat natiuitatem cuiusdem magni.* = **T7**. Ptd Günzel 1993, pp. 150–1.

67. Titus D. xxvi, 10v–11v. Calendar prognostic of the *Revelatio Esdrae* type, titled *Incipiunt signa de temporibus,* beginning *Si die .i. feria fuerint* [alt. from *fueri*] *kal. ianuarii, hiemps bona et uentosa erit.* Similar to item **32**. Ptd Günzel 1993, p. 151.

68. Titus D. xxvi, 11v–16r. A version of the *Somniale Danielis,* titled *Alphabetum somniale excerptum ex Danielis libro* by a later hand, beginning *Aues in somnis uidere et cum illis pugnare: litem significat. Aues in somno capere: lucrum significat.* Similar to **T1** but not the same; lists 151 items. Some corrections made by the rubricator. Ptd Günzel 1993, pp. 151–6.

Vespasian D. xiv (V). Ker, *Catalogue,* no. 209. Rochester or Christ Church, Canterbury, s. xii^med. This largely homiletic MS, mostly in one hand, contains two prognostics in English (items 26, 34 in Warner 1917):

1. 75v. Prognostic for the year's weather based on which day of the week the first day of the year falls (a version of the *Revelatio Esdrae*), beginning 'Ðonne forme gearesdæig byð sunendæig, hit byð god winter. and windig lænctetid. dryge sumer. god hærfest' (Frank and Cameron, 'List of Old English Texts', B23.3.5.1). Ptd Warner 1917, p. 66.

2. 103v. Thunder prognostic by month, beginning 'On Januarius monðe, gyf hit þunreð, hit bodeð toweard mycele windes, and wel gewænde eorðe wæstme. and gefiht' (Frank and Cameron, 'List of Old English Texts', B23.3.5.2). Ptd Warner 1917, p. 91.

Cotton Vitellius A. xii (Sa). Ker, *Catalogue,* no. 214. Several originally separate MSS, the first of which (fols. 5–72) is probably from Salisbury (s. xi/xii) and is closely related to Exeter, Cathedral Library, 3507.[133] Badly damaged in the Cottonian fire of 1731. Contains computistical and astronomical works by Gildas and Abbo of Fleury, Isidore *De natura rerum,* runic alphabets and short poems on scientific subjects. One prognostic is included among a series of short texts (*De septem miraculis manufictis; de duobus verticibus mundi;* a list of readings for the church year by season) not found in the Exeter MS:

1. 44rv. Note on the three critical Mondays, titled *De Diebus ægyptiacis* and beginning *Hos dies maxime obseruare debemus. In quibus nullomodo. neque ulla necessitate licet homini uel pecori sanguinem minuere.* Similar to **Æ56**.

Vitellius C. viii, fols. 22–5. Ker, *Catalogue,* no. 221; Gneuss, 'Preliminary List', no. 404. s. xi¹. Leaves are now mounted separately and bound with unrelated material; Old English material includes computistical texts, a fragment of Ælfric's *De temporibus anni,* and a private prayer. Ker notes that texts are closely related to **Vi**. Between the prayers and the Ælfrician material is one prognostic text:

---

[133] R. Derolez, *Runica Manuscripta: the English Tradition* (Brugge, 1954), pp. 222–7; see also Jones, *Bedae Pseudepigrapha,* p. 121.

1. 22rv. Lines on Egyptian days, beginning 'þry dagas syndon on geare þe we egiptiace hatað þæt is on ure geðeode plihtlice dagas on ðam nateþæshwon for nanre neode ne mannes ne neates blod' (Frank and Cameron, 'List of Old English Texts', B23.2.4). Ptd Förster 1929, pp. 271–3.

Vitellius E. xviii (Vi). Ker, *Catalogue*, no. 224; Gneuss, 'Preliminary List', no. 407. Probably from Winchester, s. xi^med. A psalter with computus, charms etc., all in same hand as the OE gloss to the Latin psalms.[134] The badly damaged leaves in the front of the psalter contain a calendar, tables, rules for finding Septuagesima etc., rules for determining the age of the moon, notes on concurrents and epacts, and the following:

1. 2r–7v. Distributed throughout the calendar are verses for two unlucky days in each month, beginning *Iani prima dies et septima fine timetur.* = **Æ18**.
2. 9r. A list of the two unlucky days in each month, titled *De diebus malis cuiusque mensis*, beginning '[T]weigen dagas syndon on æghwilcum monðe. þæt swa hwæt swa man on þæm dagum onginneð. Ne wurð hit næfre geendod' (Frank and Cameron, 'List of Old English Texts', B23.2.5.1). = **C4**. Ptd Förster 1929, p. 262.
3. 13v. Prohibition against bloodletting in the *dies caniculares*, beginning 'Eahtatina nihtum ær hlafmæssan gangeð se styrra up <se is gehaten> canes. þæt is se hara steorra' (Frank and Cameron, 'List of Old English Texts', B23.4). Ptd Henel 1934–5, p. 331.
4. 14v. The 'Sphere of Pythagoras', beginning imperfectly *..ERE [ratio spere pitagore p]hilosophi quam appollogius descripsit.*
5. 15r. A list of the three marvellous days, beginning 'Ðry dagas syndon on twelf monðum mid þrim nihtum on þam ne bið nan wif acenned' (Frank and Cameron, 'List of Old English Texts', B23.2.5.4). = **W6 C6**. Ptd Henel 1934–5, p. 346.
6. 15r. A list of three unlucky days in the year for bloodletting, beginning 'Sindon þry dagas synd on twelf monðum. þa syndon swiðe unhalwende men oððe nytenum blod to forlætenne oððe drenc to drincanne' (Frank and Cameron, 'List of Old English Texts', B23.2.5.2). = **W7**. Ptd Förster 1929, p. 273.
7. 15rv. A list of the twenty-four unlucky days for bloodletting, beginning 'þa ealdan læcas gesettan on ledonbocum. þæt on ælcum monðe beoð æfre twegen dagas. þe syndon swiðe derigendlice ænigum menn drenc to drincanne oþþe blod to lætanne' (Frank and Cameron, 'List of Old English Texts', B23.2.5.3). = **C5**. Ptd Förster 1929, p. 266.
8. fol. 16r. The 'Sphere of Apuleius', with diagram, titled DE VITA VEL DE MORTE, beginning *Spera apulei platonici de vita vel morte vel de omnibus negotiis.* Text ptd Förster 1912c, pp. 46–7.

Harley 585. Ker, *Catalogue*, no. 231; Gneuss, 'Preliminary List', no. 421. s. x/xi. Pseudo-Apuleius, Old English *Medicina de Quadrupedibus*, Lacnunga. The volume has been

---

[134] A facsimile and description are found in Pulsiano, *Anglo-Saxon Manuscripts in Microfiche Facsimile* 2. See also his 'The Prefatory Material of London, British Library, Cotton Vitellius E. xviii', *Anglo-Saxon Manuscripts and Their Heritage*, ed. P. Pulsiano and E. M. Treharne (Aldershot, 1998), pp. 85–116.

described as a 'medical *vade mecum*'[135] and contains practical remedies. The collection of herb recipes on fols. 130–93 includes one item (item 189, 190rv) in a set of material added (s. xi[1]):

1. A list of three Egyptian days, beginning 'Þry dagas syndon on geare þe we egiptiaci hatað þæt is on ure geþeode plihtlice dagas' (Frank and Cameron, 'List of Old English Texts', B23.2.4) = **Vitellius C. viii**. Ptd Cockayne 1864–6 III, 76; Förster 1929, p. 271.

Harley 3017 (F). Not in Ker or Gneuss. s. ix. Related to Fleury MSS but not from there, according to Baker and Lapidge, *Byrhtferth's Enchiridion*, p. xlii; Jones, *Bedae Pseudepigrapha*, p. 122, calls it 'an excellent example of ninth-century Fleury *computi*'. The presence of a runic alphabet free of continental influence, added on 61r, suggests that the MS may have been in England during the Anglo-Saxon period.[136] A manuscript of computistical and scientific works, including Bede's *De temporum ratione* and Isidore on words for times and seasons. Written in two hands throughout. Prognostic material includes:

1. 1rv. A fragmentary version of the *Somniale Danielis* containing seventy-six items, not all of them legible, covering objects from D to N, beginning *D . . . habere: gaudium*. Ptd Martin, 'Earliest Versions', pp. 140–1.

2. 58r. The 'Sphere of Pythagoras', with diagram, titled *Ratio spere Pithagore philosophi qua Apuleius descripsit*, beginning *Vt quacumque scire uolueris vel consulere*.

3. 58v Medical lunarium, titled *Incipit eiusdem lunaris de egris*, beginning *Luna .i. qui inciderit difficile euadit. Luna .ii. cito surgit*. = **Æ64**. Ed. Weisser, *Studien*, 1982, pp. 273–7.

4. 58v–59r. Birth lunarium, titled *Incipit Lunaris sancti Danihel de nativitate infantium*, beginning *Luna .i. qui fuerit natus uitalis erit. Luna .ii. mediocris erit*. = **Æ63**.

5. 59rv. List of the two critical days in each month for bloodletting, titled *De diebus Egiptiacis qui maledictis sunt in anno circulo*, beginning *Ian. intrante die .i. exiente die .vii. Febr. intrante die .iiii. exsiente die .iii*. The same days as **Æ18**. A note in the margin of 59v in a different hand, beginning *In his diebus. si quis in lecto occiderit, non diu uiuit. nec nullum genus periculi dimittit*, lists the ill effects of these days.

6. 59v. A second note in the margin, beginning *Incipit de aliis diebus egipticis. in quibus nullo modo nec per nulla necessitate non licet nec hominem nec pecus sanguinem minuere nec modicum inpendere*, is a warning against the three critical Mondays. Similar to **Æ56**.

7. 59v–60r. A list of various places from which to let blood on different days of the month and warning against the *dies caniculares*, beginning *Bonum est per singulos menses studium habere sicut multo auctores scripsit*. Thorndike and Kibre, *Catalogue of Incipits*, no. 180; Beccaria, *I codici*, pp. 406–7. Also found add. in the margins of **S**, 7v–8r, in a later hand.

---

[135] By A. N. Doane, in *Anglo-Saxon Manuscripts in Microfiche Facsimile* 1 (Binghamton, NY, 1994), 26.

[136] See L. Martin, 'The Earliest Versions of the Latin Somniale Danielis', *Manuscripta* 23 (1979), 131–41, and Derolez, *Runica Manuscripta*, pp. 212–17.

8. 63r–64v. A version of the *Revelatio Esdrae*, titled *Hec sunt signa quae ostendit deus Esdre prophetae*, beginning *Kal. ian' si fuerint die dominico, erit hiemps calidus. uernus humidus; estas et autumnus uentosi*. Different from the version in Æ32 and **67**.

Harley 3271 (G). Ker, *Catalogue*, no. 239; Gneuss, 'Preliminary List', no. 435. s. xi[1]. A copy of Ælfric's *Grammar* and miscellaneous materials in Latin and Old English; Latin and Old English are not distinguished in script. In the blank space at the end of the last quire of the *Grammar* (fols. 90–2) are computistical and other notes:

1. 90v–91. Old English prohibition against bloodletting and gooseflesh on unlucky days, beginning 'We gesetton on foreweardan on þysre endebyrdnesse þone monaþ martius' (Frank and Cameron, 'List of Old English Texts', B23.2.6). = the second part of **C5**. Ptd Henel 1934–5, p. 336.

2. 91r. Old English list of twenty-four unlucky days, titled *De diebus malis*, beginning 'þa ealdan læcas gesettan on ledenbocun. þæt on ælcum monðe beoð æfre twegen dagas þe syndan swyðe derigendlice ænigne drenc on to ðicgenne' (Frank and Cameron, 'List of Old English Texts', B23.2.6). = the first part of **C5**. Ptd Henel 1934–5, p. 336.

3. 102v. Bloodletting Lunarium, titled *De sanguine minuere*. Added in a different hand. = **Æ1**. Beccaria, *I codici*, no. 76.1.

4. 120v–121. Latin list of two unlucky days in each month, beginning *In principio mensis Ianuarii. dies primus. & ante eius exitum dies septimus*. = the prose portion of **Æ18a**; verses are added between lines in a different hand, beginning *hoc ipsum metrice. Iani prima dies et septima fine timetur*. Continues after the list of days with a warning against the *dies caniculares* beginning *Super omnes hos sunt etiam isti obseruabiles. Ab initio mensis Augusti. dies primus lunae* [gl. 'se forma monandæg']. = **Æ18b**. Beccaria, *I codici*, no. 76.2.

5. fol. 121. Latin warning against the three critical Mondays, beginning *Post .viii. kal. Aprilis. illa die lunae & intrante Augusto illa die lunae*. Similar but not identical to **Æ56**.

6. 122rv. Latin list of two unlucky days in each month, titled *Versus ad dies Aegyptiacos. Inveniendas*, beginning *IANI PRIMA DIES ET SEPTIMA FINE TIMETUR. In principio mensis ianuarii dies primus. hoc est kal. ianuarii, & ante eius exitum dies septimus. hoc est. viii. kal. Februarii*. = **4** above and **Æ18a**. Followed by a text closely similar to Æ18b, beginning *Super omnes hos sunt etiam isti obseruabiles*.

7. 122v. Latin warning against the canicular days, titled *De diebus canicularibus*, beginning *Est etiam istorum temporum obseruanda ratio*. Similar to **4** above, and the latter part of **Æ18b**. Beccaria, *I codici*, no. 76.3.

8. 122v. Latin warning against the three critical Mondays, titled *De tribus diebus Aegyptiaci*, beginning *Primo .viii. kal. aprilis illa die lunae. & intrante agusto illa die lunae*. Similar to **5** above. Beccaria, *I codici*, no. 76.5.

9. 122v–123. Latin list of prohibited and prescribed activities for each month, titled *Medicina Ypocratis. Quid usitare debeatur. per singulos menses*, beginning *Mense ianuarii. non minuere sanguinem. potionem contra effocationem tantum bibe*. Beccaria, *I codici*, no. 76.5.

10. 123v–124. Latin warning against bloodletting during the *dies caniculares*, titled *De Flebotomatione. mensis. Agusto*, beginning *Incipiente ortu canis vel ar`c´turi atque siri stellæ*. Mostly = **Æ58**. Beccaria, *I codici*, no. 76.6.

11. fol. 124. Latin warning against certain lunar days, titled *Quali tempora aperienda sit uena*, beginning *Quando uena aperienda sit. iii. luna erit saluberrima. & .xiiii. luna erit bona*. Very similar to the latter part of **Æ58**. Beccaria, *I codici*, no. 76.7.

Harley 3667, fols. 2–18. See **Tiberius C. i.**

Royal 2.B.v (R). The 'Regius Psalter'. Ker, *Catalogue*, no. 249; Gneuss, 'Preliminary List', no. 451.[137] Winchester, s. xi; Canterbury?, s. x. One prognostic is found at the end of a section of computistical material (and notes on the ages of the world and the sizes of various famous objects)[138] added to the end of the MS in a different hand (either Winchester or Canterbury, probably s. x/xi):

1. 190rv. Latin thunder prognostic by month of the year, beginning *Si tonitruum fuerit in mense ianuario multe conuentiones sunt. una de ouibus; alia de homibus* [sic]. December is omitted.[139] The text bears no relation to the English thunder prognostic by month in **V2**.[140] It is followed by a group of Old English prayers, in a different hand, which are also found in **T** (no. 9 in Ker).

Sloane 475 (S), fols. 125–231. Not in Ker or Gneuss, but possibly English.[141] A composite MS made up of two parts: the first, fols. 1–124, is from s. xii¹ (it is catalogued by Beccaria, *I codici*, no. 78); the second, fols. 125–231, is written in several hands (s. xi). Both parts contain medical recipes, charms, advice on health, and prognostics, mostly in Latin but two (109rv) in Anglo-Norman.[142] The prognostics in the later (first) part of the MS (nos. 1–5 below) are apparently not of English origin, as they are of a different type from those commonly found in Anglo-Saxon MSS:[143]

---

[137] Facsimile ed. P. Pulsiano, *Anglo-Saxon Manuscripts in Microfiche Facsimile* 3 (Binghamton, NY, 1994); the MS is described on pp. 57–64.

[138] The first, on the threefold incarnation of Christ, is identical to a note found in **Æ19**, ptd Günzel 1993, p. 112.

[139] Pulsiano, *Anglo-Saxon Manuscripts 3*, p. 67, says that the prognostic is 'for the months of January, March, July, and August', but this is an oversight. These months do, however, have a slightly larger capital than the others.

[140] The indications for each month are somewhat similar to those in the pseudo-Bedan *De tonitruis libellus ad Herefridum* (PL 90, cols. 609–14) surviving in Cologne, Dombibliothek, 102; see Jones, *Bedae Pseudepigrapha*, pp. 45–7.

[141] According to Beccaria, *I codici*, pp. 255–9; M. L. Cameron, 'The Sources of Medical Knowledge in Anglo-Saxon England', *ASE* 11 (1983), 135–55, at 144, notes that confusion of *n* and *r* suggests that the scribe's exemplar was in Anglo-Saxon minuscule. See also the discussion of this manuscript in Thorndike, *History of Magic* I, 723–6.

[142] Ptd T. Hunt, *Popular Medicine in Thirteenth-Century England: Introduction and Texts* (Woodbridge, 1990), p. 82.

[143] They are not catalogued in the typology of prognostics on pp. 183–90 above, but are included here for the sake of completeness.

1. 4v–6r. Dietary and health advice for each month, titled *OBSERVATIO MENSIUM SECUNDUM BEDAM*, beginning *Hoc mense bibe. iii. gulpos uini ieiunus cotidie | electuarium. accipe gingibus. 7 reupontico utem* (?). *Sanguinum ne minuere. Iani prima dies. 7 septima fine timetur. Luna .i. iiii. v. viiii. xv. egiptiaca. sunt.* Continues through twelve months. Thorndike and Kibre, *Catalogue of Incipits*, no. 632. Beccaria, *I codici*, no. 78.2.

2. 6r. A warning against the *dies caniculares*, beginning *Kal. Augusti usque .iii. non. septembris nullo modo expedit fleotomari mari propter caniculares dies. his caueas.* Also warns against letting blood or drinking medicine on the three critical Mondays.

3. 8r. Note on Egyptian days, beginning *DIES EGIPTIACI. QUI PRO TOTUM ANNUM OBSERVANDI SUNT. VT SANGUIS NON MINUETUR. NEC POTIO SUMETUR. IDEST. iiii. NON IAN. viii. KAL. FEBR.* Beccaria, *I codici*, no. 78.6. Similar to a text in two French MSS (listed in Wickersheimer 1966): Paris, Bibliothèque Nationale de France, lat. 2825 (s. x) and Reims, MS 438 (s. ix[1]); the former also includes a medical lunarium and warning against the *dies caniculares*.

4. 37r. Bloodletting lunarium, titled *QUIBUS LUNATIONIBUS BONUM EST SANGUINUM*, beginning *Luna .i. tota die bonum est. Luna .ii. similiter. Luna .iii. non est bonum.* Indications for most days are different from those commonly found in Anglo-Saxon lunaria. Beccaria, *I codici*, no. 78.14.

5. 81r–82r. Medical lunarium, beginning *Luna .i. qui decubuerit. si tertio die alleuauerit. sanus erit. Si uero quarto die grauior fuerit. cum grandi periculo euadit.* Thorndike and Kibre, *Catalogue of Incipits*, no. 838; Beccaria, *I codici*, no. 78.18 and p. 420. Ptd Weisser, *Studien*, p. 365.

6. fol. 132v–133v. Incomplete 'Sphere of Pythagoras', with space left on fol. 132v for a diagram which has not been added. The text begins imperfectly *& partiris in triginta scilicit .xxx. partes & quicquit remanserit in spera respicies & sic inuenies.* Beccaria, *I codici*, no. 78.24a.

7. A list of the best hours in each day for bloodletting, beginning *INCIPIUNT ora se quod sanguinum minuare debes. in primis die dominico hora. iī vī nona. bonum est. Die lunis hora. iiiī. primis. s. xi. bonum est.*

8. 211r–216v. General lunarium, beginning imperfectly (at day 1) *& dies utilis est omnibus rebus agendum. Puer natus erit inlustris astutus sapiens literatus. in aqua periclitabit & si euaserit posteriori etate melior erit.* Similar in some respects to **T2**. Ptd Svenberg 1936, pp. 25–83. Beccaria, *I codici*, no. 78.28.

9. 216v–217r. Verses on unlucky days, beginning *Si tenebrae egyptus grecos sermone uocantur. In die* [sic; for *inde*] *dies mortis tenebrosus iure uocamus. Bis deni binique dies scribuntur in anno. In quibus una solet mortalibus hora timeri. Mensis quoque duos captiuos posidet herum* [sic; for *horum*]. *nec simul hos uinctos homines re* [sic; for *ne*] *peste trucidant. Iani prima dies et septima sine timetur.* Printed as a Bedan text in PL 90, cols. 955–6. Thorndike and Kibre, *Catalogue of Incipits*, no. 1466; Beccaria, *I codici*, no. 78.29. The verses are those of Æ18a, though the preface is not found in that MS.

10. 217rv. Predictions for the year based on the day on which Christmas falls, beginning *Natalis domine prima dies si acciderit domenica scitote hiem en se benignum & uentososam* [sic]. *quadragessimam. estatem estatem aridam. uineas opulentas. oues. fetus. perducentes.* Similar to the English text in **H4**.

11. 217v–218r. Dreambook,[144] beginning *Aues in somnis uidere cum ipsis pugnare lites signis. Aues in somnis capere lucrum signis. Asinas qui uiderit crementis signis.* Similar to **T1** and **Æ68**. Ends imperfectly after twenty-nine items (only the letters A and B are listed); 218v is blank.

Bodley 579 (L), the 'Leofric Missal'. Ker, *Catalogue*, no. 315; Gneuss, 'Preliminary List', no. 585. NE France, s. ix²; Glastonbury, s. x²; Exeter, s. xi^med. A large service book written in France and brought to England in the tenth century.[145] Amid computistical material (38r–58r) are the following:

1. 49b–50a. A version of the 'Sphere of Pythagoras', here presented in two diagrams of *Vita* and *Mors*, each labelled, the first beginning *Collige per numerum quicquid cupis esse probandum*, the second *Spera Apulei platonice de vita de morte vel de omnibus negotus*.[146] Similar to **Th3**.
2. 56r. Lunarium, presumably for bloodletting though not so labelled, beginning *Luna prima bona est. Luna secunda bona est.*

Digby 63 (Di). Ker, *Catalogue*, no. 319, Gneuss, 'Preliminary List', no. 611. Written in the north of England (s. ix²), but at the Old Minster in Winchester by *c.* 1000 when the calendar was added (see Ker, *Catalogue*, p. 381).[147] Devoted entirely to computistical texts, including the work of Dionysius Exiguus. Jones groups the MS with examples of the 'Canterbury Computus' (including **C**) derived from early Irish computus.[148]

1. 36rv. Notes on Egyptian days, titled *INCIPIUNT. DIES. EGIPCIACHI.* and beginning *Mense jan. Intrante die primo. exxiente* [sic] *dies .vii. Mense feb. Intrante dies. vii. exsiente dies .vii.* Similar to **F5**. It is followed by a warning against the three critical Mondays, beginning *Sunt alii .iii. dies in qibus* [sic] *nullus penitus nec per nullam necessitatem non licet hominem uenire nec pocionem accipere. nec pecus sanguinem minuere.* Similar to **Æ56** and **F6**.

Hatton 115 (H). Ker, *Catalogue*, no. 332; Gneuss, 'Preliminary List', no. 639. s. xi². A collection of homilies of unknown origin; the MS was in Worcester by the thirteenth century, where it received glosses by the 'Tremulous' scribe.[149] Prognostic material is in two quires (fols. 148–55) added in twelfth century and not part of original MS. The prognostic material consists of eleven paragraphs, each introduced by a red initial letter:

1. 148r. Dream lunarium, beginning 'Ðære æresten nyhte þonne niwe mone byð ecymen. þæt mon þonne in sweofne gesihþ. þæt cymeð to gefean.' (Frank and

---

144 See Martin, *Somniale Danielis*, pp. 38–9.
145 Ed. F. E. Warren, *The Leofric Missal* (Oxford, 1883).
146 See R. Deshman, 'The Leofric Missal and Tenth-Century English Art', *ASE* 6 (1977), 145–73, at 166–8.
147 The calendar is ptd as no. 1 in Wormald, *English Kalendars*.
148 Jones, *Bedae Opera de Temporibus*, p. 112
149 A facsimile is ed. C. Franzen, *Early English Manuscripts in Microfiche Facsimile* 6 (Tempe, AZ, 1998); a description is on pp. 44–54.

Cameron, 'List of Old English Texts', B23.3.6.1). Ptd Cockayne 1864–6 III, 158–60, Förster 1925–6, pp. 90–2.

2. 148v. Birth lunarium, beginning 'Se ðe bið acenned on annihtne mona. se bið lange lifes. ond weleði. Se þe bið on .ii. nihta ealdne monan. se bid seoc' (Frank and Cameron, 'List of Old English Texts', B23.3.6.2). = **T15**, ending imperfectly in the same place (fourteen nights). Ptd Cockayne 1864–6 III, 160–2; Förster 1912c, pp. 21–4.

3. 148v22–149r. A prognostic based on the day of the week at childbirth, beginning 'Swa hwilc man swa on sunnandæg. oððe on niht acenned bið. orsorglice leofæð he. ond bið fægger' (Frank and Cameron, 'List of Old English Texts', B23.3.6.3). Ptd Cockayne 1864–6 III, 162; Förster 1912b, pp. 297–300.

4. 149r12–149v7. Weather forecast based on the day of the week on which Christmas falls, beginning 'Gif middeswintres messedeg b`i´ð on sunnandeg. þonne bið god winter. ond lengten windi. ond drige sumer. ond wingeardas gode' (Frank and Cameron, 'List of Old English Texts', B23.3.6.4). A variant of the *Revelatio Esdrae*. Ptd Cockayne 1864–6 III, 162–4.

5. 149v8–23. Predictions of misfortune based on the occurrence of wind during the twelve days after Christmas, beginning 'Her segh ymb drihtnes gebyrd. ymb þa .xii. niht hs [*sic*, for *his*] tide. Gyf se wind byoð on þa forma niht. gehadode weras sweltað' (Frank and Cameron, 'List of Old English Texts', B23.3.6.5). Ptd Cockayne 1864–6 III, 164; Förster 1912a, pp. 56–8.

6. 149v24–150r17. Predictions of good fortune based on the occurrence of sunshine during the twelve days after Christmas, beginning 'þy forma dæg drihtnes gebyrde. gyf sunne scyneð. mycel gefea byoð mid mannum. ond genihtsum' (Frank and Cameron, 'List of Old English Texts', B23.3.6.6). Similar to **W1**. Ptd Cockayne 1864–6 III, 164–6; Förster 1912a, p. 65.

(7–8. Number of masses and psalms equivalent to a fast; ptd Cockayne 1864–6 III, 166.)

9. 150v. A thunder prognostic for the days of the week, beginning 'On anwardne ger gyf hyt þunrie on sunandæg. þonne tacnað þæt micelne blodes gyte in sumere þeode' (Frank and Cameron, 'List of Old English Texts', B23.3.6.7). Similar to **T12**. Ptd Cockayne 1864–6 III, 166–8.

10. 150v10–152v3. Dreambook in Old English, beginning 'Gyf mon meteð þæt he geseo earn on his heafod unfan [*sic*] gesettan. þæt tacnað micel weorðmynd. Gyf þe þince þæt þu geseo feola earna ætsamne. þæt byð yfel nið' (Frank and Cameron, 'List of Old English Texts', B23.3.6.8). = **T9**. Ptd Cockayne 1864–6 III, 168–76; Förster 1916, pp. 270–93.

11. 152v4–153v16. General lunarium in English, beginning 'On annihte monan fær to cyninge. ond bidde þes þu wille. ge þæt gefeð gang in to him on þa þridda tid þes deges. oðð þonne þu wyte þæt sæ si ful' (Frank and Cameron, 'List of Old English Texts', B23.3.6.9). = The text found in fragmentary form in **T10**. Ends before the bottom of the page at the 17th day of the month. Ptd Cockayne 1864–6 III, 176–80; Förster 1912c, pp. 43–5.

Oxford, St John's College 17 (J). Ker, *Catalogue*, no. 360, Gneuss, 'Preliminary List', no. 683. Written at Thorney Abbey, 1110–11; containing Bede's *De temporum ratione* and other scientific and computistical texts.[150] Written by two scribes throughout, apparently in collaboration. Among the 'miscellaneous texts and tables' noted by Baker and Lapidge, *Byrhtferth's Enchiridion*, on 1v–12r are the following:

1. 3v. Latin warning against the three critical days, beginning *Hi tres dies sunt obseruandi*. Similar to Æ**56** but not identical.

2. 3v. Latin note on the three marvellous days, beginning *Tres dies sunt in quo anno cum tribus noctibus ut fertur in quibus mulierum nonquam nascitur*. = Æ**57**.

3. 4r. Bloodletting lunarium, beginning *Luna .i. Tota die bona est. Luna .ii. Non est bona. 'Bona est'*. = Æ**61**. Annotations to the list offer differing opinions on the status of each day; these often seem to follow the recommendations in the general lunarium found in **T2**.

4. 4r. Birth prognostic based on the day of the week on which a child is born, beginning *Die domenico hora diuterna* [sic] *siue nocturna qui nascentur utillimi erit & magni*. A slightly abbreviated version of Æ**62**.

5. 4r. Birth lunarium, beginning *Luna .i. Qui natus fuerit uitalis erit. Luna .ii. Mediocris erit*. = Æ**63**, but with slight differences in wording and avoiding the errors of that copy.

6. 4r. Medical lunarium, beginning *Luna .i. Qui ceciderit difficule euadet. Luna .ii. Cito consurget*. Closely similar to Æ**64** but not identical.

7. 4r. Dream lunarium, beginning *Luna .i. quicquid uideris ad gaudium pertinet. Luna .ii. Affectus erit*. Similar to Æ**65** but not identical.

8. 8v. 'Sphere of Petosiris', similar in most respects to the 'Sphere of Apuleius' or 'Pythagoras' found in other MSS. Not accompanied by instructions (for which see PL 90, cols. 963–6) or by a list of the numerical value of letters, rendering it of doubtful utility.[151]

9. 16r–21v. Distributed throughout the calendar (*Byrhtferth's Enchiridion*, ed. Baker and Lapidge, pp. 390–416) is a list of the two critical days in each month for bloodletting, in hexameters, beginning *Iani Prima dies et septima fine timetur*. = Æ**18**.

10. 40v. At the end of a section of cosmographical *rotae* and diagrams, three brief texts on Egyptian days are added to the margin of a diagram describing the Twelve Winds. (a) A list of one unlucky day in each month, beginning *Isti dies obseruandi sunt in singulis mensibus in quibus diebus maledicus est populus egyptiorum*.[152] = **Th1**. (b) List of twenty-four unlucky days in the lunar month, beginning *Sunt in unoquoque mense duo dies*. (c) List of twenty-four Egyptian days in the year, beginning *De diebus egyptiacis qui maledicti sunt in anno*. The days named are those in the verses in Æ**18**.

11. 41r. Following the cosmographical rotae and notes on unlucky days are two versions of the 'Sphere of Pythagoras', with diagram, beginning *Ratio spere phytagori*

---

[150] Described in Wallis, 'MS Oxford St John's College 17', P. S. Baker, 'Byrhtferth's *Enchiridion* and the Computus in Oxford, St John's College 17', *ASE* 10 (1981), 123–42, and *Byrhtferth's Enchiridion,* ed. Baker and Lapidge, pp. liii–lv.

[151] See further Wallis, 'MS Oxford St John's College 17', pp. 248–50.   [152] *Ibid.* pp. 456–7.

phylosophi quem apuleius descripsit (= **Th2**) and accompanied by a (now excised) diamond diagram with a caption, beginning *De quacumque re scire uoluerit uel consulere* (= **Th4**).

12. 157v–158v. Following several short works on the zodiac is a form of divination by lots, probably dice, known elsewhere as the *sortes sanctorum,* beginning *c.c.c. Animum tuum si dubitantem sentis crede primo modum deo adiuuante inpetrabis quam uis,* continuing through all permutations of three lots with six numbers on each, and ending with a brief office and prayer (*Libera nos domine de potestate tenebrarum. & de manu mortis eternae eripe nos. ut uoluntas tua sit in omnibus aperta absque ambiguitate per hoc signum fortis te nobis poscentibus*).

13. 159r. Following a text on the fifteen signs of the Last Judgement is a version of the *Revelatio Esdrae,* begins *Si prima feria kal. Ian. fuerit. frugifer annus erit. extremi hominum morientur. frumentum et uinum abundabit. Apes perficient. oues morientur. naues periclitabuntur. gentes mouebuntur. fremitur belloris erit. pugna nulla. pax breuis. in mense septembri grauis mortalitas et silue perficient.*

Junius's knowledge of the Old English poem *Durham*

DANIEL PAUL O'DONNELL

Until recently, the late Old English poem *Durham* was known to have been copied in two manuscripts of the twelfth century: Cambridge, University Library, Ff. 1. 27 (C) and London, British Library, Cotton Vitellius D. xx (V). C has been transcribed frequently and serves as the basis for Elliott Van Kirk Dobbie's standard edition of the poem in the Anglo-Saxon Poetic Records.[1] V was almost completely destroyed in the Cottonian fire of 1731. Its version is known to us solely from George Hickes's 1705 edition (H).[2]

In a recent article, however, Donald K. Fry announced the discovery of a third medieval text of the poem.[3] Like V, the original manuscript of this 'third' version is now lost and can be reconstructed only from an early modern transcription – in this case a copy by Francis Junius now in the Stanford University Library (Stanford University Libraries, Department of Special Collections, Misc. 010 [J1]). Unlike V, however, Junius's copy is our only record of this manuscript's existence. No other transcripts are known from medieval or early modern manuscript catalogues.

If Fry is correct, this copy of the 'third' *Durham* manuscript is of the greatest importance for our understanding of the poem. It offers unique alternatives for a few passages in which C and V agree in problematic forms and, by aligning itself with one or the other version on those occasions when they do not, can presumably help the editor choose between competing readings.[4] For example,

---

[1] *The Anglo-Saxon Minor Poems*, ASPR 6 (New York, 1942), 27. C is described in N. R. Ker, *A Catalogue of Manuscripts Containing Anglo-Saxon* (Oxford, 1957), p. 12 (no. 14). A facsimile of *Durham* in C can be found in *Old English Verse Texts from Many Sources: a Comprehensive Collection*, ed. F. C. Robinson and E. G. Stanley, EEMF 23 (Copenhagen, 1991), pl. 34.1.

[2] *Linguarum veterum septentrionalium thesaurus grammatico-criticus et archæologicus*, 2 vols. (Oxford, 1705) I, 178–9. Pre-fire descriptions of V can be found in T. Smith, *Catalogus librorum manuscriptorum bibliothecæ Cottonianæ* (Oxford, 1696; repr. Cambridge, 1984) and H. Wanley, *Linguarum veterum septentrionalium thesaurus* II, 240. See also Ker, *Catalogue*, p. 298 (no. 223). A facsimile of Hickes's text of *Durham* can be found in *Old English Verse Texts*, ed. Robinson and Stanley, pls. 34.2.1–2.

[3] 'A Newly Discovered Version of the Old English Poem *Durham*', *Old English and New: Studies in Language and Linguistics in Honor of Frederic G. Cassidy*, ed. J. H. Hall, N. Doane and D. Ringler (New York, 1992), pp. 83–96.

[4] A full discussion of the variation between C and Hickes's transcription of V can be found in D. P. O'Donnell, 'Manuscript Variation in Multiple-Recension Old English Poetic Texts: the Technical Problem and Poetical Art' (unpubl. PhD dissertation, Yale Univ., 1996), pp. 76–83 and n. 136. See also A. A. Jabbour, 'The Memorial Transmission of Old English Poetry: a Study of the Extant Parallel Texts' (unpubl. PhD dissertation, Duke Univ., 1968), p. 65.

231

J1 confirms C in reading *feala fisca* (C *f,'ola fisca*) for H *fisca feola* in line 5a and *ðær gepæxen is* (C *ðær gepexen is*) for H *ðere gepexen* in line 6a.[5] It also offers a unique version of the poem's problematic closing lines, following C in reading *ðe* (against H *ðær*) in line 20a while introducing a number of highly significant changes in vocabulary, metre and syntax:[6]

H

      Eardiað æt ðem eadige   In in ðem mynstre
      Unarimeda reliquia,
[20][7] Ðær monige þundrum geþurðað,   Ðe þrita seggeð,
      Mid ðene drihtnes þer   domes[8] bideð.[9]

C

      Eardiæð æt ðem eadige   in iuðem minstre,
      unarrneda reliquia,
20   ðe monia þundrum[10] geþurðað,   ðes ðe prit seggeð,
      midd ðene drihnes þer   domes[11] bideð.[12]

J1

      Eardreð 7 ðem eadige   imuðem *forte* ymb þem mynstre,
      unarimeda reliquia
20   ðe monia þundra geþyrcað,   ðes ðe prit secgeð,
      mid ðene   drihtnes andþeardnes bydeð.[13]

[5] All citations from the texts of *Durham* have been transcribed from facsimiles, except in the case of JC, T, S (see appendix) and D (see below, n. 17), where I have been able to consult the relevant manuscript or book directly. Because the misapprehension of individual letters plays an important role in determining the relationship of these transcriptions, the Insular characters þ (for *w*) and 7 (for *ond*) are retained in my citations. Spacing and word-division are irregular in these witnesses, epecially T and J2. To facilitate comparison they have been silently regularized. Spelling, capitalization and punctuation are transcribed diplomatically.

[6] On the difficulty of the lines, see Dobbie, *The Anglo-Saxon Minor Poems*, pp. 152–3. The translations that follow are based on those suggested by Dobbie on p. 153.

[7] Hickes prints and numbers his text per metrical half-line. These do not always correspond to modern editorial line-division, however, and I have followed the modern practice and numbering throughout.   [8] *per* and *domes* are run together in H.

[9] 'Uncounted relics dwell with the blessed one inside the minster, where the multitudes celebrate with miracles, as writings say, [and] await judgement with the man of the Lord.'

[10] C makes no distinction between *wynn* (þ) and *p*: the same character is used in *pycum* (i.e. *wycum*) and *deope dalum* (lines 7a and 8a).   [11] *Per* and *domes* are run together in C.

[12] 'Uncounted relics, which the multitudes celebrate with miracles, dwell, as writ says, with the blessed one inside the minster, [and] await judgement with the man of the Lord.'

[13] '† . . . *Eardreð* and with the blessed one *imuðem unless* around that minster†, uncounted relics which produce many miracles, as writ says, with the one [who] awaits the presence of the Lord.' Cf. Junius's Latin translation: '. . . circa monasterium innumerabiles reliquiæ, quæ multa miracula operantur, prout scripta testantur, in iis qui Domini præsentiam expectant vel implorant' ('. . . around that monastery innumerable relics which work many miracles, as writings testify, in those who await or entreat the presence of the Lord').

But Fry is not correct. Far from being the sole surviving transcription of a now-lost third medieval copy of *Durham*, J1 can instead be shown to derive from C through a series of flawed seventeenth-century transcriptions, beginning with the poem's first printed edition in Roger Twysden's *Historiæ Anglicanæ Scriptores X* (T).[14] As we shall see, J1 shares a number of elementary copying mistakes with these roughly contemporary transcriptions and, just as significantly, differs from them precisely in those places in which they (and in some cases C itself) are the most difficult to understand. It is, in effect, an edition of these 'editions' – one whose editor has devoted considerable ingenuity to the correction of his sources' obvious errors, but one which was almost certainly made without recourse to any medieval manuscript. Its readings are therefore of more relevance to the historian of Anglo-Saxon studies than to the editor of the Old English poem.

JUNIUS'S TRANSCRIPTIONS OF 'DURHAM'

Junius is known to have made three copies of *Durham*: J1, J2 (bound with J1 in Stanford Misc. 010) and JC (bound with 'various fragments, some of them Saxon' in London, British Library, Harley 7567).[15]

As Fry notes, J2 and JC can be linked firmly to C. For J2, the connection is via T, which Junius appears to have copied directly. The two transcriptions share a number of common errors and differ only in their orthographic details. Like T, J2 has the nonsense or unusual forms *seond* for C *geond*, line 1a; *nugerum* for C *ungerim*, line 8b; *7 ðele geferes* for C *æðele geferes*, line 13b; *ðere nine* for C *ðer inne*, line 14a; *lustun* for C *lustum*, line 17a; *Eardreð* (T *Eardreþ*) for C *Eardiæð*, line 18a; *7 ðem* for C *æt ðem*, line 18a; *imuþem* for C *in iuðem* (expected *in on ðem*[16]), line 18b; *minystre* for C *minstre*, line 18b; *perddmes* for C *perdomes* (i.e. *per domes*), line 21a–b. Of the ten readings in which J2 differs from T, eight involve variation in the use of *ð* and *þ*. Junius – like the scribe of C – prefers to use *þ* initially and *ð* medially and finally; Twysden is less consistent and often strays from his exemplar. The remaining two differences involve other minor variation in spelling: J2 *cyn* for T *Kin*, line 5a; and J2 *Cupberht* for T *Cupbert*, line 16a.

For its part, JC appears to have been copied directly from C. Leaving aside differences in spacing, word-division and layout, its main text differs from that of the twelfth-century manuscript in only twelve readings, most of which again

---

[14] *Historiæ Anglicanæ scriptores X* (London, 1652), col. 76. A corrected version of this text by W. Somner (S) is printed on an unnumbered page [Dd8v] in the same volume. It does not appear to have been consulted by Junius. I discuss Somner's corrections in an appendix, below.

[15] *A Catalogue of the Harleian Manuscripts in the British Museum with Index of Persons, Places and Matters*, 4 vols. (London, 1808) III, 536. Fry notes that the catalogue incorrectly attributes this transcription to Hickes.

[16] Cf. Hickes's transcription of the equivalent in V: *In inðem* (word-spacing not normalized) and Dobbie's note to line 18b (*The Anglo-Saxon Minor Poems*, p. 152)

involve minor differences in orthography or the correction of obvious minor errors: JC *feola fisca* for C *f,ᶜola fisca*, line 5a; JC *puniað* for C *puniad*, line 7a; JC *cyninges* for C *cynuiges*, line 11b; JC *breome* for C *breoma*, line 15a; JC *genam* for C *genom*, line 17b. In two cases, Junius makes a more substantial emendation in his main text, substituting *his pislara* for C *pislara* (i.e. *pislara*) in line 17b and *in ðem* for C *in iuðem* (expected *in on ðem*), line 18b. In line 3b, he ignores a correction now in C, reading *ymbeornan* for C *ymbeornad* (where *d* has been adapted from an underlying *n*), expected *ymbeornað*. A final four variants involve Junius's misinterpretation of individual letters in his exemplar: etymological *p* as the runic character *wynn* (*þ*) in JC *in deope dalum* for C *in deope dalum*, line 8a; Insular *s* (*ſ*) as Insular *r* (*ɼ*) in JC *arferta* for C *arfesta*, line 10a; and the minim errors: *iun* for *um* in JC *pundriun gepurðað* for C *pundrum gepurðað*, line 20a; and *ri* for *n* in JC *gemorige* for C *gemonge*, line 5b.[17]

Junius also includes six suggestions for alternative readings and corrections in notes and his Latin translation. Unlike the changes introduced into the basic transcription, all but one of these suggestions have a significant effect on sense, syntax, or metre and – as Junius explicitly cites the C form in each case before offering his alternative – are clearly intended to be understood as emendations to the received poem. Of these, four involve suggestions for the correction of obvious errors in C or of words which Junius has incorrectly copied into his transcription's main text: JC '*in deope dalum* (forte legendum *in deore dalum*)'[18] for C *in deope dalum*, line 8a; JC '*7 ðelpold* (lege *eðelpold*)'[19] for C *7 ðelpold*, line 14b; JC '*unarrneda* (forte legendum *unapemeda*)'[20] for C *unarrneda*, line 19; and JC '*drihnes* (forte *drihtnes*)'[21] for C *drihnes*, line 21a. Another two offer emendations for readings from C which are also supported by Hickes's transcription of V: JC '*on gecheðe* (lege *on geþeahte*)'[22] for C *on gecheðe* (H *On gicheðe*), line 16b; and, in a reading also included in J1, JC '*pundriun gepurðað* (lege *purcað* vel *pyrcað*)'[23] for C *pundrum gepurðað* (H *pundrum gepurðað*), line 20a.

THE 'THIRD' TRANSCRIPTION (J1)

Of Junius's three transcriptions, J1 exhibits what appears at first glance to be the most independent text of the poem. Ignoring once again differences in punctu-

---

[17] Fry incorrectly reads *gemonige* in his transcription of JC ('A Newly Discovered Version', p. 87); the medial consonant is clearly *r* in the manuscript. S. D'Ewes makes the same mistake as JC in his copy of C in British Library, Harley 533 (D), where the word is transcribed *gemœige* (129v). As this reading suggests, the mistake appears to have arisen through a misinterpretation of *on* in C as an *o* + *r* ligature followed by *i*. JC and D share a few other minor errors and unusual forms, but none which cannot be attributed to the coincidental misinterpretation of forms in their common exemplar. Both transcriptions also exhibit unique errors not found in the other copy; there is no evidence to suggest that JC was copied from D or vice versa. See also fig. 5.

[18] '*in deope dalum* (unless to be read *in deore dalum*)'.   [19] '*7 ðelpold* (read *eðelpold*)'.

[20] '*unarrneda* (unless to be read *unapemeda*)'.   [21] '*drihnes* (unless *drihtnes*)'.

[22] '*on gecheðe* (read *on geþeahte*)'.   [23] '*pundriun gepurðað* (read *purcað* or *pyrcað*)'.

ation, word-division, capitalization and *mise en page*, this transcription exhibits thirty-eight variant forms found in neither C nor its early modern descendants T, J2 and JC (fig. 3).

But the sheer amount of this variation is misleading. For despite its many unique forms, J1 nevertheless shows a strong affinity with the other members of the C–T–J2 'tradition' and with J2, its probable exemplar, in particular. It shares a number of common errors and unusual forms with these earlier transcriptions and differs from them primarily through the same type of correction and normalization we have already seen to be Junius's practice in copying J2 and JC. While J1 does occasionally reject a reading in which J2, T and C agree, these readings are themselves invariably problematic and have been frequently queried or emended by modern scholars of the poem. Given the generally poor quality of the seventeenth-century copies from which he worked, it seems likely that Junius would have thought these accurately transmitted forms to be modern corruptions.

Although it eliminates most of their more egregious errors, J1 nevertheless shares seven unusual forms with J2, T and, in two cases, C (as we shall see, several of these common forms are accompanied by suggestions for emendation or correction in J1). All seven involve the misinterpretation of relatively common Insular characters or ligatures: 7 (the Insular character for *ond*) for expected *æ* (apparently misunderstood as &, i.e. the ligature for Latin *et*) in J1 J2 T *7 ðele geferes* for C *æðele geferes*, line 13b; J1 J2 T *7 þelpold* (C *7 ðelpold*) for expected *Æðelpold*, line 14b; J1 J2 T *7 ðem* for C *æt ðem*, line 18a; Insular *re* (*ɲe*) for *iæ* (*ıæ*) in J1 J2 *Eardreð* (T *Eardreþ*) for C *Eardiæð*, line 18a; *wynn* (*þ*) for expected *h* in J1 J2 T *he þislara* (C *he þislara*) for *he his lara* (as in H), line 17b;[24] and two minim errors: J1 J2 T *ðere nine* for C *ðer inne*, line 14a; and J1 *imuðem* (J2 T *imuþem* C *in iuðem*) for expected *inon ðem*, line 18b.

In his article, Fry takes these forms to be evidence that the connection between J1 and J2 was psychological rather than textual – that is to say, to be evidence that Junius used J2 as a guide in copying J1 from the supposedly now-lost 'third' medieval *Durham* manuscript and was led into incorporating a number of its mistakes in his transcription as a result:

I suspect Junius had J2 in front of him as he wrote J1. Anyone who has transcribed a manuscript knows how such a 'pony' sets up expectations of what we see on the manuscript page, and we tend to stay (and therefore stray) with our original impression . . . I think Junius saw what his fair copy of Twysden predicted . . .[25]

---

24 While the reading in J1, J2, T and C makes sense, it is to be rejected on metrical grounds: *þis-* adds a non-alliterating lift to the beginning of an off-verse that should alliterate on /l/. The H version alliterates properly but has other metrical problems. For a further discussion of this variant, see O'Donnell, 'Manuscript Variation', p. 81.

25 Fry, 'A Newly Discovered Version', p. 94.

But the connection between J1 and J2 can also be seen when the two transcriptions differ. For not only does J1 have a few unusual forms in common with J2 and T, it also exhibits a number of readings which are best understood as responses to some of the more obvious errors in Junius's earlier copy of T. As we have seen to be his practice in copying J2 from T and JC from C, in copying J1 Junius silently normalizes a number of J2's remaining non-standard spellings and minor errors, substituting West-Saxon *æ* for non-West-Saxon *e* (J1 *clæne* J2 T C *clene*, line 16a), West-Saxon *-h* for non-West-Saxon *-ch* (J1 *burh* J2 T C *burch*, line 1a) and unstressed *-o-* for late *-e-* (J1 *breotonrice* J2 T C *breotenrice*, line 1b) to give only a few examples. As in JC, Junius also suggests a number of emendations to his received text. On two occasions, he 'corrects' the J2 form silently, substituting *secgeð* for J2 *setgeð* (C *seggeð*) in line 20b and *andpeardnes* for the nonsense form J2 *perddmes* (C *perdomes* [i.e. *per domes*]) in line 21a–b. In most cases, however, the link to his exemplar is made through the explicit citation of a form similar or identical to that in J2: J1 *'in deore dalum* vel *in deore pealdum'*[26] (J2 *in deope dalum* C *in deope dalum*), line 8a; J1 *'7 ðele geferes* forte *7 ðere geferas'*[27] (J2 *7 ðele geferes* for C *æðele geferes*), line 13b; J1 *'7 þelpold* forte *æðelpold'*[28] (J2 *7 þelpold* C *7 ðelpold*), line 14b; and J1 *'imuðem* forte *ymb þem'*[29] (J2 *imuþem* C *in iuðem*), line 18b.

A final group of innovations in J1 involves forms which are neither related to mistakes in J2 nor obvious attempts at the normalization or correction of its non-standard spellings. Instead, these replace readings in which J2 (and T) accurately transmit a more-or-less sensible and metrical form from C. In three of these examples, Junius makes the substitution without citing the form from J2, T and C: J1 *stopa* for J2 T C *steppa*, line 2a; J1 *on gechete* for J2 T *on gecheþe* (C *on gecheðe*), for expected *on geogoþe* (?), line 16b;[30] and, in a reading Fry considers preferable to those in C and H, J1 *pundra gepyrcað* for J2 *pundrum gepurðað* (C *pundrum gepurðað* T *pundrum gepurþaþ*), line 20a. In the other three cases, however, Junius follows his usual practice of citing the word he wishes to emend before suggesting his improvement: J1 *'fæstern* vel *pestern'*[31] for J2 T C *fæstern* in line 6b; J1 *'engle leo* nisi forte malis *engle leof'*[32] for J2 T C *engle leo* in line 12a; and J1 *'lustum* forte ponitur pro *lustlice'*[33] for the nonsense form *lustun* in J2 and T (cf. C *lustum*) in line 17a.

The fact that J1 explicitly cites a reading from the J2–T–C tradition in half these examples is of course strong evidence of its connection to the earlier copies. But even if we were to ignore these citations, we would not need to assume the existence of a third medieval text in order to explain the differences between

---

[26] *'in deore dalum* or *in deore pealdum'*.   [27] *'7 ðele geferes* unless *7 ðere geferas'*.

[28] *'7 þelpold* unless *æðelpold'*.   [29] *'imuðem* unless *ymb þem'*.

[30] This is the most commonly suggested emendation. It ruins alliteration, however.

[31] *'fæstern* or *pestern'*.   [32] *'engle leo* unless you prefer *engle leof'*.

[33] *'lustum* unless set down for *lustlice'*.

J1 and its likely ancestors. For while J2 and T accurately transmit the C readings in all six cases, Junius himself would have had no way of knowing this if, as seems likely, he did not yet have access to the original manuscript. Although attested by C and in some cases H as well, all six forms are notoriously difficult and have been frequently emended in modern treatments of the poem.[34] Without being able to consult the manuscript upon which his exemplars were based, Junius would have attributed them quite naturally to the same kind of incompetence which led Twysden to produce such obvious nonsense as *seond* for C *geond* and *nugerum* for C *ungerim*. Had C been lost and J1 better known, I suspect that more than one modern scholar would have been tempted to join Junius in his emendations.

THE CHRONOLOGY AND RELIABILITY OF JUNIUS'S 'DURHAM' TRANSCRIPTIONS

Despite its many unique readings, Junius's transcription of Fry's 'third' *Durham* manuscript is almost certainly a corrected copy of J2, Junius's fair copy of T, Twysden's 1652 *editio princeps* of C. The two transcriptions share a number of common errors and unusual forms and differ for the most part only in relatively minor details of orthography. Even the most innovative features in J1, more-over, can be explained as responses to difficulties in its ancestor: they either 'correct' problematic readings carried over from C in T and J2, or they attempt to fix the many nonsensical and non-standard forms introduced in Twysden's text. Apparently without access to C or V at the time he made his first two copies, Junius was probably unable to tell the difference.

Having established that J1 is most likely a copy of the same medieval version as J2 and JC, it is now possible to reconstruct a rough chronology for Junius's work with the poem (fig. 5). Of Junius's three copies, J2 is the result of what appears to have been his first contact with *Durham*, via Twysden's *Historiæ Anglicanæ Scriptores X*. Having decided for some reason to copy this edition, Junius first produced a relatively conservative transcription, regularizing – perhaps unconsciously – some details of Twysden's eccentric orthography, but otherwise retaining even the most obvious of his mistakes. Using this fair copy, J2, as his exemplar, Junius then appears to have set about trying to correct Twysden's errors in a new transcription, J1. In addition to continuing his silent correction and normalization of unusual spellings in the text, Junius also uses this copy to suggest a number of explicit emendations. In the process, he 'improves' a number of forms in which T and J2 accurately report the readings of their medieval ancestor C.

---

[34] A good line-by-line account of the poem's editorial history can be found in Dobbie, *The Anglo-Saxon Minor Poems*, pp. xliii–xlv and 151–3. To this should be added F. C. Robinson, 'The Royal Epithet *Engle leo* in the Old English *Durham* Poem', *MÆ* 37 (1968), 249–52.

Only after completing J1 does Junius appear to have consulted C. The result was JC, his third transcription of the poem and the first to be based directly on a medieval manuscript. As was his practice in copying J2, Junius seems to have aimed in the first instance at producing a substantively accurate transcription of his exemplar: apart from a few apparently inevitable examples of orthographic normalization, Junius introduces few significant variants into the base text. As in J1, however, Junius also makes a number of explicit suggestions for emendation in his notes and translation, including one – '*pundriun gepurðað* (lege *purcað* vel *pyrcað*)',[35] line 20a – adopted from J1.

The fact that J1, J2 and JC all appear to have been derived from known medieval and modern exemplars also allows us to draw some preliminary conclusions about Junius's habits and reliability as a copyist. On the one hand, it seems clear that Junius was able to copy to a relatively high degree of substantive accuracy when the purpose of his transcription or the authority of his exemplar warranted. Thus the most substantively accurate of Junius's three *Durham* transcriptions are his 'fair' copies J2 and JC. Of the eight substantive emendations from the text of C suggested in JC, all but two are accompanied by an explicit citation of the original form (or a very close variant); for its part, J2 contains no substantive variation whatsoever from the text of T. In contrast, J1, Junius's revision of J2, is far more speculative: it contains twelve substantive readings not found in the earlier transcription and associates these forms with an explicit citation from the earlier transcription little more than half the time.

On the other hand, Junius appears to have been far less interested in preserving the accidental details of his exemplars – although this too varies with their authority. In all three copies of the poem, Junius regularly corrects and normalizes minor errors and unusual or non-West-Saxon spellings – although he does so more thoroughly when he is copying from a modern edition or transcription (as in J2 and especially J1) than from a medieval manuscript (as in JC). In JC, these accidental variants include the correction C *cynuiges* to JC *cyninges*, line 11b, and sporadic normalizations such as JC *genam* for C *genom*, line 17b. In J2 and J1, similar changes are also accompanied by a programmatic adjustment in the use of *þ* and *ð*.

As these differences among the *Durham* transcriptions suggest, Junius appears to have transcribed his Old English to different standards of accuracy depending on his rationale for making the transcription in the first place. Other texts might therefore be expected to show even greater differences in their relative accuracy.

In fact this appears to be the case. Although no comprehensive study of Junius's reliability appears ever to have been attempted,[36] several scholars have

---

[35] '*pundriun gepurðað* (read *purcað* or *pyrcað*)'.

[36] For a recent discussion of this question, see K. Dekker, 'Francis Junius (1591–1677): Copyist

examined his performance in copying the *Regulae S. Fulgentii* and variant readings from London, British Library, Cotton Otho B. ii and London, British Library, Hatton 20 (copied in the margins of his transcription of the *Pastoral Care* from London, British Library, Cotton Tiberius B. xi).[37] In each case, Junius appears to have been far less conscientious in copying these texts than he shows himself to be in his *Durham* transcriptions – especially, as Logeman notes, with regard to the silent emendation of his exemplars' wording.

Junius appears to enjoy the reputation of being a faithful copyist, but when collating his copy of the so-called 'Regulae S. Fulgentii' with the MS, I observed that this reputation was entirely unfounded. He adds words not found in his MSS. He leaves out words found in his original, or transposes them. He does not distinguish between ð and þ which he consequently uses indiscriminately. He entirely disregards the punctuation of the MS and he adds numbers of chapters after his own pleasure or notions of how they ought to have been. Lastly he corrects his text without giving the reading of the MS.[38]

That the conscientiousness seen in the *Durham* transcriptions is not unusual, however, is confirmed by my own test collation from Junius's edition of *Daniel* 279–364.[39] As in J2 and J1, Junius's transcription of the control passage from *Daniel* exhibits numerous examples of the normalization of unusual spellings (in this case, almost exclusively involving the use of þ and ð; see fig. 4). In contrast to his *Durham* transcriptions, however, Junius does not mark any emendations in this text with an explicit citation of the manuscript form.[40]

---

or Editor?', *ASE* 29 (2000), 279–96. I was unable to consult Dekker's work, which was published while this article was at press.

[37] The *Regulae S. Fulgentii* is discussed by H. Logeman, *The Rule of St. Benet*, EETS os 90 (London, 1888), pp. xxxi–xxxii. The *Pastoral Care* transcriptions have been studied by H. Sweet: see *King Alfred's West-Saxon Version of Gregory's Pastoral Care*, ed. H. Sweet, 2 vols., EETS os 45 and 50 (Oxford, 1871–2) II, p. xix; K. Jost, 'Zu den Handschriften der *Cura Pastoralis*', *Anglia* 37 (1913), 63–8; *The Pastoral Care: Edited from British Museum Cotton Otho B.ii*, ed. I. Carlson, completed by L.-G. Hollander, M. Lövenberg and A. Rynell, 2 vols., Acta Universitatis Stockholmiensis: Stockholm Studies in English 34 and 48 (Stockholm, 1975–8) I, 158–60; and D. M. Horgan, 'The Old English *Pastoral Care*: the Scribal Contribution', *Studies in Earlier English Prose*, ed. P. E. Szarmach (Albany, NY, 1986), pp. 109–28.

[38] Logeman, *The Rule of St. Benet*, pp. xxxi–xxxii; similar catalogues from the *Pastoral Care* are found in Jost, 'Handschriften der *Cura Pastoralis*' and Carlson, *Pastoral Care*.

[39] F. Junius, *Caedmonis monachi paraphrasis poetica Genesios ac praecipuarum sacrae paginae historiarum, abhinc annos M.LXX Anglo-Saxonice conscripta, & nunc primum edita a Francisco Junio* (Amsterdam, 1655), pp. 81–3. In making this collation I compared Junius's edition against the facsimile in *The Cædmon Manuscript of Anglo-Saxon Biblical Poetry: Junius XI in the Bodleian Library*, ed. Sir Israel Gollancz (Oxford, 1927).

[40] Although Junius makes no substitutions in the control passage from *Daniel* he makes several in the more difficult opening lines of *Christ and Satan*. None of these are accompanied by an explicit citation of the manuscript reading.

CONCLUSION

Although, as a corrected copy of a flawed seventeenth-century edition, Junius's J1 is of no value in establishing the text of the Old English poem *Durham*, this ought not to take away from its achievement. Working with a badly flawed text and relying apparently on little more than his own sense of Old English orthography and verse, Junius nevertheless managed to construct a version of the poem which easily passes for a legitimate medieval text. That he could fool a modern scholar of Donald Fry's experience and ability is very high praise indeed.

APPENDIX

CORRECTIONS TO TWYSDEN'S EDITION BY WILLIAM SOMNER

Junius was not the first person to recognize the problems in Twysden's edition of C; a corrected version of the poem by William Somner (S) appears with a Latin translation on an unnumbered page [Dd8v] among the addenda and errata to Twysden's volume.[41]

Like Junius's J1, Somner's text appears to have been 'corrected' on internal grounds alone, without reference to C. While it removes many of T's most egregious errors, it retains some, incorrectly emends others and introduces a few new mistakes itself. Like J1, S emends the obvious errors *seond*, *nugerum*, *lustun* and *setgeþ* (lines 1b, 8b, 17a and 20b). It normalizes or corrects *gepæxen* to *gepæxen* (line 3a), *ymbeornad* to *ymbeornað* (line 3b), *pinnad* to *punað* (C *puniad*, line 7a) and *Cutberch*, *Eadberch*, *7 þelpold* and *drihnes* to *Cutberht*, *Eadberht*, *Æþelpald* and *drihtnes* (lines 10b, 13a, 14b and 21a). Emendations and normalizations not supported by C are: S *cynne* for T *Kin* (C *kyn*), line 5a; S *fæstenne* for T (and C) *fæstern*, line 6b; S *on geogoþe* for T *on gecheþe* (C *on gecheðe*), line 16b; S *inne þem* for T *imuþem* (C *in iuðem*), line 18a; and S *unarymeda* for T *unarimeda* (C *unarmeda*), line 19. Among the new forms introduced in S are: S *7 eðele geferas* for T *7 ðele geferes* C *æðele geferes* (line 13b), S *ðere inne* for T *ðere nine* C *ðer inne* (line 14a) and S *ðone* for T *mid ðene* (C *midd ðene*), line 21a. S follows T in reading *Eardreþ* incorrectly for C *Eardiæð* (line 18a) and 'improves' on a number of T's errors without correcting the underlying problem: S *7 mid ðem* for T *7 ðem* (C *æt ðem*) and S *mynistre* for T *minystre* (C *minstre*) in lines 18a and b. Unique errors in S include *þe pislara* for T *he pislara* (C *he pislara*) in line 17b; and S *þer domes* for T *perddmes* (C *perdomes*, i.e. *per domes*) in line 21a-b.

Although it is clear that Junius knew of T, he does not seem to have used S in any of his transcriptions. While J1 shares a number of emendations and normalizations with

---

[41] The corrected text is announced as: *Scriptura Saxonica de Dunelmensis urbis situ &c ad fidem codicis Ms. Simeonis, loci monachi, col. 76, exhibita, hic denuo recognita, gravioribus a mendis repurgata, & (ad verbum) Latine reddita* ('The Saxon composition "*de Dunelmensis urbis situ &c*" presented faithfully from the Codex of Simeon, monk of that place, col. 76, reconsidered here, purged of its most serious faults and – literally – translated into Latin').

Somner's text, it shows none of its unique errors and, more significantly, fails to follow it in some of its more sensible improvements. Most of the six emendations and normalizations shared by J1 and S involve the correction of relatively straightforward graphic errors or unusual spellings: S J1 *ymbeornað* for T C *ymbeornad,* line 3b; S J1 *gepæxen* for T *gepexen* (C *gepexen*), line 6a; S J1 *punað* for T *pinnad* (C *puniad*), line 7a; S *ungerim* (J1 *ungerim*) for T *nugerum* (C *ungerim*), line 8b; S J1 *Eadberht* for T C *eadberch,* line 13a; and S J1 *drihtnes* for T *drihnes* (C *drihnes*), line 21a. Of the places in which S and J1 disagree in their emendation of T, however, S frequently has a reading which is at least as good as that suggested by Junius: S *steopa* (cf. H *Steopa*), J1 *stopa* for T C *steppa,* line 2a; S *on geogope* J1 *on gechete* for T *on gechepe* (C *on gecheðe*; H *On gicheðe*[42]), line 16b; S *inne þem* J1 *'imuðem* forte *ymb þem'* for T *imuþem* (C *in iuðem* H *In inðem*), line 18a. Had Junius known the S forms in these cases, it seems reasonable to assume that he would have preferred them to the readings he cites from T – if not to his own suggestions.[43]

---

[42] The reading in H may have been influenced by S. In a footnote, Hickes refers the reader to Somner's text.

[43] I thank Kees Dekker and Sophie van Romburgh for their help in examining Junius's hand and their comments on an earlier version of this paper.

Fig. 3 Innovative readings in J1 (innovative forms marked in bold)

Line	C	T	J2	J1	H
1a	burch	burch	burch	**burh** vel **byrig**	burch
	breome	Breome	Breome	breome vel **breme**	breome
	breotenrice	breotenrice	breotenrice	**breotenrice**	breotenrice
2a	steppa	steppa	steppa	**stopa**	steppa
3b	ymbeornad	ymbeornad	ymbeornad[44]	**ymbeornað**	ymbeornað
4b	ðer inne	ðer inne	ðer inne	**ðer inne**	ðer inne
5a	f,°ola fisca	feola fisca	feola fisca	**feala** fisca	Fisca feola
	kyn	Kin	cyn	**cynn**	kinn
6a	gepexen is	gepexen is	gepexen is	**gepexen** is	gepexen
6b	fæstern	fæstern	fæstern	fæstern vel **pestern**	festern
7a	puniad	pinnad	pinnad	**puniað**	Puniað
	ðem	ðem	ðem	**ðæm**	þem
8a	in deope dalum	in deope dalum	in deope dalum	**in deore dalum** vel **in deore Pealdum**	In deopa dalum
9a	ðere	þere	þere	**ðære**	ðere
9b	gecyðed	gecyped	gecyped	**gecyðed**	geciðed
10a	ðe	ðe	ðe	**se**	Ðe
10b	arfesta	arfesta	arfesta	**arfæsta**	arfesta
	cudberch	Cutberch	Cutberch	**cuðberht**	Cuðbercht
11b	cynuiges	cynninges	cynninges	**cynninges**	cynninges
12a	engle leo	engle leo[45]	engle leo	engle leo nisi forte malis **engle leof**	Engla leo
13a	eadberch	Eadberch	Eadberch	**Eadberht**	Ædbercht
13b	æðele geferes	7 ðele geferes	7 ðele geferes	7 ðele geferes forte **7 ðere geferas**	Æðele geferes
14a	midd	midd	midd	**mid**	mid
14b	7 þelpold	7 þelpold	7 þelpold	7 þelpold forte **æðelpold**	Æðelpold
15b	abbot	abbot	abbot	**abbod**	abbet
16a	clene	clene	clene	**clæne**	clæne
16b	on gecheðe	on gecheþe	on gecheþe	on **gechete**	On gicheðe

[44] Reported incorrectly as *ymbearnad* by Fry, 'A Newly Discovered Version', p. 85. -o- is clear in facsimile.
[45] Corrected from *engle leos leo* with *leos* crossed out.

17a	lerde	lerde	lerde	**lærde**	lerde
	lustum	lustun	lustum	**lustum** forte ponitur pro **Iustice**	lustum
18b	in iuðem	imuþem	imuþem	imuðem forte **ymb þem**	In inðem
	minstre	minystre	minystre	**mynstre**	mynstre
20a	pundrum geþurðað	pundrum geþurþaþ	pundrum geþurðað	**pundra geþyrcað**	pundrum geþurðað
20b	seggeð	setgeþ	setgeð	**secgeð**	seggeð
21a	drihnes	drihnes	drihnes	**drihtnes**	drihtnes
21ab	perdomes	perddmes	perddmes	**andweardnes**	perdomes

Fig. 4   Variation in Junius's edition of *Daniel*, 279–364.[46]

Exemplar	Transcription	Line
þu	ðu	283b
þin	ðin	284b
þine	ðine	286a
þu	ðu	288a
þine	ðine	289a
þec	ðec	294a
þæs	ðæs	304b
þu	ðu	308b
þu	ðu	309a
forðam	for þam	310a
ðe	þe	310b
þu	ðu	311b
þu	ðu	315a
þu	ðu	316a
ðeah	þeah	325b
þin	ðin	326b
ðaþe	þaþe	329a
þu	ðu	330a
ða	þa	335b
ðone	þone	339b
þa	Ða	345b
hwile	while	348b
todwæsced	todwæscæd	352b
geðancum	geþancum	357a
ðeoden	þeoden	357b

[46] Citations exclude differences in word-spacing, use of abbreviation and accents. Junius has his own system of accents, which only occasionally coincide with those in his exemplar. He expands or contracts abbreviations as required by the layout of his own edition.

Fig. 5   Transmission of *Durham* in the seventeenth century

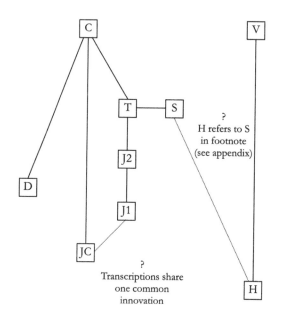

Sigla

C   Cambridge, University Library, Ff. 1. 27 (s. xii)
D   London, British Library, Harley 553 (Simonds D'Ewes)
H   George Hickes, *Linguarum veterum septentrionalium thesaurus grammatico-criticus et archæologicus* (Oxford 1705)
J1   Stanford University Library, Misc. 010 (Part 1) (Junius)
J2   Stanford University Library, Misc. 010 (Part 2) (Junius)
JC   London, British Library, Harley 7567 (Junius)
S   William Somner, Corrected Text of T (Printed in T, p. [Dd8v])
T   Roger Twysden, *Historiæ Anglicanæ scriptores X* (London, 1652)
V   London, British Library, Cotton Vitellius D. xx (s. xii)

Bibliography for 2000

DEBBY BANHAM, CARL T. BERKHOUT, CAROLE P.
BIGGAM, MARK BLACKBURN, CAROLE HOUGH, SIMON
KEYNES and TERESA WEBBER

This bibliography is meant to include all books, articles and significant reviews published in any branch of Anglo-Saxon studies during 2000. It excludes reprints unless they contain new material. It will be continued annually. The year of publication of a book or article is 2000 unless otherwise stated. The arrangement and the pages on which the sections begin are as follows:

Carl Berkhout has been mainly responsible for sections 2, 3 and 4, Teresa Webber for section 5, Debby Banham for section 6, Mark Blackburn for section 7, Carole Hough for section 8 and Carole Biggam for section 9. References to publications in Japan have been supplied by Professor Yoshio Terasawa. Simon Keynes has been responsible for co-ordination.

The following abbreviations occur where relevant (not only in the bibliography but also throughout the volume):

AAe   *Archaeologia Aeliana*
AB   *Analecta Bollandiana*
AC   *Archæologia Cantiana*

AHR	*American Historical Review*
AIUON	*Annali, Istituto Universitario Orientale di Napoli: sezione germanica*
ANQ	*American Notes and Queries*
AntJ	*Antiquaries Journal*
ANS	*Anglo-Norman Studies*
ArchJ	*Archaeological Journal*
ASE	*Anglo-Saxon England*
ASNSL	*Archiv für das Studium der neueren Sprachen und Literaturen*
ASPR	Anglo-Saxon Poetic Records
ASSAH	*Anglo-Saxon Studies in Archaeology and History*
AST	Anglo-Saxon Texts
BAR	British Archaeological Reports
BBCS	*Bulletin of the Board of Celtic Studies*
BGDSL	*Beiträge zur Geschichte der deutschen Sprache und Literatur*
BIAL	*Bulletin of the Institute of Archaeology* (London)
BN	*Beiträge zur Namenforschung*
BNJ	*British Numismatic Journal*
CA	*Current Archaeology*
CBA	Council for British Archaeology
CCM	*Cahiers de civilisation médiévale*
CCSL	Corpus Christianorum, Series Latina
CMCS	*Cambrian Medieval Celtic Studies*
CSASE	Cambridge Studies in Anglo-Saxon England
CSEL	Corpus Scriptorum Ecclesiasticorum Latinorum
DAEM	*Deutsches Archiv für Erforschung des Mittelalters*
EA	*Études anglaises*
EconHR	*Economic History Review*
EEMF	Early English Manuscripts in Facsimile
EETS	Early English Text Society
EHR	*English Historical Review*
ELN	*English Language Notes*
EME	*Early Medieval Europe*
EPNS	English Place-Name Society
ES	*English Studies*
FS	*Frühmittelalterliche Studien*
HBS	Henry Bradshaw Society Publications
HS	*Historische Sprachforschung*
HZ	*Historische Zeitschrift*
IF	*Indogermanische Forschungen*
JBAA	*Journal of the British Archaeological Association*
JEGP	*Journal of English and Germanic Philology*
JEH	*Journal of Ecclesiastical History*
JEPNS	*Journal of the English Place-Name Society*
JMH	*Journal of Medieval History*
JTS	*Journal of Theological Studies*

LH	*The Local Historian*
MA	*Medieval Archaeology*
MÆ	*Medium Ævum*
MESN	*Medieval English Studies Newsletter*
MGH	Monumenta Germaniae Historica
MLR	*Modern Language Review*
MP	*Modern Philology*
MS	*Mediaeval Studies*
MScand	*Mediaeval Scandinavia*
N&Q	*Notes and Queries*
NChron	*Numismatic Chronicle*
NCirc	*Numismatic Circular*
NH	*Northern History*
NM	*Neuphilologische Mitteilungen*
OEN	*Old English Newsletter*
PA	*Popular Archaeology*
PBA	*Proceedings of the British Academy*
PL	Patrologia Latina
PMLA	*Publications of the Modern Language Association of America*
PQ	*Philological Quarterly*
RB	*Revue bénédictine*
RES	*Review of English Studies*
RS	Rolls Series
SBVS	*Saga-Book of the Viking Society for Northern Research*
SCBI	Sylloge of Coins of the British Isles
SCMB	*Seaby's Coin and Medal Bulletin*
SettSpol	*Settimane di studio del Centro italiano di studi sull'alto medioevo* (Spoleto)
SM	*Studi Medievali*
SN	*Studia Neophilologica*
SP	*Studies in Philology*
TLS	*Times Literary Supplement*
TPS	*Transactions of the Philological Society*
TRHS	*Transactions of the Royal Historical Society*
YES	*Yearbook of English Studies*
ZAA	*Zeitschrift für Anglistik und Amerikanistik*
ZDA	*Zeitschrift für deutsches Altertum und deutsche Literatur*
ZVS	*Zeitschrift für vergleichende Sprachforschung*

Online journals cited in the bibliography are currently located at the following addresses on the internet:

Arch. Rev. [*Archaeology Review*] English Heritage
www.eng-h.gov.uk/ArchRev/
Assemblage University of Sheffield www.shef.ac.uk/assem/
Heroic Age Belleville, IL, USA
www.mun.ca/mst/heroicage/

Bibliography for 2000

Internet Archaeol. [*Internet Archaeology*] University of York
intarch.ac.uk/journal/
Marinarkæologisk Nyhedsbrev fra Roskilde National Museum for Maritime Archaeology,
Roskilde, Denmark
www.natmus.dk/nmf/nyhed/indexGB.htm

1. GENERAL AND MISCELLANEOUS

Alcock, Leslie, 'From Realism to Caricature: Reflections on Insular Depictions of
Animals and People', *Proc. of the Soc. of Antiquaries of Scotland* 128.1 (1998), 515–36
Ashbee, Paul, 'Sonia Chadwick-Hawkes, M.A., F.S.A.', *AC* 119 (1999), 430–2
Ashe, Roxi, *Spell Weaver* (New York, 1999)
Banham, Debby, Carl T. Berkhout, Carole P. Biggam, Mark Blackburn, Carole Hough,
Simon Keynes, and Teresa Webber, 'Bibliography for 1999', *ASE* 29, 297–358
Barczewski, Stephanie L., *Myth and National Identity in Nineteenth-Century Britain: the
Legends of King Arthur and Robin Hood* (Oxford) ['Robin Hood, King Arthur, and the
Rise of Anglo-Saxon Racialism', pp. 124–61]
Barnhouse, Rebecca, and Benjamin C. Withers, *The Old English Hexateuch: Aspects and
Approaches*, Publ. of the Rawlinson Center 2 (Kalamazoo, MI)
Bennett, Stewart, and Karen Charlesworth, *Lincoln's First Millennium: Romans, Anglo-
Saxons and Vikings. History and Archaeology for the School Curriculum* (Lincoln)
Berkhout, Carl T., 'Adrian Stokes, 1519–1585', *N&Q* 47, 27–8 [Laurence Nowell]
'Old English Bibliography 1999', *OEN* 33.4, 5–35
'The Old English Inscription Attributed to Roger Ascham', *N&Q* 47, 420–3
'William Lambarde and Old English', *N&Q* 47, 415–20
Berkhout, Carl T., and Patrick W. Conner, 'In Memoriam: Phillip John Pulsiano,
1955–2000', *OEN* 33.4, 3–4
Blockley, Mary, 'Philology, Linguistics: Should You Leave?: 1988–1998', *Thirty Years
More*, ed. Trahern, pp. 3–14
Bloomer, Robert K., 'Rudolf Hildebrand's Impression on Friedrich Kluge', *Amer. Jnl of
Germanic Ling. and Literatures* 12, 23–39
Boenig, Robert, and Kathleen Davis, ed., *Manuscript, Narrative, Lexicon: Essays on Literary
and Cultural Transmission in Honor of Whitney F. Bolton* (Lewisburg, PA)
Bradley, S. A. J., 'Det er hvad jeg kalder at oversætte Digte: Grundtvig as Translator',
Grundtvig Studier, pp. 36–59
Bremmer, Rolf H., Jr, 'The Anglo-Saxon Pantheon According to Richard Verstegen
(1605)', *The Recovery of Old English*, ed. Graham, pp. 141–72
Briggs, Julia, 'New Times and Old Stories: Middleton's *Hengist*', *Literary Appropriations of
the Anglo-Saxons*, ed. Scragg and Weinberg, pp. 107–21
Bruce, Alexander M., 'Strategies for Introducing Old and Middle English Language and
Literature to Beginning Students', *Stud. in Med. and Renaissance Teaching* 7.2 (1999),
33–41
Carrasco, Magdalena Elizabeth, 'The Construction of Sanctity: Pictorial Hagiography
and Monastic Reform in the First Illustrated Life of St Cuthbert', *Stud. in
Iconography* 21, 47–89

Collins, Roger, 'Britian: Anglo-Saxon', *Encyclopedia of Historians and Historical Writing*, ed. Kelly Boyd (London, 1999) I, 126–9 [historiography to present day]

Cross, Gillian, *Down with the Dirty Danes!* [children's book]

Deary, Terry, *The Smashing Saxons*, Horrible Histories (London) [children's book]

Dekker, Kees, 'Francis Junius (1591–1677): Copyist or Editor?', *ASE* 29, 279–96

'"That Most Elaborate One of Fr. Junius": an Investigation of Francis Junius's Manuscript Old English Dictionary', *The Recovery of Old English*, ed. Graham, pp. 301–44

Dockray-Miller, Mary, *Motherhood and Mothering in Anglo-Saxon England* (New York)

Donoghue, Daniel, 'Lady Godiva', *Literary Appropriations of the Anglo-Saxons*, ed. Scragg and Weinburg, pp. 194–214

Fellows-Jensen, Gillian, 'King Olaf Tryggvason and Sir Edward Elgar', *Elgar Soc. Jnl* 11, 202–18

Fisiak, Jacek, 'Studies on Old and Middle English Language in Poland (1900–2000)', *Studia Anglica Posnaniensia* 35, 3–17

Foys, Martin Kennedy, 'Above the Word, beyond the Page: the Past and Present Dilemma of Bayeux Tapestry Scholarship', *Envoi* 8 (1999), 87–103

Frankis, John, 'King Ælle and the Conversion of the English: the Development of a Legend from Bede to Chaucer', *Literary Appropriations of the Anglo-Saxons*, ed. Scragg and Weinberg, pp. 74–92

'Lawman and the Scandinavian Connection', *Leeds Stud. in Eng.* 31, 81–113

Frederick, Jill, 'The *South English Legendary*: Anglo-Saxon Saints and National Identity', *Literary Appropriations of the Angla-Saxons*, ed. Scragg and Weinberg, pp. 57–73

Gelling, Margaret, 'Aileen Armstrong FRHS', *JEPNS* 32 (1999–2000), 76

'John Field', *JEPNS* 32 (1999–2000), 77

'John Field (1921–2000)', *Onoma* 35, 363–4

German, Gary D., 'Britons, Anglo-Saxons and Scholars: 19th Century Attitudes towards the Survival of Britons in Anglo-Saxon England', *The Celtic Englishes II*, ed. Hildegard L. C. Tristram, Anglistische Forschungen 286, 347–74

Glosecki, Stephen O., 'Movable Beasts: the Manifold Implications of Early Germanic Animal Imagery', *Animals in the Middle Ages: a Book of Essays*, ed. Nona C. Flores (New York, 1996), pp. 3–23

Godwin, Parke, *Lord of Sunset* (New York, 1999) [fiction, Battle of Hastings]

Graham, Timothy, 'Early Modern Users of Claudius B. IV: Robert Talbot and William L'Isle', *The Old English Hexateuch*, ed. Barnhouse and Withers, pp. 217–316

'John Joscelyn, Pioneer of Old English Lexicography', *The Recovery of Old English*, ed. Graham, pp. 83–140

Graham, Timothy, ed., *The Recovery of Old English: Anglo-Saxon Studies in the Sixteenth and Seventeenth Centuries* (Kalamazoo, MI)

Greenman, Ben, 'Beowulf: New Prose Translations', *New Yorker*, 29 May, p. 67 [parody]

Gruber, Loren C., with Meredith Crellin Gruber, and Gregory K. Jember, ed., *Essays on Old, Middle, Modern English and Old Icelandic in Honor of Raymond P. Tripp, Jr* (Lewiston, NY)

Hadley, D. M., and Julian Richards, ed., *Cultures in Contact: Scandinavian Settlement in England in the Ninth and Tenth Centuries*, Stud. in the Early Middle Ages 2 (Turnhout)

Hargreaves, David, 'James Campbell as Tutor', *The Medieval State*, ed. Maddicott and Palliser, pp. xxiii–xxix

Harris, Oliver, '*Old English* = "Anglo-Saxon": an Instance from Sir Simonds D'Ewes', *N&Q* 47, 414

Harte, Jeremy, 'Legends of the Fall: Giants in the Anglo-Saxon Imagination', *3rd Stone: Archaeol., Folklore and Myth* 39, 5–11

Harvey, David C., 'Continuity, Authority and the Place of Heritage in the Medieval World', *Jnl of Hist. Geography* 26, 47–59 [includes uses of Anglo-Saxon tradition]

[Hill, Joyce], 'Record of the Ninth Conference of the International Society of Anglo-Saxonists, at the University of Notre Dame, 8–14 August 1999', *ASE* 29, 1–4

Howe, Nicholas, 'What Was Culture for Anglo-Saxonists Thirty Years Ago? What Is It Now?', *Thirty Years More*, ed. Trahern, pp. 29–37

Irving, Edward B., Jr, 'The Charge of the Saxon Brigade: Tennyson's *Battle of Brunanburh*', *Literary Appropriations of the Anglo-Saxons*, ed. Scragg and Weinberg, pp. 174–93

Jackson, Peter, '*Fontes Anglo-Saxonici*: a Register of Written Sources Used by Authors in Anglo-Saxon England. Fifteenth Progress Report', *OEN* 33.3, 7–9

Jayatilaka, Rohini, 'How Well Read Were the Anglo-Saxons? The World Wide Web Version of the *Fontes Anglo-Saxonici* Register', *OEN* 33.3, 12–14

Lapidge, Michael, 'Anglo-Saxon Studies at Clare', *Clare Assoc. Ann.* (1999–2000), 28–33

Lee, Stuart, 'Oxford, Bodleian Library, MS Laud Misc. 381: William L'Isle, Ælfric, and the *Ancrene Wisse*', *The Recovery of Old English*, ed. Graham, pp. 207–43

Linsell, Tony, ed., *Our Englishness* (Hockwold-cum-Wilton)

Low, Mary, *St Cuthbert's Way: a Pilgrim's Companion* (Glasgow)

Lowe, Kathryn A., '"The Oracle of his Countrey"? William Somner, *Gavelkind*, and Lexicography in the Seventeenth and Eighteenth Centuries', *The Recovery of Old English*, ed. Graham, pp. 281–300

Lucas, Peter J., ed., *Franciscus Junius: Cædmonis Monachi Paraphrasis Poetica Genesios ac praecipuarum Sacrae paginae Historiarum, abhinc annos M.LXX. Anglo-Saxonicè conscripta, & nunc primum edita*, Early Stud. in Germanic Philol. 3 (Amsterdam)

'Sixteenth-Century English Spelling Reform and the Printers in Continental Perspective', *The Library* 7th ser. 1, 3–21

Lucken, Christopher, 'La Fin des temps et la fiction des origines. L'historiographie des îles britanniques: du royaume des Anges à la terre des Bretons', *Médiévales* 38, 35–70

Luiselli Fadda, A. M., and É. Ó Carragáin, ed., *Le isole britanniche e Roma in età romano-barbarica* (Rome, 1998)

Lutz, Angelika, 'The Study of the Anglo-Saxon Chronicle in the Seventeenth Century and the Establishment of Old English Studies at the Universities', *The Recovery of Old English*, ed. Graham, pp. 1–82

Maddicott, J. R., and D. M. Palliser, ed., *The Medieval State: Essays presented to James Campbell* (London)

Marner, Dominic, *St Cuthbert: his Life and Cult in Medieval Durham* (London)

McKitterick, Rosamond, *History and its Audiences*, Inaugural Lecture (Cambridge) [including Bede]

Messent, Jan, *The Bayeux Tapestry Embroiderers' Story* (Thirsk)

Millard, John, 'Anglo-Saxons with Attitude: Bede's World, Jarrow, Tyneside', *Museums Jnl* (October), pp. 32–3

Mitchell, Sarah, 'Kings, Constitution and Crisis: "Robert of Gloucester" and the Anglo-Saxon Remedy', *Literary Appropriations of the Anglo-Saxons*, ed. Scragg and Weinberg, pp. 39–56

Morris, Jane, 'Mixing Business and Bede', *Museums Jnl* (July), p. 48 [Bede's World]

Nelson, Marie, 'Beowulf Lives – and So Do his Worthy Adversaries: Archetypes and Diction, both Old and New', *Essays on Old, Middle, Modern English and Old Icelandic*, ed. Gruber, pp. 481–509

O'Keeffe, Katherine O'Brien, 'Keeping the Conversation Going: Critical Strategies and Old English Texts', *Thirty Years More*, ed. Trahern, pp. 15–27

Otter, Monika, 'La *Vie des deux Offa*, l'*Enfance de saint Edmond* et la logique des "antécédents"', *Médiévales* 38, 17–34

Parker, Joanne Mary, 'The Apocryphal Alfred', *The Medieval World and the Modern Mind*, ed. Michael Brown and Stephen H. Harrison (Dublin), pp. 142–70

Pearson, Jacqueline, 'Crushing the Convent and the Dread Bastille: the Anglo-Saxons, Revolution and Gender in Women's Plays of the 1790s', *Literary Appropriations of the Anglo-Saxons*, ed. Scragg and Weinberg, pp. 122–37

Petheram, John, *An Historical Sketch of the Progress and Present State of Anglo-Saxon Literature in England*. With introduction and bibliographical index by Karen Thomson (Edinburgh) [facsimile of 1840 edition]

Pitt, H. G., '"Off To Do good": James Campbell as Colleague', *The Medieval State*, ed. Maddicott and Palliser, pp. xxxi–xlii

Plumer, Danielle Cunniff, 'The Construction of Structure in the Earliest Editions of Old English Poetry', *The Recovery of Old English*, ed. Graham, pp. 243–79

Postles, David, and John Insley, 'Richard McKinley 1921–1999', *Nomina* 23, 170–4

Pratt, Lynda, 'Anglo-Saxon Attitudes?: Alfred the Great and the Romantic National Epic', *Literary Appropriations of the Anglo-Saxons*, ed. Scragg and Weinberg, pp. 138–56

Pulsiano, Phillip, 'Research in Progress', *OEN* 33.4, 36–40

'William L'Isle and the Editing of Old English', *The Recovery of Old English*, ed. Graham, pp. 173–206

Purkis, Sallie, *Romans, Anglo-Saxons and Vikings Teacher's Book*, Sense of Hist., Key Stage 2 (Harlow)

Roberts, Jane, and Janet Nelson, ed., *Essays on Anglo-Saxon and Related Themes in Memory of Lynne Grundy*, King's College London Med. Stud. 17 (London)

Roy, Gopa, 'The Anglo-Saxons and the Shape of the World', *Essays on Anglo-Saxon and Related Themes*, ed. Roberts and Nelson, pp. 455–81

Sampson, Fay, *The Flight of the Sparrow* (London) [novel, seventh-century Northumbria]

Sanders, Andrew, '"Utter Indifference"?: the Anglo-Saxons in the Nineteenth-Century Novel', *Literary Appropriations of the Anglo-Saxons*, ed. Scragg and Weinberg, pp. 157–73

Schichler, Robert L., 'Understanding the Outsider: Grendel, Geisel, and the Grinch', *Popular Culture Rev.* 11.1, 99–105

Schichler, Robert L., comp., with assistance of Jennifer Kisner, 'Abstracts of Papers in Anglo-Saxon Studies', *OEN* 33.3, A1–A54

Scobie, Graham, 'The Search for Alfred: Hyde Community Archaeology Project 1999', *Newsletter: CBA Wessex* (October), 47–9

Scragg, Donald, 'Introduction. The Anglo-Saxons: Fact and Fiction', *Literary Appropriations of the Anglo-Saxons*, ed. Scragg and Weinberg, pp. 1–21

Scragg, Donald, and Carole Weinberg, ed., *Literary Appropriations of the Anglo-Saxons from the Thirteenth to the Twentieth Century*, CSASE 29 (Cambridge)

Scragg, Leah, 'Saxons versus Danes: the Anonymous *Edmund Ironside*', *Literary Appropriations of the Anglo-Saxons*, ed. Scragg and Weinberg, pp. 93–106

Shippey, T. A., 'The Undeveloped Image: Anglo-Saxon in Popular Consciousness from Turner to Tolkien', *Literary Appropriations of the Anglo-Saxons*, ed. Scragg and Weinberg, pp. 215–36

Short, Harold, 'Lynne Grundy: an Appreciation', *Essays on Anglo-Saxon and Related Themes*, ed. Roberts and Nelson, pp. xiii–xviii

Smith, Robin D., 'Language for Everyone: Eighteenth-Century Female Grammarians, Elstob, Fisher and Beyond', *History of Linguistics 1996*, ed. David Cram, Andrew Linn, and Elke Nowak, 2 vols., Stud. in the Hist. of Ling. Sciences 94–5 (Amsterdam, 1999) II, 205–13

Stanley, Eric Gerald, *Imagining the Anglo-Saxon Past: The Search for Anglo-Saxon Paganism and Anglo-Saxon Trial by Jury* (Cambridge)

'The Sources of Junius' Learning as Revealed in the Junius Manuscripts in the Bodleian Library', *Franciscus Junius F.F. and his Circle*, ed. Rolf H. Bremmer Jr (Amsterdam, 1998), pp. 159–76

Stiegemann, Christoph, and Matthias Wemhoff, ed., *799, Kunst und Kultur der Karolingerzeit: Karl der Grosse und Papst Leo III in Paderborn: Beiträge zum Katalog der Ausstellung, Paderborn, 1999* (Mainz, 1999)

Swan, Mary, and Elaine M. Treharne, ed., *Rewriting Old English in the Twelfth Century*, CSASE 30 (Cambridge)

Szabo, Vicki Ellen, 'The Use of Whales in Early Medieval Britain', *Haskins Soc. Jnl* 9 (1997), 137–57

Trahern, Joseph B., Jr, ed., *Thirty Years More of the 'Year's Work in Old English Studies'*, OEN Subsidia 27 (Kalamazoo, MI, 1999)

Wawn, Andrew, 'The Vikings and Victorian Merseyside', *Wirral and its Viking Heritage*, ed. Cavill *et al.*, pp. 100–7

Weinberg, Carole, 'Victor and Victim: a View of the Anglo-Saxon Past in Laȝamon's *Brut*', *Literary Appropriations of the Anglo-Saxons*, ed. Scragg and Weinberg, pp. 22–38

Wieczorek, Alfried, *et al.*, ed., *Die Franken: Wegbereiter Europas, 5. bis 8. Jahrhundert = Les Francs: précurseurs de l'Europe*, 2 vols. (Mainz, 1996)

Wilcox, Jonathan, ed., *OEN* 33.1–4 (Kalamazoo, MI, 1999–2000) [issue 33.2 forthcoming]

Withers, Benjamin C., 'A Sense of Englishness: Claudius B. IV, Colonialism, and the History of Anglo-Saxon Art in the Mid-Twentieth Century', *The Old English Hexateuch*, ed. Barnhouse and Withers, pp. 317–50

Wormald, Patrick, 'James Campbell as Historian', *The Medieval State*, ed. Maddicott and Palliser, pp. xiii–xxii

Zarnecki, George, 'Charles Reginald Dodwell, 1922–1994', *PBA* 105, 389–94

2. OLD ENGLISH LANGUAGE

a. Lexicon and glosses

Anderson, Earl R., 'The Semantic Puzzle of "Red Gold"', *ES* 81, 1–13

Arcamone, Maria Giovanna, 'Germanico **fehu-* "patrimonio" e germanico **laihwna-* "prestito": contributo allo studio della terminologia feudale', *SettSpol* 47, 915–47, [*feoh, læn*]

Bammesberger, Alfred, 'Zur Etymologie von westgermanisch **beur-a-*', *Sprachwissenschaft* 25, 229–31

Bately, Janet, '*Here Comes the Judge*: a Small Contribution to the study of French Input into the Vocabulary of the Law in Middle English', *Placing Middle English in Context*, ed. Taavitsainen *et al.*, pp. 255–75

Bennett, Bryan, 'House and Home', *Mod. Eng. Teacher* 8.4 (1999), 23–5 [*ham, hus, dwellan*]

Biggam, Carole P., 'Anglo-Saxon Plant-Name Survey (ASPNS). First Annual Report', *OEN* 33.3, 9–11

'*Grund* to *Hrof*: Aspects of the Old English Semantics of Building and Architecture', *Lexicology, Semantics and Lexicography: Selected Papers from the Fourth G. L. Brook Symposium, Manchester, August 1998*, ed. Julie Coleman and Christian J. Kay, Amsterdam Stud. in the Theory and Hist. of Ling. Science, ser. 4, 194 (Amsterdam), 103–25

Boutkan, Dirk, 'A New Etymology of "herring"', *Amsterdamer Beiträge zur älteren Germanistik* 53, 1–6

Breivik, Leiv Egil, and Toril Swan, 'The Desemanticisation of Existential *there* in a Synchronic-Diachronic Perspective', *Words: Structure, Meaning, Function. A Festschrift for Dieter Kastovsky*, ed. Christiane Dalton-Puffer and Nikolaus Ritt, Trends in Ling., Stud. and Monographs 130 (Berlin), 19–34

Coates, Richard, see sect. 8

Crowley, Joseph, 'Anglicized Word Order in the Old English Continuous Interlinear Glosses in London, British Library, Royal 2. A. XX', *ASE* 29, 123–51

Dance, Richard, 'Is the Verb *die* Derived from Norse? A Review of the Evidence', *ES* 81, 368–83

Davis, Garry W., 'Notes on the Etymologies of English *big* and Gothic *ga-*', *Amer. Jnl of Germanic Ling. and Literatures* 12, 41–52

Detges, Ulrich, 'Time and Truth: the Grammaticalization of Resultatives and Perfects within a Theory of Subjectification', *Stud. in Lang.* 24, 345–77 [*habban*]

Diensberg, Bernhard, 'The Etymology of Modern English *girl* Revisited', *Folia Linguistica Historica* 21, 119–24

Dietz, Klaus, 'Altenglisch *digol, digle* "verborgen, heimlich": Etymologie und Geschichte einer Wortfamilie', *Sprachwissenschaft* 25, 201–27

'Altenglisch *lign(i)an*, mittelenglisch *lighen* "leugnen, Lügen strafen"', *Sprachwissenschaft* 25, 193–200

'Sind engl. *beer* und dt. *Bier* Erb- oder Lehnwörter?', *Sprachwissenschaft* 25, 103–11

Fellows-Jensen, Gillian, see sect. 8

Feulner, Anna Helene, *Die griechischen Lehnwörter im Altenglischen*, Texte und Untersuchungen zur englischen Philologie 21 (Frankfurt am Main)

Bibliography for 2000

Görlach, Manfred, 'Conceptual and Semantic Change in the History of English', *Words: Structure, Meaning, Function. A Festschrift for Dieter Kastovsky*, ed. Christiane Dalton-Puffer and Nikolaus Ritt, Trends in Ling., Stud. and Monographs 130 (Berlin), 95–109

Gretsch, Mechthild, 'The Junius Psalter Gloss: its Historical and Cultural Context', *ASE* 29, 85–121

Hoptman, Ari, '*Finger* and Some Other *f-* and *fl-*Words', *North-Western European Lang. Evolution* 36, 77–91

Hough, Carole, 'OE *feolheard* and OE *irenheard*: Two *hapax legomena* Reconsidered', *Neophilologus* 84, 127–36

see also sects. 6 and 8

Kahlas-Tarkka, Leena, 'A Note on Non-Standard Uses in Middle English: Weak Preterites of Strong Old English Verbs', *NM* 101, 217–23

Kay, Christian J., 'Brook Symposium on the Revised OED and English Historical Lexicography: a Report', *Lexicology, Semantics and Lexicography: Selected Papers from the Fourth G. L. Brook Symposium, Manchester, August 1998*, ed. Julie Coleman and Christian J. Kay, Amsterdam Stud. in the Theory and Hist of Ling. Science, ser. 4, 194 (Amsterdam), pp. 229–39

'Historical Semantics and Historical Lexicography: Will the Twain Ever Meet?', *Lexicology, Semantics and Lexicography: Selected Papers from the Fourth G. L. Brook Symposium, Manchester, August 1998*, ed. Julie Coleman and Christian J. Kay, Amsterdam Stud. in the Theory and Hist of Ling. Science, ser. 4, 194 (Amsterdam), pp. 53–68

'Metaphors We Lived by: Pathways between Old and Modern English', *Essays on Anglo-Saxon and Related Themes*, ed. Roberts and Nelson, pp. 273–85

Koike, Kazuo, 'A Device of Description in *Beowulf*: Variations Referring to a Ship', *Obirin Stud. in Eng. and Amer. Lit.* 40, 19–48 [in Japanese]

Kortlandt, Frederik, 'Old Norse *taka*, Gothic *tekan*, Greek *tetagón*', *North-Western European Lang. Evolution* 36, 59–65 [*paccian*]

Lazzari, Loredana, 'Il lessico medico anglosassone: descrizione e classificazione delle glosse sul f. 4 del ms London, B.L., Add. 32246', *Quaderni della Sezione di glottologia e linguistica* (Chieti) 10–11 (1998–9), 159–93

Lenker, Ursula, 'The Monasteries of the Benedictine Reform and the "Winchester School": Model Cases of Social Networks in Anglo-Saxon England?', *European Jnl of Eng. Stud.* 4, 225–38

'The *West Saxon Gospels* and the Gospel-Lectionary in Anglo-Saxon England: Manuscript Evidence and Liturgical Practice', *ASE* 28 (1999), 141–78

Liberman, Anatoly, 'The Etymology of English *boy*, *beacon*, and *buoy*', *Amer. Jnl of Germanic Ling. and Literatures* 12, 201–34

Mees, Bernard, 'Celtic Influence in the Vocabulary of Hierarchy during the Common Germanic Period', *Zeitschrift der Savigny-Stiftung für Rechtsgeschichte* 115, Germanistische Abteilung (1998), 361–88

Nagucka, Ruta, 'The Spatial and Temporal Meanings of *before* in Middle English', *Placing Middle English in Context*, ed. Taavitsainen *et al.*, pp. 329–37

Rissanen, Matti, 'The World of English Historical Corpora: from Cædmon to the Computer Age', *Jnl of Eng. Ling.* 28, 7–20

256

Bibliography for 2000

Roberts, Jane, 'OE to eME: Looking Forward from the *Thesaurus of Old English*', *Essays on Anglo-Saxon and Related Themes*, ed. Roberts and Nelson, pp. 435–54

'The Old English Vocabulary of Nobility', *Nobles and Nobility in Medieval Europe*, ed. Anne J. Duggan (Woodbridge), pp. 69–84

'*Robbares and reuares þat ryche men despoilen*: Some Competing Forms', *Placing Middle English in Context*, ed. Taavitsainen *et al.*, pp. 235–53 [words for thievery]

'Two Notes on Laȝamon's *Brut*', *New Perspectives on Middle English Texts: a Festschrift for R. A. Waldron*, ed. Susan Powell and J. J. Smith (Cambridge), pp. 75–85 [*(ge)lipigian, gift*]

Roberts, Jane, and Christian Kay, with Lynne Grundy, *A Thesaurus of Old English*, Costerus 132 (Amsterdam), 2 vols. [revised reprint of 1995 edition]

Stanley, Eric Gerald, 'HWÆT', *Essays on Anglo-Saxon and Related Themes*, ed. Roberts and Nelson, pp. 525–56

Sylvester, Louise, 'Towards a Middle English Thesaurus', *Essays on Anglo-Saxon and Related Themes*, ed. Roberts and Nelson, pp. 557–69

'The Vocabulary of *consent* in Middle English', *Lexicology, Semantics and Lexicography*, ed. Coleman and Kay, pp. 157–78

Sylvester, Louise, and Jane Roberts, *Middle English Word Studies: a Word and Author Index* (Woodbridge)

Syrett, Martin, see sect. 6 [*ðegn*]

Thier, Katrin, see sect. 6

Todd, Loreto, 'Where Have All the Celtic Words Gone?', *Eng. Today* 16.3, 6–10

Zimmer, Stefan, 'Urgermanisch **þey-na-ʒ* "Gefolgsmann"', *Amer. Jnl of Germanic Ling. and Literatures* 12, 291–9 [*ðegan, ðegn*]

b. Syntax, phonology and other aspects

Bammesberger, Alfred, 'Der Vokalismus von altenglisch *fersc* und althochdeutsch *frisk*', *Sprachwissenschaft* 25, 113–15

Bergen, Linda van, 'The Indefinite Pronoun *man*: "Nominal" or "Pronominal"?', *Generative Theory and Corpus Studies: a Dialogue from 10 ICEHL*, ed. Ricardo Bermúdez-Otero, David Denison, Richard M. Hogg, and C. B. McCully, Topics in Eng. Ling. 31 (Berlin), 103–22

Buzzoni, Marina, 'La complementazione tramite *accusativus cum infinitivo* nell'inglese medievale: analisi del costrutto in dipendenza dai verbi *hatan/(be)beodan/biddan, lætan, (ge)seon*', *Linguistica e filologia* (Bergamo) 12, 47–89

Collins, Janet Duthie, see sect. 3*bi*

Crisma, Paola, 'Sintassi formale e lingue medievali: l'articolo in inglese antico', *Archivio glottologico italiano* 85, 38–84

Crouch, Tracy A., 'The Morphological Status of Old English *ge-*', *Amer. Jnl of Germanic Ling. and Literatures* 7 (1995), 165–78

Crowley, Joseph, see sect. 2*a*

Davis, Garry W., 'OE *-estre* and PGmc. **-arjaʒ*: the Origin and Development of Two Agentive Suffixes in Germanic', *Amer. Jnl of Germanic Ling. and Literatures* 4 (1992), 103–16

Díaz Vera, Javier E., 'Prolegomena to the Development of an Inventory of Synsem Features for the Old English Verb', *Miscelánea* (Zaragoza) 21, 71–85

Bibliography for 2000

Dresher, B. Elan, 'Analogical Levelling of Vowel Length in West Germanic', *Analogy, Levelling, Markedness: Principles of Change in Phonology and Morphology*, ed. Aditi Lahiri, Trends in Ling., Stud. and Monographs 127 (Berlin), 47–70

Evans, Jonathan, 'Scribal Error as Linguistic Evidence in the *Peterborough Chronicle*', *North-Western European Lang. Evolution* 37, 53–122

Fischer, Olga, 'The Position of the Adjective in (Old) English from an Iconic Perspective', *The Motivated Sign: Iconicity in Language and Literature* II, ed. Olga Fischer and Max Nänny (Amsterdam), 249–76

Fischer, Olga, Ans van Kemenade, Willem Koopman, and Wim van der Wurff, *The Syntax of Early English* (Cambridge)

Gelderen, Elly van, 'Binding Theory and Minimalist Features', *Proc. of the West Coast Conference on Formal Ling.* 18 (1999), 558–69 [reflexive pronouns]

A History of English Reflexive Pronouns: Person, Self, and Interpretability, Linguistik aktuell 39 (Amsterdam)

Getty, Michael, 'Differences in the Metrical Behavior of Old English Finite Verbs: Evidence for Grammaticalization', *Eng. Lang. and Ling.* 4, 37–67

Goh, Gwang-Yoon, 'Alternative Case Markings in Old English Texts', *ES* 81, 185–98

'Relative Obliqueness and the Contribution of Nonheads in the Subcategorization of Old English Compound Verbs', *Eng. Lang. and Ling.* 4, 13–36

Gretsch, Mechthild, see sect. 2a

Grzega, Joachim, 'Asking Why Exactly *them*, *these*, and *those*', *North-Western European Lang. Evolution* 36, 113–20

Hogg, Richard M., 'On the (Non-)existence of High Vowel Deletion', *Analogy, Levelling, Markedness: Principles of Change in Phonology and Morphology*, ed. Aditi Lahiri, Trends in Ling., Stud. and Monographs 127 (Berlin), 353–76

Kastovsky, Dieter, 'Inflectional Classes, Morphological Restructuring, and the Dissolution of Old English Grammatical Gender', *Gender in Grammar and Cognition*, ed. Barbara Unterbeck, Matti Rissanen, Terttu Nevalainen, and Mirja Saari, Trends in Ling., Stud. and Monographs 124 (Berlin), 709–27

Kish, Judith Mara, '*Æ* and *eo* Development in the Cotton Nero A.X: a New Dialect Feature', *Folia Linguistica Historica* 21, 99–117 [OE diphthongs]

Klemola, Juhani, 'The Origins of the Northern Subject Rule: a Case of Early Contact?', *The Celtic Englishes* II, ed. Hildegard L. C. Tristram, Anglistische Forschungen 286 (Heidelberg), 329–46

Kohnen, Thomas, 'Explicit Performatives in Old English: a Corpus-Based Study of Directives', *Jnl of Hist. Pragmatics* 1, 301–21

König, Ekkehard, and Peter Siemund, 'The Development of Complex Reflexives and Intensifiers in English', *Diachronica* 17, 39–84

Koopman, Willem, and Wim van der Wurff, 'Two Word Order Patterns in the History of English: Stability, Variation and Change', *Stability, Variation and Change of Word-Order Patterns over Time*, ed. Rosanna Sornicola, Erich Poppe and Ariel Shisha-Halevy, Current Issues in Ling. Theory 213 (Amsterdam), 259–83

Kortlandt, Frederick, 'Preaspiration or Preglottalization?', *Amsterdamer Beiträge zur älteren Germanistik* 53, 7–10

Kozuka, Yoshitaka, 'On the Use of Some Synonymous Expressions in the *West-Saxon*

Gospels in Relation to their Authorship', *Jnl of Lang. and Culture* (Osaka Univ.) 9, 107–26

Kroch, Anthony, Ann Taylor, and Donald Ringe, 'The Middle-English Verb-Second Constraint: a Case Study in Language Contact and Language Change', *Textual Parameters in Older Languages*, ed. Susan C. Herring, Pieter Th. van Reenen, and Lene Schøsler, Current Issues in Ling. Theory 195 (Amsterdam), 353–91

Krygier, Marcin, 'Old English (Non)-Palatalised */k/: Competing Forces of Change at Work in the "seek"-Verbs', *Placing Middle English in Context*, ed. Taavitsainen *et al.*, pp. 461–73

Laing, Margaret, '*Never the twain shall meet*: Early Middle English – the East-West Divide', *Placing Middle English in Context*, ed. Taavitsainen *et al.*, pp. 97–124

Lass, Roger, 'Language Periodization and the Concept "Middle"', *Placing Middle English in Context*, ed. Taavitsainen *et al.*, pp. 7–41

Lutz, Angelika, see sect. 4

Millar, Robert McColl, *System Collapse System Rebirth: the Demonstrative Pronouns of English 900–1350 and the Birth of the Definite Article* (Oxford)

Mottausch, Karl-Heinz, 'Das Präteritum der 4. und 5. starken Verbklassen im Germanischen', *North-Western European Lang. Evolution* 36, 45–58

Murray, Robert W., 'Syllable Cut Prosody in Early Middle English', *Language* 76, 617–54

Nagucka, Ruta, 'Conceptual Semantics and Grammatical Relations in Old English', *Studia Anglica Posnaniensia* 35, 19–32

'Is Old English a Configurational Language?', *Kwartalnik Neofilologiczny* 47, 3–13

Nevanlinna, Saara, 'A Note on the Use of Nonfinite Forms of Intransitive Mutative Verbs with the Verb *to come* in Old and Middle English', *NM* 101, 313–21

Ogawa, Hiroshi, *Studies in the History of Old English Prose* (Tokyo)

Ogura, Michiko, '*7/and/ond* in Some Old English Manuscripts', *Jnl of Humanities* 29, 327–44

'*Gewat* + Infinitive and *uton* + Infinitive', *NM* 101, 69–78

Panieri, Luca, 'Rivisitando i verbi deboli germanici della III cl.', *Linguistica e filologia* (Bergamo) 12, 25–46

Pérez Lorido, Rodrigo, 'Coordinate Deletion, Directionality and Underlying Structure in Old English', *Generative Theory and Corpus Studies: a Dialogue from 10 ICEHL*, ed. Ricardo Bermúdez-Otero *et al.*, Topics in Eng. Ling. 31 (Berlin), 125–51

Pierce, Marc, 'Constraints on Syllable Structure in Early Germanic', *Jnl of Indo-European Stud.* 28, 17–29

Ritt, Nikolaus, 'Theory, Empiry, and Textual Witnesses: Acutes in the *Lindisfarne Gospel* and Early English Vowel Quantity', *Sprachwissenschaft* 25, 497–512

Rot, Sándor, 'Old English–Old Scandinavian: Plurilinguism on the Territory of "Danelaw" and the Results of its Linguistic Interference on the Morphological Level of English', *Eastern European Contributions to Scandinavian Linguistics*, ed. Håkon Jahr, Studia Nordica 2 (Oslo, 1997), 47–61

Schwink, Frederick W., 'The Velar Nasal in the Adaptation of the Runic Alphabet', *Amer. Jnl of Germanic Ling. and Literatures* 12, 235–49

Shields, Kenneth, Jr, 'Old English "Einheitsplural": an Archaism?', *Amsterdamer Beiträge zur älteren Germanistik* 53, 11–19

Smith, Jeremy, 'Standard Language in Early Middle English?', *Placing Middle English in Context*, ed. Taavitsainen *et al.*, pp. 125–39

Steponavičius, Albertas, 'On the Phonetic and Phonological Interpretation of the Reflexes of the Old English Diphthongs in the *Ayenbite of Inwyt*', *Placing Middle English in Context*, ed. Taavitsainen *et al.*, pp. 489–504

Stockwell, Robert, and Donka Minkova, 'What Happened to Old English Clitic Pronouns and Why?', *Words: Structure, Meaning, Function. A Festschrift for Dieter Kastovsky*, ed. Christiane Dalton-Puffer and Nikolaus Ritt, Trends in Ling., Stud. and Monographs, 130 (Berlin), 289–305

Taavitsainen, Irma, Terttu Nevalainen, Päivi Pahta, and Matti Rissanen, ed., *Placing Middle English in Context*, Topics in Eng. Ling. 35 (Berlin)

Tanaka, Tomoyuki, 'On the Development of Transitive Expletive Constructions in the History of English', *Lingua* 110, 473–95

Townend, Matthew, 'Viking Age England as a Bilingual Society', *Cultures in Contact*, ed. Hadley and Richards, pp. 89–105

Venneman, Theo, 'Triple-Cluster Reduction in Germanic: Etymology without Sound Laws?', *Historische Sprachforschung* 113, 239–58

Vezzosi, Letizia, 'Portata sintattica limitata della subordinazione in anglosassone', *Archivio glottologico italiano* 85, 85–105

Waltz, Heidi, '(Im)personal Verbs of Emotion in Germanic', *IF* 105, 284–303

Wełna, Jerzy, 'Grammaticalization in Early English', *Studia Anglica Posnaniensia* 35, 43–51

'Some Remarks on the Nonprimary Contexts for Homorganic Lengthening', *Placing Middle English in Context*, ed. Taavitsainen *et al.*, pp. 475–87

Ziegler, Debra, 'The Role of Quantity Implicatures in the Grammaticalisation of *would*', *Lang. Sciences* 22, 27–61

3. OLD ENGLISH LITERATURE

a. General

Atherton, Mark, 'A Place for Mercy: Some Allegorical Readings of "The Woman Taken in Adultery" from the Early Middle Ages (with Particular Reference to Bede, the *Heliand* and the Exeter Book)', *Ciphers in the Sand: Interpretations of the Woman Taken in Adultery (John 7.53–8.11)*, ed. Larry J. Kreitzer and Deborah W. Rooke, Biblical Seminar 74 (Sheffield), 105–38

Bately, Janet, 'Uðwita/Philosophus Revisited: a Reflection of OE Usage', *Essays on Anglo-Saxon and Related Themes*, ed. Roberts and Nelson, pp. 15–36

Berthoin-Mathieu, Anne, 'Le Vol, la loi et la magie dans l'Angleterre anglo-saxonne', *Idéologies dans le monde anglo-saxon* 9 (1997), 27–37

Boenig, Robert, trans., *Anglo-Saxon Spirituality: Selected Writings*, with preface by Richard K. Emmerson (New York)

Chuprya, O. G., 'Temporum opinio v drevnem iazyke i soznanii', *Voprosy Iazykoznaniia* 1999, no. 5, pp. 87–100 [concept of time in *Beowulf*, *Elene* and other texts]

Cubitt, Catherine, see sect. 4

Eshleman, Lori, 'Weavers of Peace, Weavers of War', *Peace and Negotiation: Strategies for Coexistence in the Middle Ages and the Renaissance*, ed. Diane Wolfthal, Arizona Stud. in the Middle Ages and the Renaissance 4 (Turnhout), 15–37

Frederick, Jill, and Mary Swan, 'Old English Literature [1997]', *Year's Work in Eng. Stud.* 78, 156–93

Gatch, Milton McC., *Eschatology and Christian Nurture: Themes in Anglo-Saxon and Medieval Religious Life*, Variorum Collected Stud. Ser. CS681 (Aldershot)

Hill, John M., *The Anglo-Saxon Warrior Ethic: Reconstructing Lordship in Early English Literature* (Gainesville, FL)
'Anthropological Approaches to Old English Literature', *PQ* 78 (1999), 1–13
'Shaping Anglo-Saxon Lordship in the Heroic Literature of the Tenth and Eleventh Centuries', *Heroic Age* 3 [online]
see also sect. 3*bii*

Lutz, Angelika, see sect. 4

Magennis, Hugh, 'Conversion in Old English Saints' Lives', *Essays on Anglo-Saxon and Related Themes*, ed. Roberts and Nelson, pp. 287–310
'A Funny Thing Happened on the Way to Heaven: Humorous Incongruity in Old English Saints' Lives', *Humour in Anglo-Saxon Literature*, ed. Wilcox, pp. 137–57

Petilli, Nicola, 'Le opere in volgare del Venerabile Beda', *Città di vita* 51 (1996), 151–6

Richardson, Peter R., 'Making Thanes: Literature, Rhetoric, and State Formation in Anglo-Saxon England', *PQ* 78 (1999), 215–32

Saenger, Michael, '"Ah Ain't Heard Whut de Tex' Wuz": the (Il)legitimate Textuality of Old English and Black English', *Oral Tradition* 14 (1999), 304–20

Scarfe Beckett, Katharine, 'Old English References to the Saracens', *Essays on Anglo-Saxon and Related Themes*, ed. Roberts and Nelson, pp. 483–509

Schlosser, Donna, 'Cynewulf the Poet, Alfred the King, and the Nature of Anglo-Saxon Duty', *Comitatus* 31, 15–37

Shippey, T. A.. '"Grim Wordplay": Folly and Wisdom in Anglo-Saxon Humor', *Humour in Anglo-Saxon Literature*, ed. Wilcox, pp. 33–48

Taylor, Paul Beekman, 'Figures of Female Cover on Medieval Germanic Landscapes', *Essays on Old, Middle, Modern English and Old Icelandic*, ed. Gruber, pp. 337–59

Trask, Richard M., 'Looking Forward to Doomsday: an Old English Pastime', *In Geardagum* 21, 1–21

Treharne, Elaine, ed., *Old and Middle English: an Anthology* (Oxford)

Treharne, Elaine, and Mary Swan, 'Introduction', *Rewriting Old English in the Twelfth Century*, ed. Swan and Treharne, pp. 1–10

Wilcox, Jonathan, ed., *Humour in Anglo-Saxon Literature* (Cambridge)
'Introduction', *Humour in Anglo-Saxon Literature*, ed. Wilcox, pp. 1–10

b. Poetry

i. General

Blockley, Mary E., 'Axiomatic Implications of a Non-Occurring Heavy Verse in Old English', *Parergon* 18.1, 1–10

Bibliography for 2000

Collins, Janet Duthie, 'The Reality of the Classification "Poetry" for Old English', *LACUS Forum* 24 (1998), 389–97

Felling, Shiraz, 'The Oral Poet as "News Reporter": Taking Another Look at the Anglo-Saxon Scop', *Proceedings of the Seventh Annual Symposium about Language and Society – Austin (SALSA VII)*, ed. Nisha Merchant Goss, Amanda R. Doran, and Anastasia Coles, Texas Ling. Forum 43 (Austin, TX), 41–55

Gade, Kari Ellen, and R. D. Fulk, *A Bibliography of Germanic Alliterative Meters*, OEN Subsidia 28 (Kalamazoo, MI)

Heinrich, Bettina, *Frühmittelalterliche Bibeldichtung und die Bibel: ein Vergleich zwischen den altenglischen, althochdeutschen und altsächsischen Bibelparaphrasen und ihren Vorlagen in der Vulgata*, Europäische Hochschulschriften, ser. 1: Deutsche Sprache und Literatur 1769 (Frankfurt am Main)

Holderness, Graham, trans., *Anglo-Saxon Verse* (Tavistock)

Lutz, Angelika, see sect. 4

Meaney, Audrey L., 'The Hunted and the Hunters: British Mammals in Old English Poetry', *ASSAH* 11, 95–105

Morgan, Gwendolyn A., *Anglo-Saxon Poetry in Imitative Translation: the Harp and the Cross*, with preface by Tom Shippey, Stud. in Brit. Lit. 50 (Lewiston, NY)

Moriya, Yasuyo, 'Compounds in Old English Alliterative Meter', *ICU Lang. Research Bull.* (International Christian Univ.) 13 (1998), 59–69

'The Line Boundary of Middle English Alliterative Meter Compared To that of Old English Alliterative Meter', *NM* 101, 387–401

Muir, Bernard J., ed., *The Exeter Anthology of Old English Poetry: an Edition of Exeter Dean and Chapter MS 3501*, 2nd ed. (Exeter)

Orton, Peter, *The Transmission of Old English Poetry*, Westfield Publications in Med. and Renaissance Stud. 12 (Turnhout)

Reichl, Karl, *Singing the Past: Turkic and Medieval Heroic Poetry* (Ithaca, NY)

Rodrigues, Louis J., *'The Dream of the Rood and Cyn(e)wulf' and Other Critical Essays* (Felinfach, 1998)

See, Klaus von, 'Das Phantom einer altgermanischen Elegiendichtung. Kritische Bemerkungen zu Daniel Sävborg, "Sorg och elegi i Eddans hjältediktning"', *Skandinavistik* 28 (1998), 87–100

Stockwell, Robert P., 'Incompatibilities among Theories of Anglo-Saxon Metrics', *The Life of Language: Papers in Linguistics in Honor of William Bright*, ed. Jane H. Hill, P. J. Mistry, and Lyle Campbell, Trends in Ling., Stud. and Monographs 108 (Berlin, 1998), 473–80

Suzuki, Seiichi, 'Resolution and Mora Counting in Old English', *Amer. Jnl of Germanic Ling. and Literatures* 7 (1995), 1–28

Townend, Matthew, 'Pre-Cnut Praise-Poetry in Viking Age England', *RES* 51, 349–70

Znojemská, Helena, 'Where Ingeld and Christ Meet: The Exeter Book Elegies', *Litteraria Pragensia* 18 (1999), 27–61

ii. 'Beowulf'

Alexander, Michael, '*Beowulf* Reduced', *Agenda* 37.4, 84 [poetic abridgement]

Baldwin, Stanley P., *Beowulf*, Cliff's Notes (Foster City, CA)

Bammesberger, Alfred, 'Beowulf's Landing in Denmark', *ES* 81, 97–9

'Old English *reote* in *Beowulf*, Line 2457a', *N&Q* 47, 158–9

'The Superlative of OE *gód* in *Beowulf*', *NM* 101, 519–21

'What does *he* in Lines 1392b and 1494b of *Beowulf* Refer To?', *N&Q* 47, 403–5

Bazelmans, Jos, 'Beyond Power, Ceremonial Exchanges in *Beowulf*', *Rituals of Power, from Late Antiquity to the Early Middle Ages*, ed. Frans Theuws and Janet L. Nelson, Transformation of the Roman World 8 (Leiden), 311–75

Brown, Phyllis R., 'Cycles and Change in *Beowulf*', *Manuscript, Narrative, Lexicon*, ed. Boenig and Davis, pp. 171–92

Carver, Martin, see sect. 9*d*

Chetrinescu, Dana, 'Beowulf – an Obsolete Variant of Superman?', *Brit. and Amer. Stud.* (Timisoara) 6, 78–85

Church, A. P., 'Beowulf's "*ane ben*" and the Rhetorical Context of the "Hunferð Episode"', *Rhetorica* 18, 49–78

Day, David, '*Hwanan sio fæh ð aras*: Defining the Feud in *Beowulf*', *PQ* 78 (1999), 77–95

Downes, Jeremy M., *Recursive Desire: Rereading Epic Tradition* (Tuscaloosa, AL) ['*Worda ond worca*: Oral Epics and Preoedipal Concerns', pp. 24–60]

Evans, Jonathan D., 'The *Heynesbók* Dragon: an Old Icelandic Maxim in its Legal–Historical Context', *JEGP* 99, 461–91

Fajardo-Acosta, Fidel, '"Think of Wulfstan": the Author of *Beowulf*', *Essays on Old, Middle, Modern English and Old Icelandic*, ed. Gruber, pp. 49–71

Fanning, Steven, 'Tacitus, *Beowulf*, and the *Comitatus*', *Haskins Soc. Jnl* 9 (1997), 17–38

Glosecki, Stephen O., '*Beowulf* and the Wills: Traces of Totemism?', *PQ* 78 (1999), 15–47

Godden, Malcolm, 'The Psyche and the Self: Some Issues in *Beowulf*', *Studies in Middle English Language and Literature: Proceedings of the Vth International Conference of the Spanish Society for Medieval English Language and Literature, León, September 28th–30th 1992*, ed. J. L. Chamosa and T. Guzmán (León, 1997), pp. 49–67

Härke, Heinrich, see sect. 9*a* [weapons]

Heaney, Seamus, 'From *Beowulf*', *Amer. Poetry Rev.* 29.1, 21–8

Hill, John M., 'The Ethnopsychology of In-Law Feud and the Remaking of Group Identity in *Beowulf*: the Cases of Hengest and Ingeld', *PQ* 78 (1999), 97–123
see also sect. 3*a*

Jucker, Andreas H., and Irma Taavitsainen, 'Diachronic Speech Act Analysis: Insults from Flyting to Flaming', *Jnl of Hist. Pragmatics* 1, 67–95

Lane, Micheal Stephen, 'June 1999: St. Beowulf?', *Triumph of the Past* June 1999, pp. [1–4]

'Remembrance of the Past in *Beowulf*', *In Geardagum* 21, 41–59

Lapidge, Michael, see sect. 5

Lionarons, Joyce Tally, '"Sometimes the Dragon Wins": Unsuccessful Dragon Fighters in Medieval Literature', *Essays on Old, Middle, Modern English and Old Icelandic*, ed. Gruber, pp. 301–16

Liuzza, R. M., trans., *Beowulf* (Peterborough, Ont.)

McConchie, Roderick W., 'The Use of the Verb *maðelian* in *Beowulf*', *NM* 101, 59–68

McFadden, Brian, 'Sleeping after the Feast: Deathbeds, Marriage Beds, and the Power Structure of Heorot', *Neophilologus* 84, 629–46

Mitchell, Bruce, and Susan Irvine, *'Beowulf' Repunctuated*, OEN Subsidia 29 (Kalamazoo, MI)

Nobis, Felix, trans., *Beowulf* (Cork)

Noguchi, Shunichi, '*Beowulf* and the (In)effectiveness of the Ancient "Curse"', *Essays on Old, Middle, Modern English and Old Icelandic*, ed. Gruber, pp. 125–38

Osborn, Marijane, 'The Two-Way Evidence in *Beowulf* Concerning Viking-Age Ships', *ANQ* 13.2, 3–6

'"The Wealth They Left Us": Two Women Author Themselves through Others' Lives in *Beowulf*', *PQ* 78 (1999), 49–76

Owen-Crocker, Gale R., *The Four Funerals in 'Beowulf' and the Structure of the Poem* (Manchester)

Patterson, Lee, 'The Heroic Laconic Style: Reticence and Meaning from *Beowulf* to the Edwardians', *Medieval Literature and Historical Inquiry: Essays in Honor of Derek Pearsall*, ed. David Aers (Cambridge), pp. 133–57

Rauer, Christine, *Beowulf and the Dragon: Parallels and Analogues* (Cambridge)

Richman, Gerald, 'Poet and Scop in *Beowulf*', *In Geardagum* 21, 61–91

Risden, E. L., 'Heroic Humor in *Beowulf*', *Humour in Anglo-Saxon Literature*, ed. Wilcox, pp. 71–8

'Irony in *Beowulf*', *Essays on Old, Middle, Modern English and Old Icelandic*, ed. Gruber, pp. 139–49

Rogers, Bertha, *'Beowulf': Translation and Art* (Delhi, NY)

Sävborg, Daniel, '*Beowulf* and *Sonatorrek* Are Genuine Enough: an Answer to Klaus von See', *Skandinavistik* 30, 44–59 [see under See in sect. 3*bi*]

Smith, R. T., 'Swimming Champ Disarms Intruder?', *Shenandoah* 50.2, 163–8

Smith, Steven E., 'The Provenance of the *Beowulf* Manuscript', *ANQ* 13.1, 3–7

Soukupová, Helena, 'The Anglo-Saxon Hero on his Death-Day: Transience or Transcendence? (A Motivic Analysis of Beowulf's and Byrhtnoth's Death Speeches)', *Litteraria Pragensia* 18 (1999), 5–26

Sullivan, Alan, and Timothy Murphy, 'The Fire-Drake. The Translators' Tale, or How Many Angles Can Dance on the Head of a Finn?', *Hudson Rev.* 52, 587–95

Suzuki, Seiichi, 'The Metrical Reorganization of Type E in the *Heliand*', *Amer. Jnl of Germanic Ling. and Literatures* 12, 281–90

Thornbury, E. V., '*Eald enta geweorc* and the Relics of Empire: Revisiting the Dragon's Lair in *Beowulf*', *Quaestio* (Cambridge) 1, 82–92

Thundy, Zacharias P., 'The Dragon in *Beowulf*: Cain's Seed, Heresy, and Islam', *Essays on Old, Middle, Modern English and Old Icelandic*, ed. Gruber, pp. 201–30

Tripp, Raymond P., Jr, 'The Homiletic Sense of Time in *Beowulf*', *In Geardagum* 21, 23–40

'Humor, Wordplay, and Semantic Resonance in *Beowulf*', *Humour in Anglo-Saxon Literature*, ed. Wilcox, pp. 49–69

Wanner, Kevin J., 'Warriors, Wyrms, and Wyrd: the Paradoxical Fate of the Germanic Hero/King in *Beowulf*', *Essays in Med. Stud.* 16 (1999), 1–15

Watanabe, Hideki, 'Final Words on *Beowulf* 1020b: *brand Healfdenes*', *NM* 101, 51–7

Webster, Leslie, see sect. 9*a*

iii. Other poems

Abram, Christopher, 'In Search of Lost Time: Aldhelm and *The Ruin*', *Quaestio* (Cambridge) 1, 23–44

Amtstätter, Mark Emanuel, 'Elemente der Klanglichkeit und Sprachkomposition in der altsächsischen Genesisdichtung', *Amsterdamer Beiträge zur älteren Germanistik* 53, 87–121 [*Genesis B*]

Anderson, Earl R., 'Old English Poetic Texts and their Latin Sources: Iconicity in *Cædmon's Hymn* and *The Phoenix*', *The Motivated Sign: Iconicity in Language and Literature* II, ed. Olga Fischer and Max Nänny (Amsterdam), 109–32

Anderson, James E., and Leslie D. Schilling, 'The *begang* of Cynewulf's "Fates of the Apostles"', *Essays on Old, Middle, Modern English and Old Icelandic*, ed. Gruber, pp. 23–47

Anlezark, Daniel, 'An Ideal Marriage: Abraham and Sarah in Old English Literature', *MÆ* 69, 187–210 [*Genesis A*]

Bammesberger, Alfred, 'Nochmals zu ae. *beohata* in *Exodus* 253a', *Anglia* 118, 258–65

'The Old English *Pheonix*, l. 407b: *topas idge*', *NM* 101, 45–9

'Old English *unnan* in *Andreas*, Line 298b', *N&Q* 47, 409–11

Battles, Paul, '*Genesis A* and the Anglo-Saxon "Migration Myth"', *ASE* 29, 43–66

Breeze, Andrew, 'Sorrowful Tribute in *Armes Prydein* and *The Battle of Maldon*', *N&Q* 47, 11–14

Caie, Graham D., *The Old English Poem 'Judgement Day II': a Critical Edition with Editions of 'De die iudicii' and the Hatton 113 Homily 'De domes dæge'*, AST 2 (Cambridge)

Crawford, Robert, trans., 'The Vision of the Cross', *Stand* ns 2.2, 143–6

Davis, Craig R., 'Cultural Historicity in *The Battle of Maldon*', *PQ* 78 (1999), 151–69

DiNapoli, Robert, 'In the Kingdom of the Blind, the One-Eyed Man is a Seller of Garlic: Depth-Perception and the Poet's Perspective in the Exeter Book Riddles', *ES* 81, 422–55

Faraci, Dora, 'Sources and Cultural Background: the Example of the Old English *Phoenix*', *Rivista di cultura classica e medioevale* 42, 225–39

Frankis, John, 'Sidelights on Post-Conquest Canterbury: towards a Context for an Old Norse Runic Charm (DR 419)', *Nottingham Med. Stud.* 44, 1–27 [*Charms*]

Gilles, Sealy, 'Text as Arena: Lament and Gnome in *The Wanderer*', *The Rhetorical Poetics of the Middle Ages: Reconstructive Polyphony. Essays in Honor of Robert O. Payne*, ed. John M. Hill and Deborah M. Sinnreich-Levi (Madison, WI), pp. 206–20

Glosecki, Stephen O., '"Blow these vipers from me": Mythic Magic in *The Nine Herbs Charm*', *Essays on Old, Middle, Modern English and Old Icelandic*, ed. Gruber, pp. 91–123

Herbison, Ivan, 'Generic Adaptation in *Andreas*', *Essays on Anglo-Saxon and Related Themes*, ed. Roberts and Nelson, pp. 181–211

Hill, David, see sect. 9*h* [*Riddles* 35, 50, 87]

Hough, Carole, '*The Battle of Maldon* Line 191b', *ANQ* 13.3, 3–8

Jackson, Elizabeth, 'From the Seat of the *fyle*? A Reading of *Maxims I*, Lines 138–40', *JEGP* 99, 170–92

Jacobs, Nicolas, '*The Seafarer* and the Birds: a Possible Irish Parallel', *Celtica* 23 (1999), 125–31

Kelly, Richard J., and Ciarán L. Quinn, *Stone, Skin, and Silver: a Translation of the Dream of the Rood* (Cork, 1999)

Klinck, Anne L., 'The Oldest Folk Poetry? Medieval Woman's Song as "Popular" Lyric', *From Arabye to Engelond: Medieval Studies in Honour of Mahmoud Manzalaoui*, ed. A. E. Christa Canitz and Gernot R. Wieland (Ottawa, 1999), pp. 229–52 [*Wulf and Eadwacer*]

Laszlo, Renate, *Ewig ist der Schöpfer: Cædmons Schöpfunghymnus im Codex Exoniensis* (Marburg) [*Riddles*]

McCulloh, John M., 'Did Cynewulf Use a Martyrology? Reconsidering the Sources of *The Fates of the Apostles*', *ASE* 29, 67–83

Morrison, Susan Signe, 'Unnatural Authority: Translating beyond the Heroic in *The Wife's Lament*', *Medievalia et Humanistica* 27, 19–31

Niles, John D., 'Byrhtnoth's Laughter and the Poetics of Gesture', *Humour in Anglo-Saxon Literature*, ed. Wilcox, pp. 11–32

'*Widsith* and the Anthropology of the Past', *PQ* 78 (1999), 171–213

Ó Carragáin, Éamonn, 'The Annunciation of the Lord and his Passion: a Liturgical Topos from St Peter's on the Vatican in *The Dream of the Rood*, Thomas Cranmer and John Donne', *Essays on Anglo-Saxon and Related Themes*, ed. Roberts and Nelson, pp. 339–81

Olsan, Lea, 'The Inscription of Charms in Anglo-Saxon Manuscripts', *Oral Tradition* 14 (1999), 401–19

Osborn, Marijane, '*Dogode* in *Wulf and Eadwacer* and King Alfred's Hunting Metaphors', *ANQ* 13.4, 3–9

Page, R. I., *The Icelandic Rune-poem* (London, 1999) [originally published in *Nottingham Med. Stud.*, 1998; *Rune Poem*]

Petersen, Helle Falcher, '*The Phoenix*: the Art of Literary Recycling', *NM* 101, 375–86

Pettit, Edward, 'Some Anglo-Saxon Charms', *Essays on Anglo-Saxon and Related Themes*, ed. Roberts and Nelson, pp. 411–33

Pollington, Stephen, see sect. 3*c* [*Charms*]

Rauch, Irmengard, 'The Old English *Genesis B* Poet: Bilingual or Interlingual?', *Amer. Jnl of Germanic Ling. and Literatures* 5 (1993), 163–84

Reichardt, Paul F., 'Bede on Death and a Neglected Old English Lyric', *Kentucky Philol. Rev.* 12 (1997), 55–60 [*Bede's Death Song*]

Roberts, Jane, 'Some Relationships between the *Dream of the Rood* and the Cross at Ruthwell', *Stud. in Med. Eng. Lang. and Lit.* (Tokyo) 15, 1–25

Rulon-Miller, Nina, 'Sexual Humour and Fettered Desire in Exeter Book Riddle 12', *Humour in Anglo-Saxon Literature*, ed. Wilcox, pp. 99–126

Rust, Martha Dana, see sect. 3*c* [*Charms*]

Shippey, Tom, 'Hell, Heaven, and the Failures of *Genesis B*', *Essays on Old, Middle, Modern English and Old Icelandic*, ed. Gruber, pp. 151–76

Smith, D. K., 'Humor in Hiding: Laughter between the Sheets in the Exeter Book Riddles', *Humour in Anglo-Saxon Literature*, ed. Wilcox, pp. 79–98

Sorrell, Paul, 'Word Alchemy: a Window on Anglo-Saxon Culture', *Parabola* 25.2, 62–8 [*Dream of the Rood* and *Riddles*]

Soukupová, Helena, see sect. 3*bii* [*Battle of Maldon*]

Stanley, Eric Gerald., 'Old English Poetic Vocabulary: "The Formal Word Precise but not Pedantic"', *Essays on Old, Middle, Modern English and Old Icelandic*, ed. Gruber, pp. 177–200 [*Death of Edward* and *Seasons for Fasting*]

Weale, J. C., 'The Canonicity of Two Edgar Poems', *Heroic Age* 3 [online]

Wheelock, Jeremy I., 'The Word Made Flesh: "engel dryhtnes" in *The Dream of the Rood*', *ELN* 37.3, 1–11

Wilcox, Jonathan, see sects. 3*a* and 3*c*

Williams, Edith Whitehurst, '"An Insight of Form": New Genres in Four *Exeter Book* Riddles', *Essays on Old, Middle, Modern English and Old Icelandic*, ed. Gruber, pp. 231–61

Zehnder, Ursula, 'Hypermetrical Verse Patterns in the *Riddles* of the Exeter Book', *N&Q* 47, 405–9

c. Prose

Anlezark, Daniel, see sect. 3*biii*

Atherton, Mark, 'Quoting and Re-Quoting: How the Use of Sources Affects Stylistic Choice in Old English Prose', *SN* 72, 6–17

Baker, Peter S., ed., *MS F, The Anglo-Saxon Chronicle: a Collaborative Edition* 8 (Woodbridge)

Barnhouse, Rebecca, 'Shaping the Hexateuch Text for an Anglo-Saxon Audience', *The Old English Hexateuch*, ed. Barnhouse and Withers, pp. 91–108

Barnhouse, Rebecca, and Benjamin C. Withers, 'Introduction: Aspects and Approaches', *The Old English Hexateuch*, ed. Barnhouse and Withers, pp. 1–13

Brookes, Stewart, 'Ælfric's Adaptation of the Book of Esther: a Source of Some Confusion', *Essays on Anglo-Saxon and Related Themes*, ed. Roberts and Nelson, pp. 37–64

Brown, Jennifer Christine, '*Writing Power and Writing-Power*: the Rise of Literacy as a Means of Power in Anglo-Saxon England', *Med. Perspectives* 15[.1], 42–56 [*Apollonius of Tyre*]

Buck, R. A., 'Women and Language in the Anglo-Saxon Leechbooks', *Women and Lang.* 23.2, 41–50

Caie, Graham D., see sect. 3*biii* [*Judgment Day II*]

Chardonnens, László Sándor, 'A New Edition of the Old English "Formation of the Foetus"', *N&Q* 47, 10–11

Chiusaroli, Francesca, '*Utraque lingua*. Teoria della traduzione e letteratura vernacolare nel medioevo germanico occidentale', *Incontri linguistici* 22 (2000 for 1999), 113–28

Clayton, Mary, 'Ælfric and Æthelred', *Essays on Anglo-Saxon and Related Themes*, ed. Roberts and Nelson, pp. 65–88

Cross, J. E., 'The Notice on Marina (7 July) and *Passiones S. Margaritae*', *Old English Prose*, ed. Szarmach, pp. 419–32

'Vernacular Sermons in Old English', *The Sermon*, ed. Beverly Mayne Kienzle, Typologie des Sources du Moyen Age Occidental 81–3 (Turnhout), 561–96

Crowley, Joseph, see sect. 2*a*

Davis, Kathleen, 'The Performance of Translation Theory in King Alfred's National Literary Program', *Manuscript, Narrative, Lexicon*, ed. Boenig and Davis, pp. 149–70

Discenza, Nicole Guenther, 'Alfred the Great: a Bibliography with Special Reference to Literature', *Old English Prose*, ed. Szarmach, pp. 463–502

Donovan, Leslie A., trans., *Women Saints' Lives in Old English Prose* (Cambridge, 1999)

Earl, James W., 'Violence and Non-Violence in Anglo-Saxon England: Ælfric's "Passion of St. Edmund"', *PQ* 78 (1999), 125–49

Fernández Cuesta, Julia, and Immaculada Senra Silva, 'Ohthere and Wulfstan: One or Two Voyagers at the Court of King Alfred?', *SN* 72, 18–23

Flight, Colin, *The Earliest Recorded Bridge at Rochester*, BAR Brit. ser. 252 (Oxford, 1997) [includes bridgework text]

Frantzen, Allen J., 'Where the Boys Are: Children and Sex in the Anglo-Saxon Penitentials', *Becoming Male in the Middle Ages*, ed. Jeffrey Jerome Cohen and Bonnie Wheeler (New York, 1997), pp. 43–66

Godden, Malcolm, ed., *Ælfric's Catholic Homilies: Introduction, Commentary and Glossary*, EETS ss 18 (Oxford)

Gretsch, Mechthild, see sect. 2*a*

Griffith, Mark, 'Ælfric's Preface to Genesis: Genre, Rhetoric and the Origins of the *Ars dictaminis*', *ASE* 29, 215–34

Grinda, Klaus, 'The Myth of Circe in King Alfred's *Boethius*', trans. Paul Battles, *Old English Prose*, ed. Szarmach, pp. 237–65 [originally published as 'Zu Tradition und Gestaltung des Kirke-Mythos in König Alfreds *Boethius*' (1990)]

Grundy, Lynne, 'Ælfric's Grammatical Theology and Theological Grammar', *Essays on Anglo-Saxon and Related Themes*, ed. Roberts and Nelson, pp. 1–14

Hill, Joyce, 'Ælfric and Wulfstan: Two Views of the Millennium', *Essays on Anglo-Saxon and Related Themes*, ed. Roberts and Nelson, pp. 213–35

Horner, Shari, '"Why do you Speak so much Foolishness?": Gender, Humor, and Discourse in Ælfric's *Lives of Saints*', *Humour in Anglo-Saxon Literature*, ed. Wilcox, pp. 127–36

Hough, Carole, 'Penitential and Secular Law in Anglo-Saxon England', *ASSAH* 11, 133–41

see also sects. 2*a*, 3*biii*, 6 and 8

Irvine, Susan, 'Linguistic Peculiarities in Late Copies of Ælfric and their Editorial Implications', *Essays on Anglo-Saxon and Related Themes*, ed. Roberts and Nelson, pp. 237–57

Jackson, Peter, 'Ælfric and the Purpose of Christian Marriage: a Reconsideration of the *Life of Æthelthryth*, Lines 120–30', *ASE* 29, 235–60

'Ælfric and the "Uita patrum" in Catholic Homily I.36', *Essays on Anglo-Saxon and Related Themes*, ed. Roberts and Nelson, pp. 259–72

Karkov, Catherine E., see sect. 5

Keefer, Sarah Larratt, 'Assessing the Liturgical Canticles from the Old English Hexateuch', *The Old English Hexateuch*, ed. Barnhouse and Withers, pp. 109–43

Kleist, Aaron, 'An Annotated Bibliography of Ælfrician Studies: 1983–1996', *Old English Prose*, ed. Szarmach, pp. 503–52

Kobayashi, Ayako, Tadao Kubouchi, Harumi Tanabe, and John Scahill, 'Studies towards a Variorum *Anglo-Saxon Chronicle*', *Bull. of Tokyo Kasei Univ.* 40.1, 201–10

Liuzza, R. M., ed., *The Old English Version of the Gospels*, II: *Notes and Glossary*, EETS os 314 (Oxford)

see also sect. 5 [Gospels]

Locherbie-Cameron, M. A., 'From Caesarea to Eynsham: a Consideration of the Proposed Route(s) of the *Admonition to a Spiritual Son* to Anglo-Saxon England', *Heroic Age* 3 [online]

Marsden, Richard, 'Translation by Committee? The "Anonymous" Text of the Old English Hexateuch', *The Old English Hexateuch*, ed. Barnhouse and Withers, pp. 41–89

Meaney, Audrey, see sect. 6 [medical texts in Harley 585]

Menzer, Melinda J., 'The Preface as Admonition: Ælfric's Preface to Genesis', *The Old English Hexateuch*, ed. Barnhouse and Withers, pp. 15–39

Morini, Carla, 'La Passio S. Agathae. La tradizione medievale inglese', *Rivista di cultura classica e medioevale* 42, 49–60

Ogawa, Hiroshi, 'Some Aspects of "Wulfstan Imitators" in Late Old English Prose', *Rising Generation* (Tokyo) 146, 78–83

Studies in the History of Old English Prose (Tokyo) [collected papers plus 'Life of St Martin (MSS Junius 85–86): Text and Notes', pp. 107–26; 'Initial Verb-Subject Inversion in Some Late Old English Homilies', pp. 235–62; and 'A "Wulfstan Imitator" at Work: Linguistic Features of Napier XXX', pp. 263–85]

Pollington, Stephen, *Leechcraft: Early English Charms, Plant Lore, and Healing* (Hockwold-cum-Wilton)

Proud, Joana, see sect. 5 [saints' lives]

Pulsiano, Phillip, 'The Old English Gloss of the *Eadwine Psalter*', *Rewriting Old English in the Twelfth Century*, ed. Swan and Treharne, pp. 166–94

Richards, Mary P., 'Fragmentary Versions of Genesis in Old English Prose: Context and Function', *The Old English Hexateuch*, ed. Barnhouse and Withers, pp. 145–63

see also sect. 5

Roberts, Jane, 'The English Saints Remembered in Old English Anonymous Homilies', *Old English Prose*, ed. Szarmach, pp. 433–61

Rosser, Susan, 'Old English Prose Saints' Lives in the Twelfth Century: the *Life of Martin* in Bodley 343', *Rewriting Old English in the Twelfth Century*, ed. Swan and Treharne, pp. 132–42

Rust, Martha Dana, 'The Art of Beekeeping Meets the Arts of Grammar: a Gloss of "Columcille's Circle" ', *PQ* 78 (2000 for 1999), 359–87

Scheil, Andrew P., 'Bodies and Boundaries in the Old English *Life of St. Mary of Egypt*', *Neophilologus* 84, 137–56

Scragg, Donald, 'An Unpublished Vernacular Exhortation from Post-Conquest England and its Manuscript Context', *Essays on Anglo-Saxon and Related Themes*, ed. Roberts and Nelson, pp. 511–24

Swan, Mary, 'Ælfric's *Catholic Homilies* in the Twelfth Century', *Rewriting Old English in the Twelfth Century*, ed. Swan and Treharne, pp. 62–82

Szarmach, Paul E., 'Alfred, Alcuin, and the Soul', *Manuscript, Narrative, Lexicon*, ed. Boenig and Davis, pp. 127–48

'Ælfric and The Problem of Women', *Essays on Anglo-Saxon and Related Themes*, ed. Roberts and Nelson, pp. 571–90

Szarmach, Paul E., ed., with the assistance of Deborah A. Oosterhouse, *Old English Prose: Basic Readings*, Basic Readings in AS England 5 (New York)

Teresi, Loredana, 'Mnemonic Transmission of Old English Texts in the Post-Conquest Period', *Rewriting Old English in the Twelfth Century*, ed. Swan and Treharne, pp. 98–116

Toswell, M. J., 'Bede's Sparrow and the Psalter in Anglo-Saxon England', *ANQ* 13.1, 7–12

Waite, Gregory, *Old English Prose Translations of King Alfred's Reign*, Annotated Bibliographies of Old and Middle Eng. Lit. 6 (Cambridge)

Wieland, Gernot R., '*Ge mid wige ge mid wisdome*: Alfred's Double-Edged Sword', *From Arabye to Engelond: Medieval Studies in Honour of Mahmoud Manzalaoui*, ed. A. E. Christa Canitz and Gernot R. Wieland (Ottawa, 1999), pp. 217–28

Wiesenekker, E., 'Translation Procedures in the West Saxon Prose Psalter', *Amsterdamer Beiträge zur älteren Germanistik* 53, 41–85

Wilcox, Jonathan, 'The First Laugh: Laughter in Genesis and the Old English Tradition', *The Old English Hexateuch*, ed. Barnhouse and Withers, pp. 239–69

'The Wolf on Shepherds: Wulfstan, Bishops, and the Context of the *Sermo Lupi ad Anglos*', *Old English Prose*, ed. Szarmach, pp. 395–418

'Wulfstan and the Twelfth Century', *Rewriting Old English in the Twelfth Century*, ed. Swan and Treharne, pp. 83–97

see also sect. 3*a*

4. ANGLO-LATIN, LITURGY AND OTHER LATIN ECCLESIASTICAL TEXTS

Abram, Christopher, see sect. 3*biii* [Aldhelm]

Aggeler, Christian, 'The Eccentric Hermit-Bishop: Bede, Cuthbert, and Farne Island', *Essays in Med. Stud.* 16 (1999), 17–25

Atherton, Mark, 'King Alfred's Approach to the Study of Latin', *History of Linguistics 1996*, ed. David Cram, Andrew Linn and Elke Nowak, 2 vols., Stud. in the Hist. of Ling. Sciences 94–5 (Amsterdam, 1999) II, 15–22

see also sect. 3*a* [Bede]

Beare, Rhona, 'Godwin's Sons as Birds', *Prudentia* [Univ. of Auckland, NZ] 32.1, 25–52 [*Vita Ædwardi regis*]

Benison, Líam, 'Early Medieval Science: the Evidence of Bede', *Endeavour* 24, 111–16

Blanco Saralegui, Carmen, 'El tratado *De ortographia* de Beda: Virgilio y los gramáticos',

Actas. II Congresso hispánico de latín medieval (Léon, 11–14 de noviembre de 1997), ed. Maurilio Pérez González (Léon, 1998), pp. 269–75

Brown, George Hardin, 'The Psalms as the Foundation of Anglo-Saxon Learning', *The Place of the Psalms in the Intellectual Culture of the Middle Ages*, ed. Nancy van Deusen (Albany, NY, 1999), pp. 1–24

Brunhölzl, Franz, 'Über die Verse De Karolo rege et Leone papa', *Historisches Jahrbuch* 120, 274–83 [Alcuin]

Burns, Paul C., 'The Writings of Hilary of Poitiers in Medieval Britain from *c.* 700 to *c.* 1330', *From Arabye to Engelond: Medieval Studies in Honour of Mahmoud Manzalaoui*, ed. A. E. Christa Canitz and Gernot R. Wieland (Ottawa, 1999), pp. 201–16 [Bede *et al.*]

Charles-Edwards, T. M., '"The Continuation of Bede", *s.a.* 750: High-Kings, Kings of Tara and "Bretwaldas"', *Seanchas: Studies in Early and Medieval Archaeology, History and Literature in Honour of Francis J. Byrne*, ed. Alfred P. Smyth (Dublin), pp. 137–45

Cross, J. E., 'On Hiberno-Latin Texts and Anglo-Saxon Writings', *The Scriptures and Early Medieval Ireland*, ed. T. O'Loughlin, Instrumenta Patristica 31 (Turnhout, 1999), 69–79

Cubitt, Catherine, 'Memory and Narrative in the Cult of Early Anglo-Saxon Saints', *The Uses of the Past in the Early Middle Ages*, ed. Yitzhak Hen and Matthew Innes (Cambridge), pp. 29–66
see also sect. 6

Cünnen, Janina, *Fiktionale Nonnenwelten. Angelsächsische Frauenbriefe des 8. und 9. Jahrhunderts*, Anglistische Forschungen 287 (Heidelberg)

Dachowski, Elizabeth, 'The English Roots of Abbo of Fleury's Political Thought', *RB* 110, 95–105

D'Imperio, Francesca Sara, 'Le glosse ai quattro Vangeli nel ms. St. Gallen, Stiftsbibliothek 50', *SM* 3rd ser. 41, 549–90 [Bede]

Duncan, Sandra, '*Signa de caelo* in the Lives of St Cuthbert: the Impact of Biblical Images and Exegesis on Early Medieval Hagiography', *Heythrop Jnl* 41, 399–412

Dunn, Marilyn, 'Gregory the Great, the Vision of Fursey and the Origins of Purgatory', *Peritia* 14, 238–54

Echavarren Fernández, Arturo, 'La influencia del *Apocalipsis* de san Juan en la denuncia a los cinco reyes de *De excidio Britanniae*', *Actas. II Congresso hispánico de latín medieval (Léon, 11–14 de noviembre de 1997)*, ed. Maurilio Pérez González (Léon, 1998), pp. 401–5

Emerton, Ephraim, trans., *The Letters of Saint Boniface*, with new introduction and bibliography by Thomas F. X. Noble (New York)

Franklin, Carmela Vircillo, 'The Date of Composition of Bede's *De schematibus et tropis* and *De arte metrica*', *RB* 110, 199–203

Frantzen, Allen J., see sect. 3*c*

Fry, Donald K., 'A Bede Bibliography Preview: *Hymn 6: In Ascensione Domini*', *Essays on Old, Middle, Modern English and Old Icelandic*, ed. Gruber, pp. 73–90

Gatch, Milton McC., see sect. 3*a*

Gneuss, Helmut, 'Zur Geschichte des Hymnars', *Mittellateinisches Jahrbuch* 35, 227–47

Gorman, M., 'Bede's *VIII Quaestiones* and Carolingian Biblical Scholarship', *RB* 109 (1999), 32–74

'The Myth of Hiberno-Latin Exegesis', *RB* 110, 42–85 [Bede *et al.*]

Gouttebroze, Jean-Guy, 'Deux modèles de sainteté royale: Édouard le Confesseur et saint Louis', *CCM* 42 (1999), 243–58

Hall, Thomas N., 'The Early Medieval Sermon', *The Sermon*, ed. Beverly Mayne Kienzle, Typologie des Sources du Moyen Age Occidental 81–3 (Turnhout), 203–69

Hen, Yitzhak, 'The Early Liturgy of Echternach', *Die Abtei Echternach 698–1998*, ed. Michele Camillo Ferrari, Jean Schroeder, Henri Trauffler, and Jean Krier, Publications du CLUDEM 15 (Luxembourg, 1999), 53–64

Hill, Joyce, 'The *Litaniae maiores* and *minores* in Rome, Francia and Anglo-Saxon England: Terminology, Texts and Traditions', *EME* 9, 211–46

Hough, Carole, see sects. 2*a*, 6 and 8

Howlett, David, 'A Response to "Lighten Our Darkness"', *EME* 9, 85–92

Janes, Dominic, 'The World and its Past as Christian Allegory in the Early Middle Ages', *The Uses of the Past in the Early Middle Ages*, ed. Hen and Innes, pp. 102–13

Johnson, Richard F., 'Feasts of Saint Michael the Archangel in the Liturgy of the Early Anglo-Saxon Church: Evidence from the Eighth and Ninth Centuries', *Leeds Stud. in Eng.* 31, 55–79

Karsten, Matthias, trans., *In epistulam Iacobi expositio [Bedae Venerabilis]. Kommentar zum Jakobusbrief*, Fontes Christiani 40 (Freiburg im Breisgau)

Keefer, Sarah Larratt, see sect. 3*c*

Kleinschmidt, Harald, 'Coping with the Legacy of Universalism: Bede and the Trouble with the Roman Empire', *Storia della storiografia* 37, 27–40

Kobialka, Michal, 'Staging Place/Space in the Eleventh-Century Monastic Practices', *Medieval Practices of Space*, ed. Barbara A. Hanawalt and Michal Kobialka, Med. Cultures 23 (Minneapolis, MN), 128–48

Lapidge, Michael, 'Hagiography in the British Isles 500–1550: Retrospect (1968–98) and Prospect', *Hagiographica* 6 (1999), 69–80 [appendix by Rosalind C. Love, pp. 81–9]

'A Metrical *Vita S. Iudoci* from Tenth-Century Winchester', *Jnl of Med. Latin* 10, 255–306

Lapidge, Michael, Gian Carlo Garfagnini, and Claudio Leonardi, ed., *C.A.L.M.A. Compendium Auctorum Latinorum Medii Aevi (500–1500)*, I: *Abaelardus Petrus – Agobardus Lugdunensis archiep.* (Florence)

C.A.L.M.A. Compendium Auctorum Latinorum Medii Aevi (500–1500), II: *Agobardus Lugdunensis archiep. – Anastasius Bibliothecarius* (Florence)

Laynesmith, Mark D., 'Stephen of Ripon and the Bible: Allegorical and Typological Interpretations of the *Life of St Wilfrid*', *EME* 9, 163–82

Lenker, Ursula, see sect. 2*a*

Lutz, Angelika, 'Æthelweard's *Chronicon* and Old English Poetry', *ASE* 29, 177–214

Marocco Stuardi, Donatella, *Alcuino di York nella tradizione degli 'specula principis'*, Collana 'Gioele Solari' 29 (Milan, 1999)

Martin, Lawrence T., 'The *Catechesis Veronensis*', *The Scriptures and Early Medieval Ireland*, ed. O'Loughlin, pp. 151–61

McKitterick, Rosamond, 'Les Femmes, les arts et la culture en Occident dans le haut moyen âge', *Femmes et pouvoirs des femmes à Byzance et en Occident (VIe–XIe siècles)*, ed.

Stéphane Lebecq, Alain Dierkens, Régine Le Jan, and Jean-Marie Sansterre, Centre de recherche sur l'histoire de l'Europe du Nord-Ouest 19 (Villeneuve d'Ascq, 1999), 149–61 [Alcuin]

Orchard, Andy, 'The *Hisperica famina* as Literature', *Jnl of Med. Latin* 10, 1–45

'Wish You Were Here: Alcuin's Courtly Poetry and the Boys Back Home', *Courts and Regions in Medieval Europe*, ed. Sarah Rees Jones, Richard Marks, and A. J. Minnis (Woodbridge), pp. 21–43

Orchard, Nicholas, see sect. 5

Patzold, Steffen, 'Konflikte im Kloster Fulda zur Zeit der Karolinger', *Fuldaer Geshichtsblätter* 76, 69–162 [Alcuin, Boniface]

Pfaff, Richard W., see sect. 5

Picchi, Luigi, 'Alcuino, monaco umanista', *Città di vita* 54 (1999), 225–8

Riedel, Kerstin, 'Lateinisch-althochdeutsche Prologglossen zum *Carmen de virginitate* Aldhelms von Malmesbury', *Septuaginta quinque: Festschrift für Heinz Mettke*, ed. Jens Haustein, Eckhard Meineke, and Norbert Richard Wolf, Jenaer germanistische Forschungen n.s. 5 (Heidelberg), 295–315

Rigg, A. G., 'The Long or the Short of It? Amplification or Abbreviation?', *Jnl of Med. Latin* 10, 46–73 [lives of Æthelwold]

Rushforth, Rebecca, 'The Medieval Hagiography of St Cuthburg', *AB* 118, 291–324

Rust, Martha Dana, see sect. 3*c*

Steel, Duncan, *Marking Time: the Epic Quest to Invent the Perfect Calendar* (New York) ['The Synod of Whitby', pp. 117–27; 'The Venerable Bede', pp. 129–36]

Stevenson, Jane, 'Altus Prosator', *Celtica* 23 (1999), 326–68

Szarmach, Paul E., see sect. 3*c*

Thacker, Alan, see sect. 6

Tyler, Elizabeth M., '"When Wings Incarnadine with Gold are Spread": the *Vita Ædwardi regis* and the Display of Treasure at the Court of Edward the Confessor', *Treasure in the Medieval West*, ed. Elizabeth M. Tyler (York), pp. 83–107

Wieland, Gernot R., see sect. 3*c*

Wiseman, Howard, 'The Derivation of the Date of the "Badon Entry" in the *Annales Cambriae* from Bede and Gildas', *Parergon* 17.2, 1–10

Wood, Ian, 'The Missionary Life', *The Cult of Saints in Late Antiquity and the Middle Ages: Essays on the Contribution of Peter Brown*, ed. James Howard-Johnston and Paul Antony Hayward (Oxford, 1999), pp. 167–83

5. PALAEOGRAPHY, DIPLOMATIC AND ILLUMINATION

Babcock, Robert G., 'A Papyrus Codex of Gregory the Great's *Forty Homilies on the Gospels* (London, Cotton Titus C. XV)', *Scriptorium* 54, 280–9

Baker, Peter S., see sect. 3*c*

Barnard, J. A., 'The Boundaries of Two Anglo-Saxon Charters Relating to Land at Corscombe: a Commentary on the Paper by Grundy (1935)', *Dorset Nat. Hist. and Archaeol. Soc. Proc.* 116 (1995 for 1994), 1–9

Barnhouse, Rebecca, 'Pictorial Responses to Textual Variations in the Illustrated Old English Hexateuch', *Manuscripta* 41 (1997), 67–87
    see also sect. 3*c*

Barrow, Julia, 'Friends and Friendship in Anglo-Saxon Charters', *Friendship in Medieval Europe*, ed. Julian Haseldine (Stroud, 1999), pp. 106–23

Beall, Barbara Apelian, 'The Codex *Amiatinus* and the Significance of a Production Error', *Manuscripta* 40 (1996), 148–56

Bierbrauer, Katharina, 'Der Einfluss insularer Handschriften auf die kontinentale Buchmalerei', *799*, ed. Stiegmann and Wernhoff, pp. 465–81

Bonne, Jean-Claude, '"Relève" de l'ornementation celte païenne dans un Évangile insulaire du VIIe siècle (Les *Évangiles de Durrow*)', *Ideologie e pratiche del reimpiegno nell'alto medioevo*, 2 vols., *SettSpol* 46 (1999) II, 1011–53

Boyle, Leonard E., *Paleografia latina medievale: introduzione bibliografia*, trans. Maria Elena Bertoldi (Rome, 1999) [a translation of the 1984 English version, with a supplement compliled by L. E. Boyle and F. Troncarelli]

Brooks, Nicholas, 'Anglo-Saxon Charters: a Review of Work 1953–73; with a Postscript on the Period 1973–98', in Brooks, *Anglo-Saxon Myths*, pp. 181–215

Brown, George Hardin, 'Bede and his Monastic Library', *Ex libris* 11 (1999–2000), 12–17
    see also sect. 4

Bruderer-Eichburg, Barbara, *Les Neufs chœurs angéliques: origine et évolution du thème dans l'art du Moyen Age*, Civilisation médiévale 6 (Poitiers, 1998)

Coatsworth, Elizabeth, see sect. 9*h*

Collier, Wendy, 'The Tremulous Worcester Hand and Gregory's *Pastoral Care*', *Rewriting Old English*, ed. Swan and Treharne, pp. 195–208

Cross, J. E., see sect. 4

Crowley, Joseph, see sect. 2*a*

Cullen, Paul, 'Sussex Charters – a Handlist', *Locus Focus: Forum of the Sussex Place-Names Net* 4.1, 17–20

Currie, Christopher K., 'A Further Note on Boundaries, Commons and "Gates"', *Hampshire Field Club and Archaeol. Soc. Section Newsletters* 25 (1996), 3–4

Dekker, Kees, see sect. 1

Dodwell, C. R., *Anglo-Saxon Gestures and the Roman Stage*, CSASE 28 (Cambridge)

Fell, Christine E., 'Pedagogy and the Manuscript', *Care and Conservation of Manuscripts* 4, ed. Gillian Fellows-Jensen and Peter Springborg (Copenhagen, 1999), pp. 21–33

Ferrari, Michele Camillo, 'Der älteste touronische Pandekt, Paris, Bibliothèque Nationale de France lat. 8847 und seine Fragmente', *Scriptorium* 53 (1999), 108–14

Gameson, Richard, 'L'Arte nell'Inghilterra meridionale e in Flandria', *L'Arte dell'anno mille in Europa*, ed. L. Castelfranchi Vegas *et al.* (Milan), pp. 161–98

'Books, Culture and the Church in Canterbury around the Millennium', *Vikings, Monks and the Millennium: Canterbury in about 1000 A.D.: Two Millennium Lectures*, ed. Richard Eales and Richard Gameson (Canterbury), pp. 15–40

'The Hereford Gospels', *Hereford Cathedral: a History*, ed. Gerald Aylmer and John Tiller (London), pp. 536–43

Geddes, Jane, 'The Art of the Book of Deer', *Proc. of the Soc. of Antiquaries of Scotland* 128 (1998), 537–49

Gorman, M., see sect. 4

Gretsch, Mechthild, see sect. 2*a*

Gullick, Michael, 'The Scribal Work of Eadmer of Canterbury to 1109', *AC* 118 (1998), 173–89

Hare, Michael, see sect. 6

Hart, Cyril, see sect. 9*k* [Bayeux Tapestry]

Hill, David, 'Eleventh Century Labours of the Months in Prose and Pictures', *Landscape Hist.* 20 (1998), 29–39

Hinton, David A., 'Some Anglo-Saxon Charters and Estates in South-East Dorset', *Dorset Nat. Hist. and Archaeol. Soc. Proc.* 116 (1995 for 1994), 11–20

Hoffman, Hartmut, 'Bernhard Bischoff und die Paläographie des 9. Jahrhunderts', *DAEM* 51 (1999), 549–90

Holder, Nick, see sect. 9*l*

Huws, Daniel, *Medieval Welsh Manuscripts* (Aberystwyth)

Irvine, Susan, 'The Compilation and Use of Manuscripts Containing Old English in the Twelfth Century', *Rewriting Old English*, ed. Swan and Treharne, pp. 41–61

Jakobi-Mirwald, Christine, *Text–Buchstabe–Bild: Studien zur historisierten Initiale im 8. und 9. Jahrhundert* (Berlin, 1998)

Johnson, David F., 'A Program of Illumination in the Old English Illustrated Hexateuch', *The Old English Hexateuch*, ed. Barnhouse and Withers, pp. 165–99

Karkov, Catherine E., 'The Anglo-Saxon Genesis: Text, Illustration and Audience', *The Old English Hexateuch*, ed. Barnhouse and Withers, pp. 201–37

Keefer, Sarah Larratt, see sect. 3*c*

Kelly, S. E., ed., *Charters of Abingdon Abbey: Part I*, AS Charters 7 (Oxford)

Knight, Stan, *Historical Scripts from Classical Times to the Renaissance* (New Castle, DE, 1998) 'Searching for Roots: the Origins of Carolingian Minuscule', *Letter Arts Rev.*, 15 (1999), 32–9

Lapidge, Michael, 'The Archetype of *Beowulf*', *ASE* 29, 5–41

Lenker, Ursula, see sect. 2*a*

Liuzza, Roy Michael, 'Scribal Habit: the Evidence of the Old English Gospels', *Rewriting Old English*, ed. Swan and Treharne, pp. 143–65

Longo, Valentina, Sabina Magrini and Marco Palma, ed., *Bibliografia della Bibbia Amiatina* (Rome)

Marner, Dominic, see sect. 1

Marsden, Richard, see sect. 3*c*

Menzer, Melinda J., see sect. 3*c*

Morini, Carla, '*Horologium e dægmæl* nei manoscritti anglosassoni del computo', *Aevum* 73 (1999), 273–93

Morton, Alan, 'Late Saxon Boundaries Near Southampton', *Hampshire Field Club and Archaeol. Soc. Section Newsletters* 25 (1996), 2–3

Neilson, Christina, 'Dedications, Coronations and Royal Intrigue: the Active Social Lives of British Library, Cotton MS Tiberius A.II', *Scrittura e civiltà* 23 (1999), 133–55

Nolden, Reiner, 'Zu den ältesten Echternacher Bibelfragmenten und zum Einband einer Echternacher Handschrift in der Stadtbibliothek Trier', *Scriptorium* 53 (1999), 114–16

Olsen, Mary C., 'Genesis and Narratology: the Challenge of Medieval Illustrated Texts', *Mosaic* 31 (1998), 1–24

Orchard, Nicholas, 'St Willibrord, St Richarius, and Anglo-Saxon Symptoms in Three Mass-Books from Northern France', *RB* 110, 261–83

Page, R. I., 'The Ideal and the Practical', *Care and Conservation of Manuscripts* 4, ed. Gillian Fellows-Jensen and Peter Springborg (Copenhagen, 1999), 122–39

Pfaff, Richard W., 'The Anglo-Saxon Bishop and his Book', *Bull. of the John Rylands Univ. Lib. of Manchester* 81.1 (1999), 3–24

Pratt, C. W. M., 'The Charter Bounds of Acton Beauchamp', *Trans. of the Woolhope Naturalists' Field Club* 49.1 (2000 for 1997), 33–46

Proud, Joana, 'Old English Prose Saints' Lives in the Twelfth Century: the Evidence of the Extant Manuscripts', *Rewriting Old English*, ed. Swan and Treharne, pp. 117–131

Pulsiano, Phillip, 'The Old English Gloss of the *Eadwine Psalter*', *Rewriting Old English*, ed. Swan and Treharne, pp. 166–94

Richards, Mary P., 'Fragmentary Versions of Genesis in Old English Prose: Context and Function', *The Old English Genesis*, ed. Barnhouse and Withers, pp. 145–63

Rosser, Susan, see sect. 3*c*

Russel, Andrew D., 'Some Comments on the Southampton Evidence in C. K. Currie's "Saxon Charters and Landscape Evolution in the South-Central Hampshire Basin"', *Hampshire Field Club and Archaeol. Soc. Section Newsletters* 25 (1996), 21–2

Stagg, David, 'A Still Further Note on Boundaries, Commons and "Gates" etc.', *Hampshire Field Club and Archaeol. Soc. Section Newsletters* 25 (1996), 4–5

Story, Joanna, '"Concerning the Bishops of Whithorn and their Subjection to the Archbishops of York": Some Observations on the Manuscript Evidence and its Links with Durham', *Durham Archaeol. Jnl* 14–15 (1999), 77–83

Swan, Mary, see sect. 3*c*

Szarmach, Paul E., 'A Return to Cotton Tiberius A.III, Art. 24 and Isidore's *Synonyma*', *Text and Gloss: Studies in Insular Learning and Literature*, ed. Helen Conrad O'Briain, Anne-Marie D'Arcy, and John Scattergood (Dublin, 1999), pp. 166–81

Tedeschi, C., 'Aspetti paleografici della cristianizzazione dell'Inghilterra: l'onciale inglese e la seconda fasa della semionciale insulare', *Le isole britanniche e Roma in età romano-barbarica*, ed. A. M. Luiselli Fadda and É. Ó Carragáin (Rome, 1998), 95–108

Treharne, Elaine M., 'The Production and Script of Manuscripts Containing English Religious Texts in the First Half of the Twelfth Century', *Rewriting Old English*, ed. Swan and Treharne, pp. 11–39

Wamers, Egon, see sect. 9*j*

Willetts, Pamela J., *Catalogue of the Manuscripts in the Society of Antiquaries of London* (Woodbridge)

Wilton, Robert, 'Treloen, a Cornish Domesday Manor: its Boundaries Investigated', *Devon and Cornwall Notes and Queries* 38 (1997–99), 240–5

6. HISTORY

Abrams, Lesley, 'Conversion and Assimilation', *Cultures in Contact*, ed. Hadley and Richards, pp. 135–53

Albarella, Umberto, see sect. 9*c* [second entry]

Astill, Grenville, 'General Survey 600–1300', *The Cambridge Urban History of Britain*, I: *600–1540*, ed. D. M. Palliser (Cambridge), pp. 27–49

Bailey, Keith A., 'Clofesho Revisited', *ASSAH* 11, 119–31

'The Manor in Domesday Buckinghamshire, II: Demesnes', *Records of Buckinghamshire* 39 (1999), 45–58

'*Vendere potuit*: "He Could Sell", To Coin a Domesday Phrase', *Records of Buckinghamshire* 40, 73–87

Baker, Peter S., see sect. 3*c* [*Anglo-Saxon Chronicle*, MS F]

Barrow, Julia, 'Athelstan to Aigueblanche, 1056–1535', *Hereford Cathedral: a History*, ed. Gerald Aylmer and John Tiller (London), pp. 21–47

'Churches, Education and Literacy in Towns 600–1300', *The Cambridge Urban History of Britain*, I: *600–1540*, ed. D. M. Palliser (Cambridge), pp. 127–52

see also sect. 5

'Survival and Mutation: Ecclesiastical Institutions in the Danelaw in the Ninth and Tenth Centuries', *Cultures in Contact*, ed. Hadley and Richards, pp. 155–76

Bassett, Steven, 'Anglo-Saxon Birmingham', *Midland Hist.* 25, 1–27

'How the West was Won: the Anglo-Saxon Takeover of the West Midlands', *ASSAH* 11, 107–18

'Medieval Ecclesiastical Organisation in the Vicinity of Wroxeter and its British Antecedents', *JBAA* 146 (1992), 1–28

Bates, David, 'England and the "Feudal Revolution"', *Il feudalesimo nell'alto medioevo*, *SettSpol* 47, 611–46

Re-ordering the Past and Negotiating the Present in Stenton's "First Century", Stenton Lecture 1999 (Reading)

Batey, Colleen E., and John Sheehan, 'Viking Expansion and Cultural Blending in Britain and Ireland', *Vikings: the North Atlantic Saga*, ed. William W. Fitzhugh and Elisabeth I. Ward [exhibition catalogue] (Washington, DC), pp. 127–41

Behr, Charlotte, 'The Origins of Kingship in Early Medieval Kent', *EME* 9, 25–52

Berryman, R. D., *Use of the Woodlands in the Late Anglo-Saxon Period*, BAR British ser. 271 (Oxford)

Blair, John, *The Anglo-Saxon Age: a Very Short Introduction* (Oxford) [rept. from *The Oxford History of Britain*, ed. K. O. Morgan (Oxford, 1984), rev. ed. (Oxford, 1999)]

'Small Towns 600–1300', *The Cambridge Urban History of Britain*, I: *600–1540*, ed. D. M. Palliser (Cambridge), pp. 245–70

Bostock, Tony, 'The Origins of Over and Darnhall', *Cheshire Hist.* 37 (1997–8), 11–22

Britnell, Richard, 'The Economy of British Towns 600–1300', *The Cambridge Urban History of Britain*, I: *600–1540*, ed. D. M. Palliser (Cambridge), pp. 105–26

Brooks, Nicholas, *Anglo-Saxon Myths: State and Church 400–1066* (London) [collected papers]

Bede and the English, Jarrow Lecture 1999 (Jarrow)

'Canterbury, Rome and the Construction of English Identity', *Early Medieval Rome and the Christian West: Essays in Honour of Donald A. Bullough*, ed. Julia M. H. Smith (Leiden), pp. 221–46

Communities and Warfare, 700–1400 (London) [collected papers]

'The Legacy of Saints Gregory and Augustine in England', *Canterbury Cathedral Chronicle* 92 (1998), 45–59

Brown, Jennifer Christine, 'Writing Power and Writing-Power: the Rise of Literacy as a Means of Power in Anglo-Saxon England', *Medieval Perspectives* 15, 42–56

Campbell, James, *The Anglo-Saxon State* (London) [collected papers]

'Britain AD 500', *Hist. Today* 50.2, 29–35

'The East Anglian Sees before the Conquest', *Norwich Cathedral: Church, City and Diocese, 1096–1996*, ed. Ian Atherton *et al.* (London, 1996), pp. 3–21

'Power and Authority 600–1300', *The Cambridge Urban History of Britain*, I: *600–1540*, ed. D. M. Palliser (Cambridge), pp. 51–78

Cavill, Paul, Stephen E. Harding, and Judith Jesch, *Wirral and its Viking Heritage*, EPNS popular ser. 2 (Nottingham)

Cheney, C. R., and Michael Jones, ed., *A Handbook of Dates for Students of British History*, rev. ed., R. Hist. Soc. Guides and Handbooks 4 (Cambridge)

Collins, Roger, 'Bede, c. 672/3–735, Anglo-Saxon Chronicler', *Encyclopedia of Historians and Historical Writing*, ed. Kelly Boyd, 2 vols. (London, 1999) I, 86–7

Crick, Julia C., 'Posthumous Obligation and Family Identity', *Social Identity*, ed. Frazer and Tyrrell, pp. 193–208

'Women, Wills and Moveable Wealth in Pre-Conquest England', *Gender and Material Culture in Historical Perspective*, ed. Moira Donald and Linda Hurcombe (Basingstoke), 17–37

Cropper, Eric, 'St Wilfrid and the Moveable Feasts', *Yorkshire Jnl* 25 (1999), 66–7

Cubitt, Catherine, 'Monastic Memory and Identity in Anglo-Saxon England', *Social Identity*, ed. Frazer and Tyrrell, pp. 253–76

'Rape, Pillage and Exaggeration', *Not Angels, but Anglicans: a History of Christianity in the British Isles*, ed. Henry Chadwick and Alison Ward (Norwich), pp. 33–9

'Sites and Sanctity: Revisiting the Cult of Murdered and Martyred Anglo-Saxon Royal Saints', *EME* 9, 53–83

'Virginity and Misogyny in Tenth- and Eleventh-Century England', *Gender and Hist.* 12, 1–32

see also sect. 4

Currie, Christopher K., 'Polesden Lacey and Ranmore Common Estates, Near Dorking, Surrey: an Archaeological and Historical Survey', *Surrey Archaeol. Collections* 87, 49–84 [includes documentary and place-name studies for the Saxon period]

Cusack, Carole M., *Conversion Among the Germanic Peoples* (London, 1998; paperback 2000, under title *The Rise of Christianity in Northern Europe, 300–1000*)

Dark, Ken, 'A Famous Arthur in the Sixth Century? Reconsidering the Origins of Arthurian Legend', *Reading Med. Stud.* 26, 77–95

Dawson, Graham, 'Southwark in Domesday Book', *Surrey Arch. Bull.* 340, 5–8 [originally published in *Newsletter of the Southwark and Lambeth Arch. Soc.* 79 (1999)]

Dierkens, Alain, 'Willibrord und Bonifatius – die angelsächsischen Missionen und das fränkische Königreich in der ersten Hälfte des 8. Jahrhunderts', *Die Franken*, ed. Wieczorek *et al.*, pp. 459–65

Eales, Richard, 'Politics and Society in Canterbury around 1000 A.D.', *Vikings, Monks and the Millennium: Canterbury in about 1000 A.D.: Two Millennium Lectures*, ed. Richard Eales and Richard Gameson (Canterbury), pp. 1–13

Evison, Martin Paul, 'All in the Genes? Evaluating the Biological Evidence of Contact and Migration', *Cultures in Contact*, ed. Hadley and Richards, pp. 277–94

Foot, Sarah, *Veiled Women*, I: *The Disappearance of Nuns from Anglo-Saxon England*, and II: *Female Religious Communities in England, 871–1066* (Aldershot)

Frazer, William O., and Andrew Tyrrell, ed., *Social Identity in Early Medieval Britain* (London)

Gardiner, Mark, 'Shipping and Trade between England and the Continent in the Eleventh Century', *ANS* 22, 71–93

Garrison, Mary, 'The English and the Irish at the Court of Charlemagne', *Karl der Grosse und sein Nachwirken: 1200 Jahre Kultur und Wissenschaft in Europa* I, ed. P. Butzer, Max Kerner and Walter Oberschelp (Turnhout, 1997), 97–123

Gibbs, Ray, *Ine, the First King of Wessex* (Felinfach)

Golding, Brian, 'Britain 1100', *Hist. Today* 50.4, 10–17

Gretsch, Mechthild, see sect. 2*a*

Hadley, Dawn, '"Cockle among the Wheat": the Scandinavian Settlement of England', *Social Identity*, ed. Frazer and Tyrrell, pp. 111–35

'"Hamlet and the Princes of Darkness": Lordship in the Danelaw, c. 860–954', *Cultures in Contact*, ed. Hadley and Richards, pp. 107–32

The Northern Danelaw: its Social Structure, c. 800–1100 (London)

Hadley, Dawn M., and Julian D. Richards, 'Introduction: Interdisciplinary Approaches to the Scandinavian Settlement', *Cultures in Contact*, ed. Hadley and Richards, pp. 3–15

Hare, Kent G., 'Apparitions and War in Anglo-Saxon England', *The Circle of War in the Middle Ages: Essays on Medieval Military and Naval History*, ed. Donald J. Kagay and L. J. Andrew Villalon (Woodbridge, 1999), pp. 75–86

Hare, Michael, 'Cnut and Lotharingia: Two Notes', *ASE* 29, 261–78

Hayashi, Hiroshi, 'A Study of the Charter-Criticism of the Anglo-Saxon Period (10)', *Hogakkai Zasshi* (*Gakushuin Rev. of Law and Politics*) 35.2, 53–92

Hayward, Paul Antony, 'Saint Albans, Durham, and the Cult of Saint Oswine King and Martyr', *Viator* 30 (1999), 105–44

Haywood, John, *Encyclopaedia of the Viking Age* (London)

Higham, N. J., 'King Edwin of the Deiri: Rhetoric and the Reality of Power in Early England', *Early Deira*, ed. Geake and Kenny, pp. 41–9

Hill, David, 'Anglo-Saxon Mechanics', *Med. Life* 13, 9–13

'Athelstan's Urban Reforms', *ASSAH* 11, 173–86

see also sects. 5 and 9*c*

Hillaby, Joe, 'King Burgred, the Severn Stoke Coin Hoard and the Demise of the Mercian Kingdom', *Trans. of the Worcestershire Archaeol. Soc.* 17, 125–48

Hines, John, 'Tidlig kontakt over Nordsjøen og de bakenforliggende årsaker', *Nordsjøen: handel, religion og politikk*, Karmøyseminaret 1994 og 1995, ed. Jens Flemming Krøger and Helge-Rolf Naley (Karmøy, 1996), pp. 18–30

Hinton, David A., see sect. 9*b*

Hirst, Joyce, 'From Paganism to Christianity', *Yorkshire Jnl* 25 (1999), 17–20

Hodges, Richard, 'Charlemagne's Elephant', *Hist. Today* 50.12, 21–5 [on trade, inc. English 'emporia']

> *Towns and Trade in the Age of Charlemagne* (London)

Holt, Richard, 'Society and Population 600–1300', *The Cambridge Urban History of Britain*, I: *600–1540*, ed. D. M. Palliser (Cambridge), pp. 79–104

Hooke, Della, 'Medieval Forests and Parks in Southern and Central England', *European Woods and Forests: Studies in Cultural History*, ed. Charles Watkins (Oxford, 1998), pp. 19–38

Hough, Carole, 'Cattle-Tracking in the Fonthill Letter', *EHR* 115, 864–92

Innes, Matthew, 'Danelaw Identities: Ethnicity, Regionalism, and Political Allegiance', *Cultures in Contact*, ed. Hadley and Richards, pp. 65–88

Insley, Charles, 'Politics, Conflict and Kinship in Early Eleventh-Century Mercia', *Midland Hist.* 25, 28–42

Ishimoto, Mari, 'The Cult of Royal Saints, a Study of its Influence in Anglo-Saxon England', *Kansai Daigaku Seiyoshi Ronso (Western Hist. Essays)* 3, 35–53 [in Japanese]

Jørgensen, Torstein, 'Fra Wessex til Vestlandet: noen perspektiver på kristeningen av Norge', *Nordsjøen: handel, religion og politikk*, Karmøyseminaret 1994 og 1995, ed. Jens Flemming Krøger and Helge-Rolf Naley (Karmøy, 1996), pp. 99–108

Keene, Derek, 'London from the Post-Roman Period to 1300', *The Cambridge Urban History of Britain*, I: *600–1540*, ed. D. M. Palliser (Cambridge), pp. 187–216

Kelly, Susan, see sect. 5

Kershaw, Paul, 'The Alfred-Guthrum Treaty: Scripting Accommodation and Interaction in Viking Age England', *Cultures in Contact*, ed. Hadley and Richards, pp. 43–64

Keynes, Simon, 'Apocalypse Then (AD 1000)', *Not Angels, but Anglicans: a History of Christianity in the British Isles*, ed. Henry Chadwick and Alison Ward (Norwich), pp. 41–7

> 'Diocese and Cathedral before 1056', *Hereford Cathedral: a History*, ed. Gerald Aylmer and John Tiller (London), pp. 3–20

Kirby, D. P., '"At the End of the World": St Augustine at the Court of King Æthelberht', *Canterbury Cathedral Chronicle* 91 (1997), 15–19

Krier, Jean, 'Echternach und das Kloster des hl. Willibrord', *Die Franken*, ed. Wieczorek *et al.*, pp. 466–78

Laing, Jennifer, *Warriors of the Dark Ages* (Stroud)

Lavelle, Ryan, 'Towards a Political Contextualization of Peacemaking and Peace Agreements in Anglo-Saxon England', *Peace and Negotiation: Strategies for Coexistence in the Middle Ages and the Renaissance*, ed. D. Wolfthal, Arizona Stud. in the Middle Ages and the Renaissance 4 (Turnhout), 39–55

Lawson, M. K., 'Observations upon a Scene in the Bayeux Tapestry, the Battle of

Hastings and the Military System of the Late Anglo-Saxon State', *The Medieval State*, ed. Maddicott and Palliser, pp. 73–91

Loseby, S. T., 'Power and Towns in Late Roman Britain and Early Anglo-Saxon England', *Sedes regiae (ann. 400–800)*, ed. Gisela Ripoll and Josep M. Gurt (Barcelona), pp. 319–70

Lowe, Chris, *Angels, Fools and Tyrants: the Britons and the Angles in Southern Scotland* (Edinburgh)

Loyn, H. R., *The English Church, 940–1154* (Harlow)

Lutz, Angelika, see sect. 4

Maddicott, J. R., 'Two Frontier States: Northumbria and Wessex, c. 650–750', *The Medieval State*, ed. Maddicott and Palliser, pp. 25–45

Manco, Jean, 'Saxon Bath: the Legacy of Rome and the Saxon Rebirth', *Bath Hist.* 7 (1998), 27–54

Margham, John, 'St Mary's, Brading: Wilfrid's Church?', *Proc. of the Isle of Wight Nat. Hist. and Archaeol. Soc.* 16, 117–35

Marner, Dominic, see sect. 1

Mate, Mavis E., *Women in Medieval English Society*, New Stud. in Economic and Social Hist. (Cambridge, 1999)

Matthews, Keith J., 'Early Estate Development in Cheshire', *Cheshire Hist.* 35 (1995–6), 2–9

'Saint Plegmund: Cheshire's Archbishop of Canterbury', *Cheshire Hist.P* 36 (1996–7), 89–113

Matthews, Stephen, 'From Chester to Rome: an Early Medieval Journey', *Trans. of the Lancashire and Cheshire Ant. Soc.* 94 (1998), 136–44 [journey of Sæbeorht from the *Vita Haroldi*]

McBride, Oswald, 'The Tenth-Century Monastic Revival', *Monks of England: the Benedictines in England from Augustine to the Present Day*, ed. Daniel Rees (London, 1997), pp. 65–83

McCarthy, Daniel, and Aiden Breen, 'A propos du synode de Whitby: étude des observations astronomiques dans les Annales irlandaises', *Annales de Bretagne* 107.3, 25–56

McCarthy, Mike, 'Carlisle and St Cuthbert', *Durham Archaeol. Jnl* 14–15 (1999), 59–67

Meaney, Audrey, 'The Practice of Medicine in England about the Year 1000', *The Year 1000: Medical Practice at the End of the First Millennium*, ed. Peregrine Horden and Emilie Savage-Smith [= *Social Hist. of Medicine* 13.2], pp. 221–37

Miyazaki, Tadakatsu, 'The Naming of Anglo-Saxon Kings and the Sense of their Names', *Yokohama Shiritsu-Daigaku Ronso, Jinbunkagaku (Jnl of Yokohama City Univ., Humanities)* 51.1–2, 31–60 [In Japanese]

Moore, John S., *From Anglo-Saxon to Anglo-Norman: North Gloucestershire in Domesday Book*, Deerhurst Lecture 1998 (Deerhurst)

Moreland, John, 'Ethnicity, Power and the English', *Social Identity*, ed. Frazer and Tyrrell, pp. 23–51

Mori, Takako, 'Anglo-Saxon Rural History in Britain since 1972', *Shigaku-Zasshi (Hist. Jnl of Japan)* 109.11, 89–111 [in Japanese]

'The *Rectitudines Singularum Personarum* Reconsidered', *Kyushu Rekishi Kagaku (Kyushu Hist. Stud.)* 28, 60–82 [in Japanese]

Nonn, Ulrich, 'Zur Vorgeschichte der Bildungsreform Karls des Grossen', *Karl der Grosse und sein Nachwirken: 1200 Jahre Kultur und Wissenschaft in Europa* I, ed. P. Butzer, Max Kerner and Walter Oberschelp (Turnhout, 1997), 63–77 [Boniface *et al.*]

Oakeshott, Michael, 'Saxon South Cerney', *Trans. of the Bristol and Gloucestershire Archaeol. Soc.* 117 (1999), 119–26

Orme, Nicholas, *The Saints of Cornwall* (Oxford)

Ortenberg, Veronica, 'The Anglo-Saxon Church and the Papacy', *The English Church and the Papacy in the Middle Ages*, ed. C. H. Lawrence, 2nd ed. (Stroud, 1999), pp. 29–62

'Aux périphéries du monde carolingien: liens dynastiques et nouvelles fidélités dans le royaume anglo-saxon', *La Royauté et les élites dans l'Europe carolingienne (debut IXe siècle aux environs de 920)*, ed. Régine le Jan (Lille, 1998), pp. 505–17

Padberg, Lutz E. von, *Die Christianisierung Europas in Mittelalter*, Universal-Bibliothek 17015 (Stuttgart, 1998) [inc. Augustine, Boniface *et al.*]

Palliser, D. M., T. R. Slater, and E. Patricia Dennison, 'The Topography of Towns 600–1300', *The Cambridge Urban History of Britain*, I: *600–1540*, ed. D. M. Palliser (Cambridge), pp. 153–86

Pelteret, David A. E., ed., *Anglo-Saxon History: Basic Readings*, Basic Readings in AS England 6 (New York)

Perman, David, 'Saxon Ware and Hertford: Some New Thoughts for the Millennium', *Hertfordshire's Past* 48, 26–33

Picken, W. M. M., *A Medieval Cornish Miscellany*, ed. O.J. Padel (Chichester)

Pollington, Stephen, *Leechcraft: Early English Charms, Plantlore and Healing* (Hockwold-cum-Wilton)

Pounds, N. J., *A History of the English: the Culture of Religion from Augustine to Victoria* (Cambridge)

Proksch, Nikola, 'The Anglo-Saxon Missionaries to the Continent', *Monks of England: the Benedictines in England from Augustine to the Present Day*, ed. Daniel Rees (London, 1997), pp. 35–54

Reno, Frank D., *Historic Figures of the Arthurian Era: Authenticating the Enemies and Allies of Britain's Post-Roman King* (Jefferson, NJ)

Rielly, Edward J., 'Anglo-Saxon Chronicle', *Encyclopedia of Historians and Historical Writing*, ed. Kelly Boyd, 2 vols. (London) I, 34–5

Roberts, B. K., 'Of *Æcertyning*', *Durham Archaeol. Jnl* 14–15 (1999), 93–100 [settlement and field layout]

Roffe, David, *Domesday: the Inquest and the Book* (Oxford)

Rollason, David, ed., *Symeon of Durham: Libellus de exordio atque procursu istius, hoc est Dunhelmensis, ecclesie/Tract on the Origins and Progress of this the Church of Durham*, OMT (Oxford)

Runcie, Lord [Robert], 'The Mission of Saint Augustine', *Canterbury Cathedral Chronicle* 92 (1998), 6–20

Rushton, Neil S., 'Parochialization and Patterns of Patronage in 11th Century Sussex', *Sussex Archaeol. Collections* 137 (1999), 133–52

Schama, Simon, *A History of Britain: at the Edge of the World? 300BC–AD1603* (London)

Scharer, Anton, *Herrschaft und Repräsentation: Studien zur Hofkultur König Alfreds des Grossen*, Mitteilungen des Instituts für Österreichische Geschichtsforschung, Ergänzungsband 26 (Vienna)

Schulenburg, Jane Tibbets, *Forgetful of their Sex: Female Sanctity and Society, ca. 500–1100* (Chicago, 1998)

Sparks, Margaret, 'Gregory the Great: Apostle of England (540–604)', *Canterbury Cathedral Chronicle* 91 (1997), 19–23

Stafford, Pauline, '*Cherchez la femme.* Queens, Queens' Lands and Nunneries: Missing Links in the Foundation of Reading Abbey', *History* 85, 4–27

'Queens and Treasure in the Early Middle Ages', *Treasure in the Medieval West*, ed. Elizabeth M. Tyler (York), pp. 61–82

Story, Joanna, see sect. 5

Studd, Robin, 'Recorded "Waste" in the Staffordshire Domesday Entry', *Staffordshire Stud.* 12, 121–33

Syrett, Martin, 'Drengs and Thegns Again', *SBVS* 25, 243–71

Taylor, Martin I., *The Cradle of English Christianity: the Coming of St Augustine and St Martin's Church, Canterbury* (Canterbury, 1997)

Thacker, Alan, 'The Early Medieval City and its Buildings', *Medieval Archaeology, Art and Architecture at Chester*, ed. Alan Thacker, Brit. Archaeol. Assoc. Conference Trans. 22 (Leeds), 16–30

'In Search of Saints: the English Church and the Cult of Roman Apostles and Martyrs in the Seventh and Eighth Centuries', *Early Medieval Rome and the Christian West: Essays in Honour of Donald A. Bullough*, ed. Julia M. H. Smith (Leiden), pp. 247–77

'*Peculiaris patronus noster:* the Saint as Patron of the State in the Early Middle Ages', *The Medieval State*, ed. Maddicott and Palliser, pp. 1–24

Thier, Katrin, 'The Cobles: Celtic Boats in Anglo-Saxon Northumbria?', *Mariner's Mirror* 86, 131–9

Thompson, Victoria, 'Women, Power and Protection in Tenth- and Eleventh-Century England', *Medieval Women and the Law*, ed., Noël James Menuge (Woodbridge), pp. 1–17

Townend, Matthew, 'Viking Age England as a Bilingual Society', *Cultures in Contact*, ed. Hadley and Richards, pp. 89–105

Trafford, Simon, 'Ethnicity, Migration Theory, and the Historiography of the Scandinavian Settlement of England', *Cultures in Contact*, ed. Hadley and Richards, pp. 17–39

Truran, Margaret, 'The Roman Mission', *Monks of England: the Benedictines in England from Augustine to the Present Day*, ed. Daniel Rees (London, 1997), pp. 19–36

Turner, Sam, 'Aspects of the Development of Public Assembly in the Danelaw', *Assemblage* 5 [online]

Tyler, Elizabeth M., see sect. 4

Tyrrell, Andrew, '*Corpus Saxonum:* Early Medieval Bodies and Corporeal Identity', *Social Identity*, ed. Frazer and Tyrrell, pp. 137–55

Walker, Ian W., *Mercia and the Making of England* (Stroud)

Ward, Benedicta, *High King of Heaven: Aspects of Early English Spirituality* (Kalamazoo, MI, 1999)

'The Northumbrian Renaissance and its Missionary Dimension', *Monks of England: the Benedictines in England from Augustine to the Present Day*, ed. Daniel Rees (London, 1997), pp. 55–64 and 251–2

Ward-Perkins, Bryan, 'Why Did the Anglo-Saxons Not Become More British?', *EHR* 115, 513–33

Wareham, Andrew, '"The Feudal Revolution" in Eleventh-Century East Anglia', *ANS* 22, 293–321

Williams, Ann, 'Britain AD 1000', *Hist. Today* 50.3, 35–41

Williamson, Tom, *The Origins of Hertfordshire*, Origins of the Shire (Manchester)

Wolf, Gunther G., 'Die Peripatetie in des Bonfatius Wirksamkeit und die Resignation Karlmanns d.Ä 745/47', *Archiv für Diplomatik* 45 (1999), 1–5

Wood, Ian, 'Augustine's Journey', *Canterbury Cathedral Chronicle* 92 (1998), 28–44
  'Franken und Angelsachsen', *Die Franken*, ed. Wieczorek *et al.*, pp. 341–5

Woolf, Alex, 'Community, Identity and Kingship in Early England', *Social Identity*, ed. Frazer and Tyrrell, pp. 92–109

Yorke, Barbara, 'Political and Ethnic Identity: a Case Study of Anglo-Saxon Practice', *Social Identity*, ed. Frazer and Tyrrell, pp. 69–89

7. NUMISMATICS

Abdy, Richard, ed., 'Coin Register 1999', *BNJ* 69 (1999), 227–41 [includes sixty-nine finds of the Anglo-Saxon period]

[Anon.], 'Medieval and Post-Medieval Artefacts', *Treasure Ann. Report* 1997–8, 14–22 [includes two Anglo-Saxon finds]
  'Medieval Coin Finds', *Treasure Ann. Report* 1997–8, 39–44 [includes four Anglo-Saxon coin hoards]

Ashton, Richard, and Nicholas Mayhew, ed., 'Coin Hoards 2000', *NChron* 160, 309–67 [includes three Anglo-Saxon hoards at pp. 322–3]

Blackburn, Mark, 'Danish Silver Penny ("Sceat")', *Castle Park, Dunbar: Two Thousand Years on a Fortified Headland*, ed. D. R. Perry, Soc. of Antiq. of Scotland, Monograph Ser. 16 (Edinburgh), 168–9

Booth, James, 'Northumbrian Coinage and the Productive Site at South Newbald ("Sanction")', *Early Deira*, ed. Geake and Kenny, pp. 83–97

Byrne, Sue, 'A Wuneetton Type Thrymsa from Boulsdon, Newent', *Glevensis* 33, 43

Eaglen, Robin J., 'The Mint of Huntingdon', *BNJ* 69 (1999), 47–145

Evans, A. C., C. Paynton, B. Ager, L. Webster, H. Geake, S. M. Youngs, B. Adams, V. Porter, M. Redknap, H. Glass, and Norfolk Museums Service, 'Early Medieval Artefacts', *Treasure Ann. Report* 1998–9, 25–54 [fifty-seven gold or silver finds recorded]

Gamby, Erik, 'Olafa Rex Ancol.', *Svensk Numismatisk Tidskrift* 1991/8 (1991), 202–4 [author doubts *Ancol.* represents *Anglorum*]

Gurney, David, see sects. 9*g* and 9*i*

Harris, E. J., and D. R. Griffiths, 'Mercury Plating on Some Early English Coins', *BNJ* 69 (1999), 37–46

Hillaby, Joe, see sect. 6

Malmer, Brita, 'Om registrering av cirkulationsspår på mynt från vikingatiden', *Nordisk*

Numismatisk Unions Medlemsblad 2000, 23–6 [includes Anglo-Saxon coins]

Pagan, Hugh, 'A Missing Coin of Ælfred Rediscovered', *BNJ* 69 (1999), 199–200 [Danelaw imitation of Two-Line type, moneyer Franbald]

Pirie, Elizabeth, 'Northumbrian Stycas', *Castle Park, Dunbar: Two Thousand Years on a Fortified Headland*, ed. D. R. Perry, Soc. of Antiq. of Scotland, Monograph Ser. 16 (Edinburgh), 168

Thrymsas, Sceattas and Stycas of Northumbria. An Inventory of Finds Recorded to 1997, Northumbrian Numismatic Stud. 2 (Llanfyllin)

Sharp, Michael, 'A New Coin of Dir/Dernt', *NCirc* 107 (1999), 7 [Edward the Confessor, Small Flan type]

Stewartby, Lord, 'Ealdnod, a New Moneyer for Offa', *BNJ* 69 (1999), 199

Williams, Gareth, 'Anglo-Saxon and Viking Coin Weights', *BNJ* 69 (1999), 19–36 see also sect. 9*i*

Williams, G., C. Barclay, E. M. Besly, M. A. S. Blackburn, and D. Robinson, 'Early Medieval Coin Finds', *Treasure Ann. Report* 1998–9, 127–9 [eleven Anglo-Saxon coin hoards summarized]

8. ONOMASTICS

Ashley, Leonard R. N., 'The Saints Come Marching In: Saints' Names in the Toponymy of Cornwall', *Names* 48, 257–64

Bailey, Keith A., 'The Boundaries of Winslow – Some Comments', *Records of Buckinghamshire* 39 (1999 for 1997), 63–6

'Buckinghamshire Parish Names', *Records of Buckinghamshire* 40, 55–71 see also sect. 6 [Clofesho]

Blake, Martin, 'Assessing the Evidence for the Earliest Anglo-Saxon Place-Names in Bedfordshire', *JEPNS* 32, 5–20

Breeze, Andrew, 'A Celtic Etymology for the Name of Glazenwood, near Braintree', *Eseex Jnl* 33 (1998), 26–7

'The Celtic Name of the River Weaver', *Cheshire Hist.* 38 (1998–9), 2–4

'Eanwulf of Pennard and a Letter to Edward the Elder', *Dorset and Somerset Notes and Queries* 35, 2–3

'The Name of Cad Green, Ilton', *Dorset and Somerset Notes and Queries* 34, 355–6

'The Name of Doulting', *Dorset and Somerset Notes and Queries* 34, 349–52

'The Name of Hergest, Near Kington', *Trans. of the Radnorshire Soc.* 69 (1999), 176–7

'The Name of the River Cray', *AC* 118 (1998), 372–4

'The Name of the River Mite', *Trans. of the Cumberland and Westmorland Ant. and Archaeol. Soc.* 99 (1999), 277–8

'The Name of the River Test', *Hampshire Stud.* 53 (1998), 226–7

'The Name of the River Wear', *Durham Archaeol. Jnl* 13 (1997), 87–8

'The Name of Trunch, near North Walsham', *Norfolk Archaeol.* 43, 483–4

'The Names of Bridport, Bredv, and the River Bride', *Dorset and Somerset Notes and Queries* 34, 408–9

'The Names of Yorkshire's Cray Beck, River Balder and River Nidd', *Trans. of the Yorkshire Dialect Soc.* 19, 27–33

'Was Durham the Broninis of Eddius's Life of St Wilfrid?', *Durham Archaeol. Jnl* 14–15 (1999), 91–2

Cavill, Paul, 'Major Place-Names of the Wirral: a Gazetteer', Cavill, Harding, and Jesch, *Wirral and its Viking Heritage*, pp. 125–47

Coates, Richard, 'Dumpford Hundred', *Locus Focus: Forum of the Sussex Place-Names Net*, 2.2 (1998), 8

'Kirkford', *Locus Focus: Forum of the Sussex Place-Names Net*, 2.2 (1998), 7

'An Old English Technical Term of Woodland Management in South-East England?', *Locus Focus: Forum of the Sussex Place-Names Net*, 4.2, 17–19 [*slæf*]

'On the Later History of the Name of Lewes', *Locus Focus: Forum of the Sussex Place-Names Net*, 3.1 (1999), 18–20

'Plardiwick', *JEPNS* 32, 21–2

'The Sinodun Hills, Little Wittenham, Berkshire', *JEPNS* 32, 23–5

'Tangmere', *Sussex Past and Present* 88 (1999), 5 and 9

'Vanished Features and Coastal Place-Names: *Meeching, The Seven Charleses* and *Winchelsea*', *Locus Focus: Forum of the Sussex Place-Names Net*, 2.1 (1998), 11–14

'Vennemann on Arundel', *Locus Focus: Forum of the Sussex Place-Names Net*, 4.2, 5–6

'Wick', *Sussex Past and Present* 87 (1999), 5 and 7

Coates, Richard, and Andrew Breeze, with a contribution by David Horovitz, *Celtic Voices, English Places: Studies of the Celtic Impact on Place-Names in England* (Stamford)

Cole, Ann, '*Ersc*: Distribution and Use of this Old English Place-Name Element', *JEPNS* 32, 27–39

Cole, Ann, Janey Cumber, and Margaret Gelling, 'Old English *merece* "wild celery, small-age" in Place-Names', *Nomina* 23, 141–7

Combes, Pam, 'A Cross-Border Link: *Esledes* and *Eslede* in *Domesday Book*', *Locus Focus: Forum of the Sussex Place-Names Net*, 2.2 (1998), 6-7

'Crottebergh: Was it *Really* in Firle?', *Locus Focus: Forum of the Sussex Place-Names Net*, 3.2 (1999), 12–17

'How Many High *tūn*s were there in East Sussex?', *Locus Focus: Forum of the Sussex Place-Names Net*, 4.2, 9–16

'Now You See It Now You Don't: Firle in *Domesday Book* and Beyond', *Locus Focus: Forum of the Sussex Place-Names Net*, 1.3 (1997), 12–14

'Totnore's Talking-Point', *Locus Focus: Forum of the Sussex Place-Names Net*, 1.2 (1997), 10–12

'*Wildetone* and *Wildene* in *Domesday Book* – Settlements in the Wilderness?', *Locus Focus: Forum of the Sussex Place-Names Net*, 3.1 (1999), 17–18

Croft, R. A., and D. C. Mynard, see sect. 9*c*

Cullen, Paul, 'Courtup Farm in Nuthurst and the Den of *Curtehope* in Lamberhurst', *Locus Focus: Forum of the Sussex Place-Names Net*, 2.2 (1998), 15

Currie, Christopher K., see sect. 6

Ellerington, Enoch, 'The Lost Village of Earnshill and the Hill Called Duun Meten in Isle Abbotts', *Dorset and Somerset Notes and Queries* 34, 327–32

Fellows-Jensen, Gillian, 'Old English *sōcn* "soke" and the Parish in Scandinavia', *Namn och Bygd* 88, 89–106

'Place-Names in Context', *Archaeol. Dialogues* 4.2 (1997), 215–19

Field, John, 'Bibliography 1999–2000', *JEPNS* 32, 81–5

Fleming, Andrew, 'Patterns of Names, Patterns of Places', *Archaeol. Dialogues* 4.2 (1997), 199–214

Gardiner, Mark, '*Esteda* and the Character of Eleventh-Century Hastings', *Locus Focus: Forum of the Sussex Place-Names Net*, 3.2 (1999), 18–19

Garner, H. W., 'The Origin of the Name "Cawsand"', *Devon and Cornwall Notes and Queries* 38, 208–11

Gelling, Margaret, 'The Place-Names of South-West Shropshire', *The Gale of Life: Essays in the History and Archaeology of South-West Shropshire*, ed. John Leonard, D. Preshous, M. Roberts, J. Smyth, and C. Train (Shrewsbury), pp. 43–51

Gelling, Margaret, and Ann Cole, *The Landscape of Place-Names* (Stamford)

Hough, Carole, 'Bibliography for 1999', *Nomina* 23, 189–200

'Carolside in Berwickshire and *Carelholpit* in Lincolnshire', *Nomina* 23, 79–86

'The Field-Name *Felterrode*', *JEPNS* 32, 47–9

'ON *kill* in English Place-Names', *SN* 72, 1–5

'The Place-Name Cabus (Lancashire)', *N&Q* 47, 288–91

'The Place-Name Pitchcombe', *JEPNS* 32, 50–2

'A Sidelight on Binderton', *Locus Focus: Forum of the Sussex Place-Names Net*, 1.3 (1997), 11

'Sinkfall in Lancashire', *N&Q* 47, 168–9

Hughes, Robert, 'A Village with Two Names: The Names of Gladestry', *Trans. of the Radnorshire Soc.* 68 (1998), 96–104

Insley, John, 'Kultische Namen – England', *Reallexikon der germanischen Altertumskunde*, ed. Heinrich Beck, Dieter Geuenich, Heiko Steuer, and Dieter Timpe, 2nd ed. (Berlin) XVII, 425–37

'Länder- und Landschaftsnamen – England', *Reallexikon der germanischen Altertumskunde*, ed. Beck *et al.*, 2nd ed., XVII, 569–79

Jelley, Harry, 'Locating the Birthplace of St Patrick', *Brit. Archaeol.* 36 (1998), 10–11

Kristensson, Gillis, 'The Hundred-Name Desborough (Buckinghamshire)', *N&Q* 47, 402–3

'The Place-Name Owermoigne (Dorset)', *N&Q* 47, 5–6

'The Place-Name Yarnfield (Wiltshire)', *N&Q* 47, 4–5

Morris, P. A., 'Earnley Wood', *Proc. of the Dorset Natural Hist. and Archaeol. Soc.* 120 (1999 for 1998), 96–7

Padgham, David, 'Glesham in Beckley', *Locus Focus: Forum of the Sussex Place-Names Net*, 2.2 (1998), 16–17

'Where was Westfield Roman Villa? (With Some Thoughts on Other Westfield Place-Names)', *Locus Focus: Forum of the Sussex Place-Names Net*, 3.1 (1999), 14–16

Parsons, David N., and Tania Styles, *The Vocabulary of English Place-Names (brace – cæster)* (Nottingham)

Pile, John, 'Ora Place Names in the Portsmouth Area', *Hampshire Field Club and Archaeol. Soc. Newsletter* 33, 3–7

Reid, Bill, 'A Post-Roman Frontier in the Stroud Valleys? The Evidence from Place-Names', *Glevensis* 33, 9–16

Roberts, B. K., see sect. 6

Tew, David, 'Addenda to the Place-Names of Rutland', *JEPNS* 32, 94

Thomas, Peter W., 'The Name "Cawsand"', *Devon and Cornwall Notes and Queries* 38 (1997–99), 251–2

Tooth, Ernest E., 'The Survival of Scandinavian Personal Names in Staffordshire Surnames', *Staffordshire Stud.* 12, 1–16

Turner, Sam, see sect. 6

Watts, Victor, 'Some Place-Name Distributions', *JEPNS* 32, 53–72

9. ARCHAEOLOGY

a. General

[Anon.], 'Archaeological Notes', *Records of Buckinghamshire* 40, 109–12

  'Fieldwork and Excavation in 1999', *Med. Settlement Research Group Ann. Report* 14 (1999), 37–47

  'Research in 1992, ii: Excavations', *Med. Settlement Research Group Ann. Report* 7 (1992), 33–45

Bennet, Mark, and Naomi Field, ed., 'Archaeology in Lincolnshire 1999', *Lincolnshire Hist. and Archaeol.* 34 (1999), 24–37

Bennett, A., ed., 'Archaeology in Essex 1998', *Essex Archaeol. and Hist.* 30 (1999), 210–31

  'Work of the Essex County Council Archaeology Section, 1998', *Essex Archaeol. and Hist.* 30 (1999), 196–209 [includes report on a disc brooch by Sue Tyler]

Biggam, Carole P., see sect 2*a*

Bradley, John, and Märit Gaimster, 'Medieval Britain and Ireland in 1999', ed. Tom Beaumont James, *MA* 44, 235–354 [pre-Conquest index, pp. 240–1]

Brown, Nigel, and Jenny Glazebrook, ed., *Research and Archaeology: a Framework for the Eastern Counties*, II: *Research Agenda and Strategy*, East Anglian Archaeol. Occasional Papers 8 (Norwich)

Budd, P., B. Chapman, C. Jackson, R. Janaway, and B. Ottaway, ed., *Archaeological Sciences 1989: Proceedings of a Conference on the Application of Scientific Techniques to Archaeology, Bradford, September 1989*, Oxbow Monograph 9 (Oxford, 1991)

CBA [ed.], *Calendar of Excavations: Summaries 1974* (1974)

Cherry, John F., Clive Gamble, and Stephen Shennan, *Sampling in Contemporary British Archaeology*, BAR Brit. ser. 50 (Oxford, 1978)

Clough, T. H. McK., 'Rutland History and Archaeology in 1998–99', *Rutland Record* 20, 445–51

Corfe, Tom, 'Tynedale Before Wilfrid', *Archaeology North* 13 (1997), 24–6

Coy, Jennie, 'Birds as Food in Prehistoric and Historic Wessex', *Animals and Archaeology*, II: *Shell Middens, Fishes and Birds*, ed. Caroline Grigson and Juliet Clutton-Brock, BAR International ser. 183 (Oxford, 1983), 181–95 [suggests regional differences in early medieval fowl populations]

Dark, Ken, *Britain and the End of the Roman Empire* (Stroud)

Dark, Petra, *The Environment of Britain in the First Millennium AD* (London)

Dixon, Philip, 'How Saxon is the Saxon House?', *Structural Reconstruction*, ed. Drury, pp. 275–87

Drury, P. J., ed., *Structural Reconstruction: Approaches to the Interpretation of the Excavated Remains of Buildings*, BAR Brit. ser. 110 (Oxford, 1982)

Frodsham, Paul, Peter Topping, and Dave Cowley, ed., *'We Were Always Chasing Time': Papers presented to Keith Blood* (Newcastle-upon-Tyne, 1999) [a special edition of *Northern Archaeol.* (vol. 17/18)]

Gardiner, Julie, ed., *Flatlands and Wetlands: Current Themes in East Anglian Archaeology*, East Anglian Archaeol. Report 50 (Norwich, 1993)

Geake, Helen, and Jonathan Kenny, ed., *Early Deira: Archaeological Studies of the East Riding in the Fourth to Ninth Centuries A.D.* (Oxford)

Glass, Helen J., 'Archaeology of the Channel Tunnel Rail Link', *AC* 119 (1999), 189–220 [includes Saxon cemeteries and settlements]

Gurney, David, and Kenneth Penn, ed., 'Excavations and Surveys in Norfolk 1998', *Norfolk Archaeol.* 43 (1999), 369–87

'Excavations and Surveys in Norfolk 1999', *Norfolk Archaeol.* 43.3, 521–43

Hamerow, Helena, 'Anglo-Saxon Oxfordshire, 400–700', *Oxoniensia* 64 (1999), 23–38

Härke, Heinrich, 'The Circulation of Weapons in Anglo-Saxon Society', *Rituals of Power from Late Antiquity to the Early Middle Ages*, ed. Frans Theuws and Janet L. Nelson (Leiden), pp. 377–99

Hills, Catherine, 'Who Were the East Anglians?', *Flatlands and Wetlands*, ed. Gardiner, pp. 14–23

Hines, John, 'Welsh and English: Mutual Origins in Post-Roman Britain?', *Studia Celtica* 34, 81–104

Hines, John, Karen Høilund Nielsen, and Frank Siegmund, ed., *The Pace of Change: Studies in Early-Medieval Chronology*, Cardiff Stud. in Archaeol. (Oxford, 1999)

Holroyd, Isabel, and Jeremy Oetgen, ed., *British and Irish Archaeological Bibliography, Volume 4*, 2 vols. (London)

Horne, Barry, ed., 'Bedfordshire', *South Midlands Archaeol.* 30, 1–8

'Buckinghamshire', *South Midlands Archaeol.* 30, 9–33

'Northamptonshire', *South Midlands Archaeol.* 30, 33–43

'Oxfordshire', *South Midlands Archaeol.* 30, 43–91

Howe, Tony, Gary Jackson, Cath Maloney, and Dinah Saich, 'Archaeology in Surrey 1997–9', *Surrey Archaeol. Collections* 87, 183–218

Huggins, Peter, Kirsty Rodwell, and Warwick Rodwell, 'Anglo-Saxon and Scandinavian Building Measurements', *Structural Reconstruction*, ed. Drury, pp. 21–65

Huntley, Jacqueline P., and Sue Stallibrass, *Plant and Vertebrate Remains from Archaeological Sites in Northern England: Data Reviews and Future Directions*, Archit. and Archaeol. Soc. of Durham and Northumberland Research Reports 4 (Durham, 1995) [includes early medieval sections]

Janes, Dominic, 'Treasure, Death and Display from Rome to the Middle Ages', *Treasure in the Medieval West*, ed. Elizabeth M. Tyler (York), pp. 1–10

Lucy, Sam, *The Anglo-Saxon Way of Death: Burial Rites in Early England* (Stroud)

Martin, Edward, *et al.*, 'Archaeology in Suffolk 1999', *Proc. of the Suffolk Inst. of Archaeol. and Hist.* 39 (1997–2000), 495–531

Rahtz, Philip, 'Anglo-Saxon Yorkshire: Current Research Problems', *Early Deira*, ed. Geake and Kenny, pp. 1–9

Ramsey, C. Bronk, P. B. Pettitt, R. E. M. Hedges, G. W. L. Hodgins, and D. C. Owen, 'Radiocarbon Dates from the Oxford AMS System: *Archaeometry* Datelist 30', *Archaeometry* 42, 459–79 [includes Saxon samples]

Reece, Richard, Carolyn Heighway, and Richard Sermon, 'Britons and Saxons in Gloucestershire', *Glevensis* 33, 3–8

Reynolds, Andrew, 'Executions and Hard Anglo-Saxon Justice', *Brit. Archaeol.* 31 (1998), 8–9

Reynolds, Tim, Jeremy Parsons, Tim Malim, and Ben Robinson, 'Field-Work in Cambridge 1999', *Proc. of the Cambridge Ant. Soc.* 89, 91–101

Roskams, Steve, ed., *Interpreting Stratigraphy 8: Proceedings of a Conference Held at the Department of Archaeology, University of York on 15th February, 1996* (York, 1996)

Russell, B. E., ed., *Gazetteer of Archaeological Investigations in England 1998*, Brit. and Irish Archaeol. Bibliography Supplement 9 (Bournemouth)

Saunders, Tom, 'Class, Space and "Feudal" Identities in Early Medieval England', *Social Identity*, ed. Frazer and Tyrrell, pp. 209–32

Scull, Christopher, and Alex Bayliss, 'Dating Burials of the Seventh and Eighth Centuries: a Case Study from Ipswich, Suffolk', *The Pace of Change*, ed. Hines *et al.*, pp. 80–8

Sinclair, Anthony, Elizabeth Slater, and John Gowlett, ed., *Archaeological Sciences 1995: Proceedings of a Conference on the Application of Scientific Techniques to the Study of Archaeology, Liverpool, July 1995*, Oxbow Monograph 64 (Oxford, 1997)

Talbot, G. J., ed., *Gazetteer of Archaeological Investigations in England 1997*, Brit. and Irish Archaeol. Bibliography Supplement 8 (Bournemouth)

Tees Archaeology, *Anglo-Saxon Teesside*, Archaeol. Booklet 1 (Hartlepool)

Tyrrell, Andrew, see sect. 6

Ulmschneider, Katharina, *Markets, Minsters and Metal-Detectors: the Archaeology of Middle Saxon Lincolnshire and Hampshire Compared*, BAR Brit. ser. 307 (Oxford)

[Various], 'Archaeology in Leicestershire and Rutland, 1997', *Leicestershire Archaeol. and Hist. Soc. Trans.* 72 (1998), 156–95

'Archaeology in Leicestershire and Rutland, 1999', *Leicestershire Archaeol. and Hist. Soc. Trans.* 74, 223–60

'Excavations by Cambridgeshire County Council Archaeology Section, August 1989–August 1990', *CBA Group VII Bull.* 11 (1990), 6–10

Webster, Leslie, 'Ideal and Reality: Versions of Treasure in the Early Anglo-Saxon World', *Treasure in the Medieval West*, ed. Elizabeth M. Tyler (York), pp. 49–59

Wills, Jan, and Julian Rawes, ed., 'Archaeological Review No. 23, 1998', *Trans. of the Bristol and Gloucestershire Archaeol. Soc.* 117 (1999), 167–86

Wilson, Catherine M., 'Archaeological Notes 1970', *Lincolnshire Hist. and Archaeol.* 6 (1971), 3–17

b. Towns and other major settlements

Albarella, U., *The Late Saxon and Early Medieval Mammal and Bird Bones Excavated in 1995 from Mill Lane, Thetford, Norfolk*, Ancient Monuments Laboratory Report 5 (1999) (Portsmouth)

Andrews, Phil, Lorraine Mepham, and Rachael Seager Smith, 'Excavations at Wilton, 1995–6: St John's Hospital and South Street', *Wiltshire Archaeol. Mag.* 93, 181–204 [includes Late Saxon defences and occupation]

[Anon.], 'How Norwich Began', *CA* 170, 48–51

Astill, Grenville G., 'Archaeological Theory and the Origins of English Towns – a Review', *Archaeologia Polona* 32 (1994), 27–71

Atkin, Malcolm, 'The Norwich Survey 1971–1985: a Retrospective View', *Flatlands and Wetlands*, ed. Gardiner, pp. 127–43

Ayers, Brian, 'Anglo-Saxon, Medieval and Post-Medieval (Urban)', *Research and Archaeology*, ed. Brown and Glazebrook, pp. 27–32

Bennett, Paul, 'Christ Church College', *Canterbury Archaeol. Trust Ann. Report* 10 (1986 for 1985–6), 8 [evidence for Saxon occupation in the College grounds]

Blackmore, Lyn, 'The Origins of Lundenwic?', *Archaeol. Matters* 11, [6]

Blair, John, see sect. 6

Blockley, Paul, 'No. 41 St George's Street', *Canterbury Archaeol. Trust Ann. Report* 10 (1986 for 1985–6), 6

Booth, James, see sect. 7

Bourdillon, Jennifer, *Animal Bones Scanned from Contexts on Sites SOU 26 and SOU 169 (Saxon Southampton, Six Dials)*, Ancient Monuments Laboratory Report 59 (1986) (London)

Animal Bones Scanned from Street Contexts in the Six Dials Excavations (Saxon Southampton), Ancient Monuments Laboratory Report 57 (1986) (London)

Bowsher, David, and Gordon Malcolm, 'Excavations at the Royal Opera House: Middle Saxon London', *Trans. of the London and Middlesex Archaeol. Soc.* 50 (1999), 4–11

Carter, A., 'Sampling in a Medieval Town: the Study of Norwich', *Sampling in Contemporary British Archaeology*, ed. Cherry *et al.*, pp. 263–77

Cessford, Craig, 'Pine Marten and Other Animal Species in the Poem *Dinogad's Smock*', *Environmental Archaeol.* 2 (1998), 71–2 [supporting evidence for animal bones from Anglo-Scandinavian York]

Charles, F. W. B., 'The Construction of Buildings with Irregularly-Spaced Posts', *Structural Reconstruction*, ed. Drury, pp. 101–12 [includes Cheddar]

Colyer, Christina, *et al.*, 'Flaxengate', *Lincoln Archaeological Trust, Third Annual Report, 1974–1975*, ed. [Lincoln Archaeological Trust] (Lincoln, 1975), 13–18

Dobney, Keith, Allan Hall, and Harry Kenward, 'The Bioarchaeology of Anglo-Saxon Yorkshire: Present and Future Perspectives', *Early Deira*, ed. Geake and Kenny, pp. 133–40 [York]

Down, Alec, *Chichester Excavations VI* (Chichester, 1989) [includes addendum to Saxon gazetteer by R. R. Morgan and Alec Down]

Frodsham, Paul, 'Forgetting *Gefrin*: Elements of the Past in the Past at Yeavering', *'We Were Always Chasing Time'*, ed. Frodsham *et al.*, pp. 191–207

Hall, A. R., A. K. G. Jones, and H. K. Kenard, 'Cereal Bran and Human Faecal Remains from Archaeological Deposits – Some Preliminary Observations', *Site, Environment and Economy*, ed. Bruce Proudfoot, BAR International ser. 173 (Oxford, 1983), 85–104 [uses a sample from Anglo-Scandinavian York]

Hall, R. A., 'Anglo-Scandinavian Attitudes: Archaeological Ambiguities in Late Ninth-to Mid-Eleventh-Century York', *Cultures in Contact*, ed. Hadley and Richards, pp. 311–24

'The Decline of the *Wic*', *Towns in Decline, AD 100–1600*, ed. T. R. Slater (Aldershot), pp. 120–36

Hamilton, Bob, 'Castles and the Children of Alfred', *Assemblage* 5 [online]

Hill, David, see sects. 6 and 9*c*

Hines, John, 'North Sea and the Proto-Urban Sequence', *Archaeologia Polona* 32 (1994), 7–26

Hinton, David A., 'Decay and Revival: Early Medieval Urban Landscapes', *The English Urban Landscape*, ed. Philip Waller (Oxford), pp. 55–73

'The Large Towns 600–1300', *The Cambridge Urban History of Britain*, I: *600–1540*, ed. D. M. Palliser (Cambridge), pp. 217–43

Holder, Nick, David Bowsher, and Ken Pitt, with Lyn Blackmore, 'Across the Saxon Town: Three New Sites in *Lundenwic*', *London Archaeologist* 9.6, 151–9

Jones, Andrew K. G., *Fish Remains from Excavation at Thetford, 1964–1966*, Ancient Monuments Laboratory Report 7 (1986) (London)

Keene, Derek, 'The Medieval Urban Landscape, AD 900–1540', *The English Urban Landscape*, ed. Philip Waller (Oxford), pp. 74–98

Kenward, Harry, and Maureen Girling, *Arthropod Remains from Archaeological Sites in Southampton*, Ancient Monuments Laboratory Report 46 (1986) (London) [mostly Saxon]

Kenward, Harry, and Frances Large, 'Insects in Urban Waste Pits in Viking York: Another Kind of Seasonality', *Environmental Archaeol.* 3 (1998), 35–53

[Lincoln Archaeological Trust], ed., *Archaeology in Lincoln 1982–1983: Eleventh Annual Report of Lincoln Archaeological Trust* (Lincoln, 1983)

Lincoln Archaeological Trust Ninth Annual Report, 1980–81 (Lincoln, 1981)

Lincoln Archaeological Trust Seventh Annual Report, 1978–1979 (Lincoln, 1979)

Mainman, A. J., and N. S. H. Rogers, see sect. 9*g*

Manco, Jean, see sect. 6

Mason, D. J. P., '"And The Walls Came Tumbling Down": Excavations Adjacent to the City Walls in St John Street 1988/9', *Jnl of the Chester Archaeol. Soc.* 73 (1998 for 1994–5), 11–20 [post-Roman renewal of town defences]

Moulden, Joan, and Dominic Tweddle, *Anglo-Scandinavian Settlement South-West of the Ouse*, Archaeol. of York 8.1 (London, 1986)

Murphy, Peter, *Fishergate, Norwich (Site 732N): Environmental Studies*, Ancient Monuments Laboratory Report 38 (1986) (London)

O'Connor, T. P., *Bones from Archaeological Deposits in York: an Overview of Results to 1986*, Ancient Monuments Laboratory Report 47 (1986) (London)

Payne, A. W., *Bishop's Palace Garden, Peterborough Cathedral, Cambridgeshire: Report on Resistivity Survey, September 1996*, Ancient Monuments Laboratory Report 55 (Portsmouth) [western defences of the Saxon *burh*]

Perring, Dom, 'Early Medieval Development at Flaxengate', *Lincoln Archaeological Trust, Ninth Annual Report, 1980–81*, ed. [Lincoln Archaeological Trust] (Lincoln, 1981), 17–19

Richards, Julian, 'Defining Settlements: York and its Hinterland AD 700–1000', *Courts and Regions in Medieval Europe*, ed. Sarah Rees Jones, Richard Marks and A. J. Minnis (York), pp. 45–74

Rogerson, Andrew, 'Vikings and the New East Anglian Towns', *Brit. Archaeol.* 35 (1998), 12–13

Samson, Ross, 'Populous Dark-Age Towns: the Finleyesque Approach', *Jnl of European Archaeol.* 2 (1994), 97–129

Schofield, John, and Tony Dyson, *Archaeology of the City of London* (London, 1980)

Smith, J. T., 'The Validity of Inference from Archaeological Evidence', *Structural Reconstruction*, ed. Drury, pp. 7–19 [includes Cheddar and Yeavering]

Spoerry, Paul, 'The Topography of Anglo-Saxon Huntingdon: a Survey of the Archaeological and Historical Evidence', *Proc. of the Cambridge Ant. Soc.* 89, 35–47

Treveil, Philip, and Mark Burch, 'Number 1 Poultry and the Development of Medieval Cheapside', *Trans. of the London and Middlesex Archaeol. Soc.* 50 (1999), 55–60 [includes a Late Saxon phase]

Ulmschneider, Katharina, 'Settlement, Economy, and the "Productive" Site: Middle Anglo-Saxon Lincolnshire, A.D. 650–780', *MA* 44, 53–79

Vince, Alan, 'A Tale of Two Cities: Lincoln and London Compared', *Flatlands and Wetlands*, ed. Gardiner, pp. 152–70

Wade, Keith, 'Sampling at Ipswich: the Origins and Growth of the Anglo-Saxon Town', *Sampling in Contemporary British Archaeology*, ed. Cherry *et al.*, pp. 279–84

'The Urbanisation of East Anglia: the Ipswich Perspective', *Flatlands and Wetlands*, ed. Gardiner, pp. 144–51

Watson, Bruce, 'Excavations and Observations at Minster Court and Minster Pavement, Mincing Lane in the City of London', *Trans. of the London and Middlesex Archaeol. Soc.* 47 (1998 for 1996), 87–102 [includes a Saxo-Norman phase]

White, Roger, 'Wroxeter and the Transformation of Late-Roman Urbanism', *Towns in Decline, AD 100–1600*, ed. T. R. Slater (Aldershot), pp. 96–119 [including early post-Roman urbanism]

Wilson, Bob, *Spatial Patterning among Animal Bones in Settlement Archaeology: an English Regional Exploration*, BAR Brit. ser 251 (Oxford, 1996) [includes a chapter on Late Saxon Oxford and Abingdon]

Woodiwiss, Simon, ed., *Iron Age and Roman Salt Production and the Medieval Town of Droitwich: Excavations at the Old Bowling Green and Friar Street*, CBA Research Report 81 (London, 1992) [includes a Saxon phase]

Wroe-Brown, Robin, 'The Saxon Origins of Queenhithe', *Trans. of the London and Middlesex Archaeol. Soc.* 50 (1999), 12–16

c. Rural settlements, agriculture and the countryside

Albarella, Umberto, *The Early to Late Saxon Animal Bones Excavated in 1995 from Kings Meadow Lane, Higham Ferrers, Northamptonshire*, Ancient Monuments Laboratory Report 79 (Portsmouth)

'"The Mystery of Husbandry": Medieval Animals and the Problem of Integrating Historical and Archaeological Evidence', *Antiquity* 73 (1999), 867–75

[Anon.], 'Fishing the Saxon Way', *Essex Archaeol.* 14 (1997), ii [fish weirs]

'Oops – These Roman Wells were Saxon!', *Essex Archaeol.* 7 (1990), viii [wells near Maldon]

'Saxon Fishing Industry Discovered', *Essex Archaeol.* 15 (1998), i [fish weirs]

'Sedgeford: Exploring an Early English Village', *CA* 171, 122–9

Barnes, Ian, J. P. W. Young, and K. M. Dobney, 'DNA-Based Identification of Goose Species from Two Archaeological Sites in Lincolnshire', *Jnl of Archaeol. Science* 27, 91–100 [one site is Flixborough]

Beresford, Guy, 'The Reconstruction of Some Saxon Buildings at Goltho, Lincolnshire', *Structural Reconstruction*, ed. Drury, pp. 113–23

Berryman, R. D., see sect. 6

Butler, Chris, *Saxon Settlement and Earlier Remains at Friars Oak, Hassocks, West Sussex*, BAR Brit. ser. 295 (Oxford)

Cawse, J. L., ed., 'Field Work in Shudy Camps, 1998–9', *Jnl of the Haverhill and District Archaeol. Group* 7.1 (1999), 8–69

Champion, Timothy, 'Strategies for Sampling a Saxon Settlement: a Retrospective View of Chalton', *Sampling in Contemporary British Archaeology*, ed. Cherry *et al.*, pp. 207–25

Croft, R. A., and D. C. Mynard, *The Changing Landscape of Milton Keynes*, Buckinghamshire Archaeol. Soc. Monograph ser. 5 (Aylesbury, 1993) [includes a section on place-names by Margaret Gelling]

Cunliffe, B. W., 'The Evolution of Romney Marsh: a Preliminary Statement', *Archaeology and Coastal Change, Being the Papers presented at Meetings in London and Manchester on 27th October and 5th November 1977*, ed. F. H. Thompson, Soc. of Antiquaries of London Occasional Paper ns 1 (London, 1980), 37–55

Dobney, Keith, Allan Hall, and Harry Kenward, see sect. 9*b*

Enright, Dawn, and David Kenyon, 'The Origins of a Cotswold Village: Evidence from Recent Excavations at Lower Slaughter', *Glevensis* 33, 56–8

Ford, Steve, 'Excavation of Saxon Structures and Bronze Age Features at Bentley Green Farm, Bentley, Hampshire, 1994', *Hampshire Stud.* 52 (1997), 59–75

Foster, I. D. L., T. M. Mighall, C. Wotton, P. N. Owens, and D. E. Walling, 'Evidence for Medieval Soil Erosion in the South Hams Region of Devon, U.K.', *Holocene* 10.2, 261–71 [pre- and post-Conquest]

Green, Francis J., and Kris Lockyear, 'Seeds, Sherds and Samples: Site Formation Processes at the Waitrose Site, Romsey', *Whither Environmental Archaeology*, ed. Rosemary Luff and Peter Rowley-Conwy, Oxbow Monograph 38 (Oxford, 1994), 91–104

Hall, David, and John Coles, *Fenland Survey: an Essay in Landscape and Persistence*, English Heritage Archaeol. Report 1 (London, 1994)

Halsall, Guy, 'The Viking Presence in England? The Burial Evidence Reconsidered', *Cultures in Contact*, ed. Hadley and Richard, pp. 259–76

Hill, David, 'Offa Versus the Welsh', *Brit. Archaeol.* 56, 18–23 [Offa's Dyke]
    see also sect. 6

Huggins, P. J., 'Waltham Abbey: the Middle and Late Saxon Evidence', *CBA Group VII Bull.* 5 (1987), [37–40]

Huntley, Jacqueline P., 'Saxon-Norse Economy in Northern Britain: Food for

Thought', *Durham Archaeol. Jnl* 14–15 (1999), 77–81

Johnston, D. E., 'A Roman and Anglo-Saxon Site at Northbrook, Micheldever, Hampshire', *Hampshire Stud.* 53 (1998), 79–108

Kelsey, Jim, 'Stowical Saxons Reveal their Secrets', *Hist. Today* 49.10, 5 [West Stow]

Knight, H., 'Excavations at Colham Mill Road, West Drayton', *Trans. of the London and Middlesex Archaeol. Soc.* 49 (1999 for 1998), 99–106 [possible Late Saxon hemp-retting site]

Lane, Tom, 'The Fenland Project in Lincolnshire: Recent Evaluations', *Fenland Research* 8 (1994 for 1993), 40-2 [includes Saxon settlement in Gosberton parish]

Lane, Tom, and Peter Hayes, 'Moving Boundaries in the Fens of South Lincolnshire', *Flatlands and Wetlands*, ed. Gardiner, pp. 58–70 [includes Anglo-Saxon]

Leah, Mark, 'The Fenland Management Project, Norfolk', *Fenland Research* 7 (1992), 49–59 [includes excavations at the Middle Saxon sites of West Walton, Walpole St Andrew, and Hay Green]

Leah, Mark, and A. Crowson, 'Norfolk Archaeological Unit, The Fenland Management Project', *Fenland Research* 8 (1994 for 1993), 43–50 [includes excavations at the Early Saxon site of Tilney St Lawrence, and of a sea bank at Clenchwarton]

Linford, P. K., and M. A. Cole, *Beerway Farm, Shapwick, Somerset: Report on Geophysical Survey, 1999*, Ancient Monuments Laboratory Report 2 (Portsmouth, 1999) [includes early medieval features]

Maloney, Cath, 'Fieldwork Round-Up, 1999', *London Archaeologist* 9, supplement 2, 35–62 [includes Saxon settlement outside London]

Martin, Gerry, and Deborah Sawday, 'Excavations to the West of Orchard Lane, Great Glen (SP 655 973)', *Leicestershire Archaeol. and Hist. Soc. Trans.* 65 (1991), 89–96 [includes Saxon earthworks and pottery]

Matthews, K., 'A Futile Occupation?: Archaeological Meanings and Occupation Deposits', *Interpreting Stratigraphy*, ed. J. W. Barber (Edinburgh, 1993), 55–61 [a case study of the Saxon settlement at Rodenhanger, Herts.]

Mortimer, Richard, 'Village Development and Ceramic Sequence: the Middle to Late Saxon Village at Lordship Lane, Cottenham, Cambridgeshire', *Proc. of the Cambridge Ant. Soc.* 89, 5–33

Murphy, P., 'Environmental Archaeology: a Review of Progress', *Fenland Research* 7 (1992), 35–9 [includes Saxon sites at West Walton, Walpole St Andrew, and Terrington St Clement]

Noort, Robert Van de, 'Where are Yorkshire's "Terps"?: Wetland Exploitation in the Early Medieval Period', *Early Deira*, ed. Geake and Kenny, pp. 121–31

Palmer, Stuart C., 'Archaeological Excavations in the Arrow Valley, Warwickshire', *Birmingham and Warwickshire Archaeol. Soc. Trans.* 103 (1999), 1–230 [Saxon occupation and landscape, pp. 197–222]

Parfitt, Keith, 'Anglo-Saxon Eastry: Some Recent Discoveries and Excavations', *AC* 119 (1999), 45–53

Pearson, Trevor, 'Early Medieval Settlement of the Yorkshire Coast', *'We Were Always Chasing Time'*, ed. Frodsham *et al.*, pp. 159–64

Pelling, Ruth, and Mark Robinson, 'Saxon Emmer Wheat from the Upper and Middle Thames Valley, England', *Environmental Archaeol.* 5, 117–19

Powlesland, Dominic, 'West Heslerton Settlement Mobility: a Case of Static Development', *Early Deira*, ed. Geake and Kenny, pp. 19–26

Reynolds, Andrew, 'Yatesbury: Vikings and Villages in North Wiltshire', *CA* 171, 113–18

Richards, Julian D., 'Anglo-Saxon Settlements and Archaeological Visibility in the Yorkshire Wolds', *Early Deira*, ed. Geake and Kenny, pp. 27–39

    'Cottam: an Anglian and Anglo-Scandinavian Settlement on the Yorkshire Wolds', *ArchJ* 156 (1999), 1–110

    'Identifying Anglo-Scandinavian Settlements', *Cultures in Contact*, ed. Hadley and Richards, pp. 295–309

Rogerson, Andrew, Alan Davison, David Pritchard, and Robert Silvester, *Barton Bendish and Caldecote: Fieldwork in South-West Norfolk*, East Anglian Archaeol. Report 80 (Gressenhall, 1997)

Russell, Vivien, and Stephen Moorhouse, 'Excavation Near the Bishop's Palace at Nettleham, 1959', *Lincolnshire Hist. and Archaeol.* 6 (1971), 19–27 [includes Saxon settlement]

Saunders, M. J., and S. D. G. Weaver, 'Battlebridge Lane, Merstham: a Late Iron Age / Early Roman Settlement Enclosure with Prehistoric and Early / Middle Saxon Deposits (TQ 2872 5244)', *Surrey Archaeol. Soc. Bull.* 340, 3–5

Silvester, R. J., '"The Addition of More-or-Less Undifferentiated Dots to a Distribution Map"? The Fenland Project in Retrospect', *Flatlands and Wetlands*, ed. Gardiner, pp. 24–39 [includes Anglo-Saxon settlement]

Tingle, Martin, *The Vale of the White Horse Survey: the Study of a Changing Landscape in the Clay Lowlands of Southern England from Prehistory to the Present*, BAR Brit. ser. 218 (Oxford, 1991) [for the Saxon period, see especially pp. 68–81]

Turnbull, Deb, Martin Milner, and Patrick Hislop, 'Pyramid, Perimeters, and Poles: Timber Solutions for Modern Buildings in an Anglo-Saxon Village', *Structural Engineer* 77.15 (1999), 15–17

Twest, Melanie Van, 'Sedgeford Historical and Archaeological Project, 1999: Fourth Interim Report', *Norfolk Archaeol.* 43, 512–16 [includes Saxon settlement and cemetery]

Tyers, I., *Tree-Ring Analysis of Additional Archaeological Timbers from the AD 1979–84 Excavations at Staunch Meadow, Brandon, Suffolk*, Ancient Monuments Laboratory Report 33 (Portsmouth) [timbers associated with Middle Saxon activity]

Wade, Keith, 'Anglo-Saxon and Medieval (Rural)', *Research and Archaeology*, ed. Brown and Glazebrook, pp. 23–6

Watts, Lorna, and Philip Rahtz, 'Society Funded Research at Kirkdale', *Med. Archaeol. Newsletter* 15 (1996), 5 [the area around the Saxon church]

Whitworth, Alan Michael, *Hadrian's Wall: Some Aspects of its Post-Roman Influence on the Landscape*, BAR Brit. ser. 296 (Oxford)

d. Pagan cemeteries and Sutton Hoo

Abramson, Philip, 'A Re-Examination of a Viking Age Burial at Beacon Hill, Aspatria', *Trans. of the Cumberland and Westmorland Ant. and Archaeol. Soc.* 100, 79–88

Albone, James, and Kevin Leahy, 'The Anglo-Saxon Cemetery at Tallington, Lincolnshire', *ASSAH* 11, 143–71

[Anon.], 'Chelmsford Bronze Age and Saxon Site', *Essex Archaeol.* 1 (1984), i

'Saxon Royal Cemetary [*sic*] Discovered in Southampton', *Brit. Archaeol.* 54, 7

'Sixth Century Cemetery Points to Origins of Sutton Hoo', *Brit. Archaeol.* 54, 5 [small cemetery near Sutton Hoo]

Ashwin, Trevor, and Sarah Bates, *Excavations on the Norwich Southern Bypass, 1989–91, Part I: Excavations at Bixley, Caistor St Edmund, Trowse, Cringleford and Little Melton*, East Anglian Archaeol. Report 91 (Gressenhall) [includes Early to Middle Saxon burials]

Bethell, P. H., 'Inorganic Analysis of Organic Residues at Sutton Hoo', *Archaeological Sciences 1989*, ed. Budd *et al.*, pp. 316–18

Brugmann, Birte, 'The Role of Continental Artefact-Types in Sixth-Century Kentish Chronology', *The Pace of Change*, ed. Hines *et al.*, pp. 37–64

Buckberry, Jo, 'Missing, Presumed Buried?: Bone Diagenesis and the Under-Representation of Anglo-Saxon Children', *Assemblage* 5 [online]

Canterbury Archaeological Trust, and Wessex Archaeology, 'Saltwood', *CA* 168, 462–3 [sixth- to seventh-century burials, Kent]

Carver, Martin, 'Boat-Burial in Britain: Ancient Custom or Political Signal?', *The Ship as Symbol in Prehistoric and Medieval Scandinavia: Papers from an International Research Seminar at the Danish National Museum, Copenhagen, 5th–7th May 1994*, ed. Ole Crumlin-Pedersen and Birgitte Munch Thye (Copenhagen 1995), pp. 111–24

'Burial as Poetry: the Context of Treasure in Anglo-Saxon Graves', *Treasure in the Medieval West*, ed. Elizabeth M. Tyler (York), pp. 25–48

'Graphic Recording at Sutton Hoo: Single Instrument Remote Plotting – With No Strings Attached', *Field Archaeologist* 7 (1987), 102–3

Cave-Penney, Helena, '"Time Team" and the Saxon Cemetery at Winterbourne Gunder', *Field Archaeologist* 23 (1995), 22–3

Cessford, Craig, 'A Possible Anglo-Saxon Burial at Castle Hill, Ayrshire', *ASSAH* 11, 187–9

Dillon, John, 'Saxon Croydon', *Archaeol. Matters* 11, [5] [fifth- to seventh-century burials]

Hawkes, Sonia Chadwick, 'The Anglo-Saxon Cemetery of Bifrons, in the Parish of Patrixbourne, East Kent', ed. E. Cameron and H. Hamerow, *ASSAH* 11, 1–94

Hines, John, 'The Sixth-Century Transition in Anglian England: an Analysis of Female Graves from Cambridgeshire', *The Pace of Change*, ed. Hines *et al.*, pp. 65–79

Huggett, Jeremy W., 'Numerical Techniques for Burial Analysis', *Computer Applications and Quantitative Methods in Archaeology 1993*, ed. John Wilcock and Kris Lockyear, BAR International ser. 598 (Oxford, 1995), 183–90 [early Anglo-Saxon inhumation burials]

'Social Analysis of Early Anglo-Saxon Inhumation Burials: Archaeological Methodologies', *Jnl of European Archaeol.* 4 (1997 for 1996), 337–65

Hummler, Madeleine, and Annette Roe, 'Sutton Hoo Burials: Reconstructing the Sequence of Events', *Interpreting Stratigraphy 8*, ed. Roskams, pp. 39–53

Knüsel, Christopher, and Kathryn Ripley, 'The *Berdache* or Man-Woman in Anglo-Saxon England and Early Medieval Europe', *Social Identity*, ed. Frazer and Tyrrell, pp. 157–91

Lucy, Sam, 'Early Medieval Burials in East Yorkshire: Reconsidering the Evidence', *Early Deira*, ed. Geake and Kenny, pp. 11–18

Murphy, Peter, *Spong Hill, North Elmham, Norfolk: Plant Remains from Iron Age, Roman and Anglo-Saon Contexts (1972–84)*, Ancient Monuments Laboratory Report 39 (London, 1986)

Museum of London Archaeology Service, 'Cuxton Anglo-Saxon Cemetery', *CA* 168, 460–1 [Kent]

Newman, John, 'Return to Sutton Hoo: a New Era of Discovery', *Rescue News* 82, 1–2

O'Brien, Colm, 'Thirlings Building C: a Pagan Shrine?', *AAe* 28, 47–9

O'Brien, Elizabeth, *Post-Roman Britain to Anglo-Saxon England: Burial Practices Reviewed*, BAR Brit. ser. 289 (Oxford, 1999)

Penn, Kenneth, *Excavations on the Norwich Southern Bypass, 1989–91*, II: *The Anglo-Saxon Cemetery at Harford Farm, Caistor St Edmund, Norfolk*, East Anglian Archaeol. Report 92 (Gressenhall)

Penn, Kenneth, and Phil Andrews, 'An Early Saxon Cemetery at Brunel Way, Thetford', *Norfolk Archaeol.* 43, 415–40

Ravn, Mads, 'The Use of Symbols in Burials in Migration Age Europe: a Theoretical and Methodological Approach', *Form, Function & Context: Material Culture Studies in Scandinavian Archaeology*, ed. Deborah Olausson and Helle Vandkilde, Acta Archaeologica Lundensia, ser. in 8° 31 (Lund), 275–97 [includes Spong Hill]

Samuels, John, and Aleck Russell, 'An Anglo-Saxon Burial near Winthorpe Road, Newark, Nottinghamshire', *Trans of the Thoroton Soc. of Nottinghamshire* 103 (1999), 57–83

Sharman, Josephine, and Patrick Clay, 'Leicester Lane, Enderby: an Archaeological Evaluation', *Leicestershire Archaeol. and Hist. Soc. Trans.* 65 (1991), 1–12 [includes Saxon burials]

Stoodley, Nick, 'Communities of the Dead: the Evidence for Living Populations from Early Anglo-Saxon Cemeteries', *Authority and Community in the Middle Ages*, ed. Donald Mowbray, Rhiannon Purdie, and Ian P. Wei (Stroud, 1999), 1–17

'From the Cradle to the Grave: Age Organization and the Early Anglo-Saxon Burial Rite', *World Archaeol.* 31 (1999), 456–72

The Spindle and the Spear: a Critical Enquiry into the Construction and Meaning of Gender in the Early Anglo-Saxon Burial Rite, BAR Brit. ser. 288 (Oxford, 1999)

Turner-Walker, G., and C. J. Scull, 'Microfauna in Anglo-Saxon Graves: Entomological Evidence at Boss Hall and the Butter Market, Ipswich', *Archaeological Sciences 1995*, ed. Sinclair *et al.*, pp. 320–7

Vallet, Françoise, see sect. 9*g*

Welch, Martin G., 'The Re-Discovery of the Early Anglo-Saxon Cemetery at Croydon in 1992 and its Partial Excavation in 1999: Trials and Tribulations', *Proc. of the Croydon Nat. Hist. and Scientific Soc.* 18.6, 129–42

Wymer, J. J., and N. R. Brown, *Excavations at North Shoebury: Settlement and Economy in South-East Essex 1500 BC–AD 1500*, East Anglian Archaeol. Report 75 (Chelmsford, 1995) [includes an early Saxon cemetery]

e. Churches, monastic sites and Christian cemeteries

Alexander, Mary, 'Guildown Saxon Cemetery, Guildford', *Surrey Archaeol. Soc. Bull.* 342, 12–13 ['rediscovery' of some bones in London]

[Anon.], 'The Oldest House in England?', *Essex Archaeol.* 7 (1990), ii [Saxon church or chapel found under house in Saffron Walden]
'200 Years Younger – but Still the Oldest Timber Building in Europe', *Essex Archaeol.* 12 (1995), ii [Greensted church]

Aston, Mick, *Monasteries in the Landscape* (Stroud)

Ayers, Brian S., 'The Cathedral Site before 1096', *Norwich Cathedral: Church, City and Diocese, 1096–1996*, ed. Ian Atherton, Eric Fernie, Christopher Harper-Bill, and Hassell Smith (London, 1996), pp. 59–72

Biddulph, Edward, 'Sedgeford Historical and Archaeological Research Project, Third Interim Report (1998)', *Norfolk Archaeol.* 43 (1999), 351–2 [includes Middle Saxon cemetery in The Boneyard]

Buckberry, Jo, see sect. 9*d*

Cinthio, Maria, 'Trinitatiskyrkan i Lund – med engelsk prägel', *Hikuin* 24 (!997), 113–34 [Cnut based the Holy Trinity Church, Lund, on the pattern of the Old Minster, Winchester; in Danish with English summary, pp. 258–9]

Davidson, Carol F., 'Change and Change Back: the Development of English Parish Church Chancels', *Continuity and Change in Christian Worship*, ed. R. N. Swanson, Stud. in Church Hist. 35 (Woodbridge, 1999), 65–77

Garner, M. F., and J. Vincent, 'Further Middle Saxon Evidence at Cook Street, Southampton (SOU 567)', *Hampshire Stud.* 52 (1997), 77–87 [cemetery]

Graham, Donald, *The Saxon Sanctuary* (Wootton Wawen, Warwickshire, 1999) [St Peter's, Wootton Wawen]

Hall, Teresa Anne, *Minster Churches in the Dorset Landscape*, BAR Brit. ser. 304 (Oxford)

Hart, Diccon, 'All Hallows by the Tower', *Archaeol. Matters* 10, [1]

Hayman, Graham, 'A Late Saxon / Saxo-Norman Execution Site at Staines', *Surrey Archaeol. Soc. Bull.* 343, 2

Hoare, Peter G., and Caroline C. Sweet, 'The Orientation of Early Medieval Churches in England', *Jnl of Hist. Geography* 26, 162–73

Kroebel, Christiane, and David Pybus, 'The Saxon Church of Escomb', *Archaeol. North* 15 (1999), 41–2

Lakin, D., 'Excavations at Corney Reach, Chiswick W4, 1989–95', *Trans. of the London and Middlesex Archaeol. Soc.* 47 (1998 for 1996), 61–77 [includes undated Saxon inhumation burial]

Lucy, Sam, see sect. 9*d*

Rahtz, Philip, Lorna Watts, and Kelly Saunders, 'Appleton-le-Street: All Saints' Church', *Ryedale Historian* 20, 24–31

Robson, Shona, and Derek Hurst, 'Watching Brief at St Augustine's Church, Dodderhill', *Trans. of the Worcestershire Archaeol. Soc.* 17, 207–14 [earliest phase probably represents Saxon church]

Rodwell, Warwick, with Kirsty Rodwell, *Historic Churches – a Wasting Asset*, CBA Research Report 19 (London, 1977) [includes case studies on Rivenhall and Hadstock]

Scull, Christopher, and Alex Bayliss, 'Dating Burials of the Seventh and Eighth Centuries: a Case Study from Ipswich, Suffolk', *The Pace of Change*, ed. Hines *et al.*, pp. 80–8

Stoodley, Nick, 'Interim Report on the Excavations at the Anglo-Saxon Cemetery, Meonstoke (1998–9)', *Hampshire Field Club and Archaeol. Soc. Newsletter* 33, 10–12

Stopford, Jennie, 'The Case for Archaeological Research at Whitby', *Early Deira*, ed. Geake and Kenny, pp. 99–107

Whyman, Mark, 'Charnel and What to Do with it', *Interpreting Stratigraphy 8*, ed. Roskams, pp. 28–35 [case study of the cemetery at Ailcy Hill, Ripon]

Wilson, Barbara, and Frances Mee, *The Medieval Parish Churches of York: the Pictorial Evidence*, Archaeol. of York ss 1 (York, 1998)

f. Ships and seafaring

Carver, Martin, see sect. 9*d*

Christensen, Arne Emil, 'Viking Age Rigging: a Survey of Sources and Theories', *The Archaeology of Medieval Ships and Harbours in Northern Europe*, ed. McGrail, pp. 183–93

McGrail, Sean, ed., *The Archaeology of Medieval Ships and Harbours in Northern Europe: Papers Based on those presented to an International Symposium on Boat and Ship Archaeology at Bremerhaven in 1979*, BAR International ser. 66; National Maritime Museum, Greenwich, Archaeol. ser. 5 (Oxford, 1979)

McGrail, Sean, and Roy Switsur, 'Medieval Logboats of the River Mersey – a Classification Study', *The Archaeology of Medieval Ships and Harbours in Northern Europe*, ed. McGrail, pp. 93–115 [argues for eleventh-century date]

Marsden, Peter, 'The Medieval Ships of London', *The Archaeology of Medieval Ships and Harbours in Northern Europe*, ed. McGrail, pp. 83–92 [includes the eighth- to ninth-century New Fresh Wharf boat]

g. Miscellaneous artifacts

Behr, Charlotte, see sect. 6 [bracteates]

Brugmann, Birte, 'The Role of Continental Artefact-Types in Sixth-Century Kentish Chronology', *The Pace of Change*, ed. Hines *et al.*, pp. 37–64

Cameron, Esther A., *Sheaths and Scabbards in England AD 400–1100*, BAR Brit. ser. 301 (Oxford)

Crummy, Nina, and T. W. Cook, *The Post-Roman Small Finds from Excavations in Colchester, 1971–85*, Colchester Archaeol. Report 5 (Colchester, 1988)

Egan, Geoff, 'Material from a Millennium: Detritus from a Developing City', *Trans. of the London and Middlesex Archaeol. Soc.* 50 (1999), 29–37 [medieval, including Saxon, finds from the City and Southwark]

Eisenberg, Jerome M., 'The Art of the Vikings', *Minerva* 11.4, 13–16

Glass, Helen, 'The Saltwood Treasures: Spectacular Anglo-Saxon Finds from East Kent Excavations', *Wipowinde* 123/4, 6–7

Gurney, David, ed., 'Archaeological Finds in Norfolk 1999', *Norfolk Archaeol.* 43, 516–21 [the Saxon items include coins]
see also sect. 9*i*

Laing, Lloyd, 'The Bradwell Mount and the Use of Millefiori in Post-Roman Britain', *Studia Celtica* 33 (1999), 137–53

Liddle, Peter, 'Reports of Fieldwork', *Leicestershire Archaeol. and Hist. Soc. Trans.* 66 (1992), 188–91 [includes varied Saxon finds]

Mainman, A. J., and N. S. H. Rogers, *Craft, Industry and Everyday Life: Finds from Anglo-Scandinavian York*, Archaeol. of York 17.14 (York)

Nielsen, Karen Høilund, 'Animal Style – a Symbol of Might and Myth: Salin's Style II in a European Context', *Acta Archaeologia* 69 (1998), 1–52 [includes Anglo-Saxon material]

  'Retainers of the Scandinavian Kings: an Alternative Interpretation of Salin's Style II (Sixth-Seventh Centuries AD)', *Jnl of European Archaeol.* 5 (1997), 151–69

Saunders, Peter, 'Anglo-Saxon Jewel Found in Wiltshire', *Minerva* 11.2, 6

Schoneveld, Jan, 'De Grote fibula van Wijnaldum', *De Vrije Fries* 73 (1993), 7-24 [cloisonné work has parallels at Sutton Hoo]

Tanner, Jeremy, 'Faces Across the North Sea: Viking Art in Norway and England, AD 700–1300', *Archaeol. International* 1998–9 (1999), 27–30

Vallet, Françoise, 'Regards critiques sur les témoins archéologiques des Francs en Gaule du Nord à l'époque de Childéric et de Clovis', *Antiquités Nationales* 29 (1997), 219–44 [includes parallels at Brighthampton and Petersfinger]

Watson, Jacqui, *Identification of Mineral Preserved Organic Material Associated with Metalwork from the Anglo-Saxon Cemetery at Worthy Park, Hants.*, Ancient Monuments Laboratory 36 (London, 1986)

  Organic Material Associated with the Smith's Hoard from Tattershall Thorpe, Lincolnshire, Ancient Monuments Laboratory Report 22 (Portsmouth)

Wilson, David M., and Ole Klindt-Jensen, *Viking Art*, 2nd ed. (London, 1980)

h. Bone, stone and wood

Bradfield, Richard Maitland, *The Newent Carved Stones Unravell'd* (Newent, 1999)

Bryant, Richard, and David Viner, 'A Late Saxon Sculptural Fragment from All Saints' Church, Somerford Keynes', *Trans. of the Bristol and Gloucestershire Archaeol. Soc.* 117 (1999), 155–8

Coatsworth, Elizabeth, 'East Riddlesden Hall', *Durham Archaeol. Jnl* 14–15 (1999), 107–10 [cross shaft fragment]

  'The "Robed Christ" in Pre-Conquest Sculptures of the Crucifixion', *ASE* 29, 153–76

Coggins, Denis, and Kenneth J. Fairless, 'Wayside Crosses: Parishes of Romaldkirk and Laithkirk, Teesdale', *Durham Archaeol. Jnl* 14–15 (1999), 101–6

Crawford, Sally, 'A Late Anglo-Saxon Sculptural Fragment from Worcester Cathedral', *Trans. of the Worcestershire Archaeol. Soc.* 17, 345–8

Hill, David, and Derek Seddon, 'An Unrecorded Anglo-Saxon Cross Shaft Now at Blackden, Holmes Chapel, Cheshire SJ 789707', *Trans. of the Lancashire and Cheshire Ant. Soc.* 94 (1998), 145–9

Lang, Jim, 'Monuments from Yorkshire in the Age of Alcuin', *Early Deira*, ed. Geake and Kenny, pp. 109–19

Morris, Carole A., *Craft, Industry and Everyday Life: Wood and Woodworking in Anglo-Scandinavian and Medieval York*, Archaeol. of York 17.13 (York)

Orton, Fred, 'Rethinking the Ruthwell Monument: Fragments and Critique; Tradition and History; Tongues and Sockets', *Art Hist.* 21 (1998), 65–106

Rowe, Peter, 'An Anglo-Scandinavian Pin from South Gare, Redcar', *Archaeol. North* 17, 9 [a bone pin]

Sidebottom, P., 'The North-Western Frontier of Viking Mercia: the Evidence from Stone Monuments', *West Midlands Archaeol.* 39 (1996), 3–15

'Viking Age Stone Monuments and Social Identity in Derbyshire', *Cultures in Contact*, ed. Hadley and Richards, pp. 213–35

Stocker, David, 'Monuments and Merchants: Irregularities in the Distribution of Stone Sculpture in Lincolnshire and Yorkshire in the Tenth Century', *Cultures in Contact*, ed. Hadley and Richards, pp. 179–212

i. Metal-work

Arnold, C. J., 'Metallurgical Analysis and the Interpretation of Modes of Production: Gold Bracteates in Anglo-Saxon Kent', *Archaeological Sciences 1989*, ed. Budd *et al.*, pp. 119–24

Bayley, Justine, *Analytical Results for Crucibles from Various Sites in Saxon Southampton, Hants.*, Ancient Monuments Laboratory Report 2 (London, 1986)

'Processes in Precious Metal Working', *Archaeological Sciences 1989*, ed. Budd *et al.*, pp. 125–31 [includes Saxon items, especially from York and Lincoln]

Behr, Charlotte, see sect. 6 [bracteates]

Bennett, A., see sect. 9*a* (second item)

Blades, N. W., J. Bayley, and J. N. Walsh, 'The ICPS [Inductively Coupled Plasma Spectrometry] Analysis of Ancient Copper Alloys', *Archaeological Sciences 1989*, ed. Budd *et al.*, pp. 8–15 [using items from the Anglian cemetery at West Heslerton]

Dennis, M., *X-Ray Fluorescence Analysis of Non-Ferrous Metalworking Debris from the Royal Opera House Site, Lundenwic, 1995*, Ancient Monuments Laboratory Report 32 (Portsmouth, 1999)

Doonan, R., *Identification of Copper Alloys and Inlays from the Saxon Smith's Burial at Tattershall Thorpe, Lincolnshire*, Ancient Monuments Laboratory Report 69 (Portsmouth, 1999)

Dungworth, D., and J. Bayley, *Crucibles, Moulds and Tuyères from Mucking, Essex*, Ancient Monuments Laboratory Report 72 (Portsmouth, 1999)

Dungworth, D., and H. Stallybrass Bowstead, *Metal Working Evidence from No. 1 Poultry, London*, Ancient Monuments Laboratory Report 54 (Portsmouth)

Fell, V., and D. Starley, *A Technological Study of Ferrous Blades from the Anglo-Saxon Cemeteries at Boss Hall and St Stephen's Lane – Buttermarket, Ipswich, Suffolk*, Ancient Monuments Laboratory Report 18 (Portsmouth, 1999)

Geake, Helen, 'A Viking-Period Scandinavian Strike-a-Light Handle from Norfolk', *MA* 44, 223–4

Graham-Campbell, James, 'Rings and Things. Some Observations on the Hon Hoard', *Beretning fra attende tværfaglige viking symposium*, ed. Gillian Fellows-Jensen and Niels Lund (Aarhus, 1999), 53–64 [includes Anglo-Saxon gold finger ring]

Gurney, David, ed., 'Archaeological Finds in Norfolk 1998', *Norfolk Archaeol.* 43 (1999), 358–68 [Saxon items consist of metalwork and coins, pp. 363–6]

Hemmingson, Lars, 'Æ blaesworm – et fabeldyr fra den lavere folketro i Gorm d[en]

Gamles grav og i Sutton Hoo fundet', *Religion från stenålder till medeltid: artiklar baserade på religionsarkeologiska nätverksgruppens konferens på Lövstadbruk den 1–3 december 1995*, ed. Kerstin Engdahl and Anders Kaliff (Linköping, 1996), 18–24 [the mythological 'snake' in the grave of Gorm the Old, and at Sutton Hoo]

Hill, Paul, 'The Nature and Function of Spearheads in England c.700–1100 A.D.', *Jnl of the Arms and Armour Soc.* 16.5, 257–80

Hinton, David A., 'Anglo-Saxon Smiths and Myths', *Bull. of the John Rylands Library* 80.1 (1998), 3–21

A Smith in Lindsey: the Anglo-Saxon Grave at Tattershall Thorpe, Lincolnshire, Soc. for Med. Archaeol. Monograph 16 (London)

Hunter, Kate, 'The Anglo-Saxon Hanging Bowl from St Paul-in-the-Bail', *Lincoln Archaeological Trust Ninth Annual Report, 1980–81*, ed. [Lincoln Archaeological Trust] (Lincoln, 1981), 23–4

Inker, Peter, 'Technology as Active Material Culture: the Quoit-Brooch Style', *MA* 44, 25–52

Jones, M. U., 'Metallurgical Finds from a Multi-Period Settlement at Mucking, Essex', *Aspects of Early Metallurgy*, ed. Oddy, pp. 117–20

Laing, Lloyd, 'The Bradwell Mount and the Use of Millefiori in Post-Roman Britain', *Studia Celtica* 33 (1999), 137–53

Leahy, Kevin, 'Middle Anglo-Saxon Metalwork from South Newbald and the "Productive Site" Phenomenon in Yorkshire', *Early Deira*, ed. Geake and Kenny, pp. 51–82

Longley, David, *Hanging-Bowls, Penannular Brooches and the Anglo-Saxon Connexion*, BAR Brit. ser. 22 (Oxford, 1975)

MacGregor, Arthur, 'The Holderness Anglo-Saxon Cross', *Minerva* 11.2, 3

'A Seventh-Century Pectoral Cross from Holderness, East Yorkshire', *MA* 44, 217–22

Mann, Jenny, 'Three Small Finds from St Paul-in-the-Bail', *Lincoln Archaeological Trust Seventh Annual Report, 1978–1979* (Lincoln, 1979), 28–30 [includes Saxon strapend]

Marchant, David, 'The Aldbrough Gilt-Bronze Sword Pommel', *Minerva* 11.2, 7

McDonnell, J. G., *Lurk Lane, Beverley: Metallurgical Report on Seven Knives*, Ancient Monuments Laboratory Report 65 (London, 1986)

The Manufacturing Techniques Used in Anglo-Scandinavian Iron Artifacts from 16–22 Coppergate, York, Ancient Monuments Laboratory Report 66 (London, 1986)

Meadows, Ian, 'The Pioneer Helmet', *Med. Archaeol. Newsletter* 17 (1997), 8

Mortimer, Catherine, 'Northern European Metalworking Traditions in the Fifth and Sixth Centuries AD', *Archaeological Sciences 1989*, ed. Budd *et al.*, pp. 162–8 [East Anglian cruciform brooches]

Mortimer, Catherine, and Martin Stoney, 'A Methodology for Punchmark Analysis Using Electron Microscopy', *Archaeological Sciences 1995*, ed. Sinclair *et al.*, pp. 119–22 [discussing metalwork from the cemeteries of Barrington, Boss Hall, Tuddenham and Linton Heath]

Oddy, W. A., ed., *Aspects of Early Metallurgy*, Brit. Museum Occasional Paper 17 (London, 1980)

'Gilding and Tinning in Anglo-Saxon England', *Aspects of Early Metallurgy*, ed. Oddy, pp. 129–34

Ottaway, Patrick, *Anglo-Scandinavian Ironwork from 16–22 Coppergate*, Archaeol. of York 17.6 (London, 1992)

Parfitt, Keith, 'A Bird Mount and Other Early Anglo-Saxon Finds: Ripple/Ringwould', *AC* 119 (1999), 394–8

Parfitt, Keith, Birte Brugmann, and Arno Rettner, 'Anglo-Saxon Spur from the Mill Hill, Deal Cemetery', *Kent Archaeol. Rev.* 140, 229–30

Starley, David E., *The Analysis of Middle Saxon Ironwork and Ironworking Debris from Flixborough, Humberside*, Ancient Monuments Laboratory Report 35 (Portsmouth, 1999)

'The Variation of Inclusion Morphology and Composition in Ferrous Artefacts', *Archaeological Sciences 1989*, ed. Budd *et al.*, pp. 175–8 [includes knife blades from *Hamwih*]

Starley, David E., and R. Doonan, *The Analytical Examination of Ironworking Debris from Thetford, Mill Lane, Norfolk, 1995*, Ancient Monuments Laboratory Report 31 (Portsmouth, 1999)

Stedman, Mark, 'Three Early Anglo-Saxon Metalwork Finds from the Isle of Wight, 1993–6', *Hampshire Stud.* 53 (1998), 109–19

Stones, Mike, 'Shrewsbury Museums Service Report 1998–1999', *Shropshire Hist. and Archaeol.* 74 (1999), 89–91 [includes two silver strap tags, and two strap mounts]

Suzuki, Seiichi, *The Quoit Brooch Style and Anglo-Saxon Settlement: a Casting and Recasting of Cultural Identity Symbols* (Woodbridge)

Thomas, Gabor, 'Anglo-Scandinavian Metalwork from the Danelaw: Exploring Social and Cultural Interaction', *Cultures in Contact*, ed. Hadley and Richards, pp. 237–55

Tulp, Caroline, and Nigel Meeks, 'The Tjitsma (Wijnaldum) Die: a 7th Century Tool for Making a Cross-Hatched Pattern on Gold Foil, or a Master Template?', *Hist. Metallurgy* 34, 13–24 [includes Anglo-Saxon metalwork]

White, A. J., 'Carnforth Viking Treasure', *Contrebis* 24 (1999), 12–13

White, Robert, 'Flaxengate's Non-Ferrous Metals', *Archaeology in Lincoln 1982–1983: Eleventh Annual Report of Lincoln Archaeological Trust* (Lincoln, 1983), 28–32

Williams, David, 'A Stirrup-Strap Mount from Little Glemham, Suffolk: a Possible Import', *Proc. of the Suffolk Inst. of Archaeol. and Hist.* 39 (1997–2000), 493–4

Williams, Gareth, 'Wealth and Power in the Viking Age', *Minerva* 11.4, 46–9 [metalwork and coins]

Wilthew, Paul, *Examination of Metalworking Waste from Site A, Thetford, Norfolk*, Ancient Monuments Laboratory Report 25 (London, 1986)

Examination of Technological Material from 1964–66 Excavations at Site 5756, Thetford, Norfolk, Ancient Monuments Laboratory Report 24 (London, 1986)

j. Pottery and glass

Adams, Lauren, 'Imported Pottery of the 9th–11th Centuries from Flaxengate, Lincoln', *Lincoln Archaeological Trust Seventh Annual Report, 1978–1979* (Lincoln, 1979), 30–4

Allen, J. R. L., 'Romano-British and Early Medieval Pottery Scatters on the Alluvium at

Hill and Oldbury, Severn Estuary Levels', *Archaeology in the Severn Estuary 1997 (Volume 8)*, ed. Stephen Rippon (Exeter, 1998), 67–81

Andrews, D. D., ed., 'Church Miscellany 1998', *Essex Archaeol. and Hist.* 30 (1999), 250–7 [includes Saxon pottery from St Mary's, Broomfield]

[Anon.], 'Barking Abbey Saxon Glass Kiln', *Essex Archaeol.* 7 (1990), xi

Arnold, C. J., 'Early Anglo-Saxon Pottery: Production and Distribution', *Production and Distribution: a Ceramic Viewpoint*, ed. Hilary Howard and Elaine L. Morris, BAR International ser. 120 (Oxford, 1981), 229–42

Bayley, J., and R. Doonan, *High-Lead Glassworking and Alkali Glass Bead Making at 16–22 Coppergate and 22 Piccadilly, York*, Ancient Monuments Laboratory Report 74 (Portsmouth, 1999)

Blackmore, Lyn, 'Aspects of Trade and Exchange Evidenced by Recent Work on Saxon and Medieval Pottery from London', *Trans. of the London and Middlesex Archaeol. Soc.* 50 (1999), 38–54

Day, L, R., and D. R. J. Perkins, 'Neutron Activation Analysis of Late Roman and Dark Age Glass from Kent', *Archaeological Sciences 1989*, ed. Budd *et al.*, pp. 16–22

Foley, Kate, 'Flaxengate Glass-Working', *Archaeology in Lincoln 1981–82: Tenth Annual Report of Lincoln Archaeological Trust* (Lincoln, 1982), 27–9

Heyworth, M. P., J. R. Hunter, S. E. Warren, and J. N. Walsh, 'ICPS [Inductively Coupled Plasma Spectrometry] and Glass: the Multi-Element Approach', *Neutron Activation and Plasma Emission Spectrometric Analysis in Archaeology: Techniques and Applications*, ed. Michael J. Hughes, Michael R. Cowell, and Duncan R. Hook, Brit. Museum Occasional Paper 82 (London, 1991), 143–54 [uses Saxon glass from Winchester and Southampton]

Jackson, C. M., J. R. Hunter, and S. E. Warren, 'The Analysis of Glass from Coppergate, York by Inductively Coupled Plasma Spectrometry', *Archaeological Sciences 1989*, ed. Budd *et al.*, pp. 76–82

Kent, Oliver, 'Ceramic Finds from Archaeological Excavations at Glastonbury Abbey, 1901–1979', *Somerset Archaeol. and Nat. Hist.* 140 (1997), 73–104

Larsson, Stefan, 'Från Lincolnshire till Östdanmark: en krukmakare i Knut den Stores tid', *Artefakter – arkeologiska ting: en bok om föremål ur ett arkeologiskt perspektiv*, ed. Anders Högberg, Univ. of Lund Inst. of Archaeol. Report Ser. 71 (Lund), 69–86

Lucas, Gavin, 'Prehistoric, Roman and Post-Roman Pottery', *The Archaeology of the St Neots to Duxford Gas Pipeline 1994*, ed. J. Price, I. P. Brooks, and D. J. Maynard, BAR Brit. ser. 255 (Oxford, 1997), 49–88

Macpherson-Grant, Nigel, 'Iron Age and Later Pottery: Eastry', *AC* 119 (1999), 378–80 [includes early Saxon pottery]

'Post-Roman Pottery: Publication and Research', *Canterbury Archaeol. Trust Ann. Report* 10 (1986 for 1985–6), 36–41

Macpherson-Grant, Nigel, and Mark Gardiner, 'Society Funded Research: Pottery from Sandtun, West Hythe, Kent', *Med. Archaeol. Newsletter* 18 (1998), 7

Martin, Gerry, and Deborah Sawday, see sect. 9*c*

Mortimer, Richard, see sect. 9*c*

Schofield, A. J., 'Understanding Early Medieval Pottery Distributions: Cautionary Tales and their Implications for Further Research', *Antiquity* 63 (1989), 460–70

Sharman, Josephine, and David Mackie, 'Excavations Along an Oil Pipeline Through Rutland', *Leicestershire Archaeol. and Hist. Soc. Trans.* 65 (1991), 97–9 [includes Saxon pottery from Tickencote]

Smith, Keith, 'Reassembly of a Complete Anglo-Scandinavian Storage Vessel from Grantham Street, Lincoln', *Archaeology in Lincoln 1982–1983: Eleventh Annual Report of Lincoln Archaeological Trust* (Lincoln, 1983), pp. 38–41

Stapleton, C. P., I. C. Freestone, and S. G. E. Bowman, 'Composition and Origin of Early Mediaeval Opaque Red Enamel from Britain and Ireland', *Jnl of Archaeol. Science* 26 (1999), 913–21

Wamers, Egon, 'Insulare Kunst im Reich Karls des Grossen', *799*, ed. Stiegemann and Wemhoff, pp. 452–64

Williams, D. F., *Note on the Petrology of Some Saxon Sherds from Staple Gardens, Winchester,* Ancient Monuments Laboratory Report 13 (London, 1986)

k. Textiles and leather

Dale, V. H. M., 'Aspects of Viking (Age) Dress: a Review of the Textile Evidence', *Archaeol. Textiles Newsletter* 14 (1992), 8–9

Dyes on Historical and Archaeological Textiles, Summary of Talks: 2nd Meeting, National Museum of Antiquities of Scotland, September 1983 (Edinburgh, 1983)

Hall, A. R., 'Evidence of Dyeplants from Viking Age York and Medieval Beverley', *Dyes on Historical and Archaeological Textiles . . . 2nd Meeting*, p. 25

Hart, Cyril, 'The Bayeux Tapestry and Schools of Illumination at Canterbury', *ANS* 22, 117–67

Henry, Philippa A., 'Development and Change in Late Saxon Textile Production: an Analysis of the Evidence', *Durham Archaeol. Jnl* 14–15 (1999), 69–76

Hill, David, 'The Bayeux Tapestry: the Case of the Phantom Fleet', *Bull. of the John Rylands Lib.* 80.1 (1998), 23–31

Padden, A. Nikki, P. John, M. D. Collins, R. Hutson, and A. R. Hall, 'Indigo-Reducing *Clostridium isatidis* Isolated from a Variety of Sources, Including a 10th-Century Viking Dye Vat', *Jnl of Archaeol. Science* 27, 953–6

Pritchard, Frances, 'Evidence of Dyeing Practices from a Group of Late Saxon Textiles from London', *Dyes on Historical and Archaeological Textiles . . . 2nd Meeting*, pp. 22–4

Stevens, Helen M., 'A Practical Reconstruction of 8th Century A.D. Embroidery Techniques', *Archaeol. Textiles Newsletter* 6 (1988), 9–10

Taylor, George W., 'Detection and Identification of Dyes on Anglo-Scandinavian Textiles', *Dyes on Historical and Archaeological Textiles, Summary of Talks: 1st Meeting, York Archaeological Trust, August 1982* (York, 1982), p. 5

Walton, Penelope, 'Dyes in Early Scandinavian Textiles', *Dyes on Historical and Archaeological Textiles, Summary of Talks: 5th Meeting, York Archaeological Trust, October 1986* (Edinburgh, 1987), pp. 38–43 [includes evidence from York]

l. Inscriptions

Eisenberg, Jerome M., 'The Spring 2000 Antiquities Sales', *Minerva* 11.5, 28–37 [includes an eighth-century gold ring inscribed with a Latin blessing]

Holder, Nick, 'Inscriptions, Writing and Literacy in Saxon London', *Trans. of the London and Middlesex Archaeol. Soc.* 49 (1999 for 1998), 81–97

O'Hara, Michael Dennis, 'An Enigmatic Silver Serpent Ring with "Runic" Lettering', *Minerva* 11.3, 41–4

Page, R. I., 'Recent Finds of Anglo-Saxon Runes', *Nytt om runer* 14 (1999), 9–11

Parsons, David, 'Odda's Chapel, Deerhurst: Place of Worship or Royal Hall?', *MA* 44, 225–8 [dedication stone with Latin inscription]

Watts, Lorna, 'The Rev. D. H. Haigh and Runes at Kirkdale', *Ryedale Historian* 19 (1999 for 1998–9), 21–4 [nineteenth-century views on the runes]

10. REVIEWS

Abels, Richard, *Alfred the Great: War, Kingship and Culture in Anglo-Saxon England* (London, 1998): L. Abrams, *Speculum* 75, 887–8; B. S. Bachrach, *Albion* 32, 620–1; J. Campbell, *EHR* 115, 1258; N. G. Discenza, *Hist. Teacher* 33, 555–6; S. Hamilton, *EME* 9, 252–5; S. Miller, *JEH* 51, 128–9; B. Yorke, *AHR* 105, 595

Abrams, Lesley, *Anglo-Saxon Glastonbury* (Woodbridge, 1996): D. B. McCulloch, *Revue d'histoire ecclésiastique* 95, 729–30

Acker, Paul, *Revising Oral Theory* (New York, 1998): F. C. Robinson, *Speculum* 75, 146–7

Aird, William M., *St Cuthbert and the Normans* (Woodbridge, 1998): J. Barrow, *DAEM* 56, 379; M. Burger, *Speculum* 75, 888–90; J. Burton, *AHR* 105, 988; A. A. M. Duncan, *Scottish Hist. Rev.* 79, 244–7; G. A. Loud, *NH* 36, 166–7; S. P. Marrone, *Albion* 32, 90–2; D. Rollason, *EHR* 115, 929–30

Anderton, Mike, ed., *Anglo-Saxon Trading Centres* (Glasgow, 1999): A. Vince, *Brit. Archaeol.* 51, 30

Baines, Arnold H. J., *Lady Elgiva* (Chesham, 1999): E. V[iney], *Records of Buckinghamshire* 40 (1998–2000), 117

Baker, Peter S., and Nicholas Howe, ed., *Words and Works* (Toronto, 1998): D. Burnley, *MLR* 95, 791–2; H. Magennis, *EME* 9, 138–9; U. Schaefer, *ASNSL* 237, 165–7

Bazelmans, Jos, *By Weapons Made Worthy* (Amsterdam, 1999): C. Rauer, *Tijdschrift voor geschiedenis* 113, 240–2

Bjork, Robert E., and John D. Niles, ed., *A Beowulf Handbook* (Lincoln, NE, 1997): H. D. Chickering, *Medievalia et Humanistica* 27, 115–16; K. Kiernan, *ASNSL* 237, 167–9; P. Sorrell, *Parergon* 17.2, 177–9; P. E. Szarmach, *JEGP* 99, 440–2; D. J. Williams, *YES* 30, 271–2

Blackburn, Mark, and David N. Dumville, ed., *Kings, Currency and Alliances: History and Coinage of Southern England in the Ninth Century* (Woodbridge, 1998): B. Andreolli, *SM* 3rd ser. 41, 931–2; F. Dumas, *Revue Numismatique* 155, 343–4; D. A. Hinton, *AntJ* 80, 353–4; R. M. Koopmans, *Albion* 32, 88–9; H. R. Loyn, *MA* 44, 391–2; J. Story, *History* 85, 495–6

Bond, J. M., and T. P. O'Connor, *Bones from Medieval Deposits at 16–22 Coppergate and Other Sites in York* (York, 1999): S. Stallibrass, *International Jnl of Osteoarchaeology* 10, 158–60

Bruni, Sandra, ed., *Alcuino: De orthographia* (Florence, 1997): B. Gansweidt, *Mittel-*

lateinisches Jahrbuch 35, 145; A. A. Nascimento, *Euphrosyne* 26 (1998), 511–13; G. Silagi, *DAEM* 56, 281

Cameron, Kenneth, *A Dictionary of Lincolnshire Place-Names*, EPNS popular ser. 1 (Nottingham, 1998): C. Hough, *Nomina* 23, 183–4

Campbell, Alistair, ed., *Encomium Emmae Reginae*, with suppl. by Simon Keynes, (Cambridge, 1998): J. Jesch, *History* 85, 311–12

Carruthers, Leo, *L'Anglais médiéval* (Turnhout, 1996): L. M. Matheson, *Speculum* 75, 900–2

Cavill, Paul, *Maxims in Old English Poetry* (Cambridge, 1999): A. Harbus, *Parergon* 17.2, 190–2; K. A. Lowe, *Nottingham Med. Stud.* 44, 204–6; P. Orton, *SBVS* 25, 322–4

Cederlöf, Mikael, *The Element '-stow' in the History of English* (Uppsala, 1998): C. Hough, *Bull. of International Med. Research* 6, 47–57

Chibnall, Marjorie, *The Debate on the Norman Conquest* (Manchester, 1999): J. Campbell, *EHR* 115, 172–3; A. Curry, *Lit. and Hist.* 9.2, 80–1; L. Huneycutt, *Albion* 32, 470; D. J. A. Matthew, *AHR* 105, 1266–7; E. Mecacci, *SM* 3rd ser. 41, 941

Clark, Cecily, *Words, Names and History*, ed. P. Jackson (Cambridge, 1995): J. Insley, *Anglia* 118, 112–18

Clayton, Mary, *The Apocryphal Gospels of Mary in Anglo-Saxon England* (Cambridge, 1998): J. K. Elliott, *Novum Testamentum* 42, 408–10; J. Hill, *EME* 9, 266–7; R. Marsden, *MÆ* 69, 298–9

Clemoes, Peter, ed., *Ælfric's Catholic Homilies. The First Series. Text* (Oxford, 1997): T. Kubouchi, *Stud. in Eng. Lit.* (Tokyo) Eng. Number 42, 85–92

Cornelius, Regina, ed., *Die altenglische Interlinearversion zu 'De vittiis et peccatis'* (Frankfurt am Main, 1995): J. D. Pheifer, *Anglia* 118, 121–4

Crawford, Sally, *Childhood in Anglo-Saxon England* (Stroud, 1999): H. Hamerow, *EHR* 115, 1258–9

Crossley-Holland, Kevin, trans., *Beowulf, The Fight at Finnsburh*, ed. Heather O'Donoghue (Oxford, 1999): E. G. Stanley, *N&Q* 47, 156

Cubbin, G. P., ed., *MS D* (Cambridge, 1996): P. W. Conner, *Speculum* 75, 910–13

D'Aronco, M. A., and M. L. Cameron, ed., *The Old English Illustrated Pharmacopoeia* (Copenhagen, 1998): R. Gendre, *NM* 101, 478–9; P. Robinson, *Medical Hist.* 44, 433; A. Squires, *MÆ* 69, 122–4; P. A. Thompson, *N&Q* 47, 223–4

Dekker, Kees, *The Origins of Old Germanic Studies in the Low Countries* (Leiden, 1999): E. G. Stanley, *N&Q* 47, 488

DeVries, Kelly, *The Norwegian Invasion of England in 1066* (Woodbridge, 1999): A. Williams, *Scandinavica* 39, 219–21

Dodwell, C. R., *Anglo-Saxon Gestures and the Roman Stage* (Cambridge): J. A. Burrow, *MÆ* 69, 296–7; R. Gameson, *N&Q*, 47, 488–90

Dreuille, Christophe de, ed., *L'Église et la mission au VIe siècle* (Paris): A. G. Holder, *Jnl of Early Christian Stud.* 8, 602–4

Driscoll, Michael S., *Alcuin et la pénitence à l'époque carolingienne* (Münster, 1999): P. Collomb, *Revue d'histoire ecclésiastique* 95, 716–18

Ebersperger, Birgit, *Die angelsächsischen Handschriften in den Pariser Bibliotheken* (Heidelberg, 1999): C. Rauer, *N&Q* 47, 222–3

Everson, Paul, and David Stocker, *Corpus of Anglo-Saxon Stone Sculpture*, V: *Lincolnshire* (Oxford, 1999): C. Karkov, *MA* 44, 369–70

Faith, Rosamond, *The English Peasantry and the Growth of Lordship* (London, 1997): A. Everitt, *Rural Hist.* 11, 132–3

Fjalldal, Magnús, *The Long Arm of Coincidence* (Toronto, 1998): H. O'Donoghue, *MÆ* 69, 119–20; P. A. Jorgensen, *JEGP* 99, 91–5

Fleming, Robin, *Domesday Book and the Law: Social and Legal Custom in Early Medieval England* (Cambridge, 1998): D. Bates, *Welsh Hist. Rev.* 20, 369–71; P. Brand, *History* 85, 121–2; K. F. Drew, *Jnl. of Interdisciplinary Hist.* 30 (1999), 498–9; E. Mason, *Midland Hist.* 25, 193–5

Foley, W. Trent, and Arthur G. Holder, trans., *Bede. A Biblical Miscellany* (Liverpool, 1999): P.-M. Bogaert, *RB* 110, 161–2

Forsberg, Rune, *The Place-Name 'Lewes'* (Uppsala, 1997): R. Coates, *Locus Focus: Forum of the Sussex Place-Names Net*, 2.2, 18–20; C. Hough, *Bull. of International Med. Research* 6, 47–57; E. G. Stanley, *N&Q* 47, 287

Frantzen, Allen J., *Before the Closet* (Chicago, 1998): F. Field, *EHR* 115, 266–7; P. J. Payer, *JEH* 51, 384; R. Trumbach, *Albion* 32, 617–18

Frantzen, Allen J., and John D. Niles, ed., *Anglo-Saxonism and the Construction of Social Identity* (Gainesville, FL, 1997): C. R. Davis, *MLR* 95, 790–1; J. P. Hermann, *JEGP* 99, 114–16; P. Richardson, *Jnl of the Rocky Mountain Med. and Renaissance Assoc.* 20 (1999), 259–61

Gameson, Richard, ed., *The Early Medieval Bible* (Cambridge, 1994): J.-L. Charlet, *Latomus* 59, 189–91

St Augustine and the Conversion of England (Stroud, 1999): J. F. Kelly, *Church Hist.* 69, 876–8

The Study of the Bayeux Tapestry (Woodbridge, 1997): P. E. Bennett, *N&Q* 47, 112–13; L. Carruthers, *EA* 53, 329–30; U. Nilgen, *DAEM* 56, 826–7; S. Randles, *Parergon* 17.2, 203–5

Geake, Helen, *The Use of Grave-Goods in Conversion-Period England, c. 600–c. 850* (Oxford, 1997): J. Blair, *EME* 9, 261–2; C. Scull, *ArchJ* 156 (1999), 432–3; K. Ulmschneider, *European Jnl of Archaeol.* 3, 136–7

Glover, Judith, *Sussex Place-Names*, 2nd ed. (Newbury, 1997): R. Coates, *Locus Focus: Forum of the Sussex Place-Names Net*, 2.1, 27–8

Graham, Timothy, and Andrew G. Watson, *The Recovery of the Past in Early Elizabethan England: Documents by John Bale and John Joscelyn from the Circle of Matthew Parker* (Cambridge, 1998): A. S. G. Edwards, *The Library* 7th ser. 1, 445–6

Green, D. H., *Language and History in the Early Germanic World* (Cambridge, 1998): F. Hugus, *Speculum* 75, 470–2; H. Reichert, *Zeitschrift für deutsches Altertum und deutsche Literatur* 129, 327–38; O. W. Robinson, *JEGP* 99, 412–14; J. C. Salmons, *Diachronica* 17, 161–5

Gretsch, Mechthild, *The Intellectual Foundations of the English Benedictine Reform* (Cambridge, 1999): S. Gwara, *SM* 3rd ser. 41, 713–23; D. O'Keefe, *Downside Rev.* 118, 233–4; R. W. Pfaff, *EHR* 115, 924; G. Scott, *ES* 81, 144–5; H. Vollrath, *DAEM* 56, 720–1

Griffith, Mark, ed., *Judith* (Exeter, 1997): T. D. Hill, *Speculum* 75, 932–3; P. J. Lucas, *RES* 51, 261–4; H. Magennis, *JEGP* 99, 251–3

Gruber, Loren C., ed., *Essays on Old, Middle, Modern English and Old Icelandic* (Lewiston, NY): D. J. Schlosser, *In Geardagum* 21, 93–102

Gwara, Scott, ed., and David W. Porter, trans., *Anglo-Saxon Conversations* (Woodbridge, 1997): M. Bayless, *JEGP* 99, 253–5; A. E. Farnham, *Speculum* 75, 188–9; N. Howe, *YES* 30, 274–5; H. Sauer, *DAEM* 56, 680–1

Hawkes, Jane, and Susan Mills, ed., *Northumbria's Golden Age* (Stroud, 1999): N. James, *Antiquity* 74, 225

Head, Pauline, *Representation and Design* (Albany, NY, 1997): D. Schlosser, *ANQ* 13.1, 62–5

Heaney, Seamus, trans., *Beowulf* (London, 1999): M. Alexander, *Agenda* 37.4, 80–3; [Anon.], *Virginia Quarterly Rev.* 76.4, A144–5; S. A. J. Bradley, *Med. Life* 13, 3–8; G. Clarke, *Poetry Wales* 35.4, 61–2; N. Howe, *New Republic*, 28 February, pp. 32–7; B. I. Koerner, *U.S. News & World Report*, 20 March, p. 68; B. Murphy, *Poetry* (Chicago) 177, 211–16; H. O'Donoghue, *Translation and Lit.* 9, 231–6; J. Shapiro, *New York Times Book Rev.*, 27 February, p. 6; E. G. Stanley, *N&Q* 47, 346–8

Henderson, George, *Vision and Image in Early Christian England* (Cambridge, 1999): R. Gameson, *JEH* 51, 599–600

Higham, N. J., *The Convert Kings: Power and Religious Affinity in Early Anglo-Saxon England* (Manchester, 1997): R. Lavelle, *MA* 44, 390–1; D. W. Rollason, *History* 85, 118–19

Hill, Peter, *et al.*, *Whithorn and St Ninian* (Stroud, 1997): [Anon.], *Current Archaeol.* 167, 425–6

Hines, John, ed., *The Anglo-Saxons from the Migration Period to the Eighth Century* (Woodbridge, 1997): M. Gelling, *N&Q* 47, 108–9; N. J. Higham, *History* 85, 116–17; T. Reuter, *DAEM* 56, 698–9

A New Corpus of Anglo-Saxon Great Square-Headed Brooches (Woodbridge, 1997): H. Hamerow, *EME* 9, 130–1; B. Magnus, *Fornvännen* 95.3, 197–201

Hooke, Della, *The Landscape of Anglo-Saxon England* (London, 1998): C. Dyer, *EME* 9, 262–4, and *Agricultural Hist. Rev.* 48, 116–17; D. Hill, *EHR* 115, 679–80

Warwickshire Anglo-Saxon Charter Bounds (Woodbridge, 1999): C. Dyer, *Agricultural Hist. Rev.* 48, 116–17; J. Jenkyns, *JEPNS* 32, 78–80; B. Yorke, *LH* 30, 191

Howlett, D. R., *British Books in Biblical Style* (Dublin, 1997): C. D. Eckhardt, *Speculum* 75, 700–2

Jack, George, ed., *'Beowulf': a Student Edition* (Oxford, 1994): P. E. Szarmach, *JEGP* 99, 440–2

Jacobsson, Mattias, *Wells, Meres and Pools* (Uppsala, 1997): C. Hough, *Bull. of International Med. Research* 6, 47–57

John, Eric, *Reassessing Anglo-Saxon England* (Manchester, 1996): K. O'Brien O'Keeffe, *Arthuriana* 10.4, 77–8

Jones, Christopher A., *Ælfric's Letter to the Monks of Eynsham* (Cambridge, 1998): S. K. Elkins, *Church Hist.* 69, 646–7; S. Irvine, *RES* 51, 626–8; R. Jayatilaka, *MÆ* 69, 124–5; R. W. Pfaff, *Catholic Hist. Rev.* 86, 309–10

Keats-Rohan, K. S. B., *Domesday People*, I (Woodbridge, 1999): J. Campbell, *EHR* 115, 174–5; F. Neveux, *Le Moyen Age* 106, 197–9; E. Poulle, *Bibliothèque de l'École des Chartes* 158, 599–600

Keats-Rohan, K. S. B., and David E. Thornton, *Domesday Names* (Woodbridge, 1997): E. G. Stanley, *N&Q* 47, 287

Keefer, Sarah Larratt, and Katherine O'Brien O'Keeffe, ed., *New Approaches to Editing Old English Verse* (Cambridge, 1998): R. Hanna, *MÆ* 69, 125–7

Kelly, S. E., ed., *Charters of Selsey* (Oxford, 1998): J. Blair, *EHR* 115, 923–4; B. Yorke, *JEH* 51, 129–30

Charters of Shaftesbury Abbey (Oxford, 1996): R. Harvey, *Wiltshire Archaeol. and Nat. Hist. Mag.* 93, 265

Kiernan, Kevin, *et al.*, ed., *Electronic 'Beowulf'* (2 CD-ROMs, London, 1999): S. A. J. Bradley, *Med. Life* 13, 31–3; G. Coult, *Managing Information* 7.2, 47–8

Kittlick, Wolfgang, *Die Glossen der Hs. British Library, Cotton Cleopatra A.III* (Frankfurt am Main, 1998): E. G. Stanley, *N&Q* 47, 493–4

Knappe, Gabriele, *Traditionen der klassischen Rhetorik im angelsächsischen England* (Heidelberg, 1996): F. Quadlbauer, *Mittellateinisches Jahrbuch* 35, 122–7

Laing, Lloyd, and Jennifer Laing, *Early English Art and Architecture* (Stroud, 1996): C. E. Karkov, *EME* 9, 131–2

Lapidge, Michael, ed., *Bede and his World* ([Newcastle upon Tyne], 1994): G. Wieland, *Anglia* 118, 118–20

Lapidge, Michael, *et al.*, ed., *The Blackwell Encyclopaedia of Anglo-Saxon England* (Oxford, 1999): F. Chevillet, *EA* 53, 201–3; M. F. Smith, *Albion* 32, 273–4; E. G. Stanley, *N&Q* 47, 490–1; M. Swan, *RES* 51, 456–8

Lee, Alvin A., *Gold-Hall and Earth-Dragon* (Toronto, 1998): F. M. Biggs, *MÆ* 69, 297–8; L. Carruthers, *Arthuriana* 10.2, 113–15, and *Le Moyen Age* 106, 190–2; C. Larrington, *RES* 51, 260–1; L. McKill, *Eng. Stud. in Canada* 26, 219–23; G. Waite, *Parergon* 17.2, 222–4

Lenker, Ursula, *Die westsächsische Evangelienversion und die Perikopenordnungen im angelsächsischen England* (Munich, 1997): M. McC. Gatch, *Speculum* 75, 207–9

Lewis, Suzanne, *The Rhetoric of Power in the Bayeux Tapestry* (Cambridge, 1999): J. Collard, *Parergon* 17.2, 225–7; M. S. Singh, *Indian Economic and Social Hist. Rev.* 37, 244–5

Lindsay, W. M., *Studies in Early Medieval Latin Glossaries*, ed. Michael Lapidge (Aldershot, 1996): V. Von Büren, *Latomus* 59, 926–7

Liuzza, R. M., trans., *Beowulf* (Peterborough, Ont.): F. Kermode, *New York Rev. of Books*, 20 July, pp. 18–21; Soon-Ai Low, *Envoi* 8 (1999), 148–54

Lucas, Peter J., A. N. Doane, and I. C. Cunningham, *Latin Manuscripts with Anglo-Saxon Glosses* (Tempe, AZ, 1997): R. M. Liuzza, *Speculum* 75, 708–9

MacGregor, A., A. J. Mainman, and N. S. H. Rogers, *Bone, Antler, Ivory and Horn from Anglo-Scandinavian and Medieval York* (York, 1999): I. Riddler, *ArchJ* 156, 436

Magennis, Hugh, *Anglo-Saxon Appetites: Food and Drink and their Consumption in Old English and Related Literature* (Dublin, 1998): D. Banham, *EHR* 115, 922–3

Malim, Tim, *et al.*, *The Anglo-Saxon Cemetery at Edix Hill (Barrington A), Cambridgeshire* (York, 1998): H. Geake, *Antiquity* 74, 452–3

McCully, C. B., and J. J. Anderson, ed., *English Historical Metrics* (Cambridge, 1996): M. Redford, *Lingua* 110, 701–8

McGurk, Patrick, *Gospel Books and Early Latin Manuscripts* (Aldershot, 1998): C. A. Farr, *Libraries & Culture* 35, 581–2

McLynn, Frank, *1066: the Year of the Three Battles* (London, 1998): Q. Hawkins, *Med. Life* 13, 37

Mills, A. D., *Oxford Dictionary of English Place-Names*, 2nd ed. (Oxford, 1998): C. Hough, *Nomina* 23, 176

Mitchell, Bruce, and Fred C. Robinson, ed., *Beowulf* (Oxford, 1998): A. Bammesberger, *Literaturwissenschaftliches Jahrbuch* 41, 351–4; M. B. Bedingfield, *MÆ* 69, 120–2; R. Poole, *Parergon* 17.2, 169–71

Momma, H., *The Composition of Old English Poetry* (Cambridge, 1997): G. Russom, *Speculum* 75, 224–6

Muir, Bernard J., and Andrew J. Turner, ed. and trans., *Vita sancti Wilfridi auctore Edmero* (Exeter, 1998): J. van der Straeten, *AB* 118, 189–90; M. Winterbottom, *JEH* 51, 782

Neville, Jennifer, *Representations of the Natural World in Old English Poetry* (Cambridge, 1999): A. Squires, *MÆ* 69, 122–4

Nicolaisen, W. F. H., ed., *Proceedings of the XIXth Congress of Onomastic Sciences, Aberdeen, August 4–11, 1996*, 3 vols. (Aberdeen, 1998): S. Brendler, *Namenkundliche Informationen* 77/78, 185–7

Nielsen, Hans Frede, *The Continental Backgrounds of English* (Odense, 1998): O. Fischer, *European Jnl of Eng. Stud.* 4, 195–8; W. Koopman, *Amsterdamer Beiträge zur älteren Germanistik* 53, 243–6

Noel, William, *The Harley Psalter* (Cambridge, 1995): L. M. Ayres, *Speculum* 75, 506–8; A. A. Nascimento, *Euphrosyne* 26 (1998), 524–5

North, Richard, *Heathen Gods in Old English Literature* (Cambridge, 1997): J. Gerritsen, *ES* 81, 143–4; T. A. Shippey, *MLR* 95, 170–1

O'Brien, Bruce R., *God's Peace and King's Peace* (Philadelphia, 1999): J. C. Holt, *JEH* 51, 607–8; J. Hudson, *MÆ* 69, 340–2; P. Stafford, *EHR* 115, 428–9

Obst, Wolfgang, and Florian Schleburg, ed. and trans., *Lieder aus König Alfreds Trostbuch* (Heidelberg, 1998): E. G. Stanley, *N&Q* 47, 491–3; G. Wieland, *Anglia* 118, 118–20

Ogawa, Hiroshi, *Studies in the History of Old English Prose* (Tokyo): M. Godden, *Stud. in Eng. Lit.* (Tokyo) Eng. Number 42, 111–17

O'Keeffe, Katherine O'Brien, ed., *Reading Old English Texts* (Cambridge, 1997): D. Schlosser, *ANQ* 13.1, 62–5

Owen-Crocker, Gale R., *The Four Funerals in 'Beowulf' and the Structure of the Poem* (Manchester): G. Holderness, *TLS*, 3 November, p. 32

Padberg, Lutz E. von, *Studien zur Bonifatiusverehrung* (Frankfurt am Main, 1996): M. Th. Kloft, *Historische Zeitschrift* 270, 451–4

Bibliography for 2000

Page, R. I., *An Introduction to English Runes*, 2nd ed. (Woodbridge, 1999): K. Düwel, *Germanistik* 40 (1999), 688; E. G. Stanley, *N&Q* 47, 401

Runes and Runic Inscriptions (Woodbridge, 1995): P. Cardew, *MA* 44, 391

Pasternack, Carol Braun, *The Textuality of Old English Poetry* (Cambridge, 1995): H. Momma, *Speculum* 75, 721–3

Peddie, John, *Alfred, Warrior King* (Stroud, 1999): B. S. Bachrach, *Albion* 32, 468–9

Pfaff, Richard W., *Liturgical Calendars, Saints, and Services in Medieval England* (Aldershot, 1998): R. Godding, *AB* 118, 219

Poole, Russell, *Old English Wisdom Poetry* (Cambridge, 1998): R. Allen Rouse, *AUMLA* 94, 119–20; G. Wieland, *Anglia* 118, 118–20

Potin, V. M., *Hermitage Museum, St Petersburg*, I: *Anglo-Saxon Coins to 1016* (Oxford, 1999): H. Pagan, *BNJ* 69 (1999), 242–4

Pulsiano, Phillip, and E. M. Treharne, ed., *Anglo-Saxon Manuscripts and their Heritage* (Aldershot, 1998): S. Sato, *Stud. in Med. Eng. Lang. and Lit.* (Tokyo) 15, 77–84 [in Japanese]

Rahtz, Philip; Lorna Watts, *et al.*, *St Mary's Church, Deerhurst, Gloucestershire* (Woodbridge, 1997): A. Thacker, *Trans. of the Bristol and Gloucestershire Archaeol. Soc.* 118, 241–2

Raw, Barbara C., *Trinity and Incarnation in Anglo-Saxon Art and Thought* (Cambridge, 1997): R. Gameson, *Albion* 30 (1998), 453–4

Remley, Paul G., *Old English Biblical Verse* (Cambridge, 1996): [Anon.], *Forum for Mod. Lang. Stud.* 36, 218

Reynolds, Andrew, *Later Anglo-Saxon England* (Stroud, 1999): D. A. Hinton, *MA* 44, 368; N. James, *Antiquity* 74, 225

Roberts, Jane, and Christian Kay, with Lynne Grundy, *A Thesaurus of Old English* (London, 1995): R. Marsden, *Leeds Stud. in Eng.* 31, 293–5; P. G. Remley, *Peritia* 14, 458–61

Roberts, Jane, and Janet L. Nelson, with Malcolm Godden, ed., *Alfred the Wise* (Cambridge, 1997): M. Griffith, *N&Q* 47, 114; R. Marsden, *YES* 30, 272–4

Russo, Daniel G., *Town Origins and Development in Early England* (Westport, CT, 1998): C. Lohmer, *DAEM* 56, 335–6; D. M. Palliser, *NH* 36, 331–2

Russom, Geoffrey, *'Beowulf' and the Origins of Old Germanic Metre* (Cambridge, 1998): C. B. McCully, *Language* 76, 188–91; P. Orton, *MLR* 95, 463–4; S. Suzuki, *JEGP* 99, 249–51

Sampson, Fay, *Runes on the Cross* (London): D. Griffith, *Expository Times* 112, 63

Sato, Shuji, ed., *Back to the Manuscripts* (Tokyo, 1997): J. Gerritsen, *ES* 81, 142–3

Sawyer, Peter, *Anglo-Saxon Lincolnshire* (Lincoln, 1998): D. M. Palliser, *NH* 36, 164–5; J. Story, *History* 85, 496–7; B. Yorke, *MA* 44, 392–3

Schwab, Ute, ed., *Waldere* (Catania, 1999) [reprint of 1967 edition]: M. V. Molinari, *Linguistica e filologia* (Bergamo) 12, 194–6

Scragg, D. G., and Paul E. Szarmach, ed., *The Editing of Old English* (Woodbridge, 1994): J. S. Myerov, *Text* 13, 270–7

Shippey, T. A., and Andreas Haarder, ed., *'Beowulf': the Critical Heritage* (London, 1998): B. Yorke, *Lit. and Hist.* 9.2, 79–80

Bibliography for 2000

Smith, Jeremy J., *Essentials of Early English* (London, 1999): M. B. Bedingfield, *MÆ* 69, 351; M. Krygier, *Studia Anglica Posnaniensia* 35, 309–10

Snyder, Christopher A., *An Age of Tyrants: Britain and the Britons, 400–600* (Stroud, 1998): K. C. Grabowski, *Speculum* 75, 245–7

Spitzbart, Günter, ed. and trans., *Venerabilis Bedae Historia Ecclesiastica Gentis Anglorum*, rev. ed. (Darmstadt, 1997): W. Widhalm-Kupferschmidt, *Ianus* 21, 68

Stafford, Pauline, *Queen Emma and Queen Edith: Queenship and Women's Power in Eleventh-Century England* (Oxford, 1997): J. Campbell, *EHR* 115, 1261–2; M. A. Meyer, *Albion* 30 (1998), 464–6

Swan, Mary, and Elaine M. Treharne, ed., *Rewriting Old English in the Twelfth Century* (Cambridge): G. Holderness, *TLS*, 15 December, pp. 28–9

Szerwiniack, Olivier, *et al.*, trans., *Bede le Vénérable. Histoire écclésiastique du peuple Anglais*, I: *Conquête et conversion* (Paris, 1999): P. Bourgain, *Bibliothèque de l'École des Chartes* 158, 337–8; M. Goullet, *Revue des Études Latines* 77 (1999), 407–8; K. L. Maund, *Welsh Hist. Rev.* 20, 366–7

Taylor, Paul Beekman, *Sharing Story* (New York, 1998): P. Jorgensen, *JEGP* 99, 423–5; H. O'Donoghue, *RES* 51, 105–6; M. Clunies Ross, *Scandinavian Stud.* 72, 135–6; T. A. Shippey, *MLR* 95, 1065–6

Townend, Matthew, *English Place-Names in Skaldic Verse* (Nottingham, 1998): W. Laur, *Germanistik* 41, 30–1; H. Williams, *Namn och Bygd* 88, 199–200 [Swedish]

Treharne, Elaine M., ed. and trans., *The Old English Life of St Nicholas* (Leeds, 1997): S. Irvine, *RES* 51, 458–60

Tweddle, Dominic, Joan Moulden, and Elizabeth Logan, *Anglian York* (York, 1999): N. James, *Antiquity* 74, 225

Underwood, Richard, *Anglo-Saxon Weapons and Warfare* (Stroud, 1997): S. James, *Britannia* 31, 462–3

Walker, Ian W., *Harold, the Last Anglo-Saxon King* (Stroud, 1997): R. Abels, *Speculum* 75, 732–3

Ward, Benedicta, *The Venerable Bede* (London, 1998): R. Pollock, *New Blackfriars* 80 (1999), 477–8

Warner, Peter, *The Origins of Suffolk* (Manchester, 1996): B. Yorke, *MA* 44, 392–3

Williams, Ann, *Kingship and Government in Pre-Conquest England c. 500–1066* (Basingstoke, 1999): L. Abrams, *Albion* 32, 467–8; J. Campbell, *EHR* 115, 681–2

Williams, David, *Late Saxon Stirrup-Strap Mounts: a Classification and Catalogue* (York, 1998): G. Thomas, *ArchJ* 156, 436–7

Wormald, Patrick, *Legal Culture in the Early Medieval West: Law as Text, Image and Experience* (London, 1999): A. Harding, *History* 85, 701–2; J. Hudson, *MÆ* 69, 340–2; J. G. H. Hudson, *EHR* 115, 905–7

    The Making of English Law: King Alfred to the Twelfth Century, I: *Legislation and its Limits* (Oxford, 1999): A. Harding, *History* 85, 701–2; R. H. Helmholz, *Albion* 32, 274–5; J. G. H. Hudson, *EHR* 115, 905–7

Wyly, Bryan Weston, *Figures of Authority in the Old English 'Exodus'* (Heidelberg, 1999): M. Griffith, *N&Q* 47, 113–14; S. Love, *ES* 81, 500–1

Index to volumes 26–30

Volume numbers in italic precede page numbers

Aa, river, *28*.212
Aachen, *27*.129; Capitula of (A.D. 818/819), *30*.182n; council of (A.D. 816), *27*.107n, 248n
Aalst, family of, *28*.215n, 216
Aaron, island of: *see* Saint-Malo
Abbo of Fleury, *28*.108n; *30*.221; literary style of, *27*.28; *Passio S. Eadmundi*, *28*.71n; *29*.254n; *Quaestiones grammaticales*, *27*.17
Abbo of Saint-Germain, *Bella Parisiacae urbis*, *29*.141, 143n
Abingdon (Berks.), abbey, *30*.166; connections with Canterbury, *28*.107n; connections with France, *28*.106–7; manuscripts, *27*.141, 143n, 150, 151, 153n, 167, 168, 276; *28*.89n, 106, 109; *29*.86, 88
Abraham, biblical figure, *28*.122n, 124, 125, 127, 128, 130, 131, 139
Acca, bishop of Hexham, *26*.43
accents, and other markings for pauses, in AS manuscripts, *26*.139n; in OE verse, *29*.292; *and see* punctuation
Achadeus, count, *30*.48; psalter of (CCCC 272), *26*.162; *30*.48
Actium, battle of, *28*.17
Ad Herennium: *see* Cicero, pseudo-
Ad mensam philosophiae, *27*.15n
Adalbertus, St, *29*.69n, 268n
Adalram, bishop of Salzburg, *27*.107
Adam of Bremen, *Gesta Hammaburgensis ecclesiae*, *28*.5; *29*.261, 262n, 266–8, 272; *30*.177n
Adam, biblical figure, *28*.127
Adelard of Bath, *Quaestiones naturales*, *28*.234
Adelina, daughter of Richard of Rullos, *28*.222n
Adeliza, wife of King Henry I, *28*.213n, 223
Ademar, monk of Saint-Martial, *26*.172
Ado of Vienne, martyrology of, *29*.68, 69, 70, 71n, 72–3, 75, 76, 82; *30*.117n; *Libellus de festiuitatibus sanctorum apostolorum*, *29*.73, 75, 76, 77, 78, 79, 80, 81
Ado, founder of Jouarre nunnery, *26*.51
Adomnán, abbot of Iona, *26*.23; 'The Reliquary of Adomnán', OIr poem, *26*.31
De locis sanctis, *26*.32–3, 34, 38, 39; *27*.110; *30*.67–8; relationship with iconography in Book of Durrow, *26*.31–2; in Book of Kells, *26*.32
Vita S. Columbae, *26*.30; manuscript copies of, *27*.109; latinity of, *27*.109, 111, 113

Adoratio crucis, liturgy on Good Friday, *26*.23
Adoro te domine Iesu Christe in cruce ascendentem, Good Friday devotional prayer, *26*.123–4
Advent, *26*.57; *27*.252; *liturgica* for, *28*.153n, 160, 171, 173
Æbba, abbess: *see* Eafe
Aed, St, *29*.112, 117
Ælberht of York, *magister* of Alcuin, *27*.12
Ælfflæd, queen of Edward the Elder, *29*.119; *30*.55n; and the Cuthbert embroideries, *30*.138
Ælfgifu, abbess of Nunnaminster (Winchester), *28*.316; *29*.277
Ælfheah, St, bishop of Winchester, archbishop of Canterbury, *28*.186; *30*.139; murder of, *27*.211n; relics of, *30*.167
Ælfhelm, (lost) account of St Æthelthryth, *29*.252n
Ælfric Bata, *28*.181
Ælfric, abbot of Eynsham, *29*.89, 121; *30*.93, 98, 111n
    general: and biblical commentaries, *26*.167; and CCCC 190, *27*.242, 243; and Old Testament translations, *26*.193; and the *Excerptiones pseudo-Ecgberhti*, *29*.245n; and the OE translation of the Ely privilege, *29*.254; and the *Old English Bede*, *29*.104n; and the *Old English Hexateuch*, *28*.113, 114, 130n; Ealdorman Æthelweard as patron of, *29*.177
    literary style of, *27*.14, 23n; *29*.213; vocabulary used by, *27*.282; latinity of, *27*.248; linguistic achievements of, *29*.104n; OE vocabulary associated with, *26*.142, 167; *28*.103n; *29*.89n; his use of the word *cræft*, *26*.84, 85, 87, 88, 89; (in *Catholic Homilies*), *26*.86, 88; (in *Lives of Saints*), *26*.86; (in the OE interlinear version of Ælfric's *Colloquy*), *26*.86; (in his *Grammar*), *26*.89; his use of the word *tid*, *27*.192
    on anti-Judaism, *28*.65–7, 68–80, 85–6; on Jewish custom, *28*.71–2, 74, 76–7; on the Old Testament, *28*.72–3, 76, 84; on his vision of society, *28*.80–4, 85; on the Three Orders of Society, *28*.81–4; on the Four Types of War, *28*.82n; on liturgical books required for priests, *30*.143; on male and female saints, *30*.134n; on marriage, *29*.240, 241–50, 255, 257–9; on prognostication, *30*.196–8, 200–2, 203, 204; on the cult of the Virgin Mary, *26*.202; on the persona of Saturn, *26*.145; on the soul and body, *30*.121; on the threefold reward,

Women at the Sepulchre, *28*.51–2, 57, 62; theme of salvation in, *28*.49, 51–2; bodily presence of Christ in Hell, *28*.52–3; lyric mode of, *28*.53–4; iconography of Ps. XV.10 in the Utrecht Psalter as a source for, *28*.54–8, 59, 60, 61–3

Deus cuius dextera beatum Petrum ambulantem, prayer, *26*.125n

Deus cuius gratiam beatus Petrus mirabilis, prayer, *26*.125n

Deus qui [...] lacrimis aures, prayer, *26*.125n

Deus qui conspicis quia nos undique mala, prayer, *26*.125n

Deus qui cunctae oboediunt creaturae, Good Friday devotional prayer, *26*.123n

Deus qui inter cetera potentiae, prayer, *26*.125n

Deus qui Iohannem baptista nuntia, prayer, *26*.125n

Deus qui miro ordine angelorum, prayer, *26*.125n

Deus qui os beati apostoli tui Iohannis, prayer, *26*.125n

Deus qui Raphahele archangel, prayer, 26.125n

Deus qui unigeniti fili, Good Friday devotional prayer, *26*.123n

Deusdedit, *27*.48n

Deutz (nr Cologne), abbey, *29*.269, 270, 274, 276, 277n, 278

Devon, *26*.65

Dhuoda, *Liber manualis*, *30*.46n

dialectic, *27*.7n

Dietrich of the Nordmark, Margrave, *29*.263

Dijon, manuscripts, *30*.203n

Diomedes, *Ars grammatica*, *27*.9n

Dionysius Exiguus, computus, *30*.227

discretio, *26*.1–6

Divine Office, *26*.158, 159, 163

Dobrava, queen of Poland, *29*.263

Dolfin, 'Earl', *28*.221

Domburg (Walcheren), *28*.207

Domesday Book, *27*.39; *28*.201, 217n, 220n; *30*.3n

'Dominator Dominus', prayer: *see* Gregory the Great's *oratio*

Domine Iesu Christe filius dei unum gloriosissime conditor mundi, prayer, *26*.123n, 124

Donatus, *26*.5n; commentary on Vergil, *27*.88; *Ars maior*, *26*.6n; *27*.17; bk III (*Barbarismus*), *27*.9n, 10; knowledge of in ASE, *27*.16, 17, 18; *Ars minor*, *28*.87n

Donegal, *26*.30n

Dorbene, prior of Iona, *26*.30n

Dorchester, *30*.51; charters, *30*.52n; manuscripts, *26*.74

Dorset, and Vikings, *28*.6, 9

Dracontius, *27*.89

drama, liturgical, in the Book of Cerne, *28*.55

Dream of the Rood, The, *27*.186, 189n, 192n, 200, 201; *29*.10n; stylistic devices in, *27*.24, 26

Drogo, of St Winnocsbergen, *Translatio S. Lewinnae*, *28*.209

Druids, *28*.295, 330

Dryden, John, *26*.243

Duddo, letter to from Boniface, *30*.21n, 23

Dungal, Irish pupil at Salzburg, *26*.33n

Dunstan, abbot of Glastonbury, archbishop of Canterbury, *28*.306, 311, 316; *29*.150; *30*.74, 92; charters of, by 'Dunstan B', *30*.74; marginal annotations of, *26*.1n; *post mortem* miracles of, *27*.223; *Vita S. Dunstani*, by 'B', manuscript copies of, *27*.107n; on the Three Orders of Society, *28*.82n

Dura, biblical province, *26*.156

Dura Europos, wall-painting from, *28*.57n

Durham, OE poem, *29*.293–4; *30*.231; transmission of, *30*.231–4, 237, 240, 245; transcripts of by Junius, *30*.231, 232, 233–44; edition of, *30*.233, 237, 240–1

Durham, cathedral of, catalogues of, *27*.78; manuscripts, *27*.117, 119n, 120, 121, 125; *30*.206n

Durleigh (Somerset), *30*.10

Durley (Hants.), *30*.10

Dutch, language, *29*.284

Eaba, abbot of Malmesbury, *30*.34n

Eadberht II, king of Kent, *27*.60n

Eadberht, bishop of Lindisfarne, *27*.130n

Eadberht Præn, *30*.53n

Eadburg, abbess of Minster-in-Thanet, *27*.43, 44, 57, 63; *30*.29; translation of relics of St Mildrith, *27*.45, 60, 62; elevation of cult of St Mildrith, *27*.59, 61, 62; relations with Æthelbald of Mercia and Kent, *27*.61, 62; correspondence with Boniface, *27*.63; *30*.18, 20–2, 23–4, 28, 33n, 35, 38; trip to Rome, *27*.60

Eadburg, queen of King Æthelwulf, *30*.58

Eadfrith, teacher of Æthelwulf, *27*.130n

Eadgyth, empress to Otto I, *29*.177

Eadmer, monk, *Historiae nouorum*, on the Lucca cross, *29*.166

Eadred, king, *28*.308n, 311n; *30*.74

Eadric Streona, *30*.167

Eadric, king of Kent, law-code of, *27*.33

Eadric, reeve, *27*.223

Eadsige, expelled canon of Old Minster, Winchester, *27*.218

Eadweard, OE letter to, *29*.226

Eadwig, king, *28*.251n, 272n, 308n, 311n, 316, 334

Eadwig, ætheling, *30*.173n

Eadwig Basan, scribe, *27*.145n, 146n; *28*.169, 181; manuscripts attributed to, *30*.137, 138–9, 143; dating of his corpus, *30*.139; script associated with, *30*.139–40; influence of script, *30*.141, 143–4

Eadwine, monk of New Minster, Winchester, OE letter to Ælfsige, *29*.226, 230

Eafe, abbess, founder of Minster-in-Thanet, *27*.41, 44, 46, 47, 48–50, 51n, 52, 53, 54–5, 56–7, 58, 59, 62, 63; *and see* 'the Mildrith legend' *under* Mildrith; grants of land to as abbess of Thanet, *27*.59; Mercian connections of, *27*.61, 63

Ealdred, bishop of Worcester, archbishop of York, *28*.214; *29*.273, 277

335